DEMOCRATIC RIGHTS AND ELECTORAL REFORM IN CANADA

~

*This is Volume 10 in a series of studies
commissioned as part of the research program
of the Royal Commission on Electoral Reform
and Party Financing*

DEMOCRATIC RIGHTS AND ELECTORAL REFORM IN CANADA

~

Michael Cassidy
Editor

Volume 10 of the Research Studies

ROYAL COMMISSION ON ELECTORAL REFORM
AND PARTY FINANCING
AND CANADA COMMUNICATION GROUP –
PUBLISHING, SUPPLY AND SERVICES CANADA

DUNDURN PRESS
TORONTO AND OXFORD

Published by Dundurn Press Limited in cooperation with the Royal
Commission on Electoral Reform and Party Financing and Canada
Communication Group – Publishing, Supply and Services Canada.

Canadian Cataloguing in Publication Data

Main entry under title:
Democratic rights and electoral reform in Canada

(Research studies ; 10)
Issued also in French under title: Les Droits démocratiques et la réforme
    électorale au Canada.
ISBN 1-55002-106-0

1. Political rights – Canada. 2. Civil rights – Canada. 3. Elections –
Canada. I. Cassidy, Michael, 1937– . II. Canada. Royal Commission on
Electoral Reform and Party Financing. III. Series: Research studies (Canada.
Royal Commission on Electoral Reform and Party Financing) ; 10.

JL193.D44 1991   323'.0971   C91-090522-3

Dundurn Press Limited
2181 Queen Street East
Suite 301
Toronto, Canada
M4E 1E5

Dundurn Distribution
73 Lime Walk
Headington
Oxford, England
OX3 7AD

CONTENTS

FIGURES

TABLES

3. REFLECTIONS ON CRITERIA FOR EXCLUDING PERSONS WITH MENTAL DISORDERS FROM THE RIGHT TO VOTE

FOREWORD

THE ROYAL COMMISSION on Electoral Reform and Party Financing was established in November 1989. Our mandate was to inquire into and report on the appropriate principles and process that should govern the election of members of the House of Commons and the financing of political parties and candidates' campaigns. To conduct such a comprehensive examination of Canada's electoral system, we held extensive public consultations and developed a research program designed to ensure that our recommendations would be guided by an independent foundation of empirical inquiry and analysis.

The Commission's in-depth review of the electoral system was the first of its kind in Canada's history of electoral democracy. It was dictated largely by the major constitutional, social and technological changes of the past several decades, which have transformed Canadian society, and their concomitant influence on Canadians' expectations of the political process itself. In particular, the adoption in 1982 of the *Canadian Charter of Rights and Freedoms* has heightened Canadians' awareness of their democratic and political rights and of the way they are served by the electoral system.

The importance of electoral reform cannot be overemphasized. As the Commission's work proceeded, Canadians became increasingly preoccupied with constitutional issues that have the potential to change the nature of Confederation. No matter what their beliefs or political allegiances in this continuing debate, Canadians agree that constitutional change must be achieved in the context of fair and democratic processes. We cannot complacently assume that our current electoral process will always meet this standard or that it leaves no room for improvement. Parliament and the national government must be seen as legitimate; electoral reform can both enhance the stature of national political institutions and reinforce their ability to define the future of our country in ways that command Canadians' respect and confidence and promote the national interest.

In carrying out our mandate, we remained mindful of the importance of protecting our democratic heritage, while at the same time balancing it against the emerging values that are injecting a new dynamic into the electoral system. If our system is to reflect the realities of Canadian political life, then reform requires more than mere tinkering with electoral laws and practices.

Our broad mandate challenged us to explore a full range of options. We commissioned more than 100 research studies, to be published in a 23-volume collection. In the belief that our electoral laws must measure up to the very best contemporary practice, we examined election-related laws and processes in all of our provinces and territories and studied comparable legislation and processes in established democracies around the world. This unprecedented array of empirical study and expert opinion made a vital contribution to our deliberations. We made every effort to ensure that the research was both intellectually rigorous and of practical value. All studies were subjected to peer review, and many of the authors discussed their preliminary findings with members of the political and academic communities at national symposiums on major aspects of the electoral system.

The Commission placed the research program under the able and inspired direction of Dr. Peter Aucoin, Professor of Political Science and Public Administration at Dalhousie University. We are confident that the efforts of Dr. Aucoin, together with those of the research coordinators and scholars whose work appears in this and other volumes, will continue to be of value to historians, political scientists, parliamentarians and policy makers, as well as to thoughtful Canadians and the international community.

Along with the other Commissioners, I extend my sincere gratitude to the entire Commission staff for their dedication and commitment. I also wish to thank the many people who participated in our symposiums for their valuable contributions, as well as the members of the research and practitioners' advisory groups whose counsel significantly aided our undertaking.

Pierre Lortie
Chairman

INTRODUCTION

THE ROYAL COMMISSION'S research program constituted a comprehensive and detailed examination of the Canadian electoral process. The scope of the research, undertaken to assist Commissioners in their deliberations, was dictated by the broad mandate given to the Commission.

The objective of the research program was to provide Commissioners with a full account of the factors that have shaped our electoral democracy. This dictated, first and foremost, a focus on federal electoral law, but our inquiries also extended to the Canadian constitution, including the institutions of parliamentary government, the practices of political parties, the mass media and nonpartisan political organizations, as well as the decision-making role of the courts with respect to the constitutional rights of citizens. Throughout, our research sought to introduce a historical perspective in order to place the contemporary experience within the Canadian political tradition.

We recognized that neither our consideration of the factors shaping Canadian electoral democracy nor our assessment of reform proposals would be as complete as necessary if we failed to examine the experiences of Canadian provinces and territories and of other democracies. Our research program thus emphasized comparative dimensions in relation to the major subjects of inquiry.

Our research program involved, in addition to the work of the Commission's research coordinators, analysts and support staff, over 200 specialists from 28 universities in Canada, from the private sector and, in a number of cases, from abroad. Specialists in political science constituted the majority of our researchers, but specialists in law, economics, management, computer sciences, ethics, sociology and communications, among other disciplines, were also involved.

In addition to the preparation of research studies for the Commission, our research program included a series of research seminars, symposiums and workshops. These meetings brought together the Commissioners, researchers, representatives from the political parties, media personnel and others with practical experience in political parties, electoral politics and public affairs. These meetings provided not only a forum for discussion of the various subjects of the Commission's mandate, but also an opportunity for our research to be assessed by those with an intimate knowledge of the world of political practice.

These public reviews of our research were complemented by internal and external assessments of each research report by persons qualified in the area; such assessments were completed prior to our decision to publish any study in the series of research volumes.

The Research Branch of the Commission was divided into several areas, with the individual research projects in each area assigned to the research coordinators as follows:

F. Leslie Seidle	Political Party and Election Finance
Herman Bakvis	Political Parties
Kathy Megyery	Women, Ethno-cultural Groups and Youth
David Small	Redistribution; Electoral Boundaries; Voter Registration
Janet Hiebert	Party Ethics
Michael Cassidy	Democratic Rights; Election Administration
Robert A. Milen	Aboriginal Electoral Participation and Representation
Frederick J. Fletcher	Mass Media and Broadcasting in Elections
David Mac Donald (Assistant Research Coordinator)	Direct Democracy

These coordinators identified appropriate specialists to undertake research, managed the projects and prepared them for publication. They also organized the seminars, symposiums and workshops in their research areas and were responsible for preparing presentations and briefings to help the Commission in its deliberations and decision making. Finally, they participated in drafting the Final Report of the Commission.

On behalf of the Commission, I welcome the opportunity to thank the following for their generous assistance in producing these research studies – a project that required the talents of many individuals.

In performing their duties, the research coordinators made a notable contribution to the work of the Commission. Despite the pressures of tight deadlines, they worked with unfailing good humour and the utmost congeniality. I thank all of them for their consistent support and cooperation.

In particular, I wish to express my gratitude to Leslie Seidle, senior research coordinator, who supervised our research analysts and support staff in Ottawa. His diligence, commitment and professionalism not only set high standards, but also proved contagious. I am grateful to Kathy Megyery, who performed a similar function in Montreal with equal aplomb and skill. Her enthusiasm and dedication inspired us all.

On behalf of the research coordinators and myself, I wish to thank our research analysts: Daniel Arsenault, Eric Bertram, Cécile Boucher, Peter Constantinou, Yves Denoncourt, David Docherty, Luc Dumont, Jane Dunlop, Scott Evans, Véronique Garneau, Keith Heintzman, Paul Holmes, Hugh Mellon, Cheryl D. Mitchell, Donald Padget, Alain Pelletier, Dominique Tremblay and Lisa Young. The Research Branch was strengthened by their ability to carry out research in a wide variety of areas, their intellectual curiosity and their team spirit.

The work of the research coordinators and analysts was greatly facilitated by the professional skills and invaluable cooperation of Research Branch staff members: Paulette LeBlanc, who, as administrative assistant, managed the flow of research projects; Hélène Leroux, secretary to the research coordinators, who produced briefing material for the Commissioners and who, with Lori Nazar, assumed responsibility for monitoring the progress of research projects in the latter stages of our work; Kathleen McBride and her assistant Natalie Brose, who created and maintained the database of briefs and hearings transcripts; and Richard Herold and his assistant Susan Dancause, who were responsible for our research library. Jacinthe Séguin and Cathy Tucker also deserve thanks – in addition to their duties as receptionists, they assisted in a variety of ways to help us meet deadlines.

We were extremely fortunate to obtain the research services of first-class specialists from the academic and private sectors. Their contributions are found in this and the other 22 published research volumes. We thank them for the quality of their work and for their willingness to contribute and to meet our tight deadlines.

Our research program also benefited from the counsel of Jean-Marc Hamel, Special Adviser to the Chairman of the Commission and former

Chief Electoral Officer of Canada, whose knowledge and experience proved invaluable.

In addition, numerous specialists assessed our research studies. Their assessments not only improved the quality of our published studies, but also provided us with much-needed advice on many issues. In particular, we wish to single out professors Donald Blake, Janine Brodie, Alan Cairns, Kenneth Carty, John Courtney, Peter Desbarats, Jane Jenson, Richard Johnston, Vincent Lemieux, Terry Morley and Joseph Wearing, as well as Ms. Beth Symes.

Producing such a large number of studies in less than a year requires a mastery of the skills and logistics of publishing. We were fortunate to be able to count on the Commission's Director of Communications, Richard Rochefort, and Assistant Director, Hélène Papineau. They were ably supported by the Communications staff: Patricia Burden, Louise Dagenais, Caroline Field, Claudine Labelle, France Langlois, Lorraine Maheux, Ruth McVeigh, Chantal Morissette, Sylvie Patry, Jacques Poitras and Claudette Rouleau-O'Toole.

To bring the project to fruition, the Commission also called on specialized contractors. We are deeply grateful for the services of Ann McCoomb (references and fact checking); Marthe Lemery, Pierre Chagnon and the staff of Communications Com'ça (French quality control); Norman Bloom, Pamela Riseborough and associates of B&B Editorial Consulting (English adaptation and quality control); and Mado Reid (French production). Al Albania and his staff at Acart Graphics designed the studies and produced some 2 400 tables and figures.

The Commission's research reports constitute Canada's largest publishing project of 1991. Successful completion of the project required close cooperation between the public and private sectors. In the public sector, we especially acknowledge the excellent service of the Privy Council unit of the Translation Bureau, Department of the Secretary of State of Canada, under the direction of Michel Parent, and our contacts Ruth Steele and Terry Denovan of the Canada Communication Group, Department of Supply and Services.

The Commission's co-publisher for the research studies was Dundurn Press of Toronto, whose exceptional service is gratefully acknowledged. Wilson & Lafleur of Montreal, working with the Centre de Documentation Juridique du Québec, did equally admirable work in preparing the French version of the studies.

Teams of editors, copy editors and proofreaders worked diligently under stringent deadlines with the Commission and the publishers to prepare some 20 000 pages of manuscript for design, typesetting and printing. The work of these individuals, whose names are listed elsewhere in this volume, was greatly appreciated.

Our acknowledgements extend to the contributions of the Commission's Executive Director, Guy Goulard, and the administration and executive support teams: Maurice Lacasse, Denis Lafrance and Steve Tremblay (finance); Thérèse Lacasse and Mary Guy-Shea (personnel); Cécile Desforges (assistant to the Executive Director); Marie Dionne (administration); Anna Bevilacqua (records); and support staff members Michelle Bélanger, Roch Langlois, Michel Lauzon, Jean Mathieu, David McKay and Pierrette McMurtie, as well as Denise Miquelon and Christiane Séguin of the Montreal office.

A special debt of gratitude is owed to Marlène Girard, assistant to the Chairman. Her ability to supervise the logistics of the Commission's work amid the tight schedules of the Chairman and Commissioners contributed greatly to the completion of our task.

I also wish to express my deep gratitude to my own secretary, Liette Simard. Her superb administrative skills and great patience brought much-appreciated order to my penchant for the chaotic workstyle of academe. She also assumed responsibility for the administrative coordination of revisions to the final drafts of volumes 1 and 2 of the Commission's Final Report. I owe much to her efforts and assistance.

Finally, on behalf of the research coordinators and myself, I wish to thank the Chairman, Pierre Lortie, the members of the Commission, Pierre Fortier, Robert Gabor, William Knight and Lucie Pépin, and former members Elwood Cowley and Senator Donald Oliver. We are honoured to have worked with such an eminent and thoughtful group of Canadians, and we have benefited immensely from their knowledge and experience. In particular, we wish to acknowledge the creativity, intellectual rigour and energy our Chairman brought to our task. His unparalleled capacity to challenge, to bring out the best in us, was indeed inspiring.

Peter Aucoin
Director of Research

PREFACE

THE PAST DECADE has been marked by a series of developments that have affected the legitimacy of Canada's electoral system and eroded its structure. These include court challenges under the *Canadian Charter of Rights and Freedoms* that have struck down important sections of the *Canada Elections Act*; the rise of political parties that question some basic concepts of representative democracy; and difficulties in administering elections that, in some cases, have shaken public confidence. All of these factors have had a role in the Commission's research program on democratic rights and election administration.

Most of the authors in this volume go beyond reflection and history to develop practical proposals that, in many cases, are reflected in the Commission's Final Report. They have also sought to contend with problems of public perception that do not necessarily correspond to reality, but cannot be ignored in remaking election law.

A theme that runs through this volume is the need for policies that balance conflicting objectives, and the difficulties entailed in trying to implement ideal solutions. A test for mental competence, as suggested by Jennifer Smith, might indeed ensure that every elector casts a rational vote; at the same time it might exclude from voting many citizens who have no trace of mental illness or deficiency. The tradition of a politically neutral civil service, as the two studies on political rights demonstrate, cannot help but be in some conflict with the extension of rights entailed in the Charter.

These studies cover many areas, from voting rights and political rights to direct democracy and questions of voter registration and election administration.

In the opening study, Jennifer Smith puts the question of voting rights into a historical context; notes how these rights have been extended alongside the evolution of representative democracy; and illuminates the conflict between the concepts of virtual representation and delegate representation in a contemporary context. Her analysis leads her to take issue with an uncritical advocacy of rights, particularly with reference to voting by prisoners and persons with mental disorders. It is important, she contends, to maintain the dignity of the vote and to uphold standards of right political conduct because of the very risk involved in voting in a democratic system based on virtual representation.

The question of voting by prison inmates has been considered at length in the courts, but it has not been reviewed in depth from the standpoints of criminology, philosophy or political science. This Pierre Landreville and Lucie Lemonde attempt to do. While condemned prisoners once lost all their civil rights, the current policy of Correctional Service Canada is to limit the punishment of inmates to their actual imprisonment. In this context, they contend, there is no reason why someone should lose the right to vote by virtue of being incarcerated. Moreover, it would be arbitrary to restrict prisoners from voting when there are large numbers of persons in Canada who have also committed criminal acts but who have not been arrested, were not convicted or were not sentenced to imprisonment.

In his study, Yves Denoncourt, a research analyst with the Royal Commission, concludes that people with mental disorders – either mental illness or deficiency – could be subject to a test for competency to vote if such a test were relatively uniform among provinces, were applied by law and provided the right to appeal. He finds that tests of competency used for involuntary confinement of persons with mental illness meet these criteria, as do the legal tests applied when persons who have committed criminal acts are confined by reason of insanity.

The question of political rights for civil servants is another issue that frequently has gone to the courts – most recently with the Supreme Court's decision striking down the restrictions on political activity in the *Public Service Employment Act*. Kenneth Kernaghan and Patrice Garant, in separate studies, explore this issue in depth and arrive at differing conclusions. Professor Kernaghan judges that far more experience than one election will be needed to see whether the relaxation of rules on political activity can be sustained without harm to the political neutrality of the civil service. Professor Garant, drawing both from the Charter and from Quebec's experience with a liberal regime of political rights, concludes that the right to participate politically should have precedence over the principle of political neutrality. Both agree, however, that public servants need to show moderation in the exercise of their political rights.

The referendum has returned to the political agenda in Canada as a device for giving democracy back to the people and taking control out of the hands of the politicians and parties. David Mac Donald, a senior research analyst with the Commission, focuses on referendums held at the same time as general elections. His study casts doubt on whether this type of referendum can deliver what it promises; the parties, politicians and interest groups will almost inevitably be involved in framing the questions, in debating the referendum issues during a campaign and, finally, in implementing any measure recommended by referendum.

Peter McCormick deals with another instrument of direct democracy, the recall. While the recall has played only a minor function in American politics since its introduction 75 years ago, Professor McCormick concludes that it could serve as a safety valve in Canadian politics and that, if adopted, it might actually be used more often than in the United States because of the longer terms served by Canadian legislators and the opportunity for disgruntled electors to target a government minister or leader in a recall petition. As he notes, however, the only recall law ever enacted in Canada was introduced by the Social Credit government in Alberta (1936) under Premier William Aberhardt – then hastily withdrawn when the voters threatened to use it against Aberhardt himself.

Canada is the only major democracy that waits to register electors to vote until after the beginning of the election campaign, and its system of enumeration also puts more responsibility for voter registration on the state than other democracies. This system, which has been almost unchanged since 1938, came under increasing scrutiny in the 1980s because of the difficulties both in recruiting enumerators and in finding and registering voters. As John Courtney and David Smith demonstrate in their study, however, these difficulties are not unique to Canada. The systems of voter registration used in the countries examined fall even shorter of 100 percent coverage than does Canada's, and the problems in the Canadian system have tended to overshadow its achievements. Enumeration is worth preserving in its general form, they conclude, but the rules need to be updated to include more electors and to allow for shorter election campaigns.

In the final study in this volume, Cécile Boucher, a research analyst with the Commission, explores the linked issues of election law enforcement and the present structure of Elections Canada, the body responsible for administering Canada's elections. She reviews how elections are administered in other jurisdictions and surveys the *Canada Elections Act*'s treatment of election offences, much of it unchanged for more than a century. Drawing on a number of models, she develops a proposal for decriminalizing election offences, a goal sought by many interveners at the Commission's hearings, by creating a Canada Elections Commission capable of serving both as an administrative tribunal and as the corporate body directing Elections Canada. She demonstrates that the vast majority of election offences, contrary to public perception, can be handled by administrative means because they do not involve dishonesty or fraud.

These studies are a good example of the approach taken by the Royal Commission: careful analysis of issues based on past experience and on practice in other jurisdictions, followed by proposals tailored to Canada's experience and needs. They clearly demonstrate that differences in electoral practices between jurisdictions are much greater than a casual observer would suppose. As Professors Courtney and Smith put it with reference to voter registration, "Canada's ... system would be as unacceptable to other ... democratic states as we believe theirs would be to Canada."

In addition to these studies, the Commission carried out a substantial amount of internal research in the areas of voting, candidacy and election administration, including extensive comparative research. Much of this work is reflected in the Final Report; some is being published in a separate volume of Commission research studies. It has been my privilege to work with the four talented research analysts who carried out this work at the Commission offices in Montreal – Cécile Boucher, Yves Denoncourt, Luc Dumont and Alain Pelletier. I thank them for their cooperation and for the energy and perseverance with which they responded to the demands of the Commission. My thanks go equally to Peter Aucoin, director of research, for guiding me in a new undertaking and to Hélène Leroux, the research secretary, and all the other Commission staff for their cheerful and consistent support.

Michael Cassidy
Research Coordinator

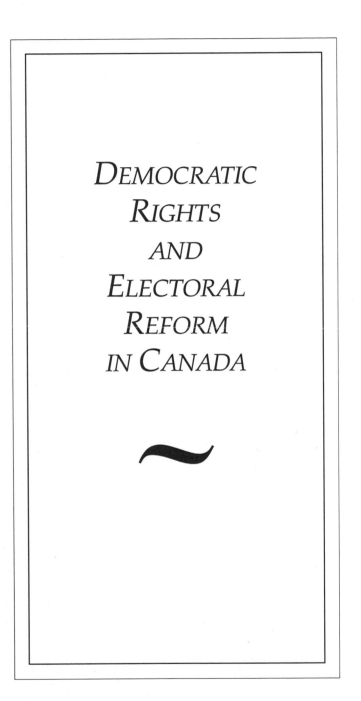

DEMOCRATIC
RIGHTS
AND
ELECTORAL
REFORM
IN CANADA

~

1

THE FRANCHISE AND THEORIES OF REPRESENTATIVE GOVERNMENT

Jennifer Smith

TODAY THE IDEA of "rights" is everywhere. As a result, people are led to believe that a right is an end in itself, one that is universally applicable and self-justifying. This belief is without foundation, but it does ensure that anyone who appropriates the language of rights has seized upon a rhetorically effective device. How does it affect current thinking about the franchise?

The franchise, the right to vote at public elections, is one of the oldest political rights. At times there has been general agreement on issues surrounding it. In his "Appeal from the New to the Old Whigs" (1791), Edmund Burke argued that property-owning members of the British Parliament should and did represent the communities and diverse economic interests of the country, and that people who lived in those communities or pursued those interests were thereby represented whether they voted or not (1960, 57–61). Most did not. The passage of the *Reform Act* in 1832 marked the triumph of the very different concept of representation by population – which means the representation of individuals, not communities or interests – and this in turn paved the way for universal manhood suffrage.

The suffragette movement in the early years of the 20th century exploded the consensus on a manhood suffrage, subject to few or no property qualifications. Once women gained the vote, a consensus re-emerged on the meaning of a universal suffrage limited only by age, citizenship and residence requirements. No one agitated to enfranchise prisoners or patients in asylums, individuals not incorporated in the word "universal." Now, in a complete reversal of the earlier view, public commentary appears to favour the idea.[1] But this is not the only development in what looks more and more like another unsettled period as far as the vote is concerned. The postwar certainty surrounding the importance and utility of the very act of voting is under scrutiny.

Feminists have expressed disenchantment with the vote. They point out that after securing the vote, Canadian women tended not to pursue public office, indeed were discouraged from doing so (Trofimenkoff and Prentice 1977). The few who did ran into barriers in party politics, many of which linger today (Brodie 1985). The implication is that the vote, far from being a central and sensitive instrument of change, is a deceptive feature of liberal democratic government, which is itself based on "male" assumptions, or assumptions that historically have favoured men. The American theorist, Carole Pateman, expresses the feminist suspicion: "The lesson to be learned from the past is that a 'democratic' theory and practice that is not at the same time feminist merely serves to maintain a fundamental form of domination and so makes a mockery of the ideals and values that democracy is held to embody" (1983, 217).

A different form of disenchantment with the vote pertains to party politics. It is argued that a political system featuring disciplined political parties blunts voters' voices because it can never reflect accurately the mix of any individual voter's preferences.[2] The preferences in question are not always marginal. In the last federal election, the few socialists who supported free trade with the United States had to consider voting for the governing Conservative party. From the point of view of the Conservatives, this was undoubtedly a source of amusement and satisfaction. It ought to have been. On the other hand, there is a problem of legitimacy for the victorious party if some of its own voters find it largely unrepresentative of their views.

In this study I want to examine some of our present discontents about the vote: Who should have it? Is it the asset that it is made out to be, at least in civic texts? My starting point in the second section of the study is the contemporary legal concept of the vote as a "constitutional right." This is a concept that turns out to be empirically accurate in the narrowest sense but is theoretically impoverished. It gives questionable direction on the difficult issues of whether prisoners and mental patients ought to vote, and the wrong direction on the special category of constituency returning officers. Accordingly, in the third section I turn to the traditional justifications of the vote.

The justifications that are reviewed range from early arguments about the relationship between political obligation (citizens obeying the law) and consent (choosing law makers) to the sociological arguments of Alexis de Tocqueville and J.S. Mill. These arguments provide some direction on the question of eligibility to vote. They also show that it is difficult to consider eligibility in the absence of an idea of citizenship. But that idea is tied closely to the system of representation. Accordingly, the fourth section is taken up with the relationship between voting, citizenship and representation, beginning with Rousseau's explanation of the dilemma of representation. He thought representation an impossibility. On the other hand, James Madison, one of the architects of the American constitution, defended representation as the key to republican government in the modern age. But Rousseau and Madison envisaged different republican governments and different republics.

In the fifth section of the study, I examine the commonly conceived forms of representation: mirror, virtual and delegate. The current disenchantment with the vote stems in part from confusion about these forms, and about the limits of representation generally under party government. I conclude by arguing that virtual representation is the natural form of the institution of representation; that this only adds to the difficulty of the task of the voter and at the same time increases the importance of general elections; and that the dignity of citizenship, which is bound up with the vote, is the proper standard by which to judge some of the issues of voter disqualification.

THE CONTEMPORARY LEGAL CONCEPT OF THE VOTE

Under the *Canadian Charter of Rights and Freedoms*, the right to vote is classified as a democratic right and is said to belong to every citizen of Canada. In addition, and by virtue of its inclusion in the Charter, the vote is also a "constitutional right" that is beyond the easy reach of ordinary law, rather than, say, a privilege conferred by legislatures.

Both the absolute language used and the fact of entrenchment seem to discourage much in the way of exceptions, which is absurd on the face of it, since children are citizens but not normally considered rationally fit, or experienced enough, to vote. The way out is the Charter's opening limitations clause, which applies to all of its provisions and thereby subjects the vote to "such reasonable limits prescribed by law as can be demonstrably justified in a free and democratic society." But it might be a narrow passage. In the spirit of the Charter, Gerald Beaudoin refers approvingly to the *Oakes* case (1986), in which the Supreme Court cast the limitations clause into the form of a test to be used to determine whether legislative limits of rights and freedoms are reasonable and justifiable. The test is tough because the objective of the limits must be "pressing and substantial," and the means used "proportional" to it, that is, precise and economical in every respect.[3] Beaudoin opines that this test will permit "very few" exceptions to the right to vote and then turns to consider those already in place.

The *Canada Elections Act* forbids the chief electoral officer (CEO) and his or her assistant to vote. Beaudoin emphasizes that these officials must enjoy the trust of the political parties, and that for this reason (presumably), the Supreme Court could find the denial of their right to be consistent with the requirements of the *Oakes* test if the court is called upon to consider the issue (Beaudoin and Ratushny 1989, 274). Not so for the returning officer in each electoral district. Beaudoin notes the rule that in the event of a tie on a recount in any constituency, the returning officer votes to break the tie. Since this act would be a public vote, in effect, he cannot see why this officer, too, is forbidden to cast a secret ballot in the election and is puzzled that the CEO has not recommended that returning officers vote like everyone else (ibid., 275). Evidently it has not occurred to Beaudoin (unlike the experienced CEO) that in the event of a tie on a recount, and with emotions running high, voters are likely to look askance at any individual who gets to vote twice. Thus the politically prudent course is to deny an ordinary vote to tie-breakers.

However, Beaudoin is following the logic of rights and the *Oakes* test, which is designed to make it difficult for legislators to violate rights. If the returning officer's right to vote is considered as being close to inalienable, then one solution is to let the officer exercise it and to deal with the rare tie vote by holding a run-off election between the two top contenders. But there are two main objections to this idea. (1) It is an uneconomic, exaggerated and ultimately unfair response to an alleged rights violation that is incomparably minor. It is uneconomic and exaggerated because any election, even a second one, is not a simple event. It uses up a great deal of time, energy and money. A run-off election is also unfair to the candidates in question, since they alone are forced, as it were, through a hoop and must perform in an *environment altogether changed* by the results of the general election. (2) It permits overt partisanship of the returning officer. Under the present system, these officials are not civil servants, but partisans serving their party in an administrative fashion during an election. Deprived of the vote, they are reminded of the responsibilities of their peculiar position – that of known partisans who are expected to act fairly, or in a nonpartisan manner. Armed with the vote, like everyone else, they confront one less restraint on their partisanship.

Where do rights logic and the *Oakes* test take Beaudoin on the wholesale denial of the vote to inmates in penal institutions in federal elections? He believes that the courts ought to assert the right of such inmates to vote. Again he is influenced by the universal language of the Charter ("every citizen") and by the Supreme Court's caution about limits, particularly the idea of proportionality, to which, as he points out, the outright denial of a right does not conform (Beaudoin and Ratushny 1989, 279). Presumably he has in mind the fact that prisoners are convicted of a wide variety of crimes, some less loathsome than others, although the implications that result from this idea are unclear.

Perhaps the most telling hint of Beaudoin's thinking is the way in which he formulates the general question: "Are the reasons which justify depriving prisoners of their freedom applicable to voting rights?" (Beaudoin and Ratushny 1989, 277). His answer is "no." Denial of the vote is not a justifiable punishment; incarceration is. The implication is that individuals who are not free should nevertheless exercise one of the greatest freedoms, which is a peculiar idea and possible to arrive at only by thinking about rights separately and serially – the way they appear, say, in the Charter. Otherwise, how is it possible to suppose that an individual whose free speech is constrained should vote? In contrast to the new rights logic, the Western tradition, heavily influenced by classical thought, holds that free speech and free association are the very ground of politics, itself constituted by equals talking. In *Jolivet v. Canada*, the British Columbia Supreme Court made the same point, stating that by definition prisoners who vote are not making a free choice or engaging in a democratic act (Boyer 1987, 392).

Beaudoin resists this argument, responding instead that the presence of electronic media solves the information problem and that in any event many free citizens decline to participate in politics. Lynn Smith, another critic of the *Jolivet* opinion (she finds it "somewhat startling"), makes the same pair of points. The electronic media, she writes, relay as much information about politics to prisoners as they do to anyone else. She adds: "Prisoners could even be said to be in a better position with more time to read, listen or watch" (1984, 381). No doubt. Like Beaudoin, she misses the point of *Jolivet* altogether because, again like Beaudoin, conceptually she dissociates political rights from politics.

The *Canada Elections Act* also forbids mental patients to vote – those who, "by reason of mental disease," are confined or are deprived of the management of their estate. Beaudoin declines to take a position on this category of individuals, although he is concerned about the lack of precise criteria to determine mental illness and cites with approval the view of Mr. Justice James McRuer that the extent of the illness, not the facts of confinement or external property management, is the proper test to apply to the right to vote (Beaudoin and Ratushny 1989, 279).

In *Canadian Disability Rights Council* (1988), Madam Justice Reed clearly states that "a requirement of mental competence or judgmental capacity" might well be a proper limitation of the right to vote. But she found the phrase "mental disease" that is used in the *Canada Elections Act* too broadly framed and therefore apt to produce arbitrary and discriminating results. For example, it might include "individuals who might suffer from a personality disorder which impairs their judgment in one aspect of their life only" (269). As a result, she ruled that the mental disease provision is contrary to the Charter, and the federal government immediately directed that arrangements be made to enable some of the individuals contemplated by the provision to vote in the November 1988 federal election.

Setting aside technical arguments about the reach and vagueness of the concept of mental disease – arguments subject to the *Oakes* test – the real question turns on the validity of the idea of a rational capacity to vote. Is it possible to determine what constitutes a minimum rational capacity in this respect? And even if it is, should that be made a requirement of the right to vote? Lynn Smith argues against such a requirement on the ground that it would disenfranchise all kinds of people who, for a variety of reasons such as geographic isolation, age and disinterest, decline to participate at all in politics (1984, 381–82). But her argument sets up a straw man, namely, an "ability to participate in the electoral process." In liberal societies, citizens are free to judge politicians by the use of the ballot – quite an effective tool. They are not required to engage in politics themselves, and in fact most do not, preferring instead to watch it whenever they can take time from their busy private lives. Thus, while a minimum rational capacity has nothing to do with engaging in politics, it might relate to responsibility.

Undoubtedly it is difficult to determine minimum rational capacity, although surely it has to do with holding an individual responsible for assessing his or her own self-interest. It is another thing altogether to abandon all conceivable standards of rationality in relation to the right to vote, because to do so cuts at the heart of the idea of individual responsibility, which is a very important part of democratic politics. It also devalues the right to vote itself.

TRADITIONAL JUSTIFICATIONS OF THE VOTE

As a mode of analysis, rights logic treats individuals as rights-bearing creatures abstracted from their environment. When a particular right is at issue, such as the right to vote, the analysis focuses on the distribution of the right among individuals rather than on the activity to which it relates. In other words, if individuals are rights bearers, then they are not equal to others, nor are they "whole," unless they bear all of the designated rights, and it is a grave matter to deny them any rights. The quality or purpose of the related activity is a secondary consideration.

Modern rights analysts, particularly lawyers, have no need to defend a concept such as the right to vote. Their task is to see that as many people as possible have the opportunity to exercise the right. In 17th-century England, however, royalist and commonwealth opponents were engaged in a fierce struggle over the very foundation of authority in the political system – did authority lie with the king or with the people? Which was sovereign? The arguments that were made then and subsequently in defence of the right of citizens to choose their governors are useful because they throw a different light on the voter disqualification issue, or at the very least suggest alternative considerations.

Consent and Obligation

The Levellers, a group that included soldiers who fought for Oliver Cromwell as well as tradesmen and peasant farmers, pressed for a radically republican government to replace the monarchy. They contended that government must be based on the consent of the governed, consent taking the form of the popular election of members of the legislature. One of their two principal arguments was that consent was the condition of the political obligation of free men. Men could not be asked to live under laws, the authors of which they had not chosen.

The other argument was the idea of the natural equality of men, which was not, however, considered the same as an equality of right. The Levellers obviously adhered to a rough notion of citizens' equality. Nonetheless, in *An Agreement of the Free People of England* (1649), a tract setting out a constitutional plan, they proposed a manhood suffrage confined to those "not being servants, or receiving alms, or having served the late King in Arms or voluntary Contributions" (The Levellers 1944, 321). They considered private property an essential condition of personal independence and a defence against corruption by political opponents and therefore a requirement of the exercise of a free vote. People without property – women, beggars, the unemployed – could not be expected to make independent judgements.

The idea that people who are wrongly denied the vote have no moral obligation to obey the laws is relevant to the situation of prisoners and the mentally handicapped. Taken alone, it is an argument for permitting prisoners to vote, since society certainly wants them to feel morally obligated to obey the laws when they leave prison and will hold them responsible for this whether or not the prisoners themselves feel the same way. Would society want to hold mentally handicapped individuals who vote fully responsible in the event that they were found to have broken the law? Is their moral obligation the same even if their capacity is different? If it is answered that their moral obligation is not the same, then what do their votes signify?

Natural Right

Natural right theory offers a different defence of the right to vote. It is argued that the natural rights of individuals derive from their natural equality. Yet how is it that individuals are natural equals, when at first glance they appear to be so radically unequal? The answer offered by both Locke and Rousseau is that individuals are free and equal in the state of nature. They become unfree and unequal (unless government is constituted properly) in civil society. To my mind, the state of nature is an abstraction, and so it is necessary to think of individuals in the abstract as free and equal in order to follow a theory that Tom Paine, the great pamphleteer of the American Revolution, did so much to popularize.

In the *Rights of Man: Being an Answer to Mr Burke's Attack on the French Revolution* (1791–92), Paine explained that natural rights are the foundation of civil rights. Natural rights (for example, intellectual rights) "appertain to man in right of his existence"; civil rights (for example, rights to security and protection) arise out of his membership in society. Paine's civil rights are not hostages to the whims of legislatures. They grow out of natural rights. In his words, every civil right is a natural right exchanged (1942, 37ff.). In *Common Sense* (1776), his hypothetical account of the origin of government, he suggests that members of a small settlement meet to make rules for themselves and that each has a natural right to attend the meeting. When population size makes this impossible, they elect representatives. Therefore the vote, a civil right in large and settled societies, is derived from a natural right in very small and young societies (1942, 2–4).

Natural rights theory seems more favourable to the claims to vote of prisoners and the mentally handicapped than the consent argument. If the vote is a civil right that is based on a natural right, then it has a kind of pre-political status and cannot be extinguished by governments established to preserve rights generally. In the case of prisoners it can be argued that disqualification means suspending the right to vote rather than extinguishing it, since it is immediately repossessed when they return to civil society. But this does not seem to apply to the mentally handicapped. Prior to the 1988 election, many in this category were not only forbidden to vote, they could *never* hope to vote. Thus the issue of mental capacity looms, and natural rights theory, in all its generality and abstractness, yields nothing on this point other than a predilection for expanding rather than contracting rights.

Utilitarianism

Utilitarianism began with Jeremy Bentham who, in *Anarchical Fallacies: Being an Examination of the Declarations of Rights Issued During the French Revolution* (1795), dismissed the language of natural rights as "rhetorical nonsense – nonsense upon stilts."[4] Since he did not believe in natural rights, how did he justify representative democracy?

Bentham made two observations about human nature: individuals prefer their own interests to those of others; and they are most likely to be the best judge of their interests. If these observations are accepted, then it follows, as Bentham held, that the happiness of one individual should count as much as that of another. People are equal insofar as they pursue pleasure and avoid pain. He held further that the proper end of government is the greatest happiness of the greatest number and that the form of government most likely to maximize happiness is one in which citizens choose their legislators. These representatives could be made especially keen to pursue the public interest, which is the sum of individuals' interests, if, as Bentham advocated, there were annual elections (1962, vol. 1, 1–4).

Even this hopelessly inadequate sketch of Bentham's principle of utility as applied to representation places the issue of voter disqualification in a different light. Bentham's standard for judging government is the greatest happiness of the greatest number, not whether it is legitimate because it is based on consent. He supposes individuals know their own interests best and therefore will assess shrewdly candidates seeking their support in elections. But he concedes that they may miscalculate from lack of information or from misinformation, or that they may be so ignorant of their interests that it is better for others to take on the responsibility. In this doctrine, then, the factor of capacity to judge one's interests so that life yields pleasures rather than pains is crucial, and a discussion of the mentally handicapped and voting would take it into account.

How does the claim of prisoners to the right to vote fare in relation to the greatest happiness of the greatest number? Not too well under Bentham, the architect of the famous "panopticon," a prison of circular design featuring a central tower from which to inspect the inmates. Bentham, who held that a primary responsibility of government was to secure private property rights, was much interested in criminal activity and in the fact that it was engaged in largely by poorer people and often against private property. In a sense he believed in what is now called rehabilitation, except that his version of it amounted to teaching criminals and would-be criminals how to calculate rationally their interests. The process of rational calculation would show that illegal behaviour yields pain, not pleasure. From this standpoint, denial of the vote is yet another penalty designed to show that criminal behaviour is not rational because it does not maximize pleasure.

Democratic Citizenship

Both Alexis de Tocqueville and John Stuart Mill drew attention to yet another aspect of the vote, namely, its function in relation to democratic citizenship. Tocqueville, perhaps the greatest student of American government, considered democracy in America a grand experiment in the attempt to construct society on the basis of "theories hitherto unknown, or deemed impracticable" (1945, 26). He was not an uncritical student, as is indicated by his warning about the "tyranny of the majority," which he considered the source of the greatest danger to American government (ibid., 278–80). And yet the American experiment gave him reason to be optimistic about the effect of democratic institutions on the cultivation of good citizenship.

In a discussion of public spirit in *Democracy in America* (1835–40), Tocqueville distinguishes between unreflective love of country and a "patriotism of reflection"; he argues that only the latter obtains in America. While it is a calculating patriotism, and for that reason less likable than the other kind, it has advantages: "It springs from knowledge; it is nurtured by the laws; it grows by the exercise of civil rights; and, in the end, it is confounded with the personal interests of the citizens" (1945, 251). A rational patriotism, then, is the mechanism to unite private with public interest in the democracies of the new world, the democracies of immigrants who, merely by emigrating, leave behind the older patriotism. And it is generated by the distribution of political rights. "I maintain," Tocqueville writes, "that the most powerful and perhaps the only means that we still possess of interesting men in the welfare of their country is to make them partakers in the government" (ibid., 252).

All men? Tocqueville was fascinated by the fact that in America the franchise was so broadly based that the poorer classes voted – although slaves, servants and paupers supported by the local governments, he noted carefully, did not – and he was deeply interested in how they chose to exercise their vote. His observations must have reassured his readers:

> It is incontestable that the people frequently conduct public business very badly; but it is impossible that the lower orders should take a part in public business without extending the circle of their ideas and quitting the ordinary routine of their thoughts. The humblest individual who cooperates in the government of society acquires a certain degree of self-respect; and as he possesses authority, he can command the services of minds more enlightened than his own. (1945, 260–61)

But he had a prudent lesson for them as well:

> I do not say it is easy to teach men how to exercise political rights, but I maintain that, when it is possible, the effects which result from it are highly important; and I add that, if there ever was a time at which such an attempt ought to be made, that time is now. Do you not see that religious belief is shaken and the divine notion of right is declining, that morality is debased and the notion of moral right is therefore fading away? Argument is substituted for faith, and calculation for the impulses of sentiment. If, in the midst of this general disruption, you do not succeed in connecting the notion of right with that of private interest, which is the only immutable point in the human heart, what means will you have of governing the world except by fear? (ibid., 255)

One of Tocqueville's readers was J.S. Mill, who regarded *Democracy in America* as the finest analysis written on the advantages and disadvantages of modern popular government. He was persuaded by Tocqueville that the effects of political participation on the participants are at least as important as the more abstract considerations of consent or equal rights or utility. Thus Mill argued that the franchise ought to be extended (to include women, for example), in part because it would encourage citizens to develop an interest in public life and to educate themselves accordingly. But Mill recognized that this could not happen overnight, and that in the meantime, there was the danger that ignorance would drown intelligence. As a result, Mill, who had no trouble determining minimum intellectual requirements, recommended that the illiterate and those unable to make elementary calculations be forbidden to vote. The same for the poor who paid no taxes, since they could have no personal stake in the expenditure of public funds.

In addition, Mill recommended an electoral system designed to maximize the voting weight of those of superior intellectual ability and general accomplishment. It included giving them extra votes and abolishing geographic constituencies in favour of a country-wide system of proportional representation. Mill was alert to the fact that the constituency system can silence the same (intellectual) minority right across the country.[5]

Contemporary ideas about the rehabilitative effects of the vote on prisoners logically stem from the view that popular participation in the conduct of public affairs, however minimal, stimulates citizen virtue or public spiritedness. The question, then, is not whether voting would convert the odd prisoner to the practice of public virtue. It is the effect of the prisoner's vote on everyone else. Tocqueville writes: "In America, the lowest classes have conceived a very high notion of political rights, because they exercise those rights; and they refrain from attacking the rights of others in order that their own may not be violated" (1945, 254). The unstated premise of the sentence, unstated because it is the message of a two-volume work, is that democracy in America is real – it matters. Tocqueville's subjects do not value rights that have no meaning or consequences. They obey the law, he says, because they help to make it. Would they obey it and love it more if those who break it help to remake it? I think not, at least not if his observations are correct.

Mill's belief in the self-educative effects of the vote, on the other hand, is a stepping-stone to a more ambitious objective, which is to raise the tone of popular politics by enabling intelligent minorities to make an imprint on the heavy weight of majority opinion. This is possible only under an electoral system, like proportional representation, that represents minority opinions as well as majority opinion and represents the variety of minority opinions. Mill aimed at a representative body, the members of which reflect the many points of view in society. He assumed that voters make rational decisions, choosing representatives who share their views about politics. It is an assumption that leads to odd consequences in the case of prisoners who continue to prefer a life of crime. It simply excludes mental patients.

THE VOTE AND REPRESENTATION

As long as the vote is considered simply a right, then under an equal rights doctrine there are not many yardsticks available to defend exceptions to it. On the other hand, once the effect of the vote on those who exercise it is taken into account, the vote itself is no longer a discrete phenomenon. It is an important but dependent element in the system of representation. Some systems require a more active citizenry than others, for example, those with a more fluid and competitive party system. Paine, Bentham, Mill and Tocqueville all wrote before the advent of the disciplined party system as we know it, and it is partly because of this that their writings evoke the image of citizens who engage in political discussion as equals and who know their own interests.

Moreover, the effectiveness of the vote from the point of view of the voter will vary from system to system. In Tocqueville's America, the vote is effective because it is ubiquitous. Elective offices abound. In Mill's ideal universe, it is effective because it is deadly accurate. Ultimately each voter's opinion about politics is mirrored in the representative assembly. Since many opinions are represented, many opinions count. In Canada, by contrast, doubts are expressed about the utility of the vote precisely because of its perceived lack of effectiveness. As indicated earlier, this is often attributed to the combined effect of a disciplined party system and a constituency-based electoral system, which leaves too many voters feeling unrepresented. The feminist critique is particularly severe because it goes to the very heart of the concept of representation. Certainly the idea that men cannot represent "women's interests" is a denial of the possibility of virtual representation, to say nothing about its legitimacy. What, then, is the dilemma of representation?

Rousseau and the Representation Dilemma

It seems indelicate to use Rousseau to probe the issue of representation in this context, since he is despised by feminists for defining woman exclusively in terms of her sexual and procreative function and concluding that she is properly subject to man, just as the will is properly subject to reason (Okin 1979, 99–194). Nonetheless, in his attack on representation, Rousseau more than any other theorist has helped maintain the ideal of the small republic in the modern mass society.

In his *Contrat social* (1762), Rousseau offers a defence of popular government and instruction on how to establish one. At the conclusion of Book I, he says that when men choose to establish civil society, they convert their natural freedom and independence in the state of nature to a moral and lawful equality, "so that however unequal in strength and intelligence, men become equal by covenant and by right" (1968, 68). As equals, they are sovereign together, and the general will is the expression of their sovereignty. The general will is the pure expression of their decisions about the common good. Rousseau says that sovereignty cannot be alienated and therefore that the sovereign can never be represented by anyone except itself. In other words, sovereign equals can never delegate their general will to a third party, only the power to carry out that will (ibid., 69–70). Why does he insist on this point? Does he mean that the human will is so complicated that it can never be understood and represented to effect? Not at all.

Rousseau is aware that citizens also possess private wills and, if left to their own devices, will exercise them in pursuit of their own interests at the expense of the common good. His argument is that in a properly constituted republic, their regard for and opportunity to act for the common good can be expanded and their pursuit of their particular goods proportionately decreased. One way is to put the policy issue to the assembled citizens in the right way. They are not asked if a given policy would benefit them personally, but whether it would promote the common good. Another is to ban representatives and the corrupt institutions that follow in their wake, namely, factions and parties, because invariably "the will of each of these groups will become general in relation to its own members and private in relation to the state" (1968, 73). Citizens must decide for themselves, undistracted by the claims of rival parties.

It follows on this account of politics that parties are corrupt by definition because they appeal to the self-interest of a part of the whole. In effect, they always represent the wrong thing. A feminist party, then, would be just as corrupt as any other, in fact more so, since it would make no pretence of pursuing the common good.

Rousseau's detractors often portray him as a naïve idealist, and yet nothing could be further from the truth. He had very little faith in human nature, which is one reason why he worked out the strict requirements of republican government mentioned above. There are others, the most important of which is the small size of the state. It must be small enough so that its citizens can assemble in one spot and know each other's characters. Aristotle made the same point, and it is the one that has put the small republic ideal beyond the grasp of democrats in the mass age. And so, Rousseau writes (the sarcasm palpable), they have had to settle for an inferior substitute, representation:

> The cooling-off of patriotism, the activity of private interest, the vastness of states, conquests, the abuse of government – all these have suggested the expedient of having deputies or representatives of the people in the assemblies of the nation. This is what in certain countries they dare to call the third estate – the private interest of two classes being there given first and second place, and the public interest only third place ... The English people believes itself to be free; it is gravely mistaken; it is free only during the election of Members of Parliament; as soon as the Members are elected, the people is enslaved;

it is nothing. In the brief moments of its freedom, the English people makes such a use of that freedom that it deserves to lose it. (1968, 141)

The Federalist and the Opportunity of Representation

The Federalist papers initially appeared in the fall of 1787 as a series of newspaper articles written by James Madison, Alexander Hamilton and John Jay in defence of the constitution drafted at Philadelphia. In No. 14, Madison takes aim at theorists like Rousseau who seemed to have persuaded people that republics had to be the size of city-states, arguing that the theorists failed to distinguish between democracies, in which citizens rule themselves, and republics. Democracies must be small enough to enable the citizens to assemble to conduct public business, but republics, on account of the "mechanical power" of the principle of representation, can be very large (1937, 81). Europe discovered representation, but the United States was the first to use it to combine elective office with large size. Thus Madison attempts to placate the democrats who fear that large nations invariably tend toward oligarchy, or worse, monarchy.

On the other side are the conservatives who are all too aware of the violent and short histories of the city-states of Greece and Italy, and they are not at all partial to popular government. In *Federalist* No. 9, Hamilton responds to their fears by citing some of the new principles of political science – one of which is the Janus-faced principle of representation – which temper the excesses (demagoguery) and imperfections (mob rule) of popular government (Madison et al. 1937, 48–49). In No. 10, however, Madison delivers the coup de grâce on this score. There he argues that the real problem of popular government is the control of faction, which is a number of citizens who form a minority or majority and who are driven by "some common impulse of passion, or of interest, adverse to the rights of other citizens, or to the permanent and aggregate interests of the community" (ibid., 54). Since faction is rooted in human nature, the only remedy open to a free society is to control its effects. Again the levers are representation and large size. Representation is particularly important against a majority faction which, after all, can lay claim to the principle of majority rule. Madison explains how it works:

> The effect ... is ... to refine and enlarge the public views, by passing them through the medium of a chosen body of citizens, whose wisdom may best discern the true interest of their country, and whose patriotism and love of justice will be least likely to sacrifice it to temporary or partial considerations. Under such a regulation, it may well happen

> that the public voice, pronounced by the representatives of the peo-
> ple, will be more consonant to the public good than if pronounced by
> the people themselves, convened for the purpose. (1937, 59)

The moderating effect of representation is intensified by the factor
of large size. The larger the population, the more able and competitive
the candidates for public office and the less likely they are to get away
with chicanery. But large size is also a factor in its own right. Again,
Madison explains: "Extend the sphere and you take in a greater variety of parties and interests; you make it less probable that a majority of
the whole will have a common motive to invade the rights of other citizens; or if such a common motive exists, it will be more difficult for all
who feel it to discover their own strength, and to act in unison with
each other" (1937, 61).

It is hard to imagine two more opposing views of representation
than those of Rousseau and the two American federalists. Rousseau
regards it as a lower-order form of popular government; they extol it
as the key to popular government in large states. He considers it a sign
of the corruption of the republic, the triumph of private will over public virtue; they consider it a remedy for the otherwise unavoidable
excesses and corruptions of democracies. But there is a point of agreement between them, made all the more striking, of course, by the fundamental difference in viewpoint. They both despise faction, or party.

As noted above, Madison, writing before the advent of the party system, refers to organized political groups that pursue objectives inimi-
cal to the rights of others and the general good of the whole. What does
he mean? He means that they pursue their own interests ahead of, and
even against, everyone else's, that they elevate the interest of a part
over that of the whole, or worse, mistake it for the good of the whole.
Rousseau sees in parties exactly the same phenomenon at work. They
appeal to individuals' self-interests, he argues, not to their opinion of
the good of the whole, which would include the good of their opponents.
Madison's remedy is a set of modern political institutions, like representation, that helps prevent any one party from becoming a permanent
majority that can defeat the minority at every turn. These institutions
ensure that parties remain fluid and shifting coalitions of interests, com-
bining and recombining on successive issues. Rousseau's very different remedy is to rid the republic of parties altogether. But he, more than
anyone, knows how difficult it is to establish a party-less republic, and
so, as a fall-back position, he too prefers many parties over a few parties: "If there are sectional associations, it is wise to multiply their number and to prevent inequality among them, as Solon, Numa and Servius

did. These are the only precautions which can ensure that the general will is always enlightened and the people protected from error" (Rousseau 1968, 73–74).

THE FORMS OF REPRESENTATION

The American federalists, not Rousseau, pointed to the future. Representation is the accepted basis of popular government in all nations, large and small. But parties are everywhere entrenched. This is an interesting development, because the 18th-century critique of them still touches a sensitive nerve. Parties have sought to respond, either by appealing to as many interests as possible (the brokerage model), or by making the claim that their policies are designed for the good of the whole (the programmatic model). But not everyone believes them. Business people do not believe that Marxist parties formulate policies with their best interests at heart. Union organizers doubt that brokerage parties can serve the interests of labour and capital and assume that in the end they will side with capital. And sometimes ordinary people just complain that parties do not represent them at all. So they blame "party politics," or they blame politicians for behaving like partisans. They rarely blame the institution of representation, and yet that is precisely the institution that stands in their way.

Rousseau is no help to them when he argues that elected representatives cannot represent the general will, that is, the people and the opinions about the public good they hold in common. How can they complain about their politicians not representing them if such a thing is impossible? According to him, their only alternative is to abandon representation altogether and rule themselves. But this brings them face to face with the problem of size. On the other hand, if they accept representation, then they confront Madison's argument about its purpose, which is to separate the people and their passions from the instruments of power. Madison supposes that people pursue their own self-interests, which they are in danger of mistaking for the interest of the whole. Only representatives, who by virtue of their election by the people are set at one remove from the people, are in a position to regard the interest of the whole, particularly if the country itself is large enough to encompass a multitude of competing interests. On this account, the institution of representation points to the practice of virtual representation.

In his "Speech to the Electors of Bristol" (1774), Edmund Burke argued the case for virtual representation, which is that elected officials are representatives simply by virtue of having been elected. Once elected, they must be free to use their own and usually better judgement in determining the issues that come before them. They have better judge-ment because they leave home and confront a variety of points of view in the capital (1960, 147–48). Today very few politicians defend this doctrine because they know that it is unpopular with voters. Nevertheless, it is rooted in the logic of Madison's observation that elections come between the electors and the elected. Left to their own devices, the two tend to go their separate ways, at least until the next election. The opposing doctrine of delegate representation resists this likelihood by requiring that representatives follow the instructions of their electors. They are conceived of as spokespersons with mandates, or mediums through which electors' demands are transmitted unal-loyed. Although the doctrine is flattering to voters, and at times of frus-tration they are inclined to promote it, it has never really taken hold. The reason is that it denies the distance between the electors and their representative, and therefore it denies outright the dignity of the rep-resentative.

The virtual and delegate doctrines focus on the function of the rep-resentative. A third idea of representation arises out of the assumption that identity is the basis of representation. The claim is made that a member of a self-defined group must be elected to represent it because only one of the group can understand and communicate its needs. There are three points to be made about this idea of "mirror" representation. (1) It has become increasingly popular in some quarters, a political con-sequence, one presumes, of the post-modern obsession with self-identity that has been going on for at least three decades. (2) It is silent on the question of function debated by the advocates of virtual and del-egate representation. Is the mirror representative expected to function as an independent or a delegate? Or does identity, in a kind of osmosis-like process, somehow dissolve that tension? And if it does, what does that suggest about the status of the voter? (3) There is the question of what the politically relevant identities might be. Ethnicity is an obvi-ous candidate and is well documented by psephologists. The so-called life-style identities appear somewhat more nebulous although, as Alan Cairns (1988) has pointed out, the ones that find themselves in the *Canadian Charter of Rights and Freedoms* gain a constitutional profile.

The three types of representation just reviewed are adaptations of Hannah Pitkin's classification and discussion in *The Concept of Representation*. Burke defined the independence-mandate debate in his Bristol speech in 1774, sometime before the appearance of political par-ties as we know them (a development on the horizon that, incidentally, he defended). As Pitkin explains, the debate has been complicated by the party system. She concludes, rightly in my view, that parties exhibit elements of both virtual and delegate representation (1967, 166). I would add the point that Canadian parties behave in ways that reflect all three kinds of representation, and in the remainder of this study I will consider what this means for the citizen as voter.

CONCLUSION

Representation and Citizen Virtue

In systems of representative government, there are few opportunities for ordinary citizens to perform acts of public virtue, that is, to serve the public in political life. This is a practical as well as a logical outcome of the system. It is logical, irrespective of whether one views the system as a corruption of republican government, as did Rousseau, or as a perfection of the republican idea, as did Madison. Either way, representation reserves the public and political life to politicians. This is a practical outcome: once they have been elevated above their peers, politicians have every reason to maintain their monopoly of the parts in the play. There seem to be very few walk-on roles, and should a person create one, he or she is usually and quickly asked to join the troupe.

From the standpoint of the voter, the consequence is a good deal of virtual representation – perhaps mostly that. In a large country that encompasses competing economic interests, the system of representation, particularly when combined with disciplined political parties, is sure to yield elected officials who are often acting like trustees. They rarely have uncontested or majority mandates from voters on specific issues. They are more likely to gain a minority mandate on the odd issue, but a minority mandate is an oxymoron as well as a political problem. Most of the time, they will find themselves facing a bewildering array of unpredictable problems on which few voters have or care to have an opinion at all. How, then, is the act of voting to be understood?

Representation and the Vote

Once it is understood that virtual representation generally carries the day, it is easy to see that political parties like to be seen to practise the other forms of representation as much as possible. If they can claim anything remotely resembling a mandate, they will. It is much easier to defend a position on the grounds that many people hold it than to defend it on its merits. The parties also practise mirror representation whenever possible. They will try to run "ethnic" candidates in "ethnic" neighbourhoods. They will run feminist candidates when they deem them to be vote getters. But the parties are circumscribed in their resort to the appeal of identity by the single-member plurality electoral system and the principle of majority rule. So long as self-defined groups remain minorities within constituencies, candidates selected from among them cannot make the group the basis of an appeal.

While Canadian politicians use the rhetoric of delegate and mirror representation as much as possible for reasons of convenience and legitimacy, in fact they practise virtual representation much of the time because it is impossible not to do so. As a result, voters are left in the position of having to rely on rhetoric for guidance on what might be expected in practice. They have to find in the forms of representation that are not practised some clues to the kind of representation that will be practised. In the end, and in addition to knowing their own interests, voters have to judge the character of candidates for office. It is an inescapable requirement of the politics of virtual representation, and it makes the task of voters very difficult. How much easier it would be if they could rely on mere identity, or on instructions to delegates.

While virtual representation requires that voters exercise good judgement, it also ensures that elections are serious and vitally important affairs. Because of the built-in unpredictability of the system, voters take big risks. But they are limited term risks, since competitive elections enforce real accountability. Bernard Crick ably makes this point:

> What is crucial to a free regime is not the likelihood that a government can be defeated every time it introduces unpopular legislation, but that it can be defeated at the polls and that it will submit itself to polls which will be fairly conducted. The competitive general election is as important as parliament – on that point Schumpeter was right. Governments are restrained as much by knowing that people know, roughly speaking, why they are making a decision, as they are by formal votes. Governments fear public opinion as it begins to crystallise in the form of the prospects for the next election. (1989, 76)

Representation and Voter Disqualification

To conceive of the vote as simply an equal right leads nowhere. Or, rather, it leads to the one democratic principle that contemporary rights theorists decline to appreciate, namely, the principle of majority rule. The majority decision-making rule is defensible only on the basis of the formal equality of citizens that is denoted by equal political rights.

Political activists like Tom Paine, who sought to extend the franchise, were compelled to defend the idea of political equality as a natural (empirically sound) and right principle before an unbelieving world. So equality looms large in Paine's account of matters. And yet there is nothing in his work to supply a single argument for extending the vote to prisoners or to those whose mental handicap is serious enough to require them to live in an institution. The same is true of J.S. Mill, who devoted considerable attention to the issue of gender equality and argued for the extension of the franchise to women. In fact, in Mill's case, mental capacity is used as a minimum standard of eligibility to vote. The point, then, is that the abstract notion of an equal right to vote gives no direction at all on the issue of voter disqualification. What does give direction is the background idea of right political conduct, of the way people ought to engage in politics, that a theorist has in mind. And this idea will drive the institutional arrangements that are recommended. Mill thought that politics ought to take the form of intelligent men and women engaged in intelligible debate. Unlike his conservative opponents, he happened to take an optimistic view of human potential in this respect.

In Canada, the fundamental institutional arrangements that support and shape the conduct of politics are those of representation and the party system. What kind of politics do they imply? Essentially there are only two answers to the question. One is the radical republican critique, and in my view no one has ever pressed it more brilliantly than Rousseau. But there is always the problem of small size, which continues to stand in the way of the small republic alternative. That leaves Madison's answer, also very brilliant, but perhaps not what people today expect to hear. Madison's analysis points to virtual representation. I have argued that his analysis is applicable to Canada and that it yields a basic but correct understanding of the Canadian conduct of politics. I have also argued that this same analysis in no way denigrates the Canadian voter or the importance of general elections. On the contrary, it shows that the voter's task is serious and difficult and that elections, always serious and important, are rather risky affairs.

The issue of voter disqualification should be determined entirely in relation to the right conduct of politics in representative regimes. This means encouraging the view that the vote is a serious responsibility of citizens. It means discouraging anything that would bring the vote into disrepute, or devalue it in citizens' eyes. It is likely that distributing the vote to prisoners would do precisely that. The vote is not a therapeutic technique available for prisoner rehabilitation. Prisoners are not equal to citizens because only free individuals are equals. If prisoners, who have been convicted of breaking the law and therefore the social contract, find themselves not free because they are incarcerated, that is their own responsibility. They will not be equals in freedom until they have served their sentence and are discharged. In the case of those who can choose to discharge their penalty by paying a fine, they are obviously free when they do so. It is true that inequities seem to arise in cases where a convicted individual has a choice of serving time or paying a fine. The poor cannot always exercise the choice. However, such an inequity is the responsibility of the legislators and judges who direct the justice system. It does not originate with the electoral system. Individuals convicted of a crime should regain the vote only when they have discharged their obligations to the state and therefore are no longer subject to the supervision of state authorities.

There is more. Elections are crucial institutions in systems that require political losers to respect political winners and require political winners to re-engage in the contest in the future. In between, the winners are entitled to promulgate some laws and to rely on their opponents to obey them. I think it is very foolish not to see that this requires an enormous degree of trust and civility among citizens. Agreeing to obey the law is an entrance requirement to the world of citizens and their politics.

It is wisest to assume, as Crick says governments do, that people know their own interests, roughly speaking, and that they make rational political choices based on the information available to them. It may well be the case that some of the mentally handicapped who are institutionalized and were forbidden previously to vote could have made such choices. Undoubtedly others could not. I would certainly recommend the use of a simple or minimum competency test, but it may well be that the questions about name and residence that are permitted now (or at least were used in the 1988 election) are sufficient to the purpose. If not, it might be enough to request additionally an expression of intent to vote – after all, people who get themselves to polling booths or request help to get there are expressing such intent by definition. I also think that the matter of political information is extremely important and that in institutions careful efforts must be made to provide it. Certainly Canadian electoral history suggests the need to be alert to the potential for the manipulation of voters in institutions. The assumption that must be made for all voters is that they make rational choices. It is an assumption that is required by the importance of the vote and the dignity of citizenship.

ABBREVIATIONS

B.C.L.R. (2d)	British Columbia Law Reports (Second Series)
F.T.R.	Federal Trial Reports
R.S.C.	Revised Statutes of Canada
S.C.	Supreme Court

S.C.R.   Supreme Court Reports

NOTES

1. Canada, Royal Commission (1990). This document is a summary that is based on briefs submitted to the Royal Commission on Electoral Reform and Party Financing and on testimony heard at the Commission's public hearings, 12 March to 13 June 1990.

2. Riker defines the paradox of voting as "the coexistence of coherent individual valuations and a collectively incoherent choice by majority rule" (Riker 1982, 1).

3. See Chief Justice Dickson's formulation of the test in *R. v. Oakes* (1986), quoted in Russell et al. (1989, 457–58).

4. Bentham is commenting on Article II of the Declaration of Rights, which states: "The end in view of every political association is the preservation of the natural and imprescriptible rights of man. These rights are liberty, property, security, and resistance to oppression" (1962, vol. 2, 501). His commentary covers every phrase, and when he arrives at the phrase "natural rights," he writes: "That which has no existence cannot be destroyed – that which cannot be destroyed cannot require anything to preserve it from destruction. *Natural rights* is simple nonsense; natural and imprescriptible rights, rhetorical nonsense, – nonsense upon stilts. But this rhetorical nonsense ends in the old strain of mischievous nonsense: for immediately a list of these pretended natural rights is given, and those are so expressed as to present to view legal rights. And of these rights, whatever they are, there is not, it seems, any one of which any government *can*, upon any occasion whatever, abrogate the smallest particle."

5. Mill did not expect proportional representation to produce a legislative assembly of the intelligentsia, but he did think it would help raise the assembly's calibre: "The natural tendency of representative government, as of modern civilisation, is towards collective mediocrity: and this tendency is increased by all reductions and extensions of the franchise, their effect being to place the principal power in the hands of classes more and more below the highest level of instruction in the community. But though the superior intellects and characters will necessarily be outnumbered, it makes a great difference whether or not they are heard" (1910, 265–66).

REFERENCES

Beaudoin, G.-A., and E. Ratushny, eds. 1989. *The Canadian Charter of Rights and Freedoms.* 2d ed. Toronto: Carswell.

Bentham, Jeremy. 1962. *The Works of Jeremy Bentham,* ed. John Bowring. Vol. 1, *Anarchical Fallacies.* Vol. 2, *An Introduction to the Principles of Morals and Legislation.* New York: Russell and Russell.

Boyer, J. Patrick. 1987. *Election Law in Canada*. Vol. 1. Toronto: Butterworths.

Brodie, Janine. 1985. *Women and Politics in Canada*. Toronto: McGraw-Hill Ryerson.

Burke, Edmund. 1960. "Speech to the Electors of Bristol," 1774, and "Appeal from the New to the Old Whigs," 1791. In *The Philosophy of Edmund Burke*, ed. L.I. Bredvold and R.G. Ross. Ann Arbor: University of Michigan Press.

Cairns, Alan. 1988. "Citizens (Outsiders) and Governments (Insiders) in Constitution-Making: The Case of Meech Lake." *Canadian Public Policy* 14:121–45.

Canada. *Canada Elections Act*, R.S.C. 1985, c. E-2.

Canada. Royal Commission on Electoral Reform and Party Financing. 1990. "Mentally Handicapped." Working document of the Royal Commission. Ottawa.

Canadian Disability Rights Council v. Canada (1988), 21 F.T.R. 268.

Crick, Bernard. 1989. "Republicanism, Liberalism and Capitalism: A Defence of Parliamentarianism." In *Democracy and the Capitalist State*, ed. Graeme Duncan. Cambridge: Cambridge University Press.

Jolivet v. Canada (1983), 48 B.C.L.R. (2d) 121 (S.C.).

Madison, James, Alexander Hamilton and John Jay. 1937. *The Federalist*. Introduction by E.M. Earle. New York: Random House.

Mill, J.S. 1910. *Representative Government*. In *John Stuart Mill: Utilitarianism; Liberty; Representative Government*. London: J.M. Dent and Sons.

Okin, Susan. 1979. *Women in Western Political Thought*. Princeton: Princeton University Press.

Paine, Thomas. 1942. *Basic Writings of Thomas Paine*. New York: Wiley Book.

Pateman, Carole. 1983. "Feminism and Democracy." In *Democratic Theory and Practice*, ed. Graeme Duncan. New York: Cambridge University Press.

Pitkin, Hannah. 1967. *The Concept of Representation*. Berkeley: University of California Press.

R. v. Oakes [1986] 1 S.C.R. 103.

Riker, William H. 1982. *Liberalism against Populism: A Confrontation Between the Theory of Democracy and the Theory of Social Choice*. San Francisco: W.H. Freeman.

Rousseau, Jean-Jacques. 1968. *The Social Contract*. Trans. Maurice Cranston. Harmondsworth: Penguin Books.

Russell, P., R. Knopff and T. Morton. 1989. *Federalism and the Charter*. Ottawa: Carleton University Press.

Smith, Lynn. 1984. "Charter Equality Rights: Some General Issues and Specific Applications in British Columbia to Elections, Juries and Illegitimacy." *UBC Law Review* 18:351–406.

The Levellers. 1944. In *The Leveller Tracts 1647–1653*, ed. William Haller and Godfrey Davies. New York: Columbia University Press.

Tocqueville, Alexis de. 1945. In *Democracy in America*, ed. Phillips Bradley. Vol. 1. New York: Random House.

Trofimenkoff, S., and A. Prentice, eds. 1977. *The Neglected Majority: Essays in Canadian Women's History*. Toronto: McClelland and Stewart.

2

VOTING RIGHTS FOR PRISON INMATES

Pierre Landreville
Lucie Lemonde

INTRODUCTION

THE RIGHT TO VOTE of prison inmates is one of the questions being examined by the Royal Commission on Electoral Reform and Party Financing. This study, carried out at the request of the Commission, explores the different aspects of this issue in the Canadian context.

Section 51(*e*) of the *Canada Elections Act* stipulates that "every person undergoing punishment as an inmate in any penal institution for the commission of any offence" is denied the right to vote (relevant sections of statutes discussed herein are given in the Appendix). Most provincial legislation contains similar provisions, although inmates in Quebec and Newfoundland are able to vote in provincial elections.

Section 3 of the *Canadian Charter of Rights and Freedoms* specifies that "every citizen of Canada has the right to vote in an election of members of the House of Commons or of a legislative assembly and to be qualified for membership therein." This right is stated in such absolute terms that a highly experienced commentator wrote, "one may accordingly wonder whether any exceptions can exist" (Beaudoin 1989, 273). Nor is it surprising that both the federal Act and the provincial acts have been challenged in court and that the decisions have often been inconsistent. Some people would like to see the *Canada Elections Act* changed to bring it more in line with the Charter.

Although the right to vote and the qualification for membership in legislative bodies, as stated in section 3 of the Charter, seem to constitute a single right, in the case of prison inmates it would appear preferable to consider them as two separate rights, allowing for them to be analysed separately. This study is confined to the voting rights of prison inmates, hereafter referred to as inmates.

The Importance of the Right to Vote in a Democracy

The right to vote is a fundamental right in a democracy. According to the Honourable James McRuer, former Chief Justice of Ontario, "in any truly democratic country, the right or power to vote should be included as a political right. In fact, it is the keystone in the arch of the modern system of political rights in this country" (Ontario, Royal Commission 1969, 1561). Similarly, Senator Gérald Beaudoin says, "After the right to life and liberty, it is one of the most fundamental rights" (1989, 268). In *Wesberry v. Sanders,* a frequently cited case, the United States Supreme Court wrote that no other right is as precious as the right to vote, because "[o]ther rights, even the most basic, are illusory if the right to vote is undermined" (1964, 17). In another case (*Reynolds* 1964, 533), the Court added that the right to vote freely guarantees the other rights and freedoms.

While control of its representatives by the people is one of the fundamental principles of the democratic system, the principle of political equality, that is, the equality of all citizens in choosing their representatives, is just as fundamental (Mayo 1960, 61–62).

Universal suffrage, the principle that gives all adult citizens the right to vote, is supported by several kinds of reasoning. Mayo points out (1960, 115–19) that universal suffrage may be seen as a fundamental right. The Charter unequivocally lends weight to this point of view in Canada. The principle of justice also supports universal suffrage: It is only fair and equitable that those who are subject to the laws (as well as the taxes) be able to participate in the appointment of those who decide the laws (and the taxes).

Self-protection is another reason for universal suffrage: "Any section of society is likely to have its opinions and interests overlooked and perhaps trampled upon unless it has the vote to ensure its share of the control of government and hence of policy" (Mayo 1960, 118). Minority or unpopular groups, therefore, should get or maintain their right to vote so they can make their political views known. There is always a danger that members of the majority or those in power may withdraw or withhold the right to vote from those who challenge authority, those who have different interests and views or those whom they see as bad citizens.

The Right to Vote of Prison Inmates

Universal suffrage came only gradually, after a long and difficult struggle. The right to vote was originally tied to property rights. Eventually, the modern and democratic trend was to broaden this right by abandoning traditional restrictions based on property, education, race and sex. The question for the Commission was whether the exclusion of judges, the mentally ill and prison inmates from voting is justified in any way.

The disenfranchisement of inmates has been justified for political, penal and practical reasons. Politically, some people argue that those who do not honour the social contract lose the right to participate in the government of the community. Anyone committing a serious offence is, therefore, morally unfit to vote. The penal reasons are linked to the objectives and principles of sentencing. Those who have committed a serious offence and have been imprisoned for it deserve the additional punishment of losing their right to vote. This penalty, others argue, helps protect society. The practical reasons relate to administrative, security or procedural issues. These include the enumeration process, the constituency in which an inmate would vote and the voting procedure itself.

The Structure of this Study

Our study centres on an analysis of the reasons for excluding inmates from voting. Before proceeding with this analysis, however, we review the current situation with respect to inmates and voting.

We begin by outlining the current situation in Canada, both from a constitutional perspective and in the light of specific federal and provincial legislation and their interpretation by the courts. We then address the situation in other countries. From these analyses, we are able to highlight the principal issues and determine where solutions may lie.

In the fourth section, we describe the selection operating in the penal system and provide a portrait of the individuals being excluded. Among these individuals are those who at some time (e.g., on election day) are in penitentiaries or provincial facilities. Although incomplete, this information represents the only existing reliable data. These data provide an overview of the characteristics of inmates, as well as their distribution among the provinces.

The next section deals with the rights and principles involved in the issue, concentrating on inmate rights, penal philosophy and prevailing correctional principles in Canada. We question whether the grounds for exclusion – political and penal – are compatible with philosophy and generally accepted principles. Finally, we recommend the principles that should be adopted.

THE SITUATION IN CANADA

After analysing the effects of including the right to vote as part of the Constitution, we present an overview of the situation in Canada, both federally and provincially. We identify the different legislative restrictions on inmate voting rights as well as how they have been interpreted by the courts.

The Constitution

When the Charter came into effect in 1982, the right to vote became a constitutional right. Section 3 states this right in absolute terms: "Every citizen of Canada has the right to vote." There are no restrictions. In the past, the right to vote was considered a political right; today, it is referred to as a fundamental or democratic right. In fact, section 3 is the first provision under the heading "Democratic Rights."

Because it is enshrined in the Charter, the right of all Canadian citizens to vote is no longer a statutory right, but a constitutional guarantee. It is no longer a privilege that may be granted or withdrawn by a legislature. Unlike some other rights (e.g., the rights to life and to liberty), the right to vote is considered so fundamental to our system of parliamentary democracy that it is not subject to the notwithstanding clause of section 33 of the Charter. Therefore, the federal and provincial governments cannot use legislation to suspend the right to vote, even temporarily. Only a constitutional amendment can set aside section 3.

Any limitation of section 3 that restricts the right of exercising the vote to certain categories of citizens, whether by statutory provision or administrative decision, must be examined in the light of section 1 of the Charter. Section 1 states that such limitations must be by enactment and that the rights and freedoms set out in the Charter are "subject only to such reasonable limits prescribed by law as can be demonstrably justified in a free and democratic society."

This statement raises the following question: "Is it reasonable in a free and democratic society to deprive inmates of the right to vote?" To answer this question, we must use the three-stage test defined by the Supreme Court of Canada in the *Oakes* (1986) decision. The author of the limitation, that is, the legislator, must first demonstrate clearly and convincingly that the request pursues an urgent and real interest of society and that this interest is sufficiently important to justify abolishing the right. If the objective is recognized, the next question is whether the means chosen to achieve it is in proportion. Is the limitation carefully drafted so as to attain the objective without being arbitrary, unreasonable or unfair? Furthermore, the means chosen must restrict the right as little as possible, and the impact of the restriction and the urgent and real interest of society must be in proportion.

This is a strict test. In the first cases in the United States that involved a limitation of the right to vote, the U.S. Supreme Court accepted as satisfactory that a legislature was pursuing a reasonable and rational interest (*Green* 1968; *Beacham* 1969). Later, the courts demanded proof of a "compelling interest" (*Kronlund* 1971; *Stephens* 1970). According to a number of authorities, the same approach should be taken in Canada because of the fundamental nature of the right to vote. Senator Beaudoin, for example, said, "We believe that very few exceptions to the right to vote can be justified under the criteria formulated in the *Oakes* decision" (1989, 273).

Does denying the right to vote to inmates in Canada satisfy an urgent and real objective? Does the absolute exclusion of this right, without distinction, meet the standard of proportionality? Excluding part of the population from voting because of their social status seems to violate the right to equality before and under the law, as guaranteed in section 15 of the Charter.

At the Federal Level

Legislation
Section 51(*e*) of the *Canada Elections Act* specifies that "every person undergoing punishment as an inmate in any penal institution for the commission of any offence" is denied the right to vote.

At first glance, this disenfranchisement does not appear to apply to people on probation or parole, since they are not detained in a "penal institution." The situation is less clear, however, in the case of people on day parole as defined in the *Parole Act*. Section 19 of the *Parole Act* states that people on day parole are continuing to serve their penitentiary sentences. According to section 21.2 of the same Act, these individuals generally stay either in community residential facilities (CRFs) managed by the Correctional Service or in community residential centres (CRCs), which are private facilities run under contract with the Correctional Service. According to the wording of section 51(*e*) of the *Canada Elections Act*, only those living in CRCs may vote, since these centres are not actually "penitentiary facilities."

It should also be noted that this exclusion from the right to vote applies only to people "undergoing punishment." Defendants awaiting trial are therefore entitled to vote in federal elections. According to the principle of the presumption of innocence, one does not punish a person who has not been convicted. To our knowledge, no mechanism allowing defendants to exercise their right to vote has been established in Canadian detention centres. The practice of not registering defendants on voters lists is therefore in direct contradiction of the

Act. To date, it has not been contested in the courts.[1]

The Canadian Bar Association, in its brief to the Royal Commission, noted a number of problems arising from this exclusion from the right to vote. First, section 51(e) of the Act is not clear on the status of inmates who, on polling day, are absent with authorization granted on a discretionary basis (i.e., either on supervised or unsupervised absence or on day parole). This ambiguity opens the door to arbitrary and inequitable application of the section. Second, the authors of the report point to the potential unfairness of the current exclusion to people who are in jail for failure to pay a fine. Those who can pay are able to vote, whereas those who cannot pay are denied the right to vote.

A number of other factors were raised before the Commission: the disparity of sentences imposed; the variety of offences that could lead to exclusion; and the disproportion between the number of crimes committed and the number of people charged, convicted and imprisoned. We return to these factors in our analysis of the individuals affected by exclusion.

Jurisprudence

The constitutionality of section 51(e) of the *Canada Elections Act* has often been challenged before the Canadian courts. In all the decided cases, the courts concluded that section 51(e) of the Act [formerly section 14(4)(e)] violates section 3 of the Charter. The discussions dealt mostly with whether it is reasonable to limit an inmate's right to vote in a free and democratic society.

In *Jolivet v. R.*, the Honourable Mr. Justice Taylor wrote, "Since the disenfranchisement of convicted persons cannot be justified for the protection of society, it seems that any use of disenfranchisement for punitive purposes must be unconstitutional. The prospect of loss of voting rights is hardly likely to operate as a deterrent to the commission of criminal offences, and disenfranchisement holds no hope of reforming offenders" (1983, 7). Mr. Justice Taylor therefore rejected the principal arguments normally used to justify the disenfranchisement of inmates. Instead, he stated that excluding inmates because of moral unfitness or as an additional punishment was not a reasonable limit within the meaning of section 1 of the Charter. He did believe, however, that exclusion might be justified where the exercise of the right was rendered impossible because of practical difficulties. He concluded that this is the case because of the conditions of imprisonment. According to the Court, the right to vote implies the right to inform oneself for the purpose of making an informed choice, that is, to have access to public debate. Because freedom of expression and freedom of association are limited in prison, the exercise of this right to inform oneself is impossible. Inmates are unable to make an informed choice because they do not have access to sufficient information. Under these circumstances, it is reasonable for a legislature or Parliament to prohibit inmates from exercising their right to vote.

In another case, an inmate applied, on 28 August 1984, for an injunction asking the returning officer and the Solicitor General to allow him to vote in the federal election of 4 September 1984 (*Gould* 1984a). The Honourable Madam Justice Reed of the Federal Court, Trial Division, granted the request, stating that the exclusion in the *Canada Elections Act* was not a reasonable limit in a free and democratic society. She ruled that the security reasons presented did not justify the loss of the right to vote. The Quebec example – inmates in that province are entitled to vote in provincial elections – shows that the exercise of this right is possible from the point of view of security. Madam Justice Reed also rejected Mr. Justice Taylor's reasoning in *Jolivet* (1983), saying that the fact that inmates are restricted in some of their rights does not justify denying them all their rights. Finally, she said, the fact that several countries limit inmate voting does not constitute proof that it is a reasonable and justified limit. "It may be no more than a vestige of that period in our history when a convicted person lost all legal status" (ibid., 1127). This decision was later reversed on appeal – not on a question of substance, but on a question of procedure. In a majority decision, the Federal Court of Appeal ruled that this matter could not be decided by a request for an injunction but should be dealt with by an action for declaratory relief in view of the importance of the right involved (*Gould* 1984b, 1133). This position was upheld by the Supreme Court of Canada (Gould 1984c, 124).

A case in Ontario also challenged section 14(4)(*e*)[now section 51(*e*)]. In *Sauvé* (1989), the Court found that the exclusion of inmates from the right to vote withstood the test of proportionality of section 1 of the Charter. According to the Honourable Mr. Justice Van Camp, Parliament in a democratic society is justified in requiring those who vote to be responsible and decent citizens. The basis of any democratic system is voluntary respect for the law. The state has a duty to maintain the symbolic exclusion of criminals from the right to vote in order to reinforce the concept of responsible citizenship. This concept of the responsible voter has been accepted, both in law and in jurisprudence, since 1430. In fact, said the judge, the disqualification is imposed on those who by their conduct have chosen to disqualify themselves. Moreover, the disqualification is not excessively restrictive in relation to the objective sought: the right to vote is restored automatically when the inmate is released from prison, and there is no loss of citizenship rights during imprisonment.

Finally, a case in Manitoba attacked this exclusionary provision in *Badger v. Canada* (1988a). The Court of Queen's Bench concluded that section 14(4)(*e*) violated section 3 of the Charter and did not constitute a reasonable limit under section 1. As a remedy, the Court granted an injunction under section 24(1) of the Charter forcing the returning officer to prepare a list of those inmates entitled to vote and to provide them with the physical facilities needed to do so.

The Manitoba Court of Appeal unanimously reversed this decision (*Badger* 1988b). The Honourable Mr. Justice Monnin concluded that it was up to the elected members of Parliament and not to the courts to decide the qualifications for voting. In addition to the reasoning of Mr. Justice Van Camp in *Sauvé* (1989), Mr. Justice Monnin justified his decision by citing the concepts of the responsible and decent citizen and of the duty of the state to maintain the symbolic exclusion of criminals from the right to vote. Mr. Justice Monnin said that this was the practice in some provinces and in some countries, such as the United Kingdom, France, Greece and the United States.

In the opinion of the Honourable Mr. Justice Lyon of the Manitoba Court of Appeal, adopting section 3 of the Charter made the traditional basic right – the way it has been known and accepted by all Canadians for 120 years – part of the Constitution, subject to the statutory limitations and disqualifications that existed at the time the Charter came into effect. The intention was not to create a new right.

The Court of Appeal also criticized the remedy ordered by lower court, saying that it was totally new and not a matter for the courts to decide but for Parliament. According to the Court, the remedy was completely out of proportion to the infringement, if in fact there had been one.

In the recent case of *Belczowski* (1991), the Honourable Mr. Justice Strayer, at the end of an action for declaratory judgement, concluded that section 51(*e*) [formerly s. 14(4)(*e*)] of the Act violated the right guaranteed under section 3 of the Charter and did not constitute a reasonable restriction in the meaning of section 1 of the Charter. Consequently, the judge declared the provision invalid.

According to the judge, none of the justifications invoked by the government in support of restricting the right of inmates to vote passes the *Oakes* (1986) test. The first justification may be summarized as follows: the integrity of the democratic electoral process requires that participants be decent, responsible and law-abiding, which is not the case for criminals. The judge saw no evidence that this was Parliament's objective in adopting the Act. Furthermore, he thought it highly questionable that a state should be allowed to impose tests of "decency" or "responsibility" on voters. The only acceptable test is that of capacity, that is, maturity and mental condition. He made the following statement:

> It is arbitrary in singling out one category of presumably indecent or irresponsible citizens to deny them a right which they otherwise clearly have under s. 3. It is self-apparent that there are many indecent and irresponsible persons outside of prison who are entitled to vote and do vote; on rare occasions some even get elected to office. On the other hand there are many law-breakers who are never charged with offences, and a high percentage of those who are are never imprisoned. Those who have been identified among the indecent and irresponsible by a sentence of imprisonment do not necessarily become decent and responsible upon release, although their voting rights automatically arise again under the *Canada Elections Act*. I therefore do not find, in the effects of this provision, a clear indication of a legitimate objective of confining the vote to the "decent" and the "responsible", nor do I find that objective sufficiently meaningful or workable to sustain a direct and expressed deprivation of a right guaranteed under s. 3 of the Charter. (*Belczowski* 1991, 108)

The second justification invoked by the government was that the realities inherent in imprisonment prevent inmates from having access to sufficient information to be able to vote with full knowledge of the facts. The Court rejected this justification as well, saying that no proof had been submitted to this effect. The evidence of the plaintiff indicated that he was able to follow public events by watching television, reading newspapers and magazines, and so on, and the government submitted no counter-evidence.

Lastly, the government pleaded that the exclusion pursued the objective of "punishment." According to Mr. Justice Strayer, this objective is much more plausible and in itself not invalid. It is well accepted that the state may punish criminals. However, the method for attaining this objective – absolute exclusion and total negation of the right guaranteed under section 3 – does not meet the criterion of proportionality. The exclusion applies regardless of the gravity of the crime committed. It also leads to arbitrary application, since it depends on "fortuitous circumstances such as the timing of federal elections in relation to the period he happens to serve his sentence. Thus someone in prison for two weeks for nonpayment of parking fines could lose his vote for four years because his sentence happened to coincide with a federal election. On the other hand, someone sentenced to prison for five years ...

and released on parole after three and one-half years might never miss the opportunity to vote. Thus there is no necessary coordination between serving of a prison sentence and the actual loss of a right to vote" (*Belczowski* 1991, 110–11).

The Court added that this exclusion conflicts with Canadian penal objectives, which in the past 15 years have been directed toward rehabilitation and the preparation of inmates for successful reintegration into society. According to the Court, "[i]n this process the element of punishment is reduced in importance and the readjustment of the inmate to society is emphasized. Voting could form part of that readjustment" (*Belczowski* 1991, 111).

In all these cases, with the exceptions of *Gould* (1984c) and *Belczowski* (1991), the courts ruled that section 51(*e*) of the *Canada Elections Act* was a reasonable limit in a free and democratic society. They came to a diametrically opposed conclusion, however, in the cases dealing with different provincial exclusions. This jurisprudence is discussed at the end of this section.

Before closing this review, a few words about other exclusions in the *Canada Elections Act* are in order.

Section 14(4)(*f*) [now section 51(*f*)], which excluded some people from voting because of mental disease, was judged invalid in *Canadian Disability Rights Council v. Canada* (1988). According to Madam Justice Reed of the Federal Court, this provision does not stand up to analysis under section 1 of the Charter because it is too vague and arbitrary. The section does not refer to judgement capacity, which might constitute a valid objective, but instead links the ineligibility to vote to mental disease. Mental disease has not been defined and may cover various personality disorders that do not affect a person's judgement at all. "Every person who is restrained of his liberty of movement or deprived of the management of his property by reason of mental disease" is covered by the exception. Some people may be very affected mentally without being committed to an institution. This limit, therefore, is arbitrary, and the presumption of general incompetence must be rejected.

Similarly, section 14(4)(*d*) [now 51(*d*)], which excluded from voting "every judge appointed by the Governor in Council other than a citizenship judge appointed under the *Citizenship Act*," was declared invalid and inoperative in *Muldoon v. Canada* (1988). The plaintiffs argued that a secret ballot allows judges to remain objective and politically neutral. The exclusion of judges does not exist in several other democracies, including the United Kingdom, Ireland, Australia and the United States. The government agreed that section 14(4)(*d*) did not constitute a reasonable limit within the meaning of section 1 of the Charter. The Honourable

Mr. Justice Walsh declared section 14(4)(*d*) invalid, taking the time to say that if evidence had been presented, it could have been argued that limiting judges' right to vote removed all possible criticism of their complete political neutrality. Furthermore, one could also make a list of democratic countries that do not allow judges to vote. The example of the United States is not conclusive, since American judges are elected and are, therefore, partisan. The Court concluded by saying that the decision could have been in favour of either of the parties if there had been an actual challenge. Unlike the matter concerning the validity of the exclusion of prisoners, these decisions were not appealed.

At the Provincial Level

Legislation
The election acts of the different provinces and territories vary widely on the question of the voting rights of inmates. In two provinces, Quebec and Newfoundland, inmates are not excluded from voting. In Prince Edward Island, Nova Scotia, New Brunswick, Ontario, Manitoba, Saskatchewan, Alberta, the Northwest Territories and the Yukon, the exclusion is similar to that of the *Canada Elections Act*: it applies to individuals in penitentiary facilities. British Columbia is the only province where the exclusion is based on the nature of the offence committed: those convicted of treason or a criminal offence are prohibited from voting. Other small differences exist between the provinces and territories. Both the Yukon and Alberta exclude inmates awaiting sentencing or appeal from voting. In Saskatchewan, those under Lieutenant-Governor warrants are excluded.

The Quebec *Election Act* specifies that inmates in that province are entitled to vote in general elections. Special provisions cover enumerating and listing inmates on the voters list, counting votes in the constituency where the inmates lived before imprisonment, and establishing advance polling stations in all detention facilities. In Newfoundland, a similar system allows inmates to exercise their right to vote.

Jurisprudence
Lévesque v. Canada (Attorney General) (1985) dealt with the exercise of penitentiary inmates' right to vote in Quebec provincial elections. As we have seen, the Quebec *Election Act* allows them to vote, but penitentiary management refused to let them, citing reasons of security. Management prevented the returning officer from establishing voters lists and opening a polling station.

An inmate presented a request for a mandamus order to compel the Solicitor General of Canada and the prison director to respect his rights and the law. The Honourable Mr. Justice Rouleau of the Federal Court concluded that there had been a violation of section 3 of the Charter and that the management's restriction was not reasonable within the meaning of section 1: this restriction was not prescribed by law, as required by section 1 of the Charter, but was an administrative decision. The Court further said that the respondents had presented no valid proof in support of the importance of the pursued objective – security. Neither administrative convenience nor security justifies depriving people of the right to vote.

The government claimed that it was immune from any mandamus and that such a writ could not be issued to a minister. The Court stated that

> [T]he Charter has not only altered existing law, but also overturned it. Accordingly, since adoption of the Charter, and in particular sections 32 and 52 of the Charter, there is no longer any doubt that the Crown is subject to the provisions of the Charter in the same way as any other individual ...
>
> If the *Canadian Charter of Rights and Freedoms*, which is part of the Constitution of Canada, is the supreme law of the country, it applies to everyone, including the Crown or a Minister acting in his capacity as a representative of the Crown ... [They] cannot take refuge in any kind of declinatory exception or rule of immunity derived from the common law so as to avoid giving effect to the Charter. (*Lévesque* 1985, 296)

In a case in British Columbia (*Reynolds* 1983), it was decided that the exclusion provision was null and without effect to the extent that it applied to individuals on probation. In another case (*Maltby* 1982), the Court ruled that the right of an accused awaiting trial to vote had been violated because no provision had been made for him to exercise this right.

The inmate Badger (who would later use the Charter to argue against his disenfranchisement, as described earlier in this study) challenged the exclusion in the Manitoba *Elections Act*. The province argued that the exclusion was reasonable and justified by the urgent and real objective of symbolically preserving the stigma attached to individuals who have breached their duty as responsible citizens. In the opinion of the lower court, this was a valid objective and the first *Oakes* (1986) criterion had been met (*Badger* 1986a, 158). The absolute exclusion of all inmates, however, was not proportionate to the objective. The lower court found no rational connection between the denial of the right to vote and the inadvertent commission of an offence against a strict or prescribed responsibility. The Court of Appeal upheld this decision. A few hours before the election, however, the Court of Appeal refused to order the implementation of the electoral machinery necessary for the exercise of this right in the penitentiaries (*Badger* 1986b). The Honourable Mr. Justice Hall referred with assent to the decision of the British Columbia Court of Appeal in *Hoogbruin* (1985), which stated that the exclusion of inmates does not constitute a reasonable limit in a free and democratic society and that this right was subject only to obvious limits like age and mental capacity.

The exclusion in the Ontario *Election Act* was successfully challenged in *Grondin* (1988). The Ontario government argued that the need to exclude symbolically those who are hostile toward the community is sufficiently important to justify the denial of the right to vote. Moreover, the number of elections in which the individual would be unable to vote was determined by the length of imprisonment and was thus proportional to the seriousness of the offence. The Honourable Mr. Justice Bowlby of the Supreme Court of Ontario said that he was unable to accept these arguments. In his opinion, the Charter not only failed to stipulate the exclusion of inmates, as the Fourteenth Amendment to the U.S. Constitution does, but also considered this right so basic that it was not made subject to the notwithstanding clause of section 33. Being able to vote is potentially important to rehabilitation and is, therefore, a step toward reintegration into society. The Court referred to the report of the Canadian Sentencing Commission (1987), which states that the sentence must foster a sense of responsibility and the opportunity to become a productive and law-abiding member of society. Participation in the electoral process clearly promotes these objectives. The Court said,

> Punishment lies in confinement, but even with the most flagrant crime must exist hope of reform. This is the philosophy of our penal system ... What greater avenue to constructive thought and hope of change of those who have contemptuously violated our laws is inherent in an interest in our democratic process and how we best will be governed? ... The "prison bars" symbolize society's contempt for the breaking of the law; the ballot, the sunrise or birth of reform, at least, in part. (*Grondin* 1988, 432)

Discussion

Inmates are prevented from voting in federal elections by the exclusion contained in section 51(*e*) of the *Canada Elections Act*. This provision has resulted in the handing down of contradictory decisions. The recent decision in the *Belczowski* case in the Federal Court, Trial Division, which invalidated this exclusion, could be the basis for substantial administrative and legislative changes.

Moreover, the current provision could be arbitrarily and unreasonably applied to people who enjoy some form of anticipated freedom during their prison term: temporary release, partial release or parole. Some people could vote even if, theoretically, they are serving a sentence. The same situation prevails for those on probation.[2]

The rules concerning provincial elections differ from one province to the other. Currently, as a result of court decisions or the abolition of exclusions, inmates are entitled to vote in Quebec, Newfoundland, Ontario, British Columbia and Manitoba. Experience has shown that the Quebec system of advance polling stations works well, whereas the Ontario system of voting by proxy has caused problems.

Based on this overview of the jurisprudence concerning the constitutional validity of excluding inmates from voting, it is obvious that regional disparities exist and that the jurisprudence is both contradictory and inconsistent.

Virtually all of the decisions[3] have upheld the constitutional validity of the federal exclusion and struck down similar provisions in provincial election acts. The logic of this distinction is difficult to understand. Courts of the same level in Manitoba and Ontario have ruled that the denial of the right to vote in federal elections is both justified on the grounds that it is a reasonable limit in a free and democratic society and not justified on the grounds that it is not a reasonable limit in such a society.

The distinction is not based on the length of the sentence, which would have made some sense. Nor is it based on the place of imprisonment (i.e., a provincial prison or a federal penitentiary, depending on the length of the sentence). The right to vote is granted or denied to all inmates without exception according to the type of election involved.

The logic for this distinction must therefore be sought elsewhere. The only possible explanation is that the Canadian courts show greater deference to the federal Parliament than they do to the provincial legislatures. They are more likely to strike down provincial legislative provisions while upholding and not interfering with the legislative choices of the central government. The judges of the Manitoba Court of Appeal expressed this concern in the *Badger* (1988b) case when they stated that it was the responsibility of Parliament, and not of the courts, to set out the qualifications or disqualifications for voting. "In cases of this nature," said Mr. Justice Monnin, "courts must show considerable restraint.

It is better to maintain the status quo until Parliament has considered, debated and resolved this issue" (ibid., 227). This statement, as well as the deferential attitude, runs counter to the teachings of the Supreme Court of Canada on the constitutional duty of the courts to analyse the validity of the legal provisions challenged under the Charter and to declare inoperative those provisions that are inconsistent with it (*R. v. Big M Drug Mart* 1985, 295).

In the *Badger* (1988b) case, the position of Mr. Justice Lyon – that the intention of section 3 of the Charter was not to create a new right, but only to give constitutional force to the right to vote as it existed at the time the Charter was adopted, that is, with all the restrictions attached to it at the time – also runs counter to all the decisions of the Supreme Court dealing with the interpretation of the Charter (*R. v. Big M Drug Mart* 1985; *Reference re s. 94(2) of the Motor Vehicle Act (B.C.)* 1985; *Hunter* 1984).

An examination of the Canadian jurisprudence on this question reveals the weakness of the arguments given for the decisions and the absence of a consistent and satisfactory analytical approach. It must be said in defence of the courts, however, that they have frequently been required to produce their decisions very quickly because of the urgency of the situation and the approaching date of elections.

In the *Big M Drug Mart* (1985) case, the Supreme Court suggested a satisfactory method of analysis in constitutional matters to be used in the event of an apparent conflict between a legislative provision and a right guaranteed in the Charter.

First, one should determine the objective of the constitutional guarantee. In the case of the right to vote, a complete historical and political analysis of this right in our system of parliamentary democracy has to be carried out. Then, one must examine the purpose of the challenged law and its effects to see if they are incompatible with the Charter. At this stage, the courts should analyse the origin of the exclusion and its impact on the guaranteed right. In the case of the exclusion we are discussing, the examination is fairly easy, since the effect of the legislative restriction is to deprive completely certain categories of people of the right to vote guaranteed in section 3 of the Charter. Since the answer to this question is positive, the next question is whether this restriction constitutes a reasonable limit in the sense of section 1 of the Charter.

As we have seen, the courts arrived at different answers to this question in the various cases referred to them. Some ruled that the restriction had an urgent and real social objective, whereas others failed to see any such objective. The courts also disagreed on whether the end was in proportion to the means. The evidence presented by the government, with respect to both the objective and proportionality, was scanty: there was mention of the need for security and the need to preserve a symbolic exclusion without actually proving the need. In the *Gould* case, the Honourable Mr. Thurlow, Chief Justice of the Federal Court of Appeal, pointed to the weak evidence presented under section 1 of the Charter and concluded: "The impression I have of it is that when that is all that could be put before the Court to show a serious case, after four years of work on the question, it becomes apparent that the case for maintaining the validity of the disqualification as enacted can scarcely be regarded as a serious one" (1984b, 1137).

Finally, it is impossible to draw definitive conclusions from this inconsistent, contradictory and unconvincing jurisprudence. The fact that several courts have found the section 51(*e*) exclusion justifiable does not mean that the Supreme Court would take the same position. The recent decision by Mr. Justice Strayer in the *Belczowski* (1991) case shows that a more complete and detailed analysis of the issue can lead to a different result and to conclusions that will be difficult to ignore in the future because of the force of its argument.[4] This decision will therefore have to be taken seriously unless it is reversed on appeal or the law relating to inmate voting is modified. However, the inconsistency and contradictions in the jurisprudence, which now lead to discriminatory application of the right to vote or which may do so in the future, illustrate the need for legislative action to bring an end to the current uncertainty.

A LOOK AT OTHER COUNTRIES

Differences in Other Countries

Whether offenders or inmates are entitled to vote varies enormously from country to country. Some countries with democratic traditions, like Italy, Norway, Sweden, Denmark, Ireland and Israel, have no restrictions, whereas others, like France, the United Kingdom, Greece, Switzerland and West Germany, do. In England, the exclusion applies to people serving a prison sentence and to those found guilty of corruption or electoral fraud during the preceding five years. It is very difficult to draw any conclusions whatsoever from these examples, since each country has its own history and traditions. In reviewing the jurisprudence, the courts repeatedly affirmed that comparative law did not offer any conclusive help because the legislative approaches to this issue differ widely. It is impossible to state that exclusions exist in the less democratic countries or that there are no restrictions in the more liberal countries.

Australia

Australia is of special interest to Canada because of the similarity of our constitutional systems. In both countries, the central government determines the qualifications for voting in federal elections. Australian state elections, on the other hand, are the responsibility of each state; there is no uniformity between the different laws, just as in the Canadian provinces. Thus, the same individual could, in some cases, be able to vote in a specific state but not in Commonwealth elections. Unlike in Canada, however, an inmate would be able to vote in federal elections but would not be allowed to do so in state elections.

The Commonwealth

For federal elections, people convicted of an offence punishable by five years or more are disqualified from voting regardless of the length of the sentence received.[5] This provision was so difficult to apply that it seems that it is no longer used in its present form. The criterion currently in use is the length of the sentence effectively imposed (Fitzgerald and Zdenkowski 1987, 15).[6]

Calculating the length of multiple sentences presents other practical problems. It is also not clear whether disqualification extends to individuals on parole.

A recent amendment to the law enables inmates who are entitled to vote to vote by mail. They must request to be placed on a list provided for the purpose. Their votes are counted in the riding of their former address if they express the intention of returning there upon release. Another option is to become registered in the constituency where they were born. If neither of these solutions is applicable, the address is that of the "subdivision with which the person has the closest connection" (Australia, *Electoral and Referendum Amendment Act*, s. 35).

The States

New South Wales   In this state, inmates sentenced to more than 12 months are disqualified while they are in prison. Those inmates who are qualified may vote by mail. Few people make use of this provision, however, because they lack information about their rights (Fitzgerald and Zdenkowski 1987, 22).

Northern Territory   A legislative amendment in 1979 granted the right to vote to all inmates otherwise qualified to vote. Voting is again done by mail, with the constituency address being that of the prison. Problems arise because of the frequency of transfers.

Queensland   The law of this state stipulates that people sentenced to more than six months in prison are not entitled to vote.

South Australia   All inmates in this state are entitled to vote. They are entitled to choose their constituency: their previous or future address or that of the prison. The correctional services have prepared an information document, *Electoral Visitation*, on the right and the duty to vote, including the mechanisms for exercising this right.[7] (Voting is compulsory in Australia.)

Tasmania   Tasmania is the most restrictive state: it excludes all inmates, regardless of the length of their sentence.

Victoria   According to the law in force, persons convicted of treason or an offence punishable by five years or more are excluded from the right to vote. These criteria have caused the same problems in state elections as in the Commonwealth ones. Voting is done by mail.

Western Australia   People found guilty of treason or sentenced to more than a year are excluded from the right to vote. The law has been interpreted as including individuals on parole. Those who are entitled to vote do so by mail. Inmates are informed of this right, as well as their right to have their name reinstated on the voters list once they have served their sentence.

Conclusion
As in Canada, there are marked differences between the various federal and state laws in Australia. However, since the federal exclusion applies only to individuals serving a sentence of more than five years, many more inmates are entitled to vote in Australia than in Canada. These differences appear both in legislative provisions and in the administration of the exercise of this right.

A number of reports condemn the Australian exclusions: the 1973 *Criminal Law and Penal Methods Reform Committee of South Australia*, the 1978 *Royal Commission into New South Wales Prisons* and the 1986 *Joint Select Committee on Electoral Reform*. All of these reports have recommended the abolition of inmate disqualification (Fitzgerald and Zdenkowski 1987).

United States
The U.S. Constitution provides that the qualifications established by the different states for their own elections also apply in presidential and senatorial elections. As a result, voter qualifications vary according to the state of residence.

With respect to inmate voting rights, the laws vary considerably from one state to another. Some states have no disqualification. Others make a distinction according to the offence committed: individuals convicted of treason, of crimes involving the loss of civil rights (e.g., banishment), of electoral fraud or of a felony are not entitled to vote. Other states use the length of the sentence or the place of imprisonment, in a federal penitentiary for instance, as the criterion for disqualification. How long the inmates lose their voting rights also varies from state to state. In some, the exclusion is effective for the time of imprisonment; in others until the restoration of civil rights is ordered in accordance with the legislation in effect. Finally, in some states, convicted persons lose their right to vote for life: ex-inmates therefore do not have the right to vote in any election.

We should not blindly import the legal arrangements of our U.S. neighbours, because fundamental differences exist between the two systems. In the United States, the disqualification of convicted persons is provided for in the Fourteenth Amendment to the Constitution. In the U.S. states that have opted for exclusion, the laws are allowed and protected by the Constitution. This is not the case in Canada, where section 3 of the Charter grants the right to vote to all citizens, without exception.

INMATES AND THE PENAL PROCESS

In 1989–90, the average number of inmates in Canadian correctional facilities was 29 555. Of these, 11 415 were in federal establishments under the responsibility of Correctional Service Canada and 18 140 were in provincial institutions (Canada, Statistics Canada 1990b, 31). These numbers represent only a small fraction of individuals in the care of the correctional services and an even smaller fraction of those who commit crimes.

This section briefly shows how inmates are screened at several stages between being charged with an offence and imprisonment, and provides an overview of the inmate population.

Selection in the Corrections System

Penal law in general and criminal law in particular are means used to counter or control damaging, reprehensible or anti-social behaviour. Many of the most reprehensible behaviours – occupation of someone else's territory, large-scale pollution, physical elimination of opponents, disregard for basic rights, contempt for the life and health of workers, breaking of contracts, shameful manipulation of financial markets, and so on – are handled by military or economic sanctions, symbolic trials, treaties, subsidy policies, the insurance system, and civil or administrative law.

Many actions that are damaging, often including those committed by people in positions of authority, are not considered to be a matter for the criminal law. Likewise, many "criminal" actions are never brought to the attention of police or punished by imprisonment.

The Size of the "Black Number"

Crimes that are never reported to the police or officially recorded make up the difference between actual crime and apparent or reported crime. This hidden figure – sometimes referred to as the "black number" – is substantial. In 1982, the Department of the Solicitor General of Canada, with the help of Statistics Canada, conducted a survey on victims of criminal activities in seven large Canadian urban centres. According to the survey (Canada, Solicitor General 1984, 3), only 42 percent of crimes[8] were reported to police; the black number – incidents not reported – thus amounts to 58 percent.

In reality, the black number is much higher, because this kind of survey does not take into account offences of which the victims are unaware (fraud, pickpocketing, etc.). Nor does it count incidents, even very serious ones, that the victims believe do not warrant the involvement of the criminal system, such as family violence or violence involving acquaintances. Commercial and white-collar crimes, like theft or fraud in businesses, banks and the public sector, are also not represented in these surveys. Therefore, the hidden figure of unreported crime is more likely at least 65 percent. Only an estimated one-third of all offences are reported or recorded in crime statistics.

The Low Clearance Rate

In 1989, the police recorded almost 2.5 million (2 431 428) *Criminal Code* violations in Canada (table 2.1). Most of these (1 444 748) were property offences. Ten percent (248 992) were offences involving violence. The police resolved or "cleared" 36.7 percent of all cases; thus, 63 percent remained unsolved. A case may be cleared in one of two ways: the police lay a charge, that is, information is laid against at least one person; or the case is without charge. In the latter case, "the police cannot lay an information even though they feel that they have identified the offender and have enough evidence to support the laying of an information. This would happen, for example, if the victim refuses to sign a complaint, or if the alleged offender dies before he/she can be formally charged" (Canada, Statistics Canada 1990c, 17–18). Less than one-quarter (24.4 percent) of the offences are cleared as a result of a charge being laid, however. The statistics show that the rate of laying charges varies considerably between categories of offences: the rate for murder, for instance, is 75 percent, whereas that for break-and-enter is 13.8 percent.

Table 2.1
Criminal Code offences recorded by the police, in Canada, in 1989

| | | Offences cleared | |
| | Total offences N | Charges laid % | Without charge % |
Category of offence			
Violent offences			
Murder	657	75.0	14.1
Attempted murder	829	79.7	5.1
Assault	217 232	49.9	29.0
Robbery	25 709	30.6	4.7
Total violent offences	248 992	48.2	26.2
Property offences			
Break and enter	349 164	13.8	7.2
Theft – motor vehicle	100 336	14.8	7.4
Theft over $1 000	86 908	8.9	5.1
Theft under $1 000	758 935	14.9	7.7
Fraud	122 739	53.4	19.9
Total property offences	1 444 748	18.9	8.4
Other *Criminal Code* offences	35 640	27.3	15.3
Total *Criminal Code* offences	2 431 428	24.4	12.3

Source: Canada, Statistics Canada (1990c, 2.1–2.5).

Note: Table does not include traffic violations.

In the 24.4 percent of offences where an information was laid, charges were laid against 598 531 persons, of whom 179 668 (30 percent) were young offenders (i.e., under 18 years of age) (Canada, Statistics Canada 1990c, 2–5).

Breakdown of Sentences

Unfortunately, not all of the information on the penalties imposed by the courts in Canada since 1970 is currently available. The most recent series of complete data on sentences (excluding Alberta and Quebec) published by Statistics Canada covers 1973.

About 35–40 percent of persons convicted of criminal offences receive a prison sentence. Only about 10 percent of convictions for offences under the *Criminal Code* that are punishable on summary conviction result in prison sentences (see table 2.2).

In summary, since about one-third of criminal offences are reported and recorded, only one-quarter of these offences are cleared by laying

Table 2.2
Breakdown of sentences for *Criminal Code* offences in Canada, in 1973
(percentages)

	Supervised or unsupervised probation	Fine	Imprisonment
Persons convicted of criminal offences	29.3	34.3	36.4
Convictions for offences punishable on summary conviction	6.3	79.5	10.0

Source: Canada, Statistics Canada (1978).

Note: Table does not include sentences imposed in Quebec and Alberta.

charges, one-third of those charged are under 18 years of age and no more than one-quarter of adults charged are sentenced to prison, one could estimate that approximately 1 percent of *Criminal Code* violations result in imprisonment. This evaluation corresponds roughly to other estimates of approximately 7.5 million *Criminal Code* violations in Canada each year and about 75 000 admissions of people sentenced to penal institutions following a *Criminal Code* violation.

The Inmates
Section 731 of the *Criminal Code* provides that persons sentenced to imprisonment for two years or more must serve their sentence in a federal penitentiary. Persons sentenced to less than two years serve their sentence in a provincial prison. Although the responsibilities of each level of government are defined by law, an exchange of services is provided between the provinces and the federal government. These agreements apply especially to female inmates. In Quebec, for instance, most women serving prison sentences in excess of two years are held in provincial facilities.

There are two ways to analyse an inmate population: study *admissions* to the system; or study the nature of the population at any given time, which produces a population *profile*. The first approach tells us who is being sent to prison in Canada. The second approach can give us data about the characteristics of the prison population at a particular moment, such as during an election.

This study is particularly interested in the latter information.

Admissions to Canadian Prison Facilities
In 1989–90, 199 897 people were admitted to Canadian provincial institutions (Canada, Statistics Canada 1990b, 122). Most of these admissions (115 114) were for individuals serving sentences, while 84 783

were for individuals under remand warrant. These numbers refer to admissions, not individuals, since individuals may be admitted twice for the same incident if they are held in custody (before or during the trial), then released and readmitted after sentencing.

Admissions to Federal Facilities During the same period, 6 586 people were admitted to federal institutions (Canada, Statistics Canada 1990b, 31). These admissions have generally already been counted as admissions to the provincial system, since federal offenders are normally held in the provincial system (either before trial or while awaiting appeal) before they are transferred.

Of the 6 586 admissions in 1989–90, 65 percent (4 274) were admissions under a warrant of committal, 22 percent were admissions following the revoking of mandatory supervision and 6 percent were admissions following the revoking of parole. The rest were transfers from a provincial facility under a federal-provincial exchange-of-service agreement, or transfers from another country.

The length of sentence for those admitted to federal institutions under a warrant of committal was relatively stable during the 1980s (table 2.3). In 1989–90, more than 40 percent of the sentences were for less than three years; 3.5 percent were for life.

From 1980–81 to 1989–90, there were slight shifts in the types of

Table 2.3
Warrant of committal admissions to federal penitentiaries by length of aggregate sentence, 1980–81 to 1989–90
(percentages)

Aggregate sentence	1980– 1981	1981– 1982	1982– 1983	1983– 1984	1984– 1985	1985– 1986	1986– 1987	1987– 1988	1988– 1989	1989– 1990
Less than 2 years	2.5	2.1	2.1	2.3	3.8	2.9	4.1	4.0	4.1	4.3
2–3 years	36.9	36.9	37.5	37.3	35.1	37.5	38.3	37.0	37.2	36.9
3–4 years	24.0	25.2	23.7	24.0	22.8	23.2	22.4	22.4	23.2	24.4
4–5 years	11.5	11.5	11.4	11.2	12.3	11.2	11.1	11.6	11.3	12.0
5–10 years	17.1	15.8	16.3	16.3	17.7	17.7	16.8	16.8	16.5	15.5
10 years or more	3.5	3.8	3.8	3.8	4.0	3.1	3.4	4.0	4.0	3.3
Life	3.3	3.4	4.1	4.4	3.7	3.9	3.6	3.8	3.4	3.5
(N)	(3 055)	(3 671)	(4 036)	(4 059)	(3 956)	(4 076)	(3 741)	(3 988)	(4 011)	(4 274)

Source: Canada, Statistics Canada (1986, 185; 1990b, 138).

Table 2.4
**Warrant of committal admissions to federal penitentiaries by offence categories,
1980–81 to 1989–90**
(percentages)

Offence	1980–1981	1981–1982	1982–1983	1983–1984	1984–1985	1985–1986	1986–1987	1987–1988	1988–1989	1989–1990
Murder	9	8	10	10	9	9	10	9	8	8
Sexual offences	9	8	9	10	10	13	3*	12	14	13
Wounding, assault	3	3	4	4	4	5	14*	5	5	5
Robbery	28	28	26	25	26	22	23	22	20	20
Break and enter	19	19	20	21	21	20	20	20	18	17
Narcotic Control Act	9	8	7	7	7	8	9	11	12	14
Other	23	26	24	23	23	23	21	21	23	23
(N)	(3 055)	(3 671)	(4 036)	(4 059)	(3 956)	(4 076)	(3 741)	(3 988)	(4 011)	(4 274)

Source: Canada, Statistics Canada (1986, 185; 1990b, 137).

*Unreliable data.

offences for which individuals were admitted under a warrant of committal (see table 2.4). The admissions for murder dropped in the last two years; those for assault and battery, on the other hand, were on the rise. The most significant changes, however, can be observed in admissions for robbery, which dropped significantly, and in those under the *Narcotic Control Act*, which increased in the last few years. Because of the substantial legislative changes with respect to sexual offences, it is difficult to interpret the changes in this area.

In Canada, especially in some provinces, the high percentage of Aboriginal people in correctional facilities is a major concern in the administration of justice. The number of Aboriginal people from the Prairie provinces who were in federal institutions is striking (table 2.5).

Of the 4 274 federal admissions, 3 percent (128) were women. This percentage varied between 2 and 3 percent, depending on the province (Canada, Statistics Canada 1990b, 98).

Admissions to Provincial Facilities As already mentioned, those admitted to provincial correctional facilities were either serving a sentence that had been imposed or waiting for sentencing. Those awaiting sentencing represented 42 percent of all admissions, a proportion that generally varied between 30 and 45 percent, depending on the province (Canada, Statistics Canada 1990b, 60).

Table 2.5
Warrant of committal admissions of Aboriginal people to federal penitentiaries, by province/territory of sentence, 1989–90
(percentage)

Province/territory of sentence	Aboriginal people
Newfoundland	2
Prince Edward Island	6 (1988–89)
Nova Scotia	1
New Brunswick	5
Quebec	1
Ontario	5
Manitoba	40
Saskatchewan	54
Alberta	23
British Columbia	14
Yukon	44
Northwest Territories	75
Total Canada	11

Source: Canada, Statistics Canada (1990b, 139–40).

In 1989–90,

> *Criminal Code* offences comprised 72% of all sentenced admissions …
> Among those provinces reporting most serious offences, the percent
> of admissions with a *Criminal Code* offence ranged from 60% in Quebec
> to 89% in Newfoundland and Labrador … Approximately 18% of all
> admissions were for Provincial Statute offences … Municipal By-laws
> accounted for 3% of all provincial admissions. This group was virtu-
> ally negligible in all provinces except Quebec, where 6% of all admis-
> sions were for Municipal By-law infractions … Fine defaulters
> accounted for 28% of all admissions to provincial facilities, ranging
> from a low of 7% in Nova Scotia to a high of 38% in Saskatchewan.
> (Canada, Statistics Canada 1990b, 66–67)

Sentences for people admitted to provincial institutions are short:
43 percent are for less than one month, and 38 percent are for 30 to 179
days. Sentences of under six months represent more than 80 percent of
admissions. The length of sentences, however, varies considerably
among the provinces (table 2.6).

Table 2.6
Sentenced admissions to provincial/territorial custody, by length of aggregate sentence and province/territory, 1989–90
(percentage)

| Province/territory | 1–29 days | Aggregate sentence | | |
		30–179 days	180–364 days	12 months and over
Newfoundland	40	38	11	11
Prince Edward Island	76	17	3	3
Nova Scotia	19	51	12	17
New Brunswick	58	35	5	2
Quebec	48	30	11	10
Ontario	46	38	8	8
Manitoba	20	49	15	13
Saskatchewan	32	45	12	10
Alberta	40	43	7	10
British Columbia	55	31	7	8
Yukon	54	41	5	—
Northwest Territories	20	50	19	12
Total Canada	43	38	9	10

Source: Canada, Statistics Canada (1990b, 123).

The percentage of Aboriginal admissions to provincial institutions is even higher than to federal penitentiaries: 18 percent (table 2.7) in the former case, compared with 11 percent in the latter (table 2.5).

Again, most Aboriginal people admitted are from the Prairie provinces. Two-thirds of the people sentenced to Saskatchewan institutions are Aboriginal people. They represent close to half of the admissions in Manitoba and close to a third in Alberta.

Finally, women account for approximately 9 200 or 8 percent of admissions of people in provincial custody. This proportion varies between 4 and 10 percent, depending on the province (Canada, Statistics Canada 1990b, 126).

Profile of Inmates in Federal Institutions
In 1989–90, the average number of inmates present in federal institutions was 11 415 persons. However, 1 227 inmates, or 10 percent of the

Table 2.7
**Sentenced admissions of Aboriginal people to
provincial/territorial custody, by province/territory,
1989–90**
(percentage)

Province/territory	Aboriginal people
Newfoundland	4
Prince Edward Island	3
Nova Scotia	3
New Brunswick	5
Quebec	2
Ontario	8
Manitoba	47
Saskatchewan	66
Alberta	31
British Columbia	19
Yukon	65
Northwest Territories	88
Total Canada	18

Source: Canada, Statistics Canada (1990b, 126).

total population, were temporarily out of custody; therefore, the average population on register was 12 652. Most of those on temporary release (67 percent) were on day parole and most were housed in private community residential centres (Canada, Statistics Canada 1990b, 92–93).

On 30 June 1990, there were 12 921 persons on register in federal institutions (tables 2.8–2.11). Correctional Service Canada produces a report that gives an overview of the characteristics of this population. Most inmates (59.9 percent) are there for the first time; 17.3 percent have previously served one sentence in federal custody. It is significant that 1 312 individuals (10.1 percent of the penitentiary population) claim native or Métis origin: 966 Amerinds (7.4 percent), 305 Métis (2.3 percent) and 41 Inuit (0.3 percent). Their presence is particularly striking in the Prairie region, where they represent 34.3 percent of the inmate population in federal custody: 22.7 percent of the total are Amerinds, 10.4 percent Métis and 1.2 percent Inuit.

Table 2.8
**Major offences for which persons were incarcerated in a
federal institution on 30 June 1990**

Offence	N	%
Murder	1 789	13.8
Manslaughter	625	4.8
Sexual assault	1 503	11.6
Robbery	2 998	23.2
Break and enter	1 778	13.7
Theft, receiving and fraud	711	5.5
Narcotic Control Act	866	6.7
Other	2 441	18.9
Missing data	210	1.6
Total	12 921	100.0

Source: Canada, Correctional Service (1990a, D0001).

Table 2.9
Sentences imposed on persons incarcerated in federal institutions on 30 June 1990

Sentence	N	%	% cumulative
Less than 2 years	537	4.1	4.1
2–3 years	2 548	19.7	23.8
3–4 years	1 957	15.1	38.9
4–5 years	1 290	9.9	48.8
5–10 years	2 877	22.3	71.1
10–15 years	1 000	7.7	78.8
15 years and longer	630	4.9	83.7
Life	1 935	14.9	98.6
Preventive detention	144	1.1	99.7
Missing data	3	0.0	
Total	12 921	100.0	100.0

Source: Canada, Correctional Service (1990a, D0002).

Table 2.10
Ages of inmates in federal custody on 30 June 1990

Age	N	%	% cumulative	Canadian population*
17–19 years	159	1.2	1.2	4.1
20–24 years	2 213	17.1	18.3	10.5
25–29 years	3 240	25.0	43.3	12.3
30–34 years	2 662	20.6	63.9	12.2
35–39 years	1 820	14.0	77.9	11.2
40 years and over	2 826	21.9	99.8	50.0
Missing data	1	0		0.0
Total	12 921	100.0	100.0	100.0

Sources: Canada, Correctional Service (1990a, D0002); Canada, Statistics Canada
(1990a, 30–31).

*Distribution of the Canadian male population aged 18 years and over.

Profile of Inmates in Provincial Custody

In 1989–90, the average number of people resident in provincial prisons
was 18 140, with another 20 percent on register (except for British
Columbia and the Northwest Territories) as being on temporary release
for medical reasons, on temporary absence or on day parole. This proportion varies between provinces from 0 to 34 percent (table 2.12),
depending on whether the province has temporary absence programs
and whether there is overcrowding. (To solve the overcrowding problem,
temporary absences are being granted to more people (Canada, Statistics
Canada 1990b, 59).) In 1989–90, of all the inmates residing in provincial
institutions, 13 947 (77 percent) had already been sentenced, whereas
4 193 (23 percent) had not.

No province except British Columbia regularly produces profiles
of the population in detention facilities. Other information on this
subject is usually incomplete or comes from one-time studies. In Quebec,
for instance, the only study characterizing the population in custody was
done in 1986 by a commission studying alternatives to imprisonment
(Quebec, Comité d'étude 1986).

This study showed that, on 7 May 1986, the official count of inmates
registered in Quebec institutions was 3 988, but only 2 733 were actually
resident in the facilities. That means 1 255 of those on register (31 percent)
were on temporary absence. Sentenced inmates accounted for 78 percent of registered inmates; those under remand accounted for 22 percent.

Table 2.11
Province/territory of residence of inmates in federal custody on 30 June 1990

Province/territory	N	%	Canadian population*
Newfoundland	149	1.1	2.1
Prince Edward Island	44	0.3	0.5
Nova Scotia	567	4.3	3.3
New Brunswick	293	2.2	2.7
Quebec	3 817	29.5	25.6
Ontario	3 484	26.9	36.8
Manitoba	642	4.9	4.0
Saskatchewan	436	3.3	3.6
Alberta	1 257	9.7	9.1
British Columbia	1 712	13.2	12.0
Yukon	16	0.1	0.1
Northwest Territories	53	0.4	0.2
Outside Canada	104	0.8	—
Missing data	347	2.6	0.0
Total	12 921	100.0	100.0

Sources: Canada, Correctional Service (1990a, D0004); Canada, Statistics Canada (1990a, 30–31).

*Distribution of the Canadian male population aged 18 years and over.

Forty-six percent were under 25 years of age, and two-thirds were under 30. Seven percent were imprisoned solely for non-payment of fines.[9] Ten percent of offenders were serving sentences of less than a month, 47 percent had sentences of less than six months and one-third had sentences of one to two years.

In 1989–90, there was an average of 1 843 inmates in British Columbia. Eighty-two percent had been sentenced, and 18 percent were under remand. Five percent were women, and 17 percent were Aboriginal people. Thirty-two percent of the population were under 25 years of age, and 52 percent were under 30. Of those sentenced, 14 percent were serving less than a month, 57 percent less than six months and 23 percent were serving one to two years.[10]

There are no available offender profile data for the other provinces.

Table 2.12
Average number of persons in provincial/territorial custody, by province/territory, in 1989–90

Province/territory	On-register count	Actual count			
		Sentenced	Not sentenced	Total	Absent (%)
Newfoundland	350	277	27	304	13
Prince Edward Island	90	79	11	90	0
Nova Scotia	470	344	55	399	15
New Brunswick	387	325	45	370	7
Quebec	4 654	1 884	1 184	3 068	34
Ontario	7 884	5 445	1 721	7 166	10
Manitoba	1 168	712	243	955	18
Saskatchewan	1 495	1 185	136	1 321	13
Alberta	3 340	1 857	404	2 261	32
British Columbia	—	1 512	331	1 843	—
Yukon	91	72	12	84	8
Northwest Territories	—	255	24	279	—
Total	19 929	13 947	4 193	18 140	

Source: Canada, Statistics Canada (1990b, 121).

Note: Figures represent the average count for the year.

Female Inmates

Federal Custody   On 30 June 1990, 305 women were in the custody of Correctional Service Canada and were serving sentences of two years or more. Most of them (161) were being held in the Penitentiary for Women in Kingston, Ontario, 29 were in other federal institutions and 115 were in provincial facilities under federal–provincial agreements covering inmate transfers. Most of the women in provincial facilities (66) were being held in a Quebec detention facility (table 2.13).

The Penitentiary for Women in Kingston accommodates women from all the provinces of Canada. However, in June 1990, there were no inmates from Prince Edward Island, and 13 were from outside Canada (table 2.14).

Close to one-third (32 percent) of the women in the care of Correctional Service Canada were imprisoned for murder or

Table 2.13
Location of women in Correctional Service Canada custody, 30 June 1990

Custody location		N	%
Kingston Penitentiary for Women		161	53
Other federal institutions		29	9
Provincial prisons		115	38
Nova Scotia	1		
Quebec	66		
Manitoba	6		
Saskatchewan	7		
Alberta	19		
British Columbia	13		
Yukon	1		
Northwest Territories	1		
Data missing	1		
Total		305	100

Source: Canada, Correctional Service (1990b).

Table 2.14
Province of residence of female inmates of the Kingston Penitentiary for Women, 30 June 1990

Province	N	%
Newfoundland	2	1.2
Nova Scotia	8	4.9
New Brunswick	5	3.1
Quebec	14	8.6
Ontario	69	42.8
Manitoba	7	4.3
Saskatchewan	3	1.8
Alberta	14	8.6
British Columbia	20	12.4
Outside Canada	13	8.0
Data missing	6	3.7
Total	161	100.0

Source: Canada, Correctional Service (1990b).

Table 2.15
Major offences for which women in Correctional Service Canada custody were incarcerated, 30 June 1990

Offence	Kingston Penitentiary for Women		Other federal institutions		Provincial prisons		Total	
	N	%	N	%	N	%	N	%
Murder	36	22.2	5	17	13	11.2	54	17.7
Manslaughter	20	12.4	6	21	18	15.6	44	14.4
Assault	13	8.0	2	7	2	1.7	17	5.6
Robbery	29	18.0	2	7	19	16.5	50	16.4
Theft, receiving and fraud	11	6.7	3	10	11	9.4	25	8.1
Narcotic Control Act	23	14.2	6	21	27	23.4	56	18.4
Other	25	15.5	3	10	22	19.1	50	16.4
Data missing	4	2.4	2	7	3	2.6	9	3.0
Total	161	100.0	29	100.0	115	100.0	305	100.0

Source: Canada, Correctional Service (1990b).

manslaughter (table 2.15). Most of those convicted of murder were held in Kingston. The proportion of female inmates (18.3 percent) to male inmates (6.7 percent) in federal prisons who had been convicted of offences under the *Narcotic Control Act* was nearly three to one (table 2.8).

On 30 June 1990, the distribution of sentences for women in the custody of Correctional Service Canada was similar to that of all inmates in federal custody (table 2.9). Women sentenced to life imprisonment were held in Kingston rather than in provincial prisons (table 2.16).

Although the average age of female inmates in federal custody did vary with place of incarceration, on average they were older than the male inmates in federal penitentiaries. While men under 30 years of age represented 43.3 percent of the population, women in that age group represented only 35 percent (table 2.17). At the other extreme, 27.2 percent of the women were 40 years of age or older, compared with 21.9 percent of the men (table 2.10).

Provincial Custody   There are even fewer data available on the profile of female offenders in provincial custody than there are for male offenders. Statistics Canada has no information on the sex of inmates

Table 2.16
Sentences imposed on women in Correctional Service Canada custody, 30 June 1990

Sentence	Kingston Penitentiary for Women		Other federal institutions		Provincial prisons		Total	
	N	%	N	%	N	%	N	%
Less than 2 years	6	3.7	1	3	4	3.4	11	3.6
2–3 years	36	22.3	6	21	28	24.3	70	22.9
3–4 years	20	12.4	6	21	25	21.7	51	16.7
4–5 years	21	13.0	3	10	11	9.5	35	11.4
5–10 years	29	18.0	6	20	27	22.6	62	19.7
10 years and longer	12	7.4	2	7	6	5.2	20	6.5
Life	37	22.9	5	17	14	12.1	56	18.3
Total	161	100.0	29	100.0	115	100.0	305	100.0

Source: Canada, Correctional Service (1990b).

Table 2.17
Ages of women in Correctional Service Canada custody on 30 June 1990

Age	N	%	% cumulative	Canadian population*
17–19 years	3	0.9	0.9	3.7
20–24 years	34	11.1	12.0	9.6
25–29 years	71	23.2	35.2	11.6
30–34 years	50	19.3	54.5	11.7
35–39 years	54	17.7	72.2	10.8
40 years and over	83	27.2	99.4	52.6
Data missing	1	0.3	100.0	0.0
Total	305	100.0	100.0	100.0

Sources: Canada, Correctional Service (1990b, A0005); Canada, Statistics Canada (1990a, 32–33).

*Distribution of the Canadian female population aged 18 years and over.

in Canada at any given time. We must refer to individual studies for these data.

In a recent report (Shaw 1990, 38) prepared for the task force on female offenders in federal custody, it was estimated that at a specific point in 1988, about 790 women were serving sentences of less than two years in provincial prisons in Canada.

To our knowledge, the last study providing a profile of female inmates of provincial prisons was done in 1982 for the Canadian Association of Elizabeth Fry Societies. It reported that in February 1982, there were 788 women incarcerated in provincial institutions (table 2.18). Two-thirds of them were serving a sentence, and one-third were under remand warrant. Of those serving a sentence of less than two years, 77 percent had a sentence of less than six months, while 11 percent had a sentence of more than one year.

In Quebec, the study conducted for the Landreville Commission (Quebec, Comité d'étude 1986) reveals that on 7 May 1986, there were 213 women on register in Quebec detention facilities, that is, 5 percent of the total. Of these 213 female inmates, 51 were serving a sentence of two years or more (ibid., 135), corresponding to the total population just described. Of the 162 women inmates under provincial responsibility, about 30 (20 percent) were under remand warrant.

On the one hand, women represented 3 percent of federal admissions but 2.4 percent of those in the custody of Correctional Service Canada in June 1990; on the other, they accounted for 8 percent of all provincial admissions but about 6 percent of those serving a sentence of under two years at any given time in these institutions. Therefore, females are generally sentenced to shorter terms than males.

Offenders Sentenced to Life Imprisonment
Of special interest are the offenders who are sentenced to life imprisonment. This sentence is reserved for those who have committed the most serious violations of the criminal law, generally murder. Some argue that anyone who has committed such a reprehensible offence, violating the social contract in such a flagrant manner, should lose the right to participate in governing the community.

But who are these inmates? Where are they from? How are they different from other federal inmates?

On 30 June 1990, there were 1 959 persons serving life sentences. Correctional Service Canada provided information about all but five. The province of residence at the time of sentencing is shown in table 2.20. Most (93.8 percent) were convicted of murder (table 2.21).

Offenders sentenced to life imprisonment differ from other inmates

Table 2.18
Number of female inmates in provincial/territorial institutions, by province/territory, and percentage who were Aboriginal people, in February 1982

Province/territory	N	% Aboriginal people
Newfoundland	8	100
Prince Edward Island	2	0
Nova Scotia	20	0
New Brunswick	17	12
Quebec	145	21
Ontario	278	17
Manitoba	38	71
Saskatchewan	60	77
Alberta	140	29
British Columbia	65	20
Yukon	3	100
Northwest Territories	12	75
Total Canada	788	25

Source: Mish et al. (1982, 4).

Table 2.19
Most serious offence for which female inmates of provincial/territorial institutions were in custody, in February 1982

Offence	%
Theft of $200 or less	13
Other *Criminal Code* offences	13
Theft over $200	11
Narcotic Control Act and *Food and Drugs Act*	10
Fraud	9
Robbery	6
Break and enter	5
Assault	4
Murder	3

Source: Mish et al. (1982, 17).

Note: Table includes only the most frequently occurring offences.

Table 2.20
Province/territory of residence of inmates sentenced to life imprisonment in Correctional Service Canada custody on 30 June 1990

Province/territory	N	%	Canadian population*
Newfoundland	26	1.3	2.1
Prince Edward Island	6	0.3	0.5
Nova Scotia	63	3.2	3.3
New Brunswick	44	2.2	2.7
Quebec	509	26.0	25.6
Ontario	590	30.2	36.8
Manitoba	86	4.4	4.0
Saskatchewan	76	3.9	3.6
Alberta	185	9.5	9.1
British Columbia	295	15.1	12.0
Yukon	3	0.2	0.1
Northwest Territories	9	0.5	0.2
Outside Canada	16	0.8	—
Data missing	46	2.4	0.0
Total	1 954	100.0	100.0

Sources: Unpublished data supplied by Correctional Service Canada; Canada, Statistics Canada (1990a, 30–31).

*Distribution of the Canadian male population aged 18 years and over.

held in federal penitentiaries. Contrary to popular belief, they are more likely than other inmates to be serving their first sentence: 70 percent of the inmates serving life sentences are in for the first time, compared with 61 percent of the general inmate population (table 2.22). Although these figures are the only indicator we have, they tend to confirm a fact that is well known in criminology: murder is often an isolated criminal act. Those imprisoned for murder have a much less extensive criminal history than other inmates.

It is evident that at any given time, offenders in extended custody are older than other inmates. On 30 June 1990, only 23 percent of the inmates with long sentences were under 30 years of age, whereas 43 percent of all other inmates fell into that age group (table 2.10). On the other hand, 38 percent of those with long sentences were 40 years of

Table 2.21

Major offences for which inmates in the custody of Correctional Service Canada serving life sentences were incarcerated as of 30 June 1990

Offence	N	%
Murder, first degree	419	21.4
Murder, second degree	1 181	60.4
Murder, capital	13	0.7
Murder, non-capital	220	11.3
Manslaughter	29	1.5
Attempted murder	27	1.4
Rape, aggravated sexual assault	14	0.7
Robbery	18	0.9
Other offences	33	1.7
Total	1 954	100.0

Source: Unpublished data supplied by Correctional Service Canada.

Table 2.22

Number of previous incarcerations in federal penitentiaries of persons in Correctional Service Canada custody on 30 June 1990

Previous incarcerations in a penitentiary	Persons sentenced to life imprisonment			All persons incarcerated		
	N	%	% cumulative	N	%	% cumulative
None	1 375	70.4	70.4	8 214	60.6	60.6
One	291	14.9	85.3	2 322	17.1	77.7
Two	172	8.8	94.1	1 387	10.2	87.9
Three or more	116	5.9	100.0	1 616	11.9	100.0
Total	1 954			13 539		

Source: Canada, Correctional Service (1990a, A0002).

age or older, compared with 22 percent for the population as a whole. Also, 9 percent of the offenders sentenced to life imprisonment were Aboriginal people, as were 10 percent of all inmates under the responsibility of Correctional Service Canada. These relatively similar percentages should not obscure the fact that Aboriginal people are overrepresented in Canadian penitentiaries.

Summary

- Only about one-third of criminal offences are reported and show up in crime statistics.
- About one-quarter of *Criminal Code* offences reported to the police are cleared by laying a charge (table 2.1).
- Two-thirds of the individuals charged are adults.
- Between 35 and 40 percent of adults convicted of indictable offences receive prison sentences. Only 10 percent of convictions for *Criminal Code* offences punishable on summary conviction result in prison sentences (table 2.2).
- Generally, less than 1 percent of *Criminal Code* offences lead to incarceration.
- In 1989–90, an average of 29 555 inmates were in correctional institutions in Canada.
- In the same year, the mean population on register in federal institutions (including people temporarily out of custody) was 12 642. Ten percent of these (1 227) were on temporary release.
- Close to 15 percent were serving life sentences. About 60 percent were serving their first sentence in a penitentiary.
- In June 1990, 305 inmates, or 2.4 percent of the population in custody, were women. Most were in the Penitentiary for Women in Kingston (table 2.13).
- At the same time, 10 percent of inmates in federal custody claimed Aboriginal or Métis origin. They made up 34 percent of the population of penitentiaries in the Prairie provinces.
- In 1989–90, an average of 18 140 inmates were resident in provincial institutions, and about 20 percent of these were temporarily out of custody (table 2.12).
- Of inmates resident in these institutions, 77 percent had been sentenced.
- In February 1982, about 800 women were serving sentences of less than two years in provincial custody; of these, 25 percent were of Aboriginal origin (table 2.18).
- The overrepresentation of Aboriginal people both for admissions (11 percent admitted to penitentiaries; 18 percent to provincial institutions) and in penal institutions at any given time (10 percent

in penitentiaries in general; 34 percent in penitentiaries in the Prairies) raises serious questions concerning the equity of the Canadian penal system.

• In June 1990, 1 959 people were serving life sentences in the custody of Correctional Service Canada. More than half of them (56 percent) were from Quebec and Ontario (table 2.20); 93.8 percent were convicted of murder (table 2.21). Of the people convicted of murder, 70 percent were first-time inmates of a penitentiary, compared with 61 percent for all penitentiary inmates (table 2.22).

THE RIGHTS AND PRINCIPLES INVOLVED

The Fundamental Rights of Inmates

Discussing the rights of inmates in correctional institutions is a fairly recent development. For some authors, this may result from an extension of the minority rights movement to encompass other groups including prisoners. Over the years, interest has not only focused on prison conditions but also has led to a reassessment of the legal status of people sentenced to prison (Kaiser 1971; see also "Colateral Consequences" 1970).

Denying criminals their civil rights and privileges is not new. Over the years, the collateral consequences of conviction have taken a variety of forms: infamy, outlawry, corruption of blood, civil death and loss of civil rights. (See the section "Historical Background" later in this study.) These additional sanctions were harsh and involved the loss of a number of rights.

Even though civil death has been abolished and the civil disqualifications to which convicted persons were subjected have disappeared, inmates have continued to be seen as having forfeited their rights. Imprisonment, according to the traditional and widespread view, necessarily leads to the loss of rights. Prisoners enjoy only certain discretionary privileges.

This traditional view has been thrown into question, however, by changes in the philosophy of imprisonment, away from punishment and vengeance and toward rehabilitation.

The questions now arising in jurisprudence are the following: To what extent are inmates deprived of the rights granted to citizens? Which civil rights do they enjoy? Do they lose all their rights, with the exception of those specifically granted to them by law or, conversely, do they retain all their rights, with the exception of those expressly or implicitly denied them by law because of imprisonment?

In *Solosky* (1980), the Supreme Court of Canada resolved this debate. Solosky, an inmate, was claiming the common law right to privileged communication between counsel and client. The court said that the question of inmate rights must be approached from a wider perspective and ruled that "a person confined to prison retains all of his civil rights, other than those expressly or impliedly taken from him by law" (ibid., 839).

In 1980, therefore, it was recognized that inmates retain all their civil rights but that some may be expressly withdrawn by the legislator. Since the *Canadian Charter of Rights and Freedoms* came into effect in 1982, even rights denied expressly by law can be reviewed or struck down by the courts. Parliament's supreme authority is no longer absolute. Any restriction or denial of rights must be reasonable in a free and democratic society. The statement of the Supreme Court in *Solosky* must be changed and should now read: "A person confined to prison retains all of his civil rights, other than those expressly taken from him by law within such reasonable limits as can be demonstrably justified in a free and democratic society."

Denying voting rights to inmates must be assessed in the light of the right itself, as well as in the light of the evolution of inmates' legal status and constitutional rights. In addition, we must consider the evolution of Canadian penal philosophy and modern correctional principles.

Penal Philosophy and Correctional Principles

There are no statements in the *Criminal Code* on the objectives and the principles of penal law or of sentencing. Such statements have to be retrieved from committee or commission reports, government documents and policy statements. Criminal law reform has, in fact, been a topic for review and continuing debate in Canada since the end of the 1960s. The following documents, listed in chronological order, illustrate the scope and quality of this debate: the report of the Canadian Committee on Corrections (Canada, Canadian Committee 1969); the work of the Law Reform Commission of Canada, a document entitled *The Criminal Law in Canadian Society* (Canada, Department of Justice 1982); the working papers of the Correctional Law Review Working Group (Canada, Solicitor General 1986–87); the report of the Canadian Sentencing Commission (1987); the Daubney report (Canada, House of Commons 1988); and, finally, the *Directions for Reform* volumes (Canada, Solicitor General 1990a, 1990b; Canada, Department of Justice 1990), a green paper tabled by the federal government in July 1990.

Objectives and Principles of Penal Law

To begin with, the green paper entitled *Directions for Reform: Sentencing* (Canada, Department of Justice 1990) subscribes to the two main objectives of penal law formulated in *The Criminal Law in Canadian Society*:

1. preservation of the peace, prevention of crime, and protection of
    the public – security goals; and
2. equity, fairness, guarantees for the rights and liberties of the indi-
    vidual against the powers of the state, and the provision of a fitting
    response by society to wrongdoing – justice goals. (Canada,
    Department of Justice 1982, 40)

Besides, one of the consistent themes characterizing all the Canadian
papers is the principle that penal law and the penal system should be
applied with moderation. The same paper says, "This notion – which
has unfortunately and inaccurately been interpreted by some as a call
for laxity and leniency – is properly understood as implying the need
to examine carefully the appropriateness, the necessity, and the efficacy of employing the criminal law, rather than these other, less intru-
sive, less coercive means of dealing with particular social problems"
(Canada, Department of Justice 1982, 41).

The principle of moderation also means "The criminal law should
be employed to deal only with that conduct for which other means of
social control are inadequate or inappropriate, and in a manner which
interferes with individual rights and freedoms only to the extent necessary for the attainment of its purpose" (Canada, Department of Justice
1982, 59).

This principle would appear to be particularly pertinent to the issue
of voting rights for inmates.

Objectives and Principles of Sentencing

The green paper *Directions for Reform: A Framework for Sentencing,
Corrections and Conditional Release* (Canada, Solicitor General 1990a)
suggests that a statement of the objectives and principles of sentencing
be included in the *Criminal Code*. These objectives and principles are
the result of 20 years of review and debate in Canada and are highly relevant to this study. They include not only the idea that the sentence
should foster a sense of responsibility, but also the principle of moderation in sentencing.

One of the objectives the courts must consider in determining an
appropriate sentence is to promote "a sense of responsibility on the
part of offenders and [provide] for opportunities to assist in their rehabilitation as productive and law-abiding members of society" (Canada,
Solicitor General 1990a, 16).

This emphasis on rehabilitating the offenders rather than punishing
them was stated forcefully by the Ouimet Committee: "The Committee
believes that the ultimate rehabilitation of the individual offers the

best long-term protection for society" (Canada, Canadian Committee 1969, 189). Fostering responsibility originates to a great extent with the Law Reform Commission of Canada: "Dispositions and sentences in the criminal process should promote a sense of responsibility on the part of the offender and enable him to understand his actions in relation to the victim and society" (Law Reform Commission of Canada 1976, 8).

Subsequently, the Archambault Commission emphasized "the accountability of the offender rather than punishment" (Canada, Canadian Sentencing Commission 1987, 154). The Daubney Committee then combined both dimensions, and said, "The purpose of sentencing is to contribute to the maintenance of a just, peaceful and safe society by holding offenders accountable for their criminal conduct through the imposition of just sanctions which ... if necessary, provide offenders with opportunities which are likely to facilitate their habilitation or rehabilitation as productive and law-abiding members of society" (Canada, House of Commons 1988, 55).

The green paper expounded upon the principle of moderation in sentencing: "A sentence should be the least onerous alternative appropriate in the circumstances" (Canada, Solicitor General 1990a, 16). This principle, to which the Law Reform Commission had assigned a great deal of importance (Law Reform Commission of Canada 1976, 8–9), is found word for word in *The Criminal Law in Canadian Society* (Canada, Department of Justice 1982, 42) and in a similar form in the report of the Archambault Commission (Canada, Canadian Sentencing Commission 1987, 169).

Correctional Principles
We now consider three correctional principles that are generally accepted in Canada today.

1. Offenders are sent to prison as punishment, but not for punishment (Canada, Solicitor General 1987, 5).

From 1955, the First United Nations Congress on the Prevention of Crime and the Treatment of Offenders recognized this principle by adopting minimum rules for the treatment of prisoners: "Imprisonment and other measures which result in cutting off an offender from the outside world are afflictive by the very fact of taking from the person the right of self-determination by depriving him of his liberty. Therefore the prison system shall not, except as incidental to justifiable segregation or the maintenance of discipline, aggravate the suffering inherent in such a situation" (United Nations 1955, rule 57).

This principle is stated in Britain as "the criminal is sentenced 'as punishment, not for punishment'" (Canada, Solicitor General 1986, 40) and is now very widely accepted. In 1977, the Parliamentary Subcommittee on the Canadian Penitentiary System recommended that the following principle should govern the actions of all officers of the system: "the sentence of imprisonment imposed by the court constitutes the punishment" (ibid.).

Some years later, the Solicitor General of Canada, the Honourable Robert Kaplan, adopted this principle when, in an information booklet for inmates published by Correctional Service Canada, he declared, "Going to prison is punishment; it is not our purpose to add extra suffering to the sentence of the court that brought you here" (1980, i).

More recently, the Correctional Law Review Working Group expressed this idea: "The punishment consists only of the loss of liberty, restriction of mobility, or any other legal disposition of the court. No other punishment should be imposed by the correctional authorities with regard to an individual's crime" (Canada, Solicitor General 1986, 40).

Here, the principle is directed toward the penitentiary authorities, but its application is much broader: the sentence handed down by the court should be the only punishment.

2. Offenders under sentence retain the rights and privileges of all members of society (Canada, Solicitor General 1990a, 17).

This principle is general, referring to "sentenced" offenders, but it is also stated with respect to imprisonment. According to the first principle adopted by the Correctional Law Review Working Group, "Individuals under sentence retain all the rights and privileges of a member of society, except those that are necessarily removed or restricted by the fact of incarceration" (Canada, Solicitor General 1986, 38). This recognition of the rights of inmates derives directly from a philosophy that requires them to become increasingly more responsible and assume the same duties and responsibilities as other citizens.

In 1975, the Law Reform Commission of Canada put this position well: "In general, the object of facilitating the offender's successful return to the community will be enhanced by permitting living conditions in prison to approximate those in the community. This is important ... [because] it assumes that the prisoner is expected to discharge the normal duties and responsibilities of all citizens" (1975, 35).[11]

This principle has been incorporated into the policies of Correctional Service Canada and a number of provincial correctional services for several years. The preface to the information manual for inmates, published by Correctional Service Canada, states, "The Correctional Service of Canada accepts the basic proposition that an inmate retains all of the rights of an ordinary citizen save those which have been removed either by law, or by the necessary implication of incarceration" (1980, 1). More recently, the same principle was adopted in the Correctional Service Canada mandate: "Offenders, as members of society, retain their rights and privileges except those necessarily removed or restricted by the fact of their incarceration" (Canada, Correctional Service 1990, 8). Similarly, Quebec correctional services stipulate that "in general, inmates must retain the same rights as other citizens. We are talking here about civil, political, legal and other rights as recognized by the Quebec *Charter of human rights and freedoms*, as well as by the Canadian Charter, with the exception of those an inmate may be deprived of by reasons prescribed in specific legislation" (Quebec, Services correctionnels du Québec 1988, 25).

3. Imprisonment must encourage the offender's rehabilitation and reintegration into the community.[12]

One of the guiding principles of the *Standard Minimum Rules for the Treatment of Prisoners* is as follows:

> The purpose and justification of a sentence of imprisonment or a similar measure deprivative of liberty is ultimately to protect society against crime. This end can only be achieved if the period of imprisonment is used to ensure, so far as possible, that upon his return to society the offender is not only willing but able to lead a law-abiding and self-supporting life. (United Nations 1955, rule 58)

The Government of Canada, in its green paper entitled *Directions for Reform: Corrections and Conditional Release*, proposes to include in a corrections administration act a statement of the aims and principles of federal corrections. That statement would say, among other things, that "the purpose of federal corrections is to contribute to the maintenance of a just, peaceful and safe society by contributing to the rehabilitation and integration of offenders into the community as law-abiding citizens through the provision of programs in penitentiaries and in the community" (Canada, Solicitor General 1990b, 49).

Even though rehabilitation has generally been rejected as a justification for imprisonment,[13] it has been accepted in Canada[14] for more than 30 years that correctional services encourage inmates "to adopt acceptable behaviour patterns and ... to prepare for eventual release and successful re-integration in society" (Canada, Solicitor General 1986, 32–33).

This principle still has a prominent place in the policy statements of correctional services in Canada. One of the basic values in Correctional Service Canada's mandate is expressed as follows: "We recognize that the offender has the potential to live as a law-abiding citizen" (1990, 10). One of the guiding principles derived from this states, "We believe that programs and opportunities to assist offenders in developing social and living skills will enhance their potential to become law-abiding citizens" (ibid.).

This rehabilitation and reintegration into the community should not be promoted solely by correctional programs but also by any other "opportunities designed to help the offender in his personal and social development," including, we believe, the exercise of democratic rights.

MODERN JUSTIFICATIONS FOR EXCLUSION

Historical Background

Historically, disenfranchisement of convicted and incarcerated people goes back to the distant past and is linked to the loss of citizenship. In ancient Greece and Rome, criminals were subject to infamy (disgrace). They were deprived of the rights associated with citizenship, such as the rights to appear in court, make speeches, serve in the army and vote. In a society where citizenship and the rights that go with it were highly valued, infamy was a potent punishment for crimes against society.

Later, in continental Europe and in England, outlawry (a concept similar to infamy) was used to punish people who committed crimes against society. Once declared an outlaw, a criminal lost all protection of the law and was exposed to harassment by the entire community. This harassment included the loss of all rights, forfeiture of property and exposure to physical harm and death.

In France at the time of the Renaissance, those convicted suffered civil death, or the absolute loss of all rights. Criminals ceased to be citizens and became persons without a country. They could not bring legal action or testify, could not transmit or inherit property, and could not make or receive donations.

Later, in England, the status of outlaw was replaced by that of "attainder." A person attainted was civilly dead. This had three consequences: forfeiture of property and lands; "tainted" blood; and loss of civil rights and the legal capacity to bring suit, testify, inherit and so on.

These different sanctions were imposed for violating social and moral norms. In every civilization, civil death or loss of citizenship served two purposes: vengeance and deterrence. According to the thinking of the time, society was justified in exacting revenge for wrong-doing by barring people who had broken these norms from participating in society. The stigma of civil death and the humiliation imposed upon the criminals and their families served as deterrents and were the means for society to prevent other crimes. Like public shows of punishment (e.g., pillory, maiming, hanging), civil death degraded criminals and isolated them from society.

These consequences were imported by the British to the colonies of North America, where offenders became attainted. Similarly, the French introduced the civil death concept of the *Napoleonic Code* to the *Civil Code of Lower Canada.*

Legal reforms have restricted the consequences of civil death. Corruption of blood was the first sanction to disappear in Upper Canada (1833). When criminal law became the *Criminal Code* in 1892, attainder status and forfeiture of property were abolished. In Quebec, civil death was replaced in 1906 (*An Act to abolish civil death*) by the loss of civil rights for those sentenced to death or to life imprisonment; such loss included the loss of the right to vote and the right to stand for election.

The loss of voting rights, that is, the loss of the right to political expression, is a relic of civil death, which by extinguishing any legal existence conferred the status of a non-person on the offender. Today, although offenders no longer lose their citizenship, they continue to lose their right to vote. Is this disqualification based on a rational penological consideration or is it merely an anachronism? We must analyse the relevance and the strength of the contemporary justifications to determine whether this exclusion is legitimate.

Modern justifications for excluding offenders in custody are not very clearly expressed. As Chief Justice Thurlow of the Federal Court of Appeal pointed out, it is difficult to define the interest the state has in exclusion (*Gould* 1984b). This interest is described in very broad terms and, in the words of an American court, often comes down to a "metaphysical invocation that the interest is preservation of the purity of the ballot box" (*Dillenburg* 1972, 1224).

In recent Canadian rulings, the courts have invoked the concept of the responsible and decent citizen and the duty to preserve a symbolic exclusion of the criminal to reinforce this concept. They have also pointed out that inmates may be unable to make well-informed and intelligent choices. Along with these moral and political reasons, some penal arguments were put forward: for example, exclusion serves to punish the offender and protect society. In addition, several practical objections were raised.

Moral and Political Justifications

The Responsible Citizen and Symbolic Exclusion
According to this concept, the exercise of the right to vote requires moral decency, a responsible way of life, and respect for the law and community standards. By breaking the social contract and acting irresponsibly, criminals become the authors of their own misfortune, excluding themselves from the right to take part in the life of the community. The state is justified in retaining the symbolic exclusion of criminals to reinforce the concept of the responsible citizen, to preserve the purity of the ballot box and to discourage any form of discredit or devaluation of the vote in the eyes of the public.

Breach of the Social Contract   In recent Canadian decisions, some courts have used the concept of the responsible and decent citizen and the voters' respect for the law to justify excluding offenders in correctional custody. For example, Mr. Justice Van Camp relied on this concept in *Sauvé* (1989).[15] This argument has been used by the American courts as well.

John Locke said that all those entering into society authorize that society to make laws for the common good and commit themselves to respect these. The 2nd Circuit Court of Appeal wrote, "A man who breaks the laws he has authorized his agent to make for his own governance could fairly have been thought to have abandoned the right to participate in further administering the compact" (*Green* 1967, 451). Exclusion, therefore, is considered the result of a deliberate decision for which the individual must suffer the consequences, not the result of an immutable characteristic like sex or race (*Wesley* 1985, 813).

This argument (based on Locke's theory) and this narrow view of the social contract are highly criticized today (see Rawls 1971; *Harvard Law Review* 1989). According to a more modern concept of liberalism, the aim of the social contract is not simply to suppress individual impulses but to promote human freedom and equality. In this sense, a one-time, isolated transgression does not repudiate the whole contract. For this transgression, the criminal pays a price – the sentence imposed.

The statement that crime is the result of a deliberate choice to break the social contract and to withdraw from society is also being questioned. Putting the blame on one individual obscures the complexity and the social dimensions of the crime (*Harvard Law Review* 1989, 1311). Exclusion from the electoral process suggests that we are preserving the distinction between the "pure" and the "impure." The person's past is not taken into account; neither are the nature and circumstances of the offence nor the prospects for rehabilitation. In addition, exclusion based on imprisonment, as it exists in Canada, does not take into account the accidental nature of this imprisonment.

Moral Unfitness　The idea of moral irresponsibility and unfitness developed from the ancient concept that the criminal is a corrupt being who must be banished, excommunicated and outlawed. In 1884, an American court expressed this view in more modern language: "The presumption is, that one rendered infamous by conviction of felony, or other base offense indicative of great turpitude, is unfit to exercise the privilege of suffrage, or to hold office, upon terms of equality with freemen who are clothed by the State with the toga of political citizenship" (*Washington* 1884, 585). The argument of moral unfitness – that criminals are not virtuous enough to vote – has been used in more recent decisions, which cited the state's interest in preserving the integrity of the electoral process and preventing those with an anti-social and destructive attitude from voting (*Kronlund* 1971, 73; *Shepherd* 1978, 115).

There is an important distinction between mental incapacity and moral unfitness. It has been repeated several times that the only restriction to the right to vote is to those with the capacity to participate intelligently in the electoral process and the maturity or mental capacity to exercise the right to vote reasonably and responsibly. Inmates are not restricted from voting because of lack of maturity or reduced mental capacity but because of an archaic notion that criminals are morally unfit. Today, the right to vote is not related to whether a voter is a good or bad citizen. A virtuous heart and mind are no longer values associated with voting. This élitist concept has been replaced by an egalitarian concept of the right to vote.

Basing the qualification for voting on the moral fitness of citizens is not only archaic and élitist but also arbitrary. It opens the door to discrimination. As demonstrated earlier, excluding inmates only affects a fraction of the "immoral" population. Moreover, people who are incarcerated are often poor, Aboriginal, illiterate or otherwise marginalized.

We therefore believe that any exclusion based on moral fitness or on the concept of the responsible citizen must be rejected. The criteria do not meet the requirements of the *Oakes* (1986) test, either in terms of rational interest or in terms of proportionality.

Purity of the Ballot Box　The justification based on the need to preserve the purity of the ballot box by keeping undesirable elements away from it derives from the preceding justification. It, too, assumes that criminals are impure people. This particular argument, however, is phrased somewhat differently. The argument given here is that criminals must be prevented from influencing the vote. Because of their moral depravity, they will vote for corrupt candidates, and the danger of electoral fraud increases.

In today's reality, these arguments are no longer persuasive and go against common sense. Those affected by exclusion are not the criminals but the inmates. Further, since there is but one vote each, no individual is really able to influence the outcome of an election. Inmates represent only an insignificant proportion of the electorate. Besides, there are much more effective ways to help a corrupt candidate.

In addressing the argument of the duty to guard against an "immoral" vote, the Honorable Thurgood Marshall, Associate Justice of the Supreme Court of the United States, wrote in *Richardson v. Ramirez*,

> Although, in the last century, this Court may have justified the exclusion of voters from the electoral process for fear that they would vote to change laws considered important by a temporal majority, I have little doubt that we would not countenance such a purpose today. The process of democracy is one of change ... [To] disenfranchise a class of voters to "withdraw all political influence from those who are practically hostile" to the existing order, strikes at the very heart of the democratic process ... The ballot is the democratic system's coin of the realm. To condition its exercise on support of the established order is to debase that currency beyond recognition. (1974, 82–83)

To disenfranchise part of the population because of the way it might vote or because of its political ideas is clearly unconstitutional (*Carrington* 1965).

Finally, the potential for increased electoral fraud is not a valid argument. In most cases, there is no relation between an offence committed and the tendency to commit offences against election laws; however, absolute exclusion does not permit this distinction to be made. Moreover, today, specific infractions are identified in different electoral acts to prevent and provide penalties for this type of fraud. The danger of electoral fraud is no longer as evident as it was in the past, when illegal practices like vote buying were not unknown. The electoral process has improved, and cases of electoral fraud are now very rare.

Symbolic Exclusion   Despite the feebleness of these foregoing justifications, the government, rather than excluding all criminals, may want to exclude inmates as a symbolic gesture to make the right to vote more attractive in the eyes of the public.

This, however, is an illusion. The value of the right to vote is certainly not endangered by granting this right to the tiny fraction of the population who are incarcerated offenders.

Furthermore, it is not clear that denying the right to vote to inmates has any symbolic value in the eyes of the public. Most Canadians, even some judges, are probably not aware that this restriction exists.

Symbolic exclusion affects only the inmates themselves. It does not affect the public. It illustrates that criminals must be isolated from the community. It is an anachronism, a relic of civil death. As has been written, "Disenfranchisement is a symbol, and it is the wrong sort of symbol to legitimate in law. It is a symbol of rejection, not reconciliation; a symbol of difference, rather than commonality; a symbol of domination instead of equality. Disenfranchisement is a symbol that should be repudiated" (*Harvard Law Review* 1989, 1317).

We believe, therefore, that the arguments of a responsible citizenry and symbolic exclusion should be rejected in our society because they no longer have any relevance and are, in fact, contrary to the present-day values of equality and fairness. This restriction is a relic of obsolete customs. Holmes said it well: "The customs, beliefs, or needs of a primitive time establish a rule or a formula. In the course of centuries the custom, belief, or necessity disappears, but the rule remains. The reason which gave rise to the rule has been forgotten, and ingenious minds set themselves to inquire how it is to be accounted for" (1881, 5).

A Free and Informed Democratic Choice

In *Jolivet* (1983), the Supreme Court of British Columbia concluded that for practical reasons related to the imperatives of imprisonment, the disenfranchisement of inmates is a reasonable limit. According to Mr. Justice Taylor, the right to vote means more than putting one's ballot into the ballot box. Voting implies the right to gather information in order to make an informed choice: in other words, to have access to public discussion. The limits that are placed on the freedoms of expression and association, inherent in imprisonment, make the exercise of this right impossible. Inmates cannot inform themselves sufficiently about politics to make an informed choice. In these circumstances, the Court reasoned, the right to vote can be denied.

This was the only instance from among the literature examined – whether Canadian or American jurisprudence or other types of legal writings – where this type of argument was used to justify the disenfranchisement of inmates. The argument, however, has been strongly criticized by commentators on the *Jolivet* (1983) case, as well as in other judicial decisions.

In the book *The Canadian Charter of Rights and Freedoms,* in his chapter entitled "Democratic Rights," Senator Gérald-A. Beaudoin says that "in today's electronic age, with the media increasingly present, this argument is not very convincing" (1989, 278). He concludes that it is not as true today to say that inmates do not have adequate knowledge of the candidates, who now appear on television and the radio. Inmates read the papers, watch television and are able to discuss the election among themselves. They are as well informed as free citizens, many of whom no longer attend public political meetings.

Lynn Smith (1984) writes that most Canadians get their political information from the media. In this respect, inmates are as well off as others. They may actually be better off, she adds, since they have more time to read, listen and watch.

The argument was also criticized in some of the reports submitted to the Royal Commission, including that of the Canadian Bar Association. In the Association's opinion, the *Jolivet* decision ignores the different levels of security in various types of correctional institutions: there is as much exchange of information and ideas in a minimum-security penitentiary as in a logging camp, for example. The authors of the report further point out that inmates in all institutions have access to television, radio and newspapers. The report concludes that exclusion on these grounds is not justified, and it refers to members of the armed forces or civilians outside the country who must rely on the media for information.

In an era when the electronic and print media are omnipresent, inmates are as able as most Canadians to inform themselves about politics. Nothing prevents them from receiving the programs of the different political parties, nor would it be impossible to hold evening sessions in penal institutions to provide political information. Several outside groups are currently going to the penitentiaries for cultural, educational, sports, therapeutic or religious gatherings.

According to the *Standard Minimum Rules for the Treatment of Prisoners,* the state has an obligation to keep inmates as close to the community as possible. Rule 39 stresses the importance of maintaining contact with the outside world:

> Prisoners shall be kept informed regularly of the more important items of news by the reading of newspapers, periodicals or special institutional publications, by hearing wireless transmissions, by lectures or by any similar means as authorized or controlled by the administration. (United Nations 1955)

Rule 57 and subsequent rules establish the principles that must guide penal system policies and objectives. The institutions should put the period of incarceration to good use, so that, upon release, offenders not only will want to obey the law and provide for their own needs but also will have the ability to do so. Rule 61 states that this treatment should not put the emphasis on excluding inmates from society but should encourage them to continue to be part of it.

Thus, the exclusion of inmates because they have insufficient access to information to be able to make an informed choice does not conform to the spirit of the rules or to today's reality. Further, basing the exercise of the right to vote on the ability to make an informed choice is both discriminatory and arbitrary: theoretically, this reasoning could be used to disenfranchise other categories of people, such as the illiterate, the disabled and the inhabitants of remote regions. Mr. Justice Strayer raised this possibility in the *Belczowski* case when he stated,

> If one were to join this particular crusade advocated by Crown counsel, it would be necessary to disenfranchise the sick and the elderly who are confined to their homes or institutions, those in hospital prior to an election, probably those out of the country during election campaigns, the illiterate, those who live in remote parts of the country and, most of all, those hundreds of thousands who live in our midst and who, according to regular polls, take no interest whatever in politics. The absurdity of this proposition throws into question the whole argument that the state has a right to choose among adult citizens of sound mind as to who is worthy to vote. (1991, 110)

According to this reasoning, few people would be entitled to vote and the constitutional guarantee would no longer have much meaning. In the words of Lynn Smith, "To build an ability qualification into the definition of the 'right to vote' is to open the door to legislation seriously infringing what most Canadians would consider to be one of their most basic rights" (1984, 381–82).

Penal Justifications

Functions of Penal Sanctions
Some people, like the Honourable Mr. Justice MacDonnell of the Supreme Court of British Columbia, believe that "prohibiting a prisoner from voting is a reasonable sanction" (*Reynolds* 1983, 336). But what objectives are served by using exclusion as a penal sanction?

In this study, we can simplify the philosophical debates on the objectives of sanctions by assuming that a sanction can be justified in one of two ways: by referring to a theory of retribution or by taking a utilitarian approach.

In the first case, it is believed that inflicting a punishment requires no other justification than the offender's guilt. In the second, it is thought that the sanction cannot be justified in itself and must draw its justification from some other end or social function.

The retribution theory assumes that a person who is guilty of an offence deserves to be punished. The severity of the sentence, therefore, should be in proportion to the gravity of the offence.

In the utilitarian approach, penal sanctions generally protect society by reducing the frequency of behaviours prohibited by criminal law. Behaviour can be controlled by (1) influencing the behaviour of the members of society in general (general prevention); and (2) influencing the behaviour of persons who have previously disobeyed the law (special prevention).

General prevention covers deterrence as well as the moral or sociopedagogical effect of the sentence. The risk of being discovered and punished serves as a deterrent. But general prevention also includes the idea that punishment is an explicit expression of society's disapproval of certain actions and a reaffirmation of certain values.

Special or individual prevention, which results from each sanction's effects on the person being punished, is carried out by intimidation, neutralization or rehabilitation.

Punishment   We rarely hear that incarcerated or convicted people should be disenfranchised because they deserve additional punishment. Still, many of those who use political or utilitarian reasons to deny inmates the right to vote are subconsciously taking a retributive approach.

The more or less conscious desire to punish and the idea that the sentence is deserved are usually found among people who believe that the exclusion of all inmates, or at least those who have committed "the most serious crimes," does not require explicit justification. For example, one group presenting a brief to the Commission wrote, "We believe that ... violent criminals, and those *without any remorse whatever* for their criminal activity, should not be qualified to vote at any time during their incarceration." This could be classified as a retributive stance. We can also see this more or less conscious desire to punish in the general public – a segment of society and some of its representatives are very reluctant to give prisoners the right to vote.

This argument, that denying the vote to inmates is a deserved punishment, is, in our opinion, contrary to the penal philosophy and the correctional principles generally accepted in Canada. This extra punishment does not conform to the principle of moderation found in penal law and sentencing that has been advocated in Canada for the past 20 years. From this perspective, it is difficult to accept that such punishment, in addition to the court's sentence, could conform to the principle that "the sentence must be the least restrictive measure that would suffice and be adequate under the circumstances."

This additional sanction is also difficult to reconcile with the proportionality between the seriousness of the offence and the severity of the sentence, which is at the heart of the retributive approach.

Finally, this extra sanction is contrary to the generally accepted correctional principle that "the sentence of imprisonment pronounced by the court constitutes the punishment."

The Protection of Society   It would be difficult to argue that disenfranchisement of inmates is an effective means of general crime prevention. The risk of losing the right to vote may not have any influence whatsoever on those members of society who are tempted to commit offences that already call for potentially lengthy prison sentences. For the deterrent or socio-educational effects of sanctions to be effective, society must be aware of them. This precondition is rarely met in the case of supplementary sanctions. Potential offenders do not know that they could lose the right to vote if they commit such and such an offence, and they certainly are not thinking about that possibility when they consider committing a crime.

On the other hand, even if they were aware, the loss of the right to vote is generally quite insignificant when compared with the main sanction, the possibility of going to prison. Because of the marginal effect of the severity of sanctions on general prevention (Beyleved 1980), disenfranchisement of inmates cannot be seen as a rational means of achieving this objective.

A similar argument can be made about instilling fear in the offender. The loss of voting rights has no additional threat over and above the threat of a prison sentence such that it would prevent a former inmate from committing another crime.

Disenfranchisement of inmates, therefore, is not an adequate means of instilling fear or of general deterrence. How effective, then, are voting rights in the social reintegration and rehabilitation of offenders?

Voting Rights as a Means of Rehabilitation
Denying voting rights neither encourages the rehabilitation of inmates nor contributes to the protection of society. On the contrary, it has long

been argued that exercising the right to vote can contribute to the inmate's moral, intellectual and political development.

John Stuart Mill, for example, attached a great deal of importance to the educational benefits of participating in the affairs of the state, even though he wasn't thinking specifically about inmate voting rights. A political scientist wrote about Mill's belief: "To give a person a share of the responsibility for governing the society of which he is a part was, Mill argued, a most effective way of contributing to his moral and intellectual development" (Pennoch 1979, 443).

Today, a number of people specifically argue that the right to vote contributes to the rehabilitation and social reintegration of inmates. It shows inmates that they are still part of the community and have the same duties and responsibilities as other citizens. At the same time, it fosters links with the outside, reduces the feelings of rejection and exclusion, and puts into practice one of the most widely accepted correctional principles in Canada, as we saw earlier in the section on correctional principles.

With this in mind, a justice of the Supreme Court of Ontario declared, "In my view, enabling convicted inmates to exercise their franchise and participate in the electoral process clearly advances those goals [rehabilitation]" (*Grondin* 1988, 432). In a submission to the Commission, the Canadian Bar Association wrote, "in fact, such a limitation [disenfranchisement] would likely have a negative impact on one of the stated goals of sentencing policy, rehabilitation" (1990, 9). Similar opinions were submitted by others interested in inmate rehabilitation.

Therefore, we can say that disenfranchising inmates is not a way to protect society, either from the point of view of general prevention or from that of instilling fear. It certainly does not promote rehabilitation and, from this perspective, even runs counter to the generally accepted principles of sentencing and correction.

Practical Objections

Administration and Security
In court rulings, in public debate and at hearings of the Commission, administrative or security considerations have sometimes been cited as reasons for disqualifying inmates from the right to vote. Whatever system is adopted, it is evident that allowing inmates to vote will create additional tasks for management and staff at custodial facilities. It is conceivable that voting, distributing campaign materials and especially allowing access to candidates might require extra security precautions.

The interveners appearing before the Commission who had experience with inmates' voting unanimously acknowledged that the administrative and security problems were minimal and that the few elections in which inmates had taken part had gone well.

In Quebec, penitentiary inmates voted in the 1980 referendum and in the provincial elections of 1981, 1985 and 1989. In the referendum, there was 40 percent participation; between 20 and 25 percent voted in the provincial elections. Jacques Diotte (1990), representing Correctional Service Canada, Quebec Region, spoke before the Commission but did not raise any particular problems. Pierre-F. Côté (1990), Chief Electoral Officer of Quebec, stated in his testimony that his office had worked in close cooperation with the authorities of Correctional Service Canada and the province of Quebec and that there had been no problems in prison facilities during the provincial elections. The organization responsible for inmate voting produced a 42-page procedures manual for voting by inmates (Lavergne 1990), "prepared for persons assigned to carry out the various operations related to inmate voting." The Services correctionnels du Québec also confirmed that there were no serious administrative or security-related problems involved in inmate voting (Simard 1991).

The only point that causes some reservations is allowing the candidates access to institutions. Neither Correctional Service Canada nor the Services correctionnels du Québec allows candidates to enter prison facilities. Still, in view of the fact that elected members have already met with some inmates in Quebec penitentiaries and many volunteer workers meet regularly with groups of inmates, well-planned meetings with representatives of political parties could take place in prison facilities under certain conditions. Such meetings, however, are not absolutely necessary to ensure that the inmates are well informed and able to exercise their voting rights in a knowledgeable manner – few Canadian voters actually meet candidates.

Procedures for Exercising Voting Rights
The main questions related to the voting procedures for inmates concern the enumeration process, determining the constituency where the vote will be exercised and the voting procedure itself. These questions may be closely related, even though we treat them separately for the purpose of this analysis.

Enumeration Preparing a voters list in each institution poses no particular problem, regardless of the riding in which the inmates are entitled to vote. The management of a facility can easily prepare a list of inmates who are voters; enter for each voter the family and given names, home address and age; and ask if the inmate wishes to be included on the voters list, as prescribed, for example, by section 274 of the Quebec *Election Act*. In his brief to the Commission, Jean-Pierre Kingsley (1990), Chief Electoral Officer of Canada, suggested that it is also easy to ask the inmates to declare their ordinary place of residence, indicating in particular their place of residence before incarceration.

Choice of Constituency There are three options: inmates could vote either in the riding of their ordinary residence or in the riding containing the institution where they are imprisoned, or they could choose between the two. The last two options raise the fear that inmates would have undue "political weight" in ridings where a large number of inmates are concentrated, such as Kingston, Ontario.

This fear could be allayed if inmates were enumerated in the riding of their ordinary residence or where they lived just before sentencing. Provincial election laws favour this choice because it avoids concentrations of inmate votes. In Quebec, for instance, in the last election of 1989, 2 194 inmates voted in 125 constituencies. This solution appears to be the best option.

Method of Voting The voting procedure for inmates is clearly more complex and controversial. To simplify it, we can combine the different possibilities into three alternative methods of voting: voting in regular polling stations located in the prisons, voting by proxy and voting at advance polls.

The first option allows inmates to vote on election day in regular polling stations located in the prisons; the candidates on the ballot are those running in the constituency where the institution is located. This procedure, which is the easiest to implement, raises the problem of the concentration of inmate votes just discussed. For this reason, it does not have many supporters.

The second option, voting by proxy, is currently in use in Ontario, and enables inmates to vote in provincial elections. Inmates authorize close friends or relatives to register them on a voters list and to vote on their behalf using proxy forms.

This procedure offers certain advantages. First, it eliminates the need to establish polling stations inside the prisons and is, therefore, the method with the fewest administrative problems. Second, it allows the inmates to vote in the constituency of their ordinary residence without their votes being identifiable. Third, it prevents a significant concentration of inmate votes in one or more constituencies.

Voting by proxy, however, presents two major problems. First, it carries a large stigma for the agents, forcing them repeatedly to identify themselves as close friends or relatives of an inmate: first when the proxy is certified, then when the voter is registered and finally when the vote is cast. In addition, to vote by proxy, inmates must have a close friend or relative who agrees to act as their agent and is able to go and vote for them in the riding in which they lived before imprisonment. Many inmates would probably be unable to find such an agent. This option, therefore, should also be rejected.

Finally, there is the option of voting at advance polls. Quebec has already had considerable experience with this method of voting. This procedure allows inmates to vote for one of the candidates running in the constituency where they lived before incarceration; they vote several days before the election. The ballot could be forwarded by mail or be placed in a ballot box that would then be delivered to the chief electoral officer, as is currently done in Quebec. The ballot could be either a blank ballot form on which the voter would write the name of the preferred candidate, as is suggested in the brief prepared by the Chief Electoral Officer of Canada (Kingsley 1990, 33), or a ballot with the specific names of the candidates standing for election in the inmate's constituency of residence, as provided for in the Quebec *Election Act*.

Voting at advance polls is the most administratively complex and burdensome for both the chief electoral officer and the prison facilities. It is also inappropriate for by-elections. It does have the advantage of allowing inmates to vote in person for a candidate in their own home riding, and it avoids the concentration of inmate votes in certain constituencies. This method of voting works very well in Quebec provincial elections and could be used without major difficulties in federal elections. It is the method suggested by Jean-Pierre Kingsley (1990, 32), Chief Electoral Officer of Canada.

CONCLUSION

Refusing to grant the right to vote to inmates must be seen as a remnant of the exclusion practices of the past.

On the one hand, these practices involved excluding criminals from society through banishment, deportation, loss of citizenship or civil death. When criminals were excluded, they lost their rights. On the other hand, universal suffrage has progressed very gradually, even in the most democratic countries. For a long time, the right to vote was restricted to specific groups of citizens. The poor, the illiterate, Blacks, Aboriginal people and women were all excluded from the democratic process. People who were convicted or incarcerated were excluded both from society and from the right to vote.

The modern trend is toward equality of rights and participation in political life by everyone, even the members of unpopular or marginal groups. Canada may be seen as one of the front runners among democratic countries when it comes to legal and political equality. As we have seen earlier, Canadian courts and correctional policies recognize that inmates retain all of their civil rights other than those expressly denied them by law. The *Canadian Charter of Rights and Freedoms* spells out the equality of rights for all Canadians, including the right to vote. Exclusions are becoming less and less acceptable, and we believe that there ought to be no exceptions to the right to vote and that the *Canada Elections Act* should be revised to grant the right to vote to all prison inmates.

In addition to these basic principles, we believe that the aims of justice – "equity, fairness, guarantees for the rights and liberties of the individual against the powers of the state, and the provision of a fitting response by society to wrongdoing" (Canada, Department of Justice 1982, 46) – and the prevailing Canadian principles in the area of penal law both point in the same direction.

The following principles deserve special emphasis:

"A sentence should be the least onerous alternative appropriate in the circumstances." (Canada, Solicitor General 1990a, 16)

"A sentence should be proportionate to the gravity of the offence." (ibid.)

"The punishment consists only of the loss of liberty, restriction of mobility, or any other legal disposition of the court." (Canada, Solicitor General 1986, 40)

In addition, for more than 30 years, almost every committee in the penal area and almost every policy statement have recognized that rehabilitation and reintegration of the offender into the community are major concerns of correctional authorities. As the Correctional Law Review Working Group recently reminded us, correctional services should encourage inmates "to adopt acceptable behaviour patterns and ... to prepare for eventual release and successful re-integration in society" (Canada, Solicitor General 1986, 32–33). We must help inmates to develop personally and socially by providing appropriate programs and "by permitting living conditions in prison to approximate those in the community. This is important [because] it assumes that the prisoner is expected to discharge the normal duties and responsibilities of all citizens" (Law Reform Commission 1975, 35). The ability to exercise their voting rights is one of the factors that could demonstrate to inmates that they are considered to have the same duties and responsibilities as all other citizens.

It might be argued that denying the right to vote to inmates is likely to be applied disproportionately to members of some socially disadvantaged groups, like Aboriginal people. The 30 000 people in prison represent only a very small proportion of those who have committed *Criminal Code* offences. The law and the penal system, unfortunately, do not observe the maxim that "all men are equal before the law." Big swindlers, white-collar criminals, chemical-weapons manufacturers, big polluters or drug producers are rarely found in prison. The people in prison are those convicted of theft ("petty theft"), drunk driving or the non-payment of fines. The poor, the disadvantaged and Aboriginal people are overrepresented in the prisons. Aboriginal people often make up more than one-third (and even more than one-half) of the prison population, especially in western Canada. Taking the right to vote away from these people accentuates this injustice and social inequality.

Finally, some argue that only those who have committed major crimes, such as inmates with life sentences, should be denied the right to vote. This approach must also be rejected, despite the arguments that are advanced to support it.

Some claim that the act committed is of such gravity that the offenders have broken the social contract and therefore have deprived themselves of the right to participate in the political process by their own action. We might ask, however, whether a single action (often an isolated one) can nullify the entire contract. It could also be argued that the prison sentence imposed by the court should be the only consequence of violating the terms of the contract. Others believe that people have certain fundamental rights and freedoms independent of the contract.

In another attempt to justify this position, some argue that those who have committed an act of such gravity have demonstrated that they are morally unfit and therefore unable to exercise a right that requires good judgement. In this case, a person's whole character is being judged on a single instance of negative behaviour. Someone who has committed murder has not only committed a very reprehensible act but is also a killer, a bad individual, immoral and so forth. This judgement of the whole person on the basis of a single action must, in our opinion, also be rejected.

Both justifications for the disenfranchisement of those sentenced to life imprisonment are all the more open to challenge because the serious acts are usually isolated criminal actions. More so than with other inmates, these people have usually led their lives as good citizens, with fewer previous incarcerations than other inmates (table 2.22).

In the final analysis, the disenfranchisement of prison inmates is an anachronistic practice that does not reasonably serve any of the aims of sentencing and is, in fact, contrary to the penal philosophy and the correctional principles prevailing in Canada. It also accentuates social inequalities which are already found in the administration of justice as well, and cannot be justified for any group of human beings.

APPENDIX
TEXT OF STATUTES

Canadian Charter of Rights and Freedoms

Article 3 — Every citizen of Canada has the right to vote in an election of members of the House of Commons or of a legislative assembly and to be qualified for membership therein.

Canada Elections Act

Article 51 — The following persons are not qualified to vote at an election and shall not vote at an election:

(e) every person undergoing punishment as an inmate in any penal institution for the commission of any offence.

Quebec *Election Act*

Article 273 — Every inmate has the right to vote at a general election.

To exercise his right to vote, an inmate must be registered on the list of electors of the house of detention in which he is detained. He shall exercise his right to vote in the advance polling station of that establishment.

His vote shall be counted in the electoral division of his domicile.

Article 274 — The director of a house of detention shall draw up the list of the inmates of that establishment who are electors. The list shall indicate the surname, given name, address of the domicile and age of each elector.

The director shall then ask every inmate if he wishes to be registered on the list of electors and verify with him the accuracy of the particulars concerning him.

The director shall transmit the list of electors to the chief electoral officer not later than the sixteenth day preceding polling day.

Article 275 — The returning officer of the electoral division in which the house of detention is situated shall establish in it, in cooperation with the director of the house of detention, as many advance polling stations as he considers necessary.

Article 276 Each authorized party may, in accordance with sections 316 and 317, designate a representative.

Article 283 After counting the ballot papers for each electoral division, the deputy returning officer shall draw up a statement of votes for each advance polling station and an abstract of the statement of votes for each electoral division.

The deputy returning officer shall then place in separate envelopes, for each electoral division, the ballot papers given in favour of each candidate, the rejected ballot papers, the spoiled or cancelled ballot papers and the unused ballot papers. He shall seal the envelopes and place them in another sealed envelope bearing the name of the electoral division concerned.

The deputy returning officer, the poll clerk and those representatives wishing to do so shall affix their initials to the seals.

The envelope, the poll book and the list of electors shall be placed in the ballot box.

Article 284 The deputy returning officer shall seal the ballot box; the latter, the poll clerk and those representatives wishing to do so shall affix their initials to the seals.

The deputy returning officer shall then give the ballot box, the statement of votes and the abstracts of the statement to the chief electoral officer or the person designated by him.

Article 285 The chief electoral officer shall immediately communicate the results of the vote to every returning officer concerned and send him the abstract of the statement of votes with which he is concerned.

Article 286 To allow inmates to exercise their right to vote, the chief electoral officer may make any agreement he considers expedient with the warden of any house of detention established under an Act of the Parliament of Canada or of Québec.

Article 316 A candidate may attend every operation related to the poll. He may also designate a person and give him a power of attorney to represent him before the deputy returning officer or the officer in charge of information and order, or before each of them.

Article 317 The power of attorney shall be signed by the candidate or his mandatary and be presented to the deputy returning officer or to the officer in charge of information and order, as the case may be. It is valid for the duration of the polling and of the counting.

Article 366 The deputy returning officer shall consider every objection raised by a candidate or the representative of a candidate in respect of the validity of a ballot paper and make a decision immediately. The objection and the decision of the deputy returning officer shall be entered in the poll book.

Newfoundland *Election Act*

Section 4 of R.S.N. 1970, c. 106 was repealed and re-enacted by S.N. 1988, c. 39, s. 25 to read only

4. The chief electoral officer is disqualified from voting.

ABBREVIATIONS

Ala.	Alabama Reports
am.	amended
art.	article
B.C.C.A.	British Columbia Court of Appeal
B.C.S.C.	British Columbia Supreme Court
c.	chapter
C.A.	Court of Appeal
C.C.C. (3d)	Canadian Criminal Cases, Third Series
Cir.	Circuit
C.R.R.	Canadian Rights Reporter
D.L.R. (4th)	Dominion Law Reports, Fourth Series
F.2d	Federal Reporter, Second Series
F.C.	Federal Court Reports
F. Supp.	Federal Supplement
F.T.R.	Federal Trial Reports
Ga.	Georgia
H.C.	Ontario High Court
Man. R. (2d)	Manitoba Reports, Second Series
M.D.	Middle District
N.D.	Northern District
O.R.	Ontario Reports
Ont. C.A.	Ontario Court of Appeal
Q.B.	Court of Queen's Bench
R.S.C.	Revised Statutes of Canada

R.S.N.	Revised Statutes of Newfoundland
R.S.Q.	Revised Statutes of Quebec
S.C.	Statutes of Canada
S.C.R.	Supreme Court Reports
S.M.	Statutes of Manitoba
S.N.	Statutes of Newfoundland
S.O.	Statutes of Ontario
S.Q.	Statutes of Quebec
s(s).	section(s)
Supp.	Supplement
T.D.	Federal Court, Trial Division
Tenn.	Tennessee
U.S.	United States Supreme Court Reports
W.W.R.	Western Weekly Reports

NOTES

This study was completed in February 1991.

In this study, quoted material that originated in French has been translated into English.

1. A similar situation was contested under Saskatchewan's *Election Act* in *Maltby* (1982); it was decided that this institutional practice of not allowing defendants to vote violated their fundamental rights.

2. One should mention, among other things, that inmates who do not have Canadian citizenship could, in principle, vote (by mail or otherwise) in elections in their own countries in accordance with the laws in force in those countries.

3. Except for the *Gould* (1984a) case (the decision was reversed on appeal on procedural grounds), the *Belczowski* (1991) case, of all the decisions handed down to date, is perhaps the most significant.

4. In our opinion, this decision will have a very significant impact because of the exceptional force of the arguments presented, certain aspects of which seem incontrovertible.

5. Before 1983, the period of possible imprisonment was one year or more. In 1983, it was increased to five years by an amendment (Australia, *Commonwealth Electoral Act*, s. 93(8)(*b*), as amended).

6. In this article, the authors, both commissioners on the Australian Electoral Commission, state that it was impossible for penitentiary authorities

to prepare a list of the inmates entitled to vote because they did not have the necessary information to meet the required criteria. In addition, it was impossible to verify the situation of persons not sentenced to prison terms. The authors conclude, "The Australian Electoral Commission has now accepted that the legislation, in its current form, is unworkable and now has regard to the *actual* sentence of imprisonment of five years or longer as the disqualifying criterion."

7. The system of voting by mail has been abandoned in favour of advance polls, which are considered more effective and expeditious. This system appears to be working well (Fitzgerald and Zdenkowski 1987, 27).

8. The eight categories of crimes covered by the survey were sexual assault, robbery, robbery with violence, breaking and entering, motor vehicle theft, theft of private property, theft of personal property and vandalism (Canada, Solicitor General 1984, 13).

9. It should be noted, however, that in 1985–86, 44 percent of offenders were admitted for defaulting on fine payments only.

10. Unpublished data provided by the Corrections Branch of the Department of the Attorney General of British Columbia.

11. This philosophy is very obvious in the *Standard Minimum Rules for the Treatment of Prisoners:*

> The régime of the institution should seek to minimize any differences between prison life and life at liberty which tend to lessen the responsibility of the prisoners or the respect due to their dignity as human beings ...
>
> The treatment of prisoners should emphasize not their exclusion from the community, but their continuing part in it ... Steps should be taken to safeguard, to the maximum extent compatible with the law and the sentence, the rights relating to civil interests, social security rights and other social benefits of prisoners. (United Nations 1955, Rules 60(1), 61)

12. This principle is formulated as follows in article 10(3) of the *International Covenant on Civil and Political Rights:* "The penitentiary system shall comprise treatment of prisoners the essential aim of which shall be their reformation and social rehabilitation" (United Nations 1976).

13. See also, among others, Law Reform Commission of Canada (1976, 26), Canada, Canadian Sentencing Commission (1987, 169) and Canada, House of Commons (1988, 63).

14. Already seen in Canada, Department of Justice (1956).

15. Upheld by the Manitoba Court of Appeal in *Badger* (1988b).

REFERENCES

Australia. *Commonwealth Electoral Act*, 1918, s. 93(8)(*b*), am. 1983, No. 144; s. 96, am. *Electoral and Referendum Amendment Act*, 1990, No. 24, s. 35.

Badger v. Canada (Attorney General) (1988)a, 55 Man R. (2d) 211 (Q.B.); reversed (1988)b, [1989] 1 W.W.R. 216 (Man. C.A.).

Badger v. Manitoba (Attorney General) (1986)a, 27 C.C.C. (3d) 158 (Man. Q.B.); affirmed (1986)b, 29 C.C.C. (3d) 92 (Man. C.A.).

Beacham v. Braterman 396 U.S. 12 (1969).

Beaudoin, G. 1989. "Democratic Rights." In *The Canadian Charter of Rights and Freedoms*. 2d ed., ed. G. Beaudoin and E. Ratushny. Toronto: Carswell.

Belczowski v. Canada (1991), 42 F.T.R. 98; affirmed [1992] 2 F.C. 440.

Beyleved, D., ed. 1980. *A Bibliography on General Deterrence Research*. Westmead: Saxon House.

Canada. *Canada Elections Act*, R.S.C. 1970, c. 14 (1st Supp.), s. 14(4)(*e*),(*d*),(*f*).

———. *Canada Elections Act*, R.S.C. 1985, c. E-2, s. 51(*e*),(*d*),(*f*).

———. *Canadian Charter of Rights and Freedoms*, ss. 1, 3, 15, 24, 33, Part I of the *Constitution Act, 1982*, being Schedule B of the *Canada Act 1982* (U.K.), 1982, c. 11.

———. *Criminal Code*, S.C. 1892, c. 29.

———. *Criminal Code*, R.S.C. 1985, c. C-46, s. 731.

———. *Narcotic Control Act*, R.S.C. 1985, c. N-1.

———. *Parole Act*, R.S.C. 1985, c. P-2, ss. 19, 21.2.

Canada. Canadian Committee on Corrections. 1969. *Toward Unity: Criminal Justice and Corrections*. Ottawa: Information Canada.

Canada. Canadian Sentencing Commission. 1987. *Sentencing Reform: A Canadian Approach*. Ottawa: Minister of Supply and Services Canada.

Canada. Correctional Service Canada. 1980. *Inmates' Rights*. Ottawa: Minister of Supply and Services Canada.

———. 1990. *Mission of the Correctional Service of Canada*. Ottawa: Minister of Supply and Services Canada.

Canada. Correctional Service Canada. Management Information Services. 1990a. *Population Profile, 06–30–90*. Ottawa: Minister of Supply and Services Canada.

———. 1990b. *Female Population Profile, 06–30–90*. Ottawa: Minister of Supply and Services Canada.

Canada. Department of Justice. 1956. *Report of a Committee Appointed to Inquire into the Principles and Procedures Followed in the Remission Service of the Department of Justice of Canada*. Ottawa: Queen's Printer.

———. 1982. *The Criminal Law in Canadian Society*. Ottawa: Department of Justice.

———. 1990. *Directions for Reform: Sentencing*. Ottawa: Minister of Supply and Services Canada.

Canada. House of Commons. Standing Committee on Justice and Legal Affairs. Sub-Committee on the Penitentiary System in Canada. 1977. *Third Report*. Ottawa: Queen's Printer.

Canada. House of Commons. Standing Committee on Justice and Solicitor General. 1988. *Taking Responsibility*. Ottawa: Queen's Printer.

Canada. Solicitor General Canada. 1984. *Le Sondage canadien sur la victimisation en milieu urbain. Bulletin 2: Crime signalés et non signalés*. Ottawa: Minister of Supply and Services Canada.

———. 1986. *Correctional Philosophy*. Correctional Law Review Working Group Working Paper 1. Ottawa: Solicitor General Canada.

———. 1987. *Correctional Authority and Inmate Rights*. Correctional Law Review Working Group Working Paper 5. Ottawa: Solicitor General Canada.

———. 1990a. *Directions for Reform: A Framework for Sentencing, Corrections and Conditional Release*. Ottawa: Minister of Supply and Services Canada.

———. 1990b. *Directions for Reform: Corrections and Conditional Release*. Ottawa: Minister of Supply and Services Canada.

Canada. Statistics Canada. 1978. *Crime Statistics 1973*. Cat. 85-201. Ottawa: Information Canada.

———. 1986. *Adult Correctional Services in Canada 1984–1985*. Canadian Centre for Justice Statistics, Cat. 85-211. Ottawa: Minister of Supply and Services Canada.

———. 1990a. *Postcensal Annual Estimates of Population by Marital Status, Age, Sex and Components of Growth for Canada, Provinces and Territories, June 1, 1990*. Vol. 8, 8th ed. Cat. 91-210. Ottawa: Minister of Supply and Services Canada.

———. 1990b. *Adult Correctional Services in Canada 1989–1990*. Canadian Centre for Justice Statistics, Cat. 85-211. Ottawa: Minister of Supply and Services Canada.

———. 1990c. *Canadian Crime Statistics*. Canadian Centre for Justice Statistics, Cat. 85-205. Ottawa: Minister of Supply and Services Canada.

Canadian Bar Association. 1990. "Responses to Questions Raised by Commissioners on the Canadian Bar Association Submission to the Royal Commission on Electoral Reform and Party Financing." Ottawa.

Canadian Disability Rights Council v. Canada (1988), 21 F.T.R. 268.

Carrington v. Rash 380 U.S. 89 (1965).

Côté, Pierre-F. 1990. Testimony of the Director General of Élections Québec before the Royal Commission on Electoral Reform and Party Financing, Québec, 30 April.

Dillenburg v. Kramer 469 F.2d 1222 (9th Cir. 1972).

Diotte, Jacques. 1990. Testimony of the representative of Correctional Service Canada, Quebec Region, before the Royal Commission on Electoral Reform and Party Financing, Montreal, 10 April.

Fitzgerald, J., and G. Zdenkowski. 1987. "Voting Rights of Convicted Persons." Criminal Law Journal 11:10–39.

Gould v. Canada (Attorney General), [1984]a 1 F.C. 1119 (T.D.); reversed [1984]b, 1 F.C. 1133 (C.A.); affirmed [1984]c 2 S.C.R. 124.

Green v. Board of Elections of City of New York 380 F.2d 445 (2d Cir. 1967); certiorari denied 389 U.S. 1048 (1968).

Grondin v. Ontario (Attorney General) (1988), 65 O.R. (2d) 427 (H.C.).

Harvard Law Review. 1989. "The Disenfranchisement of Ex-Felons: Citizenship, Criminality, and the Purity of the Ballot Box." 102:1300–317.

Holmes, Oliver W. 1881. The Common Law. Boston: Little, Brown, reprinted 1949.

Hoogbruin v. British Columbia (Attorney General) (1985), 24 D.L.R. (4th) 718 (B.C.C.A.).

Hunter v. Southam Inc., [1984] 2 S.C.R. 145.

Jolivet v. R. (1983), 8 C.R.R. 5 (B.C.S.C.).

Kaiser, G.E. 1971. "The Inmate as a Citizen: Imprisonment and the Loss of Civil Rights in Canada." Queen's Law Journal 2:208–77.

Kingsley, Jean-Pierre. 1990. Brief from the Chief Electoral Officer of Canada to the Royal Commission on Electoral Reform and Party Financing. Ottawa.

Kronlund v. Honstein 327 F. Supp. 71 (N.D. Ga. 1971).

Lavergne, F. 1990. Manuel de procédure sur le vote des détenus. Service responsable du vote des détenus. Sainte-Foy: Direction générale des élections du Québec.

Law Reform Commission of Canada. 1975. Imprisonment and Release. Working Paper 11. Ottawa: Information Canada.

———. 1976. A Report on Dispositions and Sentences in the Criminal Process: Guidelines. Ottawa: Information Canada.

Lévesque v. Canada (Attorney General) (1985), [1986] 2 F.C. 287 (T.D.).

Maltby v. Saskatchewan (Attorney General) (1982), 4 C.R.R. 348 (Sask. Q.B.).

Manitoba. Elections Act, S.M. 1980, c. 67.

Mayo, H.B. 1960. *An Introduction to Democratic Theory*. New York: Oxford University Press.

Mish, C., C. Jefferson, B. Hayes and C. Graham. 1982. *National Survey Concerning Female Inmates in Provincial and Territorial Institutions*. Ottawa: Canadian Association of Elizabeth Fry Societies.

Muldoon v. Canada, [1988] 3 F.C. 628 (T.D.).

Newfoundland. *Election Act*, R.S.N. 1970, c. 106, s. 4.

———. *Election Act*, S.N. 1988, c. 39, s. 25.

Ontario. *Election Act, 1984*, S.O. 1984, c. 54.

Ontario. Royal Commission Inquiry into Civil Rights. 1969. *Report 2*. Vol. 4. Toronto: Queen's Printer.

Pennoch, J.R. 1979. *Democratic Political Theory*. Princeton: Princeton University Press.

Quebec. *An Act to abolish civil death*, S.Q. 1906, c. 38.

———. *Charter of human rights and freedoms*, R.S.Q. c. C-12.

———. *Civil Code of Lower Canada*.

———. *Election Act*, R.S.Q. c. E-3.3, ss. 273–76, 283–86, 316–17, 366.

Quebec. Comité d'étude sur les solutions de rechange à l'incarcération. 1986. *Rapport*. Québec: Ministère de la Sécurité publique.

Quebec. Services correctionnels du Québec. 1988. *Mission, valeurs et orientations*. Québec: Ministère de la Sécurité publique.

R. v. Big M Drug Mart, [1985] 1 S.C.R. 295.

R. v. Oakes, [1986] 1 S.C.R. 103.

Rawls, J. 1971. *A Theory of Justice*. Cambridge: Harvard University Press.

Reference re s. 94(2) of the Motor Vehicle Act (B.C.), [1985] 2 S.C.R. 486.

Reynolds v. British Columbia (Attorney General) (1983), 4 C.R.R. 332 (B.C.S.C.); affirmed [1984] 5 W.W.R. 270 (B.C.C.A.).

Reynolds v. Sims 377 U.S. 533 (1964).

Richardson v. Ramirez 418 U.S. 24 (1974).

Sauvé v. Canada (Attorney General) (1989), 66 O.R. (2d) 234 (H.C.); reversed (1992), 7 O.R. (3d) 481 (Ont. C.A.).

Shaw, M. 1990. *The Federal Female Offender*. Report on a Preliminary Study. Ottawa: Solicitor General Canada.

Shepherd v. Trevino 575 F.2d 110 (5th Cir. 1978).

Simard, André. 1991. Interview with the authors, 25 January.

Smith, L. 1984. "Charter Equality Rights: Some General Issues and Specific Applications in British Columbia to Elections, Juries and Illegitimacy." *University of British Columbia Law Review* 18:352–406.

Solosky v. R., [1980] 1 S.C.R. 821.

Stephens v. Yeomans 327 F. Supp. 1182 (1970).

United Nations. *International Covenant on Civil and Political Rights*, art. 10(3). U.N. General Assembly Resolution 2200 A (XXI) of 16 December 1966; in force 23 March 1976.

———. *Standard Minimum Rules for the Treatment of Prisoners*, 1955, rules 39, 57, 58, 60(1), 61. Adopted by First U.N. Congress on the Prevention of Crime and the Treatment of Offenders, Geneva, 1955; approved by U.N. Economic and Social Council Resolution 663 C (XXIV) of 31 July 1957.

United States. *Constitution of the United States*, 1788.

———. *Fourteenth Amendment*, 1868.

Vanderbilt Law Review. 1970. "The Collateral Consequences of a Criminal Conviction." 23:939–1241.

Washington v. State 75 Ala. 582 (1884).

Wesberry v. Sanders 376 U.S. 1 (1964).

Wesley v. Collins 605 F. Supp. 802 (M.D. Tenn. 1985).

3

REFLECTIONS ON CRITERIA FOR EXCLUDING PERSONS WITH MENTAL DISORDERS FROM THE RIGHT TO VOTE

Yves Denoncourt

OVER THE LAST two centuries, there has been slow but steady progress toward a better understanding and acceptance of the issue of mental health. Because "mental illness" is the most social of all illnesses, there have been many attempts to demystify it and to strip it of its many derogatory labels. Using the terms "mental illness" and "mental handicap" promotes these prejudices. Advances in terminology alone have required major adjustments. These changes have led us to a clearer understanding of the different concepts inherent in mental health issues.

There is a fundamental distinction between intellectual impairment and mental illness. In the literature on this topic, we find various definitions of intellectual impairment, but in this study we refer to the definition proposed by Rock Gadreau of the Office des personnes handicapées du Québec (Quebec, Office 1984, 31), who describes intellectual impairment as a "loss, malformation or anomaly of an organ, a structure or a mental, psychological or anatomic function. It is the outcome of an objective pathological condition that is observable and measurable and that can be diagnosed." Impairment leads to "a cognitive functioning which is generally significantly lower than average, accompanied by difficulties in adaptation" (Grossman and Begab 1977, cited in Quebec, Ministère de la Santé 1988, 9). Today we use the term "intellectual impairment," rather than the long-used labels "mentally retarded" or "mentally handicapped."

The degree of attention to and understanding of mental health issues reflects how widespread mental illness is and how difficult it is to evaluate its pervasiveness. The World Health Organization (WHO) estimates that 3 percent of any country's population has some degree of intellectual impairment. At this rate, with a population estimated at 26 727 200, more than 801 000 Canadians would be affected by problems related to intellectual impairment. Most of these (88 percent) have only minor impairment (704 000). The other 12 percent, fewer than 100 000, are moderately, severely or profoundly impaired.[1]

The Canadian Association for Community Living estimates that in any population, 1 percent will have a significant need for special services throughout their lives (Quebec, Ministère de la Santé 1988, 9).

These figures, however, do not give an accurate indication of the problems of mental health. Mental illness, another facet of mental health, is recurrent and episodic, and it is difficult to estimate how many people are affected and how often. Mental illness can appear in a number of forms, and with the complex vocabulary used to describe it, we find it difficult to understand as a social phenomenon.

There is not necessarily a connection between mental illness and intellectual impairment. Mental illness can be the result of trauma, chromosomal aberrations, stroke, or degenerative illnesses, such as Alzheimer's disease and Korsakoff's psychosis. Based on studies done in Quebec, one person in five will be faced with a problem related to mental health in the course of their lifetime, as stated in an advertisement produced by the Association pour l'intégration sociale. Recent statistics show that in Canada "more than 200 000 people suffer from schizophrenia, and nearly 300 000 others suffer from manic-depressive psychosis" (Drapeau 1991). These data are sketchy at best, since, according to some specialists in the field, only 20 percent of mental health problems are currently being identified and treated.

Despite these statistics, which appear to paint a fairly grim picture of mental health in Canada, Statistics Canada (1989) indicates that there were only about 60 000 approved beds in specialized institutions in 1985–86: 44 percent of these were reserved for people with psychological disorders, and 29 percent were for "mentally retarded" people (the terminology then used by Statistics Canada). The remaining beds were used for treating children with emotional problems (18 percent), and alcoholics and drug addicts (9 percent).

It may appear paradoxical that after distinguishing between people with intellectual impairments and the mentally ill, we now consider them together in relation to their ability to exercise one of the most fundamental democratic rights: the right to vote. At first glance, this could be seen as a step backward toward the confusing terminology of the current *Canada Elections Act*. This outdated document groups all psychological and intellectual disorders under the label "mental disease." For the purposes of this study, we consider these two very different groups together, but only in regard to their ability to exercise the right to vote and not in regard to their ability to live "normal" lives in the community. To be able to refer to these two groups simultaneously, we had to find a term that would be as accurate as possible – the lesser evil. We decided upon "persons with a mental disorder" to refer collectively to people with intellectual impairments and those with mental illness.

People with mental disorders want society to recognize the problems related to such disorders, and to respect their integrity, as much as they want to see an end to the hurdles and obstacles placed before them. Their most fundamental rights have been restored after many years of struggle, but there are still large gaps to be filled. Those with mental disorders who reside in institutions have had the right to vote restored to them, but only after a legal battle (*Canadian Disability Rights Council v. Canada* 1988). The decision invalidated section 14(4)(*f*) (now section 51*f*) of the *Canada Elections Act*, which denies voting rights to "every person who is restrained of his liberty of movement or deprived of the management of his property by reason of mental disease."

But this did not resolve all the issues. The right to vote is a fundamental right, indeed the cornerstone of all democratic societies. According to section 1 of the *Canadian Charter of Rights and Freedoms*, rights should not be restricted except for "such reasonable limits prescribed by law as can be demonstrably justified in a free and democratic society." Many legislative texts, like the *Canada Elections Act*, are still built on archaic terminology that does not adequately distinguish who is denied the right to vote.

The Federal Court of Canada's decision added a new dimension to the issue of voting rights for persons with mental disorders. The question is no longer whether they should be allowed to vote, but rather who among them should be allowed to do so. How many of the 50 000 institutionalized patients[2] affected by one of these disorders are fit to perform an action that requires intelligence and reflection? Is it possible to deny voting rights to some and still maintain the spirit of the Charter? If so, what would be the acceptable limits of such a prohibition?

This study is based on the premise that, in accordance with the Charter, the right to vote is a fundamental and inalienable right as long as it is used to uphold the integrity of the Canadian electoral system. The exercise of this right is tangible evidence of the participation of as many Canadians as possible in the democratic life of their country.

In this study, we present some reflections on what the criteria for denying this right should be. The desire to restrict the right to vote to the smallest number possible is based on several elements that make up the arguments in support of this thesis. This view is supported by statements of the principles that guide the preparation of laws, legal recommendations and court decisions. These statements are also important in the study of provincial and foreign voting legislation as well as in the evolution of the thinking behind the terminology of rights and attitudes.

Among the justifications that are used to limit the right of those with mental disorders to vote, two are of particular interest: warrants issued by the Lieutenant-Governor and involuntary committal to a psychiatric treatment centre. The first depends upon the application of the *Criminal Code*. Although we intend to dissociate the concepts of mental health and criminal behaviour, we accept the Lieutenant-Governor's warrant as a response to unacceptable behaviour, although the suspension of certain rights may result.

All provinces and territories have laws for involuntary committal that not only protect those with mental disorders, but also deny some of them the right to vote. This second reason for exclusion is not an original proposition. The Federal Republic of Germany, Belgium and the United Kingdom have all adopted it as part of their election laws.

These approaches have not yet been considered at the federal level; thus, the text of the *Canada Elections Act* is still too vague and too restrictive.[3] In order to measure and limit the scope of the criteria we propose, we have attempted to describe those who would be affected by such a denial. We undertook a statistical study in each of the Canadian provinces, the results of which make up most of the final section of this study.

VOTING RIGHTS AND LEGISLATIVE TEXTS

Foundations of the Concept of Human Rights

The decision to grant voting rights to those with an intellectual impairment is a logical outcome of efforts, principally after the Second World War, to extend to all individuals the dignity and respect to which they are entitled. The obstacles to this goal have been overcome one by one. Legislation now recognizes and protects these human rights and reflects the underlying fundamental principles. The United Nations pioneered this struggle. Its work led to the development of the following legislative texts, which form the basis for the rights of those living with problems related to mental health and intellectual capacity:

- the 1948 *Universal Declaration of Human Rights*;
- the 1959 *Declaration of the Rights of the Child*;
- the 1971 *Declaration on the Rights of Mentally Retarded Persons*; and
- the 1975 *Declaration on the Rights of Disabled Persons*.

The *Universal Declaration of Human Rights* specifically recognized the right to vote and the right to be elected by universal suffrage without distinction. The *Declaration on the Rights of Mentally Retarded Persons* ensures that people with intellectual deficiencies have the same rights as every other human being. The declaration also specifies that when these rights must be restricted, such restriction must not be abusive and must be based on expert evaluation, be subject to periodic revision and provide for the right of appeal to higher authorities.

The Impact of the *Canadian Charter of Rights and Freedoms*

In addition to the texts listed above, Canada's Charter, civil codes and *Criminal Code* also recognize the personal dignity of all human beings and that all are equal in the eyes of the law. The right to vote arises from the fundamental principle that grants everyone the right to achieve the greatest possible autonomy, development and fulfilment.

The Charter had a great impact on rights generally and, in particular, on care and committal procedures with respect to people with mental disorders. The Charter protects the life, liberty and security of the person, but it also allows certain rights to be reasonably restricted by law, within the framework of a free and democratic society.

Deprivation of Liberty and Respect for Guaranteed Rights

Involuntary deprivation of liberty, either by warrant of the Lieutenant-Governor or by committal to a psychiatric treatment centre, must conform with the spirit of the Charter: "Deprivation of liberty can occur only in accordance with the principles of fundamental justice ... Deprivation of liberty for mental disorder in need of treatment is justifiable in a free and democratic society if to prevent serious and imminent harm to the person or to others. Deprivation of liberty for mental disorder *per se* is not" (Rodgers 1988, 86).

The Lieutenant-Governor's warrant and involuntary committal are both governed by a strict group of parameters and behaviours written into both the Canadian *Criminal Code* and the laws on mental health. Adoption of the Charter made these restrictions even more essential: "Even prior to the imposition of the Charter, the courts were clearly moving in the direction of increasing the procedural rights of involuntarily committed individuals, even in the absence of constitutional guarantees in the context of common law protections ... We had this direction before the Charter. The Charter constitutionalizes it" (Rodgers 1988, 96–97).

The Charter guarantees respect for human beings. More particularly, in the case of those with mental disorders, it protects against inadequate or even harmful decisions and medical care. Any committal procedures that do not conform to the spirit of the laws, particularly to the Charter, must be judged unconstitutional and ineffective.

Other Laws and Protection of Guaranteed Rights

The Charter is not the only constitutional guarantee. In addition to civil codes and the *Criminal Code*, the provinces and territories have laws protecting the welfare of those with mental disorders. In Quebec, for example, there is the *Charter of human rights and freedoms*, the *Act respecting health services and social services* and the *Act to secure the handicapped in the exercise of their rights*.

Although the objectives of these acts are to respect rights and to protect the person, they recognize that certain measures must be taken to protect everyone involved. Committal against a person's will is one of these measures. This action places security and life above all other democratic rights, however fundamental they may be. Does denying voting rights to those deprived of their liberty by an external decision constitute a reasonable restriction of human rights? A study of court decisions and various opinions that have been handed down on this crucial issue will certainly shed light on this matter.

COURT OPINIONS AND DECISIONS

Opinions of Advisory Bodies

The issue of excluding persons with mental disorders from voting has led to several legal challenges and has inspired a number of recommendations from organizations created by the federal government. As far back as 1968, the McRuer Royal Commission noted that "committal to a hospital or the restriction of liberty by reason of illness does not constitute adequate grounds where the right to vote is concerned" (Ontario, Royal Commission 1968, 1235–1236). The Honourable James McRuer, Chief Justice of Ontario, felt that decisions should instead be based on the seriousness of the mental illness, which would be subject to certification or to a court order when appropriate (Wagnière 1988).

The Special Committee on the Disabled and the Handicapped then released a report, *Obstacles*, in which it proposed a series of recommendations, such as: "Amend the Canada Elections Act to reduce disqualifications because of 'mental disease' – That the federal government amend the Canada Elections Act to reduce the number of persons disqualified from voting by reason of 'mental disease,' by providing clear criteria for determining the specific cases where exclusion from the democratic process is absolutely justified" (Canada, House of Commons 1981, 24).

One year later, a progress report by the Committee noted the changes that had occurred following the publication of *Obstacles*. The Committee concluded that there was still a lot to do, especially with regard to the above-mentioned recommendation that the particular criteria used to disenfranchise individuals with mental illnesses be defined. The Chief Electoral Officer of Canada acknowledged that a recommendation of this type was very difficult to put into practice, and he proposed that the question be submitted to the Speaker of the House of Commons (Canada, House of Commons 1982, 19), as the question was outside his jurisdiction.

Since that time, a number of statements have been made regarding former section 14(4)(f) (now section 51(f)) of the *Canada Elections Act*. The Chief Electoral Officer (in his 1984 statutory report) (Canada, Elections Canada 1984), the Parliamentary Committee on Equality Rights (in its 1985 report *Equality for All*) and the Commons Standing Committee on Privileges and Elections (in a 1985 motion) all expressed the opinion that it was imperative to examine section 14(4)(f). More specifically, many groups, including the Coalition of Provincial Organizations of the Handicapped, the Canadian Association for Community Living and the Canadian Mental Health Association, all demanded that this section of the *Canada Elections Act* be repealed.[4]

The debate led the government to express (in its 1986 *Toward Equality: The Response to the Report of the Parliamentary Committee on Equality Rights*) its agreement with the principle that persons traditionally denied the right to vote could exercise that right without running the risk of being exploited or compromising the integrity of the process. The trend continued with a white paper on the reform of the *Canada Elections Act* (Canada, Privy Council Office 1986), in which the federal government recommended section 14(4)(f) be repealed to allow Canadians with mental disorders [in institutions] to be enumerated and to vote. However, the white paper specified that polling stations should not be set up in psychiatric hospitals and that only a vote "in person" would be allowed, excluding the possibility of voting by proxy.

Legal Challenges in Canada

These recommendations eventually resulted in the amendment of some provinces' legislation governing elections. This was the case in

Ontario (1984) and Manitoba (1988), in particular. In a decision rendered on 17 March 1988, the Honourable Mr. Justice Glowacki of the Court of Queen's Bench of Manitoba struck down section 31(b) of the Manitoba *Elections Act* (under which persons in a hospital or an institution for the "mentally deficient" were ineligible to vote). His decision upheld the action of the plaintiff, the Canadian Mental Health Association (Manitoba Branch), against Chief Electoral Officer Richard Willis and the attorney general of Manitoba (1988), declaring that the clause in question violated section 3 of the *Canadian Charter of Rights and Freedoms*. The Charter makes the following guarantee: "Every citizen of Canada has the right to vote in an election of members of the House of Commons or of a legislative assembly." Two years later, the overly vague and general concepts of "mental retardation" and "mentally retarded" were successfully contested in the same court.

The Canadian legal system faced another important case in 1988. This time, the Canadian Disability Rights Council, acting on behalf of a number of disabled persons,[5] brought a case before the Federal Court of Canada Trial Division.

In her opinion of 17 October 1988, quoted by the Association des centres d'accueil du Québec (1990, 2), the Honourable Madam Justice Barbara Reed pointed out that "the category addressed by the legislators in fact covers those citizens who deserve the reinstatement of their voting rights despite personal difficulties, which do not, according to the experts, affect their capacity of judgement during an election." The Canadian Bar Association (1990, 17) also issued a similar opinion, emphasizing that "this disqualification is predicated not upon mental disability, but on mental disease. In addition, disqualification is restricted to two categories of 'mentally diseased' persons, namely those whose liberty of movement has been restrained and those whose property is under the control of a committee of estate. It is evident that the ... two criteria have little, if any, direct relationship with the capacity to vote." Madam Justice Reed based her decision on the following points:

[The clause in question] is more broadly framed than that. It denies people the right to vote on the basis of "mental disease." This clearly will include individuals who might suffer from a personality disorder which impairs their judgment in one aspect of their life only. There may be no reason on that basis to deprive them of the right to vote. What is more, paragraph 14(4)(f) does not deny all persons suffering from mental disease the right to vote, but only those whose liberty of movement has been restrained or whose property is under the control of a committee of estate ...

> The limitation prescribed by paragraph 14(4)(*f*) is in that sense arbitrary. If it is intended as a test of mental competency, it is at the same time both too narrow and too wide ...
>
> It is similarly a *non sequitur* to assume that psychiatric patients are necessarily incapable of voting ...
>
> An individual incapable of making particular types of decisions may be fully capable of making many others ...
>
> It is hereby declared that paragraph 14(4)(*f*) of the *Canada Elections Act* is invalid as being in conflict with section 3 of the *Canadian Charter of Rights and Freedoms. (Canadian Disability Rights Council* 1988, 624–27)

The fact that section 14(4)(*f*) of the *Canada Elections Act* was struck down is not, in itself, surprising. The decision simply substantiated what everyone already expected: the recovery of a right guaranteed by the Charter. In 1987, when Bill C-79 was being prepared – a bill that died on the order paper – the repeal of the litigious clause was recommended. However, this decision did not attempt to meet the desire on the part of many people that restrictions of voting rights be based not on a condition but on the capacity to participate in the procedure.

Legal Challenges in the United States
Savage and McKague (1987) report that the issue of voting rights for residents of institutions has also been debated before the American courts. The rulings maintain that the right to vote should be granted to such individuals on the grounds that "residency at a state facility for the developmentally handicapped does not *per se* render one ineligible to vote" (*Caroll* 1976). This question has been the subject of many court actions, some of which became precedents in the case that led to section 14(4)(*f*) of the *Canada Elections Act* being struck down.[6]

The Legal Vacuum
Although the court decisions were very useful in ensuring that the rights of persons with mental disorders were protected in this instance, they left a legal vacuum and required that legislators determine the threshold of the capacity to vote. In their ultimate intent, the decisions rendered by the various courts are simply serious attempts to reconcile respect for fundamental rights with citizens' expectations of social justice. Even though all aspects of the question have not been clarified, the opinions and decision nevertheless provide a positive answer to our initial question regarding the appropriateness of limiting the exercise of the right to vote. As well, these findings appear to corroborate our desire to consider a criterion governing exclusion – a criterion that

would be based not on illness but on the capacity to perform an act as fundamental as voting.

Before expressing opinions on the second major issue – where to draw the line concerning the capacity to vote – we believe it is necessary to study the restrictions and procedures embodied in the electoral legislation of various jurisdictions. The next section is devoted to this issue.

THE RIGHT TO VOTE: A SURVEY OF ELECTORAL LAWS

Election Acts in Canada

An examination of legislation governing elections in each of Canada's jurisdictions shows that there is no single pattern. Legislation in six provinces or territories and the *Canada Elections Act* do not grant voting rights to persons with a mental disorder if they are institutionalized, whereas legislation in seven other provinces grants this right, subject to certain exceptions. Newfoundland, Quebec, Ontario, Manitoba, Saskatchewan, Alberta and British Columbia all accord voting rights to people in this category. Their procedures differ, however, as we can see from the following brief descriptions.

Newfoundland

Voters with a mental disorder can vote at ordinary polling stations, as well as at special polling stations. Voters receiving individual care for chronic illness or undergoing treatment in health care institutions for severe illness use special methods for voting, unless the institution in question is their permanent place of residence (Newfoundland, *Election Act*, s. 10).

Quebec

Persons with a mental disorder have the right to vote, subject to section 1(4) of the Quebec *Election Act*, which denies voting rights to any otherwise eligible person who is under guardianship. Guardianship is the last of three forms of protective supervision offered to recipients of psychiatric care under the new Quebec law on public trusteeship (*Public trusteeship act and modifying the Civil Code and other legislative provisions* 1989). The other regimes, advisorship and tutorship for persons of full age, are described in more detail in a later section of this study.

Ontario

Persons with a mental disorder have had the right to vote since 1984. Section 14 of the Ontario *Election Act* proposes special measures to enable individuals in institutions (as defined in the Act) to vote at polling stations set up within their institutions. "Where an institution for the reception, treatment or vocational training of persons who have served or are serving in the Canadian Forces or who are disabled, a hospital, a psychiatric facility, a home for the aged, a nursing home or other institution of twenty beds or more, in which chronically ill or infirm persons reside or a retirement home of fifty beds or more is situate in an electoral district, a polling place shall be provided in such institution or upon the premises" (Ontario, Election Act 1984, s. 14).

Voters who reside in an institution as described in the terms of the above paragraph and who are registered on the voters list can vote in that polling station. The returning officer will ensure that the scrutineer and the poll clerk go to the patients' beds or otherwise see to it that patients receive their ballots.

Manitoba

The Manitoba *Elections Act* has been contested in the courts twice since 1988. In 1988, the validity of restricting the voting rights of persons living in mental institutions was contested successfully by the Manitoba branch of the Canadian Mental Health Association (1988). Two years later, the same court had to examine the overly vague concept of "mental retardation." The ruling was in favour of the plaintiff, the Manitoba Association for Community Living Inc. (1990), and granted persons described by law as being mentally retarded the right to vote. The decisions handed down in 1988 and 1990, which both confirm the current vocabulary as violating the *Canadian Charter of Rights and Freedoms*, have significantly lowered the number of voters deprived of the right to vote by retaining the exclusion only for those "persons who have been declared to be mentally disordered by an order of the Court of Queen's Bench made under the *Mental Health Act* and whose custody has been committed to a committee under that Act" (s. 31(c)). Given the absence of regulatory mechanisms, the Chief Electoral Officer of Manitoba was obliged to adapt the Manitoba *Elections Act* to allow persons who had until then been excluded to exercise their right to vote.

In order to implement the recent decisions, a special enumeration was held the day before the 11 September 1990 provincial election. As a result, 775 persons who were then residing in three institutions for the intellectually impaired were added to the electoral lists. Voting procedures were applied differently, depending on whether the patient's address of residence corresponded to that of the institution in which he or she resided at the time of the enumeration. In the first case, a regular ballot was issued to the voter, who had only to mark his or her preference with an X. Persons with a different address of residence used a blank ballot and were given the names of the candidates and the necessary information by election officials.

Saskatchewan

Persons with mental disorders may vote, except for those who on election day are subject to a warrant issued by the Lieutenant-Governor, under the terms of section 617 of the *Criminal Code*, and who have not been released from the application of this warrant (Saskatchewan, *Election Act*, s. 27(*d*)).

Section 617 of the *Criminal Code* stipulates that,

> Where an accused is, pursuant to this Part, found to be insane, the lieutenant governor of the province in which he is detained may make an order
> (*a*) for the safe custody of the accused in a place and manner directed by him; or
> (*b*) if in his opinion it would be in the best interest of the accused and not contrary to the interest of the public, for the discharge of the accused either absolutely or subject to such conditions as he prescribes.

Prohibitions based on warrants issued by the Lieutenant-Governor are not unique to Saskatchewan, since they are based on the *Criminal Code*. We pay particular attention to this procedure in a later section of this study.

Alberta

Persons with intellectual impairment or a mental illness can vote and may exercise this right in the same way as any other voter. However, special polling stations are set up to facilitate voting by persons residing in accredited institutions. Those wishing to vote are not enumerated but are sworn in as voters. Polling stations have flexible hours, determined by the returning officer of the electoral district.

British Columbia

Denial of the right to vote depends exclusively on court decisions. Only those committed to institutions by virtue of a court order are considered unfit to vote according to section 3(1)(*c*) of the British Columbia *Election Act*. According to the Chief Electoral Officer of British Columbia, this restriction of voting rights actually affects only 100–150 people, although this estimate is difficult to confirm.

Electoral Laws in Other Countries

Although some may object to the idea of comparing our society with

European countries because of our differing histories, cultures and political traditions, we find it useful to look at how other countries address similar problems in their laws. This overview does not pretend to be a faithful reflection of all foreign practices. It is valid only for those countries studied – the Federal Republic of Germany, France, Australia, the Netherlands, Belgium, the United Kingdom and the United States.

Federal Republic of Germany

Suspending voting rights is justified under the criterion of involuntary trusteeship and on the basis of court decisions. German citizens, therefore, can be denied voting rights if they:

- are incapacitated, or as a result of mental impairment are placed under guardianship, as long as they do not provide a statement from a trusteeship tribunal that their guardianship was ordered with their consent (Federal Republic of Germany, *Federal Elections Act*, s. 13(2));
- are committed by virtue of section 63 of the *Penal Code* to a psychiatric hospital (s. 13(3)); or
- are provisionally committed to a psychiatric hospital because of a mental illness or a mental disability following a judgement based on the judicial prescription of the region (s. 13(4)). [translation]

France

Clause 6 of section L.5 of the French *Electoral Code* denies the intellectually impaired or the mentally ill the right to vote. This restriction applies to people who have reached the age of majority and have been placed under legal guardianship because of their mental capacity.

Australia

Recent amendments (30 September 1990) to the *Commonwealth Electoral Act, 1918* reveal a greater willingness to grant all citizens the right to vote. The text of the law confirms that with regard to certain mental disorders, any person capable of meeting the minimum requirements of the voting process, that is, identification of the voter and performance of the voting act itself, must not be deprived of the right to vote. Consequently, only persons who do not possess all their mental faculties and are incapable of understanding the nature and significance of enrolment and of voting are ineligible to be registered on the voters list (s. 93(8)(*a*)).

Netherlands

Voting rights are denied to those as determined by the courts or to those who have been declared mentally unfit to manage their own affairs.

Belgium

Persons who have a mental disorder are generally not denied the right to vote. Section 7(1) of the electoral laws, however, excludes "the confined insane," those "under prolonged minority status" (by the application of the law of 29 June 1973) and "abnormal" persons.

The "confined insane" refers to those permanently committed to psychiatric hospitals. Those "under prolonged minority status" are over 18 years of age but have been declared – either by their family or a judge – incapable of managing their own affairs. The very large category of "abnormal" persons includes those with illnesses affecting their intellectual capacities, such as Alzheimer's, and whose affairs are being administered by a guardian.

United Kingdom

The amendments made to the *Representation of the People Act 1983* in 1983 now require that a distinction be made between "voluntary" and "involuntary" patients in psychiatric hospitals. According to the Act's definition, anyone in a psychiatric hospital who is not there by virtue of a warrant is a voluntary patient. These voluntary patients and those with intellectual impairments who are not institutionalized may vote. Voluntary patients must be able to provide a residential address other than that of the hospital and must fill out a declaration, as described in sections 7(4) and 7(9) of the Act, to prove their capacity to vote. Because the residential address is a criterion, these patients are limited to voting by mail.

There is no official means to measure whether those with mental disorders understand the voting procedure, nor can presiding officers make the evaluation of their capacity to vote.

United States

The situation in the United States is indicative of prevailing trends in the field of mental health. Here, the move is away from institutionalization and toward social integration through community living. This is especially true since a court decision found that keeping individuals in psychiatric institutions was unconstitutional (*Halderman* 1977). Twelve states currently grant unrestricted voting rights to those living in institutions, while another 15 restrict the rights of only those who have been judged incapable. A further 19 states base the denial of voting rights on declarations of insanity and *non compos mentis*, etc. Finally, only three states base restrictions on the right to vote on committal to an institution. Of the states already cited, only three use two criteria simultaneously: Louisiana and Wisconsin use the declaration of incapacity and declaration of insanity; Missouri uses incapacity and committal.

In most of these states, patients follow the procedures for voting by mail or for absentee voting.

In both the Canadian election laws and foreign legislation, there are many subtleties, variations and exceptions regarding the right to vote. The various permutations and combinations cause confusion in this area. Although it does not take the United States into consideration, table 3.1 attempts to summarize the general situation.

Statistical Survey of Electoral Behaviour

Because the people we are concerned with in this study have been granted voting rights so recently, we do not have an exhaustive statistical report of their electoral behaviour. Studies undertaken in several provinces show that:

- In Ontario, 55.5 percent of those with intellectual impairment living in institutions participated in the provincial elections of 1985, whereas 61.3 percent of the general public did so.
- In eight of 10 psychiatric hospitals in this province, the vote by patients favoured the same candidate as the overall vote in the local constituency.
- Also in Ontario, 61.5 percent of those in psychiatric institutions who were registered on the voters lists voted, which is about the same percentage as the general population.
- In 1987, 2 160 patients in 11 Ontario psychiatric institutions were enumerated, and 50 percent of them voted.[7]

In the Manitoba provincial election of September 1990, of the 775 patients on voters lists at three institutions for persons with intellectual impairment, 101 (13 percent) exercised their right to vote.[8] Even more remarkable is the observation made by Elections Manitoba: "It is interesting to note that the vote at each institution was evenly distributed among all candidates. There was no observable pattern to the vote, which is sometimes raised as a concern when new groups gain the right to vote."[9]

These kinds of statistics are more difficult to collect in Quebec because of the philosophy behind the law. In giving the right to vote to those with a mental disorder, this province asserts that these individuals, traditionally brushed aside, have become voters just like everyone else. No attempt is made to find out how they behave electorally; rather, there is an effort to obscure voting preferences whenever possible by setting up polling stations in locations where voters will come from both the institution and the surrounding area.

Table 3.1
Voting rights of persons with mental disorders

Jurisdiction	Yes	No	Exclusions
Canada		X	Persons whose freedom of movement is limited or who are denied the management of their own affairs for reason of mental illness; provision declared unconstitutional
Newfoundland	X		
Prince Edward Island		X	Persons whose freedom of movement is limited or who are denied the management of their own affairs for reason of mental illness
Nova Scotia		X	Persons whose freedom of movement is limited or who are denied the management of their own affairs for reason of mental illness
New Brunswick		X	Persons whose freedom of movement is limited or who are denied the management of their own affairs for reason of mental illness
Quebec	X		Persons under curatorship
Ontario	X		
Manitoba	X		Persons hospitalized in a facility for persons with mental impairments, persons declared by the Court to have mental disorders, and persons who have been placed under the care of a guardian
Saskatchewan	X		Persons subject to a warrant issued by the Lieutenant-Governor by virtue of the *Criminal Code* who have not been freed from the application of this warrant
Alberta	X		
British Columbia	X		Persons who are institutionalized by virtue of a court order
Northwest Territories		X	
Yukon		X	Persons whose freedom of movement is limited or who are denied the management of their own affairs for reason of mental illness
Federal Republic of Germany	X		Persons under guardianship without their own consent, those who are committed to a psychiatric hospital by virtue of the *Penal Code*, and those who, following a judgement, are provisionally committed to a psychiatric hospital
France	X		Persons who have attained majority and who have been placed in trusteeship

Table 3.1 (cont'd)
Voting rights of persons with mental disorders

Jurisdiction	Yes	No	Exclusions
Australia	X		Persons who, because of mental incapacity, are incapable of understanding the nature and significance of voting
Netherlands		X	Persons restricted in freedom of movement or denied the management of their affairs by a court, for reason of mental illness
Belgium	X		The confined (committed) insane, persons under prolonged minority status (inability to manage their affairs), abnormal persons (who have illnesses that affect intellectual capacity and whose affairs are managed by a guardian)
United Kingdom	X		Involuntary patients (committed by virtue of a warrant)

We should, however, look at the figures on voter registration in a few of the major psychiatric institutions in Quebec as reported by the print media just before the general election of 1989. The figures show that 216 of the 1 900 patients at the Centre hospitalier Robert-Giffard were registered on the voters list. At the Louis-Hippolyte-Lafontaine Hospital, the proportion was 373 out of 2 050.[10] The Douglas Hospital in Verdun was statistically similar, with 73 of 400 patients registered. The exception was the Albert-Prévost wing of the Sacré-Coeur Hospital, where 114 of 134 patients were on the list. These less than impressive percentages are attributed to a change in the registration process that required enumerators to meet the voters instead of drawing up a list from the patient register provided by the hospital. Another obstacle was the very novelty of this right for most patients: "After 20 years of institutionalization, when you've never voted, you don't get excited about it just like that, from one day to the next."[11]

A recent study, published in the *Canadian Journal of Psychiatry*, takes a look at the results of a survey of 272 patients in a psychiatric institution in Ontario.[12] The study concluded that the patients were very familiar with and knowledgeable about the Canadian political system. The results show that of the 198 who responded to the questionnaire, 69.5 percent were aware of the election of the Progressive Conservative Party of Canada, 85.3 percent could name the three major parties, 80.1 percent knew the names of the party leaders and 82.7 percent correctly identified the prime minister (Jaychuk and Manchanda 1991, 124).

In a comparison of the practices regarding denial of voting rights, no particular reason for exclusion stands out as being standard. Some practices are based on court rulings, while others are supported by a criminal or civil code, by a form of protective supervision such as guardianship, or by a criterion as vague as the ability to understand the significance of voting.

Basing disenfranchisement on a Lieutenant-Governor's warrant or on involuntary committal applies criteria that are sufficiently restricted and controlled to ensure that this right, guaranteed by the Charter, will be denied to very few Canadians.

DEPRIVATION OF LIBERTY AS A CRITERION FOR EXCLUSION

The first sections of this study have shown that greater understanding of intellectual impairment and mental illness is leading to the recognition of certain rights, although those struggling for recognition have often had to overcome official inertia. The development of fundamental laws such as the Charter has guided the courts, which nevertheless continue to look to legislators to establish a standard by which restrictions on rights can be judged reasonable and demonstrably justified in a free and democratic society.

Community Living and Deinstitutionalization

Community living or social integration is a logical extension to all human beings of the fundamental rights to liberty, autonomy and respect. It has been an important step in strengthening and protecting the status of people living with intellectual impairment and mental illness.

Community living evolved once society realized that institutionalizing large numbers of people with intellectual impairments was a serious error. Many studies on the impact of institutionalization agree with Blanchet (1980, 392), who wrote:

> We have even created a syndrome that bears the name "institutionitis" and can be defined as follows: a pathological condition found in an individual who has remained in an institution for a long period of time whereby the person loses his or her own identity ... [and] becomes alienated in the literal sense of the term, i.e., disconnected from him or herself. The person conforms to the expectations of the milieu, which are often minimal and dehumanizing (these attitudes are not always conscious) because the very decision to place someone in an institution and thus to deprive him or her of a part of his or her rights implies a conscious or unconscious perception of that person as inferior.

By showing the positive effects of social reintegration, these studies directly support the argument that many of those living in institutions simply require a more stimulating situation to lead more fulfilling lives.

Going out into the community encourages the development of handicapped persons. Generally speaking, handicapped persons who go
out into the community to live increase the level of their adapted
behaviours and reduce the level of their unadapted behaviours, while
those persons who remain in institutions tend to remain stagnant.
Specifically, deinstitutionalized persons improve their general level
of communication, social skills and skills related to activities of daily
living, and they increase the frequency and diversity of their activities. (Laurendeau et al. 1983, 8–9)

The industrialized countries have been working for more than 20
years toward reducing the numbers of those in institutions. This action,
according to Picard (1988, 40), is the result of three factors: "The decline
of social Darwinism and its replacement by the ideology of normal-
ization; the emergence of numerous associations for the defence and
promotion of the rights of mentally handicapped people; and the contribution of the humanities and the social sciences to the deinstitutionalization movement."

This action was more than just a large-scale effort to empty the
major mental health institutions. It also stressed that alternative living
settings should be suitable and comfortable for human beings and that
a network of services to provide support for the residents of those alternative settings should be established. Because of its benefits and the
reinstatement of rights, deinstitutionalization has played a role in
re-opening the debate over restriction of the right to vote.

Restriction of the Right to Vote

According to some authors (Luckasson 1988; Bergeron 1981), it is important to review the criteria for disenfranchisement: "While the restrictions
may be justified for a small number of persons with mental retardation, they make no sense at all for the majority of persons with the
disability and are clearly a vestige of the widespread discrimination
historically imposed on persons with mental retardation" (Luckasson
1988, 209).

While accepting this line of thought, Bergeron (1981, 193–94) nevertheless confirms that applying exclusion criteria is still difficult in practice. With this in mind, he states: "We are of the opinion, however, that
the right to vote may be withdrawn from those held under warrant,
from persons who are involuntarily committed [cure fermée],[13] and from
persons who are under the jurisdiction of a public guardian."

His proposition rests on the assumption that the act of voting,
though a fundamental right, is a gesture of intelligence and reflection,

and thus certain people may be deprived of the right to vote out of respect for the integrity of the democratic system: "To exercise the right to vote, a person must be of sound mind and able to understand the issues at stake in the political arena. The act is so important that we must not allow it to be exercised by persons who lack the ability and the means to make use of it" (Bergeron 1981, 194).

Discussion of Exclusion Criteria

Bergeron's proposals base exclusion on committal under warrant, protective supervision and involuntary committal. If we restrict ourselves to considering the situation of a single province, as Bergeron does, each of these exclusion criteria is relatively simple to apply. The laws concerning mental health, however, fall under provincial jurisdiction and differ from one province to the next. The same is true for systems of protective supervision, the scope and development of which vary significantly. For these reasons, we cannot select protective supervision as a criterion for exclusion. It seems preferable to consider other criteria, notably exclusion based on warrants issued by the Lieutenant-Governor and involuntary committal. The criteria in these two approaches can easily be applied to and integrated within the *Canada Elections Act*.

Many interested parties gave testimony at the hearings of the Royal Commission on Electoral Reform and Party Financing, and a good number of them raised the issue of mental capacity as a criterion for exclusion. We feel it is important to mention some of the opinions expressed at these hearings.

Competency Criteria

Everyone agrees that the main difficulty with respect to voting rights and intellectual capacity relates to how to determine whether a person's mental condition would permit him or her to cast a rational and informed vote. Although many believe that mental incapacity precludes any notion of personal competence, most individuals with a mental disorder do have the potential for development.

Anyone wishing to vote must be competent, but it is difficult, and very controversial, to measure the intellectual capacity necessary for voting. One suggestion is to establish a minimal test to measure the ability to understand what is at stake in political participation. This is utopian, however, since using one competency test would be not only discriminatory but also in all likelihood unconstitutional. We accept the arguments made by the Canadian Mental Health Association (Moncton Region) (1990), which raised questions about the capacity of voters generally: "We make no assumptions of the general public at large in relation to competency to vote. Without doubt, many citizens vote for candidates based on very unenlightened thinking ... If we don't test the voting competency of the public, then what right do we have to test it on certain groups or individuals such as a person who undergoes treatment in a psychiatric hospital?"

Many of those who spoke before the Commission shared the idea that voters with problems stemming from a mental disorder should not have to take a test. In their opinion, the only necessary competency test is the one currently in effect – the ability to state one's name, approximate age, citizenship and place of residence and to cast a ballot. Besides the fact that this practice ensures equitable treatment of all voters, it is also a de facto self-regulatory mechanism that permits only those whose mental condition is "adequate" to vote.

At first glance, this solution, which proposes the right to vote with no exclusions, seems to reflect the opinions of most of the members of the mental health community who appeared before the Commission. However, we note that this practice is in effect in only two of the 19 jurisdictions studied earlier. That specific exclusions still exist shows the importance governments place on the electoral process: only those presumed to be competent may vote.

Protective Supervision

The major drawback to using protective supervision as a criterion for exclusion is the inconsistency in its application. While the situation may change, guardianship seems to protect legally acts that could be harmful to those with intellectual impairments. "Rightly or wrongly, the context in which medicine is practised today obliges the physician to take all possible precautions to reduce the risk of law suits. This legitimate concern, which cannot be ignored, can lead the physician to take the safest route, even if it is perhaps not the route that is most respectful of the rights and needs of the person upon whom a system for protective supervision is imposed against his or her will" (Deschamps 1988, 195).

Intellectual capacity may play only a secondary role in the assignment of systems for protective supervision. Where two people are judged to have the same level of intellectual impairment, the one with significant assets (inheritance, pension funds, etc.) might be brought under the protection of a guardianship or trustee system, while the one with few possessions or assets might not. This situation was denounced by the Canadian Mental Health Association (Alberta Division) (1990) in its brief to the Commission: "People who are admitted voluntarily or involuntarily to psychiatric facilities often have property outside the facilities which they are unable to manage in practical terms. They are not mentally incapable of managing, but, in practical terms, it is more convenient to have the public trustee come in and deal with the landlord, to receive cash and bank cheques and to do things which they, in practical terms, cannot do."

Some members of the mental health community have even expressed the view that guardianship is at times imposed on certain individuals to force them to submit to treatments they would otherwise refuse. There is at best only a weak correlation between the form of protective supervision imposed and the person's intellectual potential. As its name indicates, protective supervision is meant to ensure protection of the individual's person or assets. At no time should it be the cause of systematic deprivation of rights: "It simply does not follow that people who are declared incapable of managing their financial affairs are necessarily incapable of understanding the nature of the right to vote and of exercising it in a rational manner" (Robertson 1987, 242).

Protective supervision should certainly not be imposed on a case-by-case basis. Such supervision must also be subject to due legal process. Nevertheless, the disadvantage of protective supervision is that its form and application vary from one province to the next. This is even more pronounced now with the *Public trusteeship act* in Quebec. The Act provides for a graduated system of three types of protective supervision for those who have reached the age of majority: advisorship, tutorship and guardianship.[14] Given that this is a recent Act, it is impossible to determine how many people are under each of these forms of protective supervision. However, in her testimony before the Commission, the Public Trustee of Quebec estimated that approximately 7 000 residents of that province would be deprived of the right to vote on the basis of the Quebec *Election Act*, which disqualifies anyone who is subject to guardianship. Since these distinctions do not exist in all provinces, it does not seem wise to base the denial of the right to vote on a concept that is applied so dissimilarly in different jurisdictions. Even if these systems could be applied uniformly, would their use lead to a systematic association of the right to vote with the ability to manage one's affairs? The primary function of these systems is to protect the individual. We would run the risk of denying a fundamental right to some individuals and once again opening the exclusion criteria to legal challenges.

The decision not to use protective supervision as a criterion for disenfranchisement at first glance seems to conform with the opinion stated earlier by many interveners: that there should be no restriction at all on the right to vote for persons with mental disorders. However, although our goal remains to deny the right to vote to as few as possible, we maintain that voting is an act of intelligence and reflection. This leads us to consider interdiction by the Lieutenant-Governor and involuntary committal as exclusion criteria.

Lieutenant-Governor's Warrant

The Lieutenant-Governor's warrant (interdiction) is a legal mechanism that deprives individuals of the exercise of their civil rights. Those rights are entrusted to a third party who will exercise them on behalf of the individual. Some authors have questioned whether the systematic use of this procedure, which leads to the deprivation of rights, is appropriate. Because the right to vote is surely among those rights that would be withdrawn, we concur with Deschamps (1988, 179), who questioned the true goals of the use of this procedure: "Considered as an infamous measure, interdiction serves to further stigmatize a person with mental illness. The fundamental question is if, in order to protect an individual, it is absolutely necessary *from the outset* to deprive him of the exercise of all of his civil rights, or if we can indeed assure his protection without necessarily restricting his exercise of those rights."

The transfer of civil rights is an important question, and the consequences of interdiction are a matter of concern. This concern is central to our view: our ultimate objective is the right to vote for all who are capable of understanding what it means to vote. In some cases, however, a declaration of interdiction could conceivably restrict this fundamental right specifically. Restriction of the right to vote based on interdiction must be decided upon through a uniform legal process. Important as it is to dissociate the concepts of mental health and criminality, it seems relevant to consider how the Canadian *Criminal Code* deals with the actions of individuals with mental disorders.

Under sections 614–19 (inclusive) of the *Criminal Code,* those facing criminal charges who also have mental disorders are subject to warrants issued by the Lieutenant-Governor. Two situations lead to such warrants: unfitness to stand trial, and acquittal by reason of insanity. In the first case, the person who is unable to stand trial because of his or her mental condition must be sent to a medical facility by the court at the pleasure of the Lieutenant-Governor. This person must be held under strict or rigorous custody until the Lieutenant-Governor issues an order to stand trial. A large majority of persons found unfit to stand trial become fit following a period of strict or rigorous custody during which they can obtain the care their mental condition requires. In the case of acquittal by reason of insanity, the person must also be sent to the medical facility, again at the pleasure of the Lieutenant-Governor. This warrant for strict custody will be changed, depending on the person's mental condition, to a conditional release order. There is no time limit on warrants. The Lieutenant-Governor authorizes the warrant to be lifted upon recommendation by the Board of Review. The warrant's only power is to limit a person's movement and does not at any time oblige the individual to accept the care that his or her condition might require. Treatment is given only with the consent of the person involved, and in cases where this person is unable to consent to the care, a substitute consent would be obtained in accordance with the powers conferred by the legislator in provincial mental health laws.

In March 1990, Lieutenant-Governor's warrants affected slightly more than 1 100 persons across the country, as shown in table 3.2.

The length of time of deprivation of rights as a result of interdiction under a Lieutenant-Governor's warrant varies. This depends on whether those receiving treatment display behaviour allowing them to be reintegrated into society. At the Institut Philippe-Pinel in Montreal, there are between 500 and 600 permanent discharges annually,[15] thus ending the period of strict custody imposed following acquittal of a charge by reason of insanity. The period of strict custody for those found

Table 3.2
Number of patients committed under a Lieutenant-Governor's warrant as of 1 March 1990

Province	Number of persons
Newfoundland	7
Prince Edward Island	4[a]
Nova Scotia	13
New Brunswick	9
Quebec	414
Ontario	405
Manitoba	34
Saskatchewan	22
Alberta	74
British Columbia	142
Total	1 124

Source: Institut Philippe-Pinel, Montreal.

[a]Prince Edward Island did not provide data to the research centre at the Institut Philippe-Pinel. As a result, this value was estimated by the centre's Dr. Sheilagh Hodgins.

unfit to stand trial also varies, but in most cases it is 30 days or less. Persons who are still unfit to stand trial after the first 30-day period are sent back for further treatment, in the hope that they will then become fit.

We propose linking the incapacity to exercise the right to vote with the periods of custody ordered by the Lieutenant-Governor's warrant. Acquittal by reason of insanity rests principally on the accused's inability to distinguish right from wrong at the moment of the misdeed. Unfitness per se, on the other hand, is an inability to understand the significance of the legal process, and by extension, to adequately communicate with a lawyer and thereby provide a defence. Consequently, it seems to us that denying the right to vote during these periods of treatment (which are intended to render a person fit to stand trial) and so-called strict custody can be interpreted as a "reasonable and demonstrably justified" limitation of guaranteed rights.

The validity of the provisions regarding automatic detention in the *Criminal Code* was challenged before the Supreme Court of Canada in *Swain v. R.* (1991). The provisions were found to violate the individual rights expressly guaranteed by section 7 of the *Canadian Charter of Rights and Freedoms* ["Everyone has the right to life, liberty and security of the person and the right not to be deprived thereof except in accordance with the principles of fundamental justice"]. According to the Right Honourable A. Lamer, Chief Justice of the Supreme Court, "the indeterminate nature of the order for rigorous custody ... restricts the right to liberty to an extent that is unacceptable." Chief Justice Lamer believes that individuals "acquitted by reason of insanity must only be detained for the time necessary to determine if as a result of their insanity they are still dangerous."

In judging this provision invalid, Chief Justice Lamer took into consideration the consequences of immediately invalidating the provision for rigorous custody, so he allowed Parliament six months to modify the *Criminal Code:* "A period of temporary validity will extend for a period of six months because of the serious consequences of striking section 542(2) [now s. 614(2)]. During this period, detention ordered under section 542(2) will be limited to 30 days in most instances, or to a maximum of 60 days where the Crown establishes that a longer period is required in the particular circumstances of the case."

To a certain extent, this decision confirms that an individual is not necessarily dangerous throughout the whole prescribed period of custody. Rejecting custody that is arbitrarily based on "the pleasure of the Lieutenant-Governor" and replacing it with more clearly defined time periods shifts the emphasis to the behaviour of each individual. The provisions for custody in the *Criminal Code* are meant to protect society from "dangerous" persons; these provisions will now also provide better evaluation of individuals under strict custody and greater flexibility in changing their status. Abolishing arbitrary custody contributes to the objective of restricting the right to vote as little as possible. In providing for more timely follow-up through mandatory evaluation of each renewal of strict custody, this procedure will put an end to arbitrary and sometimes unnecessarily long detention and the deprivation of rights.

As Chief Justice Lamer stated, "past violence and earlier mental difficulties of persons acquitted by reason of insanity do not necessarily indicate a greater probability of dangerous conduct in the future." This reinforces our goal of restricting the right to vote only during periods of strict custody.

Involuntary Committal Based on Mental Health Acts

Generally speaking, involuntary committal is meant to be an exceptional measure that can be imposed only on the basis of precise criteria and whose duration is stipulated by legislation. We will look at the suitability of this procedure as a criterion for denial of the right to vote. Given the originality in the Canadian context of considering this procedure as grounds for deprivation of a fundamental right, we shall devote significant attention to it. We will concentrate on the voluntary and involuntary aspects of committal and the procedures that govern them.

The discussion thus far of exclusion criteria only confirms the arbitrary nature of the situation. Thus, persons under protective supervision or those who have been involuntarily committed by reason of insanity are not necessarily incapable of voting. We also believe that tests of competency, in addition to being costly and difficult to administer, would almost certainly meet an insurmountable obstacle in the Charter.

We must conclude that the choice of exclusion criteria will undoubtedly require compromise among a few options that are all somewhat arbitrary. Faced with this situation, we must not forget the objectives that guide our reflections. The fundamental prerequisites for voting (reflection and intelligence) and the observance of reasonable and justifiable limits on rights expressly guaranteed by the Charter remain the underlying theme of our reflection. Added to this is our desire to consider the minimum exclusion possible; in this vein, we have attempted to identify as accurately as possible the number of individuals who could be affected by such a restriction of the right to vote.

VOLUNTARY AND INVOLUNTARY COMMITTAL

The notions of voluntary and involuntary committal are based on an individual's capacity to give informed consent to treatment for self-protection or for the protection of others. These concepts stem from the most basic of human rights: the autonomy and inviolability of the person. If voluntary consent to committal is to be recognized, it must be done in a specific context and must meet certain criteria. Under certain circumstances, however, when consent is impossible to obtain, action may have to be taken without it. Known as substitute consent, it is considered involuntary.

Capacity to Give Consent

According to Morrison (1988, 9), the capacity to give consent is a legal concept defined as "an individual's capacity to perform or refrain from performing a given act or gesture." According to the same author (ibid., 10), the concept can be clinically defined by considering the following three elements:

- Anatomically speaking, is the brain intact?
- If it is, are the perceptual and cognitive functions intact?
- If they are, is the individual's emotional condition affected?

In a less clinical and more pragmatic analysis, Morrison (ibid., 6) points out that the capacity to give consent should meet the following criteria:

- free and voluntary consent, free of any coercion;
- consent based on information given by the physician not only on the nature of the diagnostic or therapeutic action to be undertaken, but also its consequences, benefits and potential adverse effects; as a corollary, information given concerning more conservative alternative forms of intervention, as well as the consequences of no treatment; and
- consent based on the individual's capacity to agree to or refuse a diagnostic or therapeutic action.

Validity Criteria for the Capacity to Give Consent

Unless proven otherwise, anyone being considered for treatment for a mental condition is assumed to have the capacity to give consent. Without strict evaluation criteria, however, it is possible that there will be abuses and unfavourable interpretations of this capacity. As a result, as reported by Morrison (1988, 10), in Canada a series of criteria known as the "Nova Scotia criteria" was developed:

1. Does the patient understand the illness or condition for which treatment has been proposed?
2. Does the patient grasp the nature and purpose of the proposed treatment?
3. Does the patient understand the risks involved in undertaking the treatment?
4. Does the patient understand the risks involved in not undertaking the treatment?
5. Does the illness interfere with the patient's capacity to grant consent?

The right to refuse treatment is a guaranteed fundamental right for those who are presumed to be capable of giving consent. Any breach of that wish is a flagrant and direct violation of the security of the person, the consequences of which are very serious and include lawsuits, fines and jail sentences.

The capacity to grant consent, therefore, is decisive in determining the type of admission under which an individual will receive care. While in most cases admission is voluntary, compulsory admission is frequent; it remains a solution for many short and episodic behavioural crises.

Voluntary Committal

There are few problems with voluntary committal, also referred to as informal admission. It is usually little more than a formality. A study of provincial laws governing mental health sheds light on how it is applied.

Voluntary Committal Procedures in the Provinces and Territories

In most provinces, the mental health act expressly stipulates that voluntary admission to a hospital or treatment centre can be made on the recommendation of a physician and that it can be refused if hospitalization is not urgent or necessary or if adequate care and treatment are not available there (Robertson 1987, 312–13).

In Newfoundland, Quebec and Alberta, the relevant laws contain no specific sections pertaining to mental health. However, it is not impossible for an individual to claim voluntary treatment status.

Except in two provinces, none of the laws governing mental health prevent those admitted voluntarily from leaving the hospital. Only British Columbia (*Mental Health Act*, s. 19(1)) and Manitoba (*Mental Health Act*, s. 7(5)) require a waiting period before release can be authorized after a voluntary committal. In British Columbia, the maximum waiting period is 72 hours after the director of the institution has been notified. In Manitoba, there is a waiting period of 72 hours if the patient has not been admitted under one of the two systems (voluntary or compulsory admission) or has not obtained a discharge from a psychiatrist. Also, patients under voluntary treatment may be detained for 24 hours against their wishes so that they may be examined by a physician if a responsible member of the care-giving staff has good reason to believe that their health and safety are threatened.

The same waiting periods exist in many American states, in the United Kingdom and in many other countries. These measures provide a last chance for hospital staff to persuade the patient to remain in their care. It also gives the hospital administration time to begin the procedures for involuntary committal, if required.

Involuntary Committal

Involuntary committal – also known as formal or compulsory admission – is the second category by which a person can be admitted to a psychiatric treatment centre. Unlike voluntary committal, which is almost a formality, involuntary committal procedures must follow strict and precise parameters.

Basis of the Process

In Canada today, involuntary committal is a medical rather than a legal process. Until the 1950s, however, Canada relied upon a legal process, as is still the case in the United States and most other countries. In Canada the legal process is more commonly used for review and appeal. It remains in force because of the *Criminal Code*, as described earlier.

Involuntary Committal Procedures

There is a relatively uniform procedure for involuntary committal in mental health acts throughout the provinces. The first step is short-term committal, giving medical authorities the opportunity to observe and examine the mental condition of the person and to determine if treatment is necessary. If committal is called for and the person cannot give consent, the medical authorities at the institution issue a certificate requiring the patient to remain under the authority of the institution. In certain cases, the law requires that the examination be done by a physician other than the one who initiated the request for evaluation.

Many people are incapable of giving consent because they are in crisis situations, most often temporary. Authorities in the treatment centre have no choice but to proceed with involuntary committal in these cases.

Obstacles to Consent A crisis situation is the most common obstacle met by medical authorities who wish to obtain a person's consent for treatment. Although definitions exist, it is difficult to define an emergency situation. The one characteristic common to all is a danger to the life or health of the person. The Jamison decree, governing the use of treatments in California, presents this definition: "An emergency situation exists when there is a sudden and marked change in the patient's condition such that action is immediately necessary to preserve life or prevent serious bodily harm for the patient or for others and when it is impossible to obtain prior consent" (Garneau and Diener 1988, 53–54).

Committal may not be urgent but may be necessary because of the attitude a person has toward his or her own mental health. Those who deny an illness seriously limit their capacity to consent to treatment. Denial of an illness that can jeopardize the condition of a "psychotic patient" is sufficient reason to go beyond the prerequisite condition for consent.

Finally, a person's refusal to be informed about a condition or illness may permit medical authorities to proceed without consent.

Reasons for Committal
The same evaluation criteria are used for involuntary committal as for voluntary committal, except that two medical certificates may be required in some cases. In addition, the person cannot be eligible for the status of voluntary patient. Certain provinces require that one of the two certificates be from a psychiatrist. In Quebec, for example, the examination must be carried out by a psychiatrist, although in exceptional cases a physician may perform the task. If committal is deemed necessary, the person is admitted to an appropriate treatment centre for a length of time in accordance with the provisions of that province's law.

Mental Disorder Specifically, the first evaluation criterion is the observation of a mental disorder, which most provincial laws now define on the basis of the inability to function rather than on medical criteria. This is clearly seen in the definition given in section 2(*m*) of *The Mental Health Services Act* in Saskatchewan: "a disorder of thought, perception, feelings or behaviour that seriously impairs a person's judgment, capacity to recognize reality, ability to associate with others or ability to meet the ordinary demands of life, in respect of which treatment is advisable."

Not all definitions of mental disorder are so precise. In most provinces a more general meaning – such as "any disease or disability of mind" – is implied, but it can extend, as is the case in Alberta, to the broader meaning, "lack of reason or lack of control."

Potential Danger and Protection   The second criterion refers to the potential danger that people may represent to themselves and to society. It also refers to the protection that must be provided. Quoting a judge, Bergeron (1981, 107) recalls that in the broad sense the term danger "implies the idea of a risk that something may arise causing harm, loss or damage." In the context of mental health, danger refers to the fear that a crisis or illness may cause some kind of harm. The first evaluation criterion is highly contested: a considerable amount of research (e.g., Hill 1977; Rodgers 1988) questions the validity and reliability of psychiatrists' predictions of how potentially dangerous an individual will be. This was confirmed by the Law Reform Commission of Canada: "More remarkable than the bulk of this literature is its unanimity – it concludes that the clinical predictions of dangerousness are at best, suspect, and at worst, totally unreliable" (1975, 19).

Despite this serious drawback, legislation on mental health definitely refers to this potential for danger. The index of dangerousness may also be interpreted in the laws as being a way, through committal, of protecting the individual's or others' interests. Despite its reputation, this approach, known as the "Safety Test," is widely used in Canada. It uses the commission of violent acts and manifestations of mental instability as indicators. It includes the following as violent acts, listed in order of frequency:

- physical assault on other persons;
- voluntarily self-inflicted injury;
- damage to furniture or possessions;
- attempted suicide;
- sexual assault against others; and
- attempted murder.

The most common signs of mental instability are psychiatric symptoms, depression and verbal or behavioural displays of hostility.

The degree of dangerousness is not in itself an absolute indicator of the inability to perform certain actions. However, we believe that when an individual's judgement is so affected that he or she is unable to give consent to treatment that is deemed essential to protect the life of that person or of his or her family, this individual cannot meet the minimum and fundamental requirements of voting.

The Welfare Test   The "Welfare Test" is an adaptation of the "Safety Test" and is used in British Columbia and Manitoba. It is used for a person with a mental disorder "that seriously impairs his ability to react appropriately to his environment or to associate with others; and that requires medical treatment or makes care, supervision and control of the person necessary for his protection or for the protection of others" (British Columbia, *Mental Health Act*, s. 1).

Inadmissibility As a Voluntary Patient   Committal as an involuntary patient is not possible in most provinces unless the person is not admissible for voluntary committal. There are also many cases where an individual can refuse to be admitted or examined in the centre as a voluntary patient, as is the case in Prince Edward Island, New Brunswick and Alberta. The laws of Manitoba and Saskatchewan are more precise, referring directly to the refusal to undergo voluntary examination. Finally, there are those cases where an individual demonstrates an obvious mental incapacity that prevents him or her from consenting to voluntary committal, as described earlier in the section on obstacles to consent.

A brief overview of provincial legislation shows that there is a certain consistency in the grounds for committal. The tendency is to rely on medical advice to determine whether there is a serious threat to a person's own safety and the safety of others. Other criteria, such as the refusal to voluntarily undergo an examination, inadmissibility as a voluntary patient or the need for particular care, are frequently found within the mental health legislation.

INVOLUNTARY COMMITTAL IN THE PROVINCES AND TERRITORIES

General Scope of Application

Involuntary committal generally requires the opinion of a single physician, though in British Columbia, Saskatchewan, Nova Scotia and the Yukon two physicians are required to perform this task. There are exceptions, however, including cases where no qualified physician is available nearby or within a reasonable distance.

According to the legislation in several provinces, "any person who has good reason to believe that an individual must be placed under observation for evaluation with respect to his or her own safety and that of his or her surroundings" can initiate a request for committal. This applies in Nova Scotia, Prince Edward Island, Ontario, Manitoba, Alberta, the Yukon and the Northwest Territories.

In Newfoundland, Quebec, Saskatchewan, Manitoba and British Columbia, mental health laws prohibit a physician from issuing a medical certificate in the following situations: when the physician is a close relative; or when the physician is connected to the patient through other ties such as marriage, employment or partnership. The laws also stipulate that the two medical certificates must not be signed by the same person.

The procedure used in the Yukon differs from those of the provinces. It is based on the use of legal petitions to request and authorize involuntary committal.

Waiting Periods for Issuance of Certificates

Most Acts also indicate the time allowed for the completion of the certificate; this ensures that no one is subjected to unnecessarily long procedures. The amount of time varies, however, as can be seen in table 3.3. In Quebec, the *Mental patients protection act* does not stipulate the amount of time allowed but rather that examination must be made "without delay." An employee of the Ministère de la Santé et des Services sociaux du Québec (Quebec ministry of health and social services) stated that this examination must take place within 24 to 48 hours of admission, however. If not, the person must be transferred to a hospital or a community service centre.

Respect for the time periods stipulated by the provinces remains extremely important. Their violation can nullify any committal,

Table 3.3
Maximum time permitted for issuance of certificates authorizing involuntary committal

Jurisdiction	Maximum time	Legislative reference
Newfoundland	7 days	S.N. 1971, No. 80, s. 6(4)(b)
Prince Edward Island	7 days	R.S.P.E.I. 1988, c. M-6, s. 9(4)
Nova Scotia	7 days	R.S.N.S. 1989, c. 208, s. 36(4)
New Brunswick	7 days	S.N.B. 1989, c. 23, s. 7.1(3)
Quebec	Not specified	
Ontario	7 days	R.S.O. 1980, c. 262, s. 9(4)
Manitoba	2 days	S.M. 1987–88, c. 56, s. 8(3)
Saskatchewan	7 days	S.S. 1984–85–86, c. M-13.1, s. 18(4)
Alberta	24 hours	R.S.A. 1988, c. M-13.1, s. 2
British Columbia	14 days	R.S.B.C. 1979, c. 256, s. 20(3)
Northwest Territories	24 hours	S.N.W.T. 1985 (2nd), c. 6, s. 9(3)
Yukon	Not specified	

as occurred in 1984 when a person with a mental illness was awarded $500 in damages following an unnecessarily long committal
(*Ketchum* 1984).

Committal Facilities
Individuals may be committed only to treatment centres that are specifically recognized and designated by the provincial mental health acts.[16]
This legislation restricts the extension of powers concerning mental
health to a limited number of institutions.

Committal Periods
The decision to commit anyone involuntarily is not permanent. All
legislation stipulates an initial committal period to be followed by a
second evaluation of the person's mental condition. This approach
makes it possible to avoid hasty decisions based on an evaluation made
during a crisis. In fact, while many are admitted to hospitals involuntarily, few remain for extended periods. At the end of the 1980s, for
example, more than 90 percent of those committed involuntarily to the
Centre hospitalier Robert-Giffard in Quebec were there for 10 days or
less.[17] Similarly, the average period of involuntary committal in 1990
was 14 days in the Yukon and 15.5 days in Saskatchewan.

Initial Committal Period
The maximum duration for initial committal established by provincial
and territorial law is reported in table 3.4.

Renewal of Certificates
The procedures for involuntary committal offer certain flexibility while
being subject to a precise evaluation timetable. After the initial committal
period, therefore, medical personnel must issue a renewal certificate
for involuntary treatment if they determine, after examination, that
there are still grounds for involuntary committal. If committal is
renewed, it is subject to the time periods stipulated by the provincial
and territorial mental health acts (see table 3.5).

Only a small proportion of involuntary admissions are extended
beyond the initial committal period. In most cases, involuntary
committal is necessary as a result of a temporary behavioural crisis that
can be eased by time alone, by treatment or by medication. Bergeron
(1981, 147) agrees, making these comments following close examination
of the annual reports of the Commission des affaires sociales du Québec:
"In 1977–78, the Commission des affaires sociales issued a report
concerning all involuntary committals which lasted more than six

Table 3.4
Maximum duration of initial involuntary committal

Jurisdiction	Maximum duration of initial committal	Legislative reference
Newfoundland	15 days	S.N. 1971, No. 80, s. 7(2)
Prince Edward Island	1 month	R.S.P.E.I. 1988, c. M-6, s. 9(5)
Nova Scotia	7 days	R.S.N.S. 1989, c. 208, s. 34(2)
New Brunswick	14 days	S.N.B. 1989, c. 23, s. 7.1(4)
Quebec	21 days	R.S.Q. 1985, c. P-41, s. 23
Ontario	7 days	R.S.O. 1980, c. 262, s. 9(5)
Manitoba	3 weeks	S.M. 1987–88, c. 56, s. 19(4)
Saskatchewan	21 days	S.S. 1984–85–86, c. M-13.1, s. 24(3)
Alberta	72 hours	R.S.A. 1988, c. M-13.1, s. 2
British Columbia	15 days	R.S.B.C. 1979, c. 256, s. 20(6)
Northwest Territories	48 hours	S.N.W.T. 1985 (2nd), c. 6, s. 9(2)
Yukon	24 hours, unless a court order or specific warrant has been issued	R.S.Y. 1986, c. 115, s. 6(3)

months. Out of a total of 152 cases reported, it reviewed 136 files and maintained 57 of these involuntary committals. This tends to indicate that long involuntary committals are diminishing, if one considers that during the same period the Commission had received notice of 1 333 warrants for involuntary committals."

This move away from long involuntary committals, already evident in Quebec in 1978, reflects the influence of the philosophy of deinstitutionalization and respect for the fundamental rights of the person. This phenomenon can be seen as supporting our desire to limit the number of individuals deprived of the right to vote and to ensure that exclusion not be extended any longer than necessary.

Expiration of Certificates and Changes in Status

When a certificate expires and is not renewed, it is understood that the patient then has the status of voluntary patient. Any failure to follow the required procedure automatically puts an end to involuntary committal.

A system of periodically issuing certificates ensures that each person will benefit from a periodic evaluation and have a formal occasion to exercise the right to be heard. Some provinces even provide

Table 3.5
Renewal certificate provisions for involuntary committals

Jurisdiction	Renewal certificates	Legislative reference
Newfoundland	Possibility of 5 certificates, valid for periods of 1, 2, 3 and 6 months and 1 year; the last 1 can be renewed every 12 months	S.N. 1971, No. 80, s. 9(1) and s. 9(1) and 9(2)(a), (b), (c), (d), (e)
Prince Edward Island	First 4 certificates are for 2, 3, 6 and 12 months; each subsequent certificate shall be valid for 12 months	R.S.P.E.I. 1988, c. M-6, s. 14(3)(a), (b), (c), (d), (e)
Nova Scotia	First 2 certificates are for 3 months; subsequent certificates may not exceed 6 months	R.S.N.S. 1989, c. 208, s. 44(3)(a), (b), (c)
New Brunswick	First 2 certificates are valid for 1 and 2 months; third and subsequent certificates are valid for 3 months	S.N.B. 1989, c. 23, s. 13(4)(a), (b), (c)
Quebec	An examination must be made 3 months after the beginning of the involuntary committal, and at least every 6 months thereafter	R.S.Q. 1985, c. P-41, s. 23
Ontario	First 2 certificates are valid for 1 and 2 months; third and subsequent certificates are valid for 3 months	R.S.O. 1980, c. 262, s. 14(4)(b)(i), (ii), (iii)
Manitoba	Certificates are renewable every 3 months	S.M. 1987–88, c. 56, s. 19(4)(b)
Saskatchewan	Certificates are valid for periods not exceeding 21 days	S.S. 1984–85–86, c. M-13.1, s. 24(7)
Alberta	2 physicians must find that a certificate should be issued; first 2 certificates are for 1 month; subsequent certificates are valid for 6 months	R.S.A. 1988, c. M-13.1, s. 8(3)(a), (b), (c)
British Columbia	First certificate is for 1 year; the second and subsequent certificates are for 2 years	R.S.B.C. 1979, c. 256, 21(2)(a), (b)
Northwest Territories	Judge may request that committal be extended for a maximum period of 14 days until a physician rules on the case	S.N.W.T. 1985 (2nd), c. 6, s. 24(1)(a), (b)
Yukon	Not specified	

for a compulsory periodic review mechanism whereby, after a certain period, the person named in the certificate may request a review. Finally, as in the Alberta legislation, medical authorities may be obliged to advise the person in writing of any change in status.

In Ontario, New Brunswick, Prince Edward Island, Saskatchewan, Manitoba and the Northwest Territories, a change of status is possible through a decision by a review committee (upon filing of the appropriate form completed by a medical authority) or by legal decision, even if a certificate is still valid.

Review Procedures and Appeal

Every province has provisions for creating a review board. The composition of these review boards is essentially uniform across provinces, consisting of three members: usually a lawyer, a psychiatrist and one member who is neither a lawyer nor a psychiatrist. The make-up of these decision-making bodies in each of Canada's provinces and territories is shown in table 3.6.

Eligibility for Review Procedures and Appeal

The review boards are established to evaluate only the cases of involuntary committal. The right to request a review of status rests first of all with the affected person, who may request one from the time of admission, according to timetables stipulated in the provincial mental health acts. Nova Scotia and Manitoba provide automatic reviews. In many jurisdictions, another person acting on behalf of the person who is committed may also request that a decision be reviewed. An overview of the review procedure in the provinces and territories is given in table 3.7.

Grounds for Review

Each request for review must be studied carefully. This imperative has been raised to the level of a constitutional guarantee under section 7 of the *Canadian Charter of Rights and Freedoms*, which grants everyone the right to life, liberty and security (Rodgers 1988, 85).

The grounds used to refuse a change in status vary, but they usually involve a lack of self-criticism on the part of a person displaying psychotic behaviour combined with a refusal to recognize the illness. Bergeron (1981, 118) gives several examples:

- a patient who has been hospitalized several times, is suffering from a psychotic syndrome, has attempted suicide and shows no self-sufficiency;

Table 3.6
Decision-making bodies for review of involuntary committals

Jurisdiction	Decision-making body	Legislative reference
Newfoundland	With the agreement of the Lieutenant-Governor in Council, the minister names a review board composed of 3 members: a lawyer, who presides over the board meetings; a physician; and 1 who is neither a lawyer nor a physician	S.N. 1971, No. 80, s. 16(1)
	Any decision of the review board may be contested before the Supreme Court	S.N.1971, No. 80, s. 19(6)(a), (b)
Prince Edward Island	Review board must be composed of 3 members: a Supreme Court judge, who shall act as chair, a physician, and 1 who is neither lawyer nor a physician	R.S.P.E.I. 1988, c. M-6, s. 24(1) and 24(2)
Nova Scotia	Review board is named by the director of the psychiatric institution; composition of the board is not specified	R.S.N.S. 1989, c. 208, s. 48(4)
New Brunswick	Lieutenant-Governor in Council names appeal commissions, each composed of a member of the New Brunswick Bar (chair), a psychiatrist (or a physician) and 1 who is neither a lawyer nor a physician	S.N.B. 1989, c. 23, s. 30(2)
Quebec	Request for review may be made to the Commission des affaires sociales by the person concerned, a tutor or a guardian; committee consists of a member of the Commission and 2 medical evaluators	R.S.Q. 1985, c. P-41, s. 30
Ontario	Review board is named by the Lieutenant-Governor in Council who also decides upon the appropriate number of lawyers, psychiatrists and other members who are neither lawyers nor psychiatrists	R.S.O. 1980, c. 262, s. 30
Manitoba	Review board is composed of 3 members: 1 of whom is a lawyer, who chairs the board meetings, a psychiatrist, and 1 who is neither a lawyer nor a psychiatrist	S.M. 1987–88, c. 56, s. 26.4(3)
	Review board may add as a party anyone who, according to the board, has a significant interest in the question under review	S.M. 1987–88, c. 56, s. 26.5(5)

Table 3.6 (cont'd)
Decision-making bodies for review of involuntary committals

Jurisdiction	Decision-making body	Legislative reference
Saskatchewan	Review board, named by the minister, consists of 3 members, of whom 1 must be a physician and 1 a lawyer (solicitor)	S.S. 1984–85–86, c. M-13.1, s. 26.5(5)
Alberta	Review board consists of a chair and a vice-chair (who must be lawyers), a psychiatrist, a physician and a member of the general public	R.S.A. 1988, c. M-13.1, s. 34(4)(a), (b), (c), (d)
British Columbia	Committee consists of a chair, a physician and a person unrelated to the patient but who knows the patient and is named by the patient; if that is not possible, another person shall be named	R.S.B.C. 1979, c. 256, s. 21(a), (b), (i), (ii), (iii)
Northwest Territories	Decisions concerning involuntary committal may be subject to review before the Supreme Court	S.N.W.T. 1985 (2nd), c. 6, s. 27(1)
Yukon	Review board consists of 2 medical practitioners, 1 member of the Law Society of the Yukon, and 3 other persons	R.S.Y. 1986, c. 115, 8(1)

Table 3.7
Origin and frequency of requests for review of status

Jurisdiction	Origin/frequency of requests	Legislative reference
Newfoundland	Patient or any other person acting on his or her behalf may at any time request a review of status by completing the appropriate review form	S.N. 1971, No. 80, s. 17(1)
Prince Edward Island	At the time of involuntary admission or of renewal of any certificate concerning the patient, the patient or any other person acting on his or her behalf may request a review of status by making a request to the chair of the review committee, using the prescribed form	R.S.P.E.I. 1988, c. M-6, s. 25(1) and 25(2)(a), (b)
Nova Scotia	Patients' files are reviewed every 6 months during the first 2 years and once every 12 months thereafter	R.S.N.S. 1989, c. 208, s. 64
	Review of a file may be refused within 6 months of the preceding review	R.S.N.S. 1989, c. 208, s. 65(2)

Table 3.7 (cont'd)
Origin and frequency of requests for review of status

Jurisdiction	Origin/frequency of requests	Legislative reference
New Brunswick	Request may be filed at the time that any detention certificate concerning the patient comes into force; request for review of involuntary status may be made at any time by the minister, or the executive director or administrator of an institution	S.N.B. 1989, c. 23, s. 31(2) and 31(3)
Quebec	Once a decision has been made, a review may be requested by any person who finds it unsatisfactory including a tutor or guardian	R.S.Q. 1985, c. P-41, s. 30
Ontario	Review may be requested when a certificate of admission for obligatory treatment comes into force or is renewed or when a patient is placed under obligatory care after admission to a psychiatric institution	R.S.O. 1980, c. 262, 31(2)
Manitoba	Review is automatic upon the filing of the third and fourth renewal certificates, to determine if the conditions for involuntary committal are still met	S.M. 1987–88, c. 56, s. 26.3(1)
Saskatchewan	Person has no right of appeal pursuant to this section unless at least 2 new certificates have been issued	S.S. 1984–85–86, c. M-13.1, s. 34(4)
Alberta	Patient, guardian, person on his or her behalf, or a board that has made an application under this section with respect to 2 admission certificates or 2 renewal certificates may make further applications with respect to those certificates	R.S.A. 1988, c. M-13.1, s. 38(3)
British Columbia	Person admitted to a provincial mental health facility under section 20 shall at any time after the expiration of 30 days from the date of admission, on his or her request or on the request of a person on his or her behalf, be entitled to receive a hearing ... to determine whether or not detention should continue	R.S.B.C. 1979, c. 256, s. 21(4)
Northwest Territories	Review must be within a 30-day period following a decision of the Supreme Court	S.N.W.T. 1985 (2nd), c. 6, s. 30(1)
Yukon	Not specified	

- a patient out of touch with reality, who is very anxious, and whose defence mechanisms are extremely fragile;
- a patient who is passive, disorganized and who refuses medication, easily becomes aggressive and has escaped several times; and
- a patient who refuses to acknowledge his or her illness, who is not convinced of the need for treatment and who is out of touch with reality.

Bergeron (1981, 120) reports that in addition to these examples, which indicate danger to the patient, the threat of danger to others is very important. He notes that "the majority of these patients have undergone several hospitalizations, which seems to confirm the chronic and persistent nature of their illness and which may indicate future acts dangerous to others." Physical aggressiveness, lack of control in dealing with frustrations, and the absence of self-criticism in these cases are all grounds for refusal of a change in status. Finally, violent and aggressive behaviour and tendencies toward suicide, homicide or pyromania are all conditions that involve danger both to the person and to others.

Bergeron (1981, 164), in his study of requests for review of involuntary committal addressed to the Commission des affaires sociales du Québec, concluded that "the study of the Commission's decisions produces the clear impression that the patient must be docile, not cause trouble, take all medication, be aware of and accept his or her illness, try to integrate socially, be capable of tolerating frustrations in life, and finally, be able to control and organize him- or herself."

Until now, our theoretical consideration of the disenfranchisement of persons with mental disorders based on the involuntary committal procedure has confirmed how exceptional, restrictive and controlled these procedures are. We turn now to the statistics to measure the extent of this practice.

STATISTICAL OVERVIEW OF INVOLUNTARY COMMITTAL IN CANADA

Methodology

For this section we surveyed the provincial health ministries as well as other related organizations. The object of this exercise was to provide the most up-to-date report possible of the number of people who are currently involuntarily committed in Canada. However, the information collected has a flaw in those provinces where there is a distinction between institutions serving people with intellectual impairments and those treating people with mental illnesses. This is the case particularly in Ontario, where we deal with only 10 institutions, although the actual number of institutions specializing in the treatment of persons with mental disorders is more than 20. Although the statistical tables in this section are more a reflection of institutions that treat people with mental illnesses, they are nevertheless a fairly accurate reflection of our observations on involuntary committal.

This is evident from a study of the profiles of individuals who have been committed involuntarily. According to Dr. Louis Roy of the Centre hospitalier Robert-Giffard in Quebec, more than 90 percent of patients who are committed involuntarily have one or more mental illnesses; most of the others have both intellectual impairment and a mental illness.

In addition, many of the patients in centres for people with intellectual impairments are fairly elderly people who have no other resource outside these institutions and have chosen voluntarily to reside there.[18] They would therefore not represent a very high "risk" of belonging to the group of individuals usually found in the involuntary committal category.

The Yukon and the Northwest Territories did not respond to our requests for information; consequently, this section contains no statistical description of these regions.

Newfoundland

Newfoundland has one main psychiatric institution and eight psychiatric departments in other hospitals to treat persons with mental disorders. There were 3 896 such patients in 1989–90. Data in table 3.8 were provided by the Health Research and Statistics Division of the Newfoundland Ministry of Health.

The Newfoundland Health Research and Statistics Division was unable to tell us how many involuntarily committed patients were in that province. However, we were able to establish that fewer than 14 percent of those admitted to institutions, on average, did not get permission to leave that year. In the three hospitals we studied, however, no more than 8.3 percent of the patients were involuntarily committed. The statistics are shown in table 3.9.

Table 3.8
Mental health care in Newfoundland, 1985–86 to 1988–89

Year	Admissions	Discharges	No. remaining
1985–86	4 200	3 338	862
1986–87	3 882	3 324	558
1987–88	3 389	3 365	531
1988–89	3 833	3 310	523

Source: Brenda Kavanagh, Health Research and Statistics Division, Ministry of Health, Newfoundland.

Table 3.9
Involuntary committals in three Newfoundland hospitals, April 1991

Institution	No. of patients	Involuntary committals	% involuntary committals
St. Clare's Mercy Hospital	24	2	8.3
Waterford Hospital	368	28	7.6
James Paton Memorial Hospital	142	0	0

Sources: Ann D. Hyde, Health Record Analyst, St. Clare's Mercy Hospital; Dorothy Dalten, Medical Records Division, Waterford Hospital; Philomena O'Grady, Medical Records Division, James Paton Memorial Hospital.

Prince Edward Island

All mental health care on Prince Edward Island is provided at Hillsborough Hospital, which has 190 beds for in-patient care. According to the hospital's Division of Aging and Extended Care, occupancy of available beds is between 93 and 98 percent. Of the 190 beds, 135 are reserved for long-term care. On 31 March 1991, for example, there was a 94.2 percent occupancy rate, and 11 of the 179 in-patients (6.1 percent) were committed involuntarily (for statistics on committals in PEI, see table 3.10).

Nova Scotia

Two institutions in this province are accredited to admit and treat people needing psychiatric care: the Nova Scotia Hospital and the Cape Breton Hospital. In total, 435 beds are available (table 3.11), of which 373 are at the Nova Scotia Hospital.

Using information provided by the Nova Scotia Department of Health and Fitness at the end of April 1991, we identified 105 of the 373 patients as being committed involuntarily, i.e., 28.2 percent of all patients receiving psychiatric treatment during this period. The situation is shown in table 3.12.

New Brunswick

As is the case for Nova Scotia, New Brunswick has two institutions for treating people who need psychiatric care. Each of these institutions has just over 300 beds.

It is clear from table 3.13 that patients who are involuntarily committed are not evenly distributed between the two hospitals. This is because Centracare has more facilities for admitting individuals under Lieutenant-Governor's warrants, whereby the state requires detainment in a hospital.

Table 3.10
Committals by type in Prince Edward Island, 1986–87 to 1990–91

Year	Voluntary committals	Involuntary committals	Other	No. of patients	% involuntary committals
1986–87	81	56	4	141	40
1987–88	101	52	11	164	32
1988–89	143	107	6	256	42
1989–90	144	102	4	250	41
1990–91	187	117	5	309	38

Source: Michelle White, Medical Records Clerk, Hillsborough Hospital.

Table 3.11
Mental health care in Nova Scotia, 1985–86 to 1989–90

Year	No. of beds	Discharges
1985–86	456	2 712
1986–87	446	2 746
1987–88	435	2 729
1988–89	435	2 764
1989–90	435	2 586

Source: Brenda Ryan, Director, Research and Statistics, Department of Health and Fitness, Nova Scotia.

Table 3.12
Involuntary committals in Nova Scotia, April 1991

Institution	Voluntary committals	Involuntary committals	No. of patients	% involuntary committals
Nova Scotia Hospital	218	73	291	25.1
Cape Breton Hospital	50	32	82	39.0

Source: Brenda Ryan, Director, Research and Statistics, Department of Health and Fitness, Nova Scotia.

Table 3.13
Involuntary committals in New Brunswick, April 1991

Institution	No. of patients	Involuntary committals	% involuntary committals
Centracare	301	180	59.8
Centre Hospitalier Restigouche	317	27	8.5

Sources: Susan Black, Manager, Health Records Department, Centracare; Hilda Katan, Health Records Administrator, Centre Hospitalier Restigouche.

Quebec

Although our study of Quebec psychiatric institutions was incomplete, it did give us a fairly accurate description of the situation in that province. With the help of the Ministère de la Santé et des Services sociaux and the medical records sections in some of these institutions, we gathered the data shown in table 3.14.

The table presents a reasonable picture of the situation in Quebec. The estimates given in the footnote were confirmed by a chronological study at the Centre hospitalier Robert-Giffard, which shows, as indicated in table 3.15, that over the last seven years there have never been more than 30 patients confined involuntarily at any one time.

Table 3.14
Involuntary committals in selected Quebec institutions, 28 February 1991

Institution[a]	In-patient population	Involuntary committals	% involuntary committals
Hôpital Douglas	818	10[b]	1.2
Louis-Hippolyte-Lafontaine	1 964	38	1.9
Mont-Joli	468	1	0.2
Rivière des Prairies	594	0	0.0
Robert-Giffard	1 780	21	1.2
St-Julien	660	0	0.0

Source: Guy Doré, Ministère de la Santé et des Services sociaux du Québec, Direction de la Santé mentale.

[a]The six hospitals listed in this table have 80 percent of the patient population. According to two officials at the Ministère de la Santé et des Services sociaux, an extrapolation of the data suggests that the number of patients confined involuntarily is approximately 75–80.

[b]This figure was accurate on the date indicated; however, the records department of this institution reports that the number is usually 15.

The trend toward deinstitutionalization is confirmed in table 3.16. In Quebec, throughout the network of psychiatric services, the number of patients has dropped from 10 519 in 1984 to 9 146 in 1990. This is an average annual decrease of 229 patients during that period.

Table 3.15
Involuntary committals in Quebec, 31 March 1985–31 March 1991

Year	No. of patients	Involuntary committals	% involuntary committals
1985	2 207	11	0.5
1986	2 100	11	0.5
1987	2 030	11	0.5
1988	1 905	8	0.4
1989	1 799	8	0.4
1990	1 715	21	1.2
1991[a]	1 650	23	1.4

Source: Dr. Louis Roy, Directeur des services professionnels, Centre hospitalier Robert-Giffard.
[a]For 1991, data are from 27 March.

Table 3.16
Changes in number of patients in psychiatric hospitals in Quebec,
1 April 1984–1 April 1990

Year	No. of patients	Annual change
1984	10 519	—
1985	10 315	-204
1986	10 066	-249
1987	9 913	-153
1988	9 529	-384
1989	9 280	-249
1990	9 146	-134

Source: Guy Doré, Ministère de la Santé et des Services sociaux du Québec, Direction de la Santé mentale.

Ontario

There are 10 institutions in Ontario accredited to provide services to individuals with mental illness. On 20 July 1990, 3 561 persons lived in these institutions, of whom 412 (11.5 percent) were committed involuntarily. Of the 3 561 patients, 1 806 (50.7 percent) had been hospitalized for less than one year. On 1 June 1989, the proportion of patients in these institutions under involuntary committal was approximately 22 percent, or 720 out of 3 276 patients.

As in Quebec, deinstitutionalization efforts have led to a considerable drop in the in-patient population, as shown in table 3.17.

Manitoba

Psychiatric services in Manitoba are provided by three institutions (table 3.18), serving an average of 700 persons. The statistics available for voluntary and involuntary admissions are for the year 1989 only. During that year, 29.4 percent of the admissions to the two hospitals mentioned in table 3.19 were involuntary (117 of 398). Of the 456 readmissions to these two hospitals, 117 (25.6 percent) were involuntary. Research carried out through the Mental Health Division of the Department of Health showed that at the end of April 1991, 8.9 percent of the patients in the three hospitals (54 out of 607) were under involuntary committal. The breakdown by hospital is shown in table 3.20.

Table 3.17
Changes in number of in-patients in psychiatric hospitals in Ontario, 1984–85 to 1989–90

Year	No. of in-patients	Annual change
1984–85	4 372	—
1985–86	4 192	-180
1986–87	4 163	-29
1987–88	3 957	-206
1988–89	3 823	-134
1989–90	3 561	-262

Source: Roberta Stephens, Policy Analyst Coordinator, Mental Health Facilities Branch.

Table 3.18
Average annual population of psychiatric hospitals in Manitoba, 1986–89

Institution	1986	1987	1988	1989
BMHC	436.8	406.0	387.1	350.0
SMHC	323.7	308.5	295.3	301.2
EMHC	39.3	44.2	42.0	41.2

Source: Dr. Anwar Islam, Senior Planning Program Analyst, Mental Health Division.

BMHC = Brandon Mental Health Centre; SMHC = Selkirk Mental Health Centre; EMHC = Eden Mental Health Centre.

Table 3.19
Number and percentage of voluntary and involuntary admissions and readmissions in two Manitoba psychiatric hospitals, 1989

Institution	Voluntary admissions	Involuntary admissions	% involuntary admissions	Voluntary readmissions	Involuntary readmissions	% involuntary readmissions
BMHC	223	58	20.6	241	62	20.5
SMHC	58	59	50.4	100	55	35.5
Total	281	117	29.4	341	117	25.6

Source: Dr. Anwar Islam, Senior Planning Program Analyst, Mental Health Division.

BMHC = Brandon Mental Health Centre; SMHC = Selkirk Mental Health Centre.

Table 3.20
Involuntary committals in Manitoba psychiatric hospitals as of 1 May 1991

Institution	No. of patients	Involuntary committals	% involuntary committals
BMHC	259	12	4.6
SMHC	308	42	13.6
EMHC	40	0	0.0

Source: Dr. Anwar Islam, Senior Planning Program Analyst, Mental Health Division.

BMHC = Brandon Mental Health Centre; SMHC = Selkirk Mental Health Centre; EMHC = Eden Mental Health Centre.

Saskatchewan

Psychiatric care and services in Saskatchewan are divided among 11 institutions, 10 of which provide short-term treatment. The only institution accredited for long-term care has 209 beds. The other 10

Table 3.21
Saskatchewan admissions by length of stay and status, 1987–90

Year	Short-term admissions	Long-term admissions	Short-term involuntary admissions	Long-term involuntary admissions	% total involuntary admissions
1987	4 101	18	433	9	10.7
1988	4 266	15	442	14	10.6
1989	4 224	15	557	9	13.3
1990	4 160	16	1 020	16	24.8

Source: Dr. Kent Silzer, Senior Program and Policy Analyst, Mental Health Services.

Table 3.22
Proportion of in-patients under involuntary committal by length of stay in Saskatchewan, 31 March 1991

No. of short-term patients	No. of short-term involuntary committals	% involuntary committals	No. of long-term patients	No. of long-term involuntary committals	% involuntary committals
268	41	15.3	165	1	0.6

Source: Dr. Kent Silzer, Senior Program and Policy Analyst, Mental Health Services.

together have 352 beds. Both total admissions and involuntary admissions for the years 1987–90 inclusive, by length of stay, are shown in table 3.21.

A survey of psychiatric institutions confirms that involuntary committal plays a limited role in this province. On 31 March 1991, 42 patients were considered involuntarily committed. More interestingly, 41 of these were in short-term care facilities. The proportion of patients under involuntary committal by length of stay on 31 March 1991 is shown in table 3.22.

Alberta

In Alberta, there are 1 965 beds available for persons needing mental health care. They are divided among a network of 15 general hospitals (594 beds), two provincial institutions (1 053 beds) and three long-term treatment centres (318 beds). A survey of these institutions showed that at the beginning of April 1991, only 239 individuals (12.2 percent) were under involuntary committal (table 3.23).

Table 3.23
Involuntary committals in Alberta, April 1991

No. of patients	Involuntary committals	% involuntary committals
1 965	239	12.2

Source: Yvonne Collinson, Hospital Mental Health Consultant, Mental Health Division.

British Columbia

Denying the right to vote on the basis of involuntary committal is currently a problem in British Columbia. The *Mental Health Act* is under revision, and the criteria for committal may be less important than the patient's ability to pay the costs incurred during a stay at one of the centres (other than those costs directly related to treatment).

On 30 March 1991, 70 percent of the 900 patients in the principal psychiatric institution in this province were under "involuntary committal." The situation is changing, since in June 1990 this proportion had been 90 percent.

The situation tends to be closer to the norm when you look at the 700 or so patients in the psychiatric departments of the general hospitals. There, the proportion of patients involuntarily committed has been significantly less (about 25 percent) in the last five years.

In British Columbia, exclusion based on committal would disenfranchise approximately 800 people, most of whom have chronic schizophrenia.

CONCLUSION

There is no perfect way to resolve the issue of who can be denied the right to vote, as demonstrated by the different approaches found in the electoral laws of various jurisdictions. These laws all reflect a desire to maintain the right to vote for the greatest possible number of people, but the change in attitudes and perceptions is far from complete. Like all laws, electoral laws reflect the evolution of society.

The current climate favours reform of the electoral laws. Canada has an opportunity to join this trend by supporting fundamental principles that promote the rights of the individual. Accordingly, the objectives of the *Canada Elections Act* must include the presumption of competence and the promotion of individual autonomy, as these are the guiding principles behind the movement toward greater integration into society of people with mental disorders or intellectual impairment. The right to vote falls within these objectives as a means to "make choices and assume the responsibility for one's own personal, social and economic life" (Quebec, Ministère de la Santé 1988, 14).

There are those who fear that minimal restrictions on the right to vote will leave an easily influenced group of new voters vulnerable to manipulation. Although we are well aware of this risk, those with a mental disorder are not the only people who can be manipulated. The Canadian electoral system is based, above all, on the integrity of those who take part in it. The experience of Quebec, Ontario and Manitoba, although very recent, shows that those with mental disorders are quite capable of becoming voters without being unduly influenced. Our primary concern is respect for fundamental human rights, and we agree with what Bergeron (1981, 194) says: "It is better, in our opinion, to be concerned with the rights and guarantees whereby individuals are protected from interdiction or confinement ... without justification. If all formalities and precautions are taken to avoid arbitrary and unjust actions in these domains, the consequent loss of the right to vote should not concern us."

The issue of voting rights is an emotional one. Even more problematic is the inconsistency of the most frequently advanced premises behind the issue discussed here: Does the need for a guardian always signify an incapacity to vote? Likewise, does the crisis that leads to involuntary committal necessarily deprive an individual of the judgement required to perform all acts? A negative response to these two questions is perhaps the appropriate one under the circumstances. One would have to agree that this issue continues to evolve in a grey area and that compromise is necessary. Imposing a test of competency implies that persons with mental disorders do not have an a priori ability to vote. In addition, testing does not accurately demonstrate the competence of a person, unless it is a test that is specific to the electoral process. Such a test would involve considerable expense and contribute to a system that promotes inequality among individuals. We admit that the proposed exclusion criteria also contain their share of subjectivity by relying on medical or legal decisions. These medical decisions, in the case of involuntary committal, must nevertheless adhere to a strict framework that is part of a "positive developmental trend that has moved the doctor–patient relationship away from a traditional one of authority and dependence to one of mutual participation" (Garneau and Diener 1988, 49).

As for individuals committed under Lieutenant-Governor's warrants, the recent decision in the *Swain* case finally ensures that a person will not have an unnecessarily lengthy committal. As emphasized by Chief Justice Lamer, the past is not necessarily responsible for the future, and the danger represented by a person at the time of a misdeed may be absent during the committal period. Under the same logic, there may not be an absolute link between the warrant issued by the Lieutenant-Governor and the inability to vote.

The two proposed forms of exclusion are certainly not flawless. However, they conform with the two guiding principles determined by the ideological foundations of the Canadian electoral system and by the parameters imposed by the *Canadian Charter of Rights and Freedoms*. They also answer the greatest criticism of the current system: the denial of the right to vote would no longer rely solely on the illness, but also on the individual's capacity to exercise this right.

Despite our best efforts, we could not estimate accurately how many people would be deprived of the right to vote under the proposed criteria. Most of the information we collected in our survey did not distinguish statistically between involuntary committal resulting from a Lieutenant-Governor's warrant and that resulting from a behavioural crisis. For New Brunswick, for example, it was impossible to determine the status of the 180 persons who were under involuntary committal at Centracare on 5 April 1991.

Despite this confusion, we maintain that the exclusion criteria proposed here provide for carefully circumscribed limits on both procedures and the number of persons affected. The figures in table 3.24 tend to confirm these views.

Table 3.24
Estimated number of individuals affected by proposed exclusions from the right to vote

Jurisdiction	Lieutenant-Governor's warrants	Involuntary committals
Newfoundland	7	30
Prince Edward Island	4[a]	11
Nova Scotia	13	105
New Brunswick	9	207
Quebec	414	80
Ontario	405	412
Manitoba	34	54
Saskatchewan	22	42
Alberta	74	239
British Columbia	142	700
Total	1 124	1 800

[a]Estimate given by the research centre at the Institut Philippe-Pinel.

A new elections act cannot be adopted without administrative pitfalls causing implementation difficulties. Among these is the necessary disclosure of the contents of medical files in order to separate the fit from the unfit. Should privacy have priority over the establishment of voters lists? This issue was raised to a certain extent in Manitoba when voters with mental disorders were enfranchised. The position of civil liberties organizations was that granting persons the right to vote should be pursued, even if it meant access to private medical files.

We can only conclude with the wish that the right to vote be granted to persons with mental disorders, in accordance with the democratic rights guaranteed under the *Canadian Charter of Rights and Freedoms*, with the exception of those people who, for reasons defined by provincial mental health acts, are deprived of their liberty because of involuntary committal and those who, under sections 614–19 inclusive of the *Criminal Code*, are committed under a warrant issued by the Lieutenant-Governor.

ABBREVIATIONS

am.	amended (by)
App. Div.	Appellate Division
B.C.L.R.	British Columbia Law Reports
c.	chapter
F.C.	Federal Court Reports
F. Supp.	Federal Supplement
N.J. Super.	New Jersey Superior Court Reports
R.S.A.	Revised Statutes of Alberta
R.S.B.C.	Revised Statutes of British Columbia
R.S.C.	Revised Statutes of Canada
R.S.M.	Revised Statutes of Manitoba
R.S.N.	Revised Statutes of Newfoundland
R.S.N.B.	Revised Statutes of New Brunswick
R.S.N.S.	Revised Statutes of Nova Scotia
R.S.O.	Revised Statutes of Ontario
R.S.P.E.I.	Revised Statutes of Prince Edward Island
R.S.Q.	Revised Statutes of Quebec
R.S.S.	Revised Statutes of Saskatchewan

R.S.Y.   Revised Statutes of the Yukon

S.A.   Statutes of Alberta

S.C.   Statutes of Canada

S.C.C.   Supreme Court of Canada

S.M.   Statutes of Manitoba

S.N.   Statutes of Newfoundland

S.N.B.   Statutes of New Brunswick

S.N.W.T.   Statutes of the Northwest Territories

S.O.   Statutes of Ontario

S.Q.   Statutes of Quebec

S.S.   Statutes of Saskatchewan

s(s).   section(s)

T.D.   Trial Division

NOTES

This study was completed in May 1991.

In this study, quoted material that originated in French has been translated into English.

1. The intelligence quotient (IQ) is one tool used to define categories of intellectual impairment. The parameters for each category are as follows:

   Normalcy: IQ = 70–110
   Slight impairment: IQ = 55–70
   Moderate impairment: IQ = 40–55
   Severe impairment: IQ = 20–40
   Profound impairment: IQ = 0–20

2. This figure, released in 1976, is an estimate of the number of persons affected by the repeal of section 51(f) of the *Canada Elections Act*. Although over the last 20 years there has been a marked tendency toward deinstitutionalization, Statistics Canada (1989) still reports that more than 58 000 beds are available for patients receiving mental health care across the country.

3. The restrictive aspect of the *Canada Elections Act* was revealed in the 1984 election when patients at the Rideau Regional Centre in Ottawa had to present a medical certificate stating that despite their residency in a psychiatric institution, under the terms of the *Canada Elections Act* they had no mental disease. Thus, section 14(4)(f) (now section 51f) was moving toward the case-by-case era.

4. The list of these groups also included the following organizations: British Columbians for Handicapped People, the Alberta Committee of

Consumer Groups of Handicapped People, the Saskatchewan Voice of the Handicapped, and the Psychiatric Patient Advocate Office.

5. This refers specifically to Marie-Michèle Bédard, Clifford Stacey, Tom Last, Eldon Hardy and the Public Trustee of Quebec, Lucienne Robillard, acting as guardian ex officio of the person and over the property of Gilles Hawey, incapable, and Denis Duval, incapable.

6. For a detailed overview of case law concerning disqualification from the right to vote and specifically concerning individuals with a mental disorder, see: "Mental Disability and the Right to Vote" (1979).

7. These statistics, reported by the Chief Electoral Officer of Ontario, Warren Bailie, are based on statistics compiled in *Ontario Election Returns, 1987*.

8. *Le Relevé des suffrages*, published following the 11 September 1990 provincial election, showed that of the 104 ballots received, three came from staff members living at one of these three centres.

9. Reported in a document written by Judy Thompson, Elections Operations and Communication Officer for Elections Manitoba.

10. Of the 2 050 patients in this institution, 1 400 are under guardianship and thus are deprived of the right to vote, as stipulated in the Quebec *Election Act*. The number on the voters list is thus 373 out of 650, or 57.4 percent. We do not know the number of patients at the Centre hospitalier Robert-Giffard who are under guardianship, so our results are clearly limited and inaccurate.

11. Opinion of Raymond Côté of the Centre hospitalier Robert-Giffard in Quebec, reported by Paul Roy in *La Presse* (6 November 1988).

12. St. Thomas Psychiatric Hospital, St. Thomas, Ontario. The authors do not give precise information on the mental condition of the patients or on their status within the institution.

13. This is the term used in Quebec for involuntary committal, discussed later in this study.

14. The first of these systems, advisorship for adults, is intended for persons generally capable of taking care of themselves and managing their assets but who need temporary assistance or advice in certain aspects of managing their affairs. Tutorship for persons of full age is designed for persons who are partially or temporarily incapable of taking care of themselves and managing their assets. Re-evaluation of these two forms of protective supervision is mandatory every three years. Finally, guardianship for adults is a type of protective supervision reserved for those who are totally and permanently incapable of taking care of themselves and managing their assets. In these cases, the files are re-evaluated every five years.

15. According to the opinion of Dr. Jacques Lesage (1991), psychiatrist at the Institut Philippe-Pinel in Montreal, reported in *Le Soleil*.

16. In Newfoundland, the provisions of the *Mental Health Act* apply to all hospitals.

17. Opinion expressed during a telephone interview with Dr. Louis Roy, director of professional services at the Centre hospitalier Robert-Giffard in Quebec.

18. On 31 March 1991, 612 of the 1 800 patients at the Louis-Hippolyte-Lafontaine Hospital in Montreal were in psycho-geriatric units and a reception centre. The average ages of patients in these two units were 66.9 and 75.2 years, respectively. The average age of the total population was 54.2 years in 1990–91.

BIBLIOGRAPHY

Alberta. *Election Act*, R.S.A. 1980, c. E-2.

———. *Mental Health Act*, S.A. 1988, c. M-13.1.

Association des centres d'accueil du Québec. 1990. Brief to the Royal Commission on Electoral Reform and Party Financing. Ottawa.

Association for Community Living Manitoba Inc. v. Manitoba (Chief Electoral Officer) (29 August 1990), Winnipeg 90-01-48629 (Man. Q.B.).

Australia. *Commonwealth Electoral Act, 1918*, am. 1990.

Belgium. *Code électoral* (Élections législatives), Arrêté royal du 12 août 1928 et Loi du 26 avril 1929, Titre premier « Des électeurs », article 7.

———. *Loi complétant le Titre X du Livre I du Code civil en y insérant le statut de minorité prolongée*, Loi du 29 juin 1973.

Bergeron, Viateur. 1981. *L'Attribution d'une protection légale aux malades mentaux*. Montreal: Éditions Yvon Blais.

Blanchet, A. 1980. "L'Arriération mentale." In *Psychiatrie clinique: approche contemporaine*, ed. P. Lalonde and F. Grunberg. Chicoutimi: Gaëtan Morin.

British Columbia. *Election Act*, R.S.B.C. 1979, c. 103.

———. *Mental Health Act*, R.S.B.C. 1979, c. 256.

Canada. Bill C-79, *An Act to amend the Canada Elections Act*, 2nd Session, 33rd Parliament, 1986–87.

———. *Canada Elections Act*, R.S.C. 1985, c. E-2, am. 1985, c. 27 (2nd Supp.); 1989, c. 28; 1990, c. E-2.

———. *Canadian Charter of Rights and Freedoms*, Part I of the *Constitution Act, 1982*, being Schedule B of the *Canada Act 1982* (U.K.), 1982, c. 11.

———. *Criminal Code*, R.S.C. 1985, c. C-46.

Canada. Department of Justice. 1986. *Toward Equality: The Response to the Report of the Parliamentary Committee on Equality Rights.* Ottawa: Minister of Supply and Services Canada.

Canada. Elections Canada. 1984. *Report of the Chief Electoral Officer of Canada as per subsection 59(1) of the Canada Elections Act.* Ottawa: Minister of Supply and Services Canada.

Canada. House of Commons. Committee on Equality Rights. 1985. *Equality for All.* Ottawa: Minister of Supply and Services Canada.

Canada. House of Commons. Special Committee on the Disabled and the Handicapped. 1981. *Obstacles.* 3d Report. Ottawa: Minister of Supply and Services Canada.

————. 1982. *Obstacles.* 5th Report. Ottawa: Minister of Supply and Services Canada.

Canada. Privy Council Office. 1986. *White Paper on Election Law Reform.* Ottawa: Queen's Printer.

Canada. Statistics Canada. 1989. *Residential Care Facilities for Mental Disorders 1984–85 and 1985–86.* Cat. 83-238. Ottawa: Minister of Supply and Services Canada.

Canadian Bar Association. 1990. Brief to the Royal Commission on Electoral Reform and Party Financing. Ottawa.

Canadian Disability Rights Council v. Canada, [1988] 3 F.C. 622 (T.D.).

Canadian Mental Health Association (Alberta Division). 1990. Brief to the Royal Commission on Electoral Reform and Party Financing. Ottawa.

Canadian Mental Health Association (Manitoba Division) v. Manitoba (Chief Electoral Officer) (17 March 1988), Winnipeg CI 88-01 27535 (Man. Q.B.).

Canadian Mental Health Association (Moncton Region Inc.). 1990. Brief to the Royal Commission on Electoral Reform and Party Financing. Ottawa.

Caroll v. Cobb, 139 N.J. Super., 439 (App. Div. 1976).

Deschamps, Pierre. 1988. "La Réforme des régimes de protection (de représentation et d'assistance) des majeurs: perspectives." In *Consentement éclairé et capacité en psychiatrie. Aspects cliniques et juridiques, Actes du colloque tenu le 17 octobre 1986 au Douglas Hall,* ed. Pierre Migneault and John O'Neill. Montreal: Douglas Press.

Drapeau, Jacques. 1991. "Sur la trace des gènes fautifs." *Le Soleil,* 6 May.

Federal Republic of Germany. *Federal Elections Act,* 1956, am. by 5th Amending Law, 1979.

————. *Basic Law for the Federal Republic of Germany* [Constitution], 1949. Text in force in 1976.

France. *Code électoral*, 1989. Amended by basic laws 88-226 and 88-227, 1988 (financial disclosure in politics); 90-95, 1990 (limitation of election expenses and clarification of financing of political activities).

Garneau, Yvon, and Jean-Martin Diener. 1988. "La Règle du consentement éclairé et ses impasses en psychiatrie." In *Consentement éclairé et capacité en psychiatrie. Aspects cliniques et juridiques, Actes du colloque tenu le 17 octobre 1986 au Douglas Hall*, ed. Pierre Migneault and John O'Neill. Montreal: Douglas Press.

Grossman, H.J., and M.J. Begab. 1977. *Manual on Terminology and Classification in Mental Retardation*. Washington, DC: American Association on Mental Deficiency.

Halderman v. Pennhurst State School and Hospital, 446 F. Supp. 1295 (District Court of United States, Pennsylvania 1977).

Hill, Brian P. 1977. "Civil Rights of the Psychiatric Patient in Quebec." *Revue juridique Thémis* 12:503–29.

Jaychuk, G., and R. Manchanda. 1991. "Psychiatric Patients and the Federal Election." *Canadian Journal of Psychiatry* 36:124–25.

Ketchum v. Hislop (1984), 54 B.C.L.R. 327 (S.C.).

Laurendeau, M.-C., A. Blanchet and M. Coshan. 1983. "Une Évaluation de l'impact d'un programme de désinstitutionnalisation de personnes vivant avec un handicap mental." *Déficience mentale* 33:3–46.

Law Reform Commission of Canada. 1975. *The Criminal Process and Mental Disorders*. Working Paper 14. Ottawa: Information Canada.

Lesage, Jacques. 1991. "Un Cas pénible." *Le Soleil*, 16 April.

Luckasson, Ruth. 1988. "The Transition to Independent Living." In *Transitions to Adult Life for People with Mental Retardation*, ed. B.L. Ludlow, A.P. Turnbull and R. Luckasson. Baltimore: Paul H. Brookes.

Manitoba. *Elections Act*, R.S.M. 1987, c. E30.

———. *Mental Health Act*, R.S.M. 1987, c. M110.

———. *Mental Health Act*, S.M. 1987–88, c. 56.

"Mental Disability and the Right to Vote." 1979. *Yale Law Journal* 88:1644–64.

Morrison, Denis. 1988. "Consentement éclairé et capacité en pratique psychiatrique ou opinion: le consentement éclairé s'applique-t-il en psychiatrie?" In *Consentement éclairé et capacité en psychiatrie. Aspects cliniques et juridiques, Actes du colloque tenu le 17 octobre 1986 au Douglas Hall*, ed. Pierre Migneault and John O'Neill. Montreal: Douglas Press.

New Brunswick. *Elections Act*, R.S.N.B. 1973, c. E-3.

————. *Mental Health Act*, R.S.N.B. 1973, c. M-10.

————. *An Act to Amend the Mental Health Act*, S.N.B. 1989, c. 23.

Newfoundland. *Election Act*, R.S.N. 1970, c. 106.

————. *Mental Health Act*, S.N. 1971, No. 80.

Northwest Territories. *Elections Act*, S.N.W.T. 1986 (2nd Sess.), c. 2.

————. *Mental Health Act*, S.N.W.T. 1985 (2nd Sess.), c. 6.

Nova Scotia. *Elections Act*, R.S.N.S. 1989, c. 139.

————. *Hospitals Act*, R.S.N.S. 1989, c. 208.

————. *Nova Scotia Hospital Act*, R.S.N.S. 1989, c. 313.

Ontario. *Election Act*, S.O. 1984, c. 54.

————. *Mental Health Act*, R.S.O. 1980, c. 262.

Ontario. Royal Commission Inquiry into Civil Rights. 1968. *Report.* Toronto: Queen's Printer.

Picard, Daniel. 1988. *La Réinsertion sociale des personnes handicapées mentales en famille d'accueil.* Vol. 1. Quebec: Centre de services sociaux de Québec.

Prince Edward Island. *Election Act*, R.S.P.E.I. 1988, c. E-1.

————. *Mental Health Act*, R.S.P.E.I. 1988, c. M-6.

Quebec. *Act respecting health services and social services*, R.S.Q., c. S-5.

————. *Act respecting the Public Curator*, R.S.Q., c. C-81.

————. *Act to secure the handicapped in the exercise of their rights*, R.S.Q., c. E-20.1.

————. *Charter of human rights and freedoms*, R.S.Q., c. C-12.

————. *Election Act*, R.S.Q., c. E-3.3.

————. *Mental patients protection act*, R.S.Q., c. P-41.

————. *Public trusteeship act and modifying the Civil Code and other legislative provisions*, S.Q. 1989, c. 54.

Quebec. Ministère de la Santé et des Services sociaux. 1988. *L'intégration des personnes présentant une déficience intellectuelle. Un impératif humain et social. Orientations et guide d'action.* Quebec.

Quebec. Office des personnes handicapées du Québec. 1984. *À part ... égale. L'Intégration sociale des personnes handicapées: un défi pour tous.* Quebec: Gouvernement du Québec.

Robertson, Gerald B. 1987. *Mental Disability and the Law in Canada.* Scarborough: Carswell.

Rodgers, Sanda. 1988. "The Impact of the *Charter of Rights and Freedoms* on Institutional Psychiatry." In *Consentement éclairé et capacité en psychiatrie. Aspects cliniques et juridiques, Actes du colloque tenu le 17 octobre 1986 au Douglas Hall*, ed. Pierre Migneault and John O'Neill. Montreal: Douglas Press.

Roy, Paul. 1988. "Peu de malades mentaux voteront." *La Presse*, 6 November.

Saskatchewan. *The Election Act*, R.S.S. 1978, c. E-6.

———. *The Mental Health Act*, R.S.S. 1978, c. M-13.

———. *The Mental Health Services Act*, S.S. 1984–85–86, c. M-13.1.

———. *The Mentally Disordered Persons Act*, R.S.S. 1978, c. M-14.

———. *Public Trustee Consequential Amendment Act*, S.S. 1983, c. 80.

Savage, Harvey, and Carla McKague. 1987. *Mental Health Law in Canada*. Toronto: Butterworths.

Swain v. R., [1991] 1 S.C.R. 933.

United Kingdom. *Representation of the People Act 1983*, 1983, c. 2, am. 1985, c. 50; 1990.

Wagner, Frédéric. 1988. "Scrutin universel." *La Presse*, 19 October.

Yukon Territory. *Elections Act*, R.S.Y. 1986, c. 48.

———. *Mental Health Act*, R.S.Y. 1986, c. 115.

4

POLITICAL RIGHTS OF PUBLIC SERVANTS IN THE POLITICAL PROCESS

Patrice Garant

THE ROYAL COMMISSION on Electoral Reform and Party Financing studied two important issues. The first concerns the right of eligibility of public servants to run for office and relates directly to the *Canada Elections Act*. The second does not come directly under the Act, but concerns the involvement of public servants in partisan political activities during election periods. These two matters are governed by sections 32 to 34 (formerly section 32) of the *Public Service Employment Act*. They have been the subject of litigation, especially in July 1988 before the Federal Court of Appeal. The Supreme Court granted permission to appeal. The government reacted on 30 August 1988 by tabling Bill C-157 in the House of Commons. The bill proposed to add to the *Public Service Employment Act* a Part IV entitled "Political Rights."

The Ontario Law Reform Commission studied these issues in its 1986 report. The issues have also been the subject of legislative reforms at the provincial level, especially in Quebec and Nova Scotia.

Finally, there is the *Canadian Charter of Rights and Freedoms*. Section 3 of the Charter has an impact on the right of candidacy and eligibility, and section 2 on the right to freedom of expression in matters of party and electoral politics.

Our goal is to review the status of these issues as of 1990 by studying the following areas:

- the jurisprudence of the Federal Court of Canada with respect to sections 32 to 34 of the *Public Service Employment Act;*
- Bill C-157 of 30 August 1988;
- the situation in each of the Canadian provinces;
- the position and recommendations of the Ontario Law Reform Commission (1986);
- the impact of the liberalization of political rights resulting from the Quebec *Public Service Act* of 1983; and
- the impact of the *Canadian Charter of Rights and Freedoms* and the requirements of section 1 of this Charter (reasonable and justifiable restrictions within the framework of a free and democratic society).

NEUTRALITY OF THE PUBLIC SERVICE AND POLITICAL FREEDOM OF PUBLIC SERVANTS

In 1987, the Supreme Court of Canada stated that the principle of public service neutrality is based on a "constitutional convention." The Court noted that the most fundamental convention "is probably the principle of responsible government which is largely unwritten, although it is implicitly referred to in the preamble of the *Constitution Act, 1867"* (*O.P.S.E.U.* 1987, 38).

The Court then recognized the public service as an essential element of the governmental apparatus:

> It can similarly be said that the public service in Ontario is a part of the executive branch of the government of Ontario. The ministers and the executive council of Ontario would be powerless and quite incapable of administering the province if they were deprived of the public service and left to their own device. The government of a large modern state is impossible to manage without a relatively large public service which effectively participates in the exercise of political power under the supervision of responsible ministers. (*O.P.S.E.U.* 1987, 42)

The Court also recognized the provisions of the *Public Service Employment Act* concerning the political neutrality of public servants as having constitutional force, making such neutrality an essential condition for the very existence of responsible government:

> It is clear to me that those provisions are constitutional in nature in the sense that they bear on the operation of an organ of government in Ontario and that they impose duties on the members of a branch of government in order to implement a principle of government. The organ of government is the Ontario Public Service. The duty is the

one imposed upon the members of the public service to abstain from the political activities contemplated by the impugned provisions. The principle of government is the impartiality of the public service considered as an essential prerequisite of responsible government. (*O.P.S.E.U.* 1987, 41)

Nevertheless the Supreme Court reaffirmed, in the *Fraser* decision of 1985, that freedom of expression in political matters, in other words, " 'freedom of speech' is a deeply-rooted value in our democratic system of government. It is a principle of our common law constitution, inherited from the United Kingdom by virtue of the preamble to the Constitution Act, 1867" (*Fraser* 1985, 462).[1]

The Court returns to the importance of freedom of expression in other judgements, especially in the cases of *Ford* (1988), *Slaight Communications* (1989) and *Irwin Toy* (1989). In the *Ford* (1988) decision, the Court unanimously reaffirmed its statement in the *R.W.D.S.U.* judgement (1986), which is that freedom of expression constitutes "one of the fundamental concepts that has formed the basis for the historical development of political, social and educational institutions of Western society" (*R.W.D.S.U.* 1986, 583).

In *Ford v. Quebec* (*Attorney General*) (1988), the Court quoted with approval the following extract from an article by Thomas Emerson: "The values sought by society in protecting the right to freedom of expression may be grouped into four broad categories. Maintenance of a system of freedom of expression is necessary (1) as assuring individual self-fulfillment, (2) as a means of attaining the truth, (3) as a method of securing participation by the members of the society in social, including political decision-making, and (4) as maintaining the balance between stability and change in society" (Emerson 1963, 878, cited in *Ford* 1988, 766).

If these objectives are applied to the particular category of citizens who are public servants, it is easy to understand the importance of maintaining a system of free expression for them also. According to Professor Emerson (1970), freedom of expression is not only a political value but also an essential part of human dignity.

Freedom of expression is therefore confronted with the principle of public service neutrality, which also has a constitutional value. According to Mr. Justice Beetz of the Supreme Court of Canada, both are "called for by the structural demands of the Constitution" (*O.P.S.E.U.* 1987, 57).

Prior to the *Canadian Charter of Rights and Freedoms*, the Supreme Court of Canada had clearly established that we are confronted with two fundamental constitutional values: on the one hand, freedom of expression, and on the other, the requirement of neutrality for the public service. With the Charter, as Mr. Justice Beetz gives us to understand, we can expect a reinforcement of political rights: "I should perhaps add that issues like the last will in the future ordinarily arise for consideration in relation to the political rights guaranteed under the *Canadian Charter of Rights and Freedoms*, which, of course, gives broader protection to these rights and freedoms than is called for by the structural demands of the Constitution" (*O.P.S.E.U.* 1987, 57).

RIGHTS AND DUTIES OF PUBLIC SERVANTS WITH RESPECT TO ELECTORAL POLITICS

In the Federal Government

The main statutory provisions concerning the rights and duties of public servants in electoral politics are sections 32 to 34 of the *Public Service Employment Act:*

> 32. For the purposes of sections 33 and 34, "candidate" means a candidate for election as a member of the House of Commons, a member of the legislature of a province or a member of the Council of the Yukon Territory or the Northwest Territories.

> 33. (1) No deputy head and, except as authorized under this section, no employee, shall
> (*a*) engage in work for or against a candidate;
> (*b*) engage in work for or against a political party; or
> (*c*) be a candidate.
> (2) A person does not contravene subsection (1) by reason only of attending a political meeting or contributing money for the funds of a candidate or of a political party.
> (3) Notwithstanding any other Act, on application made to the Commission by an employee, the Commission may, if it is of the opinion that the usefulness to the Public Service of the employee in the position the employee then occupies would not be impaired by reason of that employee having been a candidate, grant to the employee leave of absence without pay to seek nomination as a candidate and to be a candidate for election, for a period ending on the day on which the results of the election are officially declared or on such earlier day as may be requested by the employee if the employee has ceased to be a candidate.
> (4) Forthwith on granting any leave of absence under subsection (3), the Commission shall cause notice of its action to be published in the *Canada Gazette*.

(5) An employee who is declared elected as a member of the House of Commons, of the legislature of a province or of the Council of the Yukon Territory or the Northwest Territories thereupon ceases to be an employee.

34. (1) Where any allegation is made to the Commission by a person who is or has been a candidate that a deputy head or employee has contravened subsection 33(1), the allegation shall be referred to a board established by the Commission to conduct an inquiry at which the person making the allegation and the deputy head or employee, or their representatives, shall be given an opportunity to be heard.

(2) The Commission, on being notified of the decision of the board on an inquiry into an allegation conducted pursuant to subsection (1),

(a) in the case of a deputy head, shall report the decision to the Governor in Council who may, if the board has decided that the deputy head has contravened subsection 33(1), dismiss the deputy head; and

(b) in the case of an employee, may, if the board has decided that the employee has contravened subsection 33(1), dismiss the employee.

(3) In the application of this section to any person, the expression "deputy head" does not include a person for whose removal from office, otherwise than by the termination of his appointment at pleasure, express provision is made by this Act or any other Act.

By virtue of these sections, public servants are forbidden to participate in the political activities of a candidate or political party either at federal or provincial levels. This applies both during and between elections. In fact, public servants are forbidden to work for a candidate during the period leading up to an election, and for a political party, whether an election has been called or not. Under section 33(2) of the Act, this ban does not cover attendance at political meetings or financial contributions to a candidate or party. Public servants are, however, forbidden to be candidates without having first asked and received the permission of the Public Service Commission. Permission is usually refused for upper-echelon public servants (Dussault and Borgeat 1986, 348). It can also be noted that even if the public servant has the right to resume her or his position if not elected, election means exclusion from the public service since, at the end of the term of office, the public servant does not have the right to take up the position again.

The application of these provisions has been the subject of several disputes before the Public Service Staff Relations Board. In the case of *Brewer* (1979), a senior employee of the Customs Service wished to be a candidate for the New Democratic Party (NDP) in elections in New Brunswick. Before announcing his candidacy, Mr. Brewer notified the Board of his intentions and at the same time requested a leave without pay. The Board refused to grant it, and his subsequent appeal (*Brewer* 1980) was also rejected. The Board's refusals did not alter Mr. Brewer's determination. He was finally named the NDP candidate. In spite of warnings that seeking election could cost him his job, nothing could make him change his mind. As it happened, he was not elected. He was, however, dismissed from the job for having committed a serious disciplinary error. The Public Service Staff Relations Board concluded that a severe penalty was necessary, but changed the dismissal to a one-year suspension.

The *Canada Elections Act* also prohibits federal public servants from becoming candidates in federal elections. Sections 77 and 78 of this Act (the former section 21) state who is ineligible, including

> *f*) every person who accepts or holds any office, commission or employment, permanent or temporary, in the service of the Government of Canada at the nomination of the Crown or at the nomination of any of the officers of the Government of Canada, to which any salary, fee, wages, allowance, emolument or profit of any kind is attached, during the time he so holds that office, commission or employment.

Section 78 of the Act adds, however, that:

> (1) Paragraphs 77(c) and (f) do not render ineligible ...

> *g*) an employee, as defined in the *Public Service Employment Act*, who, under that Act, has been granted and is on leave of absence without pay to seek nomination as a candidate and to be a candidate at an election.

Federal public servants are therefore doubly forbidden the right to be a candidate in a federal election, since they are liable to be dismissed if they become candidates. In addition, the very right to become candidates is denied them, since the Act makes them ineligible. This situation may, however, be avoided if the public servant makes a formal request and obtains leave from the Public Service Commission.

In Quebec

Quebec's *Charter of human rights and freedoms* establishes very broad rights, especially freedom of opinion, expression, association, the right to vote and to be a candidate in any election, as well as the right to the protection of privacy. These rights and freedoms are exercised with respect to the democratic values of Quebec as stipulated in section 9 of its Charter.

The 1983 *Public Service Act* contains three important provisions with respect to the political freedom of public servants:

> 10. A public servant shall be politically neutral in performing his duties.

> 11. A public servant shall act with reserve in any public display of his political opinions.

> 12. Nothing in this Act prohibits a public servant from being a member of a political party, attending a political meeting or making, in accordance with the law, a contribution to a political party or a local association of a political party or to a candidate in an election.

The first provision stipulates that in exercising his or her duties, the public servant must "demonstrate political neutrality." Note that the law implicitly provides that when not on duty, the public servant recovers full political freedom. It is only when on duty that the public servant must not express opinions, or even modify behaviour toward clients for political reasons.

The second provision stipulates that public administrators must "demonstrate reserve" when expressing political convictions in public. Thus, even outside working hours, a Quebec public servant must show moderation in his or her speech. The effect of this section is also linked to a regulation requiring a public servant to seek authorization for any public communication, be it verbal or in writing, directly connected to his or her work or organization's activities. If the comments in question concern other spheres of government activity, no authorization is necessary. However, the public servant must show moderation in expressing any political opinion.

A third provision establishes the right of public servants to engage actively in political activities. This recognizes their right to belong to a party, to make financial contributions to a party or to party authorities, to attend political meetings, and, as well, to be candidates for public elective office. This provision follows the rationale of the sections of the Quebec *Charter of human rights and freedoms*.

"State administrators," that is to say, very highly placed public servants such as the deputy head, associate or assistant deputy head and the president and vice-president of the Office des ressources humaines (Human Resources Board), have the same rights and duties as the others except for the right to be a candidate in any election whatever.

Sections 24 and following of the *Public Service Act* establish in addition the means of exercising the right to be a candidate. The law establishes first of all that any public servant has the right to a leave without pay if he or she wishes to be a candidate for an elective public office. Candidates in municipal or school board elections may also be granted leave. The law establishes that if a public servant is not chosen as a candidate or elected, the public servant has the right to resume her or his position within 30 days. If elected to Parliament or any other elective office, the public servant has the right by law either to a complete leave or a partial leave as needed. At the end of the term of office, the employee in question will have the right by law to resume his or her position in the same category. The public servant can also require a new assessment of his or her fitness for a position. When a public servant is elected as a member of the National Assembly, leave is valid for the entire term of office. In the case of other offices, such as federal member of Parliament, the leave is valid for only one term. Even the official agent of a candidate in a provincial election can benefit from a similar leave.

To these provisions can also be added collective agreements that can sometimes establish similar measures (Dussault and Borgeat 1986, 349). In the same way, the Quebec laws may also sometimes affect the political freedoms of certain public servants. Thus the *Election Act* of 1989 requires every employer to grant electoral leave without pay to any employee who is a candidate or intends to be a candidate, or is acting as the official agent of a candidate. This employee keeps the right to resume her or his position as well as other rights as a worker, and can complain to the labour commissioner about violations to the *Labour Code.* Moreover, section 498 of the same *Election Act* forbids employees of the chief electoral officer to "engage in partisan work." Another law specifically forbids a deputy public prosecutor, "under pain of dismissal," from being a "candidate in any federal, provincial, municipal or school election," or from engaging "in any partisan activity in favour of a candidate or political party" (Quebec, *An Act respecting Attorney General's Prosecutors*, s. 8).[2]

In a general way, if a parallel is drawn between federal measures and Quebec laws, it is evident that the latter were much more liberal than the former, up until the Supreme Court judgement in *Osborne* that quashed the ban on participation at any time in partisan activities for activities either on the federal or the provincial scene (*Osborne* 1991). As well, the combined effect of the *Public Service Employment Act* and the

Canada Elections Act makes it extremely difficult for a federal public servant to be an election candidate. In Quebec, public servants are not forbidden to participate in partisan activities; they are simply restrained by a secondary obligation imposed by the legislation. Similarly, Quebec law fully recognizes a public servant's right to be a candidate in an election. In this respect, the Quebec policy on leave can only encourage increased participation in the democratic process. There is no doubt that it conforms more closely to the *Canadian Charter of Rights and Freedoms*, discussed in the section that follows.

In Ontario

The *Public Service Act* (1980) distinguishes between two categories or classes of government agents with respect to political rights: ordinary public servants and officials (mainly managerial personnel) in the restricted category within the meaning of section 21 of Regulation 881 (1980).

Under section 12(1)*a* of the Act, a government official cannot be a candidate in a provincial or a federal election. However, an ordinary public servant may request the Lieutenant Governor in Council or the minister responsible for leave without pay, which must be granted. The Act specifies the length of this leave. If the public servant who is a candidate is elected, he or she must resign immediately from the public service. However, if the term of office is completed within five years, she or he may re-enter the public service in the position formerly held, or in another position for which she or he is qualified.

A public service official or deputy head (Ontario, Regulation 881, schedule 2) who wishes to become a candidate must simply resign with no right of returning to a job, or face dismissal. In a 1973 decision, the divisional court confirmed a decision of the Public Service Grievance Board validating the dismissal of a deputy public prosecutor who had been a candidate in a federal election (*Dick* 1973).

Leave without pay is available only to the public servant who is already a candidate, not to the public servant seeking to become one. During the period preceding the formal announcement of candidature, a public servant may obtain special leave at the discretion of superior authority, according to section 74 of Regulation 881. The Public Service Commission publishes guidelines to clarify the rights and obligations of public servants in these matters (1985, 6).

All public servants are forbidden to solicit political contributions, except those on electoral leave (Ontario, *Public Service Act*, s. 12(1)*b*).

All public servants are also forbidden to do "canvassing" (that is, engage in partisan political activity) during election periods. At any other time, all public servants except for top-level managers (deputy heads and others; see Ontario, Regulation 881, schedule 2) are allowed to undertake partisan political activity. Jurisprudence of the Public Service Grievance Board has insisted on the distinction between these two categories. An ordinary public servant can be president of a local riding association of a political party without violating either the letter or the spirit of the law (*McKay* 1981).

During working hours, the Act forbids any partisan political activity (s. 15). Similarly, a government employee, of whatever rank, may not associate his or her position in the public service with any political activity (Ontario, *Public Service Act*, s. 12(1)*c*). However, a public servant on electoral leave may mention his or her title as a public servant.

Finally, section 14 of the Act is the most problematical as concerns freedom of expression in political and electoral matters: "[A] civil servant shall not at any time speak in public or express views in writing for distribution to the public on any matter that forms part of the platform of a provincial or federal political party."

First of all, this restriction applies only to "civil servants" or departmental employees, and not to all Crown employees. In addition, it extends beyond the election period since it concerns the political programs of federal and provincial parties. This is a partial muzzling of political expression that is of doubtful constitutionality.

In the Atlantic Provinces

While New Brunswick has provisions similar to the federal Act (New Brunswick, *Civil Service Act*, s. 27),[3] the *Civil Service Act* of Nova Scotia is characterized by certain features. Before 1987, section 34(1) of the Nova Scotia law forbade all partisan work in a federal or provincial election. Public servants were also forbidden to solicit or receive political contributions.

The law said nothing about whether a public servant could obtain electoral leave, but the *House of Assembly Act* stipulated that a public servant is ineligible unless she or he resigns.

Since 1987 the law has distinguished public servants from "politically restricted employees," those in a "managerial or confidential capacity" as described in section 11 of the *Civil Service Collective Bargaining Act.* Any ordinary public servant may be a candidate in an election, work for a political party and make financial contributions to a party. However, unless the public servant is on electoral leave, she or he may not solicit funds, publish or publicize partisan positions, place policies related to employment in a partisan context, engage in politics during working hours, publicize or distribute publications or other material of a partisan nature in the workplace or during working hours.

The public servant who wishes to be a candidate must first obtain leave without pay from the Commission and from the deputy head. This leave must be granted and may begin before the date the election writ is issued.

Elected candidates have the right to an extension of leave without pay until their re-election. If they are no longer a candidate or are not re-elected, they have the right to resume their positions or those of an equivalent level if their positions have been filled or abolished.

We should mention the fact that, while the Nova Scotia law is quite generous for ordinary public servants, there is a fairly long list of those in the restricted category.

In Prince Edward Island before 1988 the prohibition of all partisan political activity was quite general and even included making or receiving partisan financial contributions. Since then, the law has distinguished ordinary public servants from "restricted employees," namely the officers (Prince Edward Island, *Civil Service Act*, s. 38). An ordinary public servant may join a political party, be a candidate in an election and engage in political activities, provided that these do not interfere with his or her duties as a public servant. To become a candidate, the public servant must request leave without pay from the deputy head, who may refuse if he or she believes that it would "seriously undermine the ability of the government to deliver a necessary or essential service to the public" (s. 40). The public servant can appeal a refusal before an appeal board established by regulation. Electoral leave applies to the first term of elective office.

It should be pointed out that public servants in the "restricted" category may not engage in any partisan political activity.

In Newfoundland, a 1975 Order in Council regulates the political activity of public servants. In general, all partisan political activity is forbidden at all times. A public servant may become a candidate provided she or he resigns. If elected, the person may at a later date request permission to resume the position, but the government has no obligation in this regard.

In the West

Manitoba
The *Civil Service Act* of Manitoba (s. 44, a provision existing since 1974) recognizes the right of all public servants, other than deputy heads or other categories designated by regulation, to declare themselves candidates in a federal or provincial election, or to support a candidate. It also recognizes public servants' right to express, in writing or orally,

opinions on election issues provided they do not divulge information obtained in the course of their duties.

A public servant may obtain electoral leave without pay from the minister responsible for granting it in order to seek nomination as a candidate or election to office. If not elected, the public servant has the right to resume the position if he or she makes a request within 90 days from the date of the election results. If elected, the public servant has the right to leave without pay for five years in order to fill his or her elective mandate.

Finally, the law prohibits any solicitation of funds for a party or a candidate.

Saskatchewan

The *Public Service Act* begins by forbidding any political pressure on public servants, then forbids them to engage in any form of political activity at work. As well, a public servant is forbidden to engage at any time in political activities in such a manner "as to impair this usefulness in the position in which he is employed" (s. 50).

Any public servant who wishes to become a candidate in an election may obtain a leave without pay of 30 days before the date of the election. In practice, a longer period of leave is normally granted. It sometimes even happens that a leave is granted so that a public servant may participate in an election campaign without actually being a candidate.

In Saskatchewan, electoral leave ceases the day the candidate is elected, unless the election is contested and annulled.

Alberta

In Alberta the *Code of Conduct and Ethics* for the Public Service (15 May 1978, 1215) that regulates this matter is a quasi-regulation. It distinguishes between two levels: officers or "executive managerial employees," and other public servants. However, both categories are not allowed to participate directly in soliciting election funds.

The Code forbids officers to be candidates in any federal or provincial election. This ban is apparently interpreted as extending to any public participation in party politics.

Ordinary public servants may, on the other hand, obtain a leave without pay during the regular election period. A candidate who is not elected has the right to resume his or her position. If elected, the person ceases to be a member of the public service.

The Code forbids public servants only to make public declarations, either written or oral, which would transmit information in violation of the oath of office that they take under section 29 of the *Public Service Act*.

British Columbia

In this province, the political freedom of public servants is regulated either by collective agreements or by the Master Agreements, three in number, or, in the case of managers, by a regulation of the Treasury Board.

The collective agreement establishes a public servant's right to public action subject to the oath of office prescribed by the *Public Service Act*. If a public servant wishes to become a candidate, she or he has the right to a leave without pay for a maximum of 90 days. If elected, the public servant has the right to a five-year leave.

As for managers, Regulation 508/79, no longer in force, used to establish that before seeking a "public position," written approval from the Public Service Commission was required. This body had to make sure that there was no conflict of interest between the public servant's duties and the post that he or she was seeking. If there was no conflict, the Commission could order the minister concerned to grant the leave without pay. The candidate who was elected had the right to a five-year leave without pay.

In the Territories

In the Yukon, under the *Public Service Commission Act* (ss. 160–70) and the Public Service Regulations, any public servant may request a leave without pay to be a candidate in a federal or territorial election. Before 1987, the Public Service Commissioner was obliged to grant this whenever the needs of the service permitted it. Since 1987, a public servant has only had to give his or her deputy head written notice. The Public Service Regulations are, as far as we know, the only texts in Canada that use the expression "political leave" (s. 180). Only deputy heads are not eligible for this leave.

Apart from deputy heads, any public servant may engage in partisan political activities during a federal election. For a territorial election, officers and "confidential" employees as well as deputy heads are forbidden all partisan activity; this is not so for ordinary public servants.

A public servant who obtains electoral leave must nevertheless abstain from divulging information obtained in the exercise of duty and from publicly criticizing government policies in which she or he participated as a public servant.

Finally, all public servants who engage in political activities cannot solicit partisan contributions. Nevertheless, with the exception of deputy heads, public servants may make partisan contributions. All public servants must abstain from partisan politics during working hours.

In the Northwest Territories, the Public Service ruling distinguishes the category of "restricted employees" from other public servants.

Any public servant, whatever his or her category, may attend political meetings, be a member of a party and make partisan financial contributions.

Any public servant other than those in the restricted category may obtain electoral leave by making a written request. Those in the restricted category may also request leave, but the minister will grant it only if convinced that "the employee's absence will not seriously interfere with the operation of the public service."

The ruling enumerates the activities forbidden respectively to ordinary public servants and to those in the restricted category. For example, the ruling mentions bans on soliciting funds for a party or candidate, on engaging in politics at work, on using government equipment or resources for partisan purposes, on distributing literature or other promotional material in the offices of the administration, on publicly criticizing government policies related to one's duties except when on electoral leave, and on acting as official agent of a party or a candidate. In addition, an officer in the restricted category may not publicly discuss issues related to the programs of the parties and the candidates, participate in a meeting as a voting delegate, act as executive officer of a federal party or association, campaign or actively work for a party or a candidate.

It is worth noting here the effort made by the Northwest Territories government to specify precisely which activities are permitted and which are forbidden.

THE IMPACT OF THE *CANADIAN CHARTER OF RIGHTS AND FREEDOMS*

The preceding sections have reviewed the judicial framework that surrounds the exercise of political freedom by public servants. In doing this, we have established the constitutional principle that a "neutral" public service is necessary, and specified the exact context of this concept. We have also examined the nature of the restrictions on government employees. The second stage of the study ascertains the compatibility of the limitations imposed on the political freedom of public servants with the rights guaranteed by the *Canadian Charter of Rights and Freedoms*.

Relevant Constitutional Provisions

Has the very nature of our political system been profoundly modified by including in our Constitution a charter of rights and freedoms guaranteeing respect for each person's fundamental rights? Has this affected some of the principles on which this political system was based? Certainly the absolute sovereignty of Parliament, cornerstone of a democratic system inspired by the British one, has been reduced, inasmuch as the role bestowed on the courts now charged with constitutional matters has been increased. Thus, measures that have had their constitutional validity doubted in the past are once again thrown into question by the *Canadian Charter of Rights and Freedoms*. An example is the concept of political neutrality in the public service and the measures taken by legislators to ensure it. Before the adoption of the Charter, this situation could not be contested, except, of course, as regards the division of legislative competence that is a feature of federalism. Thus, the Supreme Court of Canada ruled in 1987 that a provincial legislature is constitutionally competent to make laws regarding the provincial public service, including the right to make regulations restricting the political freedom of public servants, even when these apply in federal areas.[4]

In spite of the Charter and by virtue of it, parliamentary sovereignty may nevertheless be strengthened by the effect of the derogatory clause of section 33, according to which Parliament or a legislature may formally declare that a specific law will apply "notwithstanding a provision included in section 2 or sections 7 to 15 of this Charter" (Tassé 1989, 116ff., on the scope of section 33). Parliament could indisputably exclude sections 32 to 34 of the *Public Service Employment Act* from sections 2 or 15 of the Charter for a five-year period, renewable indefinitely every five years. These sections may not, however, be excluded from the application of section 3!

It is easy to identify six rights recognized by the Charter that may be restrained by legal limitations on the political freedom of public servants. These are freedom of expression as found in section 2(*b*), freedom of peaceful assembly found in section 2(*c*) and freedom of association guaranteed by section 2(*d*) of the Charter. There are also democratic rights, the right to vote and the right to be a candidate in legislative elections, granted to all citizens by section 3 of the Charter. Finally, there is the protection offered by section 15 of the Charter, which provides for the right to equality before and under the law.

We should keep in mind the terms of section 1 of the Charter, which permit these rights to be legally restricted "only to such reasonable limits prescribed by law as can be demonstrably justified in a free and democratic society."

The effect of section 1 of the Charter is accordingly to render the law in question perfectly constitutional; we will specify elsewhere the criteria that must be respected in order to conform to it. We will first examine the nature of the rights conferred by the Charter.

Freedom of Expression
Freedom of expression is one of the concepts essential to a flourishing democratic society. However, before the *Canadian Charter of Rights and*

Freedoms was adopted in 1982, the status of this concept was not well defined (Beckton 1989, 223ff.). In spite of certain judgements that worked in favour of a constitutional recognition of this liberty (*Reference re Alberta Statutes* 1938; *Switzman* 1957; Cotler 1989, 189ff.), it remained until recently at the mercy of Parliament and the legislatures.

In spite of a trend in jurisprudence that freedom of expression as protected by the Charter was only the freedom of expression in political and not artistic matters (*Rio Hotel* 1986, 670), it seems evident that the Charter covers a number of forms. Thus, as early as 1983, the Ontario High Court affirmed: "It is clear to us that all forms of expression, whether they be oral, written, pictorial, sculpture, music, dance or film, are equally protected by the Charter" (*Ontario Film* 1983, 590; see also Tremblay 1986, 285–86). From this point of view the form of the expression is protected and not only the content of what one is expressing (*Ford* 1988).

It is very difficult to describe exactly the notion of freedom of expression. By its very nature it is not an absolute value, and must be defined in such a way as to respect other equally important values. Freedom of expression can only be defined in relation to what it is forbidden to do or say. In such a context, the right to freedom of expression is limited by other rights, such as the right to reputation, to human dignity, or to other demands such as that of national security (Tremblay 1986, 287). Therefore, in spite of the constitutionalization of the right to free expression, defamation of character and the distribution of obscene material or subversive literature will likely continue to be banned.

In this context, the fundamental significance of the concept of freedom of expression has not been changed by the adoption of the *Canadian Charter of Rights and Freedoms*. However, while formerly the only limits regulating proscriptions were those on the division of legislative competences, the norm established in section 1 of the Charter now requires limits to be reasonable in a "free and democratic society" (Tremblay 1986, 288). In truth, legislators have always been subject to this norm, but they were the only judges of that apart from the electorate. Since 1982, section 33 of the Charter has given the courts the last word.

Freedom of Peaceful Assembly

Freedom of peaceful assembly is protected by section 2(*c*) of the Charter. The content of this concept is somewhat difficult to define as it can easily be confused with the freedoms of association, of speech and expression. Besides, for some people it constitutes only one particular form or manifestation (Cotler 1989, 177). It would seem that no definition has ever truly separated the freedom of assembly from the freedom of speech, since, in order to have any real meaning at all, the right of assembly necessitates the right to free expression. Similarly, the freedom of speech has no significance if one is not able to meet to exchange ideas. Thus, "in simple terms, freedom of assembly constitutes words in action, the physical act of meeting to communicate and exchange ideas and emotions" (ibid., 177–78).

Freedom of Association

Freedom of association constitutes, in the words of the Supreme Court of Canada, one of the most "fundamental" rights in a democratic society (*Reference re Public Service Employee Relations Act* 1987, 393). The different concepts of freedom of association are divided into two main tendencies. The first, an "individualist" approach, limits its effect to "the human right to associate with others, that is, mainly to belong to a group, in the case of an existing structured association" (Verge 1985, 102ff.). The second tendency adds a collective dimension to the freedom of association. Thus, in addition to the possibility that each person may belong to an association, constitutional protection would also extend to group or collective activities, the purposes of the association being equally protected (ibid., 107ff.).

The Supreme Court of Canada has, however, rejected this last view of freedom of association. According to the Court, "The purpose of freedom of association is to ensure that various goals may be pursued in common as well as individually. Freedom of association is not concerned with the particular activities or goals themselves; it is concerned with how activities or goals may be pursued" (*Reference re Public Service Employee Relations Act* 1987, 406).

From this viewpoint, freedom of association as protected by the *Canadian Charter of Rights and Freedoms* must be defined as follows:

> *Charter* protection will attach to the exercise in association of such rights as have *Charter* protection when exercised by the individual. Furthermore, freedom of association means the freedom to associate for the purposes of activities which are lawful when performed alone. But, since the fact of association will not by itself confer additional right on individuals, the association does not acquire a constitutionally guaranteed freedom to do what is unlawful for the individual. (*Reference re Public Service Employee Relations Act* 1987, 409)

For example, this is the protection offered by the Charter for the right to join together to form a union. However, the activities of this group, like strike activity, do not enjoy constitutional protection and can therefore be restrained without limit by ordinary legislators. If any strike, even a basic one, may be regulated or forbidden, it goes without saying that all political strikes or similar movements may be also.

Democratic Rights

The *Canadian Charter of Rights and Freedoms* also guarantees each Canadian citizen a body of "democratic" rights (Beaudoin 1983, 151; 1989, 307–48; Brun and Brunelle 1988, 689). It should first be noted that these rights cannot be suspended by virtue of section 33 of the Charter. The only restrictions that can affect these rights are those that can be justified under section 1 of the Charter.

Within the scope of our concerns, section 3 of the Charter is most interesting: "Every citizen of Canada has the right to vote in an election of members of the House of Commons or of a legislative assembly and to be qualified for membership therein." The right to vote as well as to be a candidate for election to the House of Commons or to a provincial legislative assembly enjoys, therefore, constitutional recognition. On the other hand, nothing guarantees such a right on the municipal or local scene. However, at the school board level, section 29 of the Charter maintains the guarantees of section 93 of the *Constitution Act, 1867*. By virtue of this Act it seems certain that the right to vote in school board elections was guaranteed, as well as the right to be a candidate for the post of school trustee or member of a school board with responsibility for denominational schools (Beaudoin 1983, 151; 1989, 307–48). Virtually the same question could be put regarding linguistic school boards, insofar as section 23 of the Charter would give the right to a school organization involving elected school commissioners (Brun and Brunelle 1988, 698ff., on the significance of section 23).

Traditionally, the right to vote and be a candidate in legislative elections has been subject to certain restrictions. These should now conform to the limits imposed by section 1 of the Charter.

Some people have wondered if these democratic rights were less fundamental than the "fundamental freedoms" established by section 2 of the Charter. Mr. Justice Grant of Nova Scotia gave the opinion that the two categories are equally important: both are included in the same constitutional document and are "a necessary component of the democratic process" (*Fraser* 1986, 353). We share this point of view entirely, inasmuch as the rights in section 3 are even more intangible because of section 33 of the Charter.

The Right to Equality

The Supreme Court of Canada had occasion to give a ruling on section 15 of the Charter and the meaning of the requirement for equality. In the *Andrews* (1989) judgement, the Court begins by warning us that equality is a difficult concept to grasp, one that does not have a precise definition: "It is a comparative concept, the condition of which may only be attained or discerned by comparison with the condition of others in the social and political setting in which the question arises" (*Andrews* 1989, 164).[5]

What must be considered is above all the "impact of the law on the individual or the group concerned" in the search for "full equality before and under the law":

> Recognizing that there will always be an infinite variety of personal characteristics, capacities, entitlements and merits among those subject to a law, there must be accorded, as nearly as may be possible, an equality of benefit and protection and no more of the restrictions, penalties or burdens imposed upon one than another. In other words, the admittedly unattainable ideal should be that a law expressed to bind all should not because of irrelevant personal differences have a more burdensome or less beneficial impact on one than another. (*Andrews* 1989, 165)

It is, however, not sufficient for persons in similar situations to be treated in a similar manner for there to be equality. That "does not afford a realistic test," as "[c]onsideration must be given to the content of the law, to its purpose, and its impact upon those to whom it applies, and also upon those whom it excludes from its application" (*Andrews* 1989, 168), for there are distinctions or differences in treatment before the law which undermine the guarantee of equality in section 15 of the Charter, while others do not.

According to the analysis proposed by the *R. v. Big M Drug Mart* judgement (1985, cited in *Andrews* 1989, 168), in order to determine which distinctions or differences undermine section 15 of the Charter it is necessary to establish the meaning of the right in question by considering the purpose of such a guarantee according to the interests protected. Now equality in the sense of section 15 of the Charter has a more precise purpose than the simple elimination of distinctions. It aims to eliminate discrimination. But what is discrimination?

Mr. Justice McIntyre tells us that this presents few difficulties, as the Supreme Court of Canada, in several cases under the provincial charters of rights, had to describe situations of discrimination. According to him:

> [D]iscrimination may be described as a distinction, whether intentional or not but based on grounds relating to personal characteristics

of the individual or group, which has the effect of imposing burdens, obligations, or disadvantages on such individual or group not imposed upon others, or which withholds or limits access to opportunities, benefits, and advantages available to other members of society. Distinctions based on personal characteristics attributed to an individual solely on the basis of association with a group will rarely escape the charge of discrimination, while those based on an individual's merits and capacities will rarely be so classed. (*Andrews* 1989, 174–75)

More recently, on 4 May 1989, the Court once again clarified its thinking: "The guarantee of equality before the law is designed to advance the value that all persons be subject to the equal demands and burdens of the law and not suffer any greater disability in the substance and application of the law than others" (*Turpin* 1989, 1329).

However there is the "internal qualification in s. 15 that the differential treatment be 'without discrimination.' " Equality must have been violated "with discrimination" (*Turpin* 1989, 1331). In order to determine whether there has been discrimination based on the personal characteristics of an individual or a group, it is necessary to examine not only the legislative provisions but also examine "the larger social, political and legal context" (ibid.).

Unanimously, the Court added the following: "[S.] 15 mandates a case by case analysis as was undertaken by this Court in *Andrews* to determine 1) whether the distinction created by the impugned legislation results in a violation of one of the equality rights and, if so, 2) whether that distinction is discriminatory in its purpose or effect."

Limits Established by Section 1 of the Canadian Charter of Rights and Freedoms

As noted previously, section 1 establishes that it is possible to set certain restrictions on the rights and freedoms guaranteed by the *Canadian Charter of Rights and Freedoms*. These must, however, be such as may be justified "in a free and democratic society." The Supreme Court of Canada has determined in the *Oakes* case (1986) the type of test to be applied in order to establish compatibility with the Charter as regards section 1. In *R. v. Edwards Books and Art* (1986, 768 and 769; *Ford* 1988, 770), it reformulated this test and gave it a definitive form.

When it has been established that a rule of law restricts a right protected by the Charter, the government must demonstrate that the provision has objectives that are important enough to justify a restriction to this right: "First, the objective, which the measures responsible for a limit on a Charter right or freedom are designed to serve, must be 'of sufficient importance to warrant overriding a constitutionally protected right or freedom' " (*Oakes* 1986, 138).

What is "of sufficient importance"? "It is necessary, at a minimum, that an objective relate to concerns which are pressing and substantial in a free and democratic society before it can be characterized as sufficiently important" (*Oakes* 1986, 138–39).

Once this first step has been taken, the government must demonstrate the reasonable nature of the contested measure and its justification. There should be a certain proportion between the measure adopted and the objective sought. According to the Court, this criterion of proportionality comprises three aspects:

> First, the measures adopted must be carefully conceived to attain the objective in question. They should be neither arbitrary nor inequitable, nor founded on irrational considerations. Briefly, they must have a rational link with the objective in question. Second, even supposing that there is such a rational link, the means chosen must be such as to impair "as little as possible" the right or freedom in question (*R. v. Big M Drug Mart Ltd.*, already cited, 352). Thirdly, there must be a sense of proportion between the *effects* of the measures restricting a right or a freedom guaranteed by the Charter and the *objective* recognized as "of sufficient importance." (*Oakes* 1986, 140)

THE CONSTITUTIONALITY OF RELEVANT LEGISLATION

Sections 32 to 34 of the *Public Service Employment Act*

There are two kinds of restrictions established by sections 32 to 34 of the Act (formerly section 32 of the same Act). First, public servants are forbidden to work for or against a candidate in a federal or provincial election or for or against a political party or in its name. Second, public servants are forbidden to become candidates unless they have received the authorization from the Public Service Commission.

Section 32 was attacked in the Federal Court of Canada in 1984 in three cases in connection with the federal election of September 1984. The Court gave its judgement on 26 August 1986, confirming the constitutional validity of the provision (*Osborne* 1986, Walsh J.). However, the Federal Court of Appeal partially reversed this judgement in a decision of 15 July 1988, which was upheld in June 1991 by the Supreme Court of Canada.[6]

The facts of the three cases are similar. They did not concern public servants who held executive positions. Two cases were concerned with members of a political party who wished to be delegates to a party convention. Their immediate superior indicated to them that this was partisan work forbidden by sections 32 to 34 of the Act and that they must either resign from the public service or cease all partisan activity under threat of disciplinary action. The third case concerned several public servants who contested the fact that sections 32 to 34 of the Act forbade them all partisan work, although their duties did not entail any contact with the public and the proposed partisan work was of secondary importance.

In a very elaborate judgement, Mr. Justice Walsh of the Federal Court of first instance avoided attempting "to generalize" (*Osborne* 1986, 237). He limited the debate to two areas. First, was the partisan activity in question really forbidden by sections 32 to 34 of the Act? Second, are the restrictions imposed by sections 32 to 34 of the Act really reasonable and justifiable in view of section 1 of the *Canadian Charter of Rights and Freedoms*? In two of the cases studied, the judge felt that for someone simply to be a delegate to a political convention did not undermine sections 32 to 34 of the Act. The judge likened this occasion to the kind of participation at a political meeting already allowed by sections 32 to 34 of the Act. This is, in our opinion, a very debatable interpretation!

The second aspect is the compatibility with the Charter of the ban on partisan work. The judge applied the criteria of the *Oakes* (1986) decision in the following way. First, the objective pursued is sufficiently important in that it concerns the principle of public service neutrality recognized in the *Fraser* (1985) decision. Second, the means adopted are not disproportionate to the objective pursued. On the contrary, if in addition to what was already permitted, any partisan work was freely authorized, "there would be nothing left to preserve the tradition of political neutrality" (*Osborne* 1986, 242–43) established by the Supreme Court of Canada in the *Fraser* (1985) decision.

The Federal Court of Appeal, for its part, concentrated on the "reasonable" nature of the limitation imposed on partisan work, taking as guide a pronouncement of Mr. Justice Hugessen in the *Luscher* (1985) judgement of the same Court:

> In my opinion, one of the first characteristics of a reasonable limit prescribed by law is that it should be expressed in terms sufficiently clear to permit a determination of where and what the limit is. A limit which is vague, ambiguous, uncertain, or subject to discretionary determination is, by that fact alone, an unreasonable limit. If a citizen cannot know with tolerable certainty the extent to which the exercise of a guaranteed freedom may be restrained, he is likely to be deterred

from conduct which is, in fact, lawful and not prohibited. Uncertainty and vagueness are constitutional vices when they are used to restrain constitutionally protected rights and freedoms. While there can never be absolute certainty, a limitation of a guaranteed right must be such as to allow a very high degree of predictability of the legal consequences. (*Luscher* 1985, 89)

We should point out that the Supreme Court of Canada expressly confirmed this statement of principle by Mr. Justice Hugessen in a judgement in 1990 (*Reference re Criminal Code*).

The Federal Court of Appeal sought to establish in what measure the Public Service Commission itself had been able to specify what is to be understood by partisan work. However, in its different reports or directives, nothing precise is to be found. The Commission finished by proposing (*Osborne* 1988, 228–29) a teleological criterion: abstain from all that could compromise your impartiality in the eyes of others! The Court concluded that section 33(1)(*a*), (*b*) of the Act does not impose a limit to the freedom of expression and association of public servants that could be considered reasonable because this limitation is too imprecise.

On the other hand, the limitation imposed on candidature is precise. But is it justifiable on the application of the test of the *Oakes* (1986) judgement? The Court replied in the affirmative. On the one hand, the objective pursued is important. Citing the *Fraser* (1985) judgement, the Court affirmed that it was in the public interest to have a neutral public service; political debate during an election period is incompatible with the impartiality required of a public servant. As for the means used, it is rational, reasonable and equitable. However, the Court considered that the Act contains two anomalies. First, the investigation provided for in section 34(1) of the Act can be requested from the Commission only by a candidate or an elected member in the election in question. Secondly, the Court judged excessive the absolute right of a defeated candidate to re-enter the public service.

The Court concluded accordingly that only section 33(1)(*a*), (*b*) of the Act is contrary to the Charter, except for the case of deputy heads.

This decision of the Federal Court of Appeal contains positive aspects but also notable weaknesses. On the first point, which is the ban on partisan work, the Court is certainly right to consider that the means used constitutes an imprecise measure. To forbid all partisan work without regard for the nature of the work in question, its visibility, the rank of the public servant, the nature of the duties performed and the public servant's relations with the public, is unreasonable and especially cannot be justified in a democratic society that constitutionalizes the right to freedom of expression. The Court was furthermore right to exclude the deputy heads, but it offers no explanation. Any explanation that could be given would be just as valid for the other senior officers.

On the second point, the *Osborne* (1988) judgement is particularly weak and open to criticism. It raises the question of the invalidity of section 33(1)(c) of the Act, which forbids any public servant to be a candidate in an election, and which expressly contradicts section 3 of the *Canadian Charter of Rights and Freedoms*. However, the ban is not absolute as the Public Service Commission may, upon request, permit such a candidature if the Commission believes that, as regards the public service, the effectiveness of an employee would not suffer from his or her political commitment. This is a very wide discretionary power given to the Commission according to criteria that are not conspicuous for their clarity and precision. Referring to the judgement of Mr. Justice Hugessen in the *Luscher* (1985) case, is this not a limit that is vague, ambiguous, unspecified or subject to a discretionary interpretation? How can public servants know the exact scope of the limitation imposed on as fundamental a right as this in a democracy? We are very far from the "very high degree of predictability" of which Mr. Justice Hugessen speaks (ibid., 90).

The Federal Court of Appeal poorly applied the test of the *Oakes* (1986) decision. Certainly the objective is sufficiently important. But what about the means used? Were the means carefully conceived to attain the objective? Is there a rational link with the objective? If one exists, is it likely to cause the least possible harm to the right enshrined in the Charter? Finally, is there some sense of proportion between the effects of the measure restricting the right and the objective sought?

The rational link that must exist between the means and the objective, the effectiveness of the official in the position he or she occupies as regards the public service and that sufficiently important objective, which the political neutrality of the public service represents, is not evident. The objective of effectiveness is an objective of another order that must not be confused with the constitutional principle of neutrality recognized in the *Fraser* (1985) decision. The legislator seems to feel that the Commission will, by forbidding a candidature, be able to avoid a situation where a defeated candidate would be unable to resume his or her post in an "effective" manner, that is, to implement the objective of neutrality of the public service. It is on the basis of this conjecture that a public servant would be denied a constitutional right recognized in section 3 of the Charter! It seems to us that the question has been badly put. In our opinion, it is necessary to distinguish between a public servant's right to be a candidate and to resume his or her post on the one hand and, on the other, the solution of disciplinary or adjustment problems resulting from the public servant's return to the public service, which respect for the principle of political neutrality might entail.

With the present legislation it is very difficult to evaluate the proportional aspect of the effects of the ban on a particular public servant or the permission granted to another, on maintaining the political neutrality of the public service. However, the fundamental reason that leads us to maintain that sections 32 to 34 of the Act are contrary to the Charter is that the legislator's criteria, both in the case of partisan work and in that of candidatures, are fuzzy, vague and imprecise, and tantamount to the absence of criteria noted by the Supreme Court of Canada in the decision of *R. v. Morgentaler* (1988) regarding decisions of hospital committees on the subject of abortion. In this case, three of the judges considered that the absence of criteria was contrary to the principles of fundamental justice of section 7 of the Charter.

Section 15 of the Charter has also been invoked in arguing that sections 32 to 34 of the Act are discriminatory. Mr. Justice Walsh of the Federal Court of first instance rejected the argument on the grounds that this provision "does not discriminate in any way against any individual public servant" (*Osborne* 1986, 235). The argument was not submitted again before the Federal Court of Appeal. The Supreme Court has upheld, by a majority decision, the Federal Court of Appeal judgement invalidating paragraphs 33(1)(*a*) and (*b*), except with respect to deputy heads. In an Instruction dated June 1991, the Public Service Commission noticed that the state of law has been modified only insofar as to give effect to the Supreme Court judgement.

The Former Section 34 of the Nova Scotia Law

The Supreme Court of Nova Scotia had occasion in 1986 to pronounce on quite similar provisions of the *Civil Service Act* of Nova Scotia (*Fraser* 1986). This Act forbade in particular all deputy heads or public servants to engage in partisan work with respect to federal or provincial elections, as well as to give or to collect partisan contributions. However, it allowed any public servant who was not a deputy head or officer designated by regulation to be a candidate in a municipal or school election, provided that she or he had no affiliation to a provincial or federal political party, that the candidature did not interfere with the execution of duties as a public servant, and did not conflict with the interests of the government.

Mr. Justice Grant of the Supreme Court of Nova Scotia considered that the objective pursued was important but, applying the test of the *Oakes* (1986) decision, he concluded that the three contested restrictions to political freedom were disproportionate and excessive. In a long and rather analytical decision where the legislation of all provinces is reviewed, the judge notes that in several of them, the objective of political neutrality of the public service seems to have been attained without difficulty with a much more permissive legislation. The judge concludes, therefore, that this objective may be achieved by less radical measures.

The incompatibility with section 15 of the Charter had already been raised before the Court. The judge admitted that the contested disproportion created inequality, besides representing a violation of sections 2 and 3 of the Charter, that is, a restriction on certain fundamental or assimilated rights; he accordingly concluded that the same test must be applied (*Fraser* 1986, 353).

Mr. Justice Grant concluded his judgement with reflections on the diverse manifestations of the freedom of political expression. The learned judge held, for example, that a public servant could express himself, with moderation, in public at political meetings, but that it would not be desirable to appear on radio or television!

The Quebec Law

On 22 June 1989, the Commission de la fonction publique du Québec (Quebec Public Service Commission) began considering a case concerning the right of a provincial public servant to be a candidate. The person came under section 8 of the *Act respecting Attorney General's Prosecutors*, forbidding this category of public servant "se porter candidat à une élection fédérale ou provinciale" [translation: from "being a candidate in a federal or provincial election"] (*Tremblay* 1989, Commission Roberge). The public servant had declared himself a candidate in the election of November 1988, and had been dismissed in conformity with the Act. The Commission considered in the first instance that the ban on becoming a candidate decreed by section 8 of the Act did not impinge on the fundamental right enshrined in section 3 of the *Canadian Charter of Rights and Freedoms*, which is concerned only with the eligibility, that is, the legal aptitude to be elected. Rather, according to the Commission, section 8 of the Act creates an incompatibility between the fact of becoming a candidate and the status of deputy public prosecutor. On the other hand, even if one admitted that section 8 of the Act restricts the right enshrined in section 3 of the Charter, this restriction passes the test of the *Oakes* (1986) judgement. Since such prosecutors "exercent des fonctions quasi-judiciaires" [translation: "exercise quasi-judicial functions"] the purpose of section 8 of the Act is "de promouvoir le maintien de l'autorité, de la neutralité, de l'impartialité réelle et apparente et de l'intégrité du système judiciaire, en particulier en matière de justice criminelle et pénale" [translation: "to promote the maintenance of the authority, of the neutrality and the true and apparent impartiality and the integrity of the judicial system, particularly in matters of criminal and penal justice"] (*Tremblay* 1989, 222).

In our opinion, the Commission's concept of the right of eligibility is too restrictive, and is contrary to the wide and liberal interpretation recommended by the Supreme Court of Canada in its principal judgements on the Charter (*Law Society of Upper Canada* 1984; *Southam Inc.* 1984; *Big M Drug Mart* 1985) as well as to the body of jurisprudence on section 3 of the Charter itself (*Osborne* 1988; *Fraser* 1986; see also the case law cited in Beaudoin 1983). As for the application of the criteria of the *Oakes* (1986) judgement, the Commission applied the test of proportionality in a satisfactory manner. Certainly the measure is radical, but it is all the same softened by the fact the the public servant may request to be reclassified to another area of the public service and then to benefit from a leave without pay. On the other hand, the Commission shows the extreme importance of the objective pursued by the Quebec legislator – the neutrality and integrity of the system of criminal and penal justice, something which clearly distinguishes the situation in question from the one dealt with by the Federal Court of Appeal in the *Osborne* (1988) decision. The Commission should have made a better distinction between these two situations.

The Superior Court of Quebec, in the *Tremblay* (1990) judgement, reversed the commissioner's decision. According to the Court, section 8 of the *Act respecting Attorney General's Prosecutors* is not of a nature such as to cause the least possible harm to the right of eligibility guaranteed by section 3 of the Charter. The government had not "démontré de façon beaucoup plus convaincante que l'administration de la justice courrait un risque réel d'être irrémédiablement entaché par la candidature d'un substitut du procureur général" [translation: "demonstrated in a much more convincing manner that the administration of justice ran a real risk of being irremediably tainted by the candidature of a deputy public prosecutor"] (*Tremblay* 1990, 1402). The objective of the legislator can be achieved by less restrictive means, notably by granting a leave without pay. The Court cited with approval the *Fraser* (1986) decision of Nova Scotia.

The Court set out the fact that both the white paper on electoral reform of June 1986 and Bill C-70 of June 1987 abolished the prohibition on candidacy that applied to bailiffs, justices of the peace and Crown prosecutors.

The Court added that certain restrictions could be justified "au nom de l'impartialité, de la neutralité et de l'intégrité," but that that did not authorize "des mesures trop draconiennes ... imposées outrancièrement," when other "plus flexibles" measures would enable the same objective to be reached. There exists "un aménagement possible qui tienne compte du statut hiérarchique particulier du candidat."[7]

As to whether section 8 of the *Act respecting Attorney General's Prosecutors* violates section 15 of the Charter, the Court analysed the jurisprudence of the Supreme Court of Canada (*Andrews* 1989; *Turpin* 1989). The Court decided that if there were a disadvantageous distinction, it was discriminatory only if it rested on the personal characteristics of an individual or group. However, here a measure as drastic as dismissal means, for all practical purposes, that a prosecutor cannot become a candidate, while other public servants can benefit from a leave without pay. Following the *Andrews* (1989) decision, the Court added that section 15 of the Charter protects groups disadvantaged socially, politically and judicially, so that a heavy responsibility rests on the government to justify the discrimination.

The Ontario Law

On 5 August 1988 the High Court of Ontario rendered judgement in a dispute over similar provisions of the Ontario *Public Service Act* (*O.P.S.E.U.* 1988, Eberle J.).[8] The judge concluded that the clause providing for leave without pay for the ordinary public servant conformed with the *Canadian Charter of Rights and Freedoms.* He found it normal that the public servant not be paid and that the leave last for the duration of the election campaign. The question of deputy heads and officers who do not have rights in this regard was not raised. The judge considered that once a public servant was elected, it was normal for that person to resign.

Section 12(1) of the Act forbids a public servant not on electoral leave to solicit electoral or partisan funds or to associate his or her position with political activities. However, the Ontario judge ruled that nothing would be more harmful to the impartiality and integrity of the public service than to permit this. The judge also ruled that section 13(1) of the Act, which forbids all public servants to campaign for a candidate in an election period, is justified within the framework of a democratic society because of the high degree of "visibility" such activity entails. It would be disastrous for the impartiality and integrity of the public service if a public servant campaigned among people he or she administered and dealt with in the performance of his or her duty.

The Court next turned its attention to section 14 of the Act, which forbids any public servant to express opinions in public or in a document destined for public distribution concerning any issue that is part of the platform of a federal or provincial political party. To allegations that the criteria of section 14 of the Act were too vague, the judge replied that no one had presented convincing proof of real difficulties that could result from its application. Nevertheless, he concluded that section 1 of the Charter salvages this provision:

> The involvement of public servants in public controversy over current political issues would, in my view, be a serious breach of that political neutrality and impartiality which it is so important to maintain. Once that neutrality and impartiality and the integrity of the public service has been eroded or even if, in the eyes of the public, those qualities appear to have become eroded, it would surely be a most difficult, lengthy and perhaps even impossible task to restore them. (*O.P.S.E.U.* 1988, 709)

This judgement of the High Court is interesting because the judge considers that each of these provisions is part of a whole, a "regulatory scheme" taking its inspiration from a philosophy referred to by the Supreme Court of Canada itself. However, he places himself on the side of the right to free expression and not of section 3 of the Charter. The judge even adds that, as far as he is concerned, the question of electoral leave has nothing to do with the right of eligibility (*O.P.S.E.U.* 1988, 707).

BILL C-157: PROPOSED AMENDMENTS TO THE
PUBLIC SERVICE EMPLOYMENT ACT

The decision of the Federal Court of Appeal of 15 July 1988 (*Osborne*) did not leave the government indifferent. The government proposed a bill that was tabled on 30 August 1988, a little while before the November election was called that year.

For several reasons, Bill C-157 occupies a special place in the evolution of the former section 32 of the *Public Service Employment Act*, replaced by sections 32 to 34 of the present Act. First of all, the bill was a government proposal, unlike previous bills that were only the result of parliamentary initiatives. Second, since it followed up on the decision of the Federal Court of Appeal, it may be considered as the government response to the search for compatibility between the imperatives of the *Canadian Charter of Rights and Freedoms* and those of government policy. Third, this is not a simple amendment, but a veritable codification of about 30 sections constituting a rather ambitious chapter dealing with the political rights of public servants. They form a new Part IV, called "Political Rights."

The bill was tabled for first reading by the president of the Privy Council right in the middle of the pre-election period; therefore, it may be considered a trial balloon. However, the bill, completely forgotten, was not at stake in the election campaign that followed from September to November 1988.

The bill begins by firmly linking two principles, namely to recognize the "freedom of public servants to engage in political activities and to maintain the principle of political neutrality in the Public Service." The legislator has preferred to speak of the principle of impartiality within the public service rather than that of the neutrality of the public service, a fact that appears significant to us. Indeed, this is a more concrete approach, avoiding the controversy that could be raised by the very mention of the idea of public service neutrality. In a certain sense, since the public service is a government service, it cannot be politically neutral toward government; it is part of the governmental apparatus. Furthermore, if the idea of political neutrality is maintained, it is in the sense of a neutrality with respect to partisan politics. It is for the public servant, while participating by right in political life, to practise a form of political impartiality. The public servant's aim, as the bill specifies, is to ensure that, in exercising his or her functions, the public servant acts independently of political convictions and avoids any undue influence. As well, in the same manner, the public servant advises ministers or implements policies, programs or government services. In addition, appointments must be made according to the merit principle.

The principle of the right to participate in political life is recognized for all public servants, as is noted in section 32.11 of the bill, but restrictions are imposed by the maintenance of the principle of impartiality. These restrictions will concern either certain types of political activity or certain categories of public servant.

It should first be noted that the bill mentions only federal and provincial elections. When it mentions political parties it only deals with parties registered in conformity with section 27 of the *Canada Elections Act*, and the corresponding provisions of any provincial law.

At the outset, the bill distinguishes between two categories of public servant, general and "restricted." It identifies four types of political activity.

The first type of political activity, open to all public servants, includes the right to vote in an election, to participate in a peaceful meeting, to contribute to the funds of a political candidate or party and to be a member of such a party.

A second type of activity includes other activities exercised for or against a political candidate or party; according to section 33 of the bill, such activities would be determined by government regulation.

A third type of activity, forbidden to "restricted" public servants, consists of holding a position within a political party, or soliciting or collecting or managing funds for a political candidate or party, where the deputy head decides in writing that this activity is incompatible with the duties of the public servant concerned. This public servant can, however, appeal the decision before a review committee established by the Public Service Commission. This is, in fact, an appeal committee that can review the soundness of a decision, and either confirm, modify or set it aside.

The two latter types of activity are therefore subject to restrictions that must undergo the test of section 1 of the Charter. In a case where the government is empowered to regulate, it is impossible to say in advance whether this is a rule of law that restricts freedom of expression, and to what degree it is restricted. As long as such a ruling is not made, it is not possible to evaluate whether it constitutes a reasonable and justifiable rule of law within the framework of a free and democratic society. In our opinion, sections 32.1 and 33 of the bill are not incompatible with section 2(*b*) of the Charter. On the contrary, section 1 of the Charter allows the parliamentary or governmental legislator to place restrictions on established rights and freedoms.

In the case of the third type of activity, the capacity of a deputy head to forbid it is not a matter left entirely to his or her discretion. A norm has been provided for, to wit, incompatibility with the duties exercised by the public servant in question. Is this norm too imprecise and is it equivalent to an absence of a norm, as stated in the analysis of the Supreme Court of Canada in the *Morgentaler* (1988) judgement, or that of the Federal Court of Appeal in the *Luscher* (1985) case? Certainly it is not a question of a rigid or exact norm that excludes all subjective evaluation. However, we consider that it is not such as to render unconstitutional section 32.11(3) of the bill, which decrees it. There are three reasons for this. First, the decision the deputy head must make is quite circumscribed: the deputy head must check whether, in the light of the two objectives of the law in question, there is incompatibility between the specific duties carried out by a particular public servant, and four specified means of participating in the life of an accredited political party. Second, the person to whom this decision is entrusted is a highly credible authority, who cannot be accused of involvement in partisan politics, and who offers the best guarantees of expertise. Third, this decision is subject to appeal before a quasi-judicial tribunal, which may review its cogency in an objective manner.

Moreover, the third type of activity is absolutely forbidden to deputy heads, associate deputy heads and "restricted" public servants. These public servants may not therefore play an active or visible role in directing or financing parties.[9] There is a rational link with the objective pursued, but is the measure too radical? The interdiction is universal, but it is not easy in these matters to establish a gradation between the positions occupied within a party according to their importance. As for the first subcategory of senior officers, the measure seems to us to be justified. However, the second subcategory to be designated by the Treasury Board may appear radical. The legislator fears that these public servants without high rank in the hierarchy may not be impartial in exercising their duties or that their impartiality may be doubted because of their involvement with a political party. This fear is not unfounded because of the high degree of "visibility" attached to certain forms of political militancy. Moreover, the measure does not forbid other forms of partisan political activity. Such a public servant may be active in a party, or be active behind the scenes. Finally, the Treasury Board must proceed to make designations "having regard to the purpose of this Part" and an appeal to the Public Service Commission is possible. Treasury Board's discretionary power is therefore clearly circumscribed. For these reasons we consider sections 32.11(3) and 32.12(2) of the bill to be compatible with the *Canadian Charter of Rights and Freedoms* as concerns possible political militancy.

The fourth type of activity consists of activities expressly forbidden by section 32.16 of the bill, namely

32.16 A public servant shall not:
a) make any public statement in conflict with the duties of the public servant; or
b) engage in any political activity:
    (i) during the course of or at the place of the public servant's employment; or
    (ii) in a manner that calls attention to the public servant's employment as a public servant.

These restrictions may be viewed differently with respect to section 1 of the Charter. On the one hand, the ban on a public servant making public declarations conflicting with his or her professional capacity is precise, clear and, a priori, does not appear abusive. To allow any public servant to make public declarations concerning his or her role would create such absurd situations that the opposite appears normal in a constitutional system like ours. We even find the expression "in conflict" a bit restrictive. In our opinion, conflict is not necessary; the ban should normally cover all that concerns the professional capacity of the public servant. We support, however, the provision as written. The concept of conflict of interest is the determining factor here, as the report of the Ontario Law Reform Commission (1986, 299), as well as the report of the Task Force on Conflicts of Interest (1984, 43), remind us.

The restriction stated in section 32.16(*a*) of the bill seems to be better circumscribed than what the report of the Ontario Law Reform Commission (1986, 301) calls the "home department criticism." American constitutional jurisprudence has judged the ban on public servants commenting on everything that concerns their department too wide (*Pickering* 1968). What it is important to define is "job-related criticism" as opposed to "non-job-related criticism." It is not a question here of following American jurisprudence, but of situating the issues in the context of the *Canadian Charter of Rights and Freedoms*.

The ban forbidding all public servants to engage in political activities while performing their duties or in the workplace does not raise any problems. Indeed, the contrary would be surprising and would make maintaining a climate of impartiality and neutrality within the government illusory. On the other hand, the ban on engaging in an activity in such a way as to draw attention to one's employment as a public servant is more imprecise. What seems to be aimed at is the public servant's use of his or her title or status when engaging in a political activity. Therefore a public servant's behaviour is the key factor rather than the perception the public and the media could have of it, or even the manner in which the latter could exploit it. On the whole, it seems to us that this ban does not violate the *Canadian Charter of Rights and Freedoms*, because fundamentally it is as a private person or citizen that the public servant is constitutionally protected in his or her political rights.

For the purposes of participation in political life, Bill C-157 creates two classes of public servant: the general class, and the "restricted class," which has more limited political rights. Which public servants are included in this restricted class, and what are the limitations imposed on their political involvement?

The restricted category contains two subcategories. According to the bill, the first includes:

32.12(1)

a) deputy heads and associate deputy heads;

b) employees in the Management Category established under section 7 of the *Financial Administration Act*;

c) employees whose duties normally include any of the following responsibilities, namely,

(i)   directly advising a Minister of the Crown, a deputy head, an associate deputy head, an assistant deputy minister, or a person in a position equivalent to any of those positions, on the development of policies, programs and services, and

(ii)   the preparation or use of confidences of the Queen's Privy Council for Canada that are excluded from the application of the *Access to Information Act* under section 69 of that Act.

The second subcategory includes public servants who will be designated by Treasury Board regulation, either by name or by virtue of their position:

32.12(2)
a)   Any employee whose duties normally include the exercise of significant discretion in

(i)   deciding whether a penalty should be imposed or a prosecution commenced or continued under an Act of Parliament,

(ii)   negotiating or approving a grant or contribution or the conferral of a benefit or advantage of any kind by the Government of Canada,

(iii)   negotiating or approving a contract or agreement to which Her Majesty in right of Canada and any other person, government or governmental agency are parties, or

(iv)   the selection of persons for employment opportunities outside the Public Service; or

b)   any employee employed as a personnel administrator or in a managerial or confidential capacity, within the meaning of the *Public Service Staff Relations Act*, other than an employee who is considered to be employed in that capacity solely by virtue of hearing grievances at the first level in the grievance process provided for by that Act.

The first subcategory raises few difficulties. These are senior officers of the public service and advisers to ministers and high officials, as well as officials involved in the confidential activities of the Privy Council. These public servants are very close to government policies, so close that it would be difficult to suppose they could concurrently play an active role in a political party, especially an opposition party.

On the other hand, the second subcategory, to be determined by Treasury Board regulation, raises certain questions. This concerns public servants called to intervene directly in the relations between the administration and the citizen, either in awarding contracts, subsidies or other advantages, or in awarding positions outside the public service, or in the institution of criminal or civil proceedings. The legislator aims to preserve impartiality within the governmental apparatus by forbidding certain public servants a political involvement that would hinder them in making the objective decisions their positions require. It is the same for the other subcategory, those officials occupying positions as personnel administrators or persons engaged in management or in confidential functions, in the meaning of the *Public Service Staff Relations Act.*

The questions we have regarding the two last subcategories, especially about the ban proposed in section 32.11(3) of the bill, come from applying the criteria of the *Oakes* (1986) judgement. Would this measure cause "the least possible harm" to the right or freedom in question? Is there proportionality between the effects of the measure restricting political freedom and the objective validated by the *Canadian Charter of Rights and Freedoms*? The legislator takes it for granted that the public servant who negotiates or approves subsidies or contracts and who, as a citizen, occupies a position in a political party or solicits funds for one, will not be able to set aside his political prejudices. The same lawmaker does not have this fear when the same public servant is a member of the same party and makes his own contribution to the funds of this party. What seems to make the difference is the "visibility" of the political involvement.

In section 32.12(2) of the bill, the legislator is inspired by the techniques of judicial and administrative law, according to which, in the exercise of judicial or quasi-judicial functions, it is not enough that justice be done, but justice must also appear to have been done. It is therefore sufficient if a reasonable fear of partiality or prejudice (reasonable apprehension of bias) exists (Garant 1985, 753–97).

In addition, the legislator adds certain precautions to the designation decreed by Treasury Board regulation. First, there must be an assurance that the public servants affected by the designation be advised in writing, explaining the reasons. Second, dissatisfied public servants may ask the Public Service Commission to review this designation. The Commission then constitutes a committee of inquiry that proceeds along quasi-judicial lines in the manner of an appeal committee. If the committee recommends the invalidation or modification of the designation, the Treasury Board must modify the regulation accordingly. Because of these procedural precautions, we are inclined to think that the restrictions imposed on the two subcategories targeted by section 32.12(2) of the bill are compatible with the *Canadian Charter of Rights and Freedoms*.

Finally, Bill C-157 regulates the right of candidature in federal and provincial elections, incidentally a right constitutionally enshrined in section 3 of the Charter, which stipulates that "every citizen of Canada has the right ... to be qualified for membership" in the House of Commons or a legislative assembly.

The bill creates three categories of public servant and subjects them to three different sets of regulations. First, the deputy head and the associate deputy head may be election candidates, but they then cease to be part of the public service. Second, public servants of the restricted category who wish to be candidates may make a written request that the Commission grant leave without pay. It is surprising that section 32.21 of the bill mentions only nomination by a party, thus does not appear to cover those who might wish to be independent candidates. We believe this is an inadvertent omission. The Commission will grant leave if it considers that "being a candidate would not impair the ability of the applicant to perform the duties of the applicant's employment" on returning to the position he or she occupies. Finally, all other public servants may seek to be nominated and in all likelihood be candidates, even without party nomination. However, they must notify the appropriate deputy head in writing before making any public announcement. Leave without pay is granted as soon as they make public their intention to seek election.

If the test developed by the Supreme Court of Canada under section 15 of the Charter is applied, some would be tempted to conclude that, on the face of it, sections 32.20, 32.21 and 32.22 of the bill create a situation that discriminates between the three categories of public servant. However, we must ask ourselves whether the distinction rests on "personal characteristics" or rather on the position's requirements with respect to the duties exercised by these persons. The Court considers that there are three ways of determining whether there is discrimination; the one that must be used under section 15 of the Charter is "the method of listed or similar reasons." Now, can the reason that appears to cause the legislator to make the previously mentioned distinction be compared, or is it analogous to one or more of the reasons listed in section 15 of the Charter? Obviously not! This is not a case of discrimination based on the reasons listed, or on similar ones. In fact, the distinction made by the legislator rests on the nature and importance of the duties and responsibilities of senior officers, and not their age, their social status or their political opinions. In the 1990 *Tremblay* decision, the Superior Court of Quebec contents itself with affirming that deputy public prosecutors constitute "un groupe défavorisé" [translation: a "disadvantaged group"]; "il s'agit d'une mesure arbitraire et injustifiée dont l'effet préjudiciale est certain" [translation: this is "an arbitrary and unjustified measure whose prejudicial effect is certain"] (*Tremblay* 1990, 1411). The Court affirms that section 8 of the *Act respecting Attorney General's Prosecutors* is motivated by the danger that a deputy public prosecutor may be loyal to a political party and compromise the legislative objective of neutrality, impartiality. Here the judge confuses the legislator's objective and the reason for the discrimination, which is the criterion or basis.

Mr. Justice Grant of Nova Scotia applies section 15 of the Charter to election conventions in an imprecise manner. He merely considers that there is "inequality in the protection and benefit of the law through the infringement and denial of the fundamental freedom under s. 2(*a*), (*c*) and (*d*) and the democratic right of candidature under s. 3 of the Charter" (*Fraser* 1986, 353).

Finally, we should remember that Mr. Justice Walsh of the Federal Court thought that section 15 of the Charter is not applicable for the following reason: if we consider the entire public service as an employment category that needs certain restrictions on political activity, sections 32 to 34 of the *Public Service Employment Act* establish no discrimination as regards a specific public servant, even if we extend the term "discrimination" beyond the categories explicitly provided for in section 15(1) of the Charter (*Osborne* 1986, 235). This opinion was upheld by the Supreme Court of Canada in June 1991.

CONCLUSION

Sections 32 to 34 of the *Public Service Employment Act*, already partially invalidated by the Federal Court of Appeal, are, as a whole, in our opinion unconstitutional. Certainly the legislator's objective is valid and sufficiently important to justify a restriction of fundamental or assimilated rights enshrined in sections 2 and 3 of the Charter. Upholding the public neutrality of the public service is a constitutional principle that the Supreme Court of Canada expressly recognized in the *Fraser* (1985) judgement as directly deriving from the very principle of responsible government. However, the ban on all partisan political activity for all public servants without distinction and in all circumstances seems excessive and unjustified within the framework of a democratic system. This system essentially depends on the participation of every citizen in the political and electoral process, in a system where political parties play an essential role. The ban on "working" for or against a candidate or a party is both imprecise and much too broad. There is a flagrant disproportion between the scope of the ban and the objective pursued. This is not a measure that will cause "the least possible harm" to the fundamental rights enshrined in the *Canadian Charter of Rights and Freedoms*, and precisely stated by the Supreme Court of Canada.

Our point of view can only be confirmed by the attitude recently taken by the Supreme Court of Canada in the *Ford* decision (1988) regarding the requirement to post public signs in French only, decreed by Quebec's *Charter of the French language*. This requirement was considered a prejudicial attack on freedom of expression as recognized by section 2(*b*) of the *Canadian Charter of Rights and Freedoms*. Certainly the objective of the Quebec legislator was valid, but the means taken to reach this objective was judged too radical. The Court invalidated the relative provisions of the *Charter of the French language* as not being such as to cause the "least possible harm" to freedom of expression, even though only commercial communications were involved.

As for the relative ban forbidding all public servants to become candidates in a federal or provincial election, it does not respect the fundamental right recognized in section 3 of the Canadian Charter; it subjects this right to the discretionary power of the Public Service Commission, which must apply a criterion that has no rational link with the objective of the legislation. On the other hand, the law has no other criteria both valid and precise enough to indicate to the public servant the limits imposed on his or her fundamental right to be a candidate. We are very far from the "very high degree of predictability" that Mr. Justice Hugessen spoke of in the *Luscher* (1985) decision.

Legislation that would fully satisfy the spirit of the *Canadian Charter of Rights and Freedoms* should deal only with the restrictions to rights by making appropriate distinctions and qualifications. A first distinction should identify the nature of the political activity, whether it be partisan or nonpartisan politics. A second distinction should deal with the time and place where the public servant engages in this political activity with respect to the duties carried out. A third distinction should deal with the link (or absence of one) between the political activity a public servant is contemplating and his or her job. A fourth distinction would be necessary to establish categories of public servants according to rank and the kind of duties performed.

However, whatever the form of political freedom the public servant adopts, he or she should act with moderation, out of loyalty to the employer (the government) and to maintain a general climate of neutrality and impartiality in the public service; that is, a public servant should act with "reserve," the expression used by the Quebec legislator.

The first distinction prompts us to define clearly the notion of partisan political activity in the sense usually understood, namely that which is linked to party politics, to the party programs, to the support of parties or of the ideas of candidates who are their spokesmen or spokeswomen, etc. On the other hand, nonpartisan politics is any public expression of opinion or participation in activities of a political nature without apparent or real links with political parties or electoral commitments. Nonpartisan political expression may take the form of critical comment on government policy or government action (Ontario Law Reform Commission 1986, 296).

The second distinction aims to separate the occasions when the official is in the public service from private life as an ordinary citizen. It is easy to imagine that when he or she is on duty at work, a public servant may not engage in politics of any kind. This is a vital minimum for the constitutional principle of the political neutrality of the public service and for the impartiality that must be shown by every public servant in applying government laws and policies, and in his or her official relations with citizens.

The third distinction is important in cases where political activity takes the form of comments or criticism regarding government policies or existing legislation. Thus, it must be considered inadmissible for a public servant to criticize in public the government policy or legislation that he or she must apply. One must also consider that the member of an organization or a public servant exercising quasi-judicial functions, especially in cases involving government, should not indulge in any public criticism or comment that might put his or her impartiality in doubt. Indeed this is a requirement following from the principles of natural justice.

A notable illustration of the fourth distinction was proposed in Bill C-273 of 26 November 1987; it is equally inspired by the situation of present-day British law. Without going into exaggerated details or subtleties, the public service can be divided into three categories. First there are people in senior positions (Group A), corresponding to senior executive positions (EX) and senior management (SM). These public servants work very closely with the political leaders. They are very close advisers; by delegation, they exercise executive positions in the governmental apparatus. Second, there is Group B, namely middle management and the seven categories of professionals identified by the designations CO (commerce), PM (program management), PG (purchasing and supplies), LA (law), ES (economics, sociology and statistics), IS (information services) and PE (personnel management). Third, there are all the other public servants, white-collar or blue-collar workers.

Some people, including the Chief Justice of the Supreme Court of Canada in the *Fraser* decision (1985, 466), have proposed another criterion for differentiation, namely the "public visibility of the public servant." Chief Justice Dickson considers that a job in the public service comprises two dimensions, one relating to the employee's task and the other to the manner in which the public perceives the job (ibid., 492). This perception depends on the job's visibility. Therefore "the degree of restraint which must be exercised is relative to the position and visibility of the civil servant" (ibid., 466). In theory, one could agree with such a criterion, but in practice it is difficult to apply. Is being visible a question of dealing with subordinates or the public, or having to make individual decisions in response to requests from citizens? But tens of thousands of public servants assigned to these tasks nevertheless remain completely anonymous. It is rare for public servants, except for those in senior positions, to be really known by the public because they are visible. In our opinion the criterion of visibility cannot really be used to single out categories of public servants whose rights would be restricted relative to others.

Therefore, a public servant has, under section 3 of the Charter, the right not only to be a candidate but also not to lose his or her job. This conclusion implicitly supposes that the public servant be put on temporary leave of whatever form (vacation, special leave, leave without pay, etc.). It is a necessary implication that the constitutional right of a public servant to be eligible would include the right to be available to campaign, that is, to obtain electoral leave.

In our opinion, the failure to grant leave for purposes of candidature strikes a blow at section 3 of the Charter. Additionally, we must ask whether this restriction, in the case of deputy heads as well as that of the restricted class, responds to the criteria of section 1 of the Charter.

In the *Fraser* (1986) decision, Mr. Justice Grant seems to consider the establishment of categories within the public service to be justifiable; he cites the English example, where the system apparently functions satisfactorily. However, in Canada we must apply the test of the *Oakes* (1986) judgement.

The objective pursued by the legislator is always the same: the impartiality or neutrality of the public service, established by jurisprudence as a constitutional principle. Does the measure have a rational link with the objective? Are its effects disproportionate to the objective? Does the measure restrict as little as possible the right enshrined in section 3 of the Charter?

It is easy to admit that there is a rational link between the ideal of neutrality of the public service and the necessity for top-ranking public servants to leave the service when they make the leap into politics. But it is not easy to respond to the other two questions. Is the measure too radical?

The legislator seems to give the reason for the measure in section 32.21(2) of Bill C-157, which aims to ensure that a public servant's candidacy will not harm his or her effectiveness on returning to the job. In the case of deputy heads and associate deputy heads, the legislator decrees that participating in an election campaign will harm their effectiveness as public servants; in the other cases, the Public Service Commission will apply the criterion. Nonetheless, the reasons that argue in favour of permitting these public servants no return are more complex.

Deputy heads and associate deputy heads are senior public servants closely linked to political power. They advise ministers and even define policy. They are directly responsible to Cabinet or to a minister whose confidence they must have. The ministers are responsible for their actions or their management to Cabinet and to public opinion. In spite of that, it is difficult to maintain with absolute certainty that their return to the public service after an election campaign would be harmful. Certainly a senior public servant's return to the same position is perhaps not desirable, or even thinkable, especially if the deputy head in question campaigned for an opposition party. But the return of senior public servants to the public service in other posts corresponding to their aptitudes, taking circumstances into account, poses much less of a problem. Is total exclusion from the public service a measure that causes the least possible harm to the constitutional right of section 3 of the Charter? We may doubt that. The measure is radical, and it is difficult to demonstrate that it is indispensable to attaining the objective of an impartial and neutral public service.

Therefore we would opt for a solution more respectful of the Charter, to wit, maintaining the link with the employer (the public service) for all public servants, but without necessarily the right for a public servant to resume the same position. However, the public servant should return to a suitable position according to his or her aptitudes and taking into account the criterion of effectiveness mentioned in section 32.21(2) of the bill.

We would apply the same norm to the other public servants of the restricted class. These public servants would not have to obtain permission from the Commission. However the Commission would have to assign a new post to the public servant upon his or her return after an election campaign, following a re-evaluation of her or his aptitudes and an evaluation of the question of effectiveness.[10] This solution resembles that envisaged by the Quebec minister of justice in the *Tremblay* (1990) affair mentioned previously.

Kernaghan concludes his 1986 study in the following way: "Thus, a substantial expansion in the political partisanship of public servants may erode the reality and appearance of a politically neutral public service by such means as increasing patronage appointments, expanding public comment by public servants, reducing public service anonymity, and diminishing job security" (Kernaghan 1986, 650).

According to Kernaghan, the present situation at the federal level constitutes a compromise between two extremes; it is located in the middle of a continuum: "Viewed in the light of the rationales for limiting and permitting political partisanship and of policies and practices in other governments, section 32 of the *Public Service Employment Act* places the existing federal regime about halfway along the continuum between unrestricted political activity and prohibited political activity" (Kernaghan 1986, 650).

The federal situation would therefore represent a happy medium. Moreover, Kernaghan likens the Quebec situation to the federal one, which is surprising.[11]

In our opinion, the Quebec situation is very different from the federal one. The province's *Public Service Act* of 1983 in no way limits the political activity of public servants except in the exercise of their duties, where they must show political neutrality, and in the public display of their political opinions, where they must show reserve. As for the right to be a candidate, this is unconditionally granted to all public servants except for government administrators, namely very senior officials. The public servant who becomes a candidate has the right to a total or partial leave without pay, and reinstatement into his or her post if he or she is not elected, or upon completion of his or her first term of office, or upon completion of successive terms of office if he or she is elected to the National Assembly. The public servant has the right to resume his or her position with the same classification.

This Quebec system, much more liberal and more in conformity with the *Canadian Charter of Rights and Freedoms*, has not, since it came into force, caused the erosion of the constitutional principle of the neutrality of the public service in Quebec. It has not increased the number of patronage appointments and promotions, has not increased public criticism by its public servants, has not reduced the anonymity of the public service, nor reduced security of employment. There was a change of government in Quebec in 1985, and nothing unusual occurred.

Kernaghan and his followers, whose utterances Cassidy (1986, 655) calls "the conventional mandarin's wisdom," fear above all that the affirmation of the political freedom of public servants under the impact of the charters may provoke a frenzy of political partisanship. Certainly, historically, in the course of the 20th century we have passed from the spoils system and the complete politicization of the public service to the merit system and the political sterilization of public servants. However, if it were necessary for the merit system to remain, political sterilization would not be justified in a context of greater political maturity and respect for human rights.

At its annual general meeting on 18 August 1986, the Institute of Public Administration of Canada adopted a declaration of principle that seems to us, in one of its provisions, to conform to the jurisprudence of the Supreme Court of Canada and to the *Canadian Charter of Rights and Freedoms:* "Public employees should enjoy the fullest possible measure of political rights that is compatible with laws, regulations and conventions designed to preserve the political neutrality of the public service" (Institute of Public Administration 1986, 349).

Other provisions of the declaration are more questionable, but this declaration is only a guide whose objective is to encourage public servants not to abuse this freedom, and to practise great "reserve."

We have attained in Canada a degree of political maturity that does not make us fear the impact of the charters. The fears raised by people opposed to granting public servants greater freedom of expression seem to us exaggerated and pessimistic. The Charter poses a challenge that the community of government employees will know how to handle; we are optimistic.

The question we must ask ourselves in 1990 is no longer whether, under the Charter's influence, it is desirable, suitable or useful that public servants engage in political activity compatible with the neutrality of the public service. What is fundamental is the political freedom considered by constitutional jurisprudence to be the keystone of our democratic system. The constitutional principle of the neutrality of the public service is important but subordinate. Political freedom, in its diverse modes of expression and for citizens as a whole, is vital to democracy. Restricting it should accordingly be considered only with the greatest circumspection. This applies as much to the freedom of political expression enshrined in section 2(*b*) of the Charter as to the rights to vote and to be a candidate set out in section 3 of the Charter, which are intimately related to it. We believe that many good or pious reasons, often advanced to protect the neutrality of the public service against public servants who might possibly abuse their freedom, no longer hold. It is the same for arguments based on the credibility of the public administration, on the image of the public service, on the susceptibility of political bosses, on respect for tradition, etc.

The 1986 report of the Ontario Law Reform Commission is of primordial interest, but its constitutional scope is very limited. It is true that the first significant decisions of the Supreme Court of Canada under section 2(*b*) of the Charter and under section 15 of the Charter are of a later date. The report certainly poses good questions, but its responses are questionable. We will attempt to make a summary inventory of the recommendations that appear open to criticism with respect to the Charter for the reasons we have previously explained.

First, the report recommends the ban on all political activity at work and in the workplace; on all political activity that would result from coercion of the public servant as such; on all public activity that would result in an improper advantage for the official; on all political activity that would conflict with the interests of the government in relation to the public servant's duties; and on all political activity that would arouse in the public a reasonable fear of partiality resulting from decisions taken relating to the functions of adjudication, allocation or evaluation. These recommendations provide for mechanisms to warn and punish violators of these bans.

Second, the report deals with "critical comment," namely political criticism, approving or disapproving, made in "public" by public servants "in their private capacities," that is, as individuals or citizens. All public servants must abstain from commenting on government policies or actions in four circumstances: if the comment creates a direct conflict of interest between the interests of the government and the exercise of duties; if the comment creates a reasonable fear of partiality related to decisions taken by the public servant; if the comment creates a reasonable fear that "working relationships within the public service involving the employee, or the employee's ability to perform his duties effectively will be significantly impaired" (Ontario Law Reform Commission 1986, 183); if the comment concerns the ministry or the body to which the public servant reports except if the policy or action commented on affects him or her personally.

The dominant criterion that should motivate these restrictions should be the link with the exercise of duties. From this point of view, the measure can be justified with respect to the sufficiently important objective of the neutrality of the public service. In addition, the measure must be sufficiently precise as to indicate the exact scope of the ban. However, the third statement is far from precise: it is a prime example of a norm that would be declared "void for vagueness" in a court of justice. It is a much too impressionistic norm! As for the fourth statement, one can express some doubts. Some departments have quite wide and varied responsibilities, while many public servants perform very precise functions of a technical nature. When there is no link with the exercise of duties we doubt that such a ban passes the test of the *Oakes* (1986) judgement, as we explained previously.

Third, the report proposes the division of the public service into two categories, namely the general and the "restricted" category. It is necessary, we believe, with respect to the test of the *Oakes* (1986) decision, to consider each subcategory of the restricted category (the subject of the restriction) from the viewpoint of the envisaged activities (the object of the restriction). It is not possible to proceed globally.

Bill C-157 is certainly less deficient than the proposals of the 1986 report of the Ontario Law Reform Commission. However, we believe that some rectification is necessary in order to avoid new disputes under the *Canadian Charter of Rights and Freedoms*. On the one side, the provisions of sections 32 to 32.19 of the bill seem to us on the whole acceptable, but this is not the case for the others.

The provisions regarding the right of candidature should be reworked to allow all public servants an electoral leave with right to return to the public service, although not necessarily to the same positions. Sections 32.20, 32.21 and 32.22 of the bill would become:

32.20(1) Deputy heads, associate deputy heads as well as employees of the restricted category who intend to seek nomination are required to give the Commission written notice of their intention before announcing it publicly.

(2) Any other employee who intends to seek nomination is required to advise the deputy head of the department before making a public announcement.

(3) When this notice is received, the public servant is placed on electoral leave without pay.

32.21 The employee whose electoral leave is terminated for any of the reasons mentioned in 32.23(1) resumes his or her post.

32.22 The deputy head, associate deputy head or public servant of the restricted category whose electoral leave is terminated for one of the causes mentioned in 32.23(1) must submit to an evaluation of his or her aptitudes and capacities by the Commission who assigns that public servant another post in the public service, taking into account his or her effectiveness and objectives.

We have therefore reduced to a strict minimum the restriction on democratic rights and we have given the maximum scope to section 3 of the Charter without putting in peril, we believe, the two essential objectives, namely "the principle of political impartiality within the Public Service" and the right of "public servants," including deputy heads and those of the restricted class, "to engage in political activities." However, these two objectives are not both on the same footing. The more important one, which is derived from the requirements of sections 2(*b*) and 3 of the Charter, is the right to participate in political life. The other, of a constitutional nature also, is, in our opinion, subordinate. If the legislator must take a risk, he or she must take it in favour of political freedom, which is the foundation and the keystone of our constitutional democracy. As Chief Justice Dickson pointed out in 1985: "Our democratic system is deeply rooted in, and thrives on, a free and robust public discussion of public issues. As a general rule, all members of society should be permitted, indeed encouraged, to participate in that discussion" (*Fraser* 1985, 467).

This political freedom must be encouraged and, moreover, limited "the least possible," according to the requirements of the *Oakes* (1986) decision. In addition, there must be proportionality between the effects of the measure restricting political freedom and the objective recognized as sufficiently important. Here the attack on political freedom of public servants is serious because this freedom is essential to the quality of citizenship in a democracy. Therefore to attain his or her goal – neutrality of the public service – the legislator should limit him- or herself to restrictions that appear truly necessary. It must be a question of conditions that are sine qua non, and it is up to the government to demonstrate that necessity. The government is not required to prove such necessity beyond all doubt, but its demonstration must be convincing. Up to now, each time a legislator has liberalized the exercise of political rights for public servants, there has been no disturbance as a result, according to inquiries made by the Ontario Law Reform Commission (1986). We do not anticipate any such disturbances if the *Canadian Charter of Rights and Freedoms* is applied in a generous manner.

ABBREVIATIONS

am.	amended
c.	chapter
C.A.	Court of Appeal
C.E.S.G.B.	Crown Employees Grievance Settlement Board
Div. Ct.	Divisional Court
D.L.R.	Dominion Law Reports
D.Y.T.	Decree of the Yukon Territory
F.C.	Federal Court Reports
L.A.C.	Labour Arbitration Cases
N.S.T.D.	Nova Scotia Trial Division
O.I.C.	Order in Council (Yukon Territory)
O.R.	Ontario Reports

R.D.C.F.P.	Recueil des décisions de la Commission de la fonction publique
Reg.	Regulation
R.J.Q.	Recueil de jurisprudence du Québec
R.R.O.	Revised Regulations of Ontario
R.S.A.	Revised Statutes of Alberta
R.S.B.C.	Revised Statutes of British Columbia
R.S.C.	Revised Statutes of Canada
R.S.M.	Revised Statutes of Manitoba
R.S.N.B.	Revised Statutes of New Brunswick
R.S.N.S.	Revised Statutes of Nova Scotia
R.S.O.	Revised Statutes of Ontario
R.S.P.E.I.	Revised Statutes of Prince Edward Island
R.S.Q.	Revised Statutes of Quebec
R.S.S.	Revised Statutes of Saskatchewan
R.S.Y.T.	Revised Statutes of the Yukon Territory
R.Y.T.	Regulations of the Yukon Territory
S.C.R.	Supreme Court Reports
S.N.S.	Statutes of Nova Scotia
S.N.W.T.	Statutes of the Northwest Territories
S.Y.T.	Statutes of the Yukon Territory
s.(s)	section(s)
U.S.	United States Supreme Court Reports

NOTES

This study was completed in May 1991.

1. See also Mr. Justice McIntyre of the Supreme Court of Canada in the *R.W.D.S.U.* (1986) judgement: "Prior to the adoption of the Charter, freedom of speech and expression had been recognized as an essential feature of Canadian parliamentary democracy. Indeed, this Court may be said to have given it constitutional status" (ibid., 584).

2. This provision was first applied to the election of November 1988 and was later judicially contested.

3. It is necessary to have the Commission's authorization to become a candidate; this will be granted if the public servant's "efficacy" in his or her position is "in no way compromised." Only deputy heads do not have this right.

4. The Ontario statutory restrictions on political activities of Ontario public servants were considered valid before the *Canadian Charter of Rights and Freedoms* came into force in the *O.P.S.E.U.* (1987) case.

5. All the judges supported this definition by Mr. Justice McIntyre.

6. *Osborne v. Canada,* [1988] 3 F.C. 219 (Mahoney, Heald and Lacombe JJ.); affirmed (1991), 82 D.L.R. (4th) 321 (S.C.C.).

7. Translation of paragraph: The Court added that certain restrictions could be justified "in the name of impartiality, neutrality and integrity," but that that did not authorize "too draconian measures ... outrageously imposed," when other "more flexible" measures would enable the same objective to be reached. There exists "a possible arrangement which takes into account the particular hierarchical status of the candidate."

8. The question of the involvement of provincial public servants in municipal politics with respect to the *Canadian Charter of Rights and Freedoms* is also dealt with in the *O.P.S.E.U.* (1988) judgement. Other Ontario judgements have dealt with the involvement of municipal or local public servants in municipal politics (*Jones* 1988, Reid J.; *Rheaume* 1989, McKein J.).

9. In certain well-known democratic countries, such as France, public servants in general may occupy posts within political parties but they must nevertheless constantly practise an attitude of "reserve." However, senior officers named by decree and ministerial advisers in the hands of the government are in a special situation. On these questions as a whole, see Stefano (1979, 35ff., 122ff. and 149ff.).

10. In countries like France, senior officials, whether at the central, regional or departmental levels, are subject to relative ineligibility. Only ministerial advisers must abandon their posts. All other eligible public servants have the right to an electoral leave taking various forms. Even during an election campaign, however, the obligation of "reserve" persists, although it is attenuated, according to well-established jurisprudence of the Conseil d'État (Stefano 1979, 167ff.).

11. "Regulations on political activities in other provinces (e.g., New Brunswick, Quebec, Ontario) are similar to federal regulations."

REFERENCES

Alberta. *Public Service Act,* R.S.A. 1980, c. P-31, s. 29.

Alberta. *Code of Conduct and Ethics.* In Legislative Assembly, *Debates,* 15 May 1978, 1215.

Andrews v. Law Society (B.C.), [1989] 1 S.C.R. 143.

Beaudoin, Gérald-A. 1983. "Les droits démocratiques." *Canadian Bar Review* 61:151–56.

————. 1989. "Democratic Rights." In *The Canadian Charter of Rights and Freedoms.* 2d ed., ed. Gérald-A. Beaudoin and Ed Ratushny. Toronto: Carswell.

Beckton, Clare F. 1989. "Freedom of Expression." In *The Canadian Charter of Rights and Freedoms.* 2d ed., ed. Gérald-A. Beaudoin and Ed Ratushny. Toronto: Carswell.

Brewer v. Canada (Treasury Board), Public Service Staff Relations Board, No. 161-25354, 11 April 1979; [(1980), 27 L.A.C. (2d) 201 (Can. P.S.S.R.B.)].

British Columbia. *Public Service Act,* R.S.B.C. 1979, c. 343.1.

Brun, H., and C. Brunelle. 1988. "Les statuts respectifs de citoyen, résident et étranger, à la lumière des Chartes des droits." *Cahiers de droit* 29:689–731.

Canada. Bill C-70. *An Act to amend the Hazardous Products Act and the Canada Code, to enact the Hazardous Materials Information Review Act and to amend other Acts in relation thereto.* 2nd Session, 33rd Parl. 1986–87–88. First reading 22 June 1987.

————. Bill C-157. *An Act to amend the Public Service Employment Act and the Auditor General Act in consequence thereof.* 2nd Session, 33rd Parl. 1986–87–88. First reading 30 Aug. 1988.

————. Bill C-273. *An Act respecting rights of public employees.* 2nd Session, 33rd Parl. 1986–87–88. First reading 26 Nov. 1987.

————. *Canada Elections Act,* R.S.C. 1979, c. 14 (1st Supp.).

————. *Canada Elections Act,* R.S.C. 1985, c. E-2, ss. 21, 27, 77–78.

————. *Canadian Charter of Rights and Freedoms,* ss. 1–3, 7–15, 23, 29. Part I of the *Constitution Act, 1982,* being Schedule B of the *Canada Act 1982* (U.K.), 1982, c. 11.

————. *Public Service Employment Act,* R.S.C. 1970, c. P-32, s. 32.

————. *Public Service Employment Act,* R.S.C. 1985, c. P-33, ss. 32–34.

————. *Public Service Staff Relations Act,* R.S.C. 1985, c. P-35.

Canada. Task Force on Conflicts of Interest. 1984. *Ethical Conduct in the Public Sector.* Ottawa: Minister of Supply and Services Canada.

Cassidy, Michael. 1986. "Political Rights for Public Servants: A Federal Perspective." *Canadian Public Administration* 29:653–64.

Cotler, Irwin. 1989. "Freedom of Conscience and Religion." In *The Canadian Charter of Rights and Freedoms.* 2d ed., ed. Gérald-A. Beaudoin and Ed Ratushny. Toronto: Carswell.

Dick v. Ontario (Attorney General) (1973), 2 O.R. (2d) 313 (Div. Ct.).

Dussault, R., and L. Borgeat. 1986. *Traité de droit administratif,* vol. 2. Quebec: Presses de l'Université Laval.

Emerson, Thomas. 1963. "Toward a General Theory of the First Amendment." *Yale Law Journal* 72:877–956.

———. 1970. *The System of Freedom of Expression*. New York: Random House.

Ford v. Quebec (Attorney General), [1988] 2 S.C.R. 712.

Fraser v. Nova Scotia (Attorney General) (1986), 30 D.L.R. (4th) 340 (N.S.T.D.).

Fraser v. Public Service Staff Relations Board, [1985] 2 S.C.R. 455.

Garant, Patrice. 1985. *Droit administratif*. 2d ed. Montreal: Les Éditions Yvon Blais.

Institute of Public Administration of Canada. 1986. *Statement of Principles Regarding the Conduct of Public Employees*. In Kenneth Kernaghan, "Political Rights and Political Neutrality: Finding the Balance Point." *Canadian Public Administration* 29 (1986): 639–52.

Irwin Toy v. Quebec (Attorney General), [1989] 1 S.C.R. 927.

Jones v. Ontario (Attorney General) (1988), 65 O.R. (2d) 737 (H.C.).

Kernaghan, Kenneth. 1986. "Political Rights and Political Neutrality: Finding the Balance Point." *Canadian Public Administration* 29:639–52.

Law Society of Upper Canada v. Skapinker, [1984] 1 S.C.R. 357.

Luscher v. Deputy Minister of National Revenue (Customs & Excise), [1985] 1 F.C.. 85 (C.A.).

McKay v. R. (1981), 28 L.A.C. (2d) 441 (Ont. C.E.G.S.B.).

Manitoba. *Civil Service Act*, R.S.M. 1987, c. C-110, s. 44.

New Brunswick. *Civil Service Act*, S.N.B. 1984 c. C-5.1, s. 27.

Northwest Territories. *Public Service Act*, S.N.W.T. 1965, c. 9.

Nova Scotia. *Civil Service Act*, S.N.S. 1980, c. 3, s. 34.

———. *Civil Service Act*, R.S.N.S. 1989, c. 70, ss. 38–40.

———. *Civil Service Collective Bargaining Act*, R.S.N.S. 1989, c. 71.

———. *House of Assembly Act*, R.S.N.S. 1989, c. 210.

Ontario. *Public Service Act*, R.S.O. 1980, c. 418, ss. 12–15; R.R.O. 1980, Reg. 881; am. O. Reg. 38–84, ss. 1, 14, 74, Sched. 2.

Ontario Film and Video Appreciation Society v. Ontario (Board of Censors) (1983), 41 O.R. (2d) 583 (Div. Ct.); affirmed (1984), 45 O.R. (2d) 80 (C.A.).

Ontario Law Reform Commission. 1986. *Report on Political Activity, Public Comment and Disclosure by Crown Employees*. Toronto: Ministry of the Attorney General.

Ontario. Public Service Commission. 1985. "Political Activity: What's Allowed." *Topical*, 12 April, 6.

O.P.S.E.U. v. Ontario (Attorney General), [1987] 2 S.C.R. 2.

O.P.S.E.U. v. Ontario (Attorney General) (1988), 65 O.R. (2d) 689 (H.C.).

Osborne v. Canada, [1988] 3 F.C. 219 (C.A.), reversing in part [1986] 3 F.C. 206 (T.D.). Affirmed (1991), 82 D.L.R. (4th) 321 (S.C.C.).

Pickering v. Board of Education 391 U.S. 563 (1968).

Prince Edward Island. *Civil Service Act*, R.S.P.E.I. 1988, c. 8, ss. 38–40.

Quebec. *Attorney General's Prosecutors, An Act respecting*, R.S.Q. c. S-35, s. 8.

———. *Charter of the French language*, R.S.Q. c. C-11.

———. *Charter of human rights and freedoms*, R.S.Q. c. C-12.

———. *Election Act*, R.S.Q. c. E-3.3, s. 498.

———. *Labour Code*, R.S.Q. c. C-27.

———. *Public Service Act*, R.S.Q. c. F-3.1.1, ss. 10–12, 24.

R. v. Big M Drug Mart Ltd., [1985] S.C.R. 295.

R. v. Edwards Books and Art Ltd., [1986] 2 S.C.R. 713.

R. v. Morgentaler, [1988] 1 S.C.R. 30.

R. v. Oakes, [1986] 1 S.C.R. 103.

R. v. Turpin, [1989] 1 S.C.R. 1296.

Reference re Alberta Statutes, [1938] S.C.R. 100.

Reference re Public Service Employee Relations Act (Alta.), [1987] 1 S.C.R. 313.

Reference re ss. 193 and 195.1(1)(c) of the Criminal Code (Man.), [1990] 1 S.C.R. 1123.

Rheaume v. Ontario (Attorney General) (1989), 63 D.L.R. (4th) 241 (Ont. H.C.).

Rio Hotel v. New Brunswick (Liquor Licensing Board) (1986), 29 D.L.R. (4th) 662 (N.B.C.A.); affirmed [1987] 2 S.C.R. 59.

R.W.D.S.U., Local 580 v. Dolphin Delivery, [1986] 2 S.C.R. 573.

Saskatchewan. *Public Service Act*, R.S.S. 1978, c. P-42, s. 50.

Slaight Communications Inc. v. Davidson, [1989] 1 S.C.R. 1038.

Southam Inc. v. Hunter, Director of Investigation and Research, [1984] 2 S.C.R. 145.

Stefano, A.D. 1979. *La participation des fonctionnaires civils à la vie politique*. Paris: Librairie générale de droit et de jurisprudence.

Switzman v. Elbling, [1957] S.C.R. 285.

Tassé, R. 1989. "Application of the Canadian Charter of Rights and Freedoms." In *The Canadian Charter of Rights and Freedoms*. 2d ed., ed. Gérald-A. Beaudoin and Ed Ratushny. Toronto: Carswell.

Tremblay, André. 1986. "La liberté d'expression au Canada: le cheminement vers la marche libre des idées." In *Perspectives canadiennes et européennes des droits de la personne*, ed. Gérald-A. Beaudoin and Daniel Turp. Cowansville: Les Éditions Yvon Blais.

Tremblay v. Public Service Commission, [1990] R.J.Q. 1386.

Tremblay v. Quebec (Minister of Justice) (1989), 6 R.D.C.F.P. 145.

United Kingdom. *Constitution Act, 1867*, 30 & 31 Vict., c. 3, s. 93.

Verge, P. 1985. *Le droit de grève : fondements et limites*. Cowansville: Les Éditions Yvon Blais.

Yukon. *Public Service Commission Act*, R.S.Y.T. 1986, c. 141, ss. 160–70.

———. *Public Service Commission Regulations*, R.Y.T. 1976/165, s. 180; am. O.I.C. 1987/75.

5

THE POLITICAL RIGHTS OF CANADA'S FEDERAL PUBLIC SERVANTS

Kenneth Kernaghan

THE ISSUE

T HE PRIMARY ISSUE examined in this study is the extent to which federal public servants should be permitted to exercise political rights. This issue involves a search for the optimum balance between promoting the individual rights of public servants and preserving the political neutrality and efficiency of the public service. While the focus of this study is on the political and managerial dimensions of the political rights debate, some reference is necessarily made to legal and constitutional implications.[1]

The issue of political rights for public servants is more complex and has more far-reaching ramifications than many commentators seem to recognize. There is often a "knee-jerk" reaction in favour of expanding political rights by those who do not understand, or who minimize unduly, the implications for the political system. Similarly, there is frequently an instinctive resistance to expanding these rights by those who wish to preserve the status quo in the face of changing political and constitutional circumstances.

The most vigorous advocates of expanding the political rights of public servants have been the New Democratic Party and the public service unions. Other major participants in the political system have supporters on both sides of the issue, but it is notable that most public service executives and managers oppose significant expansion of political rights.

While the public debate on this issue centres on considerations of individual rights and political neutrality, it must be recognized that other objectives are also being pursued. For example, public service managers want to avoid the administrative hassles of dealing with a more politically active workforce; some politicians want public servants to be able to work for them in a more high-profile way both during and between election campaigns; and public service unions want to enhance their political power. One public service union, in a research report on political rights, began by asserting that "wage controls, government cutbacks, layoffs and legislation limiting collective bargaining ... are political attacks on provincial government workers ... If provincial workers do not take a more active political role their voice will not be heard and they will continue to be pawns in their employers' political games" (National Union of Provincial Government Employees, undated, 1).

The first part of this study explains the meaning of the terms "political rights" and "political neutrality" and the evolution of political neutrality in Canada. This is followed in the second part by an examination of the rationales for limiting and permitting the exercise of political rights by public servants. The third part contains a brief examination of lessons to be learned from the experience of other government jurisdictions, both in Canada and elsewhere. The final part provides an analysis of section 33 of the *Public Service Employment Act* (*PSEA*) and of proposals for amending this section.

It is important to note that the political partisanship section of the *PSEA*, which was formerly section 32, is now section 33, R.S.C. 1985.

The Meaning of Political Rights

The term "political rights" refers here to the right to engage in partisan political activity and in public comment on government decisions and proposals.

Partisan Political Activity

Participation in partisan political activity includes the following broad range of activities:

- voting in elections;
- seeking election to public office;
- being a member of a political party or organization;
- working in a campaign office;
- holding an office in a political party or organization;
- attending political meetings, rallies and conventions;
- speaking in support of or in opposition to a particular candidate at political meetings, rallies or conventions;
- serving as a delegate or alternate to a political party convention; and

- campaigning for or against a political party or candidate by such means as making a financial contribution; soliciting financial or other contributions; door-to-door canvassing; distributing campaign material, wearing political badges, displaying lawn signs, etc.; working at the polls in a partisan capacity; and transporting voters to the polls on behalf of a political party or candidate.

These partisan political activities can be grouped into two broad categories: *low-profile* activities, such as belonging to a political party and attending political meetings, and *high-profile* activities, such as canvassing door-to-door and soliciting financial contributions.

The term "political activity" covers a broad range of activities. "A variety of activities, covering a spectrum of commitment and involvement, may justifiably be regarded as political. At one end of the continuum, a person may run for office as a candidate of a party during a federal or provincial election; at the other, a person may simply donate funds anonymously to a political cause that is unrelated to a particular political party. In between are a host of different political activities involving varying degrees of commitment, action, and publicity" (Ontario Law Reform Commission 1986, 74). Thus it is useful, but not always easy, to distinguish between *partisan* political activities and *nonpartisan* political activities. Nonpartisan political activities are activities that do not specifically relate to a federal or provincial political party, but as we shall see below, activities intended to be nonpartisan may be perceived as partisan.

Public Comment

Participation in public comment normally involves speaking or writing for public consumption on issues of government policy or administration or on matters of political controversy. While the term "public comment" covers both criticism and praise of government, most of the debate on the limits of appropriate public comment for public servants focuses on criticism of government.

The rights to engage in partisan political activity and in public comment are separate, but related, rights. Clearly, involvement in high-profile partisan politics often requires the public expression of personal or partisan views on government policies or programs. It is, however, often difficult to distinguish between public criticism of government that is motivated by partisan considerations and criticism that is motivated by other considerations. Public comment can be of either a partisan or nonpartisan nature. Public servants, who are not normally permitted to campaign in a high-profile manner for political parties or candidates, must avoid involvement in public criticism of government that is, or appears to be, partisan in nature.

There are several forms of public comment, and it is not easy to draw a precise line between those forms that are required or permissible and those that are questionable or prohibited (see appendix B). This explains in part why so few governments provide clear rules on the permissible limits of public comment. Public servants are often obliged to seek guidance by referring to conventions, understandings and practices rather than written rules. There is, therefore, room for differences of opinion on what constitutes permissible public comment. This situation can have a chilling impact on the participation of public servants in legitimate forms of public comment.

Public servants, especially at senior levels, have traditionally been restricted in the expression of public criticism of government, regardless of their motivation. The *Statement of Principles* of the Institute of Public Administration of Canada (IPAC) (1986) provides general guidance in this area by asserting that "public employees should not express their personal views on matters of political controversy or on government policy or administration when such comment is likely to impair public confidence in the objective and efficient performance of their duties." The statement also notes that "it is the responsibility of public employees to seek approval from the appropriate governmental authority whenever they are uncertain as to the legality or propriety of expressing their personal views." Similarly, the Supreme Court of Canada has stated that we have a "tradition surrounding our public service" that "emphasizes the characteristics of impartiality, neutrality, fairness and integrity ... [E]mployment in the public service involves acceptance of certain restraints. One of the most important of those restraints is to exercise caution when it comes to making criticisms of Government" (*Fraser* 1985, 471).

Section 33 of the *PSEA* makes no explicit reference to any form of public comment. By restricting certain partisan political activities, however, it implicitly restricts public comment of a partisan nature.

The Meaning of Political Neutrality

Political neutrality is a constitutional convention. It provides that public servants should avoid activities likely to impair, or to seem to impair, their political impartiality or the political impartiality of the public service.

In the context of Canada's parliamentary–cabinet form of government, the interpretation of "political neutrality" as simply the avoidance of partisan politics and public comment is unduly narrow. This narrow interpretation can be used manipulatively to obscure important aspects of the political rights debate. Such restrictive usage is more appropriate in the U.S. presidential–congressional system, which has no element of ministerial responsibility and in which public service anonymity is less important.

The full meaning of political neutrality is encompassed by the ideal model of political neutrality provided below.[2] The model sets out the requisites for an absolutely politically neutral public service in Canada's federal and provincial governments. The current state of political neutrality in various governments – and the desirability and feasibility of reform – can be assessed by examining the extent to which policies and practices in these governments depart from this model. The requirements of the model are as follows:

- Politics and policy are separated from administration; thus politicians make policy decisions and public servants execute these decisions.
- Public servants are appointed and promoted on the basis of merit rather than of party affiliation or contributions.
- Public servants do not engage in partisan political activities.
- Public servants do not express publicly their personal views on government policies or administration.
- Public servants provide forthright and objective advice to their political masters in private and in confidence; in return, political executives protect the anonymity of public servants by publicly accepting responsibility for departmental decisions.
- Public servants execute policy decisions loyally irrespective of the philosophy and programs of the party in power and regardless of their personal opinions; as a result, public servants enjoy security of tenure during good behaviour and satisfactory performance.

The centrality of these requirements in contemporary Canadian government is demonstrated by the federal government's recent statement on the unchanging values that "have characterized the Public Service since early in this century" (Canada, Public Service 2000, 1990, 14). These values include:

- loyalty to the duly elected government;
- honesty, integrity and nonpartisanship; ...
- faithfulness to the principles of fairness and impartiality; [and]
- professionalism in carrying out their duties. (Ibid.,13)

The model of political neutrality serves three purposes. First, it shows that the requirements of political neutrality are interrelated; thus, a change in one of them may well influence one or more of the others. For example, the reality or the appearance of senior public servants participating in high-profile partisan politics or in public criticism of government may undermine their security of tenure. Second, the model makes it obvious that there has been a gradual evolution in the inter-pretation and application of the convention of political neutrality; the current policies and practices of governments in Canada depart substan-tially from some of the model's requirements. Finally, the model indi-cates the close relationship between the concept of political neutrality and several issues of enduring importance in public debate, including the political rights of public servants.

The Evolution of Political Neutrality

In Canada, political neutrality has long been a central convention of the Constitution. According to the Ontario Court of Appeal, "[c]learly there was a convention of political neutrality of Crown servants at the time of Confederation and the reasoning in support of such conven-tion has been consistent throughout the subsequent years." Moreover, "the political neutrality or impartiality of Crown servants is a neces-sary and fundamental doctrine of the Canadian Constitution, adopted from the Constitution of the United Kingdom" (*O.P.S.E.U.* 1980, 330). This convention of political neutrality was reinforced early in this century by statutory provisions on the political activities of public servants. Mr. Justice Beetz of the Supreme Court of Canada has asserted that federal and provincial legislation on the partisan political activi-ties of public servants forms an "integrated scheme [that], considered as a whole, is meant to protect the principle of responsible government which is common to both orders of government" (*O.P.S.E.U.* 1987, 53).

Historically, limits on the partisan political activities of public servants have resulted primarily from the desire to promote merit and efficiency in the public service by reducing patronage appointments. For several decades after Confederation, the federal government was riddled with appointments based on partisan political affiliation rather than on merit. To increase merit and efficiency, the *Civil Service Act* of 1918 introduced competitive examinations and restricted partisan political activity. Section 32 of the Act provided that no public servant could "engage in partisan work in connection with any ... election, or contribute, receive or in any way deal with any money for party funds." Over the next 40 years, the number of patronage appointments grad-ually declined, so that by the 1960s political patronage was no longer considered a major impediment to merit and efficiency in the federal public service. This development led in part to the significant expansion of the political rights of public servants contained in section 32 of the 1967 *PSEA*. The continuing restrictions after 1967 on high-profile partisan political activities were motivated by a desire to preserve the political neutrality and efficiency of the public service.

The Current Meaning of Political Neutrality

The present status of the convention of political neutrality can be explained by a summary statement of the extent to which governments in Canada have, in general, departed from the requirements of political neutrality outlined in the model described above.[3]

First, politics, policy and administration are closely interrelated, not separated. Politicians and public servants are involved in both the making and implementation of policy decisions. Elected officials, notably cabinet ministers, make final decisions on major policy matters, but public servants influence these decisions and make decisions of their own under authority delegated by Cabinet and the legislature.

Second, the vast majority of public service appointments are made on the basis of merit, or fitness for the job. A substantial number of appointments are based on contributions to the governing political party, but at a senior level, most of these political appointments are made to agencies, boards or commissions rather than to regular government departments. Patronage appointments continue to be made at relatively low levels of the public service in some Canadian jurisdictions.

Third, public servants do participate in certain partisan political activities. In some jurisdictions, this participation is limited to low-profile activities such as making financial contributions to, and holding membership in, a political party. In others, public servants who wish to stand for public office are required to seek permission for a leave of absence. In still others, public servants are specifically forbidden to engage in partisan political activity while at work, and their political and administrative superiors are forbidden to coerce them into performing partisan work.

Fourth, in most governments, public servants are restricted, usually by convention rather than by written rules, in the expression of personal views on government policies or administration. Moreover, they are forbidden both by law and convention to engage in forms of public comment in which they make use of confidential information to which they are privy by virtue of their official position. Many public servants are, however, required to engage in public comment during the performance of their official duties. The difficulty of drawing a clear line between permissible and unacceptable forms of public comment prompts public servants to be cautious when speaking or writing for public consumption.

Fifth, public servants provide their ministers with objective advice in confidence. In return, ministers normally fulfil their responsibility to protect the anonymity of public servants by shielding them from public criticism. Public service anonymity has been diminished to some extent by the role that public servants are required to play in explaining policies and programs to the public and to legislators. In playing this role, public servants must be careful not to infringe on their minister's sphere of responsibility by justifying, or speculating on, government policy.

Sixth, public servants are expected to carry out the decisions of their minister loyally, whether they agree with the decisions or not. In return, public servants can usually expect to enjoy permanence in office, except in the event of staff cut-backs, unsatisfactory performance or bad behaviour. With a change of government, however, public servants who are political appointees are likely to lose their positions.

THE RATIONALES FOR LIMITING AND EXPANDING POLITICAL RIGHTS

Informed commentators argue for neither the completely unfettered exercise of political rights nor the absolute prohibition of these rights. Rather, they seek a balance between the need for political rights on the one hand and the need for a politically impartial and efficient public service on the other. However, considerable disagreement remains on where the balance should be struck.

The IPAC *Statement of Principles* captures the challenge in its assertion that "public employees should enjoy the fullest possible measure of political rights that is compatible with laws, regulations and conventions designed to preserve the political neutrality of the public service." Then, to elaborate this general principle, the Statement enjoins public servants to refrain from partisan political activities that are likely to impair their political neutrality and to avoid public comment that "is likely to impair public confidence in the objective and efficient performance of their duties." Similarly, with specific reference to political partisanship, Mr. Justice Walsh of the Federal Court (Trial Division) has concluded that "a public servant in entering the public service must or should realize that the political neutrality required will necessarily result in some curtailment of his or her partisan political activity even if this involves some restriction of freedom of speech or freedom of association. These restrictions should be as few as possible and no more than are necessary to attain the objective of political neutrality" (*Osborne* 1986, 682).

The rationales for and against expanding the political rights of public servants presented below apply to both partisan political activity and public comment.[4]

The Rationale for Limiting Political Rights

The arguments for limiting the political rights of public servants centre on preserving political neutrality, but also include concerns about public service efficiency. The major arguments are as follows:

1. *To preserve public trust in government, public servants must be – and must appear to be – politically impartial in the development and implementation of public policy. Members of the public must be assured that political affiliation is not a consideration in any dealings they may have with public servants.*

It is argued that the involvement of public servants in high-profile partisan politics and in public criticism of government can diminish public confidence in the impartiality of the public service and that this can have damaging effects on the public's faith in government as a whole. In support of this argument, the federal Task Force on Conflict of Interest stated that "the public interest demands the maintenance of political impartiality in the public service and of confidence in that impartiality as an essential part of the structure of government in this country" (Canada, Task Force 1984, 46). The reality and the appearance of impartiality have become more important as the general public has become more aware of the power and influence of public servants in the formulation and implementation of public policy.

In opposition to this view is the argument that only senior-level public servants exercise significant power and influence and that limits on political rights are, therefore, needed only at that level. Moreover, most of the interaction between citizens and public servants is at the middle and lower levels of the public service. The usual response to this argument is that many public servants below the senior levels of the administrative hierarchy make discretionary decisions that significantly affect the rights and livelihood of individual citizens. Some commentators go further by arguing that the involvement of large numbers of public servants in partisan politics, regardless of their level in the hierarchy, will damage the credibility and integrity of the public service. One commentator argues that "with 75 per cent of the public service exempt from restrictions on partisan political activities and with a large number of these public servants actively engaged in one form or another of partisan politics, the public at large could no longer have confidence in the impartiality of the public service" (Gallant 1986, 666). In this connection, it is notable that 30.8 percent of the 1 100 public servants surveyed for the federal Public Service Commission indicated that they would participate more actively in partisan politics if the current restrictions were eased (Carleton University 1985).

A commentator on the other side of the political rights issue agrees that the liberalization of political rights may lead some employees to "become more open in their political activity." But he doubts that "the proportions involved will greatly increase ... Some federal employees will choose to remain politically neutral even if the law changes because of how they see the requirements of their job. Many will remain uninvolved for the same reasons that most Canadians in the private sector do not participate in politics: lack of interest, or other claims on their time" (Cassidy 1986, 657).

The convention of political neutrality requires that public servants avoid the *appearance*, as well as the reality, of involvement in activities that impair their political impartiality or that of the public service as a whole. This point is related to the earlier reference to the difficulty of distinguishing partisan from nonpartisan activity and of discerning the motivation for criticism of government. For example, public servants who criticize government policies or personalities in public may undermine public confidence in their impartiality, regardless of the motivation for their action.

> 2. *Public servants must be – and must appear to be – politically impartial in order to retain the trust of their political superiors, who are dependent on them for objective policy advice and for effective policy implementation.*

As explained above, political neutrality is closely related to two other constitutional conventions: ministerial responsibility and public service anonymity.[5] The federal government, in its white paper on the renewal of the public service, states that "the principle of ministerial responsibility governs the Public Service ... ministers are *elected to decide* whereas officials are *appointed to administer and advise*" (Canada, Public Service 2000, 1990, 7–8).

Collective ministerial responsibility requires that Cabinet answer to Parliament for both the content and the administration of government policies and that the Cabinet resign if it loses a vote of confidence in Parliament. Ministers are expected, on pain of resignation, to maintain cabinet solidarity by refraining from public criticism of government policies and proposals. *Individual* ministerial responsibility requires that ministers answer to Parliament for all of the administrative errors of their department in that they must resign in the event of serious error by their departmental subordinates; and that ministers explain and defend before Parliament the actions of their departments. The ministers' acceptance of public praise and public blame for all of the activities of their departments helps to preserve the anonymity of public servants by protecting them from public visibility and attack. Public servants are, for their part, expected to retain their anonymity by providing impartial advice to ministers in private and in confidence and by avoiding activities that impair their ability to carry out their duties in a politically impartial manner.

Despite gradual modifications in practice of the conventions of ministerial responsibility and public service anonymity, they remain central elements of the Canadian Constitution. It is not surprising, therefore, that ministers should be concerned about the involvement of public servants in highly visible partisan politics and public comment. Can ministers reasonably be expected to refrain from public debate with public servants who criticize individual departments or the government as a whole and, thereby, affect adversely the ministers' electoral fortunes? Under these circumstances, will ministers have sufficient confidence in the political impartiality of public servants? Will ministers be tempted to punish their detractors and reward their supporters by resorting to patronage appointments and promotions? Will security of tenure for public servants be undermined?

In this connection, a federal deputy minister recently advised that "having the legal right to work for a political party does not guarantee that no penalties of *any* kind will be incurred by those who choose to exercise this right. Despite the fact that partisan activity by federal public servants has been prohibited by law for decades, it has not been uncommon for incoming Ministers to feel a need to satisfy themselves that their officials really are neutral, and for this purpose, to have inquiries made about possible political linkages of various individuals" (Kroeger 1991, 9).

It must be recognized that the actions of the ministers themselves have endangered the tradition of political neutrality. They have helped to politicize the public service by making patronage appointments, by using public servants for partisan purposes and by seconding public servants to their political staffs (Jackson 1989). These actions suggest that some ministers, at least, are not so much concerned about having neutral public servants as they are about having loyal public servants.

3. *Opposition parties must have trust in the political impartiality of public servants so that there will not be a politically motivated turnover of public servants with a change of government.*

The concerns of opposition members of the legislature about the political activities and public comment of public servants are similar to those of members on the government side noted above. Security of tenure for public servants normally requires that they carry out policy decisions loyally, regardless of the policies of the governing party and of their personal views. When an opposition party becomes the governing party, can it be expected to have confidence in the loyalty of public servants who have campaigned in a high-profile way for other political parties?

During the last decade, senior officials in some governments have been removed following a change of government, not only because they engaged in partisan political activity, but merely because they were perceived to be too closely associated with the policies of the former governing party. There is a tendency for an incoming government to distrust high-level officials who have served the previous government. Indeed, during recent election campaigns, there have been strong calls for the replacement of senior career public servants with partisan political appointees. While most governments have resisted pressures to politicize the senior levels of the *departmental* public service, a large number of political appointments have been made to semi-independent agencies, boards and commissions. These appointees are likely to be replaced by supporters of the incoming party in the event of a change of government. Another consideration is that politically active public servants who appear before legislative committees are more likely to be subjected to partisan attacks by legislators of a different partisan stripe.

On the basis of these considerations, it is argued that high-profile participation in partisan politics by public servants below the senior echelons of the departmental public service could have two consequences. First, opposition parties would have less trust in the loyalty and political impartiality of public servants. Second, ministers of a new government would be tempted to make partisan appointments to senior public service posts to ensure the loyalty of at least their most senior advisers. These considerations are closely related to the next argument for limiting political rights.

4. *The expansion of political partisanship may result in the re-emergence of the patronage system of hiring and promotion with a consequent decline in merit and in public service efficiency and effectiveness. Both the public and public servants must be assured that appointment and advancement in the service are based on merit rather than on party affiliation.*

The stringent restrictions on the political rights of public servants before 1967 were based on the desire to minimize political appointments to, and promotions within, the public service and thereby to enhance administrative efficiency. The question to be answered now is whether the restrictions contained in the *PSEA* of 1967 can be loosened without bringing about an increase in political and bureaucratic patronage.

As noted above, the involvement of more public servants in more high-profile partisan politics would tempt ministers to expand patronage appointments and, with a change of government, to replace the political appointees of the former government with their own supporters. Moreover, the more partisan working environment resulting from increased political partisanship could result in greater *bureaucratic* patronage in the appointment process. Many public servants have different political views and allegiances from their administrative superiors. Relationships on the job could be aggravated by the more active and public manifestation of these differences. Public service managers might be more inclined to appoint people who share their political views or affiliations. Bureaucratic patronage would be even more likely if senior public servants themselves were patronage appointees.

Many appointments could be based more on partisan considerations than on the merit principle of selecting the candidate best qualified for the job. Public service executives and managers would be challenged to avoid adverse effects on public service efficiency and the notion of a career public service. In the survey of public servants mentioned earlier, 28.1 percent of those interviewed believed that permitting public servants to be more active in partisan politics would increase conflicts and confrontation with the people they work with on a day-to-day basis. As many as 52.8 percent felt that there would be more problems between employees and management. Finally, 46.3 percent of the respondents thought that the career prospects of public servants would be affected, and 65.5 percent of these respondents believed that the area most affected would be job promotion prospects (Carleton University 1985). It is significant that two of the central principles of career public service are that appointments to, and within, the public service are based on merit, in the sense that the person appointed is the one who is best qualified; and that appointments are free from partisan political considerations.

5. *Public servants must be protected against financial or other forms of exploitation by political or administrative superiors who are affiliated with a specific political party or candidate. Public servants can both*

> *suffer and prosper unfairly from actively supporting a political party*
> *other than that to which their political superior belongs or with which*
> *an administrative superior is affiliated.*

This argument also relates to the career prospects of public servants. The concern here is that if public servants have the right to participate in partisan political activities, they are vulnerable to being pressured by political and bureaucratic superiors into participating in a specified direction. "The freer the employees are to engage in voluntary political activity, the greater is the possibility that they will be coerced into involuntary political activity" (Bolton 1976, 13). An expansion of political rights may mean that public servants are no longer able to refuse to participate, even in highly visible partisan politics, by referring to statutory constraints on their participation. They are, therefore, more exposed to exploitation by people wishing to support particular political parties or candidates.

To discourage such exploitation, the IPAC *Statement of Principles* (1986) provides that public servants "should not be compelled to engage in partisan political activities or be subject to threats or discrimination for refusing to engage in such activities." The potential for abuse in this area is so great that some governments provide specific statutory protection against coercion to participate in political activities.

In the United States, the argument is often made that the expansion of political rights for public servants can lead to political exploitation not only by hierarchical superiors but also by the *public service unions*, to which the great majority of public servants belong.

The Rationale for Expanding Political Rights

The major arguments for expanding the political rights of public servants are as follows:

1. *Public servants should be permitted to exercise the fundamental rights of freedom of expression and of association guaranteed to all citizens; they should not be treated as second-class citizens.*

This is the primary reason given for enhancing the political rights of public servants. Section 2 of the *Canadian Charter of Rights and Freedoms* guarantees to everyone the fundamental freedoms of expression and association. It is argued that limits on these freedoms, including limits on the full exercise of political rights, must meet the requirement of section 1 of the Charter that these limits be "such reasonable limits prescribed by law as can be demonstrably justified in a free and democratic society."

The differences of opinion among politicians, public servants and academics on what constitutes reasonable limits are shared by the judges of our highest courts. In 1986, Mr. Justice Grant of the Supreme Court of Nova Scotia struck down sections of the *Civil Service Act* of that province because certain limits on partisan political activity contained therein were deemed incompatible with the Charter's guarantees of fundamental freedoms (*Fraser* 1986). But in the same year, Mr. Justice Walsh of the Federal Court (Trial Division) upheld the political partisanship section of the federal *PSEA* because of the need to preserve the tradition of political neutrality (*Osborne* 1986, 662). This decision was partially reversed by the Federal Court of Appeal in 1988 and was heard on appeal by the Supreme Court of Canada in 1990. In June 1991, while this study was in production, the Supreme Court struck down the political partisanship section of the *PSEA*. The Court acknowledged the importance of the principle of political neutrality and ruled that the political rights of federal public servants were unduly restricted. The Court declined to specify where the balance between political rights and political neutrality should be struck; the task of redrafting the section was explicitly left to Parliament (*Osborne* 1991). In 1988, the Ontario High Court of Justice upheld the political activity section of the *Ontario Public Service Act* as compatible with the *Canadian Charter of Rights and Freedoms* (*O.P.S.E.U.* 1988).

Proponents of the expansion of political rights acknowledge that some limits are necessary, but they argue that the limits are often unduly restrictive. They note first that fears about the negative impact of increased political rights on the reality and perception of the political neutrality of the public service are exaggerated. For example, "even if a citizen knows the political stripe of the person who sells wine and spirits, or clears snow from the highway, or operates a word processor, there is little rational cause for any member of the public to think that the service thus being performed is in any way affected by those political leanings" (Ontario Law Reform Commission 1986, 261).

The argument is also made that limits need to be applied only to those public servants at fairly senior levels who provide policy advice and who perform duties in such sensitive areas as regulation and personnel management. Moreover, there is a very large number of public servants who have no face-to-face contact with the public and whose political activities could not reasonably be viewed as undermining public confidence in the impartiality and integrity of the public service. Most public servants are "secretaries, clerks, technicians, or blue-collar workers. In other words, they have jobs similar to other average Canadians and it is steadfastly wrong to deny them the rights other Canadians have. Even where the responsibilities of some public employees are more sensitive, the law is still too restrictive and too arbitrarily applied" (Cassidy 1986, 664). It is on the basis of this reasoning that some governments divide all public servants into two or three categories according to the need for restrictions on their political activities.

> 2. *Limits on the political rights of public servants deprive both the general public and political parties of valuable information and insights on public affairs.*

There is no doubt that the public service, especially at its middle and senior levels, contains a large number of well-educated and knowledgeable people. Moreover, the average public servant is likely to be better informed than the average Canadian citizen about public affairs and is, therefore, in a better position to make a useful contribution to political debate. This argument is even more persuasive if the issue being debated is directly related to the public servant's department or responsibilities. Isn't one of the best people to comment on the quality of environmental protection an employee involved in environmental regulation? Isn't one of the best people to comment on problems of food poisoning an inspector for the Department of Agriculture? If it should be considered inappropriate for such employees to comment on these matters in a partisan context either during or between election campaigns, couldn't such comment be permitted in a nonpartisan context?

It is helpful to examine this argument in the sphere of public comment. As explained earlier, it is difficult to distinguish partisan from nonpartisan public comment, and public servants who speak out publicly against government policies and programs can embarrass their minister and their department. Moreover, the Supreme Court has ruled that the freedom of public servants to criticize the government is not an absolute freedom and that public criticism of policies with which public servants are directly involved is *more* problematic than comment on other policies because it might affect their ability to perform their duties effectively or the public's perception of that ability (*Fraser* 1985, 470).

Yet, the Court indicated that public comment by public servants is appropriate in certain circumstances. The Court observed that "whereas it is obvious that it would not be 'just cause' for a provincial Government to dismiss a provincial clerk who stood in a crowd on a Sunday afternoon to protest provincial day care policies, it is equally obvious that the same Government would have 'just cause' to dismiss the Deputy Minister of Social Services who spoke vigorously against the same policies at the same rally" (ibid., 468). Advocates of expanding political rights contend that the rules should be clear so that those public servants whose ability to perform their duties would not be affected by certain forms of public comment or political activity can exercise their rights more fully.

3. *Limits on the political rights of public servants restrict the involvement in partisan politics and public comment of a large percentage of the labour force.*

This assertion is closely related to the two previous arguments. At present, the political rights of the 225 000 federal public servants who are subject to the *PSEA* are limited to some extent. It is argued that these limits create a large group of second-class citizens with respect to political rights and that they deprive the political system of the contributions of a significant number of knowledgeable citizens. Differential treatment of public servants according to their level and responsibilities in the service would expand the political rights of a considerable number of employees.

The additional argument is made that those who are freed for more political activity and public comment are unlikely to participate vigorously enough to diminish significantly the reality or image of public service neutrality. According to Michael Cassidy, a former member of Parliament, "despite the relatively tolerant attitude to political participation in the Ottawa area, only a very small proportion of public employees actually participate directly in election campaigns ... I would guess that no more than 5 per cent of federal employees in the capital area played a direct role in any election campaign, with perhaps another 5 per cent marginally involved through such activities as making a contribution or putting up a campaign sign" (Cassidy 1986, 656).

Moreover, some public servants are unlikely to take advantage of increased political rights because they realize that their career prospects could be detrimentally affected. It may be prudent for those who wish to be promoted to policy making and sensitive positions to refrain from political activities and public comment that may jeopardize their reputation for impartiality. While some commentators argue that the political rights of public servants should be limited to guard against this possibility, others argue that public servants should be free to use their own best judgement on the matter. In this regard, a federal deputy minister has observed that "in cases where individuals are identified, or even suspected, of having party connections of the wrong kind, there is only so much that Deputy Ministers can do to protect them ... The law prohibits such officials being fired or demoted, but is of only limited use when it comes to a variety of other, more ambiguous situations that can arise, for example, making a choice between two individuals for a particular assignment where all factors are more or less equal, except that one individual is openly allied with the Official Opposition" (Kroeger 1991, 9).

A final consideration here is that the size of the permanent public service is declining as the public service becomes increasingly populated by part-time and contract employees. Will it be practicable to impose significant restrictions on the political rights of these employees?

4. *The application of the merit principle protects the public service against political or bureaucratic patronage based on the partisan affiliation or public comments of public servants.*

The argument here is that fears about an upsurge of political and bureaucratic patronage resulting from an expansion of political rights are unwarranted. In particular, it is argued that the merit *principle,* which requires selection of the best qualified person for any job, is well established in the federal government. Moreover, while the merit *system,* which is the administrative mechanism for implementing the merit principle, permits some departures from the absolute application of the principle, these departures will not be permitted on grounds of partisan politics. Thus, public servants can feel secure that their involvement in permissible political activities will not affect their career prospects adversely. In addition, public servants can appeal against appointment or promotion decisions suspected of being based on partisan considerations.

The case of Sant P. Singh illustrates this issue well. Mr. Singh, an economist employed by the federal Department of Health and Welfare, received a leave of absence to run as a Progressive Conservative candidate in the 1974 federal election. Mr. Singh was not elected, so he returned to the public service. A few months later, when he was denied a promotion and pay increase, he filed a grievance with the Public Service Staff Relations Board claiming that he had been punished for his political activities. The Board concluded that he had been the victim of political bias and awarded him damages in the amount of $9 300 (*Singh* 1979). This case indicates that the merit principle cannot provide complete protection against political bias but that in such instances the appeal system can provide relief if the allegations can be proven.

However, some commentators contend that the merit principle cannot ensure sufficient protection against *covert* partisanship. The application of the merit principle permits the exercise of much discretion in human resource management, and subtle pressures to engage, or not to engage, in political activities can be exerted by superiors. There can be "hidden consequences for the careers of public servants who participate in political activity that is legally permissible but that is nonetheless frowned upon by political or administrative superiors" (Ontario Law Reform Commission 1986, 19). In response to this contention, the argument can be made that "the possibility that people who publicly display strong political views, or indeed strong views of any kind, might be discriminated against because of those views can scarcely argue for a suppression of those views" (ibid., 263).

5. *Knowledgeable and skilled persons whose talents are needed in government will be unwilling to accept employment in the public service if their political rights are unduly restricted.*

Given that the public service must compete with the private sector for skilled employees, it is argued that the public service should make government employment as attractive as possible; excessive restrictions on political rights would work against this objective. A related argument is that liberalizing the constraints on political rights would attract competent, politically active people to join the public service.

This argument is of secondary importance. There are few data available to confirm or deny its validity. Moreover, it is unlikely to be the decisive argument in determining the appropriate measure of political rights.

The Problem of Evidence

Another argument for expanding political rights is that the expansion of these rights in various jurisdictions has not diminished the confidence of the public and of politicians in the impartiality of the public service. This argument is considered separately because it raises the important question of the nature of the evidence available to support arguments on each side of the political rights issue and to enable an appropriate balance to be struck between them. The Ontario Law Reform Commission's conclusion about Ontario is applicable also to the federal scene. The Commission notes that "the balancing exercise that we are required to perform is not susceptible of scientific accuracy. There is really no method to measure the impact that a particular amendment will have upon the overall behaviour of so large and diverse an organization as the Ontario public service. It is a question of judgment whether a particular reform will ease the undue restrictions on individual freedom without a deleterious effect upon the principles of political neutrality" (Ontario Law Reform Commission 1986, 260).

Some officials from provinces with relatively liberal political rights regimes have asserted that there has been no apparent negative impact in the form of reduced public and government confidence in the impartiality of public servants (Decter 1986). Yet this author has received reports from officials in several provinces about employees whose career prospects have suffered as a result of their supporting an opposition party, about a polarization of public servants among the major political parties, and about links between political partisanship and the leaking of government information. A good deal of anecdotal evidence can be collected to support the view that the liberalization of political rights does have such consequences, but it must be recognized that the plural of anecdote is not data.

Saskatchewan has long had comparatively liberal rules on political rights. Concern about the application of these rules arose when, after a change of government in 1982, a large number of public servants were dismissed, some of them on the grounds of actual or alleged affiliation with, or support for, the "wrong" political party (Michelmann and Steeves 1985). A few years later, the province's most senior public servant expressed serious concerns about the political rights rules in that province. He said that whereas in the federal sphere and in a number of provinces the political rights rules "have dictated that their public services are, for the most part, perceived [as] politically neutral, this does not appear to be the case in respect of the Saskatchewan Public Service" (Riddell 1986, 1). He said also that the broad interpretation of the province's rules "has resulted in public servants at all levels running for office or actively campaigning for a particular party or candidate ... If one believes as I do in [the] British Parliamentary tradition of the neutrality of the public service, it is fairly clear that the present legislation and policy framework does little to contribute to preserving this tradition in Saskatchewan" (ibid., 3). Finally, he announced that Saskatchewan would develop a code of conduct for public servants to help achieve the objective of a nonpartisan public service and that among the questions to be considered was whether there should be restrictions on soliciting funds for political parties, holding office in a political party, and making public statements on government policy.

It is significant also that the Government of Saskatchewan intervened in an action before the Supreme Court of Canada in 1990 to argue that section 33 of the federal *PSEA* is compatible with the *Canadian Charter of Rights and Freedoms* (Saskatchewan 1990).

The head of a public service union has argued that even though section 33 of the *PSEA* was not in force during the 1988 federal election, "public service employees showed good judgment in deciding what political activity was appropriate. No one has claimed that public service neutrality or the merit system of promotion has been undermined" (Craig 1989, 20). But section 33 was struck down just before the election was called (*Osborne* 1988), and a single election campaign provides little evidence of the possible long-term effects of removing restraints on political partisanship. It is noteworthy also that election experience does not speak to the impact of the separate, but related, issue of extending the rights of public servants to comment publicly on government policies and programs between elections. A much longer period and the experience of several elections are needed for a proper assessment of the impact of liberalizing political rights. In Great Britain, the effects of an expansion of political rights for public servants in 1949 were formally assessed by means of a public inquiry in 1976, which led to a further expansion of these rights.

There is a need for a rigorous examination of the consequences of expanding the political rights of public servants in certain provinces so that self-serving claims on both sides of the issue and impressionistic evidence can be replaced with hard data.

THE COMPARATIVE DIMENSION

It is important to be careful about transplanting a political rights regime from one government jurisdiction to another (for example, from British Columbia to the federal government or from Great Britain to Canada). There are good descriptions of the formal rules in the provinces and in various other countries, but there is relatively little information on actual practices, which can depart considerably from the formal rules. It is important to recognize also that the political rights regime in each jurisdiction is the product of historical, political, constitutional, cultural and social conditions that are not shared, or are shared only partly, by other jurisdictions. The Attorney General of Newfoundland has observed that "there is no one approach to achieving a politically neutral and impartial public service. Recognition must be given to differences between jurisdictions in respect of the political history, the evolution of politics and the political realities associated with governing. Given these differences, there is no one scheme that would ensure a climate of reliance and trust fundamental to the carrying out of governmental functions and the accessing of services by the public. Indeed, the objective may properly be achieved through a variety of schemes in different jurisdictions" (Newfoundland 1990, 7).

Descriptions of the political rights rules in Canada's provincial governments and in certain other countries (the United States, Australia and New Zealand) are not provided here because they are available elsewhere (Ontario Law Reform Commission 1986, 123–57, 192–218, 244–52, 254–55). For quick reference, however, the chart in appendix C provides a summary of the provincial rules. In addition, appendix D contains an account of the political rights regimes in selected countries (Germany, France, Sweden and Japan) whose experience is relevant to the Canadian debate. A detailed treatment of the British political rights regime is provided below because this regime is so often recommended as a model for the Canadian government.

The British Model

Britain's political activity rules take the form, not of a statute, but of regulations contained in the *Civil Service Pay and Conditions of Service Code*.[6] The opening words of the political activities section of the Code are worth quoting because of their relevance to the tension between political rights and political neutrality and their similarity to a recent statement by the Canadian government.

> Civil servants owe their allegiance to the Crown. In its executive capacity, the authority of the Crown is exercised through the government of the day. Civil servants are therefore required to discharge loyally the duties assigned to them by the government of the day of whatever political persuasion. For the Civil Service to serve successive governments of different political complexions it is essential that ministers and the public should have confidence that civil servants' personal views do not cut across the discharge of their official duties. The intent of the rules governing political activities by civil servants is to allow them the greatest possible freedom to participate in public affairs without infringing these fundamental principles. (United Kingdom, *Civil Service Code*, para. 9923)

The Canadian government used a similar statement in its 1990 white paper on the renewal of the public service (Canada, Public Service 2000, 1990, 7–11) with the commitment that "the Government will take whatever measures may be necessary to maintain the confidence of the public and of successive Governments in the professionalism and nonpartisanship of the Public Service. Provided this essential principle is fully respected, the Government will be prepared at the appropriate time to consider further the exercise of political rights by particular categories of Public Servants" (ibid., 64).

The British code identifies 10 types of political activity. The five activities of national or international scope it cites are as follows:

a. public announcement as a candidate or prospective candidate for Parliament or the European Assembly
b. holding, in party political organisations, offices which impinge wholly or mainly on party politics in the field of Parliament or the European Assembly
c. speaking in public on matters of national political controversy
d. expressing views on such matters in letters to the press or in books, articles or leaflets
e. canvassing on behalf of a candidate for Parliament or the European Assembly or on behalf of a political party. (Para. 9924)

The five activities at the local level it cites are as follows:

a. candidature for, or co-option to, local authorities
b. holding, in party political organisations, offices impinging wholly or mainly on party politics in the local field
c. speaking in public on matters of local political controversy
d. expressing views on such matters in letters to the press or in book articles or leaflets
e. canvassing on behalf of candidates for election to local authorities or a local political organisation. (Para. 9925)

For purposes of participation in these political activities, British public servants are divided into three categories. First, the *politically free* group makes up about 26 percent of the civil service. It consists of "industrial" civil servants and "non-office" personnel, that is, low-profile groups like messengers, cleaners, photocopiers. This group is permitted to take full part in all political activities. Second, the *politically restricted* group, which makes up about 4 percent of the service, consists of everyone at the level of principal and above, administration trainees and higher executive officers. Members of this group are completely barred from national political activities but can seek departmental permission to participate in local activities. Finally, there is an *intermediate* group, which makes up about 70 percent of the civil service and consists of clerical and executive officers and professional employees below the level of principal. Employees in this intermediate group are eligible to participate in all political activities except candidature for Parliament or the European Assembly. They must, however, seek departmental permission for such participation, and whether permission is granted depends on the nature of their current duties. Permission to participate is specifically forbidden to:

- employees providing policy advice to ministers and senior officials or working in areas that are especially sensitive in political or national security terms;
- employees "who regularly speak for the government or the department in dealings with commercial undertakings, pressure groups local government, public authorities," etc. and who may appear to these bodies as having influence over them;
- employees "who represent [the] Government in dealings with overseas Governments"; and
- employees "whose official duties involve ... significant ... face-to-face contact with individual members of the public and who make, or may seem to the public to be involved in making decisions affecting them, and whose political activities are likely to be (or become) known to those members of the public (eg., those whose work involves them or may seem to the public to involve them in both intimate knowledge and direct contact with members of the public in regard to their personal affairs, and decisions affecting their personal lives" (Para. 9929).

With respect to posts in the intermediate category that do not fall within these sensitive areas, departments are encouraged to grant "standing permission" for employees to engage in political activities.

It is important to note that all employees in the restricted and intermediate categories, even if they have received permission individually or *en bloc*, are subject to a Code of Discretion. The Code provides that "a civil servant's political views should not constitute so strong and so comprehensive a commitment to the tenets of one political party as to inhibit or appear to inhibit loyal and effective service to Ministers of another party." Permission to participate in political activities is subject to the following Code of Discretion:

a. individuals in the intermediate and politically restricted groups undertaking political activities should bear in mind that they are servants of the Crown, working under the direction of Ministers forming the government of the day. While they are not debarred from advocating or criticising the policy of any political party, comment should be expressed with moderation, particularly in relation to matters for which their own Ministers are responsible, and indeed all comment avoided if the departmental issue concerned is controversial. Personal attacks should be avoided

b. every care should be taken to avoid any embarrassment to Ministers or to their departments which could result, inadvertently or not,

from the actions of a person known to be a civil servant who brings
himself prominently to public notice in party political controversy

c. permission to participate only in local political activities is granted
subject to care being taken by the officer concerned not to involve
himself in matters of political controversy which are of national
rather than local significance. (Para. 9934)

This Code of Discretion reinforces the importance of the reality and appearance of a politically neutral public service. The Code is likely to encourage the roughly 70 percent of employees in the intermediate category to exercise caution, even in their involvement in permissible political activities.

Any public servant who has been refused permission to participate in political activity may appeal to the Civil Service Appeal Board. The Board can only recommend to the head of the relevant department that the activity be permitted; if the department head disagrees with this recommendation, the final decision is taken by the minister.

Lessons from Comparative Analysis

In addition to this British model, the political rights regimes in Australia, New Zealand and the United States are especially relevant to Canada. The Commonwealth countries have in common the British model of parliamentary–cabinet government, and the political heritage of the United States is largely British; its political culture is more similar to that of the developed Commonwealth states than it is to other developed democratic states in Europe and Asia. In assessing the political activity rules in such countries as Germany, France, Sweden and Japan, it is useful to keep in mind the influence of their distinctive governing institutions and political cultures. A cursory analysis of these rules in several western European countries (e.g., Germany, France and Sweden) reveals considerable permissiveness compared with the rules in the United States and the developed Commonwealth countries. A detailed analysis would show that this permissiveness is a product of unique national circumstances and that permissiveness, especially in Germany and France, is associated with a significant degree of politicization of the public service.

Compared with the political activity rules in other developed democratic countries, the federal rules in Canada fall approximately halfway along a political activity continuum from complete permissiveness to complete prohibition. A comparison of the rules in these various countries places Sweden closest to the pole of unrestrained political activity, with Germany, France, New Zealand, Australia and Britain falling progressively closer to the middle of the continuum. Governments in Canada are grouped around the mid-point of the continuum. Compared with the federal rules, the rules in Alberta, British Columbia, Manitoba, Quebec and Saskatchewan are more permissive; those in Newfoundland and Prince Edward Island are more restrictive. The rules in the other provinces (New Brunswick, Nova Scotia and Ontario) are similar to the federal rules. Finally, the rules in the United States, Eire and Japan place those countries closer to the pole of completely prohibited political activity.

In several of these countries, the formal rules provide only a rough picture of the actual operation and impact of the rules. Moreover, one cannot say with confidence that rules that are effective in one country can be successfully applied in countries with different political and administrative systems. Nevertheless, some lessons can be learned.

Public servants in Sweden, Germany and France enjoy a broader range of political rights than most government jurisdictions in Canada. Sweden's political and administrative institutions and culture are very different from those in Canada. Similarly, the political and legal framework within which public servants in Germany and France work differs from that in Canada, but experience in these two countries suggests that the politicization of the senior public service is likely to filter down to lower levels of the service. This experience suggests also that a public service based formally on merit and neutrality may in practice be characterized by a good deal of political patronage.

In this regard, it is important to note the conclusions of a Canadian scholar who has done a careful study of political rights in Germany and has drawn specific lessons for Canada (Michelmann 1988). He asserts that "the normative assessments of the effects of politicization are not necessarily directly relevant in the Canadian context" but "one needs only to examine these effects and determine whether they are desirable in Canada" (ibid., 27). He concludes that broad political rights for public servants have had negative ramifications in Germany, especially "for the functioning of the public service itself" (ibid., 29). In particular, he notes that "there is no evidence that partisanship enhances competence, although there is evidence of the danger that partisanship can, in the absence of strict vigilance and the proper motivation by those who make personnel decisions, replace merit as the primary consideration" (ibid.). In conclusion, he cautions Canadians "to listen to senior public servants in Germany who in interviews with the author wished they were operating in a context such as the Canadian where party political considerations do not play the role in the public service that they do in the FRG. Their advice was not to go toward the slippery slope of expanding public servant political rights for fear of introducing into the Canadian setting the escalating partisan influence that is becoming increasingly attacked in Germany for its detrimental effects on the public service" (ibid, 31). In this context, it is notable that two German experts have concluded that "the German civil service has become clearly politicized – in a party political sense – over the past 20 years" (Mayntz and Derlien 1989, 386).

The Canadian public service, unlike that of Germany or France but like that of the Commonwealth countries, operates within a constitutional framework in which the conventions of ministerial responsibility, political neutrality and public service anonymity are of central importance. Compared with Canada, the rules on political activity in the Commonwealth countries are somewhat less restrictive. However, while it is difficult to compare the overall commitment to a politically neutral public service of one country with that of another, the tradition of political neutrality appears to be somewhat stronger in Britain and Australia than in Canada. The extent to which public servants will take advantage of permissive rules on political activity depends to a considerable degree on the importance generally attached to a politically neutral public service and, therefore, to the avoidance of political patronage and partisan politics. In Britain, "professional ethics of bureaucrats and self-imposed restraints of politicians serve as guidelines that safeguard the civil servants' political neutrality" (Etzioni-Halevy 1979, 141), and in Australia, "the principle of political neutrality is not fully defined in statutes and regulations ... Rather, it is part of a code of conduct to which public servants are socialized and which is re-enforced by self-selection" (ibid., 159–60). It is significant in this context that public servants in Britain and Australia do not participate very actively in partisan politics.

It is notable also that in Britain, Australia and New Zealand, the rules outlining the permissible political activities of public servants are accompanied by generally worded caution clauses that emphasize the importance of preserving the political neutrality of the public service. Such clauses can have a considerable inhibiting effect on the partisan political activity of public servants, regardless of how permissive the rules otherwise appear to be. Nevertheless, experience suggests that these clauses are usually necessary because of the difficulty of covering every possible contingency with detailed rules.

The political activity rules in Canada's provinces provide ammunition for both advocates and opponents of the expansion of the permissible political activities of federal public servants. Compared with the federal sphere, the rules in some provinces are more restrictive, but in other provinces, they are less restrictive. Some of the provinces with permissive rules appear to make a comparatively greater number of patronage appointments at both the highest and lowest levels of the public service; however, some governments with restrictive rules also appear to make a significant number of patronage appointments, especially at the lower levels of the public service.

Very few jurisdictions, in Canada or elsewhere, provide much specific guidance on the matter of public comment – in large part because it is difficult to provide specific guidance to cover the broad range of possible forms of public comment (see appendix B) and it is difficult to distinguish clearly between partisan and nonpartisan comment. There is a tendency in many jurisdictions to make statutory provision for political activity but to rely on traditions, conventions and understandings for regulating public comment. The federal government could make a valuable contribution by devising rules on public comment that could serve as a model for other jurisdictions.

SECTION 33 OF THE *PSEA* – CONTENT AND PROPOSALS FOR CHANGE

Section 33 of the Act, which is reproduced in part in appendix A, permits federal public servants to attend political meetings and to contribute money to support a political candidate or a political party.[7] Public servants are free to choose whether or not to participate in these permissible activities. These activities are low-profile activities that, compared with highly visible activities, pose little threat to the preservation of political neutrality. Section 33 also provides that with the exception of the permissible activities outlined above, public servants shall not work for or against a political candidate or political party. The prohibited activities are high-profile activities (for example, soliciting financial contributions, door-to-door canvassing), which are more likely than low-profile activities to attract public and media attention and to raise questions about the political neutrality of the public service.

Section 33 also provides that with the exception of deputy ministers and other public servants in senior and sensitive positions, public servants can obtain a leave of absence to seek election to public office so long as their usefulness in the public service would not be impaired by such activity.[8] Public servants who are elected to public office must leave the public service, and no provision is made for their reinstatement in the service after they leave elected office.

The Public Service Commission has issued regular bulletins over the years to inform public servants and others of the Commission's interpretation of what political activities are permissible. In May 1988, before section 32(1) of the *PSEA* was struck down (*Osborne* 1988), the

Commission issued a statement (Canada, Public Service Commission 1988) providing an up-to-date picture of its view of permissible political activities. Advocates of increased political rights sought to go beyond those activities set out below (see appendix E for the full text). A useful comparison may be made between these federal rules and the more restrictive rules in the United States, summarized in appendix F.

Permissible Political Activities (under the *PSEA*)

Public servants, in addition to having the right to vote, may engage in various political activities outside working hours and off the employer's premises. For example, they may

- sign the official nomination paper of a candidate;
- express personal views on public issues without making public statements to the media, orally or in writing, of a partisan political nature, thereby directing public attention to themselves as an active supporter of a political party;
- speak as a member of the public at all-candidates meetings and question candidates on policy issues;
- attend political meetings;
- contribute funds to a political party or candidate;
- hold membership in a political party;
- participate in discussions relating to the development of the policies of a political party without directing public attention to themselves as an active supporter of a political party;
- seek to be elected as a delegate to a leadership convention;
- attend, as a delegate, leadership conventions;
- provide assistance to a candidate or party in ways that do not attract public attention to themselves and that would not be perceived as imperilling their ability to discharge their public service responsibilities in a politically neutral manner, such as by addressing correspondence and stuffing envelopes; and
- apply to the Public Service Commission for leave without pay to seek nomination as a candidate and, provided such leave is granted, to be a candidate for election as a member of the House of Commons, a member of the legislature of a province or a member of the territorial councils.

In July 1988, the Federal Court of Appeal struck down section 32(1)(*a*) (now section 33(1)(*a*)) of the *PSEA,* which prohibits public servants from engaging in work for or against a candidate or a political party. The Court decided that this paragraph was too vague, ambiguous and open to discretionary application. The Court did confirm the validity of the other provisions of the section, including the need to obtain permission from the Public Service Commission for leave of absence to seek election to public office. The Court also acknowledged the convention of political neutrality; it pointed out that in the interest of an impartial public service, public servants have a duty to be loyal to the Government of Canada, as opposed to a political party, and that certain political activities may be incompatible with that duty. In June 1991, while this study was in production, the Supreme Court of Canada upheld the decision of the Federal Court of Appeal.

Section 33 and Bill C-157

There are various views on the extent to which section 33 of the *PSEA* strikes an appropriate balance between political rights on the one hand and political neutrality and public service efficiency on the other. The options range from no change to very fundamental change.

There is considerable support for the view that the current content of section 33 is entirely appropriate. For example, the Federal Task Force on Conflict of Interest concluded that the present arrangements constitute "an acceptable balance between individual freedom and the requirement for a politically neutral public service" (Canada, Task Force 1984, 236).

The proposals for change range from minor amendment of section 33 in the form of fine-tuning (e.g., providing greater specificity), through a modest expansion of political rights to a substantial expansion of these rights. Some of the proposals are based in broad outline on the British model: public servants are divided into two or three tiers or categories according to the political rights they are permitted to exercise. This is the approach that was recommended for the federal government by the D'Avignon Committee (Canada 1979, chap. 11) and the Daubney Committee[9] and for Ontario by the Ontario Law Reform Commission (1986, chap. 6).

The influence of the British – or tiered – model of political rights was also evident in Bill C-157, a government bill that was tabled in the House of Commons on 30 August 1988.[10] The bill was introduced six weeks after the decision of the Federal Court of Appeal bearing on section 32 of the *PSEA* and died on the order paper when the federal election of 21 November 1988 was called. This bill, which takes the form of an amendment to the *PSEA*, is much longer and more detailed than the current provisions on political partisanship. It merits careful consideration in that it may be used as a basis for future federal legislation on political rights.

Bill C-157 illustrates the point made at the beginning of this study that the issue of political rights is complex and has far-reaching ramifications. Any bill dealing with political rights should take careful account of the concerns raised in the section of this study on the rationales for and against the expansion of political rights. As explained below, Bill C-157 does not take adequate account of some of these concerns.

Purpose of the Bill

The government signalled a shift of emphasis on the political rights issue by replacing the previous heading of "Political Partisanship" with that of "Political Rights." But the stated purpose of the bill acknowledges a dual objective – "to recognize the freedom of public servants to engage in political activities and to maintain the principle of political impartiality in the Public Service." Moreover, although the term political neutrality is not specifically used, the elaboration on this main objective is closely linked to the principles of the political neutrality model outlined earlier. The bill's intention is to ensure that

- public servants, in the course of their employment, act impartially and without regard to political persuasion or any improper influence;
- public servants advise ministers of the Crown and implement the decisions, policies, programs and services of the Government of Canada impartially and without regard to political persuasion or an improper influence; and
- public servants are appointed to and from within the Public Service according to merit.

A remarkable, and undesirable, feature of the Bill is that it unnecessarily confuses the terms political activity and political freedom. A number of activities normally described as political activities are described in this Bill as political freedoms.[11] Political activity is defined as "any activity for, on behalf of or against a political candidate or a political party," but it does not include any activity described in the Political Freedom section (32.11) of the bill, namely, voting, participation at a political meeting, contributing money to a political party and being a member of a political party. These activities, which are presumably to be described as *freedoms*, are permissible for all employees. Other activities in the same section of the bill – holding office in a political party and soliciting, collecting or managing funds for a political candidate or party – are presumably to be considered *political activities*. Moreover, all other activities of a partisan political nature, which are not specified in the bill, are apparently to be deemed political activities. The bill would be more comprehensible if the conventional meaning of the term political activity was used.

It is notable also that the bill mentions most, but not all, forms of political activity. It is not clear, for example, whether public servants are permitted to work at the polls in a partisan capacity or transport voters to the polls on behalf of a political party or candidate. Are those political activities not specifically mentioned in the bill permissible or prohibited? Given the criticism that the political activity provisions of the current Act are too vague, it is desirable to provide for the clarification of what is permissible and prohibited, either in the Act itself or in associated regulations or guidelines.

Categories of Public Servants

The bill provides that a deputy head of a department may forbid a public servant who is not in the restricted category (described below) to hold office in a political party or to solicit, collect or manage funds if the deputy head determines that such activities are incompatible with the public servant's duties. A public servant may apply to the Public Service Commission for a review of this determination, in which case the Commission will establish a board of inquiry to "confirm, vary or set aside" the determination.

The bill makes explicit provision only for a restricted class of employees (section 32.12), but it actually creates three classes of employees: a restricted class; a politically free class; and, as noted above, a class that is politically free except for the right to hold office or to solicit, collect or manage funds.

The restricted class consists of

- deputy heads and associate deputy heads;
- employees in the management category; and
- employees responsible for directly advising ministers or officials at the levels of deputy, associate and assistant deputy minister on the development of policies, programs and services and for preparing or using confidential cabinet documents.

In addition, the Treasury Board may designate as restricted those employees who exercise significant discretion in such areas as imposing penalties and commencing prosecutions, negotiating or approving government grants or other benefits, negotiating or approving contracts, and selecting persons for employment opportunities outside the public service, as well as those public servants employed as personnel administrators or in a managerial or confidential capacity.

Employees placed in the restricted category may appeal this designation to the Commission, which is required to establish a board to confirm, amend or revoke the designation.

The bill creates considerable complexity and confusion by providing so many separate mechanisms for designating employees whose activities are to be restricted. These mechanisms are the designations in the bill itself, Treasury Board regulation, designation by the deputy head, and the boards set up by the Public Service Commission. In addition, it will be unclear to many employees whether they are subject to all of the restrictions or to only some of them.

Prohibited Activities

Under section 32.16, a public servant is forbidden to

(a) make a public statement in conflict with the duties of the public servant; or

(b) engage in any political activity

(i) during the course of or at the place of the public servant's employment, or

(ii) in a manner that calls attention to the public servant's employment as a public servant.

The admonition that public servants should refrain from public statements that clash with their official duties is the sole provision bearing directly on the important issue of public comment. The issue is touched on indirectly in that where public servants are restricted in their political activity, they are also restricted in public comment associated with that activity. And they are specifically forbidden to engage in political activity, presumably including public comment of a partisan nature, that brings attention to their status as public servants. However, as explained earlier, a distinction can be made between partisan and nonpartisan public comment. The bill fails to specify adequately the appropriate boundaries of the nonpartisan variety of public comment. Public servants are likely to interpret this "conflict with their duties" in different ways. This provision could have a chilling effect on those public servants who are uncertain about what the provision means in concrete circumstances; it could also have an unduly liberating effect on other public servants who might interpret it as a licence to comment publicly on a broad range of issues. Given the varying interpretations of the provision, public servants should at the very least be advised to consult their superiors when they are uncertain about the limits of permissible public comment. Ideally, careful provision would be made to ensure that public servants know what forms of public comment are permissible and whom to consult in the event of uncertainty. A broadly worded clause on public comment could be supplemented with more specific regulations and guidelines that could be adapted quickly to changing circumstances.[12]

Under section 32.19, the bill correctly prohibits any person from intimidating, threatening or coercing a public servant, either for participating or refusing to participate in partisan politics. This provision helps meet the concern that public servants may be rewarded or punished by political and administrative superiors for involvement, or lack of involvement, in political activity.

Section 32.17 provides that public servants in the restricted category may not participate in any political activity, except during a leave of absence granted under section 32.21. It appears from this provision that employees in this category can seek leave of absence to participate in political activities that are otherwise forbidden to them. Yet section 32.21 states that a restricted employee can seek a leave of absence without pay to be a political candidate; there is no mention of leave for other political activities. If this apparent contradiction were resolved to permit restricted employees to seek leave for participation in otherwise prohibited activities, the political rights of these employees would be somewhat expanded.

Candidature for Public Office
Deputy heads and associate deputy heads must resign if they wish to become a political candidate. Employees in the restricted category must seek permission for a leave of absence, which will be granted if being a candidate will not impair the employees' ability to perform their duties if they return to the public service after their leave. All other public servants are free to take a leave of absence without pay to seek nomination and election to public office. If an employee is defeated for nomination or election, he or she is entitled to return to the public service in the same or an equivalent position. If elected, the public servant ceases to be an employee. Under this arrangement, most public servants would not have to request permission to stand for nomination and election to public office. Since, under the current act, most public servants are granted such permission, it seems unlikely that this change alone will result in a significant increase in the number of public servants seeking elected office.

Complaints
Anyone who believes that a public servant has violated the Act may present a written complaint to the Public Service Commission. If, after

investigating the complaint, the Commission determines that an inquiry is warranted, it will set up a board of inquiry to determine whether the public servant has contravened the Act. The Commission will report those who are found to have contravened that Act to the deputy head of the relevant department in the case of all employees except deputies and associate deputies, who are reported to the Governor in Council.

Boards of Inquiry
These boards are to consist of three persons: a representative of the government; a representative of the public servant who is the focus of the inquiry; and a person chosen jointly by these first two persons or, failing this, by the Chair of the Public Service Commission and the Chair of the Public Service Staff Relations Board. If the public servant is a member of a bargaining unit for which an employee organization is the certified bargaining agent, it is that bargaining agent who provides a list of prospective members to represent the public servant's interests on the board. Otherwise, the public servant provides his or her own list.

These latter two provisions seem inappropriate. First, public servants are placed in a position where they are not free to decide who will represent them. Some public servants may not want to involve their bargaining agent in matters relating to their political activities. They may, for example, have very different political views from those of the bargaining agent. Second, for public servants who are free to submit their own list, the task of determining persons who are likely to represent their interests well could be a difficult one.

The redress mechanism provided by these boards of inquiry is inconsistent with the other redress mechanisms provided in the Act, and it is unnecessarily complex. The involvement of the employer, the employee's bargaining agent and the Public Service Staff Relations Board is similar to the process used in the staff relations area for setting up conciliation boards. This seems inappropriate because the Act deals with individual rights of Canadian citizens, not with the right to associate for the purpose of bargaining collectively. Moreover, the mechanism proposed here differs from those provided elsewhere in the Act. This mechanism for establishing the boards of inquiry is complex and time-consuming and is likely to result in the kinds of delays that arise in matters brought before the Public Service Staff Relations Board. Redress matters managed by the Public Service Commission are usually handled more quickly.

A final, and major, concern about Bill C-157 deserves special attention. The status of the Public Service Commission as a politically independent body responsible for guarding the merit principle is eroded by this bill. The Commission reports to Parliament, not to the government of the day, to ensure that appointments to, and within, the public service are made on the basis of merit and are free from partisan political considerations. Yet section 32.12 of this bill gives to the Treasury Board the regulatory authority to designate the categories into which public servants should fall for purposes of political activity. As a result, an important element of the political rights regime would be controlled by a body that does not have an "arm's-length" relationship with the government of the day. Given the division of opinion on the political rights issue, it is preferable to ensure that matters of merit, political rights and political neutrality are handled by a politically neutral body.

Moreover, to ensure that public servants understand clearly the limits of their political rights and that these rights are enjoyed uniformly across the public service, there is need for a body, like the Commission, to provide information on, and consistent interpretation of, the legislation. While Bill C-157 is more specific than the current section 33, it still, necessarily, leaves room for interpretation. It is very difficult to provide an exhaustive list of permissible and prohibited political rights. Research in the United States, where there is a long list of do's and don'ts (see appendix F), has shown that some public servants still do not know whether certain activities are permissible.

In general, Bill C-157 requires reworking if it is to serve as an adequate means of providing for the political rights of federal public servants. It is worth noting that the government's enthusiasm for legislative action to expand political rights seems to have diminished somewhat since the 1988 election. The government asserted recently that it would be inappropriate to introduce legislative amendments dealing with political rights pending the outcome of the Supreme Court's decision on the constitutionality of section 33. Moreover, the government is "firmly of the view that the Public Service must retain its scrupulously nonpartisan character if it is to be professional and effective in supporting the Government of the day and providing service to Canadians" (Canada, Public Service 2000, 1990, 63).

CONCLUSIONS

The issue of whether the political rights of federal public servants should be expanded beyond their current level has significant constitutional, political and managerial dimensions. The *constitutional* dimension focuses on where the balance should be struck between the constitutional convention of political neutrality and the Charter freedoms of expression and association. Impartial observers are likely to conclude that the arguments on each side of this question are fairly evenly balanced. Can the same be said for the *political* and *managerial* dimensions of the debate?

Let us consider first the consequences for the political system. Those in favour of expanding political rights can point to the prospect of a larger number of comparatively knowledgeable and well-educated Canadians possessing more political rights and, if they wish, playing a more high-profile role in partisan politics and making public statements on political and policy issues. Those in favour of limiting political rights contend that a significant expansion of these rights will tend to undermine the constitutional convention of political neutrality and the related conventions of ministerial responsibility and public service anonymity. Ministers and legislators on the government side, opposition members, public service managers and the public will tend to have less confidence in the political impartiality of the public service. It is argued also that there would more likely be an increase in patronage appointments and turnovers in personnel with a change of government.

For public service management, the costs of a significant expansion of political rights seem likely to outweigh the benefits. It can be argued that the morale and, therefore, the efficiency of certain public servants may be enhanced if their permissible political rights are increased. As explained earlier, however, available evidence suggests that the likely outcome is a more partisan working environment, with negative effects on the morale, efficiency and possibly the career prospects of public servants. The gradual change in the culture and ethos of the public service that would result from having more employees engaged in more high-profile political activity and public comment would present new challenges to public service executives and managers. The natural tension in employer-employee relations could also be exacerbated by an overlay of partisan considerations.

In conclusion, it is worth noting again that the balancing exercise involved in determining the optimum measure of political rights is "not susceptible of scientific accuracy." Thus, if it is decided that an expansion of political rights is, in general, desirable, it is sensible to proceed carefully and gradually. The process used in Great Britain is instructive in this regard. If experience shows that political rights have been expanded too much too soon, it will be extremely difficult to reduce these rights. Thus, consideration of changes to section 33 of the *PSEA* should be based on an exhaustive weighing of the rationales for expanding and for limiting political rights.

APPENDIX A

SECTIONS 33(1)–(3) AND 34 OF THE *PUBLIC SERVICE EMPLOYMENT ACT*

33. (1) No deputy head and, except as authorized under this section, no employee, shall

    (*a*) engage in work for or against a candidate;

    (*b*) engage in work for or against a political party; or

    (*c*) be a candidate.

  (2) A person does not contravene subsection (1) by reason only of attending a political meeting or contributing money for the funds of a candidate or a political party.

  (3) Notwithstanding any other Act, on application made to the Commission by an employee, the Commission may, if it is of the opinion that the usefulness to the Public Service of the employee in the position the employee then occupies would not be impaired by reason of that employee having been a candidate, grant to the employee leave of absence without pay to seek nomination as a candidate and to be a candidate for election, for a period ending on the day on which the results of the election are officially declared or on such earlier day as may be requested by the employee if the employee has ceased to be a candidate.

    ...

34. (1) Where any allegation is made to the Commission by a person who is or has been a candidate that a deputy head or employee has contravened subsection 33(1), the allegation shall be referred to a board established by the Commission to conduct an inquiry at which the person making the allegation and the deputy head or employee, or their representatives, shall be given an opportunity to be heard.

  (2) The Commission, on being notified of the decision of the board on an inquiry into an allegation conducted pursuant to subsection (1),

    (*a*) in the case of a deputy head, shall report the decision to the Governor in Council who may, if the board has decided that the deputy head has contravened subsection 33(1), dismiss the deputy head; and

    (*b*) in the case of an employee, may, if the board has decided that the employee has contravened subsection 33(1), dismiss the employee.

  (3) In the application of this section to any person, the expression "deputy head" does not include a person for whose removal from office, otherwise than by the termination of his appointment at pleasure, express provision is made by this Act of any other Act.

APPENDIX B

FORMS OF PUBLIC COMMENT BY PUBLIC SERVANTS[13]

The forms of comment listed below move from those that are generally expected, required or permissible to those that are questionable, risky or prohibited:

1. providing information and analysis of a scientific or technical nature for consideration primarily by their professional colleagues within and outside government;

2. describing administrative processes and departmental organization and procedures;

3. explaining the content, implications and administration of specific government policies and programs;

4. discussing, within the framework of governmental or departmental policy, the solution of problems through changes in existing programs or the development of new programs;

5. discussing issues on which governmental or departmental policy has not yet been determined;

6. explaining the nature of the political and policy process in government;

7. advocating reforms in the existing organization or procedures of government;

8. commenting in a constructively critical way on government policy or administration;

9. denouncing existing or potential government policies, programs and operations; and

10. commenting in an overtly partisan way on public policy issues or on government policy or administration.

APPENDIX C
COMPARATIVE ANALYSIS OF REGULATION OF POLITICAL ACTIVITIES IN CANADA

Table 5.C1
Comparative analysis of regulation of political activities in Canada, 1985

Jurisdiction	Source	Candidature for federal or provincial election	Canvassing	Fund-raising	Other activities prohibited	Safeguard of service
Canada	Public Service Employment Act, R.S.C. 1985, c. P-33, s. 33	Must apply for leave to seek nomination; leave may be granted without pay if usefulness not impaired; if elected deemed to resign	Apparently prohibited	Apparently prohibited	Working for candidate in federal or provincial election or political party	
British Columbia	Collective agreement (master agreement)	Non-management employees; when nominated as candidate entitled to leave without pay to campaign. If elected, entitled to five-year leave; if defeated, entitled to return. If elected as a member entitled to five-year leave without pay; if appointed a minister, employment deemed terminated	Not specified	Not specified	No restrictions specified except oath of office	

Table 5.C1 (cont'd)
Comparative analysis of regulation of political activities in Canada, 1985

Jurisdiction	Source	Candidature for federal or provincial election	Canvassing	Fund-raising	Other activities prohibited	Safeguard of service
Alberta	Code of Conduct and Ethics established pursuant to Public Service Act, R.S.A. 1980, c. P-31, s. 23	Non-management personnel must take a leave of absence without pay once nominated; if elected, must resign; if defeated entitled to return Management personnel: prohibited	Non-management: permitted Management: prohibited	Prohibited except when on leave	Non-management personnel: oath of office only restraint Management personnel: excluded from holding office in political parties and constituency associations; general rule requiring discretion; active public participation prohibited	
Saskatchewan	Public Service Act, R.S.S. 1978, c. P-42, s. 50	Employees entitled to leave of absence to become candidate; deemed to have resigned if elected	Not specified	Not specified	Using position to influence political action of any other person All political activity banned in working hours Activities that impair usefulness banned	Prohibition against compelling public servant to take part in political activity or make contributions to political party; prohibition against threats and intimidation for refusal to take part in political undertaking

Table 5.C1 (cont'd)
Comparative analysis of regulation of political activities in Canada, 1985

Jurisdiction	Source	Candidature for federal or provincial election	Canvassing	Fund-raising	Other activities prohibited	Safeguard of service
Manitoba	Civil Service Act, R.S.M. 1987, c. C110, s. 44	All except deputy ministers and designated staff entitled to leave of absence without pay to seek nomination Entitled to reinstatement and continuous service benefits if defeated; if elected entitled to leave without pay for five years	Permitted except for designated staff	Prohibited for all	Oath of office only restriction except for designated staff	Prohibition against coercing or intimidating employees into supporting a political party or candidate
Ontario	Public Service Act, R.S.O. 1980, c. 418, ss. 11–16	All but senior staff, entitled to leave of absence without pay, reinstatement and continuous service benefits	Prohibited except on leave	Prohibited except on leave	Speaking out on party platform prohibited except on leave Associating position in service of Crown with political activity	

Table 5.C1 (cont'd)
Comparative analysis of regulation of political activities in Canada, 1985

Jurisdiction	Source	Candidature for federal or provincial election	Canvassing	Fund-raising	Other activities prohibited	Safeguard of service
Quebec	Public Service Act, S.Q. 1983, c. 55, ss. 10–12, 24–31	Entitled to leave without pay to be candidate Entitled to reinstatement if not elected	Not specified	Not specified	Public servant to be neutral and act with reserve in public display of political opinions	
New Brunswick	Civil Service Act, S.N.B. 1994, c. 5.1, s. 27	Employee required to seek leave of absence without pay to seek nomination; may be granted if adjudged usefulness not impaired; if elected, deemed to have resigned	Prohibited	Prohibited	Engaging in work for or against a political party or candidate	
Nova Scotia	Civil Service Act, R.S.N.S. 1989, c. 70, ss. 35–41	Not permitted	Prohibited	Prohibited	No partisan work permitted nor contribution or receipt of party funds	

Table 5.C1 (cont'd)
Comparative analysis of regulation of political activities in Canada, 1985

Jurisdiction	Source	Candidature for federal or provincial election	Canvassing	Fund-raising	Other activities prohibited	Safeguard of service
Prince Edward Island	Civil Service Act, S.P.E.I. 1988, c. C-8, s. 38	Partisan election work prohibited	Prohibited	Prohibited	Using official position to influence political action of another person or during working hours engage in political activity or at any time take part in activities impairing his or her usefulness or engage in partisan work in election	Employees cannot be compelled to take part in political undertaking or contribute to party or be threatened or discriminated against for refusing to take part in political undertakings
Newfoundland	Order in Council 951-75, Aug. 18, 1975	Must resign to seek nomination; no obligation to re-employ	Partisan activity prohibited	Partisan activity prohibited	May not use position to influence political action of another person; participate in action that would impair usefulness; or engage in partisan election activity at any time	Employees cannot be compelled to take part in political undertaking, contribute to any political party, or be threatened or discriminated against for refusing to take part in political undertakings

Source: O.P.S.E.U. and Ontario (Attorney General). Undated. *Respondent's Factum* before the Supreme Court of Canada, Appendix I, 76–80, as updated.

APPENDIX D
POLITICAL RIGHTS REGIMES IN FOREIGN STATES

To provide some perspective on Canadian practice, policies concerning political rights for public servants in Germany, France, Sweden and Japan are described below.

The Federal Republic of Germany

In Germany, the Basic Law (the Constitution), as well as several statutes, suggests that the public service is a neutral and nonpartisan one. In practice, compared with the public services in the Commonwealth countries, the public service in Germany is highly politicized, especially at its senior levels.

The scope of political activities in which German public servants are permitted to participate is very broad. Federal public servants are granted a leave of absence, without pay, if they wish to seek election to political office. If they are elected to the federal Parliament, they must resign their public service post, but they are entitled to be reinstated when they leave political life. The rules on political activity in the governments of the *Länder* are broadly similar to those of the federal government.

When participating in partisan politics, federal public servants are required by statute to carry out their duties in an impartial manner and to show moderation and restraint appropriate to the responsibilities of their position. Nevertheless, the statutory provisions regarding the need for discretion in personal political activity and "neutrality" no longer reflect reality. Patronage appointments are by no means confined to the top echelons of the public service, but there is a much higher percentage of such appointments at that level.

France

The great majority of public servants in France enjoy a wide range of political rights. Most public servants are permitted to join political parties and to participate in party activities. Moreover, relatively few public servants are restricted from expressing their personal views in public on government policy and administration. Those public servants who are in senior or sensitive positions are expected to be more reserved than other public servants when exercising their political rights; they are not supposed to disclose that they are public servants and they must not use information that they have acquired by virtue of their official position. Most public servants are allowed to seek election to national or local public office. If they are elected to Parliament, they are not obliged to resign; rather they are placed on inactive status and can return to the public service when they leave their political office.

As a result of these permissive rules on political activity, the influence of partisan politics is quite pervasive in the French public service. The fact that a considerable number of former public servants hold political office increases the likelihood of effective political control over the administration; however, the politicization of the senior echelons of the service has led to frequent leaks of confidential information aimed at embarrassing the government and to strained working relations within the service itself. There is a polarization of partisan political feeling within the public service, since Gaullist supporters predominate at the senior levels of the service and supporters of the left at the lower levels.

Sweden

The rules on political activity for public servants in Sweden must be viewed within the framework of its unique government institutions and political culture. Ministerial responsibility, in the sense of ministers being individually responsible to Parliament for all the administrative acts of their departmental subordinates, is virtually non-existent. Given this fact and the presence of a strong tradition of open government, it is not surprising that the Swedish approach to political rights is a permissive one. Public servants in Sweden can exercise virtually the same political rights as other citizens. They are permitted to be members of political parties, to participate in partisan politics and to stand for election to public office. They are also allowed to criticize publicly the government of the day and their administrative superiors.

Swedish public servants are prohibited, however, from engaging in any activities that would impair confidence in the impartiality with which they discharge their official duties or that would impair the reputation of the authority for which they work. Moreover, they are not permitted to coerce other public servants into engaging in partisan political activities.

Japan

The severe restrictions on the political activities of public servants in Japan are a striking contrast to the rules in the western European countries discussed above. Public servants are prohibited from exercising virtually all political rights, except the right to vote. They are not permitted to make contributions of any kind to a political party or to stand for elective office. The public service regulations contain a long list of prohibited political activities. The rules on political activity in Japan appear to be more restrictive than those in the United States.

It is significant that these rules limit the political activities of the vast majority of public servants, but at the senior level of government the distinction between politicians and public servants is blurred. Career public servants often perform functions that would be restricted to political appointees in most other developed countries. Also, senior public servants in Japan retire earlier than their counterparts elsewhere, and many of them then run successfully for public office.

APPENDIX E

CURRENT INTERPRETATION OF SECTION 32 OF THE
PUBLIC SERVICE EMPLOYMENT ACT (MAY 1988)*

In February 1984, the Commission provided guidance to public servants regarding their participation in political activities. Since then, the Federal Court has rendered a decision on political rights as defined under Section 32 of the *Public Service Employment Act* (*PSEA*). That decision is now under appeal. Moreover, the issue of political activities of public servants is currently the object of a bill being reviewed by Parliament. Finally, there is increased public debate on this matter resulting in a certain amount of uncertainty as evidenced by the numerous requests for information and for clear and current guidance on permissible political activities. To respond to this need, the Commission is issuing the following guidelines, which take into account the Federal Court decision.

Principles

The Public Service Commission believes that federal public servants should be guided by the following principles:

- To ensure public trust in government, public servants must be, and must appear to be, both politically impartial and free of undue political influence in the exercise of their duties.
- The Canadian public has a right to expect that federal public servants will provide full assistance and services required by legislation and government policies and programs, in an impartial manner, serving everyone equitably.
- The Canadian Government at all times has the right to receive from ... federal public servants objective and impartial advice, based on professional competence, and to expect federal public servants to implement loyally all decisions of the Government regardless of their personal political persuasion or affiliation.
- Subject to the provisions of Section 32 of the *PSEA*, federal public servants should remain as free as other Canadian citizens to take part in the political affairs of their country.

General Rule concerning Political Activity

Public servants should exercise caution and prudence, avoid directing public attention to themselves as being active supporters of a given party or candidate and refrain from conduct which might compromise or be perceived to compromise their ability to carry out their duties in a politically impartial manner. They should also be mindful that, in conducting any political activities, the perception of their political impartiality will depend upon many circumstances

* This policy was updated in August 1988 and again in June 1991 as a result of court decisions. The June 1991 statement appears immediately following.

unique to them, such as the nature and public visibility of their political activities and their public service duties, their place of work and their level of responsibility as government employees.

Permissible Political Activities

Public servants, in addition to having the right to vote, may engage in various political activities outside working hours and off the employer's premises. For example, they may:

- sign the official nomination paper of a candidate
- express personal views on public issues without making public statements to the media orally or in writing of a partisan political nature, thereby directing public attention to themselves as an active supporter of a political party
- speak as a member of the public at all candidates' meetings and question candidates on policy issues
- attend political meetings
- contribute funds to a political party or candidate
- hold membership in a political party
- participate in discussions relating to the development of policies of a political party without directing public attention to themselves as an active supporter of a political party
- seek to be elected as a delegate to a leadership convention
- attend, as a delegate, leadership conventions
- provide assistance to a candidate or party in ways which do not attract public attention to themselves and which would not be perceived as imperilling their ability to discharge their public service responsibilities in a politically neutral manner, such as by addressing correspondence and stuffing envelopes
- apply to the Public Service Commission for leave without pay to seek nomination as a candidate and, provided such leave is granted, to be a candidate for election as a member of the House of Commons, a member of the legislature of a province, or a member of the territorial councils.

Advice and Assistance

Public servants who are uncertain about how to proceed in respect of specific political activity situations they might encounter should direct their enquiries to the Public Service Commission's Executive Secretariat at (613) 995-5923. When the request is for leave without pay to seek nomination and to be a candidate, the Commission will consult the employee's deputy head and will grant leave if it is of the opinion that, as a result of having been a candidate for election, the employee's usefulness in his/her current position would not be impaired.

Update

Should the courts provide a different interpretation of Section 32 of the *PSEA*, or should Parliament legislate in the matter of political activities of public servants, the Public Service Commission will provide revised guidelines in this matter.

Source: Canada, Public Service Commission (1988).

POLITICAL ACTIVITIES OF PUBLIC SERVANTS

Judgment of the Supreme Court of Canada

Public Service Commission v. Millar, Osborne and others

Section 33 of the *Public Service Employment Act*

June 1991

In 1986 a number of employees asked the Trial Division of the Federal Court to set aside section 33 (formerly section 32) of the *Public Service Employment Act*. Among other things, this section prohibited employees and deputy heads from engaging in work for or against a candidate or political party. Their ground was that section 33 was contrary to the *Canadian Charter of Rights and Freedoms*.

Since they were not successful, they appealed to the Federal Court of Appeal and in June 1988, that court struck down paragraphs 33(1)(a) and (b) with respect to public servants – it still applied to deputy heads. The reason given by the Court for its judgment was that the wording in these paragraphs was vague and open to discretionary application.

The Public Service Commission appealed to the Supreme Court of Canada and its judgment, handed down on June 6, 1991, confirmed the judgment of the Federal Court of Appeal.

The Supreme Court

In its judgment, the Supreme Court

- ruled that the prohibition against public servants working for or against a candidate or political party violated their freedom of expression as set out in section 2(b) of the *Charter;*
- recognized the importance of the political neutrality of the Public Service and of public servants;
- stated that the present provision, in banning political activities without distinction and without regard for the nature of the work performed by the public servant, went further than necessary;
- stated that legislation could be enacted limiting the political activities of public servants and gave some indication of how future legislation might be framed in order to achieve the objective of a neutral Public Service.

Although the Supreme Court alluded to section 33 in its entirety, it maintained the judgment of the Federal Court of Appeal, setting aside paragraphs 33(1)(a) and (b) except with respect to deputy heads.

Consequences of the Judgment for Public Servants

1. The statutory prohibition in the *Public Service Employment Act* against working for or against a candidate or a political party has no force.
2. At the same time, employees should be aware that the principle of a politically neutral Public Service remains intact. Therefore, in engaging in political activities, they should exercise judgment and consider their specific circumstances, particularly with due regard to the loyalty they owe to the Government and to their obligation to act, and be seen to act, impartially when dealing with the public.
3. The requirement in subsection 33(3) of the *Public Service Employment Act* to obtain leave from the Public Service Commission to seek candidacy and to be a candidate still applies.
4. The judgment did not deal at length with the expression of specific political views or criticism of government policy. On such issues, the Supreme Court's decision in the Neil Fraser case in 1985 should be consulted.

New Legislation

Should the Government decide to proceed with new legislation, public servants will be advised accordingly.

...

[signed]
Robert J. Giroux, Chairman
Gilbert H. Scott, Commissioner
Ginette Stewart, Commissioner

APPENDIX F

THE GOVERNMENT OF THE UNITED STATES
POLITICAL DO'S AND DON'TS FOR FEDERAL EMPLOYEES

Employees may not:

- be candidates for public office in partisan elections;
- campaign for or against a candidate or slate of candidates in partisan elections;
- make campaign speeches or engage in other campaign activities to elect partisan candidates;
- collect contributions or sell tickets to political fund-raising functions;
- distribute campaign material in partisan elections;
- organize or manage political rallies or meetings;
- hold office in political clubs or parties;
- circulate nominating petitions; or
- work to register voters for one party only.

Employees may:

- register and vote as they choose;
- assist in voter registration drives;
- express opinions about candidates and issues;
- participate in campaigns where none of the candidates represent a political party;
- contribute money to political organizations or attend political fund-raising functions;
- wear or display political badges, buttons, or stickers;
- attend political rallies and meetings;
- join political clubs or parties;
- sign nominating petitions; or
- campaign for or against referendum questions, constitutional amendments, municipal ordinances.

Source: United States, Office of the Special Counsel (undated, 4).

ABBREVIATIONS

c.	chapter
D.L.R. (4th)	Dominion Law Reports, Fourth Series
Fed. T.D.	Federal Court, Trial Division
N.S.T.D.	Nova Scotia Trial Division
Ont. H.C.	Ontario High Court
O.P.S.E.U.	Ontario Public Service Employees Union
O.R. (2d)	Ontario Reports, Second Series
P.S.S.R.B.	Public Service Staff Relations Board
R.S.A.	Revised Statutes of Alberta
R.S.C.	Revised Statutes of Canada
R.S.M.	Revised Statutes of Manitoba
R.S.N.B.	Revised Statutes of New Brunswick
R.S.O.	Revised Statutes of Ontario
S.C.	Statutes of Canada
S.C.C.	Supreme Court of Canada
S.C.R.	Supreme Court Reports
S.M.	Statutes of Manitoba
S.P.E.I.	Statutes of Prince Edward Island
S.Q.	Statutes of Quebec
s(s).	section(s)
S.S.	Statutes of Saskatchewan

NOTES

This study was completed in April 1991; material concerning *Osborne* was updated to June 1991.

1. For a discussion of the legal and constitutional dimensions of the issue, see Garant (1990).

2. For elaboration on this model, see Kernaghan (1976) and D'Aquino (1984). The explanatory value of this model has been cited with approval in *Stopforth* (1978, 272–73) and in *Osborne* (1986, 678–79).

3. This statement is adapted from Ontario Law Reform Commission (1986, 24–25), which is an expanded version of Kernaghan (1979, 393).

4. The wording of most of the rationales is drawn from Kernaghan (1986).

5. For elaboration on the arguments in this section, see Kernaghan (1979).

6. Civil Service Order in Council 1969, art. 5, as amended by Code Memorandum CM/662, 28 September 1987.

7. For an examination of the early history of section 32 (now 33) of the *PSEA*, see Brown-John (1974).

8. Between 1967 and 1985, about 90 percent of such requests were granted. During 1988, the Public Service Commission received 16 requests for leave, of which 14 were for the federal election and 2 for the Manitoba provincial election. Two of these requests were withdrawn; all of the rest were approved (Canada, Public Service Commission 1989, 26).

9. Bill C-273 was a private member's bill introduced, and subsequently withdrawn, by David Daubney, MP (Canada, House of Commons, 1988).

10. Canada, *An Act to amend the Public Service Employment Act and the Auditor General Act in consequence thereof,* First reading, 30 August 1988.

11. See the explanation of political rights, partisan political activity and public comment earlier in this paper.

12. Possible models for provisions in this area are Great Britain's *Civil Service Pay and Conditions of Service Code* and Australia's *Guidelines on Official Conduct of Commonwealth Public Servants.*

13. Drawn from Kernaghan (1976, 449).

REFERENCES

Alberta. *Public Service Act,* R.S.A. 1980, c. P-31, s. 23, Code of Conduct and Ethics.

Australia. *Guidelines on Official Conduct of Commonwealth Public Servants.*

Australia. Public Service Board. 1982. *Personnel Management Manual.* Vol. 3. *Guidelines on Official Conduct of Commonwealth Public Servants.* Canberra: Australian Government Printing Office.

Bolton, James R. 1976. *The Hatch Act: A Civil Libertarian Defense.* Washington, DC: American Enterprise Institute for Public Policy Research.

Brown-John, Lloyd. 1974. "The Political Activity of Federal Public Servants." *Public Administration* 52:79–93.

Canada. Bill C-157, s. 32 ¶¶ 11, 12, 16, 19, 21. *An Act to amend the Public Service Employment Act and the Auditor General Act in consequence thereof.* 2nd Session, 33rd Parl. 1986-87-88. First reading 30 Aug. 1988.

———. *Canadian Charter of Rights and Freedoms,* s. 2, Part I of the *Constitution Act, 1982,* being Schedule B of the *Canada Act 1982* (U.K.), 1982, c. 11.

———. *Civil Service Act,* S.C. 1918, c. 12, s. 32.

———. *Public Service Employment Act,* S.C. 1967, c. 71.

———. *Public Service Employment Act,* R.S.C. 1970, c. P-32, s. 32.

———. *Public Service Employment Act,* R.S.C. 1985, c. P-33, ss. 33, 34.

Canada. House of Commons. Legislative Committee on Bill C-273, An Act Respecting Political Rights of Public Employees. 1988. *Minutes of Proceedings and Evidence,* March–April.

Canada. Public Service Commission. 1988. Current Interpretation of Section 32 of the Public Service Employment Act. Ottawa: PSC.

———. 1989. *Annual Report 1988.* Ottawa: Minister of Supply and Services Canada.

Canada. Public Service 2000. 1990. *Public Service 2000. The Renewal of the Public Service of Canada.* Ottawa: Minister of Supply and Services Canada.

Canada. Special Committee on the Review of Personnel Management and the Merit Principle. 1979. *Report.* Ottawa: Minister of Supply and Services Canada.

Canada. Task Force on Conflict of Interest. 1984. *Ethical Conduct in the Public Sector.* Ottawa: Minister of Supply and Services Canada.

Carleton University. School of Journalism. 1985. *Report on Attitudes of Public Servants to Political Restrictions on the Public Service.* Ottawa: Carleton University, School of Journalism.

Cassidy, Michael. 1986. "Political Rights for Public Servants: A Federal Perspective (1)." *Canadian Public Administration* 22:653–64.

Craig, Iris [President of the Professional Institute of the Public Service]. 1989. "Political Rights for Public Service Employees." *Policy Options* (November): 20.

D'Aquino, Thomas. 1984. "The Public Service of Canada: The Case of Political Neutrality." *Canadian Public Administration* 37:14–23.

Decter, Michael B. 1986. "Political Rights: A Manitoba Perspective." *Canadian Public Administration* 29:668–69.

Etzioni-Halevy, Eva. 1979. *Political Manipulation and Administrative Power.* London: Routledge and Kegan Paul.

Fraser v. Nova Scotia (Attorney General) (1986), 30 D.L.R. (4th) 340 (N.S.T.D.).

Fraser v. P.S.S.R.B., [1985] 2 S.C.R. 455.

Gallant, Edgar. 1986. "Political Rights for Public Servants: A Federal Perspective (2)." *Canadian Public Administration* 29:665–68.

Garant, Patrice. 1990. "La Liberté politique des fonctionnaires à l'heure de la Charte canadienne." *Cahiers de droit* 31:409–76.

Germany. *Basic Law for the Federal Republic of Germany* [Constitution], 1949.

Institute of Public Administration of Canada. 1986. *Statement of Principles Regarding the Conduct of Public Employees.* Toronto: IPAC.

Jackson, Robert. 1989. "The Politicization of the Public Service? Bureaucracy and Democracy in Canada." In *Politicization and the Career Service*, ed. G.R. Curnow and R. Page. Canberra: Canberra College of Advanced Education N.S.W. Division of the Royal Australian Institute of Public Administration.

Kernaghan, Kenneth. 1976. "Politics, Policy and Public Servants: Political Neutrality Revisited." *Canadian Public Administration* 19:432–56.

———. 1979. "Power, Parliament and Public Servants in Canada: Ministerial Responsibility Reexamined." *Canadian Public Policy* 3:383–96.

———. 1986. "Political Rights and Political Neutrality: Finding the Balance Point." *Canadian Public Administration* 29:639–52.

Kroeger, Arthur. 1991. "Reflections on Being a Deputy Minister." Speech to the Canadian Club of Ottawa, 15 January.

Manitoba. *Civil Service Act*, R.S.M. 1987, C-110, s. 44.

Mayntz, Renate, and Hans-Ulrich Derlien. 1989. "Party Patronage and Politicization of the West German Administrative Elite 1970–1987 – Toward Hybridization?" *Governance* 2 (October): 384–404.

Michelmann, Hans J. 1988. "Politicization in the German Federal Bureaucracy." Paper presented at the Annual Meeting of the Canadian Political Science Association, Windsor.

Michelmann, Hans J., and Jeffrey S. Steeves. 1985. "The 1982 Transition in Power in Saskatchewan: The Progressive Conservatives and the Public Service." *Canadian Public Administration* 28:1–23.

National Union of Provincial Government Employees. Undated. *Provincial Legislation: Restrictions on the Political Rights of Provincial Government Workers.* Research Report No. 5. Ottawa.

New Brunswick. *Civil Service Act,* S.N.B. 1984, c. C-5.1, s. 27.

Newfoundland. 1990. *Factum of the Attorney General of Newfoundland, Intervenor, in the Supreme Court of Canada, in The Public Service Commission and Randy Barnhart et al.* 2 October.

Newfoundland. Order in Council 951-75, 18 Aug. 1975.

Nova Scotia. *Civil Service Act,* R.S.N.S. 1989, c. 70, ss. 35–41.

Ontario. *Public Service Act,* R.S.O. 1980, c. 418, ss. 11–16.

Ontario Law Reform Commission. 1986. *Report on Political Activity, Public Comment and Disclosure by Crown Employees.* Toronto: Ministry of the Attorney General.

O.P.S.E.U. v. Ontario (Attorney General) (1980), 31 O.R. (2d) 321 (C.A.).

O.P.S.E.U. v. Ontario (Attorney General), [1987] 2 S.C.R. 2.

O.P.S.E.U. v. Ontario (Attorney General) (1988), 52 D.L.R. (4th) 701 (Ont. H.C.).

Osborne v. Canada (Treasury Board) (1986), 30 D.L.R. (4th) 682 (Fed. T.D.); reversed in part (1988), 52 D.L.R. (4th) 241 (Fed. C.A.); affirmed (1991), 82 D.L.R. (4th) 321 (S.C.C.).

Prince Edward Island. *Civil Service Act,* R.S.P.E.I. 1988, c. C-8, s. 38.

Public Service Commission v. Millar, Osborne and others. See Osborne v. Canada (Treasury Board).

Quebec. *Public Service Act,* S.Q. 1983, c. 55, ss. 10–12, 24–31.

Riddell, Norman. 1986. "Policies on Political Leave in Saskatchewan." Paper presented at the National Conference on Public Sector Management, Victoria, 22 April.

Saskatchewan. *Public Service Act,* R.S.S. 1978, c. P-42, s. 50.

Saskatchewan. 1990. *Factum of the Attorney General of Saskatchewan, Intervenor, in the Supreme Court of Canada, in The Public Service Commission and William James Millar et al.,* 4 October.

Singh v. Canada (Treasury Board), P.S.S.R.B., 4 June 1979.

Stopforth v. Goyer (1978), 20 O.R. (2d) 262 (H.C.).

United Kingdom. *Civil Service Pay and Conditions of Service Code,* Civil Service Order in Council 1969, art. 5; am. Code Memorandum CM/662, 28 Sept. 1987.

United States. Office of the Special Counsel. U.S. Merit Systems Protection Board. Undated. *Political Activity and the Federal Employee.* Washington, DC: The Board.

6

PROVISION FOR THE RECALL OF ELECTED OFFICIALS
Parameters and Prospects

Peter McCormick

THE RECALL (or, as its 19th-century proponents called it, the "imperative mandate") is a device whereby elected officials are subject at any time to the direct review of the electors whose votes put them in office. This review is triggered by a citizen petition (typically calling for a recall election) that, if successful, leads to a special election to fill the now-vacant office. Conceptually, it resembles the notion of impeachment,[1] which also removes a representative in mid-term, although the recall usually lacks the overtones of legal impropriety; one is *impeached* for crimes and misdemeanours, but one is typically *recalled* for failing to respond to the wishes and preferences of the electors.[2] In North America, the recall has been advocated sporadically for over a century; many of the U.S. states allow the recall of elected state officials and most allow the recall of elected local officials (Price 1983, 1988), but the only Canadian example was a short-lived and ill-starred experiment in Alberta.

> The referendum repeals "unjust" laws, the initiative establishes "needed" and "desired" legislation, and the recall replaces the "unresponsive" or "corrupt" officials. These forms are perhaps the purest forms of direct democracy remaining to the people today. (Sheldon and Weaver 1980, 11)

The recall is the junior member of the direct democracy family, the optional extra in the direct democracy three-pack. Referendum (binding public vote on specific pieces of proposed legislation or constitutional amendments) is the most familiar and common device of direct democracy, and a consideration of the varieties and implications of referendum procedures dominates the direct democracy literature; initiative (whereby the citizens themselves can directly initiate the question that is sent to a referendum) ranks a fairly distant second, but the recall is a remote third.

This comparative neglect carries over to the literature of direct democracy; in contrast to the plethora of writings on democratic referendums and the extensive examination of the theory and practice of the initiative, the literature on the recall is limited. Typical is a Library of Congress bibliography on the recall, referendum and initiative compiled in 1983 (Stewart 1983): the title notwithstanding, there is not a single entry dealing directly with the recall. Similarly, a recent book on direct democracy (Tallian 1977), breathlessly promising a careful consideration of recent experience with the recall, referendum and initiative, contains only a passing one-line reference to the fact that the Swiss recall is almost never used, before devoting hundreds of pages to recent North American experiences with the initiative and referendum.

Revolutionary in its appearance and its potential, the recall in practice is typically a damp squib of infrequent use and limited direct impact. Most recall petitions fail to gain the necessary signatures; many recall elections fail to unseat the incumbent; some recalled politicians promptly win the special election and therefore replace themselves. Oddly, this relative disuse meshes with the historical expectations of supporters of the recall, who "were convinced that the existence of the recall would be a sufficient deterrent to unrepresentative behaviour that there would be little need to employ the recall" (Zimmerman 1986, 106).

Fears that the recall inevitably would lead to a revolving-door legislature,[3] and that elected legislators would tremble in fear under the uncertainty of an indefinite and revocable tenure, are completely at odds with the actual experience of those jurisdictions that have implemented such measures. More aptly, it occasionally happens that elected representatives who flout public opinion on controversial issues, or who drift out of touch with the opinions of their constituents on questions that are extremely important to them, suffer the indignity of a recall petition or a recall election or a removal from office. To what extent this marginal threat modifies their actual behaviour (that is, to what extent they are not removed because the fear of removal prevents them from acting in a way that would justify their removal) is of course a moot point. Even to its more optimistic proponents, the recall makes its contribution from the margin, not from the centre, of daily political activity.

THE NEED FOR THE RECALL:
DIRECT AND REPRESENTATIVE DEMOCRACY

The historic beginnings of democracy (even the etymological origins of the word, from *demos*, "people" and *kratos*, "rule" or "authority") are Greek, and the democracy of the ancient Greek *polis* was direct democracy. The citizens met and exercised power directly in the assembly, joining in the debate and resolution of the major (and minor) issues of the day. The problems of scale – in the double sense of geographic area and population size – meant that the rediscovery of democracy in the 18th century could not be a rediscovery of direct democracy. The new democracy was, indeed had to be, representative democracy. The assembly was no longer the gathering of all citizens but the place where their elected representatives met to act in their name and on their behalf. Representative democracy is the great modern makeshift that permits popular rule even where numbers preclude a true assembly of all citizens. As well, it permits the extension of the privileges and powers of citizenship even to those who lack the leisure time the Greeks took for granted as a prerequisite – the shift from class democracy to mass democracy. It carries, however, its own dangers and problems, including the question of the accountability of representatives between elections.

The problem can be seen in terms of two different models of representation, which are at the same time two different theories of democracy. The first (what we might call the arm's-length model) sees the electors as constituting a genuine community that chooses a person from within its ranks for his or her judgement and wisdom. Once elected, the representative exercises that judgement to formulate national policy (whether or not any given number of the electors might agree with the behaviour that follows from that judgement on any specific issue) and gives a general accounting to constituents in the process of seeking a new mandate at the next election. The second (the hands-on model) reduces the representative to a mouthpiece to promote the will of the people; what democracy requires is the most immediate and direct accountability of elected representatives to their electing citizens and the narrowest possible definition of the discretion enjoyed by individual representatives. Hence, the 19th-century Chartist cry for annual parliaments (the two-year term for members of the U.S. House of Representatives is a direct modern descendant) and for the prompt accounting and the endless campaigning this entails.[4]

The emergence of the political party cuts both ways: at one and the same time, it facilitates and hampers accountability. Its advantages are twofold: first, a political party presents a coherent package of commitments and an organized team of candidates to promote them, making it more likely that voting choices can lead directly and predictably to policy outcomes. Second, the party's continuing existence makes accountability more real; although candidate X may gain personal immunity from electoral retribution by declining to run again, the party will present a new candidate to carry the party banner and reap the political harvest. However, the disadvantage is that the elected representative can be caught between the demands of the party and the preferences of constituents.

The evolution of disciplined parties within a system of responsible government represents a major victory for the arm's-length model of democracy, aptly symbolized by the way the elected members of the democratic assembly sustain in office an appointed cabinet that enjoys a virtual monopoly on effective political initiative. Whether one attributes motives that are selfish (the desire for the perks of patronage and power) or idealistic (a strong commitment to the party's principles and an acceptance of the discipline that alone permits their achievement), the outcome is the same: voters seethe in frustration while their representative votes contrary to their desires. The power to "turn the rascals out" at the next general election is small consolation when that next election is years away, and when important and virtually irrevocable decisions are being made in the meantime.

For democrats more attached to the will of the people than to the practical demands of political organization, the recall is a way of making representatives more accountable. Unlike initiative and referendum, which end run representative democracy itself and make the elected assembly a passive bystander, the recall is directed to making representative democracy more effective and more representative by rendering the member less accountable to the party and more accountable to the citizens. The device is therefore more congenial to the looser organization of U.S. parties than to the tightly disciplined Canadian version.[5]

In terms of more closely approximating the accountability and "hands-on" control of direct democracy, modern technology presents the prospect of some truly radical innovations, from interactive cable television to computer networks. The cybernetic future could be a radically democratic future, although like all technologies cybernetics can be used for quite different purposes as well, and every vision of a democratic utopia can be balanced by the nightmare of an electronic and totalitarian dystopia. The decision as to what use we make of these new potentials is one that will set the political tone of our society for generations to come. In this context, the recall is not an extreme or radical remedy, but a rather modest and traditional one. It is an old-fashioned, crude and highly limited way of calling elected officials to

account, at a time when practical experience and technological potential alike raise the question of whether democratic participation can
usefully continue to be focused primarily on the periodic election of
territorial representatives.

HISTORICAL BACKGROUND: THE RECALL IN NORTH AMERICA

Although historical allusions are sometimes made to the 18th-century
U.S. Articles of Confederation, the ideological context of the demand
for the recall in North America was clearly the populist (or Progressive)
movement.[6] Populism, as much a mood or syndrome as a systematic
philosophy (Wiles 1969), is built on a number of factors: a common-
sense celebration of the average citizen, a preference for direct democracy devices (recall, referendum, initiative) to allow direct ongoing
influence by the electors, an identification with small-scale business
capitalism (family farms and small business), a tendency to blame outside forces (sometimes sinister in nature) for economic and social problems and to see solutions in simple or even simplistic terms (such as the
recurrent conspiracy theories), a strong feeling of community and traditional values that borders on nativism and xenophobia, and a project of reform rather than revolution to solve economic and social ills.
The "we-they" dichotomy which is invariably at the core of populist
rhetoric – we the common people versus they the special interests –
generates a focus on the democratic franchise as the weapon of choice
for reform and fuels a feeling of betrayal and outrage at any perceived
blockage of the popular will.

The movements built on these sentiments tend to be regional in
their origin (the rural areas of the American Midwest and South, and
the Canadian Prairies), but they are not necessarily narrowly regional
in their appeal, and the recurrent waves of North American populism
are an element that the more traditional political forces must accommodate rather than extirpate. The organizational core from which political action flows is typically a farmers' movement (the Grangers or the
Farmers' Alliance in the United States; the United Farmers or the
Farmers' Union in Canada) with tenuous connections to an urban labour
movement. In the United States, populism was a significant political
force in the closing decades of the 19th century, culminating in the
People's Party of the 1890s. By the turn of the century, it had been largely
replaced by the Progressive movement, which made major inroads in
the western and midwestern states.

Populism/progressivism advocated a wide range of direct democratic devices. The particular attraction of the recall, and the pragmatic
impetus carrying it through into practice, grew from its usefulness as

a weapon against corrupt elected officials, or more generally against the frustration resulting from the control of state legislatures by moneyed special interests. "The recall in the United States ... had its origins in a notably corrupt political system. None of its advocates ever viewed it as a substitute for representative government" (Cronin 1989, 131).

In many states, the enduring legacy of the Progressives includes the recall. The geographical sweep of recall measures adopted before the First World War (Schaffner 1908; Barnett 1912, 1915) clearly reflects the regional concentration of Progressive strength;[7] the three interwar adoptions were also in states where the Progressive tradition was strong. The devices of direct democracy are "clearly a Western phenomenon" (Sheldon and Weaver 1980, 9). The revival of popular interest in the recall in the 1970s is less easy to explain; in addition to the adoption of the recall in Montana and Georgia[8] in 1976 and 1978 respectively, a recall provision was narrowly defeated by the voters in Utah[9] and another was narrowly rejected by a 1978 state constitutional convention in Hawaii. Although the recall is clearly a product of the Progressive outburst in the early 20th century, it just as clearly cannot be written off as a spent force. Sentell suggests that the argument for the recall can also be derived from "the rampant mood of consumerism [that] seeks to require that advertising be substantiated, that promises be fulfilled, and that performance be perfected" (Sentell 1976, 883).

The first major wave of Canadian populism[10] took place immediately after the First World War, as Progressive candidates contested federal and provincial elections under a bewildering variety of labels.[11] In federal politics, they briefly supplanted the Conservatives as the second largest grouping in the House of Commons, but rejected official opposition status as part of the hated party system; after 1921, they faded steadily as a political force. In provincial politics (under the United Farmers label) they formed governments in Alberta, Manitoba and (briefly) Ontario.

The rhetoric of the Progressives stressed grassroots democracy, delegate control and the devices of direct democracy. In practice, the exigencies of governmental office and the demands of leadership undercut commitment to these principles, and little was done about recall, referendum and initiative.[12] The tension between responsible government on the one hand and delegate democracy on the other was an ongoing problem for the Progressives in power, but it was fought out within the ranks of the movement without taking legislative form, and the locus for attempts to establish grassroots democratic control was the local association.

Legislative fulfilment for the recall did not occur until the second wave of Canadian populism, in the form of the Social Credit and Co-operative Commonwealth Federation movements of the 1930s.[13] Social Credit, stressing its continuity with the Progressive movement, included the recall among its 1935 campaign promises, and the Aberhart government passed the *Legislative Assembly (Recall) Act* on 3 April 1936. The legislation was closely modelled on the U.S. examples, although the signatures required for a petition (two-thirds of eligible voters) were almost triple the normal U.S. state requirement. This seems unworkably high, but the voters in Premier Aberhart's own riding were soon well on the way to having the necessary signatures, and the Premier responded by retroactively repealing the legislation in October 1937 (while keeping the recall deposit) (Elliott and Miller 1987, 285) and by running in the multi-member Calgary riding in the next general election.

The political circumstances were, to say the least, unusual. Beset by the Depression and racked by a sex scandal involving the Premier (heady stuff for the 1930s), the United Farmers of Alberta were wiped out in the 1935 election. Social Credit swept to a landslide victory (56 seats in a legislature of 63) in its first election, and high school principal and preacher William Aberhart, the party's charismatic leader with his command of the new electronic medium of radio, became premier. Since Aberhart had declined to run in the general election, a seat had to be opened up for a by-election, and he chose Okotoks–High River.[14] The legislative session was far from dull; a virtually bankrupt government was caught between the provincial and federal establishment (who found the Premier's actions much too radical) and the true believers among its own ranks (who thought the Premier much too cautious). To Aberhart's supporters, the striking down of Social Credit legislation by means of reservation, disallowance and court rulings of unconstitutionality proved the strength of the sinister establishment that held the people down; to his critics, the disregard for traditional rights and liberties in legislation such as the *Alberta Press Act* demonstrated the dangerous demagoguery of Aberhart and his Social Credit movement. Rhetoric on both sides was unrestrained; comparisons of Aberhart to Mussolini and Hitler were routine.

The appearance before a legislative committee of the founder of Social Credit, Major C.H. Douglas, and his naming of two experts[15] to keep an eye on the Alberta experiment, added to the controversy and the confusion. One consequence was a backbenchers' revolt without precedent in Canadian politics, as a bloc of dissidents defied the Premier (who was not even able to move adjournment for several days) but refused to vote with the opposition to defeat him and force a new election. Aberhart survived, but controversy and dissatisfaction resurfaced when he purged the Cabinet of some of the more radical Douglas followers who had encouraged the backbenchers.

The combination of "business antipathy to the government's interventionism on the one hand, and popular disillusionment with the government's timidity on the other" (Finkel 1989, 70) flared up in the Premier's own riding, and a recall petition was circulated. Although there is no firm evidence to support it, Aberhart's contention was that oil company executives were bribing and intimidating their workers to support the recall attempt, that the "Eastern big-shots" he had attacked so vigorously were trying to deny Alberta the relief that only Social Credit ideas could offer. Certainly, no premier has been more vigorously or consistently vilified by the popular press.[16] More prosaic factors played a role as well. Aberhart was, to put it mildly, not distinguished for his constituency service and was clearly not at home in the oilfields. Certainly it was unwise, when oilfield workers claimed that Imperial Oil was ignoring Social Credit legislation, to tell them to take their problems to the Labour Bureau and stop complaining to him (ibid.).

As has often been pointed out (e.g., Macpherson 1953; Laycock 1990), it is anomalous that it should have been Aberhart's Social Credit that gave even temporary access to the recall, because among the strands of populism, Social Credit is the one most supportive of the role of the expert and most inclined toward plebiscitary rather than participatory democracy. Canada's only provincial experiment with the recall of elected officials did not end auspiciously, although the Premier's casual, almost careless, selection of a riding in which to run, and his high-handed treatment of those he purported to represent, unnecessarily aggravated an already difficult situation. It dramatically demonstrates the special vulnerability of premiers and other central cabinet ministers, a major problem for the recall under responsible government for which the American experiences offer nothing in the way of relevant wisdom or advice.

HOW THE RECALL WORKS: THE AMERICAN EXPERIENCE

Fifteen different states[17] have adopted the recall for elected state officials. Six of these states exempt elected state judges from the reach of the recall, while a single state (Montana) makes appointed state officials also subject to the recall.[18]

The recall is not in effect for any federal officials, elected or appointed, with one heavily qualified exception:

> In addition to the regular recall, Arizona uses the "advisory recall,"
> a device by which candidates seeking election to Congress *may* file a

statement indicating a willingness or unwillingness to resign if not
re-elected at a recall election. Candidates may refuse to file any statement. In any case, a recall vote itself cannot remove a member of
Congress from office, since the U.S. Constitution does not recognize
the procedure. (Maddox and Fuquay 1966, 331 fn.)

There is a considerable degree of diversity in the procedures and regulations surrounding the recall provisions in the various states. What
follows is a general summary of the major elements of the recall and an
indication of some of the variety.[19]

There are three basic patterns of recall procedure. The first requires
two elections, the people voting on the question of removal on the first,
and (if affirmative) then holding a second election to choose a replacement; this is the standard and most common form, used in almost all

Table 6.1
Provisions for recall of state officials

State	Year	Officials affected	Petition requirements
Oregon[a]	1908	all elected	15% votes
California[a]	1911	all elected	12%/20% votes
Arizona	1912	all elected	25% votes
Colorado	1912	all elected	25% votes
Nevada	1912	all elected	25% voters
Washington	1912	all elected, except judges	25%/35% voters
Michigan	1913	all elected, except judges	25% votes
Kansas	1914	all elected, except judges	40% votes
Louisiana	1914	all elected, except judges	25% voters
North Dakota[a]	1920	all elected	25% votes
Wisconsin	1926	all elected	25% votes
Idaho[a]	1933	all elected, except judges	20% voters
Alaska	1959	all elected, except judges	25% voters
Montana	1976	all elected and all appointed	10%/15% voters
Georgia	1978	all elected	15%/30% voters

Source: Adapted from table 5.16, The Book of the States (1986, 217).

Notes: Votes = votes cast at previous election. Voters = eligible voters at previous election.
10%/15% = requirement for statewide/district elections.

[a]Successful use of recall.

jurisdictions. The second calls for citizens to vote simultaneously on removal and replacement (the latter counting only if the first is decided in the affirmative). This is the procedure in Colorado and Wisconsin. "A third variation simply requires the person against whom a recall petition has been filed to run against other candidates whose names have been placed on the ballot" (Maddox and Fuquay 1966, 332). This is the procedure in Arizona and Nevada; it was initially adopted by Oregon, the first state to employ the recall for state officials (Barnett 1912, 41), but an Oregon Supreme Court decision in 1914 held that the two questions of recall and replacement must be treated separately, and the procedures were changed accordingly (Cronin 1989, 151). The first procedure is to be preferred "for several reasons, not least of which is that the official 'runs' against his record rather than against others seeking his position" (ibid.).

The proportion of voter signatures necessary for a petition varies from 10 percent (for statewide officials in Montana) to 40 percent (in Kansas). The most common figure, used in nine of the 15 jurisdictions, is 25 percent. Nine states base the requirement on the eligible voters for the office in question during the most recent election; six base it on the number of votes actually cast in that election. Given the low and variable rates of turnout in state elections, the latter is considerably more permissive.

Eight states (Alaska, Arizona, California, Georgia, Idaho, Kansas, Oregon and Washington) require filing and public notice of intent for a recall petition; two of these (Alaska and Kansas) call for a modest filing fee of $100. Some states give a maximum time for the circulation of the petition, from 60 days in Wisconsin to 270 days in Washington;[20] most have no such limit, although in practice the two-year term of most state legislators limits the time as effectively as any formal regulation would.

In Kansas, Washington and Pennsylvania the recall is a quasi-judicial procedure, limited to cases of malfeasance, misconduct, incompetence or failure to perform legal duties; a petition not based on such an accusation is invalid. Elsewhere, the recall is a political question: an elected official can be recalled for any reason that a large enough body of voters thinks appropriate. Several states will not allow a recall petition at the beginning of a term, the immune period varying from two months (Montana) to 90 days (California) to six months (Arizona, Colorado, Oregon) to one year (Wisconsin). An official is also immune after an unsuccessful recall election for a period varying from three months (Wisconsin) to 18 months (Louisiana), although some states will waive this if the new petitioners reimburse the state for the costs of the previous unsuccessful recall vote.

Michigan is the only state that bars the recalled officer from running again in the special replacement election; more typically, recalled officials are automatically candidates for their own replacement unless they formally indicate otherwise. It is not infrequent (but neither is it the normal outcome) for the recallee to be elected as his or her own replacement. Some local charters stipulate a minimum turnout (typically 50 percent) for a recall election to be valid; no state has a comparable provision.

As Maddox and Fuquay indicate, recalls are not frequent:

> The recall has been used much less frequently than the initiative and referendum. The only instance of its successful use to remove officers elected on a statewide basis occurred in North Dakota in 1921, when the governor, attorney general and secretary of agriculture were recalled. (Governor Frazier, oddly enough, was elected to the United States Senate the following year by the same electorate that had recalled him from the governor's chair!) (Maddox and Fuquay 1966, 332–33)

The removal of state legislators has not been much more common, "including two in California in 1913, two in Idaho in 1971, two in Michigan in 1983 and one in Oregon in 1988" (Cronin 1989, 127). A California state senator was successfully recalled in 1919 (Zimmerman 1986, 127). Most recall petitions against state officials (in some estimates, more than 90 percent) fail to gain the necessary signatures; the success rate for recall elections seems to be closer to 50 percent, although this estimate includes local as well as state experiences.

IMPLICATIONS OF THE RECALL: ARGUMENTS PRO AND CON

The literature suggests a number of standard arguments for and against the recall; the list is not intended to be inclusive, and clearly not all are of equal weight or validity. Briefly, these arguments may be summarized as follows:[21]

Some of the arguments in favour of the recall are:

1. Arguments from democratic principles:
   a. The recall strengthens popular control of government by allowing voters to remove public officers who are corrupt or incompetent, or who fail to reflect accurately the views of the electorate on major issues.
   b. The availability of the recall increases citizen interest in public affairs and reduces alienation by providing for continual accountability, allowing them to act when they have lost confidence in their representatives.

2. Arguments based on fear of corruption and special interests:
   a. The recall provides a backstop when the normal processes of the electoral system fail to produce accountable and responsive public officers.
   b. The recall reminds public officers that corruption and inefficiency will not be tolerated.
   c. The recall helps check undue influence by narrow special interests, by allowing voters to act promptly when such influence manifests itself.
3. Arguments stressing ancillary benefits:
   a. The recall increases the willingness to remove restrictions on the actions of public officers because it provides a recourse against officers who betray their trust.
   b. The recall encourages the electorate to accept longer terms of office for elected officials.
4. Arguments suggesting restraint of democracy:
   a. The recall offers a safety-valve mechanism for intense feelings.

The arguments against the recall include:

1. Arguments based on democratic principles:
   a. The very premise of the recall is antagonistic to representative principles, especially to the idea of electing good lawmakers, allowing them a chance to govern until the next election, and then judging them on the package of their accomplishments.
2. Arguments based on suggestions of redundancy:
   a. There are other ways of removing public officers when it is necessary to do so, and these ways do not suffer the disadvantages of the recall.
3. Arguments suggesting the unavoidable dangers of possible misuse:
   a. The use of the recall for ideological or partisan reasons is both unavoidable and undesirable.
   b. Frivolous recall petitions can be circulated to harass conscientious public officers.
   c. The recall may be abused by well-organized and well-financed organizations to achieve their special interests.
   d. The recall may be used to remove individuals from public office for petty or transient reasons; that is, recall in haste, repent at leisure.

4. Arguments stressing harmful side-effects:
   a. The recall will restrain innovative and energetic public officers.
   b. The recall will discourage highly qualified men and women from seeking office when controversial issues call for difficult decisions.
   c. The recall increases governmental costs with the need for recall elections and special elections.
   d. Recall elections are divisive, disruptive, polarizing and subject to many abuses; they are often confusing, and they place too much burden on the voters to keep informed between elections.

For many of the arguments, both for and against, the response is an obvious one: because the recall in fact is not used frequently even in those jurisdictions that permit it, its capacity for good or ill should not be overstated. As Bird and Ryan concluded, "Twenty-five years of the operation of the recall in the state of its first adoption[22] have realized neither the highest hopes of its sanguine originators nor the darkest prophecies of its cynical opponents" (Bird and Ryan 1930, 342). Nothing in the ensuing 50 years, in California or any of the other states that allow the recall, would require any revision of this judgement. At most, the recall softens the edges of the political system; it does not, cannot and was never intended to provide the basic contours.

A CANADIAN RECALL? SPECIFICS AND PROBLEMS

It is possible to pull these strands and threads together, to build on the American experience to outline a Canadian recall proposal, although some comments will end with questions rather than answers.

A critical problem for a Canadian recall is the importance of the solidarity of the party that maintains in power the government of the day. It seems unlikely that the major focus of recall efforts would be members of the opposition, who normally enjoy greater freedom to articulate the preferences of their constituents even when they are at odds with party policy, although it is easy to devise scenarios in which particular highly controversial issues might trigger these as well. Government members, however, normally have much less freedom to manoeuvre and are sitting targets for the frustration that governments normally endure. Equally serious, Cabinet members are not elected separately on a nationwide ballot but are appointed from among (with the rarest of exceptions) the ranks of the elected members; theirs is a dual role of constituent representative as well as legislator and political executive, and this has no direct American counterpart.

Linked to this is the particular importance of party in the Canadian parliamentary system. It is usually the case that voters cast their ballots for particular candidates less because of any special attractiveness of person or position than to express support for the candidate's party or party leader; once elected, members find themselves part of a disciplined and organized team, built around loyalty to party and leader, and buttressed by the petty (and sometimes not so petty) perks and punishments of legislative life. Both questions are considered in more detail later.

The catalogue that follows is intended as a canvass of some significant issues and problems rather than an encyclopedic resolution of them; the point is simply to give some feel for what a Canadian recall would look like and how it would operate.

Recall provisions usually recognize a "honeymoon" period, a short initial period of immunity after a general election. In U.S. jurisdictions this varies in length from two months to one year, and the relatively long time (in American terms) between Canadian elections makes the higher end of this range preferable. The logic of this is that it prevents the recall from being used for a quick "second shot" by narrowly defeated opponents. As well, it gives new members time to develop a personal track record to which electors can react, while for incumbents the slate has been wiped clean once the general election confirms them in their elected office. With similar logic, there is a parallel immunity after an unsuccessful recall election, but not after an unsuccessful recall petition.

In some American jurisdictions, there is also an immune period toward the term's end, but the indefinite life of a Canadian Parliament makes this difficult, and perhaps undesirable, to operationalize. Indeed, recall would provide a democratically satisfactory answer to the problem posed by Parliament's power (by vote of an unusual majority) to extend its own life beyond the normal maximum of five years.

The petition requirements must be set high enough to discourage frequent or frivolous challenges, but low enough not to be a deterrent to serious and widespread discontent. The most plausible figure, drawn from American experience, is 25 percent of eligible voters.[23] In the average federal riding, this would mean about 15 000 signatures, a hurdle that is neither inconsequential nor prohibitive. Because the outcome of a recall petition is potentially very serious, there must be some verification of signatures; yet because the number of signatures is so high, it is not feasible to verify them all. The compromise in many of the U.S. states that use the recall is the official verification of a statistical random sample of all signatures.

Although voter dissatisfaction with the government is often diffuse, it is desirable to focus the discontent by requiring the petitioners to provide a brief statement (in U.S. practice, typically 200 words or fewer) of the reasons for the recall petition, and to elicit a comparably tersely worded response from the challenged representative. Both the charges and the response are printed on the ballot, and they promote both a logical centre of gravity for the campaign and a clearer significance to the outcome, favourable or unfavourable.[24] However, "the problem of providing for more specificity in recall charges probably remains the most frustrating aspect of the recall," the difficulty being to avoid "vague or flimsy charges, or even charges different from those that really motivated the recall" (Cronin 1989, 154).

Requiring a recall petition to be linked to a particular grievance against the incumbent also suggests the desirability of a time limit for petitions, the cogency of the attack suffering attrition over time as the particular occasion for the complaint fades into the political background and out of the unprompted consciousness of citizens. The scenario that clearly supports the idea of the recall is an unusually unpopular or outrageous action by a representative, an action so repugnant to the bulk of the electors that a recall petition quickly succeeds, followed by a successful recall election. Much less attractive is the scenario of a petition initiated early in the incumbent's term, slowly accumulating signatures and finally achieving the magic number years later, after the grievance has become such stale news that it can no longer be credibly addressed as the focal issue. The time limits in various U.S. jurisdictions vary widely (60 days in Wisconsin, 270 days in Washington). During the interval between petition and recall vote, the targeted representative remains a full member of the legislative body, exercising all the powers and privileges this implies; only a successful recall vote creates a vacancy.

There are two major alternatives for a recall procedure. The first is to vote at the same time on both the recall and the replacement, the second part of the ballot becoming irrelevant if the first is decided in the negative. The second alternative is to vote on the question of the recall and to conduct a separate vote at another time to choose a replacement. The advantage of the single vote option is economy of time and public money, as it deals with the relevant questions in a single trip to the polls. Its flaws, however, are equally clear and even more cogent: it commits any replacement candidates to a strangely conditional campaign (vote for me *in case* the recall succeeds), and it creates confusion between the backward-looking vote of the recall vote itself and the forward-looking vote of the special replacement election.[25] Two separate votes seems the better choice.

A successful recall petition places the impugned incumbent in an uncertain and unsettling position, the more so because the high petition threshold demonstrates a strong and hostile public opinion. U.S. states typically require a prompt vote on the recall, although some observers (e.g., Cronin 1989, 154) recommend as a useful reform a cooling-off period between the petition and the vote on the recall. Allowing the emotional momentum of the petition drive to dissipate promotes a cooler second thought and gives the challenged representative time to organize an effective response. A successful recall vote creates the need for a by-election that is little different from those that occur from time to time in any system, although it might be desirable to place some restrictions on the timing of the special election, to limit the capacity of the governments in the parliamentary system to manipulate the timing of by-elections to their own advantage. Most U.S. state jurisdictions require a special election within a period of 30 or 40 days. There seems no reason to follow the practice of some U.S. states in barring the recalled candidate from seeking re-election.

The filing of a petition creates the presumption that there is a group that could be treated as an umbrella organization for funding the recall attempt; formal limitations and reporting requirements for campaign financing would provide some protection against the possible vulnerability of direct democracy to the efforts of those with the deepest pockets. At the very least, moneyed interests would have to identify themselves to launch the attack; the recall would not be a political weapon that could be fired from cover.[26] A comparable umbrella organization would organize the opposition to the recall. Partial public subsidy of expenses could be pegged to achievement of a specific level of support (say, 40 percent) in the recall election. Should the recall succeed, the result would simply be another federal by-election subject to the same regulations on candidacy, participation, financing and subsidy.

One attraction of the recall is that it appears logical, clean and neat, a simple assertion of voter choice exercised between normal elections through carefully defined procedures. This appearance is an illusion; as a U.S. academic has concluded, "Whatever the merits or demerits of recall, all agree that few topics constitute a more popular target for litigation" (Sentell 1976, 886). The recall is unlikely to be seriously invoked except for a major and politically charged controversy, with both sides hotly engaged and prepared to use all available weapons. A procedure as new as the recall cannot fail to stir legal concerns and ruffle Charter feathers, leaving an inevitable hiatus while the courts establish a jurisprudence of recall: the privileged status of recall charges; the niceties of timing, notice and validation of petitions; the treatment of recalls against elected members who are also national officials; the status of voters' lists; and so on. The problem is not draughtsmanship; rather, it grows out of the controversial and litigation-prone nature of the situations the recall tries to resolve and often further compounds.

THE RECALL IN A PARLIAMENTARY SYSTEM

There is one important respect in which American experiences, however extensive, cannot answer the questions or resolve the problems of a Canadian recall – specifically, the fact that Canada lives under a parliamentary system. In Canada, but not in the United States, members of the cabinet are not separately elected but are drawn from among the members of the House of Commons (or, more rarely, the Senate), leading a dual existence as members of the political executive and members of the elected legislature. The U.S. solution of "double-tracking" recall procedures – a statewide recall for elected state officials, and more localized recall procedures for those elected officials with a geographically more restricted mandate – is therefore not available or workable north of the border. It is surely not by chance that Canada's only experience with the recall of an elected official at the provincial level was an attempt to recall an MLA who was also the premier, although it is also relevant that it occurred with a unique combination of extremely unusual circumstances.

Of the three possible solutions to this problem suggested above, two are sufficiently flawed that they can be ruled out. The first possibility – a national recall procedure for those elected members who are also national officers – is an unnecessarily big solution for what I will argue is a small problem. The American experience suggests that statewide recall procedures are so difficult that they almost never succeed; the entire list of successful statewide recalls includes a single series of events in North Dakota in 1921. Even adding the 1978 Arizona episode, where a recall was cut short only by a successful impeachment, gives only two successes in 950 state-years of opportunity.[27] The hill of a nationwide recall is unlikely to be less steep or more climbable. More seriously, however, the retreat to a nationwide recall threatens the very danger it pretends to prevent, by creating a political momentum that would make it impossible for a government to carry on; a successful national recall would carry implications lacking in a purely local process. Such circumstances would indeed constitute a confidence process outside the confidence chamber of the Commons and would irrevocably transform responsible government; they would maximize, rather than minimize, the incompatibility of the recall and the parliamentary system.

The second possible solution – immunizing Cabinet members from the reach of a recall that affects all other elected representatives – would also be a cure worse than the disease. It would accentuate the growing gulf between elected representatives and public officials that is one of the greatest problems of a functioning democracy in this last half of the 20th century; by suggesting that our leaders think themselves too important to risk the accountability of their own backbenchers, this solution would demonstrate precisely the arrogance and hubris that critics find so outrageous. If a popular recall were adopted, the self-serving partiality of executive immunity might well prove only a temporary makeshift, untenable in the long haul.

Simply leaving Cabinet members subject to the same recall process as other members of the Commons – resolving the duality of elected representative and public official by exposing only the first half to such direct voter accountability – is in the end the least problematic of the three alternatives. Members of the Cabinet, especially those in the senior portfolios, enjoy a special vulnerability as a tempting target for a recall. The reverse side of the coin, however, is that they enjoy special advantages in resisting such attacks, not least of which is the pride that electors feel in the prominence of their own representatives (not unmixed with expectations of more immediate and concrete benefits flowing from this prominence). Any disgruntled group can and will start a recall petition, but gathering the signatures that are required to force a recall ballot, and then mustering the voters to recall the incumbent, is a different proposition altogether. The American experience does not suggest that the recall can be used casually by small groups with petty grievances; rather, it demonstrates how little of the antigovernment grumbling so ubiquitous in a democratic society can stand the harsh test of petition and election.

The further advantage of retaining local recalls even for those elected representatives who are also national officials is that it contains the possible damage of a successful recall. For a prime minister or senior cabinet ministers to lose their seats in such a fashion would be profoundly embarrassing but by no means politically fatal to either the individual politicians or the government of which they were a part. Not even the most panicky governor general could read it as a question of confidence suggesting the need for a new government or an immediate election; on such questions, governors general are quite properly myopic (unable to see beyond the Commons itself) and hard of hearing (unable to hear anything other than formal confidence votes in that chamber). To use the obvious and precisely analogous case: in 1989, the Alberta Conservatives called a provincial election and held 60 of the 84 seats, although their leader, the provincial premier, failed to be re-elected in his own constituency. There is no doubt that Premier Don Getty was profoundly embarrassed by this development, but there was even less doubt that the Conservatives remained the provincial government and that Getty himself remained premier. Precisely the same would be true of a prime minister recalled by unappreciative constituents in that single riding.

(The remoter fear – that a series of recalls could deprive a government of its majority and thereby force a general election – is less cogent and suffers from a double flaw. First, the principle it invokes logically requires us also to exempt a government with a painfully small majority from the risks involved in the normal by-election process; and perhaps requires us to allow government MPs to vote even if they are not physically present in the House, lest an influenza epidemic should topple a government. Second, and more fundamentally, it places a higher value on the survival of a government than on the reasoned voting preferences of the citizens, even when those preferences are expressed through formal and legally established procedures. If citizens are not to be trusted to exercise their democratic powers reasonably and wisely, then what is in doubt is not just the recall but the whole noble and dangerous experiment of representative democracy itself.)

Confidence is one of the two most overblown and overworked words in the democratic vocabulary (mandate is the other one), capable of absorbing as much or as little meaning as the government of the day wants to load onto it. To use the obvious pun: Canadian politics is a confidence game. The short leash on which our government backbenchers are kept is the product of the deliberate policy of a generation or more of governments; one of its consequences is the extremely high rate of turnover in the Canadian Commons, the product more of "backbench burnout" than of electoral volatility. The institutions of Canadian responsible government – the single-member plurality vote electoral district, and the concept of the confidence of the House sustaining the government of the day – represent a particularly rigid form of the practices that evolved in Britain in and before the 19th century. In Westminster itself, the Westminster model has softened considerably, and British governments have discovered that they can periodically, even routinely, accommodate without constitutional crisis backbench discontent resulting in significant amendments to major government legislation. (The contrast between the two countries is well caught by the story of Prime Minister Thatcher advising an incredulous Prime Minister Trudeau that she could not guarantee that her backbenchers would vote to pass a unilaterally imposed federal constitutional package; had the situations been reversed, the warning would have been both unnecessary and inaccurate.) Even in Canada, under the impact of recurrent minority governments during the 1960s, the rhetorically brittle conventions of responsibility have been found to have unexpected flexibility,[28] although the awareness seldom survived the election establishing the next majority mandate.

The recall would have an impact on the role of the individual representative and might more often (but not necessarily very often) tilt the balance between party and constituents in favour of the constituents. The knee-jerk reaction that responsible government could not possibly survive this adjustment is as predictable as it is unconvincing. Canadian governments could surely learn to tolerate (although never to enjoy) more outspoken critics within their own ranks and could back away from the pretence that the survival of the government hangs in the balance on every single Commons vote, or that minorities within its own caucus must choose between silence and expulsion. It might not be a bad thing if some of the disagreements aired in caucus should spill over into the Commons itself, or if the collaboration of some government backbenchers permitted amendments to government legislation; the gains in popular feelings of efficacy and representation could easily outweigh the costs.

The recall clearly presents potentially greater problems for a parliamentary than for a congressional system, but these problems should not be exaggerated in the light of the American experience that recalls are seldom attempted and even more rarely succeed. Cabinet members may suffer more than their share of challenges, a shaky government with a paper-thin majority may fall, and some government backbenchers may become marginally more ready to speak out and to ignore the party whips, but none of these are wounds that cut to the heart of responsible government.

THE RECALL AND THE PARTY SYSTEM

With the British parliamentary system, Canada has inherited the disciplined political parties that are necessary to make it function, aptly symbolized in the party officials melodramatically styled party whips. Indeed, in recent decades there have been serious grounds for thinking that Canada has gone the British one better, and Westminster itself now functions with political parties less rigidly disciplined than those that Canadian politicians believe to be logically entailed by the Westminster model.[29]

How well has Canada been served by this system? Certainly it has created general political stability over a century plus: only one government (John A. Macdonald's, because of the Pacific scandal) has left office because it was abandoned by its own members after winning an election, although Diefenbaker came close in the 1960s, and defections to the Bloc québécois have recently eroded Brian Mulroney's majority. But this stability has been purchased at a price, much of which is paid by the private members, or backbenchers. They are held in line by a combination of psychological subordination (most know that they were elected on the prime minister's coat-tails), party solidarity (only the prime minister has a national mandate), petty patronage (beginning with committee and office assignments) and the threat of sanctions (such as expulsion from caucus or removal from choice committees – and there have been recent examples of both).

One logical consequence of the disciplined parties is the decline of debates in the Commons, which seldom rises above partisan posturings and sterile confrontation. The televising of Commons proceedings may have improved the way that the members dress, but it has hardly enhanced their public stature and reputation, heckling not being a widely appreciated art. (It is generally held that debates in the Senate, which nobody watches, are much better, although the later stages of the GST debate showed that the Senate is capable of the same levels of puerility as the Commons.) Disciplined parties mean that every vote is a foregone conclusion; public unfamiliarity with the niceties of parliamentary procedure means that opposition tactics are usually misunderstood as obstruction. The popular focus is on Question Period where contrived indignation on both sides of the floor provides a preview of the next general election. Seldom does parliamentary debate edify or inform; usually, it is irrelevant.

A second direct consequence is the high turnover in the House of Commons from one election to the next, caused less by electoral volatility than by voluntary retirement. After each election, the proportion of rookies within the Commons is one-third or more (after a landslide turnover such as that of 1984, it rises much higher) and this is unusually high for Western democratic assemblies; most of those rookies will serve for only one or two parliaments, usually leaving in frustration and disillusionment. Pierre Trudeau had it absolutely backward when he taunted that his opposition backbench hecklers were "nobodies" once they were away from Parliament Hill; quite the contrary, MPs are individuals of some stature (often gradually turning into notoriety) in their own constituencies, but they are "nobodies" within the tightly disciplined hierarchies of Parliament.

Perhaps a third consequence is the rather disturbing recent trend toward a massive collapse of governmental popularity after an increasingly brief initial honeymoon. Diefenbaker, Trudeau and Mulroney are variations on a single theme: after an initial surge of enthusiasm and excitement, the government begins a protracted slide in the polls, each in turn reaching the lowest levels of public popularity in the history of Canadian polling before being swept from office as the cycle begins again. The Prime Minister's Office becomes a bunker, caucus meetings become pep rallies where members are exhorted to toe the party line, rather than being clearing-houses of grassroots information; MPs are reviled as sheep when they defend the government and as traitors when they convey the doubts of their constituents in caucus; and the government lurches toward an election in which the private members are the cannon fodder who pay the price of the general's mistakes. In less dramatic language, the downward arrows of command overwhelm the upward arrows of communication within the elected party hierarchy.

It is far from an original idea to suggest that there is something of an institutional misfit between the disciplined parties and inherent centralization of the British parliamentary system and the regionalism that is both presupposed and encouraged by federalism. In this context, it is unfortunate that the trend in Canada has been toward even more disciplined parties and an even less accountable centralized leadership. (Given Canadian practices, Margaret Thatcher would have led her party through at least one more election, probably more.) In the interests of stability, something has to give, and it is unlikely to be federalism and regionalism. The question is therefore less whether a step toward a less tightly disciplined party is necessary, than whether the small tiptoe of the recall will be enough to make a difference.

What would be the impact of the recall on the disciplined machinery of the national parties? Clearly it would, at least on occasion, make the individual MP more concerned with constituents and less concerned with party. Loyalty to party would not necessarily be a guarantee of job security and possible upward mobility; on the contrary, too automatic a loyalty might simply expose the member to the threat of removal and call forth a more nuanced position than silent conformity and lock-step obedience.

We know that the practice of monolithic party unity masks the diversity within the broker parties that characterizes our politics; we know from research surveys that members want to serve their ridings and are frustrated by their constricted opportunities; and we know from British experience that responsible government can survive backbench factions and the occasional defiance of prime-ministerial preferences. The recall could provide the incentive (or perhaps merely the excuse) for individual members to assert a more independent role; it could open up the discipline of Canadian political parties by putting backbench members more frequently in positions where they might feel they could not afford to bow to the party whip, and where the party whip would have to acknowledge the significance of these cross-pressures. It might be open to argument whether this would be an improvement, but certainly many voters think it would be, and the British experience in the 1960s and 1970s suggests that parliamentary government is compatible with a greater degree of backbench freedom (e.g., Richards 1972).

Recent years have seen a persistent and growing trend toward greater democracy within the national parties. At one time, party nominations were the gift of a small élite within each riding; now they are conferred by the vote of party members at public meetings that sometimes get very large indeed, in many ways the functional equivalent of the U.S. party primaries. (The noisy wrangles and complaints that often follow these extravaganzas simply remind us that democracy in action is seldom neat and sometimes not very pretty.) Incumbent members are frequently challenged and sometimes denied renomination, something we can see as a crude intraparty version of the recall that suffers several defects compared with its more formal and public counterpart. First, only party members can be involved in the process, and although modern parties are far from closed, there are still practical limitations to access. Second, like general elections themselves, these occasions take place only once every four years or so, with the member having some discretion on timing and access. Third, there is a delayed action effect, in that the member continues to serve until the House is dissolved for the next general election; indeed, in some cases the result might be to make members more loyal in the hope of future patronage now that their elected political career has been cut short. Finally, the high turnover in the House of Commons is often the product of members simply declining to stand again, removing them from the impact of the sanctions of renomination and re-election alike.

Recent decades have not been kind to Canada's major national parties. Indeed, until recently it could be doubted that any of the major parties had survived as truly national parties at all, the Liberal's extreme weakness in the West and the long-standing unpopularity of Conservatives in Quebec reducing both to the status of regional parties. The Mulroney victories of 1984 and 1988 suggested a dramatic and welcome turnaround, although recent public opinion polls hint that the changes may be more transient than permanent. At least in some parts of the country (specifically the West), disciplined parties are part of the problem rather than part of the solution. Mulroney's western MPs, like

Trudeau's before him, have paid the price in popularity for loyally toe-ing the party line regardless of constituent pressure, for appearing to be messengers *from* rather than *to* Ottawa. As the Canadian practices rigidify, they amount to offering the MPs little more than the choice of the method of their execution: expulsion from the party caucus now, or defeat at the hands of angry constituents later. What is gained in one dimension of governability (the capacity of the federal executive, once a decision has been reached, to know with certainty that it can be enacted) is lost in another (the capacity to "sell" these programs as desirable and acceptable to all regions of the country, to take action now without simply sowing the seeds for a harvest of bitterness and resentment later).

It can be suggested that the problems of Canadian governance in recent years stem less from a lack of ability to take action than from a lack of ability to generate a consensus to accept or support that action; if that is the case, then there might be some benefit in putting the MPs in a position where sometimes they must be bargained with rather than commanded, given unusually aggressive public opinion on that issue in their region. The capacity for immediate decisive action is not the only political virtue; it was not for nothing that one of Canada's most successful politicians had the nickname Old Tomorrow.

It is clear that the recall would dent the discipline of the parties, complicate the work of the whips, and make the role of the individual member more complex; it is not clear that any of this would irrepara-bly damage responsible government or that the gain in accountability, responsiveness and popular efficacy would not enhance democratic practice in Canada. In many ways, it can be seen as completely con-sistent with the evolution of the Canadian parties themselves from cadre organizations dominated by notables to more democratic mass organizations answering to a broader membership and giving that membership a more pervasive and visible role in the way decisions are made.

CONCLUSION

> The recall is sometimes called the "gun behind the door" that keeps officials responsive, yet in practice the "gun" is heavy, complicated, and requires countless people to aim and fire it. And, like a gun, it occasionally backfires. (Cronin 1989, 155)

The recall of elected officials has been part of the politics of a number of U.S. states for 75 years. During that period, it has performed a minor but significant function: rarely (but not never) has it removed corrupt or unresponsive elected officials; frequently it has served as a safety valve allowing concerned citizens to let off steam (to no avail if not enough join them, but to some purpose if they are, as they believe themselves to be, in the forefront of public opinion); and perhaps sometimes (who can know how often) it has provided additional incentive for elected officials to listen to the complaints and respond to the concerns of citizens. There is one solid indicator of its overall value: 15 American states have voluntarily moved themselves onto the list of states providing for the recall, but not one has ever moved back in the other direction. This does not prove that the recall has been of large (indeed, of any) benefit, but it does strongly suggest that at the very least it has caused no harm.

Nor is the discussion entirely academic, because the issue of the recall is again being raised from political platforms. The 1980s have seen a revival of western populism that seems to be making at least some impact on the public opinion polls, and some traditional populist issues, including the recall, are once again part of political rhetoric on the Prairies.[30] To be sure, it is more than premature to anticipate a repeat of the populist tidal wave after the First World War; populism's traditionally rural social base is badly eroded, and the practical solidarity it engendered is a thing of memory rather than everyday reality. Distant bureaucrats and their left-leaning advisers are a poor stand-in for the "Fifty Big Shots" and bloated bankers of the Progressive bestiary, and neither the National Energy Program of the 1980s nor the Goods and Services Tax of the 1990s in any way replicates the recession after the First World War or the Great Depression. The mood of populism, however, is rather more pervasive, and its appeal is enduringly perennial; the dichotomy of (grassroots) *we* versus (distant) *they* has a powerful pull whenever an unpopular government pursues policies that mesh poorly with regional priorities, while hiding behind the rhetorical wall of its five-year mandate. The fact that two American states recently adopted, and two others narrowly rejected, recall proposals suggests that some of the direct democracy mood of populism remains relevant even as its original historical social setting fades.

The transplantation of the recall from the congressional system of the United States to the parliamentary system of Canada poses problems that should be neither overlooked nor exaggerated. Canada's lower level of political activism (beyond the simple act of voting) suggests that we might use the recall opportunity less often than Americans, but there is also some reason to think that Canadian voters might use the recall more often. First, the normal life of Parliament is four years, compared with the two years that is standard in the United States; Canadians would have twice as long to become annoyed with their representative and to organize to do something about it. Second, party solidarity makes individual members sitting targets for local resentment, obliging them to follow in public a party line they may have sharply opposed in the privacy of caucus, and to take the fall for something over which they may have had very little choice. Third, Cabinet members supply a national target for a local recall, an opportunity for a visible impact on policy that will reverberate far beyond the constituency boundaries. Fourth, the practices of responsible government mean that a string of successful recalls may, on occasion, result not simply in the replacement of representatives but in the fall of a government.

All this is just another way of saying that the recall might be effective, that it might give a way for voter choice to mean something and for public opinion to have an impact, not just when the government chooses to present itself for an election but whenever the voters feel strongly enough about public affairs that they want to press their point. Sometimes governments are wise and voters foolish and short-sighted, but it is also true that sometimes governments are arrogant and self-important and voters sensible. If the case is strong, the recall election and the by-election that follows its success furnish the opportunity to present it; if the case is weak, then perhaps the government deserves to see its majority whittled away as its popularity dwindles. The arguments work even better, of course, in reverse: if voters are incapable of responding to a sensible argument, if they vote spleen over head and petulance over common sense, then they clearly deserve what they get and these just deserts are an important part of what democracy is all about.

The recall is in an important way the least radically revisionist of the direct democracy devices. Initiative and referendum essentially ignore the role of the elected representatives, doing an end run around them by forcing issues and resolving questions in ways that make elected assemblies irrelevant. The recall, by way of contrast, takes the role of the elected representatives seriously, providing a way in which their constituents can call them to account, can oblige them to explain why they have behaved a certain way. If the petition fails, the representative and his or her critics alike know that the resentment is not in fact widespread; if the petition succeeds but the subsequent explanation satisfies, either in the recall election or in the subsequent by-election, then the member has received a new mandate and the voters have been persuaded of something that was not clear or not acceptable to them before. The recall can expand the dialogue between citizens and representative, while ensuring that the latter has ample incentive to pay attention.

The second half of the 20th century has not been kind to elected legislatures, especially in parliamentary regimes. The weight of executive domination (in the form both of Cabinet and bureaucracy) has hemmed in the role of the individual member, even while disciplined parties throw the focus on the front benches by turning debates into dry runs for the next general election. The recall remembers, and might do something to revive, a time when the local member deserved and received more respect.

Recent Canadian politics has been highly controversial and unusually divisive. The major issues of the last five years – free trade, extension of the *Official Languages Act*, Meech Lake, and the Goods and Services Tax – have swung public opinion so often that the pollsters' graphs look like blueprints for a roller-coaster. It is unlikely that these levels of polarization and controversy will become standard fare, and it is therefore unrealistic to extrapolate from the government's present popularity to a scenario in which the use of the recall frequently swings the political balance of power. Even if this were the case, even if the recall often made a difference, we would have traded a certain degree of governmental efficiency for enhanced citizen efficacy, neither an unreasonable nor an unworthy exchange in a democracy.

What is at least as likely to be of relevance is the cathartic power of the recall. At a time when voter cynicism and regional alienation flare fitfully and smoulder long, the value of a political device that serves as a safety-valve, directing public discontent and resentment into formal channels with their own built-in validity checks, should not be downplayed.

ABBREVIATION

S.A.   Statutes of Alberta

NOTES

1. See Parsons (1986), which stresses both the interchangeability of the two devices ("Alone among the 50 states, Oregon has never had the impeachment process for dealing with misconduct in office by high officials, using instead recall elections and the customary procedures of the courts") and the more satisfactory results for the recall ("State experiences with impeachment over the past 15 years are not encouraging").

2. Confusion between the purposes of the two, resulting in the courts treating the recall as a quasi-judicial proceeding exactly parallel to impeachment, complicates the use of the recall in some American states (see

Fordham 1977). In general, the courts have distinguished between the more political device of the recall and the more legal device of impeachment, although some local recall legislation (Pennsylvania is an example) complicates the issue by requiring proof of "malfeasance" on the part of the official targeted for recall.

3. Most U.S. state legislators are elected for two-year terms, so the door is already revolving pretty fast.

4. In the American literature, the connection between length of term and the use of the recall is frequently explicit: one of the virtues suggested for recall provisions is that they allow a longer elected term without the loss of accountability (see Zimmerman 1986, 125).

5. It could also be that the looseness of the U.S. parties disarms the recall option by permitting the representative to vote against party and with constituents on high-profile and emotionally charged issues; in the disciplined Canadian parties, the member must stand tight and take the lumps, loyalty itself contributing to the resentment that fuels the momentum of a recall attempt.

6. The best collection of essays on populism is Ionescu and Gellner (1969); for a more theoretical approach, see Canovan (1981). The classic treatment of Canadian populism is Morton (1950); and an excellent recent addition is Laycock (1990). See also Sinclair (1975), Conway (1978, 1979) and Wood (1975).

7. See, for example, Sheldon and Weaver (1980, 8): "The initiative, referendum and recall processes were added to Washington's Constitution in 1912 during the height of the Progressive Movement." See also Zimmerman (1986, 106): "The recall was a product of the populist and municipal reform movements that were in sympathy with the Jacksonian distrust of government officials."

8. The revival of interest in the recall in Georgia grew out of a major lawsuit arising from an exercise of the local recall; the Supreme Court of Georgia settled the legal and constitutional questions, while the case gave the idea considerable favourable publicity. See Sentell (1976, 915). Sentell's article predates the approval of the recall for state officials in Georgia.

9. No specific date is given, but it was spoken of as "recent" in a 1989 account. The Utah state constitution since 1900 contains permissive but not self-executing provisions for the direct democracy devices; what has been attempted unsuccessfully on several occasions is the passage of legislation that would bring this into effect.

10. "Major" is the important and somewhat judgemental qualifier; populist movements can be identified even earlier (see Cook 1984).

11. On the "waves" of third-party – and basically populist – assaults on the two-party system, see McCormick (1984).

12. Indeed, the only legislative experiments with initiative and referendum in the Prairie provinces predate the Progressive period; in Alberta (1912), Saskatchewan (1913) and Manitoba (1916), Liberal governments introduced the legislation.

13. The casual juxtaposition of Social Credit and the CCF may seem anomalous in contemporary politics, but the description is apt for the 1930s; the transformation of Social Credit into a right-of-centre good-business party took place in the 1940s and 1950s under Manning and should not be read back into the origins of the party.

14. This was allegedly so that he could represent the Prince of Wales, whose ranch was in the riding (see Elliott and Miller 1987, 217).

15. One of these experts was subsequently convicted of defamatory libel and sent to jail for his vilification of the banking interests.

16. The feud between Aberhart and the *Calgary Herald* was particularly acrimonious, the Premier at one point calling on the citizens of Alberta to boycott the paper (Elliott and Miller 1987, 182).

17. Plus the District of Columbia, Guam, the North Mariana Islands and the Virgin Islands.

18. In which case the petition requirement for the recall of an appointed official derives from the eligible voters for the election of the appointing authority.

19. The comments in this section are drawn mostly from Zimmerman (1986), Cronin (1989) and Maddox and Fuquay (1966).

20. This applies to statewide offices; the time limit is 180 days for other offices.

21. The arguments that follow are summarized and paraphrased from Cronin (1989, chap. 6) and Zimmerman (1986, chap. 5). The grouping into categories is my own.

22. The reference is to the first adoption of the recall by any North American government in the Los Angeles City Charter of 22 January 1903, applying to elected *local* officials; Oregon was the first state to adopt the recall for *state* officials.

23. Alternatively, in many jurisdictions, 25 percent of the votes cast in the previous general election for the office in question; the normally high rate of turnout in Canadian general elections makes this distinction somewhat less significant in Canada than it is in the United States.

24. In American law, the content of these arguments for and against recall enjoys the same absolute privilege as comments made by elected members in the legislature: the content cannot be the basis for a libel action, regardless of the truth of the remarks or the intentions of those who make them.

25. A third alternative (used in Arizona and Nevada, and in Oregon before 1914) has an election following automatically from the successful petition; this seems the least attractive of the three and the most subject to misuse.

26. Researchers question whether moneyed interests can "buy" an election simply by outspending opponents; consider, for example, the following summary comments about referendum and initiative: "Across different times and locations, money has been much more successful in defeating ballot proposals than in insuring their success. Numerous scholars have found that it is easier to use money to cast doubts on ballot measures than to get citizens to vote affirmatively. Using money to try to convince voters to support a particular proposition may be more easily portrayed as benefiting a particular special interest" (Shockley 1985, 393).

27. That is, Oregonians have had the opportunity to use the recall for 82 years, Georgians for 12 years, and so on for all the states adopting the device in between.

28. In the most dramatic example, during the 1960s the government lost a vote on a major money bill but created its own precedent by convening the House to ask if it really intended to withdraw confidence, and by accepting the determination that it did not. See Hogg (1985, 204 fn.); Hogg notes that a similar practice has been adopted in the United Kingdom as well.

29. British parliamentary politics has been characterized for at least 30 years by blocs within both parties that are willing on specific issues to defeat or amend government action without leaving the party; and it is difficult to imagine any Canadian counterpart to the process whereby the British Conservatives ousted leader Margaret Thatcher.

30. The reference, of course, is to Preston Manning and the Reform Party (see McCormick 1990).

REFERENCES

Alberta. *Legislative Assembly (Recall) Act*, S.A. 1936, c. 82.

Barnett, James D. 1912. "The Operation of the Recall in Oregon." *American Political Science Review* 6:41–53.

———. 1915. *The Operation of the Initiative, Referendum and Recall in Oregon.* New York: Macmillan.

Bird, F.L., and F.M. Ryan. 1930. *The Recall of Public Officers: A Study of the Operation of the Recall in California..* New York: Macmillan.

The Book of the States. 1986. Vol. 26. Lexington, KY. Council of State Governments.

Canovan, Margaret. 1981. *Populism*. London: Junction Books.

Conway, J.F. 1978. "Populism in the United States, Russia and Canada: Explaining the Roots of Canada's Third Parties." *Canadian Journal of Political Science* 11:99–124.

———. 1979. "The Prairie Populist Resistance to the National Policy." *Journal of Canadian Studies* 14:77–91.

Cook, Ramsay. 1984. "Tillers and Toilers: The Rise of Populism in Canada in the 1890s." *Historical Papers*, presented at the Canadian Historical Association annual meeting.

Cronin, Thomas E. 1989. *Direct Democracy: The Politics of Initiative, Referendum and Recall*. Cambridge: Harvard University Press.

Elliott, David R., and Iris Miller. 1987. *Bible Bill: A Biography of William Aberhart*. Edmonton: Reidmore Books.

Finkel, Alvin. 1989. *The Social Credit Phenomenon in Alberta*. Toronto: University of Toronto Press.

Fordham, Jefferson B. 1977. "Judicial Nullification of a Democratic Political Process – The Rizzo Recall Case." *University of Pennsylvania Law Review* 126:1–18.

Hogg, Peter. 1985. *Constitutional Law of Canada*. 2d ed. Toronto: Carswell.

Ionescu, Ghita, and Ernest Gellner, eds. 1969. *Populism: Its Meaning and National Characteristics*. London: Weidenfeld and Nicolson.

Laycock, David. 1990. *Populism and Democratic Thought in the Canadian Prairies, 1910 to 1945*. Toronto: University of Toronto Press.

Macpherson, C.B. 1953. *Democracy in Alberta: Social Credit and the Party System*. Toronto: University of Toronto Press.

Maddox, Russell, and Robert Fuquay. 1966. *State and Local Government*. 2d ed. Princeton, NJ: Van Nostrand.

McCormick, Peter. 1984. "Is the Liberal Party Declining? Liberals, Conservatives and Provincial Politics 1867–1980." *Journal of Canadian Studies* 18:88–107.

———. 1990. "The Reform Party of Canada: New Beginning or Dead End?" In *Party Politics in Canada*, 6th ed., ed. Hugh Thorburn. Scarborough: Prentice-Hall Canada.

Morton, W.L. 1950. *The Progressive Party in Canada*. Toronto: University of Toronto Press.

Parsons, Malcolm B. 1986. "Checking Abuse of Power: Does Impeachment Work?" *National Civic Review* 75:219–24.

Price, Charles M. 1983. "Recalls at the Local Level: Dimensions and Implications." *National Civic Review* 72:199–205.

———. 1988. "Electoral Accountability: Local Recalls." *National Civic Review* 77:118–23.

Richards, Peter G. 1972. *The Back-Benchers*. London: Faber.

Schaffner, Margaret A. 1908. "The Initiative, the Referendum and the Recall: Recent Legislation in the United States." *American Political Science Review* 2:32–42.

Sentell, R. Perry, Jr. 1976. "Remembering Recall in Local Government Law." *Georgia Law Review* 10:883–915.

Sheldon, Charles H., and Frank P. Weaver. 1980. *Politicians, Judges and the People*. Westport, CT: Greenwood Press.

Shockley, John B. 1985. "Direct Democracy, Campaign Finance, and the Courts: Can Corruption, Undue Influence, and Declining Voter Confidence Be Found?" *University of Miami Law Review* 39:377–428.

Sinclair, Peter. 1975. "Class Structure and Populist Protest: The Case of Western Canada." *Canadian Journal of Sociology* 1:1–17.

Stewart, Alva. 1983. *The Initiative, Referendum and Recall: Theory and Applications*. New York: Vance Bibliographies.

Tallian, Laura. 1977. *Direct Democracy: An Historical Analysis of Initiative, Referendum and Recall Processes*. Los Angeles: People's Lobby.

Wiles, Peter. 1969. "A Syndrome, not a Doctrine: Some Elementary Theses on Populism." In *Populism: Its Meaning and National Characteristics*, ed. Ghita Ionescu and Ernest Gellner. London: Weidenfeld and Nicolson.

Wood, Louis Aubrey. 1975. *A History of Farmers' Movements in Canada: The Origins and Development of Agrarian Protest*. Toronto: University of Toronto Press.

Zimmerman, Joseph P. 1986. *Participatory Democracy: Populism Revived*. New York: Praeger.

7

REFERENDUMS AND FEDERAL GENERAL ELECTIONS IN CANADA

David Mac Donald

A RENEWED WAVE of populist sentiment has appeared in Canada in the 1990s, reaching a level of intensity not seen for nearly seven decades. It is manifesting itself in increased support for the instruments of direct democracy – the popular initiative, the referendum and the recall – and through disenchantment with the institutions of representative government, which is directed not just at Parliament and political parties but at the electoral process itself.

This populist revival[1] has already found expression in the Canadian electoral process with the use of referendum questions in the most recent provincial elections in British Columbia and in Saskatchewan. In British Columbia, voters endorsed by large majorities the use of the recall by constituents dissatisfied with the performance of their elected representatives, and the use of the citizen-initiated referendum as a device for enacting legislation. In Saskatchewan, voters were asked questions about balanced budget legislation, public financing of abortion procedures and the use of referendums to ratify constitutional amendments. The Reform Party of Canada, as part of its policy platform, endorses a statutory recall provision for members of Parliament and the use of citizen initiatives to instruct Parliament as to which laws should be passed.

In addition to the Reform Party, a number of individuals and organizations are in favour of having referendum questions posed during federal general elections. Such a practice, it is argued, would force parties and candidates to establish positions on important policy issues, thereby giving voters more precise indications of what their government will do, once elected.

This study will argue that, regardless of the apparent strengths of referendums,[2] these strengths cannot be preserved if referendums are held concurrently with elections. Referendums and elections place conflicting demands on voters, and therefore mixing the two will impede rather than advance the process of governing. First, this study will provide a historical review and a critical assessment of populism in Canada. Much of the recent support for referendums and for other instruments of direct democracy draws from populist sentiments that are critical of current patterns of political and economic decision making. Second, the use of referendums in Canada and in the provinces will be highlighted. Although there is a fairly rich tradition of referendums in Canada, they have normally been held separately from elections, with the exception of municipal elections and the recent provincial elections in British Columbia and Saskatchewan. Third, the role of the referendum as an instrument of political decision making in other nations will be reviewed, and the experience of other national jurisdictions where referendums have been held concurrently with general elections will be examined. Finally, the study will examine what could occur if referendums were held simultaneously with federal general elections.

POPULISM AND PARLIAMENTARY GOVERNMENT IN CANADA

The perceived inadequacies of representative and parliamentary government in Canada have given rise to two waves of populist, anti-party movements, the first in the 1920s and 1930s and the second in the early 1990s. Each outbreak of populism has been accompanied by unabashed calls for the use of direct democracy.

In the first wave, agrarian movements obtained electoral successes both federally and provincially with platforms that opposed the idea that political parties were the primary agents of representation, that assailed established patterns of political and economic decision making and that promised to make citizens key participants in the governing process. Promises of direct democracy were bandied about freely.

The reappearance of organized populism in the 1990s (as represented, for example, in the platform of the Reform Party of Canada) has been prompted, in part, by widespread dissatisfaction with the legitimacy and capacity of our political institutions to respond to the representational needs of Canadians. Populists argue that Canadians want empowerment and more control over their political leaders; they do not want backroom policy compromises that serve a narrow range of interests. The electorate want their politicians to listen, and they want the existing rigidities of the party system dismantled. The depth and extent of current support for direct democracy were documented most recently by the Citizens' Forum on Canada's Future (the Spicer Commission). It concluded that the support for direct democracy "originate[s] in a desire [among Canadians] for a more responsive and open political system, whose leaders – they think – are not merely accountable at election time but should be disciplined swiftly if they transgress greatly" (Canada, Citizens' Forum 1991, 135).

These contemporary views echo the sentiments of the earlier populist movement. Populists view direct democracy as a quick, efficient way for affirming majoritarian principles, whereby important policy decisions are based on what most citizens want, not on the use of compromises and log-rolling to accommodate the concerns of specific regions, provinces or interests. As well, populists do not want citizens' preferences mediated or reinterpreted by political actors, such as parties, or by MPs, who are seen as too submissive to the tradition of party discipline. The instruments of direct democracy are seen as mechanisms for countering the excessive control that a small number of actors have over government policies. The use of the recall and the referendum, for example, would require governments and elected representatives to respond directly to their constituents.

A short case study of the populist movement in the 1920s suggests that, even when groups come to power on a platform of dismantling the primary trappings of parliamentary government, they soon accept that the exigencies of governing cannot be met through the instruments of direct democracy.

In the immediate post-World War I period, Canadian agrarian interests, taking their cues from the populist/progressive movements in the United States, organized themselves politically to challenge the two traditional parties, both federally and provincially. These groups won elections in Ontario and Alberta, formed the official opposition in several provinces, and, through the Progressive Party, won 65 federal seats in 1921, displacing the Conservatives as the second largest party in Parliament. While the groups tapped into different ideological and populist strains, they shared a common dislike of the party system (Laycock 1990). Political parties were seen as possessing two unwanted characteristics. First, there was the problem of party discipline, the bane of all good populists. The farmers' groups charged that party discipline prevented elected representatives from doing what their constituents wanted. Second, these populists argued that traditional party élites, and governments in general, were too beholden to economic interests from eastern Canada. The Liberal and Conservative parties were seen as spending too much time catering to big business to respond to the needs of farmers and workers.

In Alberta, the United Farmers of Alberta (UFA) and the Social Credit came to power, in part, by selling themselves as anti-party and anti-cabinet governments, although neither party did much to upset these institutions when they formed their respective governments. The speed and ease with which these parties accepted the workings of parliamentary government have been documented by C.B. Macpherson in *Democracy in Alberta: The Theory and Practice of a Quasi-Party System.*

The UFA came to power in 1919. Among other policies designed to advance the social and economic interests of farmers, the UFA called for tariff protection against American imports and for a more extensive regime of farm subsidies. Under the stewardship of Henry Wise Wood, the UFA advocated the doctrine of group government.[3] Economic groups or classes, not parties, were seen as the basic unit of politics. Communities would be organized into these groups and their wishes would be transformed into public policy by elected representatives. The party system would be replaced by the political organization of occupational or industrial groups, and each group would nominate and elect its own representatives to the legislature.

> The party-divided legislature would become an industrial group legislature, artificial opposition and party discipline would disappear, issues would be decided on their merits as judged by the various groups, the cabinet would be made up of representatives of the groups in proportion to their numbers in the legislature, each group would thus bear a share of the responsibility of government, and the conventions of party government such as the resignation of a government on the defeat of a government measure would be discarded. (Macpherson 1953, 45)

Each member of the elected legislature was to be directly responsible to his or her constituency association. The cabinet and the caucus were secondary, and there was to be no party discipline. "It was emphasized [in UFA campaign literature] that the elected member's responsibility to the constituency organization was to be so direct as to rule out cabinet domination of the legislature" (Macpherson 1953, 71).

Despite its critique of party and cabinet government, the UFA leadership did not reject the practices of responsible government, whereby the government needed a legislative majority in the provincial legislature to introduce its program. Wood made it clear that if the government lost a significant vote in the legislature, it would have to resign, and either be replaced or call an election. The UFA leadership would decide whether the government should resign or not. "It did not appear to occur to [H.W. Wood], or to anyone in the U.F.A., that to take this responsibility was to accept the conventions of the cabinet system" (Macpherson 1953, 73). On the few occasions when the caucus did disagree with the party leadership the UFA premier used the threat of dissolution to obtain the necessary support. Cabinet control of the caucus, which came about in the first year or two of the UFA administration, went unchallenged during the 14 years of UFA government.

The UFA leadership was able to dominate its legislative caucus effortlessly. For Macpherson,

> what compelled the members to give up their freedom was the need of the U.F.A. to prove its ability to govern and to finance the province ... In order to make a success of independent political action they had to support their government; in order to support the government they had to dispense with those principles of group government which conflicted with the cabinet system. Specifically, the primary responsibility of the member to his constituency association had to give way to his responsibility for maintaining the government, that is, to his responsibility to the cabinet. (1953, 80)

In 1935, the Social Credit Party (Socreds) of Alberta used more or less the same tactics the UFA used to obtain power in 1919 (Morton 1967). Social Credit campaigned against the domination of eastern economic interests, the pervasive nature of parliamentary government and the suffocating influences of party government. It argued that the domination big business had over government could be contained through the Social Credit theories of under-consumption and the use of the A + B theorem, which led to the empowerment of individual consumers (Macpherson 1953, 149–60). Like the UFA, the Social Credit tapped into local farmers' organizations to recruit volunteers and resources. The evangelistic appeal of the Social Credit leader, William Aberhart, brought aboard local religious groups. Albertans were seduced by Social Credit's unique monetary and social policies. Aberhart's candidates and supporters were enticed by the promise of plebiscitarian and delegate democracy.

Once in power, the Social Credit leadership abandoned the promise of plebiscitarian democracy. "The cabinet, or more accurately the premier and those other members of the cabinet who were also leaders of the party ... established their supremacy over both the legislature and the [party] convention to an even greater degree than any U.F.A. cabinet had done. Legislature and convention were not only subordinated; they were rendered almost vestigial" (Macpherson 1953, 198).

Macpherson argues that, on attaining office, the UFA and Social Credit leaderships became quite orthodox, both in their economic policies and in their practice of democracy. This orthodoxy occurred as a result of "the exigencies of governing a society of independent producers, in revolt against outside domination but not against property." These exigencies brought out the conservatism inherent in petit bourgeois agrarian radicalism. What Macpherson does not say is that the use of traditional instruments of parliamentary government allowed the party leaderships to advance and entrench this conservatism. The UFA and the Social Credit party wanted to show Albertans that they could govern. They believed they could do this by offering consistent, predictable policies, and by staying clear of radical policies involving substantial risk (as measured by popular reaction to them). The elected representatives of both parties looked to the leadership and the cabinet to protect them from unwanted constituency demands. Even the highly radical elements in the parties realized there would be electoral repercussions if voters were uncertain about the capacity of the UFA or the Social Credit to govern. A party that cannot govern cannot protect the interests it claims to represent.

The UFA and the Socreds were committed to ideologically based programs. The effective implementation of their programs depended on the prudent management and coordination of the various agencies of the provincial government. For these movements wanting to implement a specific policy agenda, parliamentary government was an ideal system. It provided the government and the provincial cabinet with control over both the legislature and the bureaucracy. Direct democracy as a basis for governing, on the other hand, could not have accommodated the subtle and shifting linkages among different policy areas and government departments. The UFA and the Socreds were forced to accept that they could not implement the programs they had campaigned for if they used direct democracy.

The experience of these two agrarian, populist parties points to a conclusion that is now part of political science folklore: that direct democracy is incompatible with the traditions and conventions of parliamentary democracy. Parliamentary government in the Westminster tradition, it is argued, rests on the constitutional principle that sovereignty is vested in the monarch and exercised through Parliament. It is seen as being anti-populist and anti-plebiscitarian, in contrast to the American political system where sovereignty belongs to the people through a written constitution.

Some opponents of direct democracy who support the Westminster model of representative government argue that devices such as the referendum violate the principle of parliamentary supremacy insofar as they can result in laws being made by citizens and not by the legislature (Johnson 1981, 23). Others argue that the grand achievement of parliamentary government has been its institutional capacity to blend local and minority interests into national compromises through the intermediation of parties and strong political executives. As well, because parliamentary government is responsible government, the use of referendums would undermine the constitutional right of the Cabinet to design and present legislation based on its majority support in the House of Commons (Butler and Ranney 1978, chap. 1). These arguments are telling, but they have little credibility for those who support or are sympathetic to the use of referendums based on populist sentiments.

The orthodox arguments used to support or debunk referendums make scant reference to political parties, because many of these arguments draw from the American and Swiss experiences with direct democracy. The feasibility of using referendums in a system of parliamentary government cannot be addressed, however, without a critical assessment of political parties. Parliamentary government as it has evolved since the mid-19th century in Canada is now party government. The historical role of party has been to liberate local representatives from the many competing demands of their constituents. The presence of party has allowed local representatives to be more than mere delegates of their constituents.

Parliamentary government ignores rather than resolves Pitkin's oft-quoted dilemma of representation. Pitkin said: "Representation, taken generally, means the making present *in some sense* of something which is nevertheless *not* present literally or in fact. Now, to say that something is simultaneously both present and not present is to utter a paradox, and thus a fundamental dualism is built into the meaning of representation" (Pitkin 1967, 8–9). Parliamentary government is not about a "fundamental dualism" between what is and what is not present. Through the institution of party there is literal representation of that which is meant to be represented. Party ideas and policies are both the intended and the real essence of representation. While his 1774 Bristol speech serves as the benchmark for assessing whether elected representatives should be delegates or trustees, Edmund Burke ran for Parliament as a member of the Whig Party. He was not a virtual representative of his Bristol constituents – he was a party man. In the 1780 general election, Burke took his name off the ballot before polling day. He believed that the Whig platform was unpopular enough to ensure his defeat (Eulau 1978).

The debate about whether elected representatives are delegates or trustees of their constituents within parliamentary government is misplaced. Elected representatives are primarily delegates of parties, not voters. The populist critique of party and party discipline assumes that the local representative is tied to his or her party through coercion, which is administered by the party leadership and establishment. This is a misleading assumption. The use of patronage, coercion and manipulation does not fully explain why party members, ranging from local constituency workers to financial backers to party officials and to members of Parliament, submit so willingly to party discipline. Applying coercion to so many people in so many locations is beyond the resources and skills of most leaders.

Astute and ambitious politicians understand that their electoral survival is more likely if they belong to cohesive, disciplined parties. The presence of party protects politicians from the many petty demands of their constituents. These demands can be weighed against the needs and dictates of the party and the electorate as a whole. Party helps to stabilize the politicians' world. Burke understood this. "Above all, freedom from local connections and instructions was for Burke a necessary and very practical condition to work for a parliamentary party ... and accept the commitment of a party man. Burke never envisaged the possibility that his own judgment and his party's policies could ever come into conflict" (Eulau 1978, 47). Party offered predictability, order, allies, resources and rewards for all its members (Hockin 1979).

The partisan's need for party is missed by writers like Franks, who assume that discipline is brought about by coercion only, and by writers like March who believe that Parliament can be more responsive to the public if it is made up of independent legislators (Franks 1987; March 1974). However, Franks does note that it is a mistake for those who want parliamentary reform to see the lessening of party discipline as a technical issue only. Party discipline is not just the way Parliament operates: it is based on social and institutional and political mores that condition the collective behaviour of MPs. Changes in the rules and procedures of the House of Commons alone will not change these mores.

Those groups or individuals who believe that the removal of or assault on party discipline through direct democracy will be a welcome liberation for individual representatives are mistaken, and those who support direct democracy as a way to dilute the supposed coercive influence parties have over elected representatives do not always understand the forces shaping the party system in Canada.

CANADIAN REFERENDUMS

Federal

Canada has held two national referendums (they were called plebiscites at the time), but in neither case were they initiated in response to populist pressures or in order to appease widespread populist demands for direct democracy. The referendums were used by the federal government when the normal legislative process was unable to develop a satisfactory approach to resolving contentious issues. The first referendum was held in 1898 on the issue of prohibition. While prohibition was endorsed by a small majority of Canadians, fewer than half of the registered voters participated in the vote. The federal government took the unprecedented step of holding a national referendum on prohibition because previous efforts to resolve this volatile issue, including the use of a royal commission, had not provided a credible resolution. The outcome of the vote was virtually meaningless, however, since responsibility for liquor laws went to the provinces shortly after the referendum. In 1942, the Mackenzie King government held Canada's second referendum to see if it could be excused from its earlier promise not to impose conscription. The divisive outcome of the referendum has been well documented (Boyer 1982; Lemieux 1985). A majority of English-speaking Canadians said yes; a majority of French-speaking Canadians said no; conscription was implemented, and Quebec nationalism was inflamed.

The role of referendums in national politics has not been limited to the votes of 1898 and 1942. For example, while leader of the Liberal opposition, Sir Wilfrid Laurier saw the use of the referendum as "a possible way out of pending collision between English-speaking Canada and Quebec over conscription for military service in World War I" (Boyer 1982, 51). Laurier's suggestion was not accepted by the Borden government. In the 1960s, the use of the referendum was given brief but cursory consideration during the negotiation of the Fulton–Favreau constitutional amending formula.

The Trudeau government introduced the *Canada Referendum Act* in 1978–79. Bill C-40 was given first reading in April 1978, and became Bill C-9 in the fall session. Bill C-9 was the Trudeau government's response to Quebec's 1978 *Referendum Act*. Trudeau stated that any fundamental changes to Canada's constitutional configuration could not be decided by popular ratification in a single province. Such changes, it was suggested, should only be achieved through a national ratification process.

Bill C-9's provisions for the administration of a national referendum campaign drew from provisions of the *Canada Elections Act*. As stipulated in the draft legislation, the referendum question had to be approved by the House of Commons and the Senate. Registered parties and "referendum committees" could participate in referendum campaigns subject to spending limits, broadcast restrictions and the assignment of official agents. Certain referendum expenses could be reimbursed by the federal government. Referendums were not, however, to be held during a federal general election. When Parliament was dissolved for a general election in May 1979, Bill C-9 died on the order paper. Trudeau's initial 1980–81 constitutional reform package included provisions for the use of national referendums to ratify constitutional amendments. These measures were withdrawn when several provincial governments balked at the use of them.

Various members in the House of Commons have made periodic efforts to pass a national referendum bill but these proposals have gone nowhere. In the fall of 1989, Patrick Boyer, MP, introduced a private member's bill on the holding of national referendums and plebiscites (Bill C-257) into the House of Commons. Boyer's bill, the *Canada Referendum and Plebiscite Act*, would allow the federal cabinet to submit policy issues or constitutional amendments to a plebiscite or referendum for consideration. The question to be placed on the ballot would have to be approved by both Houses of Parliament. Citizen-initiated referendums could be implemented if 10 percent of the voters at the last general election "who are of the opinion that a question of national and public importance within the jurisdiction of Parliament should be submitted to a direct vote of the electors ... petition the Prime Minister to that effect" (Canada, Bill C-257, s. 14(1)). The draft legislation stated that general elections and referendum or plebiscite campaigns were not to be held concurrently. Boyer has lobbied for public support for a national referendum act in Canada through various publications and media interviews (Boyer 1988–89; 1991a; 1991b).

Referendums have become part of the strategic arsenals of the federal and Quebec governments in the design and ratification of constitutional amendments (Canada, Parliament 1991). In June 1991, the Beaudoin–Edwards Special Joint Committee on the Process for Amending the Constitution of Canada recommended that national consultative referendums be held, in order to receive citizen input on constitutional amendments. In late 1991, the Progressive Conservative government of Prime Minister Brian Mulroney gave conflicting public commitments as to whether or not it would introduce legislation enacting a national referendum procedure. The Mulroney government has had to balance pressures for more citizen participation in the constitutional reform process through national referendums with Quebec's historical distrust of such referendums (McGillivray 1991). Commentaries from the editorial writers for the larger newspapers showed a stark division of opinion as to whether national referendums would be divisive or integrative, and whether popular ratification of complex constitutional amendments was feasible or of dubious merit.

There has been a recent transformation in the language and discourse used to assess the role of referendums in Canadian national politics. Previously, with the exception of various arguments put forth by private members in defence of their draft bills sponsoring national referendum legislation in Canada, the role of the referendum as an instrument of direct democracy and, therefore, as a corrective to the perceived weaknesses of representative democracy, received little attention in national political debate. The referendum was seen as a device that expedited the resolution of a single, extraordinary issue. Support for and references to referendums did not draw on populist sentiments or on a well-articulated defence of direct democracy. Since the late 1980s, however, support for referendums as an integral facet of the policy-making process has received greater currency. Much of this support, expressed primarily through the Reform Party of Canada, is hostile to the traditional institutions of representative government and is suspicious of the role that political and economic élites have in the governing process (Blais and Gidengil 1991).

Provincial

In response to populist pressures from the farmers' movements and their critique of party government, each of the western provinces enacted direct legislation acts in the early 20th century. Between 1913 and 1919, the provincial legislatures of British Columbia, Alberta, Saskatchewan and Manitoba passed legislation that allowed for both referendums and citizen-initiated referendums. The *Direct Legislation Act* of 1919 in British Columbia, however, was never proclaimed by the provincial cabinet. Similar legislation in Saskatchewan failed to win popular endorsement when it was submitted to voters in the form of a referendum question in 1913. The Manitoba *Initiative and Referendum Act* was declared unconstitutional by the Judicial Committee of the Privy Council (JCPC) in 1919 (Manitoba *Reference* 1919). The JCPC ruled that the Act excluded the Lieutenant Governor from the legislative process since legislation, as a result of binding citizen-initiated referendums, could be enacted without his consent. (The *Constitution Act, 1867* prevents provincial legislatures from unilaterally changing the powers of the office of Lieutenant Governor.) Finally, the *Direct Legislation Act* in Alberta was never used by Albertan voters, and was repealed by the Social Credit government of Premier E.C. Manning in 1958 (Boyer 1982).

Every province except New Brunswick has held a provincewide referendum. Most of the referendum questions involved prohibition of liquor sales. There have been approximately 40 referendums conducted by provincial governments since Confederation, 31 of them in the four western provinces (*Edmonton Journal* 1991). Although all the referendums have been advisory, provincial governments have normally abided by the results.

Four provinces – Prince Edward Island, Saskatchewan, British Columbia and Quebec – have enabling legislation allowing for province-wide referendums initiated by the provincial cabinet. Only Saskatchewan has legislation that provides for citizen-initiated referendums. Ontario, Nova Scotia and Manitoba do not have statutory provisions for provincewide referendums on general public policy issues. In the remaining provinces, referendums must be held either under provincial electoral law or under specific legislation.

The Prince Edward Island *Plebiscite Act* was passed in 1954, and was used most recently in 1989 by the provincial government to seek public input on the feasibility of building a fixed link to New Brunswick. Fifty-nine percent of voters supported the link. The *Plebiscite Act* requires referendum campaigns to be conducted by the same rules and procedures used to administer provincial elections. In Saskatchewan the *Referendum and Plebiscite Act* (1991) was approved by the legislative assembly a few months before the 1991 provincial election. Under this legislation the provincial cabinet can submit either referendum or plebiscite questions to the electorate at its discretion. If more than 60 percent of voters casting ballots vote "Yes" to a referendum question, the results are "binding" on the government (assuming at least 50 percent of qualified voters cast ballots). Section 5 of the legislation states that if the results are binding, "the government that initiated the referendum shall, as soon as practicable, take any steps within [its] competence ... that it considers necessary or advisable to implement the results of the referendum" including changing existing programs, introducing new programs, and "introducing a Bill in the Assembly during its first session after the results of the referendum are known."

Plebiscite questions, initiated by the Cabinet to obtain "an expression of public opinion ... on any matter of public interest or concern," are always advisory in nature. If at least 15 percent of the registered voters in the last Saskatchewan general election request through petition that a particular policy question be put to a plebiscite, the provincial cabinet is obliged to do so.

If referendums, whether initiated by the government or through a citizen petition, are held during an election period, "all expenditures incurred by a registered political party or a candidate to promote or oppose a question put to electors ... are deemed to be election expenses." The rules and administration of the referendum campaigns are the responsibility of the provincial chief electoral officer.

The British Columbia *Referendum Act* of 1990 allows the cabinet to hold provincewide referendums if it "considers that an expression of public opinion is desirable on any matter of public interest or concern." Referendum results are "binding" on the government if more than 50 percent of the validly cast ballots are for or against the referendum question. When the results are binding, the government can amend or introduce legislation "it considers necessary or advisable to implement the results of the referendum." (The use of referendums during the October 1991 provincial elections in British Columbia and Saskatchewan will be discussed below.)

In 1969, Premier Bertrand introduced legislation that permitted the Quebec cabinet to hold referendums on political and constitutional questions. The bill was never passed. In 1978, the government of Premier René Lévesque passed the *Referendum Act* of Quebec. Passing the Act was the first step in Lévesque's commitment to hold a referendum on Quebec's status in Confederation. A referendum on sovereignty-association was held on 20 May 1980. The "Yes" side favouring sovereignty-association won 40.4 percent of the vote, while the federalist "No" option captured 59.6 percent.

In August 1991, Bill 150 was enacted by the Quebec National Assembly. Bill 150 (entitled *An Act respecting the process for determining the political and constitutional future of Quebec*) requires that a referendum on sovereignty be held between 8 June and 22 June 1992 or between 12 October and 26 October 1992. The decision on when to hold the referendum will be made by the provincial cabinet, and will be based, in part, on the credibility and scope of constitutional reforms proposed by the rest of Canada. Section 1 of the Act states that "[i]f the results of the referendum are in favour of sovereignty, they constitute a proposal that Québec acquire the status of a sovereign State one year to the day from the holding of the referendum."

Quebec referendums are managed and administered by a Referendum Council, which is composed of three Provincial Court judges. Questions to be vetted through a referendum are decided by the Cabinet and approved by the National Assembly. Individuals or groups wanting to participate in a referendum debate must do so through "Yes" and "No" umbrella organizations. With the exception of Britain in 1975, during the Common Market referendum, no other democracy has conducted referendums under a statutory framework of umbrella organizations (Boyer 1982, 206). Political parties and pressure groups are not allowed to spend money or campaign independent of the appropriate umbrella organization. The laws regulating referendum expenses and campaigning are similar to those in place for provincial elections. The umbrella organizations are subject to legal spending limits of 50 cents per elector in the aggregate of the provincial electoral districts. Each organization is required to set up a "referendum fund," and only expenses authorized by the official agent can be made. The National Assembly can decide if the umbrella organizations will receive public funding.

Several critical points can be extracted from recent provincial experience with referendums. Provincial governments have used the referendum device as an extension of their efforts to seek support on controversial issues. The referendum was held in Prince Edward Island after the provincial cabinet was unable to develop a satisfactory or credible policy on an outstanding issue that had been a permanent fixture of the public policy agenda. The results, however, did not lead to a precise legislative response to the issue. The feasibility of a fixed link with New Brunswick continues to be debated in Prince Edward Island.

The Lévesque government in Quebec was criticized for offering a fuzzily worded question on the issue of sovereignty-association during the referendum vote of 1980. Critics argued that the government soft-pedalled the issue to obtain the support of Quebeckers who were unhappy with Canadian federalism but did not want separatism. Ranney, however, has argued that the wording of a referendum question is secondary to the particular values and views voters bring to the issue. He suggests that voters must use their own interpretative prisms to decide how to vote, rather than take specific cues from the referendum question itself (Ranney 1981b). The drafting of the referendum question in Quebec does indicate the sensitivities that are involved in determining how a critical and volatile issue can be presented to voters in the form of a short, simple question, and whether the prerogative to do so should belong to the legislature or to the political executive.

While the result of the Quebec referendum was "No," there was concern that a simple majority of 51 percent opposed to the referendum question would have been of dubious legitimacy if a majority of French-speaking Quebeckers had voted "Yes." A 51 percent "No" vote could have been obtained with support from a majority of English-speaking and a minority of French-speaking Quebeckers. The fact that 60 percent of voters voted "No" to the possible future negotiation of sovereignty-association was interpreted as a decisive victory, effectively preventing the Lévesque government from pursuing this issue before the next provincial election. In contrast, in Prince Edward Island, support from 60 percent of the electorate casting ballots was not seen as a sufficient level of public support to proceed immediately with the fixed link project. The population of PEI was seen as being essentially divided on the issue. The contrasting interpretations of the referendum results in PEI and Quebec suggest that while support for the use of referendums draws from the appeal of majoritarian principles, the interpretation of results goes beyond the mere counting of ballots.

REFERENDUMS IN OTHER JURISDICTIONS: A COMPARATIVE OVERVIEW

Referendums are not widely used as instruments of decision making by national governments; they are used most often at the state and local levels (Butler and Ranney 1978). Most regimes use advisory referendums infrequently to decide extraordinary issues. Three nations – the United States, the Netherlands and Israel – have never held a national referendum of any sort (Butler 1981, 74). Despite several Congressional attempts to draft legislation, the United States has no legislative provisions for national referendums (Cronin 1989, chap. 7; Barber 1984).

Britain held its only national referendum in 1975 on the question of whether it should remain in the European Economic Community (EEC). British voters stated overwhelmingly (67 percent voted "Yes") that Britain should stay in the Community. The referendum campaign was conducted under the rubric of two umbrella organizations, and each side received a small measure of public assistance. Perhaps the "most remarkable special aspect of the referendum was the government's agreement to differ: 16 members of the Cabinet campaigned for EEC membership and seven against. The normal rules of collective responsibility, by which all ministers must support government policy or resign, were relaxed for three months with respect to this one question" (Butler 1978, 214). Cabinet solidarity was relaxed, in part, to prevent "the Labour party from tearing itself asunder," since the party was divided on the desirability of continued membership in the EEC (ibid.).

Regional referendums were held in Great Britain in 1979 on the question of whether Scotland and Wales should be given more political power. The results of the referendums did little, however, to clarify the preferences of voters on devolution. In Scotland, 51.6 percent of voters casting ballots supported devolution, but this majority represented only 33 percent of the Scottish electorate, thus falling below the 40 percent threshold that Parliament had set for the devolving of greater political power to the Scottish legislature (Bogdanor 1981, 155–56). In Wales, the vote was four to one against further devolution, although Bogdanor suggests that the results "did not finally settle the issue. It is always possible for supporters of devolution to argue that a simpler and cleaner bill, or one presented in a different political atmosphere, could have secured majority support" (ibid., 156).

The rapid and tumultuous embrace of democracy and sovereignty in several of the former republics of the Union of Soviet Socialist Republics in the early 1990s has been achieved through both legislative and popular measures. A declaration of independence by the Ukrainian republic in the summer of 1991 was ratified by a referendum in December 1991. Approximately 90 percent of Ukrainians voting in the referendum supported the declaration of independence, and only after the referendum had been conducted successfully and fairly did Canada give diplomatic recognition to Ukraine (MacPherson 1991).

Since the creation of the Fifth French Republic in France in 1958, the French president can call constitutional advisory referendums on important issues of the state. French presidents have used national referendums periodically to mobilize public support as a way of countering resistance from the National Assembly to their legislative programs. The results of French referendums are seen as a test of the president's credibility and popularity. Charles de Gaulle resigned as president in 1969 after his plans to change the French Senate and strengthen the role of regional governments were rejected in a referendum. As a result, later French presidents have found it prudent to use their constitutional power to call national referendums sparingly. President François Mitterrand has indicated recently that he may call a national referendum on several constitutional amendments, including reducing the tenure of the French president from seven years to five.

A few national governments are required to hold mandatory referendums as part of their constitutional amendment process. Constitutional amendments in Australia, Austria, Japan, Switzerland and Ireland must be ratified by voters. In Australia, two majorities are required: a national majority and a majority of the states (i.e., four out of six). Since the early 1900s, approximately 40 constitutional amendments have been submitted for ratification; 17 of the referendums have been held on election day (Adamson 1991, 39). Only eight amendments have received the necessary double majorities. Referendums are seldom used for matters other than constitutional change in Australia.

Very few nations allow citizen-initiated referendums at the national level. Most referendums are initiated by the central authority or national government. Switzerland and Italy are notable exceptions. A hundred thousand Swiss voters can seek constitutional amendments. Constitutional amendments in Switzerland can vary from changing the size of old age pensions to enacting environmental protection laws, and they all must be ratified through referendums. Legislation in Switzerland involving international treaties and a variety of budgetary matters must also be approved through mandatory referendums. As well, when legislation is passed by the Federal Assembly, it must be approved or rejected in a national referendum if, within three months, 50 000 citizens sign a petition supporting popular ratification.

Switzerland conducts referendums at both the national and canton level. From 1848 to 1990, about 350 national referendums have been held in Switzerland (Aubert 1978; Adamson 1991). Proposals submitted by the national parliament for popular ratification through mandatory referendums are normally accepted. When voters propose legislation through a citizen initiative, the legislation is usually rejected. Legislation that has been passed by the federal legislature and then submitted to voters through a referendum is usually ratified. The legislature and Federal Council have no discretion if the legislation is rejected in a referendum (Sigg 1987, 33).

Voter turnout rates are very low in Switzerland (Black 1991), falling below 50 percent since the early 1960s for general elections, and dropping to 35 percent for referendums and initiatives in recent years (Sigg 1987, 28). Those citizens who do vote represent a select sample of the Swiss population. Voters tend to be between the ages of 40 and 60, male, well educated and affluent. Public opinion surveys have shown that non-voters in Switzerland have low levels of political efficacy. This widespread sense of "political helplessness" is anomalous in a nation where the role of the individual citizen is the foremost concern of the governing process (ibid., 25). The referendum and initiative process is dominated by highly organized pressure groups committed to specific legislation and programs.

Italy also allows national initiatives. If certain petition requirements are met, Italian voters can pass judgement on legislation passed by the National Assembly. In 1974, as a result of a popular initiative, Italians voted not to repeal the divorce law enacted by the National Assembly (Adamson 1991). The citizen initiative is seldom used in Italy. With the exception of the initiative procedure, referendum questions, the campaign rules and interpretation of the results in Italy are the prerogatives of the central government.

Far more referendums and initiatives are held in the American states than in all other jurisdictions combined. As Cronin notes:

> More than 200 measures of one kind or another reached the state ballot via citizen-initiative petition during the 1980s. Several hundred others failed to obtain the appropriate signatures or, in the case of perhaps

a dozen or so measures, were ruled off the ballot by the courts. About
1,000 additional measures were referred to the voters by state legislatures or constitutional procedures ... Thousands of additional
measures were voted on by citizens at the local level ... Only about
20 percent [of petition drives] qualify to get on the ballot in recent
years. (Cronin 1989, 203, 205)

Of the 50 American states, Arizona, California, Colorado, North Dakota,
Oregon and Washington use direct democracy devices most frequently
(Barber 1984, 281). The predominant policy area for the use of referen-
dums and initiatives is tax measures.

The results of referendums, whether nationally or subnationally,
tend to be neither consistently conservative nor consistently progressive. Butler and Ranney argue that the results reflect the dominant ideological and political currents of the day. The evidence "suggests that
the referendum is neither an unfailing friend nor an implacable enemy
of either left or right. As is the case with most electoral arrangements,
the policies that referendums produce depend on the state of public
opinion at the time the vote is taken, and in a democratic polity the
voters observably lean right on some occasions and left on others"
(Butler and Ranney 1978, 85). Based on an examination of various
studies of voting patterns for referendum outcomes in the American
states, Cronin concluded that there was "about an even split between
liberal and conservative wins, suggesting again that most voters are
less concerned with whether a measure is 'liberal' or 'conservative'
than with whether they think it is right or wrong" (1989, 201).

With the exception of those nations where mandatory referendums
are required by the constitution, most referendum results are not binding
on national governments. Nonetheless, the distinction made by students
of referendums between mandatory and advisory referendums is often
misplaced (Butler and Ranney 1978; Zimmerman 1986). Even when
referendum results are not legally binding, political leaders typically
have not been willing to act contrary to the desires of voters. Advisory
referendums, then, do not necessarily give the national governments
greater discretion in the implementation of the results than do mandatory referendums. Consequently, national governments tend to use the
advisory referendum cautiously.

REFERENDUMS: AN ASSESSMENT

Many arguments are used to defend referendums.[4] First, it is said that
if citizens can initiate referendums or if governments are required to
call them to seek ratification of certain pieces of legislation, elected
representatives will need to be responsive to popular sentiments.

Citizens will not have to wait for elections to have a say about which policies should be adopted. Johnson says that there is "considerable force in the case for the referendum as a means of popular democratic control" (1981, 26). The case for popular consultations may be "reinforced by the growing complexity and remoteness of modern government, as a result of which many people feel alienated from their political institutions and suspicious of the decisions taken through them on their behalf" (ibid.).

Second, referendums can increase citizens' sense of political efficacy by allowing them to have an impact on what governments do. Referendum results are highly visible. A government's response to how its citizens voted can be more precisely measured.

Third, referendums can commit governments to consulting citizens on the credibility of constitutional amendments that can rearrange the institutional or political fabric of a nation.

Fourth, if the legislature is stalemated on a piece of extraordinary legislation, it can seek a resolution to the impasse by going to the people for direction through a referendum.

Fifth, since governments consistently engage in informal consultation through extensive public opinion polls, referendums are a defensible extension of this process. As Lemieux notes, "a poll does not provide for public debate, as the referendum does. It also limits the right to 'vote' to a sample of electors, however representative they may be" (Lemieux 1985, 140).

Sixth, legislation ratified by citizens directly enhances the legitimacy of public policies and laws. In turn, confidence in the democratic process is increased.

> People may or may not trust legislators, cabinets, and prime ministers, but they certainly trust themselves most of all. Hence a decision in which all have participated (or at least had a full opportunity to participate) is more legitimate in their eyes than one in which they have not participated. Moreover, decisions in which popular participation is direct and unmediated by others, as in referendums, produce more accurate expressions of [citizens'] will than do decisions in which they participate only by electing others who make the decisions for them, as in acts of parliaments and cabinets. (Butler and Ranney 1978, 25)

It is this potential for legitimacy that prompted Vincent Lemieux to support the increased use of referendums in Canada. For him, greater use of referendums could "promote a greater sense of attachment, on the part of Canadians, to the central institutions of the country, as well as a stronger feeling of participation in the decisions that concern us all" (Lemieux 1985, 139).

In summary, advocates of the referendum say that citizens can be trusted to make prudent decisions on public issues, and that there is no "divine right" of elected representatives. Periodic elections should not be the only instrument available to citizens to make certain that politicians are responsive to their constituents (Zimmerman 1986, 55–56).

The arguments against referendums are essentially a defence of representative government. First, it is argued that access to the referendum can make politicians reluctant decision makers. Rather than provide direction or leadership on controversial or volatile issues, politicians will use the referendum to obfuscate or shun responsibility.

Second, advocates of unadulterated representative democracy argue that citizens are too ill-informed to make deliberative decisions on complex issues. Emotion is more likely to triumph over reason, leading to unworkable legislation.

Third, "the referendum is based on the unrealistic assumption there is a simple 'yes' or 'no' answer to complex questions, and sets up a confrontation between supporters and opponents of a proposition" (Zimmerman 1986, 57). "There is no opportunity for continuing discussion of other alternatives, no way to search for the compromise that will draw the widest acceptance. Referendums by their very nature set up confrontations rather than encourage compromises. [Referendums] divide the populace into victors and vanquished" (Butler and Ranney 1978, 226).

Fourth, referendum results do not reveal the popular intensity behind "Yes" and "No" votes. For example, a small majority of voters may endorse a referendum question even if they are relatively indifferent to the results, compared to a minority of voters who may be passionately dedicated to a certain outcome.

Fifth, the referendum process can be captured by wealthy special interest groups. These groups can use the referendum process to advance a host of narrow and often competing policies, and mobilize popular support through the adroit use of money and the media.

Sixth, the indiscriminate and frequent use of the referendum can lead to democracy without responsibility. Johnson has argued that "the striking thing about consultation and the right to vote on this or that is that the person consulted or voting bears no responsibility for the decision and what follows. [The individual] has no duties laid on him [or her], cannot be held accountable, and may not be affected in any way by the consequences of his [or her] behaviour" (Johnson 1981, 32). Johnson's concerns are especially pertinent in the case of citizen-initiated referendums. Experience in the United States and Switzerland shows that the repeated use of the referendum device tends to undermine, rather than enhance, its usefulness as a way of seeking public input into important public policy issues. The referendum process is often overloaded with numerous questions that range from the trivial to the substantive. In his recent volume on American direct democracy, Thomas Cronin concludes that a national referendum and a national citizen-initiative process in the United States would be undesirable. Cronin argues that the adoption of either process at the national level "would involve making national laws based on general public opinion at a particular moment" or would "reduce some aspects of political leadership and policymaking in a large and diverse nation to a Gallup-poll approach to public policy" (1989, 194). Cronin suggests that "those who are dissatisfied with Congress should find ways to make it more responsive, accountable, and effective rather than inventing ways to bypass or supplement it with these potentially dangerous devices" (ibid., 195). He presents these conclusions in a study that is highly supportive of the use of the instruments of direct democracy at the state and local level.

Much of Cronin's scepticism of a national referendum process is implicitly directed at the majoritarian principles that often drive the use of referendums. Cronin is concerned, as are many critics of referendums, that if vindictive majorities are provided with the opportunity through a referendum to undermine or assault the rights and interests of various minority interests, they will do so. What Cronin and those who share his views mean is that the resort to unfettered majoritarian principles is too blunt an approach to develop and implement national public policies that are required to balance different representational and legislative needs.

A critique of the inherent risks of majority rule should not, however, lead to a rejection of the referendum as a device in the legislative and governing process. Much can depend on how the rules for holding referendums are structured. The referendum process in Switzerland, for example, is designed to provide minorities with considerable influence in the legislative process. Referendums on legislation that has been passed by the Swiss federal assembly can, as noted, be sought if 50 000 qualified voters or eight legislatures of 23 sovereign cantons make such a request. If the referendum proposal is defeated by Swiss voters, the legislation has no effect.

The presence of the referendum device in Switzerland and the ready access voters have to it require Swiss legislators to engage in extensive consultation among different linguistic and religious groups in order to ensure that their various representational needs are affirmed in the legislative process (Rogowski 1974, 127–33). As a result, legislation enacted by the Swiss federal parliament is often based on carefully crafted compromises designed to discourage specific groups from using the referendum device to stall or interfere with policies supported by competing groups. In this sense, the politics that surround the referendum device in Switzerland are an extension of the various consociational devices used to forge consensuses among competing interests. The use of referendums in Switzerland, therefore, is not simply an affirmation of majoritarian principles. Instead, referendums are one facet of a broad institutional configuration designed to allow minorities in Switzerland to promote their representational needs.

The Swiss experience shows that the divisive or integrative impact of a referendum result takes place in the same political and cultural environment as does the legislative process. Many critics of the use of a national referendum in Canada make frequent reference to the depth and extent of regional and linguistic cleavages in the country. They argue that the use of referendums to resolve controversial issues could result in situations where a national majority of voters could vote "Yes" or "No" for a referendum question while a minority of voters in a single region could vote the opposite way. This dilemma could be resolved, however, by tying the interpretation of referendum results to a formula more complex than a vote by a national majority of voters. For example, the acceptance or rejection of a referendum could be based on a formula similar to one found in the *Constitution Act, 1982*, whereby general constitutional amendments require endorsement from 7 out of 10 provincial legislatures, making up at least 50 percent of the population. Such an approach would help ensure that referendum proposals would not be endorsed unless they were supported by both a national majority of voters and a majority of regions. Australia, as noted, uses a double majority procedure to ratify constitutional amendments. The central point to be made here is that the referendum process does not have to be based exclusively on promoting majoritarian principles. The rules governing the use of referendums can be tailored in some degree to respect the institutional context in which legislators and governments function, in order to forge stable consensuses among competing minorities and majorities.

What criteria should be used to decide if the use of referendums and initiatives are desirable and defensible? If the objective is to empower individual citizens, instead of elected representatives, with the right to make decisions, referendums and initiatives can be effective in achieving this. If the motivation is to give credence to the argument made by advocates of direct democracy that citizens are intellectually equipped to make rational policy choices, there is evidence to suggest that this is also obtainable. The Swiss and American use of direct legislation (the phrase used to describe laws made through referendums and initiatives) suggests that citizens will not support frivolous or reckless legislation. In fact, citizens in both jurisdictions are more likely to support legislation offered by the legislature than laws supported by special interest groups. If the goal is to ensure that elected representatives are more or fully responsive to citizen likes and dislikes, however, then the use of referendums for such purposes is open to question. Where legislation must be ratified through referendums, governments have shown themselves to be adroit at crafting an appropriate referendum question, and at shaping the referendum debate and campaign to ensure a favourable outcome (Butler and Ranney 1978). As well, citizens presented with referendum questions seem more willing to take policy cues from elected representatives than from pressure groups and other policy actors.

REFERENDUMS AND ELECTIONS: A COMPARATIVE OVERVIEW

Outside the United States, only a few jurisdictions have any substantial experience with the simultaneous holding of referendum questions and general elections. As Butler and Ranney note, "the great bulk of referendums have taken the form of a single question put to the elector in an isolated contest" (1978, 16). One exception to this rule is New Zealand, where referendum options on liquor licensing policy have been an idiosyncratic tradition at every general election since before the nation's independence in 1907. The referendum results are applied locally rather than nationally, so that if one community in a town or city votes for prohibition and an adjoining community votes against liquor sales, the option receiving the majority in each community becomes the legal liquor licensing policy.

In 1937, a new Irish constitution was submitted to voters for popular ratification by Prime Minister Eamon De Valera in a general election. De Valera's objective in holding the constitutional referendum simultaneously with the general election was to use the popularity of his political party as a basis for mobilizing support for the new constitution, which he supported. The draft constitution was approved by Irish voters. "Although 74.7 percent of the electors expressed a choice between parties, only 68.4 percent marked their referendum ballot" (Manning 1978, 199). In 1959, De Valera, having served as prime minister of Ireland for approximately 25 years between 1932 and 1959, announced that he was going to resign and seek the Irish presidency in the forthcoming general election. As in 1937, De Valera also stated that a constitutional referendum on whether the existing Irish electoral system of proportional representation should be replaced with a single-member plurality system would be held concurrently with the general election of 1959. Opposition parties "immediately claimed that De Valera was personalizing the issue and appealing to sentiment and emotion, and that it would be difficult for many people to refuse this 'last request' of a great leader" (ibid., 203). De Valera's strategy of linking his electoral popularity to his support for a referendum question was unsuccessful. Although he won the presidency by a small majority in 1959, the proposal to replace proportional representation was defeated.

From 1906 to 1988, Australian voters have been presented with 42 national constitutional amendments through national referendums; only eight of these amendments have received the necessary "double majorities." Former prime minister Robert Menzies has remarked that "to get an affirmative vote from the Australian people on a referendum proposal is one of the labours of Hercules."

Of the 42 referendums, 21 have been held concurrently with general elections. Only three constitutional referendums held on election day, in 1906, 1910 and 1946, have been ratified by Australian voters. Aitkin concludes that although governments in Australia prefer to hold constitutional referendums at the same time as a general election to save money and to conduct their affairs more efficiently, "it seems pretty clear, however, that this timing is likely to result in the referendum's failure because of high party temperature at election times" (Aitkin 1978, 132). Partisanship remains the foremost determinant of voting choices in Australia, and most constitutional referendum campaigns are structured around the positions established by the various political parties.

The political jurisdiction with the most extensive and varied experience with citizen-initiated referendums held concurrently with elections is the state of California.[5] California is especially fond of initiatives. "The institution [of the initiative] appears as firmly grounded in the political culture of the state as the legislature itself. Indeed, the initiative may be more widely employed and by more people in the state than in any other democratic society in the world" (Lee 1978, 88). In the November 1990 mid-term elections there were 20 questions on the California ballot. Every Californian household was sent a 144-page booklet, which explained the referendum questions. In California, statutes and constitutional amendments developed by the legislature and submitted for popular ratification tend to be approved; citizen initiative legislation is much more likely to be defeated (ibid., 89–92).

Political parties are weak in California. Elections are candidate-centred. Individual candidates establish their own campaign and fund-raising organizations. Seldom do candidates in California seek election to the state legislature on the basis of well-defined programs. Frequently, the position that candidates take on specific referendum questions provides the most reliable measurement of their policy preferences.

California elections do not produce governments; in the American congressional system, cohesive political parties do not run a slate of candidates dedicated to a common set of policies and ideas that provide cues to voters on what to expect from their governments once elected. Nor do parties serve as the promoters or brokers of competing policy alternatives. For the most part, parties in California and throughout the United States provide candidates with labels, some logistical electoral support and some campaign funds. Unlike political parties in parliamentary democracies, American parties do not serve as disciplined collectivities that organize the processes of opposition and government, and they do not accommodate the various representational interests of elected officials. Candidates target their own constituents through elaborate media campaigns and through the use of modern communication technologies.

The relative weakness of parties as primary political organizations in California makes the referendum process a more critical vehicle for various interests and minorities seeking to influence or have representation in the legislative process. This weakness has allowed specialized interest groups to emerge as the primary organized participants in Californian elections and referendum campaigns. These groups can spend as much money as they raise (American courts have ruled that state legislatures cannot enact spending limits for interest group electoral activity). Interest groups play a key role in getting issues on the ballot: they hire paid professional circulators to get the required number of signatures on the initiative petition; structure and manage the initiative campaigns; saturate the airwaves with "Yes" and "No" advocacy advertising; and compete vigorously for voter support. In short, the process of citizen initiatives is "big business"; initiatives belong mostly to public relations firms, media consultants, public opinion pollsters and direct mail specialists.

Pressure groups use initiatives to advance a narrow set of objectives that have been either rejected by or not presented to the state legislative process. The so-called citizen-initiative process has become a potent arrow in the quiver of interest groups seeking to influence or capture the legislative agenda. The irony here is obvious: the progressives supported the recall, the initiative and the referendum during the populist fervour of the early 1900s to break the power that special interest groups supposedly had over the state legislatures, and now special interests have captured the instruments of direct democracy (Cronin 1989, 145–46; Shockley 1985).

Voter turnout is very low in California; this is the case throughout the United States. The turnout rate for California in the mid-term congressional elections in 1990 was 37 percent. It is difficult, however, to establish the causal relationship between extensive use of direct democracy and voter turnout. The contributing factors may be "voter fatigue" and indifference. Frequent voting opportunities may make it difficult for citizens to distinguish between critical and routine issues, and repeated voting on a range of issues may diminish the value of the vote as an act of civic virtue. Yet those states that use the initiative or the referendum tend to have slightly higher turnout rates than those that do not. On average, the voter turnout between 1978 and 1984 in those American states that do not have initiatives on their election ballots was 41.5 percent, compared to 46.4 percent for those states with initiatives (Cronin 1989, 227).

American voters who cast ballots in elections represent a subset of the general population – they tend to be more educated and more affluent than non-voters. Tellingly, voters who take part in referendums and initiatives in American states tend to be even more educated and more affluent than voters who cast ballots for candidates seeking elected office.

Two Canadian provinces have had very recent experience with the use of referendums held concurrently with elections. The Saskatchewan *Referendum and Plebiscite Act* was used by the Progressive Conservative government of Grant Devine in the October 1991 provincial election to present three advisory plebiscite questions to voters. Questions were presented on balanced budget legislation, whether changes to the Constitution should be approved by Saskatchewan voters and whether the government of Saskatchewan should pay for abortions. Approximately 80 percent of voters casting ballots voted for balanced budget legislation and for a statutory requirement that constitutional amendments be approved by Saskatchewan voters through referendums. On the third plebiscite question, the issue of funding for abortions, 63 percent of voters agreed that the provincial government should not pay for abortion procedures.

As in Saskatchewan, British Columbian voters were presented with referendum questions in the provincial election of October 1991. Voters were asked to consider statutory provisions for the recall of members of the provincial legislature and the use of citizen-initiated referendums. The recall and citizen-initiated referendums were endorsed by 81 and 83 percent of voters, respectively. The results of the referendum questions, as provided for in the British Columbian legislation, were binding only on the government that initiated them. In the British Columbian and Saskatchewan provincial elections, the incumbent government was defeated.

Referendum and plebiscite questions were introduced, in part, by the provincial governments to accommodate vibrant populist sentiments. Each incumbent government had a low standing in public opinion polls. The referendums and plebiscites were strategic offerings to voters who had become dissatisfied with the responsiveness of their governments. In examining the holding of referendums during a British Columbian provincial election, a national newspaper columnist suggested that "there would seem to be considerable advantages for an incumbent government, especially an unpopular one required by law to call an election in the next few months, to sugar-coat the vote with referendums. If nothing else, this allows it to direct the substance of the campaign away from past events ... toward the subject of its choice" (Sheppard 1991).

Whatever the strategic or tactical motives of the incumbent governments in British Columbia and Saskatchewan, the presence of referendum and plebiscite questions during the recent provincial elections had no discernible impact on the flow and substance of the respective campaigns. In neither province did the candidates or leaders of the larger parties expend much energy or resources in debating the referendum and plebiscite questions. In British Columbia, the dominant election issues were the record of the incumbent government and the state of the provincial economy. In Saskatchewan, the pre-eminent issue was the provincial agriculture crisis. Both election campaigns were structured around the programs, leaders and candidates of the larger parties. The only exception was the plebiscite question in Saskatchewan, which dealt with whether or not the provincial government should pay for abortion procedures. A few interest groups staked out adversarial positions on this issue, but very little of the attending debate was channelled through the political parties.

The defeat of each incumbent government created a paradox unique in Canadian electoral history. Newly elected governments came to power with explicit popular mandates to implement specific pieces of legislation; in British Columbia, there was convincing support for the adoption of statutory recall and citizen-initiated referendums. Saskatchewan voters wanted legislated balanced budgets and to ratify constitutional amendments, and did not want their government paying for abortion procedures. These policies were not, however, part of the election campaigns of the winning party, even in a marginal sense. Nor did the new government contribute to the design of the referendum and plebiscite questions. In fact, it is reasonable to suggest that the populist sentiments and sensitivities that led to the posing of the referendum and plebiscite questions during the provincial elections were incompatible, or at least inconsistent, with the ideological underpinnings of the newly elected New Democratic governments in both British Columbia and Saskatchewan.

The one-time holding of referendums and plebiscites concurrently with elections in the two provinces provides too small a sample to measure if the impact on voter turnout was comparable to the experience in the United States and Switzerland, where the generous use of direct democracy devices is accompanied by low levels of electoral participation. The voter turnout rate for the 1991 Saskatchewan election was 83 percent, a level consistent with the average turnout for provincial elections of 83.1 percent in the 1980s. Voter turnout in British Columbia, in contrast, declined to 71.2 percent, compared with the provincial average in the 1980s of 77.4 percent.

Comparative experience with the simultaneous holding of referendums and general elections suggests that when the referendum is initiated by the government of the day, it is not used to receive unadulterated public input on important public policy issues. Instead, it is used by the government as an extension of its electoral strategy.

In political systems where electoral competition and public debate on policy issues are structured and ordered by political parties, the presence of referendum questions during general elections does not disrupt traditional patterns of political discourse. The debate surrounding referendum questions is either dominated or manipulated by political parties, and therefore it is often indistinguishable from the general election campaign; this has been the experience in Australia. Conversely, when political parties shun or ignore the presence of referendum questions during elections, the questions receive minute attention and do not serve as instruments to effectively engage citizens in deliberative public policy discussions; this has been the recent experience in several Canadian provinces.

In jurisdictions such as California and other American states where referendums are supposedly initiated by citizens, the referendum questions and campaigns are structured by well-financed pressure groups to pursue specific policy objectives, and the voters who decide these referendum questions tend to be unrepresentative of the general population. It is the structural incapacity of the American electoral process to produce governments dedicated to a cohesive set of policies and ideas that makes the referendum process one of the few institutional mechanisms that voters in the United States have to assess the precise policy preferences of candidates seeking elected office.

REFERENDUMS AND CANADIAN FEDERAL GENERAL ELECTIONS

The recent support for referendums suggests that Canadians are impatient with the delicate and often imprecise accommodation of conflicting interests so critical to representational politics, the essence of which involves blending competing interests and agendas into stable compromises and consensuses. Political parties can achieve this by offering policies and ideas that are flexible enough to capture shifting consensuses and views. These continuous pressures often mean that the processes of representational politics are not necessarily as precise, responsive or timely as some would wish. These essential characteristics of representation come into question when there are groups or citizens who either reject the established compromises or feel excluded from them. Frequently, these groups do not want compromises – they want immediate, measurable responses to their needs.

Referendums are appealing because many people believe that they offer Canadians qualities that are missing from representational politics: immediacy and control. Referendums produce results – "Yes" and "No" votes are unequivocal. The results cannot be massaged or reinterpreted by politicians; their clarity cannot be muddled. The Reform Party's support for the referendum has drawn so much popular appeal because the device provides disenchanted citizens with opportunities to inject themselves into policy debates from which they consider themselves otherwise excluded: official bilingualism, multiculturalism and Ottawa's apparent excessive responsiveness to Quebec's constitutional agenda (*Globe and Mail* 1991c). Representatives from the Reform Party told the Royal Commission on Electoral Reform and Party Financing that:

> The process of resolution of an issue is too often an accommodation
> to a particular region, pressure group or an attempt to gain the favour
> of a province. Referenda ensure that the resolution of an issue is public.
> The debate over issues is subject to the cleansing agent of public
> scrutiny. The doubts and concerns that many Canadians feel about
> the process of government would be allayed by a referendum or
> plebiscite. (Reform Party of Canada 1990, 6)

The use of referendums is seen as a way for citizens to state their likes and dislikes on specific policies, supposedly unencumbered by parties, leadership politics and by slick media campaigns (Meisel 1991, 191).

The Royal Commission on Electoral Reform and Party Financing received a few briefs supporting referendums as defensible instruments of citizen participation in a parliamentary democracy. Most interveners advocating referendums suggested that they could be used to establish public legitimacy for certain policies, to give citizens a more direct say in how they are governed and to offset the perceived dominance special interest groups have over the governing process. Most of the interveners said that referendums should be held on election day. The Reform Party of Canada provided the most detailed defence for holding referendums and elections concurrently, arguing that such an approach would be much less expensive than holding the two separately.

Although it can be demonstrated that referendums have a number of strengths, if they were to be held on the same day as federal general elections they could have the peculiar result of joining what individuals like about referendums with what they do not like about representational politics. Elections in parliamentary democracies are about linkages. Voters must select from the policies and values of competing parties. The decision to vote is based on a judgement of the past, the present and the future – will a party's future performance be consistent with its past performance, and, if so, is this party a better alternative to the other parties? The voting decision is one that must stand for several years. Referendums, however, sever linkages. Voters make isolated decisions, unrelated to the various and complex stratagems of representative government.

In *Absent Mandate: Interpreting Change in Canadian Elections*, Clarke et al. (1991) argue, with lament, that Canadian election results are not about policy mandates. Canadian voters seldom elect governments based on precise policy choices:

> Part of political mythology is that elections are called to resolve policy differences. When the smoke of battle has cleared, it is expected that an incoming government will have a mandate to implement specific policies. But cases in which this actually happens are extremely rare. More often, elections turn on only the most general of issues ... or on a multiplicity of smaller issues which together provide only the fuzziest of electoral mandates. "Leadership," often important in elections, provides a mandate not for a set of policies but only for a set of actors. The mandate given a political leader in an election is a potentially fleeting one, lacking any real substance. (1991, 148)

It could be argued that the policy imprecision evident in the Canadian electoral process is one reason that more referendums should be held. Referendums would require parties and politicians to articulate clear positions on specific issues. Voters could determine more precisely where parties stand and could engage in more substantive policy debates with their governors.

Such an argument makes sense. Voters should be able to determine what policies parties support and do not support. Parties should make firmer policy statements, enabling them to "fulfil their assigned tasks of organizing choice and mobilizing change" (Clarke et al. 1991, 156). But would this reasonable objective be achieved if referendums were held on election day? The important question becomes, of course: what are elections about? Are they about precise policy mandates? If referendums were held on election day, a certain symbolic threshold would be crossed, and elected representatives would have limited legitimacy to manage critical issues of the day without direct endorsement from a majority of voters. Under such circumstances, governments would have insufficient discretion to establish priorities, to make choices, to affirm the value of minority interests, and to respond to changing political and economic events – in short, to do what governments are supposed to do.

Elections are not just about political parties seeking periodic voter approval to implement campaign promises. Elections are also about mandates to govern; they are about voters accepting the need for their governments and governors to have the capacity to exercise discretion over changing circumstances and to respond to unanticipated issues and concerns. Elections are not about placing governments in policy strait-jackets that prevent them from addressing the dynamic representational needs of Canadians. It cannot be suggested that the apparently fuzzy policy environment of Canadian elections prevents voters from critically assessing the performance and credibility of their governors. Since 1945, a federal election has been held in Canada every 3.1 years, and of the 15 general elections held, 6 have resulted in minority governments. Further, compared to the United States, there is a high level of legislative turnover in Canada (Blake 1991; Young 1991). From 1974 to 1988, a period that saw four general elections, on average 25.7 percent of MPs seeking re-election were defeated. The comparable figure for the United States House of Representatives was 6 percent.

In Canada, the presence of both a single-member plurality system and a vibrant, competitive multi-party system means that a political party can be elected to form the government even if it has less than a majority of votes cast in a general election. This feature of electoral competition raises the periodic concern that governments in Canada have a questionable or restricted mandate to implement extraordinary policies; however, the view that the Canadian electoral process does not bequeath clear mandates to political parties that win a majority of seats in the House of Commons but not a majority of votes has been traditionally latent. Following the 1988 general election, this concern has become manifest, flared by the intensive debate among the three larger parties over the Canada–United States Free Trade Agreement. While the Progressive Conservative party formed a majority government with 169 out of 295 seats and 43 percent of the popular vote, there was a widely held assumption that it did not have support from a majority of voters to proceed with the implementation of the agreement.

It has been suggested that, if a referendum question on free trade had been presented to voters during the general election, they would have had the opportunity both to elect a government and to explicitly reject or accept the agreement. The suggestion that political parties forming a government with less than 50 percent of the popular vote do not have a legitimate mandate to govern – in the broadest sense of the term – constitutes a fundamental and problematic re-assessment of the electoral process in Canada; and, while the argument that the apparent flaws of the electoral process can be readily corrected through the simultaneous holding of referendums and general elections is intuitively appealing, the practical consequences of such a measure need to be carefully scrutinized.

In an issue paper for the Report of the Commission, entitled "A New Proposal for Reviving the Spirit of Canadian Democracy," Lawrence LeDuc (1990) stated that the declining legitimacy of Canada's primary political institutions could be arrested by increasing citizen participation in the governing process through referendums and citizen initiatives. Under the LeDuc proposal, direct legislation could be achieved in one of two ways: "Parliament itself could decide to place a question on the ballot, or it could be petitioned to do so by a certain minimum number of citizens." LeDuc suggested that 3 percent of the voters enumerated in the previous general election, with the same minimum applying across at least five provinces, would be a workable formula. An all-party parliamentary committee would make the final decision to hold a referendum and would decide on the question to be asked. The chief electoral officer would be responsible for the referendum campaign. Like the members of the Reform Party, LeDuc believes that referendums and elections should be held on the same day. "In this way, the referendum question would not involve the expense and disruption of a special election, but would simply be a part of the normal electoral process" (1990, 26–27).

LeDuc suggests that his proposal would "enhance the value of elections by clarifying rather than confusing the choices presented to the voter" (1990, 28). Clarity, however, has costs. The outcome of the 1942 referendum was clear: English-speaking Canadians wanted conscription, French-speaking Canadians did not. Given Canada's charged regional and linguistic sensitivities, clarity in the electoral process can be more onerous than comforting. Elections, in contrast, "serve to legit-imize the authority of the state and to resolve peacefully social conflicts; majority and minority groups alike are more willing to accept exercises of the state's coercive powers and to obey state laws when the state offi-cials have been chosen by the people in a fair process" (Harvard Law Review Association 1975, 1114–15). The holding of referendums on impor-tant policy issues could impair the integrative qualities of elections.

LeDuc correctly states that the voting choices of Canadians in the 1988 federal election were based on a number of factors, including the record of the Mulroney government and the credibility of John Turner's leadership of the Liberal party (Clarke et al. 1991, chap. 4). LeDuc thinks, however, that the results of this election were somehow illegitimate because the Conservatives did not have an explicit mandate from a majority of voters to implement the Free Trade Agreement. "The 1988 election was, for all of its moments of high political drama, a straight-forward contest for political power in which the critical issue of the campaign was carefully manipulated by nearly all concerned for short term political advantage" (LeDuc 1990, 1).

LeDuc cannot have it both ways, however. He cannot argue, on the one hand, that the 1988 election results as related to the Free Trade Agreement were of dubious legitimacy and then, on the other hand, state that a large number of voters held ambivalent views about the agreement (LeDuc 1990, 14). If LeDuc is concerned that election campaigns in Canada are too slick and glib, the presence of the free trade debate as a substantive issue should have been welcomed.

Tom Kent has a different interpretation of the 1988 election. First, he says, "an election is not a referendum." Then, he argues, contrary to Clarke et al.:

> The 1988 election ... confirmed what has been apparent from many recent elections as well as public opinion surveys – a relatively educated public now has a firmer grasp of what an election is about than do many of our politicians. It is not to choose the politicians who will govern as they think best when in office. It is to choose the politicians whose declared policies and apparent capabilities best embody the direction of public policies as a whole that most Canadians favour for the next four years. (Kent 1989, 10–11)

Individuals and groups who support the use of referendums on election day offer contradictory interpretations of what role political parties should have. At one level, there is an undeniable anti-party sentimentality to the support for referendums. Parties are seen as distorting rather than advancing the representation of specific interests. It is believed that voters, through referendums, would be able to express their views on various policy issues without parties having intermediary roles. Alternatively, referendums are seen as a means of forcing parties to accept public policies they would prefer to ignore or reject. This perspective contains an implicit assumption that parties are pivotal players in the structuring and presentation of policy choices. Referendums should be used during elections to allow voters to determine more precisely how parties will exercise their representational functions.

Any assumption that parties would have a minimal presence if referendums were held with elections is probably misplaced. Debate on the referendum questions would be dominated by political parties. They would stake out positions, advise supporters how to vote and then compete for the undecided. Voters would not be able to escape party. So while current support for referendums in Canada draws in part from anti-party sentiments, those who say that referendums and elections can be held on the same day give parties the same prominence they so freely denounce. The comparative experience in Australia, where referendum questions are presented to voters at the state and national level on election day, suggests that, unless referendum issues are of extraordinary importance, they are likely to be overshadowed by the general election campaign and the electoral strategies of the political parties (Mackerra, Interview 1991).

Conversely, if political parties, through collusion or collective abstinence, decided to give cursory attention to the referendum questions, it is probable the attending issues would have a marginal presence in the election campaign. In such circumstances, voters would have moderate opportunities to assess the different positions of the individual parties. The widespread concern that current federal election campaigns do not involve substantive policy debates would not be appeased. Recent experience in the provincial elections in Saskatchewan and British Columbia indicates the degree to which public debate on referendum questions is very much dependent on the substance and style of the parties' election campaigns.

It could be argued that the dominance of party would be diluted if organized pressure groups were allowed to participate freely in referendum campaigns. But participation by a large number of competing interest groups would not bring voters any closer to the acquisition of greater control over what happens in politics. Comparative experience shows that pressure groups use the instruments of direct democracy to advance specific objectives that have been rejected by the mainstream legislative process.

CONCLUSION

This study has suggested that referendums, if used sparingly and prudently, can contribute to the structuring and ordering of choices in complex political systems. The use of the referendum device may involve a number of potential pitfalls, however. Comparative experience shows that governments attempt to use referendum questions and campaigns to advance their self-interest, and often this is achieved independently of whether the result is a "Yes" or "No" vote. In jurisdictions where direct legislation is used frequently, voters are more likely to reject than accept citizen-initiated referendums. No matter when referendums are held, they are dominated by political parties, pressure groups or both; thus, referendums as an instrument of direct democracy do not necessarily lead to the empowerment of individual citizens. In jurisdictions where referendums and initiatives are common, voter turnout tends to be the lowest, and those who do vote are usually more affluent and better educated, and so represent a specific subset of the general population. Conversely, where referendums are used less frequently (or sparingly) and are kept separate from elections, parties and pressure groups are less likely to dominate, and the empowerment of individual citizens is more likely.

Holding referendums and elections concurrently would exacerbate rather than attenuate the complexities of the referendum process. The critical question to be asked in assessing the consequences of holding referendums on election day is: would the objectives of those individuals and groups who support such a proposal be achieved? Referendums held on election day would strip elections of some of their meaning and value. Elections must be about voters trusting their own informed choices to pick governors who can judge, reflect, deliberate, compromise, lead and respond; they must be about accepting the need for governance. At times, governance will mean controversial compromises, indecision, unpopular measures and unadulterated mistakes. The holding of referendums on election day would not lead to the kind of unfettered, immediate kind of decision making by citizens that is promised by the advocates of populism. It would be an inadequate substitute to voters making deliberative, careful choices about those they elect to be their governors.

ABBREVIATIONS

A.C.   Appeal Cases

c.   chapter

R.S.C.	Revised Statutes of Canada
R.S.M.	Revised Statutes of Manitoba
R.S.O.	Revised Statutes of Ontario
S.A.	Statutes of Alberta
S.B.C.	Statutes of British Columbia
S.C.	Statutes of Canada
S.M.	Statutes of Manitoba
S.P.E.I.	Statutes of Prince Edward Island
S.Q.	Statutes of Quebec
s(s).	section(s)
S.S.	Statutes of Saskatchewan

NOTES

This study was completed in December 1991.

I would like to thank Peter Aucoin, Herman Bakvis and Michael Cassidy for their helpful comments on various drafts of this study. In particular, Michael Cassidy and Herman Bakvis provided some very useful editorial and analytical comments.

1. The concept of populism is used in this essay in a broad sense to capture the well-documented negative attitudes that many Canadians now express about their political institutions and elected representatives. Populism can be burdened with a number of competing ideological and political ideas; it does not consistently reflect views from either the left or the right. As Laycock notes, however, all strains of populism tend to be based on "practically oriented and critical democratic thought" (Laycock 1990, 3). According to Shils (1956) populism subsumes two cardinal principles: the supremacy of the will of the people and the desirability of a "direct" relationship between people and leadership, unmediated by political institutions. These two principles imply, first, a desire that politics somehow be brought back to the people at the grass roots and, secondly, a distrust of "experts" (Blais and Gidengil 1991).

   In a public attitudinal survey conducted for the Royal Commission on Electoral Reform and Party Financing, Blais and Gidengil presented respondents with two statements to measure the level of populism among Canadians: "We would probably solve most of our big national problems if decisions could be brought back to the people at the grass roots" and "I'd rather put my trust in the down-to-earth thinking of ordinary people than the theories of experts and intellectuals" (Blais and Gidengil 1991). Three-quarters of the respondents agreed with the first statement, and almost two-thirds agreed with the second.

   More serious attention is now being given to the utility of referendums because of the presence of a strong populist dimension in contemporary

Canadian political discourse, although this phenomenon does not account solely for popular and élite support for referendums. This study does suggest, however, that the presence of a fervent populist undercurrent exacerbates the sober assessment of referendums as instruments in political decision making, and their use in accommodating certain populist pressures could compromise whatever attributes they may have.

2. The citizen initiative, the referendum and the plebiscite all involve the submission of specific questions via ballot to voters for popular ratification or rejection. There are two forms of initiatives – direct and indirect. The direct initiative allows voters to propose statutes, constitutional amendments and bond issues by petition. If the petition procedure has the required number of signatures, the proposal must be submitted directly to the voters for their approval or rejection. With an indirect initiative, a successful petition by citizens means that the issue is sent to the legislature for consideration. If the legislature does not provide a satisfactory response, the original proposal is put to a ballot for popular consideration. For the purposes of this study, these devices will be referred to generally as citizen-initiated referendums. Citizen-initiated referendums can be either binding or advisory. If they are binding, governments are required by law to enact legislation that affirms the results of the referendum vote. If the referendum results are considered advisory, governments use their own discretion to determine what, if any, response they will make to the vote. The other class of referendums is those initiated by the government or the appropriate legislature. As is the case with citizen-initiated referendums, there are two types of government-initiated referendums – mandatory and advisory. Mandatory referendums require the government to submit specific pieces of legislation or statutes for popular ratification. The legislation cannot be proclaimed into law unless it has been approved by a majority of qualified voters. These matters commonly involve constitutional amendments. Advisory referendums are also known as plebiscites, although this term is used less frequently than in the past.

3. While the recognized leader of the United Farmers movement in Alberta, Wood declined to become premier following the election victory of 1919. Based on a nomination from Wood, H.H. Greenfield was made premier of Alberta. Wood continued, however, to direct the activities of the UFA inside the provincial legislature (Morton 1967, 217–18).

4. It should be noted that the various arguments in favour of and in opposition to referendums, as presented in the literature, do not consistently distinguish between political systems that use referendums infrequently and those that use them freely as an integral part of the legislative and policy-making processes. For example, the argument that the repeated use of referendums could lead to lower voter turnout and possibly voter fatigue would be less relevant to a political system where the referendum device was used by the national government to resolve extraordinary issues. As

well, the American experience with citizen-initiated referendums and legislature-initiated referendums is a political phenomenon distinct from the European tradition, in which referendums are used to affirm the legitimacy or popularity of the central government. The most notable exception, of course, is Switzerland.

5. Forty-nine states require constitutional amendments to be ratified by referendums; registered voters in 25 states may petition for a referendum on a law enacted by the state legislature. The filing of the required number of petition signatures suspends the law, except appropriations and emergency ones in several states, until the electorate determines whether the law should be approved. Citizen initiatives may be used in 23 states to place proposed constitutional amendments or laws on referendum ballots. The initiative in 21 states may be employed in the process of enacting ordinary statutes; the veto power of the governor does not extend to voter-approved initiated measures. In 17 states, the initiative may be used to amend the state constitution. Citizen initiatives are ratified far less frequently than are referendums sponsored by state legislatures (Cronin 1989, 197). Of the 1 500 citizen-initiated referendum questions considered by American voters at the state level, 35–40 percent have been approved. In contrast, of the several thousand referendums sponsored by state legislators, at least 60 percent have won voter approval (ibid.).

INTERVIEW

Mackerra, Malcolm. March 1991.

REFERENCES

Adamson, Agar. 1991. "Direct Democracy Has Its Place, But Not on the Day We Elect Our MPs." Paper prepared for the Royal Commission on Electoral Reform and Party Financing. Ottawa.

Aitkin, Don. 1978. "Australia." In *Referendums: A Comparative Study of Practice and Theory*, ed. David Butler and Austin Ranney. Washington, DC: American Enterprise Institute for Public Policy Research.

Alberta. *The Direct Legislation Act*, S.A. 1913, c. 3.

Aubert, Jean-François. 1978. "Switzerland." In *Referendums: A Comparative Study of Practice and Theory*, ed. David Butler and Austin Ranney. Washington, DC: American Enterprise Institute for Public Policy Research.

Barber, Benjamin. 1984. *Strong Democracy: Participatory Politics for a New Age*. Berkeley: University of California Press.

Black, Jerome H. 1991. "Reforming the Context of the Voting Process in Canada: Lessons from Other Democracies." In *Voter Turnout in Canada*, ed. Herman Bakvis. Vol. 15 of the research studies of the Royal

Commission on Electoral Reform and Party Financing. Ottawa and Toronto: RCERPF/Dundurn.

Blais, André, and Elisabeth Gidengil. 1991. *Representative Democracy: The Views of Canadians.* Vol. 17 of the research studies of the Royal Commission on Electoral Reform and Party Financing. Ottawa and Toronto: RCERPF/Dundurn.

Blake, Donald E. 1991. "Party Competition and Electoral Volatility: Canada in Comparative Perspective." In *Representation, Integration and Political Parties in Canada,* ed. Herman Bakvis. Vol. 14 of the research studies of the Royal Commission on Electoral Reform and Party Financing. Ottawa and Toronto: RCERPF/Dundurn.

Bogdanor, Vernon. 1981. "Referendums and Separatism II." In *The Referendum Device,* ed. Austin Ranney. Washington, DC: American Enterprise Institute for Public Policy Research.

Boyer, J. Patrick. 1982. *Lawmaking by the People: Referendums and Plebiscites in Canada.* Toronto: Butterworths.

———. 1988–89. "Plebiscites in a Parliamentary Democracy." *Canadian Parliamentary Review* (Winter): 2–4.

———. 1991a. "Canadians Needn't Fear National Referendum." Montreal *Gazette,* 27 May.

———. 1991b. "Give the People a Say." Montreal *Gazette,* 10 December.

British Columbia. *Direct Legislation Act,* S.B.C. 1919, s. 21 [Assented to 29 March 1919; not proclaimed].

———. *Referendum Act,* S.B.C. 1990, c. 68.

Butler, David. 1978. "United Kingdom." In *Referendums: A Comparative Study of Practice and Theory,* ed. David Butler and Austin Ranney. Washington, DC: American Enterprise Institute for Public Policy Research.

———. 1981. "The World Experience." In *The Referendum Device,* ed. Austin Ranney. Washington, DC: American Enterprise Institute for Public Policy Research.

Butler, David, and Austin Ranney, eds. 1978. *Referendums: A Comparative Study of Practice and Theory.* Washington, DC: American Enterprise Institute for Public Policy Research.

Canada. Bill C-9. *Canada Referendum Act,* 4th Session, 30th Parliament, 1978. First Reading 18 October 1978.

———. Bill C-257, s. 14(1). *Canada Referendum and Plebiscite Act,* 2nd Session, 34th Parliament, 1989. First Reading 26 September 1989.

———. *Canada Elections Act,* R.S.C. 1970, c. 14 (1st Supp.).

———. *Canada Elections Act,* S.C. 1960, c. 39.

————. *Constitution Act, 1982,* being Schedule B of the *Canada Act 1982* (U.K.), 1982, c. 11.

Canada. Citizens' Forum on Canada's Future. 1991. *Citizens' Forum on Canada's Future. Report to the People and the Government of Canada.* Ottawa: Minister of Supply and Services Canada.

Canada. Parliament. Special Joint Committee of the Senate and the House of Commons on the Process for Amending the Constitution of Canada. 1991. *Report.* Ottawa: Queen's Printer.

Clarke, Harold D., Lawrence LeDuc, Jane Jenson and Jon H. Pammett. 1991. *Absent Mandate: Interpreting Change in Canadian Elections.* 2d ed. Toronto: Gage.

Cronin, Thomas. 1989. *Direct Democracy: The Politics of Initiative, Referendum, and Recall.* Cambridge: Harvard University Press.

Edmonton Journal. 1991. "Direct Democracy." 12 January.

Eulau, Heinz. 1978. "Changing Views of Representation." In *The Politics of Representation: Continuities in Theory and Research,* ed. Heinz Eulau and John C. Wahlke. Beverly Hills: Sage Publications.

Eulau, Heinz, and John C. Wahlke. 1978. *The Politics of Representation: Continuities in Theory and Research.* Beverly Hills: Sage Publications.

Fisher, Douglas. 1991. "We're Running Out of Time," *Ottawa Sun,* 29 November.

Franks, C.E.S. 1987. *The Parliament of Canada.* Toronto: University of Toronto Press.

Globe and Mail. 1991a. "Bourassa Looking at 'Referendum Election'." 25 May.

————. 1991b. "Chrétien Continues Push for Constitutional Reform." 2 December.

————. 1991c. "The Widening Appeal of the Reform Party." 5 April.

Harvard Law Review Association. 1975. "Developments in the Law – Elections." *Harvard Law Review* 88:1111–339.

Hockin, Thomas. 1979. "Flexible and Structured Parliamentarianism: From 1848 to Contemporary Party Government." *Journal of Canadian Studies* 14:8–17.

Johnson, Nevil. 1981. "Types of Referendum." In *The Referendum Device.,* ed. Austin Ranney. Washington, DC: American Enterprise Institute for Public Policy Research.

Kent, Tom. 1989. *Getting Ready for 1999: Ideas for Canada's Policies and Government.* Halifax: Institute for Research on Public Policy.

Laycock, David. 1990. *Populism and Democratic Thought in the Canadian Prairies, 1910 to 1945.* Toronto: University of Toronto Press.

LeDuc, Lawrence. 1990. "A New Proposal for Reviving the Spirit of Canadian Democracy." Issue Paper presented to the Royal Commission on Electoral Reform and Party Financing. Ottawa.

Lee, Eugene C. 1978. "California." In *Referendums: A Comparative Study of Practice and Theory*, ed. David Butler and Austin Ranney. Washington, DC: American Enterprise Institute for Public Policy Research.

Lemieux, Vincent. 1985. "The Referendum and Canadian Democracy." In *Institutional Reforms for Representative Government*. Vol. 38 of the research studies of the Royal Commission on the Economic Union and Development Prospects for Canada. Toronto: University of Toronto Press.

McGillivray, Don. 1991. "Constitution Taking Its Toll on Joe Clark." *Ottawa Citizen*, 29 November.

Macpherson, C.B. 1953. *Democracy in Alberta: The Theory and Practice of a Quasi-Party System*. Toronto: University of Toronto Press.

MacPherson, Don. 1991. "Not as Clear-cut as in Ukraine." Montreal *Gazette*, 3 December.

Manitoba. *Initiative and Referendum Act*, S.M. 1916, c. 59.

———. *Liquor Control Act*, R.S.M. 1988, c. L160.

———. *Reference re Initiative and Referendum Act*, [1919] A.C. 935 (P.C.).

Manning, Maurice. 1978. "Ireland." In *Referendums: A Comparative Study of Practice and Theory*, ed. David Butler and Austin Ranney. Washington, DC: American Enterprise Institute for Public Policy Research.

March, Roman. 1974. *The Myth of Parliament*. Scarborough: Prentice-Hall.

Maser, Peter. 1991. "Chrétien Proposes National Referendum." *Ottawa Citizen*, 22 April.

Meisel, John. 1991. "Decline of Party in Canada." In *Party Politics in Canada*. 6th ed., ed. Hugh Thorburn. Scarborough: Prentice-Hall Canada.

Morton, W.L. 1967. *The Progressive Party in Canada*. Toronto: University of Toronto Press.

Noel, S.J.R. 1987. "Dividing the Spoils: The Old and New Rules of Patronage in Canadian Politics." *Journal of Canadian Studies* 22 (Summer): 72–96.

Ontario. *Municipal Act*, R.S.O. 1980, c. 302.

Paul, Alexandra, and Donald Campbell. 1991. "Referendums Picked by Most Voters in Poll." *Winnipeg Free Press*, 10 May.

Pitkin, Hanna F. 1967. *The Concept of Representation*. Berkeley: University of California Press.

Prince Edward Island. *Plebiscite Act*, S.P.E.I. 1954, c. 26.

Quebec. *Process for determining the political and constitutional future of Quebec. An Act respecting*, S.Q. 1991, c. 34, s. 1.

———. *Referendum Act*, S.Q. 1978, c. 6.

Ranney, Austin. 1978. "United States of America." In *Referendums*, ed. David Butler and Austin Ranney. Washington, DC: American Enterprise Institute for Public Policy Research.

———, ed. 1981a. *The Referendum Device*, ed. Austin Ranney. Washington, DC: American Enterprise Institute for Public Policy Research.

———, 1981b. "Regulating the Referendum." In *The Referendum Device*, ed. Austin Ranney. Washington, DC: American Enterprise Institute for Public Policy Research.

Reform Party of Canada. 1990. "Strengthening Democracy in Canada." Brief to the Royal Commission on Electoral Reform and Party Financing. Ottawa.

Rogowski, Ronald. 1974. *Rational Legitimacy: A Theory of Political Support.* Princeton: Princeton University Press.

Saskatchewan. *The Direct Legislation Act*, S.S. 1912–13, c. 2.

———. *Referendum and Plebiscite Act*, S.S. 1991, c. R-8.01, s. 5.

Sheppard, Robert. 1991. "Answer, Yes, No, Maybe or Phooey." *Globe and Mail*, 28 May.

Shils, Edward. 1956. *The Torment of Secrecy: The Background and Consequences of American Security Policies.* London: Heinemann.

Shockley, John S. 1985. "Direct Democracy, Campaign Finance, and the Courts: Can Corruption, Undue Influence, and Declining Voter Confidence Be Found?" *University of Miami Law Review* 39:377–428.

Sigg, Oswald. 1987. *Switzerland's Political Institutions.* 2d rev. ed. Zurich: Pro Helvetia Division Documentation-Information-Press.

United Kingdom. *Constitution Act, 1867*, 30 & 31 Vict., c. 3, s. 92¶1.

Young, Lisa. 1991. "Legislative Turnover and the Election of Women to the Canadian House of Commons." In *Women in Canadian Politics: Toward Equity in Representation*, ed. Kathy Megyery. Vol. 6 of the research studies of the Royal Commission on Electoral Reform and Party Financing. Ottawa and Toronto: RCERPF/Dundurn.

Zimmerman, Joseph. 1986. *Participatory Democracy: Populism Revived.* New York: Praeger.

8

REGISTERING VOTERS
Canada in a
Comparative Context

John C. Courtney
David E. Smith

THIS IS A STUDY of voter registration for federal elections in Canada. The study describes the enumeration system currently in place (its history, procedures, practices, problems and shortcomings), evaluates the adequacy of the system and presents some options for its reform. To help to identify the unique characteristics as well as the strengths and weaknesses of Canada's voter enumeration, part of the study examines and evaluates other voter registration processes, both provincial and foreign. By understanding the attributes of alternative forms of registering the electorate (of which no two, it can safely be said, are identical), Canadians should be better able to judge and to improve their own system.

Why and how are citizens registered to vote in a political system? Is one method of registering voters preferable to another? Is one fairer and more likely to be complete than another? There are no simple answers to such questions. Different values, cultural attitudes and institutional practices have created a variety of voter registration systems around the world. Each is country-specific and has its own distinctive characteristics, problems and shortcomings, and its own critics and defenders. No country's system is perfect, at least in the sense that any registration list can be said with certainty to constitute a totally complete and accurate registry of all eligible voters. But some procedures have proved more capable than others of producing a greater measure of reliability and thoroughness, and of engendering greater public confidence in the larger context within which elections are fought.

Voter registration is at the very heart of the democratic process: without it, citizens could not legitimately cast the ballot to which they are constitutionally entitled. If a voter registration system is to be judged appropriate to a free and democratic society, it must be designed according to three principles. It must enable all qualified citizens to be included on the list; prevent electoral abuse and fraud by individuals, special interest groups, political parties and governments; and be widely accepted as an authoritative and legitimate means of cataloguing the electoral population and of settling disputes. To provide universal accessibility, to safeguard both the individual's and the public's interest and to be widely perceived as fair and reasonable – these in our view are the three essentials of a sound and equitable system of registering voters.

This study will assess some of the alternative approaches to voter registration that are employed in both provincial and foreign political systems and compare them to the approach used in Canadian federal elections. It is our view that if Canadians are provided with an evaluation of such data, they will be better able to judge their enumeration process and to assess the appropriateness of suggested reforms. This study shows that Canada's registration system, like others, is not without its share of problems. These range from difficulties in hiring the necessary number of enumerators once an election is under way to allegations of failure to enumerate large concentrations of urban voters and to provide adequate time for additional names to be added to the revised voters lists. Whatever solutions are reached to such problems, they will have to fit the Canadian political context. They will have to reflect the extent to which, at the federal level, the attitudes and expectations of voters have been shaped by decades of experience with an election-driven, state-operated system that is based on personal contact between individual enumerators and citizens. The solutions will also have to take into account the increasingly litigious context within which recent elections have been fought and enumerations conducted – a context attributed by some to Charter-driven litigation.

At the outset it is best to note some of the constraints under which this research has been conducted. Comparative work of the sort that we have undertaken is deceptive. At first glance the data that are being compared seem relatively simple to obtain and to contrast, whether they be rules and procedures, lists of voters, turnout figures or costs. In fact, nothing could be further from the truth. Caution must be used in interpreting the results of any comparative research. Not only do such factors as the items that are included in costs, the rules that govern voter eligibility, and the procedures that are followed in administering and interpreting the enumeration or registration provisions of electoral acts differ from one jurisdiction to another, but the comparability of data and of information provided by the various authorities is open to question. Without exception we have found electoral officials at both the federal and provincial levels as well as abroad to be totally supportive of our research, and invariably willing to provide us with whatever information they could to facilitate our task. None the less, executive, legislative and judicial officials operate in discrete arenas for which they naturally design rules and interpret laws that are unique to their particular jurisdiction. The "non-comparability" phenomenon is thus one of which we have been mindful in attempting to reach helpful conclusions about the experience with enumeration and registration in several different jurisdictions.

It is also true that the statistics gathered by government agencies and electoral offices rest upon assumptions that are not always the ones that we would have chosen to make. The figures were sometimes available in forms that were not entirely compatible with our needs and that required further assumptions on our part. Data on population mobility, demographic patterns, completeness of lists and voter turnout come immediately to mind as ones that had to rest on carefully reasoned assumptions if they were to be useful for our analysis. While we ourselves are satisfied that the assumptions that we made are correct within the context of this study, others may disagree.

In its treatment of the problems and shortcomings of the current Canadian enumeration system, the study notes that part of the difficulty in assessing the accuracy of any enumeration or registration of voters stems from the absence of totally reliable information on population size. This absence helps to explain why claims made by critics of the federal enumeration in some constituencies in 1988 were at marked odds with those of Election Canada officials. It also underscores a fundamental problem inherent in any study of a population of indeterminate size. It is far from reassuring that there can be conflicting interpretations of the results of a process that is billed as being purposefully inclusive and that is designed to use relatively uniform procedures to capture the largest possible share of the population.

The most problematic of the data-gathering questions proved, not surprisingly, to be that of enumeration and registration costs. Electoral officials themselves agree that they are some considerable distance from having a satisfactory measure of uniformity in computing election costs. What is included as an enumeration or registration cost in one jurisdiction is not necessarily calculated in the same manner in another. The fact that we have little evaluation to offer on the matter of the comparative costs of compiling voters lists reflects our conviction that little of any great use would result from the effort.

Finally, a word of caution about the terminology of this study. To speak of an "enumeration" is to speak of a census, a headcount. Implicit in the term is a precise and exact measure of the total population that no demographer or statistician would accept without qualification. No census is ever totally complete or reliable; there are only degrees of completeness and reliability. By the same token, the term a "permanent list" suggests a lasting quality that simply cannot be demonstrated or supported in actuality. As more than one official told us, social demography makes a "permanent list" outdated virtually from the moment that it is completed.

What is needed, therefore, is a measure of scepticism about claims of completeness and permanence. It is unrealistic to think that all potential voters would be included on the electoral lists if only the right system could be designed. For whatever reasons, some individuals choose to ignore repeated contacts and advertisements to become listed while others remain unwilling to allow their names to be included on lists of any sort. Moreover, as every enumeration or registration system invites human error or oversight at some stage, a share of the total electorate is bound to be missed, regardless of the system employed. These and other considerations must be borne in mind as we explore voter enumeration and registration both in Canada and elsewhere.

POST-CONFEDERATION HISTORY OF VOTER REGISTRATION IN CANADA

Registering Voters: 1867–1938

> A voters' list, on the face of it, is an innocuous thing. It comprises the names and addresses of qualified electors, so that the only apparent problems are to discover what persons are entitled to vote, and to write down their names in alphabetical or possibly geographical order ... Canadian experience with voters' lists is a far cry from this routine procedure.[1] (Ward 1963, 189)

For the first 50 years after Confederation the federal franchise and voters lists were manipulated in a blatantly partisan fashion by both national parties. From 1867–85 there were no federal voters lists as such. Instead, the lists that were compiled by the various provinces for provincial and municipal elections were also used for federal elections. The qualifications for electors differed according to the various provincial laws.

In the colonial period the franchise in the early post-Confederation years was generally restricted to male property owners. Local assessment rolls typically served as the principal source of names for the lists; revisions and corrections were carried out at the local level as well. In Ontario, changes to the lists were made by county court judges, whereas in Quebec, Nova Scotia and New Brunswick, various municipal officials performed similar duties. In practical terms, the franchise was not necessarily what the law specified it to be. Electors' names might or might not appear on the lists depending upon such factors as the political circumstances in a riding, the party in control of the local election machinery and the known political allegiance of the individual voter (Ward 1963, 179; Courtney 1988, 834).

As can be seen from table 8.1, all voters lists were "closed" for many years following Confederation. After a period set aside for compilation and revision, no list could be altered, even on polling day. Omission from a list automatically disqualified an elector from voting. As early as 1870 the prime minister, John A. Macdonald, introduced a bill that was designed to put in place a federal system of enumeration based on a uniform franchise across the Dominion. This bill specified that voters lists would be compiled by an appointed board of registrars in each district, and judges would be given the responsibility of revising the lists. The system of creating federal voters lists based on provincial lists had been widely perceived as inefficient and capable of producing outdated information: individuals qualified to vote in one province were not necessarily eligible in another, and some lists used in 1867 had not been revised since 1861. The prime minister's proposal failed, however, because the Opposition feared, with some reason, that the Conservatives would merely replace provincial control of the election lists with federal Tory control.

From 1867–85, provincially compiled enumeration lists continued to be used for federal elections. Beginning in 1882, bills to establish federal lists were introduced in Parliament annually but were never passed. It was not until the comprehensive election reforms of 1885, which prompted one of the great debates on Canada's electoral laws in the House of Commons, that the system was finally changed. The Conservative government's bill (the *Franchise Act*) contained four basic features: there would be one federal franchise; a government-appointed revising officer (either a judge, or a lawyer of five years' standing at the provincial bar) would compile and revise each list for each district; there would be no readily accessible system of appeal from the compilation and revision process; and names could be removed or added to the list at the revising officer's discretion. The Act as eventually passed

Table 8.1
Preparation of voters lists for federal elections, 1867–1990

Years	Federal or provincial lists	Open or closed[a]
1867–85	Provincial	Closed
1885–98	Federal (annual revision)[b]	
1898–1917	Provincial	
1917–20	Federal (provincial lists basis for enumeration)	
1920–29	Provincial[c]	Open for voters in centres <2 500 in population; changed to <5 000 in 1925, and <10 000 in 1929
	Enumeration in centres <2 500 in population	
	Personal and voluntary registration in centres >2 500 in population; changed to enumeration in centres <5 000 in population with personal and voluntary registration in centres >5 000 in population in 1925; changed to enumeration in centres <10 000 in population with personal and voluntary registration in centres >10 000 in population in 1929	
1929–34	All lists prepared through federal enumeration; provincial lists no longer basis for federal lists	
1934–38	Federal enumeration with annual revision	Closed
1938–	Federal enumeration with preparation and revision of lists after the issue of writs of election	Closed (urban lists only) Open (rural lists only)

Source: Information derived from Ward 1963, chap. 10.

Notes: [a]"Closed" signified that after a period set aside for compilation and revision, no list could subsequently be altered, even on polling day. "Open" signified that qualified electors not yet included on the list could swear themselves in on polling day after having been vouched for by another elector.
[b]Revisions occurred only in 1886, 1889, 1891 and 1894.
[c]If existing lists in a province were over two years old, voters in all centres >1 000 in population were required to register personally at a registrar's office to have their names added to the list.

required revising officers to compare the voters lists from the previous year with the last assessment of rolls, and to use this information, and any other, in order to compile and revise the lists. Perhaps most important, the legislation accepted "the fundamental principle of having voters lists compiled and revised by a government appointee" (Ward 1963, 193).

The Liberals vehemently opposed the Act. They were convinced that the Conservatives would manipulate the system in such a way that Conservative voters would more easily be placed on the lists than

Liberal voters. Not only was there apprehension that judges, who may have been partial, were to revise the voters lists, but also that their decisions would be absolute and could not be questioned. Since appeals were not permitted, judges might exercise their power in such a way as to abuse the system. George Casey, a Liberal member for Elgin, noted that an elector who had been left off the list had to obtain legal advice before applying to be included, when in fact it ought to have been his right to be included in the first place (Ward 1963, 195).

The statute that the revising officers were called upon to administer was so loosely worded that it was open to various interpretations. The Act was called "one of the most expensive, cumbrous, and generally unsatisfactory ever put upon a statute book" (Ward 1963, 197). The revising officers across the country (some of whom were lawyers) used diverse and inconsistent criteria before accepting applications from electors who wanted their names included on the list. Some officers added names without having received proper applications; others placed disqualified voters on the lists with the expectation that they would soon become qualified; still others allowed the names of dead voters on the lists, or added the names of minors.

More than $1 million was spent on voters lists between 1885 and 1896. The federal government tended to suspend revision periods, which were intended to occur annually, whenever it was expedient to do so. As a result "annual" revisions occurred only sporadically – in 1886, 1889, 1891 and 1894. One major problem was that voters who moved to a different constituency during the period between the last revision and the ensuing election became disenfranchised in their new district. This represented a serious shortcoming in the system, especially as there was a large turnover of population in some urban areas and agricultural districts. The *Franchise Act* of 1885 thus failed to solve any of the problems associated with the voters lists; if anything, it increased the problems. In 1892, the newspaper *The Week* commented on the experience to date with the new legislation: "The Act is very complicated and expensive in operation, it affords facilities for 'stuffed lists', it tempts strongly to perjury, it works wholly in favour of the wealthier party, and in practical operation it undoubtedly results in the omission from the lists of many good citizens whose right to vote is beyond question, and in placing and retaining on the lists many who are without a shadow of qualification" (Ward 1963, 198). The Conservative government admitted the weakness of the Act and proposed abandoning the federal franchise and returning to the provincial one.

Nothing came of the Conservative proposal before they were defeated in 1896, and it fell to the Liberals to bring about a return to the provincial franchise and list system. No doubt as a reflection of their belief in provincial autonomy, the Liberals enacted new legislation in 1898. But it too had its problems. The legislation called for the adoption of various provincial laws and machinery about which the Liberal ministers knew little, if anything. Moreover, inconsistent with the Liberals' demand in 1885 that persons be allowed to appeal a revising officer's decision was the fact that, in the Maritimes at least, reversion to provincial lists meant that no such appeal would be allowed.

Federal candidates kept a close watch on the preparation of provincial lists. As most provincial governments were Liberal by 1900, there were few disputes between federal and local governments over the voters lists. But less than a decade later some provinces had Conservative governments, and the federal Liberals decided that the voters lists in British Columbia and Manitoba were unsatisfactory for their purposes. Accordingly in 1908 they attempted, without success, to reinstitute federal lists in these provinces. The opposition Conservatives staunchly opposed this move and these sections of the government's bill were withdrawn. However one provision that was important in terms of our current enumeration process was retained: the compilation of the federal voters lists in areas not under provincial jurisdiction (at that time this included only unorganized parts of Ontario) would be carried out by enumerators (Ward 1963, 200).

A general federal enumeration took place for the first time in Canada under the 1917 *War-time Elections Act*. This, along with the *Military Voters Act*, brought great changes to the franchise in Canada, including the enfranchisement of the female relatives of Canadian or British soldiers and servicemen and the disenfranchisement of those of enemy alien birth. The *War-time Elections Act* required the Governor in Council to appoint federal enumerators in each province, even though in practical terms for most of Canada provincial lists provided the basis for the enumerators' compilation.The new enumeration system received relatively little attention during the general furore of the 1917 election, except for the Liberals' concern that enumerators would be patronage appointments.

In 1920, the Conservative government returned to the system in place since 1898 of relying on provincial lists for federal elections. If lists in any province were over two years old, a measure was adopted whereby voters in all centres exceeding 1 000 people had to register in person at a registrar's office to become listed. Once judicial revision occurred, the lists were final. In rural areas, enumerators prepared the lists, but without judicial appeal. For the first time, "open" enumeration was permitted, in that qualified rural electors not yet included on the list could be sworn in on polling day after having been vouched for by another elector.

In 1922, the chief electoral officer (an office created in 1920 and one that helped to establish the conditions for the centralization of voter registration in Canada) apprised the Speaker of four major weaknesses of the provincial list system: at times the law required the use of provincial voters lists that the province itself considered obsolete; as provincial and federal polling divisions were different, creating a list for one purpose from lists compiled for another was difficult; it was nearly impossible to transfer names from one list to another because of the large population turnovers; and it was legally impossible to remove dead or disqualified electors from provincial lists (Ward 1963, 202). Only later in the decade would these concerns be addressed in a reformed franchise act.

As can be seen in table 8.1, the enumeration system was gradually extended to more areas during the 1920s. In 1921, enumerations were held in all towns under 2 500 in population. In 1925 this figure was raised to towns of 5 000 in population and in 1929, to those of 10 000. For electors residing in centres exceeding these respective populations, personal and voluntary registration was required on the voter's part. As a consequence, the voters lists for this period do not indicate the total qualified electorate for areas other than the rural ones.

In 1929, it ceased to be necessary for electors to register in large cities. Provincial lists were abandoned as a means of preparing federal lists, and for the first time all urban voters were registered through state-operated personal enumeration. The most complete lists ever compiled in Canada to that date were introduced with the 1930 election when enumerators, representing each of the major parties and working in pairs at the level of the polling district, carried out a door-to-door enumeration.

Although the chief electoral officer was of the opinion that the enumeration system that was in place at the time of the 1930 election was very satisfactory, the Conservative government scrapped much of it in 1934. The Dominion franchise commissioner (a newly created position), was given responsibility for overseeing the compilation of voters lists. The basic lists were still to be drawn up through an enumeration of voters and in every constituency revising officers (registrars) were to be appointed to conduct an annual revision. The lists were "closed," even in the rural areas, enabling only those electors whose names were on the annual list to vote.

In 1937, the Special Committee on Elections and Franchise Acts denounced this voter registration system, which had been employed for the first and only time in the 1935 election. A report of the Special Committee on Elections and Franchise Acts stated that:

> Experience has shown that the basic lists prepared in 1934 were almost obsolete within six months after they were completed, and that the Annual Revision held in the year 1935 was not adequate to remedy the situation. The conclusion arrived at is that the yearly revision under the provisions of the Dominion Franchise Act, 1934, could not produce satisfactory results, and that only through voluntary efforts on the part of Members of Parliament, candidates and political organizations, involving great cost in time and money, could the lists of electors be brought up to date and thoroughly purged. [The] Committee is unanimously of the opinion that it would be advisable to return to the system of preparation and revision of the lists of electors immediately after the issue of the Writs of Election, with closed lists in urban polls, and open lists in rural polls, as in 1930. (Canada, House of Commons 1937, vi–vii)

These recommendations were accepted in Parliament and became part of the *Dominion Elections Act, 1938.*

On another matter, the Special Committee decided that it could not favourably recommend either compulsory registration or compulsory voting. In the Committee's view, compulsory registration "could not be enforced without continuous registration, a large staff of permanent officials, an annual house-to-house check of the names of electors on the lists" or by other methods. After examining compulsory voting in Australia and other places, and "in view of the high percentage of electors who voted in Canada at the last two general elections, and of the doubtful value of compelling unwilling electors to cast their votes," the Committee unanimously rejected that proposal as well (Canada, House of Commons 1937, vi).

To Norman Ward, the system designed in 1938 minimized the possibilities of unfairness and abuse and proved to be a fitting conclusion to seven decades of trial and error with various methods of compiling lists. Writing in 1950 about the development of Canada's enumeration process, Professor Ward drew two conclusions from his research that he thought might well serve as guides for future policy:

> The first is that any scheme of "standing" lists, which are kept up-to-date by regular revisions, apparently cannot work in a country which has heavy internal movements of population. The Canadian experiments of 1885 and 1934 were both total failures, and put the ultimate

burden of compiling accurate lists not on the state, but on interested individuals and organizations. The second conclusion augments the first: any system which puts the onus on individuals and organizations is certain to produce inaccurate and unsatisfactory lists, for the circumstances governing the actual compilation of the lists will inevitably tend to be irrelevant to the lists' purpose. Eighty years of Canadian experience have furnished conclusive evidence that the making of voters lists is a proper state function; seventy of those eighty years were required to prove the point. (Ward 1963, 204)

Voter Enumeration since 1938

Few of the details of voter registration have changed since 1938. The fundamentals that were put in place at that time largely define the system today. As will be seen in the more detailed description of the current enumeration system that follows, two enumerators are to be appointed by the constituency's returning officer for every urban polling division, and one for every rural one. It is the enumerators' responsibility to compile as complete a list of voters as possible in their particular polling division. Revisions and additions are provided for in the Act, but within carefully prescribed limits. Party patronage is implicitly recognized as being part of the system. Enumerators are, in effect, to be chosen by the two most successful parties in each constituency at the time of the previous federal election. This might be faulted on the grounds that lists of voters are to be compiled by political rather than state ("neutral") officials. But it is argued by supporters of the scheme that representation from competing party interests taken together with payment to each enumerator based on the number of voters registered is intended to ensure that there are both individual and political incentives in the system aimed (ideally at least) at guaranteeing the compilation of as complete a list as possible.

A brief description of the process in place since 1938, together with an abbreviated list of the timetable for federal elections, shows how federal enumerations and revisions are to be carried out in Canada (see appendix A for the important features of the returning officer's election timetable for the enumeration of voters and revision of lists).

The federal system of voter enumeration in Canada is the product of a complex system of laws and regulations, administered by a central office (Elections Canada) in Ottawa. Responsibility for enumeration rests with the returning officers appointed by the Governor in Council (the Cabinet) in each of the country's current 295 constituencies. The *Canada Elections Act* sets a minimum campaign period of 50 days (a change introduced in 1982 over the former generally accepted minimum

60-day period) between the issuance of the election writ and voting day. The Act says nothing about a maximum period, which means that governments are able to call elections with longer campaigns should they so desire, as did the Turner government in 1984, for example, with a 57-day campaign.

As appendix A makes clear, all election scheduling and directions are calculated on the basis of the 50-day period, counting backwards from election day. Thus, by Day 45 (that is, 45 days before the election) in an urban polling area, the candidates who, at the last preceding election in the electoral district, received the highest and the next highest number of votes, are to nominate one enumerator each for every poll in the district. Enumerators are then appointed by the returning officer from these two lists to carry out the enumeration in each poll.[2] In a rural poll there is only one enumerator, who is selected and appointed by the returning officer as soon as possible after the writ of election has been issued. On Day 38 enumeration begins in both urban and rural polls. In the former, the two enumerators must ascertain by a joint house-to-house visitation and from such other sources of information as may be available, the name and address of every person entitled to have his or her name on the list. A notice signed by both enumerators is detached from the enumerators' record book and left at the residence. When they are unable to secure this information, they must leave a notification card stating when they will return, as well as the name, address and telephone number of one or both of them. By Day 31, both urban and rural enumerators will have prepared a preliminary list of voters, and by Day 26 the returning officer will have sent a notice of enumeration to each elector whose name appears on the preliminary list.

Days 31 to 17 constitute a period of revision when the names of qualified electors that were omitted from the preliminary list may be added to the list. While there are further details with regard to revision, it can be said in summary that by Day 11, the returning officer should have received the additional information gained through revision and thus the official list of voters is now completed. Urban electors cannot be added to the list after the close of revision (Day 17), but rural electors may vote on polling day even if their name does not appear on the official list. They do this by being vouched for, in person, by an elector who has been enumerated for the same rural polling division, and by taking an oath in the prescribed form at the polling station.

The registration portion of the "Electoral Hourglass" prepared by Elections Canada following the November 1988 federal election shows the number of voters captured in each of the two phases of registration (see appendix B). During the week-long door-to-door canvass,

17 161 413 electors were enumerated, 97.6 percent of the total number ultimately registered for the election. The remaining 2.4 percent (419 467) were added from Days 31–17, that is, during the revision period. As the number of electors added to the list in rural polls on election day is not released, it is impossible to know how many voters are in fact sworn in at the time of voting. Our best guess is that it is small in both absolute and relative terms. Even so, as the number of electors entitled to vote through such a procedure is added to the numerator but not to the denominator of the turnout equation, it should be remembered that the 75.2 percent turnout of registered voters shown for the 1988 election is, however slightly, an inflated figure.

Three points should be kept in mind regarding the years between the 1957 and 1988 elections and the changes that occurred in Canada's political system. First, the country experienced a record number of federal elections – 12 – over a 30-year period. Second, the electorate virtually doubled in size, from 8.9 million to 17.6 million registered voters (this was in part because the voting age was lowered from 21 to 18 years of age and in part because of natural growth and immigration following the Second World War). Third, the growth in the urban electorate vastly outpaced the rural (see table 8.2). Taken together, these demographic and political developments placed the enumeration system under great stress, particularly during the 1970s and 1980s in the large metropolitan centres. Designed in a period of Canadian history when elections were less frequent and when voters were both fewer in number and less concentrated in urban areas, the process of registering the electorate adapted to Canada's changed political and social environment remarkably well, although not without problems.

The registration system has proved that it is capable of responding fairly to instances of unanticipated crisis. For example, when the Clark government was defeated in the House of Commons late in 1979 and an election was called for February 1980, Elections Canada chose not to conduct a door-to-door enumeration – the only such occurrence during the post-1938 period. Instead, some 656 000 electors (or 4.1 percent of registered voters) were added through revision, a record for Canadian elections (see table 8.3). The process, more fully described below, was designed in response to an unexpected development and a unique set of circumstances. It was judged a success at the time. There were few complaints voiced by the voting public, and Elections Canada proved that it could respond competently with a special set of procedures on short notice.

Nevertheless, signs of weakness had already begun to appear. For example, from the early 1970s, periodic warnings had been sounded by the chief electoral officer about difficulties in finding, training and

Table 8.2
Number of electors on official lists

	Electors on lists			
Year	Urban	Rural	Total electors	Electoral districts
1957	5 183 482	3 718 643	8 902 125	263
1958	5 433 959	3 697 241	9 131 200	263
1962	6 036 440	3 663 885	9 700 325	263
1963	6 241 393	3 669 364	9 910 757	263
1965	6 606 769	3 668 135	10 274 904	263
1968	7 186 323	3 674 565	10 860 888	264
1972	8 691 921	4 308 857	13 000 778	264
1974	9 134 989	4 485 364	13 620 353	264
1979[a]	10 429 580	4 721 562	15 234 997	282
1980[b]	10 894 859	4 913 653	15 890 416	282
1984	11 705 719	5 692 294	16 775 011	282
1988	12 584 452	5 054 549	17 639 001	295

Source: Canada, Elections Canada, various official reports.
[a]Does not include 82 511 Special Voting Rules (SVR) electors or those given Certificates to vote.
[b]Does not include 82 014 SVR electors.

retaining enumerators. Two different federal reports in 1968 and 1986 addressed the adequacy of Canada's method of enumeration and revision. Nelson Castonguay, federal Representation Commissioner at the time and former chief electoral officer, completed a report in 1968 in which he investigated a variety of methods of registering voters and of absentee voting (Canada, Representation Commissioner 1968). The study examined permanent voters lists that were used in the United Kingdom and France, and in Canada from 1934–38, and continuous electoral rolls in British Columbia, Trinidad and Tobago, and Australia. It concluded that, while the length of federal election campaigns could be reduced by 30 days (from the standard of 60 days that was used at the time) if Canada adapted Australia's system of a continuous electoral roll, the move would entail substantially increased costs for operations and maintenance. The report also recommended that computers and electronic equipment be used to prepare lists of electors, and that a form of absentee or postal voting be adopted in Canada for voters unable to attend at a polling station. There were no subsequent legislative initiatives based on the Castonguay recommendations.

Table 8.3
Canadian elections, 1965–88

Categories	Nov. 1965	June 1968	Oct. 1972	July 1974	May 1979	Feb. 1980[a]	Sept. 1984	Nov. 1988
Electors registered								
Enumeration	10 200 367	10 860 888	12 818 806	13 358 576	14 861 736	15 152 486	16 164 636	17 161 413
Revision	74 537		181 972	261 777	290 740	656 126	527 046[d]	419 467
SVRs[b]	n.a.	n.a.	n.a.	n.a.	82 511	81 014	83 329	58 121
Total[c]	10 274 904	10 860 888	13 000 778	13 620 353	15 234 987	15 889 626	16 775 011	17 639 001
Percentage added during revision	0.7		1.4	1.9	1.9	4.1	3.1	2.2
Average number of electors per poll	195	212	212	211	214	225	245	303
Costs of registration (dollars)	4 982 382	5 049 506	6 554 817	9 872 558	17 333 934	9 440 232	23 741 146	27 791 142
Number of electoral districts	263	264	264	264	282	282	282	295
Average cost per district (dollars)	18 944	19 127	24 829	37 396	61 468	33 476	84 188	94 207
Average cost in constant 1986 dollars			74 330	93 724	100 767	49 815	91 113	86 747

Source: Canada, Elections Canada, various official reports. Table prepared by Margaret Woodley for the Royal Commission on Electoral Reform and Party Financing.

[a]There was no enumeration in 1980; 1979 official list used as preliminary list.

[b]This figure does not contain dependants or veterans. Number of veterans enumerated in 1980 was 3 796. SVRs = Special Voting Rules.

[c]This total does not include voting day registrants as this information is sealed in poll ballot boxes and destroyed with other election material.

[d]Revision extended by 11 days during which 82 300 added. Without this addition, revision would have been 2.7% total.

n.a. = not available.

The *White Paper on Election Law Reform* was tabled in the House of Commons in June 1986. Accepting the premise that if election laws "are flawed or unnecessarily restrictive, they can undermine democracy," the white paper noted that various problems had surfaced both in the treatment of voters and in the enumeration process during the course of some previous federal elections (Canada, Privy Council 1986, i). Several of these will be discussed later in the study. It can be noted here, however, that the white paper signalled (as did the chief electoral officer in his 1989 statutory Report) the apparent conflict between provisions of the *Canada Elections Act* and the *Canadian Charter of Rights and Freedoms*, the shortage of trained enumerators with which some returning officers were having to contend, the different statutory treatment of eligible electors in rural and urban polls, effective "administrative" disfranchisement of some eligible voters, and a host of other difficulties with the current enumeration system.

The white paper marked a break with post-1938 Canadian enumeration history. Until about 20 years ago the public record suggests that the system generated few complaints from the people it served and from the returning officers, enumerators and revising officers whose responsibility it was to make it work. By the mid-1980s this was clearly no longer the case. Starting in 1972 with his comment that political parties could not always be counted on to provide enough enumerators, the chief electoral officer in his statutory Reports had drawn the attention of both the public and Parliament to a growing number of difficulties with the process of enumeration and revision. Acceptance by Parliament of Bill C-79, introduced in the House of Commons in 1987 and based largely on the recommendations contained in the 1986 white paper, would have helped to correct a number of the faults and shortcomings of the existing system. The Bill was not enacted prior to the dissolution of Parliament in 1988. Had Bill C-79 been passed, it would have led to some practical and overdue improvements in the operation of Canada's enumeration system, clarified important responsibilities of election officials and generally liberalized the franchise and the enumeration system. In our view these reforms would have reduced or eliminated a number of the criticisms of election officials and of the registration process that were voiced at the time of the 1988 federal election.

SHORTCOMINGS OF CANADA'S ENUMERATION SYSTEM
The registration of a country's electorate is a mammoth task if the lists of eligible voters produced are to instil confidence among the citizens in the outcome of the subsequent election. The Canadian system of

voter registration is unique, because all its stages are carried out in the period following the announcement of the election date and because the list of electors is compiled in most instances by door-to-door visitation. Immense organizational demands are placed on the officials responsible for voter registration. In the last general election, there were 53 338 polls across the country (35 589 were urban, defined as an area wholly within an incorporated city or town having a population of 5 000 or more, and 17 749 were rural) and there were close to 89 000 enumerators. Despite the fact that the number of urban polls has doubled during the last 30 years while the number of rural polls has declined (in 1957, the respective numbers of each were 18 659 and 18 728), the average number of electors per poll has steadily increased (in 1988, there were 325 electors per urban poll and 264 per rural poll). In a country where constituencies vary in size from 3 433 165 km^2 (Nunatsiaq) to 8 km^2 (Rosemont), where there are two official languages but an ethnically heterogeneous culture spread across six time zones, and where the population is one of the most mobile in the world, establishing an accurate voters list prior to every general election is a major achievement. But this achievement is not free of difficulty or criticism.

Finding Enumerators

All systems of voter registration share common problems – concern about coverage and accuracy are two of them – but finding an army of persons to enumerate successfully presents a unique difficulty. Evidence to support this claim is readily apparent in the briefs and testimony received by the Royal Commission on Electoral Reform and Party Financing, excerpts of which are summarized in Working Documents (for example, No. 41, "Enumeration Issues").[3] The primary concern expressed in these documents is, without question, the quality of enumeration and the frustration of electors, parties and candidates that results from inaccurate lists or from the exclusion of individuals from voting because of the current registration process. A major source of this multiple discontent is the challenge of finding qualified enumerators.

Evidence of this challenge comes from local constituency party associations and, at the centre of Canada's electoral process, from the chief electoral officer. According to Professor R.K. Carty: "Preliminary reports from a new survey of local associations indicate 20 percent said that they could not find enough enumerators while another third said they found 'barely enough.' Assessing the 1988 enumeration in their riding, about a third reported it had major problems or was a real mess, and more than 70 percent favoured the adoption of a permanent voters list" (Carty 1991, 8). Nor is this a particularly recent observation. One experienced returning officer (RO) who needed 500 enumerators for her constituency in the 1979 election noted:

> The whole system has broken down. It is more and more difficult to find people who are willing to work. The housewives on whom we used to depend are now a part of the regular labour force. People on UIC or welfare won't work for fear that it will jeopardize their benefits. The names given to us by the political parties were a joke. The lists received from the three major parties produced a total of 76 enumerators. At the same time, if we were to appoint enumerators from our own sources before the deadline, we could be in deep trouble. This is both unreasonable and unfair. If the parties are not prepared to cooperate, they should untie our hands. (Canada, Elections Canada 1979, 4)

In his 1989 statutory Report (Canada, Elections Canada 1989b, 33), the chief electoral officer documents the fact that he had to invoke his discretionary powers under section 4(2) of the *Canada Elections Act* to extend the deadline to complete the enumeration in 104 polling divisions, to double the number of enumerators in four polling divisions, to have urban enumeration carried out by only one enumerator (instead of two as prescribed by the Act) in six polling divisions, to authorize the RO to appoint enumerators who had not reached the age of 18 years in 10 polling divisions and to authorize the RO to appoint enumerators who did not meet the residence requirement in 177 polling divisions. Perhaps as a result of these problems, in recent years there has also been a need to extend the time allocated to revision (48 electoral districts in 1988) and to appoint additional revisal agents (59 agents, also in 1988).

Furthermore, in the Royal Commission Working Document No. 6 ("Staffing and Pay of ROs and Election Staff"), it is reported that "intervenors criticized having candidates appoint enumerators and recommended that alternatives be found." Among the alternatives suggested were that "enumerators be appointed and even trained before the election," that there be "one enumerator per [urban] poll ... and that 16 and 17 year olds ... should be permitted to work as enumerators."

Such comments attest to the difficulties of finding enumerators and completing an accurate enumeration when they are not found, or when it is necessary to use incompetent or inadequately trained persons. There is, however, less unanimity on the reason why the problem exists. Among the explanations commonly offered and conveniently summarized in Working Document No. 41 ("Enumeration Issues") are the following:

The parties were less interested in finding enumerators and found that this interfered with the need for election workers at the start of the campaign; enumerators were hard to find because more women were working; people were afraid to enumerate in certain areas for reasons of personal security; people could not be reached because they were away from their homes both day and night; the polls had grown too large; the pay was too low. It was also difficult to get two enumerators to find time to work together or to match enumerators with the right language skills in bilingual or multilingual areas.

In Working Document No. 6 remuneration "for ROs and election staff and enumerators" was referred to as "the single greatest issue." Significantly, similar "concern was not expressed with respect to the pay of DROs [deputy returning officers] and poll clerks working on election day." To emphasize the obvious in this discussion, enumerators, who under the Canadian system of voter registration are necessarily temporary workers, were perceived to be less temporary than election day workers (those persons who staff the polls on the day of balloting). Significantly, too, finding election day workers did not appear to constitute a serious problem for the parties or the DROs in their itemization of difficulties. There appears to be a big difference in the availability of people who will commit one day to participating in the conduct of an election and those who will agree to act as enumerators for four or five days (at "about 90 cents per name on the voters list"), which in an average poll of 325 voters amounts to less than $300 remuneration. Commission research shows that except for 1979, the pay for enumerators has been lower than the average industrial weekly wage aggregate, and generally amounts to between 50 and 60 percent of this aggregate (see table 8.4). When expressed in constant dollars, enumerators' pay rose until 1979 and has dropped since that time.

Compared with the situation in the provinces, Canada is the only jurisdiction that does not pay enumerators a base rate. The main advantage of incorporating a base rate into the pay calculation rather than using only the number of names obtained lies in the fact that the enumerators are paid for their work even if they are met with closed doors. The problem of recruiting workers is not limited to remuneration per se, but extends to the penalties imposed by various government organizations when an individual declares earnings from paid work. Beneficiaries of income security or unemployment insurance payments may find their benefits cut if they act as enumerators.

Money or, more accurately, an inadequate amount of money in the form of enumerators' pay may explain – as much as any reason offered

Table 8.4
Enumerators' pay, 1965–88
(% average industrial weekly earnings)

Election year	Pay based on 300 electors ($)	Industrial earnings ($)	Pay as a % of industrial earnings	Pay in constant 1986 $
1965	62.00	97.49	63.6	—
1968	62.00	117.61	52.7	—
1972	65.00	159.67	40.7	194.61
1974	98.00	190.55	51.4	245.61
1979	185.00	308.42	60.0	303.28
1980*	—	—	—	—
1984	200.30	498.35	40.2	216.77
1988	259.00	579.45	44.7	238.49

Source: Pay determined from Gaston Latour, Elections Canada; industrial weekly wages from Labour Division, Statistics Canada.

Note: Because of improvements in sampling technology, all figures on weekly earnings available prior to 1983 had to be adjusted by a formula to permit accurate comparisons.

*No enumeration.

above – the problem of finding enumerators. This is not to discount the contribution that changes in occupational or living patterns may have made but to suggest the possibility of another, more basic explanation. Without some empirical evidence, however, the relative importance of any of these suggestions is not known. The perception of a problem is certainly revealed in the testimony before the Royal Commission and in its Working Documents as well as in the headlines of newspaper articles written about the enumeration period over the last decade, for example, "Enumerators Quit Jobs, Head for the Beaches" (Halifax *Chronicle-Herald*, 13 August 1984), "Forgotten Voters Angry" (*Calgary Herald*, 22 November 1988) and "Enumerators Said Often Afraid to Enter Poor Neighbourhoods" (Saskatoon *Star Phoenix*, 30 May 1990). And certainly, some eligible voters are omitted from the lists through careless enumeration.

The question to be asked, therefore, is to what degree are these problems a function of the lack of enumerators? The chief electoral officer reported that in 1988 he had to bend the rules for enumeration in 301 polls, but that is less than 1 percent of the 53 000 polls across the country, or an average of one polling division per constituency. When it is recalled that 85 percent of the ROs were inexperienced because they had been recently appointed following boundary adjustments, these relatively few deviations from the provisions of the *Canada Elections Act* seem less convincing as proof of a crisis in the system of voter registration than the foregoing criticism implies. Arguably, such a high turnover of ROs is not without precedent: there were 183 new ROs in 1962, 204 in 1968 and 153 in 1979. This could affect the training given enumerators as much or more than the quality of persons chosen for the position. Finally, the pressure of getting a campaign going from scratch in a short time, which is one of the reasons the system has depended upon political parties for nominations of enumerators, is another practical constraint on efficiency that is quite separate from the quality of personnel.

To summarize: there is a problem finding enumerators in some constituencies, but the problem is not new nor, on the basis of existing evidence, has its magnitude increased. The problem appears to be confined almost totally to urban polls, but it is not common to all or even most of them. While there is much speculation as to its cause, there are no empirical data available to evaluate the respective importance of one explanation against another. Enumerators (and certain other election officials) are poorly paid, although there is a general lack of awareness of this issue, which helps account for the failure to address the problem. Inadequate pay appears particularly relevant in view of the difficult job enumerators face in certain urban electoral districts where the population mobility is high and its demographic characteristics are heterogeneous.

Accuracy and Coverage of Enumeration

If the problem of finding enumerators is specific to Canada's system of voter registration, questions about accuracy and coverage are common to all systems. The object of voter registration is presumably to enrol the largest possible proportion of eligible voters – or is it? It might be argued that accuracy should take precedence to completeness in a political system where there is concern about voter fraud or the potential of voter fraud. As this study has already revealed, that concern was much in the mind of Canadian politicians as they struggled in the 19th and early 20th centuries to find a system of voter registration on which they could agree. They and their counterparts today would concur with the sentiment of William C. Kimberling, Deputy Director, National Clearinghouse on Election Administration, U.S. Federal Election Commission, that "the right to vote in a democracy must be accompanied by the right to have one's vote counted without being diluted by votes fraudulently cast" (Kimberling 1991, 2). Yet, of the problems and shortcomings of Canada's system of enumeration catalogued by its critics, fraud is not one that figures. Why this should be so, and why the system is perceived as fundamentally honest (if at times procedurally flawed) is worth investigating. However, part of the explanation may lie in the openness of a voter registration system that operates largely on the trust of those who claim to be eligible electors, those who compile the lists, and those who staff the polls on election day. The subject is raised only to note that in a discussion of accuracy and coverage, the matter of fraud (which Kimberling defines as "the dilution of the vote by those who [are] unqualified") is considered of slight importance in modern election practices in Canada.

To the fundamental question of what percentage of eligible voters is registered through enumeration in Canada, there is no easily verifiable answer. There are several reasons for this: first, there are no available data to determine the number of persons who are enumerated but who are in fact not eligible for inclusion on the voters list. One study that was carried out in 12 by-election ridings in 1978 determined that 98.1 percent of the names on the voters list were eligible electors; the error rate was just under 2 percent (Canada, Bureau of Management Consultants 1979). To be an elector, a person must be 18 years of age on polling day, possess Canadian citizenship and reside in Canada on the first day of enumeration. Proof that these qualifications are met by electors is not required, since enumerators are only enjoined to "exercise the utmost care in preparing the list" (Scheds. IV and V, Rules 7 and 18, *Canada Elections Act*). Second, rural voters who are not on the voters list may vote through vouching, but because the numbers of those persons who avail themselves of this option are not separately reported by Elections Canada (the poll books are sealed with the ballot box on election night), a further uncertainty arises about the quality of enumeration. Finally, even if there were no vouching, it is not possible to state conclusively what percentage of the eligible electorate is enumerated in any single election because a totally reliable figure of persons eligible to vote at any one time is impossible to obtain.

Census data from Statistics Canada are not designed to distinguish citizens from noncitizens in the Canadian population. Elections Canada, however, estimates that in 1988, there were 717 500 non-Canadian citizens of 18 years of age and over in Canada's population of that age of 19.3 million. To that should be added 50 000 prison inmates and 20 000 of the most severely mentally handicapped persons, for a total of 787 500 persons in the "population old enough to vote" category who were, in fact, ineligible to vote. This constitutes 4 percent of Canada's total population 18 years of age and over.[4]

Acknowledging these qualifications to the available data, Elections Canada has found that in "198[8], as in 1962 and 1972, registered voters constituted approximately 90 percent of the population old enough to vote, and a still higher percentage of *citizens* of voting age" (Canada, Elections Canada 1989a). How much higher, in light of the preceding qualifications, is open to question, although in another communication (see note 4), Elections Canada calculated that the percentage of registered electors reached 95.08 in 1988. Slightly more than 900 000 eligible electors were omitted, which averages just over 3 000 per district, or 16 per poll. Equally problematic is any comparison of data compiled over an extended period of time. The qualifications for those who are statutorily qualified to vote have changed over the last 30 years. British subjects other than Canadian citizens were eligible to vote up to 1968 and those who were eligible in that election continued to be eligible to vote in federal elections until 1975. Again, federally appointed judges and individuals classified as mentally handicapped were disqualified before the 1988 election.

The number of electors added to the voters list through the process of revision is one indication of the accuracy and coverage of enumeration, although the information is not reported in a particularly helpful form. At the last general election 2.6 percent of the total number of electors on the official lists (excluding those entitled to vote under the *Special Voting Rules* (Sched. II of the *Canada Elections Act*), which apply to, among others, armed forces electors in Canada and armed forces and public service electors posted abroad (along with their spouses and dependants) gained admission to the lists via the process of revision (Canada, Elections Canada 1989b, 57). Data are not available on the characteristics of those electors who avail themselves of this opportunity, nor is there any indication why only a small number of those eligible take advantage of the process.[5]

Even assuming that the present system of enumeration and revision produces a list that is 97 percent accurate in registering eligible voters, close to one-half million Canadians are missed during enumeration and revision (Canada, Elections Canada 1976, 16–17). Yet there are relatively few complaints about omission (they number at most in the thousands, if not fewer). Is the reason for this discrepancy apathy or ignorance?

The information available as a result of complaints about eligible electors omitted from the list tells researchers little, for it is fragmentary and contradictory. If the focus is fixed on the last general election (1988), however, two diametrically opposed responses are elicited: either thousands or dozens of voters were omitted. Immediately following the

1988 election, defeated NDP candidate and former member of Parliament, Cyril Keeper (Winnipeg North Centre) said "hundreds of voters in six apartment blocks and dozens of homes were missed," while "Liberal David Walker, who defeated Keeper ... said as many as 5 000 of the 45 000 eligible voters may have been missed." In evidence before the Royal Commission in 1990, Mr. Keeper said "at least 1 000 people were left off the voters list in his former riding," while Mr. Walker repeated the 5 000 figure. In answer to the original criticisms by Mr. Keeper and Mr. Walker, Richard Rochefort of Elections Canada said that "it turned out only 13 were missed [in Winnipeg North Centre]." The discrepancy in such different estimates requires some explanation. In the heat of a campaign, statements critical of enumeration achieve a prominence which can be assumed to shape perceptions of this system of voter registration. Unless the statements are investigated, perceptions may assume the status of fact.

Mr. Rochefort was also quoted by the *Winnipeg Free Press* as suggesting that "candidates [make the claim] to be noticed, to stand out from the rest of the candidates in an election geared to national issues." Other suggested reasons for complaints about enumeration were "a high-interest election" and "the Charter of Rights and Freedoms."[6] The validity of the reasons offered by Elections Canada for this discrepancy in estimates of omitted voters cannot be evaluated here. Nevertheless, the contradiction does require an answer, for the figures are so disparate as to lead to totally different perceptions of the adequacy of the enumeration process.

The publicity attending the charges against the enumeration system appears to help establish as fact what is only an unsubstantiated claim. In the process, it may even depreciate the magnitude of the problem of "noncoverage." For instance, according to Working Document No. 41 ("Enumeration Issues"), the Royal Commission was told by Dr. Alexander Kholopov, at the Halifax hearings, that "he had found that 340 000 Canadians were not enumerated and were therefore disenfranchised in the 1988 election." Dr. Kholopov told one of the authors of this study that the source of the figure was the Halifax *Chronicle-Herald* (25 November 1988). That figure is found nowhere else in the media's accounts of enumeration problems in 1988. More to the point, if it were accurate, then Elections Canada's most optimistic claim of 97 percent coverage would have to be revised upward to 98.1 percent of the eligible electorate.[7]

Among eligible electors in any country, one group which proves especially resistant to voter registration efforts is that which encompasses the disabled and the disadvantaged. These persons experience unique problems in getting registered and in exercising their franchise because of poverty, homelessness, illiteracy, illness or disability. Working Document No. 12 ("Homeless and Poverty Issues") noted:

> Because enumeration is based on where people live, the homeless tend to be excluded until it comes time for revision; also, people who are homeless may be illiterate and have little access to television or newspaper information about how to be registered. This was the reason for recommending special programs of outreach to the poor and homeless through community agencies or through Elections Canada. The Boyle Street Co-op, Edmonton, recommended that Elections Canada study voter turnout after each election and develop a plan to increase participation of low turnout groups.

As it operates currently, Canada's enumeration system makes few concessions to the needs of these people; for instance, Elections Canada does not allow people to be enumerated without a street address. Likewise, as Working Document No. 12 observed, "special training was recommended [by interveners] for enumerators in poor areas," where concerns about personal security and unfamiliar surroundings frequently arose. None the less the claim was made by some groups, such as the National Anti-Poverty Organization in its brief to the Royal Commission, that enumeration had the potential for incorporating those with special needs into the eligible electorate. Conversely, concern was expressed that "any system that shifts, even marginally, the responsibility for voter registration from the state to the elector will have a discriminatory impact on lower income Canadians" (National Anti-Poverty 1990, 17).

The advantage of enumeration was perceived to lie in the human contact created between the potential voter and the compiler of the voters list. Adopting this positive perspective on enumeration led several briefs to suggest that Elections Canada consider employing nontraditional enumeration processes to reach these potential voters. Suggestions included involving community agencies, which had experience and understanding of the special problems of poor, illiterate or new citizens, in the enumeration process or experimenting with videos, cassettes, technical devices, logos and special graphics to reach visually impaired, hearing-impaired or illiterate voters. A substantial number of persons would benefit from these innovations; the brief of the Canadian Association of the Deaf cited 270 000 profoundly deaf citizens and 2.5 million hard-of-hearing people in Canada; the brief of the National Anti-Poverty Organization, citing the 1987 Southam literacy survey, stated that 24 percent of Canadians are functionally or basically illiterate, while the same brief reported that "conservative estimates indicate that 130 000 to 250 000 Canadians are homeless over the course of a year."

Part of the argument for favouring enumeration over a permanent voters list for the homeless is that the movement of this portion of the population is too fluid to be captured by a permanent list. The same applies to other components of Canada's population: those who are highly mobile (in Vancouver, for example, 52 percent of the total population five years of age and older moved once during the years 1981– 86 (Canada, Statistics Canada 1988, 94:128)) and native peoples who live part of each year in remote areas hunting or trapping, or who move back and forth between towns and their homes on reserves. Don Ursaki (1990), a native Canadian and former candidate in Cariboo–Chilcotin, estimated that "between 3 000 and 4 000 [of 9 000 status Indians of voting age] missed getting on the voters list because of problems in the enumeration." For those people the chance timing of the election and the enumeration preceding it determined if their names would be available to be placed on the voters list.

In summary, it is not possible to state with certainty what proportion of the total eligible population of electors is placed on the voters list through enumeration and revision, because that total population is unknown; Elections Canada's claims to more than 90 percent coverage cannot be authenticated. On the other hand, the comparatively small number of eligible persons who avail themselves of the revision process suggests that there is no massive omission of voters in the compilation of the preliminary lists; as well, the episodic, fragmentary and contradictory complaints about both enumeration and revision offer little evidence that the accuracy and completeness of the system is fundamentally flawed; while enumeration does not currently serve "special-needs" voters particularly well, it has the potential for doing so because of its flexibility and because the onus for reaching such people remains with agents of the electoral system and not on the voters themselves.

Public Perception of Enumeration
Media coverage of Canada's system of voter registration has tended to focus on perceived problems, which in turn has influenced public perceptions of enumeration. Newspaper comment on individual (and isolated) cases of eligible electors who were omitted from the voters list is uniformly critical; indeed, the Royal Commission has come about, in part, because of such criticism. Yet, as previously noted, references to such problems as the claim that large numbers of voters were omitted

from the list in Winnipeg North Centre are difficult to substantiate. Where data do exist, such as for the instances in 1988 when the chief electoral officer used his discretionary power to complete the enumeration, they suggest that problems in constituencies are infrequent, if not rare. How, then, does the perception arise that enumeration as a system of voter registration is badly flawed?

The first explanation derives from the uniqueness of enumeration itself. Among Western democracies the Canadian government alone assumes responsibility for sending voter registration officials (enumerators) to the home of every potential elector in the country. As a consequence, eligible electors who are omitted from the voters list believe that they have grounds for harbouring a grievance against the election administration, a belief not shared by citizens elsewhere. In countries where the onus for becoming listed rests on the individual citizens, it would be perverse for them to blame others for their own failure to register.

A second explanation can be traced to recent publicity about other voting-rights questions that are, in fact, unrelated to enumeration – for instance, whether judges, prisoners and patients in mental hospitals have the right to vote, or whether rural and urban voters are treated in a discriminatory manner when it comes to being permitted to be sworn in and vote at the polls on election day (the former can; the latter cannot). These are problems that arise from specific provisions of the *Canada Elections Act* and which, since the adoption of the *Canadian Charter of Rights and Freedoms*, appear now to be in conflict with the guarantees of equal treatment found in the Charter. In seeking to reform Canada's present system of voter registration, it is important to be precise about the nature of its flaws. There is no profit to be gained from indicting enumeration on false charges.

Perhaps the most important reason for the negative public perception of enumeration derives from a conflation of elements of the previous two explanations: that is, the interaction of enumeration with the provisions of the Charter. That development can best be appreciated by looking at public perceptions of enumeration in the 20 years since the 1972 election. From the outset through to the most recent federal election, a feature of the process continuing to elicit critical comment has been the administrative and procedural inadequacies of the actual door-to-door enumeration process. The basis for attacking that process, however, has changed with time. In the 1970s the concerns typically expressed were system-specific: the training, ability and competence of enumerators featured prominently in the attacks, but there was scant notice taken of those who, because of the system's weaknesses, entered the ranks of the un-enumerated.

Such concerns, of course, continued to be expressed in the 1980s. But to them were added the person-specific complaints that became so much a part of the 1988 campaign and of the presentations made to the Royal Commission itself in its hearings across the country. The charges of incomplete and inaccurate lists were bound to be seen in a different light when the particulars of a case made the news reports. The case being reported may well have been one that had been brought before the courts by an allegedly aggrieved elector or group of electors, something that would have been virtually unthinkable in earlier years. It was only a question of time before the electorate learned of the value of pursuing matters related to the franchise and the enumeration process through litigation. As had been anticipated by the chief electoral officer in his statutory Reports of the mid-1980s, the Charter-driven cases of 1988 presented a host of problems for Elections Canada. These ranged from charges that whole blocks of electors had been overlooked by enumerators to last-minute challenges from urban voters who wanted the same election day vouching privileges as rural voters enjoyed under the *Canada Elections Act.*

What must be remembered about the larger issue of the enumeration process, however, is that whole blocks of voters may have been overlooked in earlier elections as well, and urban envy of a rural voting option may have been around since the distinction between "closed" and "open" electorates was first introduced in 1938. Lacking the constitutional tools or, indeed, the knowledge that others such as the deaf, the handicapped and the homeless also faced similar problems, individuals and groups in the past tended neither to seek nor to gain the degree of attention that they have received during recent elections. Thus, while the *percentage* of the total eligible electorate enumerated may not have changed to any significant degree over time, the electorate itself is now more aware of its rights and of the shortcomings of the enumeration system as it has operated in Canada for some time. As can be seen, many of these concerns came to a head in 1988 and formed an important part of the submissions made to the Royal Commission in 1990.

Length of Campaigns

While public criticism of Canada's system of voter registration has focused on the quality of the enumeration and on the perception of poor lists being produced with, as a consequence, eligible electors being excluded from voting, there is another criticism among some close observers of the election process. Enumeration (which begins after the issue of the writs) is said to take too long (or, more correctly, to take too much time at the wrong time, that is, during the election campaign).

It thus lengthens the period of the campaign. This view was reflected in the very large number of briefs to the Commission (120) which advocated a permanent voters list, and which gave as their major reasons for support problems with enumeration and "the desire to reduce the length of Canadian elections" (Canada, Royal Commission 1990, Working Document No. 43).

The Government of Canada considered this matter more than 15 years ago: "In 1975, the possibility of establishing a permanent electoral list as a means of shortening the electoral period was raised by Cabinet" (Canada, Bureau of Management Consultants 1979, 1), while in the same year "the President of the Privy Council asked the Chief Electoral Officer for Canada to try and find a way to shorten the campaign" (Carty 1991, 6). Presumably as a result of this request, the standard 60-day campaign, between issuance of the election writ and voting day, was reduced in 1982 to the current 50-day minimum. In his 1991 paper, subtitled "The Case of the Missing Voters List," Professor Carty comments on the "adverse" effects that flow from the absence of a permanent voters list, among which, he says is "the truth [that] Canadian election campaigns are too long" (ibid.).

Judged by British or Australian standards, this statement is certainly true; judged by American standards, it is not. The usual justification for 50-day campaigns rests on the length of time needed to compile the voters lists. Without the period set aside to hire and to train enumerators and to carry out the enumeration itself, critics allege that possibly as much as three weeks could be lopped off the 50-day campaign. A frequently repeated claim of the last two decades is that a permanent voters list would remove the principal obstacle to a shortened campaign. If that change were put in place, it is argued, then the problem of a lengthy campaign would be solved.

Nonetheless, in a list of problems and shortcomings of Canada's voter registration system, the length of the election campaign to which enumeration contributes, must be ranked low. In our study of recent statutory Reports made by the chief electoral officer, as well as of newspaper comments and items in Elections Canada's publication *Contact* from 1973 to 1990, we can confirm that length of campaign was not seen as a principal issue requiring reform. As already noted, the primary concern for the public has consistently rested on the quality of enumeration and the exclusion of eligible voters from the list when quality is not maintained.

Since a majority of Canada's provinces and territories follow the federal practice of using enumeration to compile their voters lists, it is germane to conclude this section by asking whether similar concerns also arise in these jurisdictions. As a general statement, it would appear that they do not. Working backwards in the above list of problems and shortcomings, the situation appears as follows. Arguments over length of campaign have less practical significance in the provinces and territories since the minimum campaign period in each is shorter than that set out in the *Canada Elections Act* (generally closer to 30 days, although the range extends from Newfoundland at 21 to Quebec at 47). Public perception of these systems appears more positive: consider, for instance, that there were almost no complaints about enumeration in Ontario during the last election (1990) (one in which the enumeration took place at the door when people were away during the summer) despite the fact the system used was similar to the federal system. Consider, too, the evaluation on Manitoba's experience with enumeration, made before the Royal Commission by Richard D. Balasko, then Acting Chief Electoral Officer for the Province of Manitoba. Citing with approval a 1979 study of the system by the Manitoba Law Reform Commission that judged enumeration to produce a complete and accurate list at relatively low cost and in a short space of time, he noted that the Commission found "a final bonus" in enumeration, which was that it *"induces community participation which is important during an election"* (Balasko 1990, 23, emphasis added).

As to accuracy and coverage of enumeration in the provinces and territories, this will be covered in greater detail in the next section of this study. It is significant, however, that most provincial acts extend the period of revision closer to election day than does the *Canada Elections Act*. Ontario, for instance, makes it easy for people to get on the list up to the eve of the election, whereas revision ends in a federal election 17 days before election day. This different practice would seem to go far toward explaining the absence of criticism of provincial enumeration. The greater openness of revision reduces the probability of irrevocable omissions from the voters list. It is not clear to what extent, if at all, this practice aids in the initial process of enumeration. It can be said, however, that the central problem of federal enumeration – assuring high quality enumeration – seems to be equally dominant in provincial and territorial election campaigns.

ENUMERATION AND REGISTRATION OF VOTERS IN THE PROVINCES AND TERRITORIES

This section describes some of the main features of the provincial and territorial systems of registering voters, notes problems mentioned by election officials at the provincial level, compares cost data provided by the provinces and territories, and concludes with an evaluation of the completeness of the various lists.

Provincial and Territorial Registration Systems

The information contained in table 8.5 presents a comparative picture of the different jurisdictions in seven categories: qualifications of electors; maximum and minimum duration of election period; preparation of lists of electors; enumerators; revision of lists of electors; confirmation of enumeration; and voting if not on list on election day. It is designed to provide a full comparison of all federal, provincial and territorial jurisdictions under these seven headings.[8]

What is immediately apparent in table 8.5 is that no two systems of compiling and revising lists of voters are identical. There are obvious similarities among a number of the jurisdictions, but clearly each has established its own set of standards, rules and procedures. The least variation occurs in the qualifications to be an elector. Canadian citizenship is standard, with a few exceptions for British subjects. Eighteen-year-olds are eligible in all systems except for British Columbia and the Northwest Territories where the voting age is 19. A six-month residency within the province is common to all provinces; it is twice that length in the two territories.

The far greater variations among the systems arise as a result of the different lengths of the election period and the way in which the lists of voters are prepared and revised. The length of campaign varies from a minimum of 21 days in Newfoundland to 47 days in Quebec, with an average for the 12 jurisdictions of 33 days and a median of 30 days. All but three of the provinces and territories (Newfoundland, Alberta and British Columbia) use a door-to-door enumeration at the time of an election to prepare their voters lists. At one extreme, names can be added to the list through revision no later than 17 days before the election (Manitoba), and at the other, as late as the eve of the election (Ontario). Manitoba, however, permits electors to vote on election day even if their names are not on the list simply by producing identification and swearing an oath. For its part, Ontario permits no voting by unlisted urban electors. Of the provinces, only Quebec and British Columbia do not allow at least some of their unlisted electors to vote by declaration or oath at a polling place on election day. It is of interest to note that Manitoba is the sole federal, provincial or territorial jurisdiction to record and publish the number of electors sworn in at the polls on election day. At the time of the April 1988 provincial election in Manitoba, 28 890 (approximately 4 percent) of the total electorate of 728 319 was sworn in on the day of the election. In the 1990 election the figure was 4.7 percent.

A new elections act is being drafted in Newfoundland. As of mid-1990 the province could hold a separate enumeration at any time

Table 8.5
Voter registration features of federal, provincial and territorial election systems in Canada

Item	Canada	P.E.I.	N.B.	N.S.	Nfld.	Que.	Ont.	Man.	Sask.	Alta.	B.C.	Yukon	N.W.T.
1. Qualifications													
Elector age	18	18	18	18	18	18	18	18	18	18	19	18	19
Nationality	Canadian	Canadian	Canadian; British subject in N.B. prior to 01/01/79	Canadian; British subject	Canadian; British subject	Canadian	Canadian	Canadian	Canadian; British subject in Sask. 23/06/71	Canadian	Canadian	Canadian	Canadian
Residency	Resident in Canada on Day 38	6 months	6 months	6 months	6 months	6 months	6 months	6 months	6 months	6 months	6 months	12 months	12 months
2. Duration of election period	Minimum 50 days	26–32 days	28–38 days	36 days+	21 days+	47–53 days	37–74 days	35–50 days	29–34 days	29 days	29 days	31 days+	45 days+
3. Preparation of lists of electors													
Type of enumeration	At election with revision	Enumeration at election	Enumeration at election	At election with revision	Separate from election	At election with revision	At election with revision	At election with revision	At election	Annual, beginning 2nd calendar year after election	Continuous list with enumeration	At election with revision	At election with revision

Table 8.5 (cont'd)
Voter registration features of federal, provincial and territorial election systems in Canada

Item	Canada	P.E.I.	N.B.	N.S.	Nfld.	Que.	Ont.	Man.	Sask.	Alta.	B.C.	Yukon	N.W.T.
Duration and when	7 days, Days 38–32	5 days, beginning 2 days after writ	4 days, Days 28–24	6 days, Days 31–26	At any time	4 days, Days 39–35	4 days as set by chief election officer (CEO)	Immediately after writ to 3 days before nomination (Day 21)	Within 10 days from writ	5 days, Sept. 15–30	Begins 1st Monday in May in 3rd year after election	13 days from writ	4 days, Days 33–30
4. Enumerators													
How many	Urban; population more than 5 000	2 per poll	Urban: 2 per poll; rural: 1 per poll	2 per poll	1 per poll	2 per poll	2 per poll	1 per poll; CEO can increase number	1 per poll	Urban: 2 per poll; rural: 1 or 2 at discretion of RO	1 or 2 at discretion of RO	1 or 2 at discretion of RO, CEO	1 per poll
Designation	2 per poll, parties nominate; rural, 1 per poll, returning officer (RO) nominates	RO nominates	Parties nominate in both	Parties nominate	RO nominates	Parties nominate; Directeur général des élections (DGE) can alter at his/her discretion	Parties nominate	RO nominates	RO nominates	Parties nominate	RO nominates		RO nominates

Table 8.5 (cont'd)
Voter registration features of federal, provincial and territorial election systems in Canada

Item	Canada	P.E.I.	N.B.	N.S.	Nfld.	Que.	Ont.	Man.	Sask.	Alta.	B.C.	Yukon	N.W.T.
5. Revision of list of electors When, by whom	Urban: Days 19–17 by revising officer; rural: any time after enumeration finishes to Day 19, by enumerator	Days 17–14 by RO	Urban: Day 13 by revising officer; rural: Day 13 by enumerator	Days 12–11 by 2 revising agents or revising officer	Any time set by RO	11 days, Mon.–Thurs. 3 weeks before and Fri.–Wed. 1 week before polling day by Revising Committee	Up to and including Day 1 by RO	Days 18–17 by revising officer (can be RO)	Day 4 by enumerator	For enumeration: Thurs.–Sat. 2nd week of Oct.; for election: 5th day after writ to Sat. before advance poll by RO	Revision decided by Court of Revision	18th and 19th days after writ by revising officer (can be RO)	Day 19 by RO or enumerator
6. Confirmation of enumeration	Card mailed plus lists posted rural	Nil	Card mailed	Card mailed	Lists posted	List mailed	Card mailed, plus lists posted urban	Lists posted	Lists posted	Lists posted	Voter ID cards	Nil	Nil

Table 8.5 (cont'd)
Voter registration features of federal, provincial and territorial election systems in Canada

Item	Canada	P.E.I.	N.B.	N.S.	Nfld.	Que.	Ont.	Man.	Sask.	Alta.	B.C.	Yukon	N.W.T.
7. Voting if not on list on voting day	Urban: cannot vote; rural: vouching at poll	Takes oath at poll	Urban: must get certificate of qualification from RO; rural: vouching or by oath	Urban: (5 000 or more) by oath, votes in returning office or poll; rural: takes oath at poll	By oath at poll	None	Urban: no voting if not on list; rural: vouching	By oath and ID at poll	By declaration at poll	By oath and ID	Discontinued; used in 1983, 1986 elections	None	By oath at poll

Sources: Information provided by election officials in all jurisdictions, July 1990; Canada, Elections Canada 1990a, 1990c.

between elections. This normally occurred once every four years, typically 12 months or less before an election. In future, the list of electors obtained in the September–October 1988 enumeration will be retained as a semi-permanent list. The province intends to update the list annually using compatible databases from its Registry of Vital Statistics and, on a volunteer basis, from places of work. Drivers' licence renewal forms will include an Electoral Registration Information form with which the individual can volunteer the needed information. Registration forms will be included in pay cheque envelopes, unemployment insurance payments, welfare payments and telephone and utility bills. This registration will be voluntary and will be advertised to make people aware of it. Revisions may take place at any time at the discretion of the returning officer in both rural and urban polling divisions.

Alberta has an annual enumeration from 15 September to 30 September in the second calendar year following the year in which the last general election was held and in each succeeding year if no general election is held in the interim. In the year of the establishment of an electoral boundary commission or in the following year, the chief electoral officer may at his or her discretion not proceed with an enumeration. In Alberta, revisions are possible on three days of the second full week of October of an enumeration year and at the time of an election from the fifth day after the writ until the Saturday before the advance polls.

British Columbia has a continuous list based on individual application for registration. In the third year following a general election, a provincewide, house-to-house enumeration is held on the first Monday of May, at which time the enumerators are provided with the names of those voters currently registered on the continuous voters list. The voter is expected to update the registration in the event of a move or a change of name. Voter registration applications are gathered in the 60 government agency and access offices located throughout the province and channelled to six regional offices responsible for the day-to-day maintenance of the permanent list. The regional offices in turn feed the information into a computerized data bank at BC Systems, a Crown corporation. Qualified electors receive an identification card in the mail. An estimated 10 000 cards, on average, are issued each month for new registrants or address or name changes.

Problems Noted by Election Officials

From our discussions with provincial and territorial officials,[9] we were impressed by the extent to which they share similar experiences in the process of registering electors. The problems they face and the solutions they adopt tend to be alike. For the majority of them, the difficulty in finding and retaining competent urban enumerators has become their principal concern. That problem is more acute in the inner-city polls of large metropolitan areas than elsewhere. Officials cite language proficiency, difficulty in gaining access to buildings and concerns about personal safety as the leading contributors to the shortage of inner-city enumerators. The problem is common in varying degrees to all provinces with sizable metropolitan centres and door-to-door enumerations (Nova Scotia, Quebec, Ontario and Manitoba). Even Alberta found it harder to get enumerators for large inner-city areas in 1988 than previously, despite the fact that enumeration was conducted at a time other than during an election. As a result, 11 of Alberta's 83 returning officers were allowed to extend the time for their enumeration.

British Columbia, with its continuous roll, is the exception on this point. For its triennial door-to-door canvass, it has so far experienced little difficulty in recruiting enumerators. Election officials believe that because their enumeration is carried out separately from an election, they are not competing with political parties for people to go from house to house. Moreover, they are neither compelled to go to parties for names nor constrained by the names that parties propose. Advertisements calling attention to the need for enumerators are used with success, as are lists of past enumerators. As the British Columbia enumeration operates on a fixed timetable, recruiting and training of enumerators can take place well in advance of the census day. The fact that the enumeration is held early in May makes it possible to hire university students for the door-to-door canvass.

The provinces facing shortages of urban enumerators have relied largely on the same solutions to the problem. In some cases enumeration deadlines have been extended so that individual enumerators can be assigned to a further canvass once they have finished their own. Enumerators have been hired who are under the age set out in the provincial elections act or who reside outside the poll for which they are responsible. Both of these practices are technical violations of the act in some jurisdictions. Election officials have moved beyond complete reliance on political parties for names, in some cases actively soliciting for enumerators through advertisements in different languages. They have also resorted to using only one enumerator in some cases when two are officially called for.

Finding enumerators for rural polls is not said to pose a problem. It would seem that the party patronage system and other traditional sources of recruitment work well enough to ensure a pool of names sufficient to the task in rural areas. Without the social, operational and linguistic constraints that now affect recruiting for inner-city polls, returning officers in rural polls say they have experienced few difficulties in reaching their necessary complement.

The quality of enumeration in the large cities of Quebec and Ontario appears to be the second-ranked problem faced by election officials in those provinces. Quebec in particular noticed an increase in the number of complaints at the time of the last election (1989), largely as a result of the increased number of names left off the voters list in large centres. Inadequate training, careless work habits and lack of interest in the task are cited as explanations by provincial officials.

The problems of inadequate or improperly prepared lists and of the failure to get some eligible voters on the list are generally resolved in one of two ways in most provinces. As can be seen in table 8.5, electors in Ontario have until the election eve itself to become listed, by the local enumerator or the returning officer. The more popular option is to allow election day registration (nine of the twelve provincial and territorial jurisdictions permit some variation of this). Only British Columbia, Quebec and Yukon do not allow at least some voters to take an oath or declaration or to be vouched for at the poll on election day. (British Columbia's brief experience with election day registration is noted below.) In eight of the nine jurisdictions (Ontario being the exception) any eligible elector, urban or rural, who is not on the revised list is permitted to vote upon presentation of acceptable identification and by taking an oath, being vouched for or taking a verbal declaration or oath.

It is possible that the acknowledged increase in the number of complaints in Quebec in 1987 was tied to that province's failure to allow either registration on election day or additions to the list through revision immediately before election day. It is clear from comments of election officials in other provincial jurisdictions that they receive few complaints from electors on the grounds of not being able to vote. Once the process for ensuring election day registration, or in Ontario's case election eve registration, has been explained to aggrieved electors whose names have appeared neither on the preliminary nor the revised lists, the way has been cleared for electoral participation.

Registration Costs of Provinces and Territories

Figures for the cost of enumeration and revision have been provided by each of the federal, provincial and territorial jurisdictions under consideration (see table 8.6). We strongly urge caution in interpreting and in comparing those data. Among all the provinces (excluding British Columbia), the estimates of per voter costs vary from $0.60 for Manitoba's April 1988 election to $2.91 in Prince Edward Island. The comparability question obviously surfaces when costs are examined, for what is included in one jurisdiction may be excluded or calculated differently in another. In Manitoba, as noted earlier, 4 percent of the voters were counted on the final list of electors as a result of having been sworn in when they came to vote on election day, yet the cost of "registering" those voters would not be itemized as such, but it would become part of polling day operations. Prince Edward Island may be on the high side because fixed costs associated with enumeration would have a particularly heavy impact on averages computed with small electorates, and Manitoba may be low because over 60 percent of the province's eligible voters are located within a single metropolitan area. Such are only a few of the variables that are apparent in comparing jurisdictional cost figures.

Table 8.6
Federal, provincial and territorial enumeration and revision costs, 1986–89

	Number of electors registered			% added at revision	Enumeration costs ($)	Cost per elector ($)
	Enumeration	Revision	Total			
Canada Nov. 1988	17 219 534[a]	419 467	17 639 001	2.2	27 791 142	1.58
Ont. Sept. 1987	5 814 009	253 369	6 067 378	4.2	9 012 019	1.49
Que. Sept. 1989	4 508 921	161 768	4 670 690	3.5	8 330 914	1.78
N.S. Sept. 1988	608 201	15 385[b]	623 586	2.5	906 927	1.45
N.B. Oct. 1987	501 646	6 883	508 529	1.4	547 508	1.08
P.E.I. May 1989	88 941	299	89 240	0.3	260 000	2.91
Nfld. April 1989			361 913		725 100	2.00
Man. April 1988	683 481	44 838[b]	728 319	2.2	421 736	0.60
Sask. Oct. 1986	647 903	21 813	669 716	3.3	605 149	0.90
Alta. March 1989	1 471 826	79 041[b]	1 550 867	5.1	3 317 041[c]	2.25
B.C. 1989	1 707 838				5 876 966[d]	3.44
Yukon Feb. 1986	13 965	1 128	15 093	7.5	70 000	4.63
N.W.T. Sept. 1987	22 222	129	22 351	3.6	26 698	1.19

Sources: Canada, Elections Canada, various official reports and data provided by Elections Canada officials.

[a]Includes Special Voting Rules electors.

[b]Includes 28 890 sworn in at polls on election day.

[c]1988 enumeration costs to get preliminary list.

[d]1989 enumeration only. Does not include annual registration costs or election year registration.

The cost of British Columbia's continuous list is the most difficult to compute. In our view a figure of nearly $6.00 is closer to the actual per voter cost than the $3.44 listed in table 8.6. Because the province maintains a continuous electoral roll, the per voter cost of registration should include some of the continuous costs associated with the maintenance of that roll. In table 8.7, we have estimated the British Columbia enumeration costs. It should be noted that in British Columbia cost savings totalling several hundred thousand dollars are claimed by municipalities contracting to use the provincial list for municipal elections in preference to conducting their own door-to-door enumeration. In any comparison of interprovincial costs of provincial and municipal enumerations, that benefit of the British Columbia system would have to be included.

It is difficult to make conclusions from the comparative cost figures of table 8.6. A jurisdiction's population has apparently little to do with the per elector cost of enumeration, as seems obvious when the figure in the Northwest Territories ($1.19) is compared with that in Yukon ($4.63), and the figure in New Brunswick ($1.08) with that in Prince Edward Island ($2.91). Such discrepant amounts suggest that differences must be explained largely on other grounds: size of polls, number of enumerators, pay scales of enumerators, revision costs and a whole host of direct and indirect or fixed and variable costs that we have not attempted to gather for this study. The political culture and personal expectations of partisan activists would also have to be taken into

Table 8.7
British Columbia enumeration costs
(in dollars)

Electors enumerated May–June 1989	1 707 838
Enumeration costs, 1989	5 876 966
Per elector cost	3.44
Annual budget*	2 800 000
Expenditures for compilation and maintenance of lists, 1987–90	
1987 (ordinary year)	1 400 000
1988 (ordinary year)	1 400 000
1989 (enumeration year)	5 876 966
1990 (ordinary year)	1 400 000
Total	10 076 966
Average per year	2 519 241
Average per year over four-year cycle	5.93

*Assume registration process and maintenance of rolls account for one-half of budget.

account. It is obvious that the provinces with enumeration and registration drives at times other than elections (Newfoundland, Alberta and British Columbia) have higher costs than all other provinces (except Prince Edward Island), but it is difficult to generalize on their experience since each of these three provinces has a system that is distinct from the other two. Allowing for the differences among all the jurisdictions, about all that can be said is that the two largest provinces (Ontario and Quebec) and one other (Nova Scotia) are within the per elector range of $1.45 to $1.78 and that none of these three is more or less than $0.20 per voter from the 1988 federal enumeration cost of $1.58. To the extent that there is any clustering of enumeration and revision costs, it is within this group of the federal and three provincial jurisdictions.

How Complete Are Enumeration Lists?

The principal question to be addressed in evaluating the various provincial and territorial approaches to enumeration of voters is the comprehensiveness of the lists that they produce. If one system's approach leads to a more comprehensive list than another, that clearly warrants consideration. Where this is also accomplished at less cost, there is an additional bonus, but as just noted, the cost comparisons among jurisdictions should be treated with some care. To examine the comprehensiveness of the various provincial and territorial lists, we have included data for comparative purposes from the November 1988 federal election (table 8.8). The enumeration and revisions for that election were carried out in the weeks following issuance of the writs on 4 September 1988.

A word of explanation is in order about the differences in the voter eligibility criteria of the provinces and territories and the federal system (see table 8.5). The major difference relates to residency requirements. Apart from Canadian residency on the first day of enumeration, there is no federal requirement. The provinces all require 6 months residency in the province, however, and the territories' requirement is 12 months. A few provinces also require a minimum length of residency in the polling district or subdivision. The other major difference in eligibility is age; British Columbia and the Northwest Territories have a minimum voting age of 19, while in all other jurisdictions it is 18.

What impact these differences have on the voter enumeration figures at the two levels of government is difficult to establish with any certainty, but we estimate that the remarkably few variances in the eligibility criteria do not lead to major or significant differences. As the statistical information included on British Columbia in appendix C reveals,

Table 8.8
Lists of voters by province from provincial and federal enumerations, 1986–89

Province and date of last provincial election		Number of electors on provincial list at time of last election (or at latest enumeration)	Number of electors on federal list for province at time of November 1988 election
Nfld.	20 April 1989	361 913 (Oct.–Nov. 1988)	384 236
P.E.I.	29 May 1989	89 240 (May 1989)	89 546
N.S.	6 Sept. 1988	623 586 (Aug. 1988)	644 353
N.B.	13 Oct. 1987	508 529 (Sept.–Oct. 1987)	508 741
Que.	25 Sept. 1989	4 670 690 (Aug.–Sept. 1989)	4 740 091
Ont.	10 Sept. 1987	6 067 378 (Aug.–Sept. 1987)	6 309 375
Man.	26 April 1988	699 429 (March–April 1988) 728 319 (includes electors sworn in on polling day)	729 281
Sask.	20 Oct. 1986	669 716 (Oct. 1986)	675 160
Alta.	20 March 1989	1 471 826 (Sept.–Oct. 1988) 1 550 867 (March 1989) (revised)	1 557 669
B.C.	22 Oct. 1986	1 707 838 (May 1989)	1 954 040
Yukon	20 Feb. 1989	15 093 (Feb. 1989)	16 396
N.W.T.	5 Oct. 1987	22 351 (Sept. 1987)	30 113
	Total	16 907 589 (Oct. 1986 to March 1989)	17 639 001

Sources: Information derived from Canada, Elections Canada 1988, table 3; 1990c, 5. Provincial total list uses the enumerated, not the revised, lists for Manitoba and Alberta.

approximately 44 000 residents of British Columbia (not all of whom would be Canadian citizens) turn 19 years of age each year. We also know from our mobility analysis of Canada's population 20 years of age and over that in a recent five-year period, 412 580 persons moved to Canada and 851 505 changed provinces. This total of nearly 1.3 million averaged 260 000 individuals per year, some of whom would be eligible to vote on citizenship grounds. Those who moved frequently would undoubtedly be counted twice and might not have resided in a province for the necessary six months at the time an election was called. But to impose the most extreme conditions on those mobility data is unnecessary, for as table 8.8 shows, there were only 12 provincial and territorial elections spread over the three-year period under examination. Distributing the 260 000 individuals annually among the 12 jurisdictions more or less in accordance with known population distributions and settlement patterns, and then dividing that distribution among the

four provinces and territories typically having an election each year
leads us to conclude that the impact of the six-month residency requirement cannot be great in most jurisdictions. This means that any sizable
differences between federal and provincial enumeration figures in most
provinces are almost certainly not explainable on the basis of the six-
month residency requirement. It is conceivable that the 12-month residency requirement in the territories, combined with their highly mobile
populations, may lead to lower enumeration rates for territorial than
for federal elections there.

A word of explanation is also needed with respect to the three-year
timespan covered in table 8.8 and the different populations to be counted
at the provincial and territorial levels if their enumerations were held
considerable time before or after the November 1988 federal election.
Seven jurisdictions carried out an enumeration within six months of
the federal enumeration: Newfoundland, Prince Edward Island, Nova
Scotia, Manitoba, Alberta, British Columbia and the Yukon. Of those,
three provincial enumerations (Newfoundland, Nova Scotia and Alberta)
were virtually coterminous with the federal one. Additionally, as annual
Statistics Canada data have shown, a majority of the provinces had
very little population growth during the period under examination.
This includes Newfoundland, Prince Edward Island, Nova Scotia, New
Brunswick, Quebec, Manitoba, Saskatchewan and Alberta. The lion's
share of the new population growth during the 1986–89 period went to
two provinces – Ontario and British Columbia.

Table 8.8 reveals a great deal about the comprehensiveness of the
various enumerations between 1986 and 1988. Four provinces with
little or no population growth (Prince Edward Island, New Brunswick,
Manitoba and Saskatchewan) had virtually identical provincial and
federal counts during the period under consideration (Manitoba's total
of 728 319 includes the 28 890 voters sworn in on election day).
Remarkably, the combined provincial totals differed by only 6 924 from
the federal total of 2 002 728 for those particular provinces. In each case,
the provinces held an enumeration once an election was called, as was
true, of course, federally.

So did Nova Scotia, a fifth province with limited growth in its population. But Nova Scotia was 20 767 names short of the federal enumeration total in 1988, even though the enumerations were carried out
within two months of one another. This discrepancy seemingly challenges the close fit between the federal and provincial totals established
in the four other slow-growth provinces. Yet there is a logical explanation for Nova Scotia's smaller provincial figure that derives from the
fact that it was based on a summer count, with both the enumeration

and the revision held in August 1988 for the province's 6 September election. Summer enumerations are known to have a noticeable impact on the number of names that appear on the official lists, as is borne out by a comparison of Nova Scotia's latest and penultimate federal and provincial enumerations. In 1988 the provincial enumeration and revision of August produced a total of 623 586 names, while the federal count of October–November gathered 644 353 names. In 1984 the comparable provincial figures from the October enumeration and revision were 614 899 compared with 613 964 from the federal enumeration of the summer months (with its extended period of revision in urban areas) – a difference of fewer than 1 000 voters.

By contrast, Newfoundland, another small province with a relatively stable population, conducts its enumeration on average once every four years as a separate event that is completed in a nonelection timeframe. Within days of the 1988 federal enumeration and revisions, Newfoundland carried out a provincewide enumeration that was 22 323 names short of the federal total of 384 236. It is improbable that the six-month residency requirement can explain much of the variance in a province with a generally stable population. Instead the explanation may well rest with the inability of the provincial authorities to generate sufficient public interest in an election exercise during a non-election period to ensure maximum citizen participation.

What of the country's four largest provinces? Each in its own way offers an opportunity to test the comprehensiveness of competing systems. Quebec's enumeration, which was carried out a year after the federal count in September 1988, fell short of the federal total by some 70 000 voters, even though inmates and non-residents of Quebec were eligible for enumeration provincially but not federally. The six-month residency requirement may, of course, account for part of the shortfall. It is also possible that the province's numbers would have been higher at the time of the provincial election if Quebec had had a provision allowing for some measure of swearing in on election day. Quebec was alone among the provinces at the time (British Columbia has now joined it) in not allowing at least some form of election day registration and voting. If the Manitoba election day figure of 4 percent is accepted as a reasonable guide to additional participation in the electoral process (and we have every reason to believe that as the election day nears, more and more eligible voters, whether enumerated or not at that stage, wish to participate on polling day), then the federal numbers of the previous year would have been more than met in Quebec in 1989. But another plausible explanation, as in Nova Scotia in 1988, lies with the timing of Quebec's 1989 enumeration – it took place in the month of

August. As found with the two federal by-elections of 13 August 1990, enumeration and revision capture fewer voters if they take place during the summer months.[10]

Ontario, on the other hand, was 240 000 short of the federal totals when it carried out its enumeration a year before the 1988 federal count. In this instance it is probable that the residency requirement had a measurable impact on the size of the voting list, if the requirement was taken at all seriously by provincial enumerators as they made their rounds and by citizens as they responded to enumerators' questions. Moreover, as noted above, Ontario was one of two provinces with major population growth between 1986 and 1989. We know by comparing the federal enumerations of 1984 and 1988 (16 775 011 compared with 17 639 001) that the national electorate grew by approximately 216 000 per year. As Ontario was the principal beneficiary of that growth, it is not surprising that its electoral population was markedly higher in 1988 than a year earlier.

Unlike Quebec and Ontario, both of which have election period enumerations, Alberta holds its enumeration between elections. The enumeration of September 1988 was the first since the May 1986 provincial election and it ran almost simultaneously with the federal enumeration. (Indeed complaints were registered by voters left off the federal lists who mistakenly thought they had been enumerated for the federal election when provincial enumerators came to their door.) Yet as is seen in table 8.8 the provincial efforts fell short of those of their federal counterparts. The provincial lists contained 86 000 fewer names than the federal ones. Not until the revisions to Alberta's provincial lists were carried out at the time of that province's election in March 1989 were the provincial numbers more or less equal to the federal ones of 1988. It is hard to conceive that at a time of very little growth in the province's population, as many as 86 000 Albertans had been disqualified provincially because of the residency requirement in the fall of 1988, only to become eligible for the first time at the time of the provincial election the following March.

Like Alberta, British Columbia enumerates at nonelection times. The purpose of its continuous roll is to keep Elections British Columbia abreast of changes, deletions and additions in order to ensure that the list is as up-to-date as possible. However, as table 8.9 shows, the provincewide enumeration of May 1989 produced a list that was nearly 250 000 short of the 1988 federal list. The reason for this discrepancy rests partly in the different age qualifications. Yet only about 44 000 residents of British Columbia (not all of whom are Canadian citizens) turn 19 years of age each year. Part of the remaining shortfall can be

explained by British Columbia's increasing population and the application of the six-month residency requirement. But the province did
not grow each year by 200 000 Canadian citizens over 19 years of age.
The explanation must lie elsewhere.

For that we turn to table 8.9, which is derived from the 1986 British
Columbia provincial election. Table 8.9 shows the dramatic impact of
registration drives on voters lists once elections have been called. In
the first 10 days of the 1986 campaign, 79 334 net additions were made
to the British Columbia writ day list of 1 575 385. That was the net result
of some 209 603 total transactions of deletions, changes and additions
to the list over those 10 days. On election day, 22 October 1986, another
115 281 names were added to the list, with no central record having
been kept of deletions or address changes on that day. The province
has since moved to end election day registration, possibly as a result of
the administrative difficulties created at the polls when fully
6.5 percent of the electors chose to become listed on the last day
possible.[11] Interestingly, the 1986 election day total of 1 770 000 names
on the voters lists was more than 60 000 names higher than that compiled
in the provincewide enumeration two-and-a-half years later in May
1989. The British Columbia experience, like that in Alberta, suggests
that a significant portion of the electorate needs the stimulus of an election to ensure that their names appear on the voters lists.

As a general conclusion about the comprehensiveness of enumeration lists, it should be noted that a comparison of total federal and

Table 8.9
Enumeration for British Columbia election, 1986

Names on list, writ day (24 Sept. 1986)	1 575 385
Registration drive added net new registrants during first 10 days of campaign[a]	79 334
	1 654 719
Net additional names election day (22 Oct. 1986)[b]	115 281
Total election day	1 770 000

Source: Information provided by Linda M. Johnson, Manager of Administrative Operations,
Elections British Columbia, Victoria, 1 August 1990.

[a]In that 10-day period there were:		
	additions	134 886
	deletions	54 778
	changes	19 939
	Total transactions	209 603
	Net additional names	79 334

[b]No election day figures for deletions or changes.

provincial electoral populations suggests that there is a difference between those provinces using an election-only enumeration and those using some other means to compile their lists. From October 1986 to March 1989 provincial and territorial enumerations and registrations included a total of 16 907 589 names. In the last quarter of that two-and-a-half-year period (September–October 1988) the federal enumeration listed 17 639 001 individuals, or about 850 000 more eligible voters in 1988 than in the previous federal election in 1984. (The data from 1980 to 1988 confirm that on an annual basis, the total eligible Canadian electorate grew by approximately 200 000 persons.) Part, but not all, of the 1986–89 "shortfall" of the provincial lists can be explained by the six-month residency requirement. Summer enumerations, as in Quebec and Nova Scotia (and indeed in the federal enumeration of 1984) can also take their toll. But the overall impression with which we are left is that provinces with election-driven enumerations and revisions, and with the attendant publicity and general excitement of an impending provincial election, have more success in compiling a comprehensive list at that time than those provinces approaching the electorate in a nonelection context. It is also probable that, based on British Columbia's 1986 experience, the high numbers of voters who registered at the last minute reflect the inevitable outdating of a permanent list in a highly mobile society. We find it difficult to generalize about costs, but with the possible exception of Newfoundland, the provinces using an enumeration or registration system in a nonelection context are among those at the higher end of the costs per pre-registered voter over a three- or four-year period. Those generating lists only when an election is called are generally at the lower end. It might also be noted that two provinces (Prince Edward Island and Quebec) experimented with a permanent voters list system in the 1970s but returned to election enumerations in the 1980s, in part because of the high costs associated with their former systems.

VOTER REGISTRATION IN A COMPARATIVE CONTEXT

Voter Registration in the United States

In contrast to virtually every other electoral registration system in the Western world (with the notable exception of France), the system that is used in the United States places the responsibility for enrolment on the individual rather than on the state. The burden is squarely on the shoulders of the voters themselves to ensure that their names are on the electoral registry. This approach differs from that employed in most other liberal democracies, including Canada, where in one form or another governments have assumed the responsibility for drawing up the voters lists.

The American system differs from the Canadian in another fundamental respect: there is an absence of a national electoral registration law. Each state makes its own laws governing elections from the presidential to the municipal levels. Accordingly, the laws and regulations vary from one state to another and, in some cases, within a state itself. This lack of uniformity has resulted in a maze of registration laws, each with separate eligibility requirements and registration procedures. In a 1990 report for Congress, the Congressional Research Service of the Library of Congress noted that the "election system in the United States, while embracing a number of common principles, encompasses a vast array of details which vary considerably from one State to the next" (Coleman et al. 1990, 39).

Not surprisingly, both the voluntary registration system and the absence of a national registration system have become the objects of informed criticism. According to one observer:

> A system of personal voter registration which imposes the burden on the individual to qualify himself rests on a set of critical assumptions: that everyone can register with equal ease; that everyone eligible to vote is able to register; and that everyone eligible to register will do so. None of these conditions is now in effect in the United States, and although it is easier to register in some localities than in others, millions of Americans otherwise eligible to vote are excluded from taking part in local, state and national elections because they may be too timid, poor, unschooled or culturally disconnected to register. (Kimball 1974, 18)

Although procedures vary among the different states, some form of permanent registration is now used in all of them, except for North Dakota, a state without a voter registration list.[12] Three states – Maine, Minnesota and Wisconsin – currently allow registration on election day. In the remaining states, the residency requirement for registration has now been set at no more than 30 days before the election, the average being about 20 days. Until a few years ago it was typically 50 days or more.

It is widely agreed that voter turnout in the United States has reached a worryingly low level, having dipped to a modern low of 50.15 percent of the total national voting-age population in the 1988 presidential election. Since 1960, the share of eligible voters who have registered has also declined in the order of 10–13 percentage points.

One critic has noted that whatever its specifics, an early cut-off date for registration effectively disenfranchises those eligible persons who "realize their interest in a particular election only during the increasing exchange of ideas that accompanies the approach of an election and therefore negatively impacts on voter turnout" (James 1987, 1615). In their study of voter turnout, Raymond E. Wolfinger and Steven J. Rosenstone confirm this. They demonstrate that the closing date for registration is the most important legal variable influencing voter turnout. Based on their study of the 1972 presidential election, they established that "an early closing date decreases the probability of voting. If one could register until election day itself, when media coverage is widest and interest is greatest, turnout would increase by about 6.1 percentage points." They estimate that a seven-day registration cut-off would have led to a 4.5 percent higher turnout of voters in the 1972 election (Wolfinger and Rosenstone 1980, 77–78). Turnout figures from the states (three or four depending upon the year) with election day registration and from the state without any registration requirement lend support to the view that the later the registration cut-off date the higher the voter turnout.[13]

Ironically the decline in both voter registration and electoral participation has occurred during the period of the greatest liberalization of registration laws and the most concerted efforts to encourage registration (especially among racial minorities and in the South) in American history. One scholar has summarized the developments of the past 30 years in the following terms:

> In 1960, most states required a year's residency in the state, 60–90 days in the county, and 30 days in the district ... The Supreme Court's ruling in *Dunn v. Blumstein* (1972) requires all but two states to keep their registration books open until 30 days before an election. Almost all states now allow absentee registration, most allow deputy registrars to enroll new registrants, half permit registration by mail, some have mobile registrars, at least 15 permit nonelection agency state or local government agencies to register citizens, six keep their registration books open as late as 10 days before the election, and three allow election-day registration.
>
> Data from several sources, nevertheless, show that a smaller percentage of the public is registered than in the early 1960s and, more important, that a smaller proportion of registrants is voting. (Bennett 1990, 167)

Although a spirited debate remains in the literature over the link between voter registration and turnout figures, the conclusions reached by Wolfinger and Rosenstone about the negative impact of early registration cut-off dates are, in our view, the most persuasive and significant findings for the purposes of our study.[14]

Registration at the State Level

To appreciate the variation in registration laws, practices will be examined in four of the largest states with distinctive systems: California, New York, Florida and Texas.[15]

In California, the closing date for registration is 29 days before a general election, with a minimum state residence requirement of 29 days. Mail registration has been allowed for all voters since 1976, and all voters are also eligible for absentee registration through the mail. Registration can also take place in the registrar's office or in such field locations as fire stations and public libraries. California's electoral list is not purged of non-voters after a certain number of years. Instead postcards are mailed out to those on the list, the return portion of which is to be sent back to the registration office. If the card is returned as undeliverable, it is presumed that the voter has moved or died and the name is then dropped from the list. On election day, a voter's identity is verified by comparing the voter's name with the registration list.

New York's closing date for registration is 30 days before a general election, with a minimum state residence requirement of 30 days. Mail registration was first used in the 1978 election. Absentee registration provisions exist for the disabled and for those voters who are temporarily out of the jurisdiction on election day. The names of electors who fail to vote after four years are automatically dropped from the list. As in California, confirmations are also mailed to those on the list. If they are undeliverable and further verification procedures are unsuccessful, registration is cancelled. To verify the voter's identity on election day, the same provisions exist as in California; the voter's signature may also be compared with the one in the registration records.

Unlike New York and California, Florida does not have mail-in registration provisions or any minimum state residency requirement, except that the closing date for registration is 30 days before a general election. Florida's absentee registration provisions are quite extensive. Voters who are absent on business, those prevented by employment from registering, those absent for religious reasons, students, persons with disabilities and those temporarily out of the jurisdiction are all able to utilize the absentee registration provisions. Any voter who fails to vote after two years has his or her name automatically removed from the list. Verification of a voter's identity on election day is done in a way similar to New York's process. In Florida, as in New York, non-voters are first notified by mail of the impending purge of their names from the registry and are provided an opportunity (by returning a postcard) to prevent their removal.

In Texas, registration closes 30 days before a general election, and the minimum state-residence requirement is 30 days. Mail-in registration was first used in the 1976 election. Since 1986, Texas has permitted absentee voting by registrants during the three-week period prior to the election. Unlike Florida and the majority of other states, there is no automatic cancellation of registration if a voter fails to vote after a certain number of years. Confirmation forms are sent to voters on the list as a means of verifying their registration. On election day the voter's identity is verified by procedures similar to those in New York and Florida, or the voter can take an oath or provide a written statement.

It is clear from such examples that voter registration in the United States is both jurisdictionally decentralized and distinctive. Not surprisingly, the absence of national registration standards has led to periodic attempts in Congress to change the system. The latest of these was Bill H.R. 2190 (the *National Voter Registration Act*), which came before the 101st (1989–91) Congress. The bill would have required all states to provide three forms of registration for eligible voters – operators' licence registration (which would have allowed a driver's licence application to serve as well as an application for voter registration), mail registration, and registration through certain state, federal and private sector offices such as welfare agencies, libraries, post offices and banks.[16] In several states all three forms of voter registration are already provided for. Although Bill H.R. 2190 was approved in the House of Representatives by a vote of 289 to 132, a similar bill narrowly failed in the Senate (*New York Times* 1990). A virtually identical bill has been introduced in the 102nd Congress, but as of June 1991, its fate is uncertain.

One concern central to any system using a permanent list is the removal of names of those who should no longer be on the roll. The "deadwood" (voters who have died or moved) are commonly estimated to range between 10 and 20 percent of the total number of names on state registration lists (Bennett 1990; Wolfinger 1991). If such names are not eliminated from the list, the size of the total electorate is inflated and the electoral turnout figures reflect a lower than actual turnout of voters. Procedures for the timely removal of names from the lists vary among the different states and even on occasion among the counties of a single state. In many instances they have been found wanting. In Rhode Island, a state that purges the names from the registry of those who have not voted for five years, an experimental statewide election mailing in 1983 led to the discovery that 100 000 of the 530 000 addressees no longer lived at their official voting address. In California, an official estimate of "deadwood" registrations in 1986 placed the number at 9 percent (Squire et al. 1987, 46–47).

In 42 states, the names of electors who have not voted in an election after a certain period of time are deleted from the list (Coleman et al. 1990, 43). This practice has been criticized on the grounds that it discourages voters who do not vote in every election and because of the self-motivated re-registration required to get back on the list. The Committee for the Study of the American Electorate (CSAE) estimated that the practice of purging non-voters may have eliminated as many as two million electors who might otherwise have voted (CSAE 1990, 12). In some cases, voters lists are also purged by cross-referencing them with mortality records and with the records of changes of address maintained by post offices in order to remove the names of voters who have died or moved. In most states, the courts are also required to notify registration officials of any person who is convicted of a felony or judged insane whose name is to be removed from the list. However well-structured the process and well-intended the officials, it seems to us that the satisfactory removal of names from the lists remains a largely unresolved problem of the American registration system.

Countless political observers have expressed concern over the low turnout of American voters. At best, little more than 50 percent of voting-age Americans now vote in presidential elections; in non-presidential election years the figure has slipped to the 36–40 percent range over the last 15 years. Some political analysts have argued that basing measures of turnout on the total voting-age population produces misleading figures. Glass et al. (1984), for example, suggest that the percentage of *registered* voters is a more appropriate measure, since compared with total voting-age population, an equation denominator composed of registered voters excludes those who are ineligible to vote.[17] On that basis they found that in the 1980 election the United States compared much more favourably with other nations. It ranked 11th among 24 countries, with an astonishingly high turnout figure of 86.8 percent of registered voters, rather than 23rd of 24 when using the traditional method of computing turnout as a share of total voting-age population (ibid.). According to others, an average, long-term turnout figure based on registered voters shows "that between 75 and 80 percent of those citizens who are registered vote in presidential elections" ("Voter Registration" 1990, 192; Gans 1990, 176).

Such figures demonstrate that once they voluntarily register, a substantial majority of American electors actually cast a ballot in presidential elections. This leads Glass et al. to argue that the real problem is not the often-cited one of low turnout, but rather one of low registration. The American system clearly captures far less than 100 percent of the eligible voters through its various registration systems – often only about 60 percent in some states and between 65 and 69 percent nationwide (Canada, Privy Council 1986, 39; "Voter Registration" 1990, 103; Squire et al. 1987, 45). Reformers claim that if more Americans were registered, turnout would be improved. They argue that attention should be directed at the registration process because whatever the other causes of low turnout (such as weak parties or voter alienation), the registration system is one that clearly can be changed through legislative action.

Virtually all states, even some of those with election day registration, separate the act of registration from the act of voting. Maine allows election day registration, but the voter must register at one location and vote in another. In 1980, Oregon also had election day registration provisions, but voters had to register at the county clerk's office which often meant a long drive for people in rural areas. The inconvenience of having to register at a location so far removed from both the voter's home and polling place proved to be an obstacle to registration for some potential voters. An added problem is that registration deadlines and regulations are often so obscure that many voters are unaware of the process involved. As noted earlier, any elector who moves must remember to register again. The process itself may be confusing or frustrating if the county or state to which the elector moves has markedly different procedures. With one of three voters moving every two years, it is not surprising that many of the more mobile are unfamiliar with local registration procedures and practices. Even in North Dakota, the one state with no registration requirement, part of the electorate seemed oblivious of their own good fortune: one-third of the non-voters claimed in their responses to the National Election Study that they did not vote because they were not registered (Glass et al. 1984, 53).

In conclusion, it should be noted that the American voter registration system impacts differentially on the American public. Those least likely to register are the young, the poorly educated, the racial and ethnic minorities, and those who have recently moved (Squire et al. 1987, 45–56). These are among the electorally disadvantaged in part because of institutional and social factors that are beyond the scope of this study, but in some measure as well because of the registration laws (Powell 1986). To motivate individual eligible voters in these groups is an immense challenge for the numerous voluntary, commercial, union, church, party and other organizations that are actively involved in the registration process. Yet Americans concerned about the perceived failures of their registration system never seem to explore the option of a system that is uniform, nationwide and federally operated – either a door-to-door enumeration, as is now the case in Canada, or some variant of a permanent voters list or roll, as is the case in most other countries.[18]

No doubt the explanation for the unwillingness to consider such a radical departure from the voluntary, decentralized American system is complex. It is in keeping with the laissez-faire, 18th-century Lockean liberalism that typifies the approach taken by Americans to various governmental institutions. But that said, it is not a model to be emulated in Canada. In commenting on the generally accepted (but in their own view inadequate) explanation of voter apathy, the League of Women Voters posed the critical question that Americans must address in evaluating their voter registration system: "If the government can find a citizen to tax him or draft him into military service, is it not reasonable to assume that the government can find that same citizen to enroll him as an eligible voter and include him in the active electorate?" (1972, 12).

Voter Registration in Great Britain

Modern British voter registration law rests in the *Representation of the People Act, 1948*, and subsequent amending legislation. A cardinal feature of that law is a permanent voters list that is revised each year. Unlike the Australian system, where additions, corrections and deletions are allowed at any time up to a fixed date before election day, there is in Britain a stipulated time for registration or changes in registration, after which the lists are in force for all elections (i.e., local, European Parliament and parliamentary) during the period of as long as one year beyond a given date. Thus, while both Australia and Great Britain may be said to have permanent voters lists, the Australian list is open, that is, subject to continuous change, while the British lists are closed.

The use of the plural "lists" indicates another significant feature of the British system, and one that again sets it apart from countries such as Australia. While in the latter country there is a single Commonwealth list, which is shared by all but two of that federation's six states, in Great Britain voter registration is the responsibility of local authorities who, for this purpose, work under the control and supervision of the Home Office. Each of the kingdom's 650 electoral districts in England, Scotland and Wales has its own electoral registration officer (ERO) – the clerk of the respective town, borough or county council in England and Wales and normally the regional valuation assessor in Scotland – who has the responsibility to maintain an up-to-date list. In Northern Ireland the register is compiled for the whole province by a single official, the chief electoral officer. The Home Secretary has the power under section 52(1) of the *Representation of the People Act 1983,* "to require an electoral registration officer to comply with any general or specific directives he may give in connection with the registration of electors." As recently as 1983, it was reported that "the Home Secretary's legal power to give binding instructions has never, to the Government's knowledge, been exercised" (Pinto-Duschinsky and Pinto-Duschinsky 1987, 30).

The compilation and maintenance of Britain's permanent voters lists are therefore decentralized to an extreme degree when compared to the lists of many other European countries or to those of Australia or Canada. The uniformity of the British system resides primarily in the fixed timetable for compilation and maintenance of the lists as it is set down in national legislation and regulations and applicable to all local authorities. The timetable for England, set out below, applies to Scotland and Wales as well.

England: Timetable for Preparation of the Annual Register

Sometime in late August or early September of each year the town clerk in each parliamentary constituency distributes an official registration form [Form A] by mail or by hand to each household. If the mail response is not satisfactory, door-to-door canvassers are sent out.
August–September

Qualifying date. Any British subject, citizen of the Commonwealth, or any Irish citizen living in Britain, who is at least 18 is entitled to vote where he resides on the qualifying date.
October 10

Publication of Electors Lists. The town clerk must publish the results of the annual canvass on this date.
November 28

Claims and Objections. During this period eligible voters missed by the canvass can add their names to the list and ineligible voters can be challenged.
November 28 to December 16

Publication of the Register. On this date the new register is published and the list is formally closed. No one may be added to it until the start of the next annual canvass. The list is effective for all elections through the following February 15.
February 15

Source: Carlson (1974, 17).

For Northern Ireland the qualifying date is 15 September, while claims and objections must be made by 15 December. The principal difference between voter registration procedures in Northern Ireland and the rest of the country is the existence in Northern Ireland of a residence requirement of three months prior to the qualifying date.

Once the list is closed, as of 15 February, no additions or alterations can be made to take account of changes in a voter's residence or status (for example, marriage or naturalization). However, since 1981 it has been possible to apply to the ERO at any time during the year (but before the last day for nominating candidates) "to get electors names added for people who qualified on 10 October but for some reason did not get included" (Todd and Eldridge 1987, 2). Despite this liberalization of the registration process, the Home Affairs Committee reported in 1983 that "surprisingly little use is made in Great Britain, as opposed to Northern Ireland, either of the established claims procedure or, it appears, of the new facility for lodging late claims" (United Kingdom, Parliament 1983, vii).

The "tight electoral timetable" (21 days) and strong support for the "traditional relationship between candidates at general or local elections and the voters whose support they are seeking to enlist" habitually discouraged exceptions to the principle that the right to vote in Great Britain was limited to those on the list and who appeared in person at the ballot box (United Kingdom, Parliament 1983, xvii). Provision is made, however, for proxy and postal votes, and for those whose occupation takes them away from home at election times or who are prevented by physical incapacity from attending the polling station. The right to a postal vote also exists for those who change electoral districts after the list is closed, but available evidence, although dated, indicates that only about a quarter of those entitled to do so exercise this right (Gray and Gee 1967, 14).

The reason for suspecting that this piece of dated evidence has not been confounded by recent practice rests in the debate during the last decade on the growing inaccuracies to be found in the permanent voters list in Great Britain. Suspicion about the comprehensiveness of the list has increased in the wake of such publications as that by the Pinto-Duschinskys, which reveals a doubling in the number of errors in the electoral registers in England and Wales between 1966 and 1981. By 1981, say these authors, the register contained "over 5 million inaccuracies," a figure derived from a major survey made by the Office of Population Censuses and Surveys that found "2.5 million eligible electors (6.7 percent of the total) were left off the register" and another "2.6 million names were wrongly included (7 percent of the total)"

(Pinto-Duschinsky and Pinto-Duschinsky 1987, 3). More troubling still was the finding that "nearly two thirds of the increase in the number unregistered resulted from the growing percentage of over 21s who omitted to register" (ibid., 38). In other words, the unregistered were not concentrated in any particular age group, such as 18- and 19-year-olds who traditionally and in most electoral systems participate less frequently than older citizens, nor were they concentrated among ethnic minorities. The Pinto-Duschinskys report that "a variety of partial evidence [suggests] that ethnicity is a relatively minor cause of non-registration," a conclusion corroborated by another recent study of electoral registration in inner-city areas (ibid., 19; Todd and Eldridge 1987, 11).

Inaccuracy is inescapable in a system of voter registration where the list is compiled and closed four months before it comes into force. Moreover, the magnitude of that inaccuracy grows daily since the list remains in force for another 12 months. If it is assumed that two-thirds of 1 percent of those registered will move every month, then the register is "already 3 percent out of date (i.e. 4 1/2 x 2/3 percent)" when it comes into force (Gray and Gee 1967, 13).[19]

Gray and Gee (1967) estimated that if the register was 96 percent accurate when it was compiled in October – an optimistic assumption – the proportion of eligible voters registered and still at the qualifying address would have fallen to 93 percent when the new register came into force the following February with 89 percent in August, halfway through the life of the register. If an election was called the next February before the register ran out, it would accurately record only 85 percent of the eligible voters.

Yet the decline in the register's accuracy – to a level that Dr. David Butler of Nuffield College, Oxford, and Professor Bryan Keith-Lucas of the Hansard Society described in 1983 as showing "an alarming degree of inexactitude" – indicates not an improvement but a deterioration over the last two decades in the compilation of Britain's voter register (United Kingdom, Parliament 1983, vi). Indeed this downward trend is now acknowledged in social science research. Ivor Crewe, director of the Social Science Research Centre Survey Archive and co-director of the British Election Study (both at the University of Essex) has said:

> In Britain, for example, it is increasingly common for political scientists to adjust the official turnout figure to the age of the register at the time of the election. One formula is + 3.4 percent (not registered) – 1.0 percent (registered twice) – 15m percent (effect of deaths) – 0.67m percent (effect of removals), where m = months from the date of the

register's compilation. Applying the formula can make a difference: thus the official statistics show quite sharply fluctuating turnout in Britain's last three general elections (78.1 percent, 72.8 percent, 76.0 percent), while the adjusted figures suggest serene stability (79.1 percent, 78.7 percent, 78.6 percent). The formula itself, however, probably needs renewing from time to time. It is generally agreed, for example, that the electoral register in Britain has declined in accuracy over the last ten years. (Crewe 1981, 233)

Part of the explanation for its decline may rest in the growth of voter apathy as evidenced by the failure of eligible voters omitted from the register to utilize the changes in the law after 1981 to apply for inclusion on the register. But part of it also rests in the lack of a uniform procedure whereby the list is revised. The detrimental effect of entrusting this responsibility to hundreds of local authorities is indicated in a description of the procedure taken from Todd and Eldridge's study (1987):

One of the decisions that the electoral registration officer has to make is what to do for those households for which no up-to-date information has been obtained. If the address is removed from the register then some people who are eligible to vote may be disfranchised. If the electors for that address are carried forward to the next year's register then some of the names on the register may be redundant because the people concerned may have moved away or died, and other people who currently live there may be eligible but not included.

Electoral registration officers have to decide what to do in such circumstances; some authorities have a policy of not carrying names forward at all, some carry names forward but limit the number of years that electors at an address would be carried forward, and some carry forward electors names indefinitely (Todd and Eldridge 1987, 2). [The Pinto-Duschinskys report that only 7.7 percent of authorities do not carry names over; 18.1 percent carry them for one year and 7.4 percent carry them indefinitely, while the practices of 26.6 percent of authorities is unknown. Pinto-Duschinsky and Pinto-Duschinsky 1987, tables 4, 6 and 11.]

In a system where "one third of households fail to return Form A and a considerable minority also omit to reply to reminders," the need for some form of canvass "to contact non responding households" appears essential as well as desirable (Pinto-Duschinsky and Pinto-Duschinsky 1987, 5). There is strong evidence that "reminder canvassing" is extremely effective: in the Metropolitan District of Sunderland, which has 230 000 electors, the introduction of canvassers increased the return of information "from 70 percent to 93 percent of households." Canvassing is also cost-effective, since the costs associated with it "are largely, if not totally, offset by savings in postal charges" (ibid., 5, 8). The Pinto-Duschinskys estimated that at British rates of pay, the cost of an individual household visit is from 20 to 25 pence. Postal charges, even with discounts, vary between 18 and 27 pence per household depending on whether a reminder is needed. A more recent survey for the Office of Population Censuses and Surveys states that "overall the median budget [devoted by EROs to voter registration] had increased from 58 p per elector in 1987 to 73 p per elector in 1989" (Young, undated, viii). Pinto-Duschinsky (1991) puts the cost of registration at an average of 90 p ($1.65) per year.

Canvassing requires canvassers and, to date, where they are employed their recruitment, training and supervision are the responsibility of the individual ERO. As has been the experience elsewhere – in Australia with its habitation review and in Canada with its enumeration – finding qualified personnel is difficult, but without them and the information they provide, the registration system operates in the absence of information. In Britain, for instance, it is reported that "a considerable proportion of registration offices have no idea of the effectiveness of their procedures. Twenty-nine percent of districts were unable to give any indication of the percentage of households which either returned Form A or were canvassed" (Pinto-Duschinsky and Pinto-Duschinsky 1987, 14).

The problems associated with inadequate knowledge are compounded in inner-city electoral districts, where residents are highly mobile and where many structures house multiple occupants. In 1981, for example, the rate of omission from the register in inner London was estimated to be 14 percent. In 1987 the omission rate in at least one area of the metropolis was estimated to reach 17 percent (Todd and Eldridge 1987, 8). It is statistics such as these that have led some observers to question "whether electoral registration officers in some London boroughs are fulfilling their basic statutory duties ... to conduct a 'house to house or other sufficient enquiry ... as to persons entitled to be registered' " (Pinto-Duschinsky and Pinto-Duschinsky 1987, 27).

Voter Registration in Australia

Compared to the countries with which it has the closest historical and political ties – the United Kingdom, Canada and New Zealand – Australia's voter registration system is unique in maintaining a continuous electoral roll. Since 1911, enrolment (the Australian term for registration) has been compulsory, a feature that was introduced "as a means of ensuring 'clean' electoral rolls: if everyone were on an electoral roll then there was little potential for the sudden 'stacking' of a roll just prior to an election in the interests of one or other candidate" (Aitkin and Jinks 1982, 127). Compulsory voting, another feature of Australia's electoral system that is unique to a country of British political origin was introduced in 1924. This measure was intended to reverse a trend to low voter turnout that was apparent in the early years of the Commonwealth's history and that reappeared in the election of 1922, when turnout sagged to 59 percent.

As early as 1914 divisional returning officers or DROs (the equivalent of Canada's returning officers) were appointed to the Electoral Branch of the Department of Home Affairs. They were responsible for all subdivisions (similar to a Canadian polling division, although usually much larger, on average 5 000 voters) within their electoral division and were charged with maintaining the electoral rolls for these districts. In testimony before the Joint Standing Committee on Electoral Matters (JSC), in 1989, the Australian electoral commissioner noted that as regards divisional areas "the organization had experienced minimal change since about 1914 when the position of DRO had become full time" (Australia, JSC 1989, 96). Currently, there are 148 divisions with an average staff complement of 3.5 persons; altogether approximately 60 percent of the total Australian Electoral Commission (AEC) staff of 784 is employed in divisional offices (Australia, JSC 1988, 11; AEC 1989b, 155).

Divisional offices report to one of seven Australian electoral officers, in each of the state capitals and the Northern Territory, who in turn are responsible to the Australian Electoral Commission in Canberra. An Australian electoral officer is appointed temporarily for the Australian Capital Territory during federal elections and referendums. In 1983, following amendments to the *Commonwealth Electoral Act, 1918,* the Commission became an independent statutory authority. Its functions may be grouped into two broad categories: the conduct of parliamentary elections and referendums and the conduct of industrial and analogous elections. Voter enrolment (registration) and roll maintenance fall within the former category. In this context it should be noted that for most of the country's history, the federal and state governments have entered into agreements to administer voter enrolment jointly. Thus, common electoral rolls exist for the Commonwealth and all states except Western Australia, where separate rolls are maintained but with the Commonwealth providing the data, and Queensland, where separate rolls are also maintained but with the data for each being secured through a common enrolment form. For the Northern Territory, a de facto joint roll exists.

By Canadian standards, the AEC is exceptional for the number of its full-time personnel and for their distribution down to the divisional level. Unlike Elections Canada, which is centralized in Ottawa, the AEC has a second level of administration – the Australian electoral officers in each of the states and now in the Northern Territory. The AEC is also responsible for the conduct of nonparliamentary elections, such as industrial elections involving trade union representation and strikes. Financial pressures, especially salaries for divisional office staff, have recently led the Commission to advocate regionalization, that is, the grouping together of divisional offices. Echoing the findings of an Efficiency Scrutiny Report on the operation of the AEC, the electoral commissioner has advocated the amalgamation of divisional offices. To the JSC he described the divisional structure as "an inflexible system which did not allow the effective deployment of personnel." In support of his claim, he cited the requirement for uniform staffing: in reality there were unbalanced workloads between, say, rural and urban divisions, or episodic workloads, that might range from normal office routine (where 15 visits from electors per week to an office was exceptional) to short periods of severe pressures and deadlines.

Despite the employment of permanent staff, "excessive overtime" remained a feature of the system. The electoral commissioner questioned the claim often made that divisional offices and their staff possessed a superior knowledge of local conditions and persons which helped them in their important task of roll maintenance (Australia, JSC 1988, 25–26). The JSC accepted the argument that greater management efficiency might be achieved through the grouping of up to three metropolitan divisional offices to form regional offices without at the same time "adversely affecting service to electors and the tasks of roll maintenance and election management." In rural areas, where transport and communications infrastructures were weaker, the JSC believed that regionalization would undermine the AEC's primary electoral tasks (ibid., 59–60).

Compulsory enrolment means that every person who is entitled to be enrolled as an elector is obliged by law to apply for enrolment within 21 days of becoming so entitled. To be qualified a person must be 18 years of age, an Australian citizen (or a British subject who was on the electoral roll on 25 January 1984), and have lived at the time of enrolment for one month within a subdivision (or division, if it is not subdivided) at his or her current address. Excluded from enrolling are those of unsound mind (defined as persons who are incapable of understanding the nature and significance of enrolment and voting) or those who are convicted and under sentence for an offence that is punishable by imprisonment under Commonwealth, state or territory law for five years or longer; as well, persons convicted of treason and who have not been pardoned are excluded.

Claims for enrolment are made on an electoral enrolment form, signed by the claimant and a witness, who must be enrolled or entitled to be enrolled. Cards are available at any office of the AEC or at any post office. Physically handicapped persons may, on the production of a medical certificate, ask another person to fill in and sign a claim form on their behalf. Once filled in and witnessed the card is sent to the DRO. If all is in order the DRO will enter the claimant's particulars onto the electoral roll and notify the elector accordingly.

Enrolment applications may be rejected by the DRO if the claimant does not qualify, but the claimant must be notified in writing of the reason and informed of the right to a review of the decision. In addition "objection action" can be taken by the DRO against a name already on the roll. Such action may also be taken by an elector whose name is on the same roll on payment of a Aust.$2.00 deposit.

A request for a review of the decision may be made by the claimant within 21 days of notification. In the first instance review is by the Australian electoral officer for that state; an appeal may be made to the Administrative Appeals Tribunal and, in states where there is a joint roll, to state bodies such as a magistrate's court. In 1989 the JSC recommended, for reasons of uniformity in decision-making, that the Administrative Appeals Tribunal be the sole agent to hear appeals (Australia, JSC 1989, 20–21).

The primary source of objection actions is where the habitation review – the biennial house-to-house call conducted by divisional offices as part of their effort to maintain the rolls – reveals that the status of the claimant has changed in such a way as to invalidate his or her enrolment. For example, the review conducted between mid-October and the end of December 1990 in the state of Queensland saw 15 500 net enrolments, which were the result of 32 500 additions and 17 000 deletions (AEC 1991, 2).

Those electors who are placed on divisional lists through the above process become ordinary voters. However, Australian law makes special enrolment provision for several other categories of voters: Antarctic electors, eligible overseas electors and itinerant electors. It is also possible for persons aged 17 to apply for enrolment to ensure that they will be able to vote if they turn 18 after the close of the rolls but before polling day. This is called a provisional enrolment. There were

16 842 provisional electors in 1987, of whom 6 537 turned 18 before polling day and were able to vote (AEC 1988a, app. 2; 1989a, 12). There are penalties for failure to enrol or to register a change of address or other vital particulars once a person is enrolled. Today, the penalty is a fine not to exceed $50, although in the 1950s and 1960s penal provisions for such failures also existed (AEC 1985, 12).[20] The revised enforcement provisions reflect a change in attitude toward compulsion that is evident in Australia as in other jurisdictions; they do not reflect a depreciation in the importance of the roll maintenance. Indeed, as shall be noted below, at the end of the 1980s imputations of laxness in maintaining the roll and publicity about "cemetery voting" (allowing the names of deceased persons to remain on the list) and multiple voting appear to have reawakened the kind of debate that gave birth to compulsory enrolment in 1911.

Roll maintenance requires several crucial steps: first, a cross-check following an election to determine which voters on the list voted; then, a follow-up campaign to see that missing electors are contacted or, if appropriate, as in the case of death, culled from the list. Australia's population is extremely mobile; between one in five and one in six divisions recorded greater than 50 percent population turnover at each of four successive censuses taken at five-year intervals between 1971 and 1986, while only five divisions in 1986 recorded a turnover of less than 33.3 percent. Interelection investigation in the form of habitation reviews is thus essential in order to maintain accuracy (AEC 1988d, 3).

The cross-check (or "mark-back," as it is called in Australia) referred to above has traditionally been carried out manually by thousands of casual staff throughout Australia. Some indication of the magnitude of the task is gained from the following description by the AEC's director of operations policy and coordination:

> Within Australia there are nearly 8 500 small and large polling places used on polling day. Some 65 000 polling officials are employed.
>
> When Australians go to vote they have their names marked on a list of electors for one of 148 electoral divisions. There are 25 000 such lists of electors used in polling – each carrying in the vicinity of 75 000 names.
>
> After each election the Australian Electoral Commission is required to mark-back the lists of electors used in polling to one master list in order to determine who voted, who did not vote, and the very few who appear to have voted more than once.
>
> From this master list of voters and non voters compulsory voting action is taken. (Farrell 1988, 1)

In the 1987 election the AEC used an optical scanner to read marks for the first time, with polling officials marking voters' names off the lists with special pens to allow for accurate reading by the scanners. Up to that time the checking process had consisted largely of calling out names: "In some areas the task resembled bingo. A local hall was hired, a caller read names from a stage to an audience each holding a list, or lists, o[f] electors." The new system is more accurate than the old one while at the same time, because of the nature of the database created, it provides an opportunity for analysis of non-voters by age and geographic location. None the less, the number of non-voters discovered in 1987 approximated the long-term average of 600 000 (Farrell 1988, 1).[21]

This finding in 1987 may in part be explained by the early call of the election that year, which interrupted the completion of the biennial habitation review. Because there was no opportunity for objection action, "departed electors identified by the habitation review" remained on the rolls. According to the AEC, the number of persons in this category totalled 1 175 745 (AEC 1988c, 10). The magnitude of such figures for non-voters and for "departed electors" elicits the question, "How accurate are the rolls?" In reply to that and to a further question as to whether all persons eligible to be electors are enrolled, the electoral commissioner has said that "it is impossible to answer such a question when there can be no sufficiently exact estimate of the number of people who are eligible to enrol" (AEC 1988d, 1). The difficulty lies in disaggregating the minority of persons eligible to enrol from the large number who are ineligible because they are under age or are not citizens. Perhaps the greatest imponderable is the one-month residency requirement in a subdivision; the electoral commissioner has said that "no data are known to be available for periods of residence so short" (ibid., 2).

Significantly, the electoral commissioner has also said that "house-to-house inquiries, as in the electoral roll review, are probably the only effective method and their reliability is uncertain." That uncertainty originates in the conflict between the requirement for a habitation review at least once in every period of two years and the calling of a federal election on average once every 2.5 years (Australia, JSC 1988, 14). It also reflects the manner by which these reviews are carried out. In rural areas local officials (for example, postal officials) are appointed as electoral agents by the AEC on recommendation of the DRO. In urban areas the DRO selects and instructs two to six revision officers to make the house-to-house inquiry. Through the notation of pertinent facts, the information gathered may lead to the purging of the lists of names of persons no longer living at the houses visited. It does not, however, lead to the addition of names of persons who are eligible but are not enrolled. That remains the duty of the individual concerned, although with the information gathered through the review, the DRO may now contact the delinquent by mail.

Australian electoral officials work actively to promote the inclusion rather than the exclusion of eligible or potentially eligible electors. Advertisements are placed in the real-estate sections of newspapers, reminding voters who move to notify the respective divisional offices. Enrolment of new citizens is a live issue; there are suggestions for a provisional enrolment scheme of new citizens that would see the Commonwealth departments responsible for citizenship obtain and forward to the AEC the information that is required on an enrolment form at the time that an application is made for citizenship. The Information and Education Branch of the AEC in part directs its energies to making young people more aware of their electoral rights and responsibilities. The need for this activity became evident following the 1983 election, "when a survey indicated that one in three 18–19 year olds who were entitled to enrol had, in fact, not done so" (AEC, 1989b, 2).

Despite all of this activity, it is customary for large numbers of last-minute enrolments to occur when a general election is announced. For instance, in 1990, between the announcement of and the closing of the rolls, 159 719 new enrolments and 434 893 other enrolment transactions occurred. These figures constitute 5.5 percent of the total electorate of 10 795 635 in 1990.

Such a volume of transactions is not an exceptional occurrence; in 1987, the transactions totalled more than 700 000. Thus, it is a matter of some concern to Australians that an interval of at least one week elapse between the dissolution of Parliament and the issue of the writs for election. The Constitution (section 32) sets an outside limit of 10 days between the two events. In 1983 the writs for the election were issued the day following the dissolution of Parliament, which was also the day the prime minister first indicated that there would be an election. At that time the *Commonwealth Electoral Act* provided that the rolls would close on the day the writs were issued. As a consequence of a number of otherwise eligible voters being disenfranchised because of lack of time to correct their registration, the Act was amended in 1984 to provide for seven days to pass between the issue of the writs and the close of the rolls. In other words, the existence of a continuous electoral roll has not guaranteed that considerable numbers of voters may not be disenfranchised if denied time to correct their voter registration.

Allegations of roll-stacking or multiple voting were made following the 1987 election. Instances of apparent multiple voting increased dramatically in the elections of 1983, 1984 and 1987 (5 410, 7 399 and 11 525 respectively). To what extent the rise between 1984 and 1987 was a result of the first-time use in 1987 of the optical scanner instead of the traditional manual mark-back procedures is open to question. Dr. Colin A. Hughes, then electoral commissioner, stated that "multiple voting is not thought to be a significant problem; it is not a threat to the integrity of election outcomes." His conclusion was based on the fact that of the 11 525 cases recorded of apparent multiple voting, 6 363 were disposed of because a match could be made between the apparent multiple voter and an apparent non-voter, while another 4 717 cases failed to proceed because of inconclusive evidence. Suggestions that Australia should consider more extensive use of computers (down to every polling place) or that it reinstitute voting at specified polls (as is done in Canada) as a means of checking personation have not found favour with the AEC. Amendments in 1984 to the *Commonwealth Electoral Act* allow voters to cast their ordinary (as opposed to postal) votes at any polling place within their division. While computerization on a massive scale is viewed as unattainable, proposals to reinstitute poll voting represent, said the former electoral commissioner, "a misplaced reliance on a tattered and threadbare security blanket" (AEC 1988d, 6).

Cemetery voting, "the ultimate absentee vote" (AEC 1988b, 5) or other possible abuses of the Australian continuous roll are beyond the concern of this study except as they demonstrate that no system of voter registration is immune to abuse or perceptions of abuse.

Voter Registration in France
In one fundamental and determinative respect, the system of voter registration in France is like that of Great Britain. There is in France a permanent list that is updated annually according to a fixed timetable and that is closed on a predetermined date (the last day of February). But in contrast to Britain, it is possible in France for the following classes of citizens to register after the list has closed: those who have turned 18, those who have been naturalized, those who have moved because of their jobs as civil servants, or those who, as discharged military personnel, have changed their domicile on their return to civilian life. As in Britain, the compilation and maintenance of France's voters list is a local responsibility, but where in Britain the task falls to an official of the local government, in France it is undertaken by a three-person special municipal commission composed of the mayor (or representative of the mayor), an appointee of the prefect of the Department and a delegate chosen by the municipal council. The basic unit of local government for electoral

registration purposes in France is the *commune*, although large cities may be divided into several election districts (bureaux de vote), with Paris, for example, having more than 30 such subdivisions.

The timetable for the municipal commission's work is shown in table 8.10.[22]

As is evident from this timetable, the sequence of activity resembles that followed by British authorities in compiling their voters lists. The principal difference is that while in Britain the local authorities work with information collected from the return of registration forms sent annually to each householder in the constituency, the French officials depend upon individual applications made at the town hall by the applicant in person or by mail if the applicant is ill, infirm or absent from the country. Personal application for initial registration and for thereafter maintaining the currency of that registration is the bedrock of France's voter registration system. For this reason, the French system is described by commentators as "volitional" and analogies are thus drawn between it and "the personal registration systems of the United States" (Carlson

Table 8.10
Deadlines for various operations involved in revising voters lists [translation]

	Time required	Deadline	Reference section code
Submission of registration applications		All year until last working day in December; Saturday is considered a working day	R. 5
Registration and deletion operations by the administration commission	4 months	From 1 September to last working day in December	R. 5
Time period granted to prepare corrective table	9 days	1–9 January	R. 5
Deadline for ruling on observations prepared in application of sections A.23 and R.8, subsection (2)	—	9 January	R. 5
Submission and publication of corrective table	—	10 January	R. 10
Time period for claims before trial court	10 days	11–20 January	R. 25
Final close of lists	—	28 February, or 29 February in a leap year	R. 16

Source: France, Ministère 1989b, annexe 1, 29.

1974, 27). The document entitled *Instruction relative à la révision et à la tenue des listes électorales* begins with the statement that "enrolment on the voters list is compulsory," but no analysis of the French system treats this as more than a patriotic exhortation, since there is no penalty for non-registration and voting is not compulsory.

During the period when new names are being added to the list, the municipal commission also strikes off the names of people who have died, who have been deprived of the franchise ("by judicial decision") and who have moved. None the less, the culling of the list is cautiously pursued, for once on the list there is "a presumption that can be overturned only when there is absolute proof that the name does not belong under any category that would entitle it to remain on the list" [translations].

For this reason, those who study the French system of voter registration "estimate that approximately 8 percent of voters whose names appear on the list do not qualify for registration" (Toinet and Subileau 1989, 176). Some of this inaccuracy is a result of fraud, they say, but a proportion of it "reflects on the inefficiency of the system in removing voters from the list" [translations] (ibid.; see also Percheron and Mayer 1990, 398–401).

Voluntarism and localism are apparent hallmarks of the French system but they are significantly qualified by the participation of the central government in the maintenance of the voters list. In this regard, France diverges markedly from the United States or Great Britain. Written 16 years ago the following description remains accurate except for the existence today of a single list in Paris rather than several regional lists:

> The voters lists are kept centrally as well as at the level of the commune. The National Institute of Statistics and Economic Studies (INSEE), a division of the Ministry of Finance, maintains lists of eligible votes in each of its 18 regional offices and serves as a clearing-house for information on voters. When a registered voter moves to a new commune and registers there, a notice is sent to the INSEE office which notifies the mayor in the former place of residence and the name is purged from the list there. The INSEE is notified by the Ministry of Justice of people who are convicted of crimes that disqualify them as voters. This information is passed to the communes where the disqualified voter is registered and his name is stricken from the rolls. If a registered voter dies outside the commune where he is registered, a similar process is followed. In these ways the INSEE helps to maintain accurate rolls and to provide an indirect form of supervision over the registration process. (Carlson 1974, 29)

In addition to this element of centralism, the French system of voter registration also differs in another crucial respect from that found in the Anglo-American democracies: each duly registered elector receives a voter's card that is valid for three years for use in national and local elections and referendums. The card includes the following information: the name and address of the voter, the date of birth, the electoral registration number and the location of the poll at which the voter is to cast his or her ballot. The card is presented to officials at the polling booth to establish the elector's right to vote, although in *communes* of more than 5 000 inhabitants, an additional piece of identification is required, such as a driver's licence or the equivalent of a social insurance card. Each time the voter votes, the card is stamped.

Despite the imprimatur of authority that the card appears to represent, there is some doubt among scholars as to its utility, since its presentation is not a necessary condition for voting:

> Several authors note that one does not have to have a voter's card in order to vote. Under no circumstances would the card compensate for nonenrolment on the voters list, and in practice enrolment on the voters list and proof of identity are sufficient. Another author adds that presentation of the card at the poll is not compulsory and that a poll could not rightfully bar a voter from voting if the voter did not have his or her card. On the other hand, the poll can turn back a voter who does not have a card and cannot offer proof of identity. André and Francine Demichel state that "for each election, particular measures are taken to ensure that voters who have lost [their card] can vote without it [A. and F. Demichel 1973]," and conclude that there is a risk the card could become less and less needed and indeed even unnecessary in exercising one's right to vote. [translation] (Massicotte 1989)

Of the countries whose voter registration systems are examined in this study, France alone uses a voter's card. Other European countries that issue a similar document are Belgium, Greece, Sweden, Italy and a majority of the Swiss cantons. The relevance of the card is none the less suspect in any debate over the respective merits of enumeration versus a permanent voters list. First, French experience suggests that the card does not supplant other forms of identification, since in certain *communes* French citizens are required to provide supplementary identification. Second, the card does not act as a substitute for a voters list, since compilation of that list (or some such enrolment) must precede the issuance of a card. Thus, the voter's card appears to be something of a red herring in any evaluation of France's voter registration system.

It does not appear to contribute in any measurable way to the completeness, currency or cost-effectiveness of the French system.

Despite concerted attempts to secure reliable information on France's system of voter registration, considerable uncertainty as to its comprehensiveness remains. For instance, while INSEE acts as a clearing-house on the movements of registered voters, its data say nothing about those persons who are eligible to vote but are not registered. The initiative to get on the list in the first instance rests with the individual and then upon the diligence of the local authorities in transmitting that information to INSEE. Similarly, the accuracy with which INSEE maintains its central registry depends upon the citizen and the local authority playing their part by informing INSEE of changes in a registered voter's location or status. In an interview with a researcher of the Royal Commission, Marie-France Toinet, a professor of political science in Paris, estimated that about 9 percent of eligible electors are not registered, largely because of administrative requirements.[23] Other students of French politics note that among persons under the age of 25, the proportion of non-registered voters may reach 40 percent (Masclet 1989, 63).

The difficulty we face is that without more information on such other subjects as the number of eligible voters to be enrolled in France, the efficiency of municipal commissions in carrying out their responsibility of maintaining the *commune* list, and the decline in the list's accuracy once it is closed at the end of February – in other words, the type of information used to evaluate the permanent voters list in Great Britain – there is no basis upon which we can evaluate or compare France's system of "volitional" registration.

Voter Registration in the Federal Republic of Germany

All German citizens are eligible to vote in a community if they are 18 years old as of election day and have resided in the community for at least three months prior to election day. German citizens residing in foreign countries are eligible to vote if they fall into one of the following categories: they are working on behalf of the Federal Republic of Germany in a diplomatic or military posting; they are dependent members at least 18 years old living with the immediate family of the individual posted abroad; they are German citizens living in a country of the Council of Europe, prior to which they lived for at least three months (since February 1949) in the Federal Republic of Germany; or they are German citizens living for no more than 10 years in a country outside the Council of Europe, prior to which they lived for at least three months (since February 1949) in the Federal Republic of Germany.

The creation and maintenance of the electoral list is, by German law, a municipal responsibility. Local authorities are required to make a voting list for each municipal ward. Wards are created by the local municipality and typically consist of approximately 2 500 inhabitants. As transfer payments and financial aid are tied to population figures, it is in the interest of a municipality or community to ensure that the list is as complete as possible. It is the individual's responsibility, however, to ensure that his or her name is on the list. Failure to register is punishable by fine, but it is an open question how seriously the authorities enforce that aspect of the law.

The registration system has been described in the following terms:

> The compilation of lists of eligible voters in the German Federal Republic is only one part of a general system of population registration which is carried out by municipal officials. Within each municipality there are usually three offices whose activities contribute to the creation and maintenance of the electoral rolls. The municipal registrars' office records all births, deaths and marriages. The registration office records each new arrival and departure, including people arriving from or leaving for a foreign country. The election office uses the data gathered by these offices to compile lists of eligible voters. This is done automatically by the election office and does not have to be requested by the individual. (Carlson 1974, 30)

Forms in triplicate are to be filed with the local authorities by an individual, either at the time of leaving one municipality and of moving to another one or at the time of moving within the same municipality. One of the three copies of the registration form is filed with the local election office, and that serves as the individual's entry on the new electoral roll and removal from the previous electoral roll for municipal, state and federal elections. As national identity cards (which all German citizens are required by law to have) are stamped by the local authorities in which the new residence is located, they too provide another source of information for the electoral roll.

Because the electoral list is basically a by-product of the municipal registrar's records of births, deaths, marriages and population movements, German citizens are not directly approached by the state to enter their names on the list. There is no door-to-door enumeration or registration drive carried out by the state. If the system is working as it should, the names of eligible voters are automatically placed on the electoral list as part of the local registration process. It is the individual's obligation to ensure that the papers have been properly filed; it is the community's responsibility to ensure that the list has been properly drawn up.

The list, composed of those voters automatically entitled to registration, is closed 35 days before the election and posted in central and public locations from the 20th to the 15th days before the election. During this period every voter has the opportunity to raise an objection to the entries on the voters list. By the 21st day before the election all communities are to notify those on the list that they have been included. The authorities usually send a special postcard to the voter, listing the voter's name and address, the times and day of voting and the location of the polling station.

Changes to the voters list can be made until the final closing day, the date of which may vary from one constituency, and indeed from one ward, to another, as this is left up to the local authorities to determine. Authorities are allowed to close the list sometime between the third and the last day before the election. In exceptional cases a potential voter who is not on the list after the closing day has the opportunity to vote if, after the closing day, he or she can prove that it was impossible (on the grounds of health, for example) to apply for registration before the 21st day before the election or to raise an objection within the 20th to 15th days. In such a case it is the voter's responsibility to ensure that he or she has applied to vote no later than noon on the election day.

It is difficult to imagine a more decentralized and discretionary registration system, at least in determining deadlines for closing the local lists. As a consequence, relevant statistics and data that might help to complete the picture of the German system are apparently unavailable and unlikely to be compiled. That makes answers to important questions concerning the coverage and costs of the German system impossible to obtain. We have been unable to determine the share of the total possible electorate missed from the lists, the number of changes (additions, removals and the like) that typically take place in the course of one year, and the portion of the total local registration costs that can be reasonably attributed to the compilation of the electoral lists. That is unfortunate, as a full assessment of what appears to be a logical and rigorously maintained system is not feasible.

Evaluation

It would be presumptuous to evaluate any one of these foreign systems of voter registration in terms of how adequately it serves the needs of its particular society. But in light of our earlier discussion of the problems and shortcomings of enumeration in Canada, it is relevant to ask if these systems, or parts of them, might be useful in resolving the difficulties that Canada faces in registering its voters. From that perspective, then, the appropriate evaluative criterion is whether the registration practices of the United States, the United Kingdom, Australia, France or Germany offer answers to Canada's problems of finding enumerators, increasing the accuracy and coverage of enumeration, improving public perceptions of Canadian voter registration practices or reducing the length of Canadian electoral campaigns.

Since each of these foreign jurisdictions uses some variant of a permanent voters list, none is confronted by Canada's periodic need to enlist tens of thousands of enumerators. Instead, each of these jurisdictions has a voters list ready at the call of an election. The one exception to that general statement that could be relevant for Canada is Australia's use of a habitation review every two years to identify new electors, deceased electors and electors who have moved. From the perspective of a Canadian, the habitation review of each household in Australia looks very much like an enumeration, except that the onus still remains on the elector to see that he or she is properly registered. The habitation review is vital to the maintenance of the voters list in Australia and, therefore, the quality of this "census" depends very much on the quality of the persons who conduct it. The most recent habitation review carried out in late 1990 and early 1991 is perceived by the Australian Electoral Commission to be a major success. It is of some interest, therefore, to read in a 1991 issue of *Scrutiny: The Newsletter of the Australian Electoral Commission* that "this success is substantially due to the increase in the Review Officer's payment from $0.50 to $1.05 for each completed form returned" (AEC 1991, 2).

As to the second "problem," is there a lesson to be learned for Canada in the accuracy and coverage of these other systems of registration? From the American evidence, the answer would appear to be no. As one group of experts there has stated (in noting that 31 percent of all Americans failed to register for the 1980 presidential election), the United States' "dismal showing in international comparisons of turnout is due in large measure to [its] registration system, in which the individual, not the government, bears the responsibility for establishing one's eligibility to vote" (Squire et al. 1987, 45). High turnout in countries like Germany and France could be interpreted as a function of an efficient registration system (Jackman 1987, 419). It could also be the result of both civic diligence and the fact that the state (in Germany at least) takes a good deal of responsibility for making up the lists as a by-product of the civil registration system, whereas in the United States, the process of voter registration is isolated from other governmental activity, except in a number of states like Michigan that have a "motor voter" program of registration at licence bureaus. For France and

Germany the information on the completeness of their voters lists is too fragmentary or contradictory to permit those systems to be cited with confidence as models for Canada to emulate. Moreover, both systems rely on a degree of state involvement, such as the issuance of national or voter identity cards, that does not conform to Canadian political traditions.

Nor do the traditions of Great Britain conform either, where police registers and compulsory identity cards are viewed as incompatible with individual freedom. Without them but with a permanent voters register that is becoming increasingly inaccurate (partly as a result of its decentralized administration), the British system of voter registration offers no improvement on the accuracy and coverage of Canada's practice of enumeration. The Pinto-Duschinskys found that between 1966 and 1981 the number of eligible electors omitted from the voting rolls in England and Wales had doubled. Such deterioration of the voters list has not been cited by critics of Canada's enumeration system.

In Australia, too, pressures are growing to tighten up the existing system of voter registration. The "general philosophical approach" of recent years – to make "it easier for electors to vote" – is being rivalled at the outset of the 1990s by, at the very least, concerns about inaccurate enrolment and at worst about "allegations of electoral malpractice" (Australia, JSC 1989, 110–11). To "restore public confidence in the integrity of the electoral system," "a savage increase in penalties for [among others] enrolment offences" has been contemplated by the electoral commissioner, while some members of the JSC have expressed support for reintroducing both a three-month residency requirement for enrolment in an electoral district and the requirement that electors vote at specified polls rather than "anywhere within the Division in which they are enrolled" (ibid., 88–89, 110–11). These pressures for more stringent oversight of the enrolment process appear to be increasing as Australia's mobile population grows more heterogeneous.

The massive number of transactions required to keep the roll accurate, the widespread bureaucracy to record and communicate these transactions (in the form of the AEC itself and other agents, such as the Registrar of Births, Deaths and Marriages, who supply it with information) and the customary influx of new enrolments when an election is called all bear witness to the organizational demands that accompany the maintenance of a continuous electoral roll. In short, the continuous roll, as it functions in Australia, is not a system that automatically adds to or deletes from the list the names of persons who become or cease to be eligible electors. While the state (the public sector) compiles and maintains the list, the onus for inclusion on it remains with the voter.

Evidence of public perception of voter registration systems is at best inferential. Outside of the United States, where organizations such as the League of Women Voters, labour unions and minority groups pose awkward questions about the status quo, few citizens seem to be aware of voter registration as a preliminary step to casting their ballots. Even academic political scientists, with the possible exception of those in the United States who regularly lament low voter turnout, tend not to see registration as a significant issue.

The difficulty experienced by the authors of this study in securing information on registration in France and Germany might be interpreted as evidence of greater contentment with those systems. Data from Great Britain suggest that even where the system of voter registration fails to enrol large numbers of eligible electors, and where those numbers are growing, little public attention to the problem results. (More mysterious in this instance is the question of why the political parties who are directly affected by the exclusion of voters from the list are so silent.) Significantly, however, in the last two years in Britain public interest in the voter register has been raised, but for a reason unconnected to voting. The permanent voters list has been associated with the introduction of the poll tax or community charge (now scheduled to be abolished), either as an instrument to implement the levy or as a means of verifying its implementation (Lambie 1990; *The Times* 1987). While a separate register was compiled for the community charge, the Home Office recognized the contamination that controversial policy might have on revisions to the permanent voters list. Moreover, while it sought to assure the public that the two lists were distinct, it also admitted that the electoral register was "open to the public" and that there was no "guarantee that the information [contained in it] won't be looked at by others" (United Kingdom, Home Office 1988, app. 3).

The concern that the permanent voters list may be used for purposes other than determining voter eligibility has arisen recently in Australia where the *Privacy Act 1988* was enacted to protect personal information that is collected by government departments. The AEC has a "long-established practice of supplying non-public information held in the electoral roll data base to other government departments and agencies" (AEC 1989b, 4–5). To date, there is no evidence that Australia's voter registration practices have been detrimentally affected by the *Privacy Act* or that there is a decline in public support for them. This is not to say that Australians are well acquainted with voter registration. A recent AEC survey found "widespread lack of information about the mechanics of continuous enrolment," with "less than 40 percent of respondents remember[ing] a visit from an electoral roll review officer at their home" (ibid., 10).

In none of these foreign jurisdictions does the compilation of the voters list begin with the call of the election, although in some, such as Germany, registration may continue into the electoral period. For this reason (in contrast to Canada), voter registration is not perceived to contribute to the length of the campaign in these countries. That perception is confined to Canada and explains the attraction of Britain's permanent (closed) register with the resulting shorter electoral campaigns. Unlike Canada, there is no need for a period of enumeration after the issue of the writs and, unlike Australia, there is none of the labour and expense of a permanent bureaucracy to maintain a continuous roll. But as the foregoing discussion has illustrated, convenience is purchased at the price of accuracy.

On this matter of the linkage between duration of campaigns and the registration of voters, it is relevant to note that despite its permanent list, Australia has had to extend the minimum election period. Part of this extension came about because of a JSC recommendation that the *Commonwealth Electoral Act* be amended "to provide that the Governor-General shall, by proclamation, announce the intention of dissolution and the dates proposed in connection with the election at least 7 days before the issue of the writ and therefore the closing of the rolls" (Australia, JSC 1983, 110). This proved necessary to guard against a repetition of what had happened in the general election of 1983, when the writs followed dissolution by only one day and when the *Commonwealth Electoral Act* then required the roll to close on the same day as the writs were issued. Great concern was expressed at the disenfranchisement of hundreds of thousands of voters who had failed to keep their enrolment current (Lindell 1983). It is coincidental that Australia's extension of its minimum election period should have occurred only one year after the *Canada Elections Act* was amended to reduce the minimum period to 50 days.

In conclusion, we have reservations about each of the non-Canadian systems examined in so far as they offer help to alleviate the problems and shortcomings Canada experiences with enumeration. In the United States, the registration system is too decentralized and diverse to satisfy the requirements of organizational and procedural uniformity that have come to define voter registration for Canadian national elections. There is also evidence to suggest that the turnout rates in the United States are adversely affected by the registration systems there. We would not want to see a similar drop in voter participation in Canada. For its part, the United Kingdom's permanent roll has been found wanting as it is incomplete and not current. Costs vary substantially in such a local-ized system, but are substantially higher than the cost of enumeration in Canada over a four-year cycle. Nor does Australia's system of a continuous roll commend itself to us. It is suffering from a loss of public confidence; it is heavily bureaucratic, costly by Canadian standards, and requires something akin to our enumeration to maintain its currency. For both France and Germany we lack independent evaluative studies to enable us to judge the completeness of their registration systems. Neither, however, can be recommended: the German system relies heavily on individual action combined with a measure of state involve-ment that would almost certainly not sit well with Canadian voters unaccustomed to state regulations of that sort. France, like Britain, relies on a permanent voters list. The system presumably suffers from the same problems as does the British system, and it relies on a volitional registration which, like the American system, leaves the intiative for enrolment with the individual.

ALTERNATIVES TO ENUMERATION

There are two alternatives to enumeration as it is currently conducted in Canada. In place of what is really a census of eligible voters compiled during the campaign, there is either a permanent voters list of two vari-ants or what might be called anticipatory enumeration. The permanent list is either closed yearly at a specified date without regard to the date of the next election (as in Britain or France), or is a form of continuous roll (as in Australia and British Columbia). In anticipatory enumera-tion, the compiling of the preliminary voters list is removed from the tumult of the election campaign and prepared at some pre-selected time before the writ is issued.

In light of the problems and shortcomings discussed earlier in this study, there are obvious advantages to either one of these alternative schemes of voter registration. The permanent list alleviates the need to recruit large numbers of enumerators immediately prior to the elec-tion, or at any time, since the list once constructed remains intact albeit subject to periodic amendment. Anticipatory enumeration does not remove the need for enumeration per se, but it does remove the rush once the writ is dropped, a rush both to nominate and train enumera-tors and then to compile a preliminary list. Nor does anticipatory enumeration remove the need for revision, although that can be accom-plished through a supplementary or topping-up enumeration after the election call. It is possible, of course, to have election day registration either with a permanent list or in a scheme of anticipatory enumeration.

These alternatives to enumeration remove both the task of compiling a voters list and the need to recruit an army of persons to carry it out during the heat of the election campaign. Thus, they have the potential for contributing to shorter campaigns. While the length of the campaign in Canada may be a secondary concern, it is none the less an issue that government, some academics and the chief electoral officer have commented upon negatively and that was raised relatively frequently before the Commission in connection with demands for a permanent list of electors.

Because of these attractive features, both alternatives to the present scheme of voter registration warrant closer examination. To provide comparability, the following analysis will consider how far each scheme goes in meeting the perceived shortcomings of enumeration as well as offer an assessment, to the extent possible, of the different systems' comparable costs and of their suitability as electoral procedures in a political system that is experiencing a profound change in values. This last requirement, which recognizes the determinative influence of the *Canadian Charter of Rights and Freedoms* and its enunciation of Canada as a free and democratic society, has been the source of past challenges to the *Canada Elections Act* (for instance, with regard to the exclusion of certain categories of persons such as judges as eligible voters) and, if unchanged, could lead to future challenges over the Act's discriminatory treatment of rural and urban electors in the matter of election day registration (the former but not the latter may be sworn in at the poll).

Permanent List

Enumerators are not required where a permanent voters list is used for the simple reason that under a permanent list the onus to place a name on the register is transferred from the state to the elector. It is true that in systems like those found in Great Britain and in Australia, canvassers or electoral roll review officers may be employed to verify or track down missing voters. It is also the case that in both of those countries, there is substantial evidence that if this additional stage is not incorporated into the registration process, a considerable number of eligible electors will be omitted from the list. Because Australia has a continuous system of registration that provides for a seven-day period after the announcement of the election writ during which Australians who have failed to keep their registration current may rectify errors, the Australian permanent list is more comprehensive than the British electoral register which allows no alterations to the list after the register is published on 15 February each year. In fact, the only changes that can be made in Britain after the qualifying date of 10 October are to correct erroneous information on eligible voters as of that qualifying date. Any qualifications or exceptions that may be noted, however, underline the general principle in a permanent list system – the responsibility to be registered rests with the voter. For that reason enumerators are not a necessary condition to the compilation of the list.

But even if enumerators are not necessary, does enumeration as opposed to the permanent list increase the accuracy or coverage of the list compiled? An answer based on empirical evidence is at best tentative, for as noted earlier, the completeness of the Canadian voters list is itself suspect. More than a decade ago Elections Canada made the claim that enumeration and revision produced a list that was 97 percent complete (Canada, Elections Canada 1979, 16–17), and more recently, it has cited the figure 95 percent (Canada, Elections Canada 1990b). Yet these are at best informed estimates. Comparable statistics from Australia are equally disputable, for there, as in Canada, "the citizenship criterion" among the general populace is not easily identified, while a further complication has been a short residency requirement on the part of the enrolled voter. These factors and the possibility, the AEC has said, of "differing standards of roll maintenance activity" in different parts of the country may explain the varying levels of coverage across electoral districts. In a country where both registration and voting are compulsory, anything below an 85 percent enrolment–population ratio is treated as "low" (in 1988, this occurred in seven divisions), 85 to 95 percent is treated as "below expected performance" (32 divisions), and above 95 percent is considered as "expected" (AEC 1988d, 3).

Great Britain is the other country for which there are statistics on the completeness of the electoral register. Surveys of voter registration there during the 1980s confirm a deterioration in the completeness of the register, with a national average of 6.7 percent eligible electors omitted and another 7 percent wrongly included. The rate of omission of eligible electors from the register in areas of inner London has reached as much as 17 percent of the total eligible electors (Todd and Eldridge 1987, 8). These statistics take account only indirectly of the aging of the register in a closed system of permanent registration. As noted earlier in this study, it is estimated that the British list increases in error as much as two-thirds of 1 percent every month, because of electors on the register moving (Gray and Gee 1967, 13).

Like enumeration, permanent lists, be they closed or open, must contend with mobile populations and the problem this creates for the registration of voters. How they contend is largely determined by the willingnesss of authorities to compromise on the goal of complete coverage of registered voters. While the particular references might require amendment for different countries, the nature of the choice confronting voter registration officials is captured in the following observations of the AEC: "An enrolment system for Australia must recognize the very high mobility of the population though whether that recognition takes the form of easy enrolment procedures, or accepting less [greater?] under-enrolment as inevitable, or draconian penalties for non-compliance is a matter of choice and legislative policy" (AEC 1988d, 3). Whether talking of the inner districts of London, the electoral divisions of Sydney and Melbourne or constituencies found in Toronto or Vancouver, the problem created by population mobility is similar.

In Canada, the 1981 census showed that of the 4.5 million Canadians 20–29 years of age, 73 percent had moved at least once during the previous five years. The comparable mobility figures for the 30–34, 35–44, 45–54, 55–64 and 65 and over age categories were 67, 47, 31, 27 and 26 percent respectively (Canada, Statistics Canada 1983). In terms of the demographics of the electoral system, this means simply that the younger the voter the greater the likelihood that he or she will have moved from one location to another between elections.

As is apparent from figure 8.1, nearly one-half of all Canadians 20 years of age or more (48.8 percent) in 1981 had relocated on at least one occasion in the previous five years. Of these, slightly more than one-half (52.3 percent) remained within the same census subdivision, a category Statistics Canada labels "non-migrants." Of the "migrants" 89 percent were intra-Canadian movers, with three-quarters of these being within the same province. Some rapidly growing urban areas are the scene of much greater population mobility than is true of the nation as a whole. In the Vancouver metropolitan area, as already noted, 51 percent of the *total* population five years of age and older moved at least once during the years between 1981 and 1986 (Canada, Statistics Canada 1988, 94:128). How much higher this percentage would be for young and newly eligible Canadian voters in and around Vancouver can be easily imagined.

One study of population mobility for a time period shorter than the five-year intervals of Canada's census found that 9.7 percent of all Canadians had lived at their current address for less than six months, 20.9 percent for less than one year, and 30.2 percent for less than two years.[24] These figures are basically similar to data from the United States showing that 16.6 percent of Americans of voting age had moved in a one-year period and 32.8 percent in a two-year interval (Squire et al. 1987, 48). In practical terms what an annual population mobility rate of 20.9 percent means is that 3 650 000 entries (based on the 1988 electorate of 17.6 million) would be needed every year to keep a

Figure 8.1
Mobility status of population 20 years and over, Canada 1976 and 1981

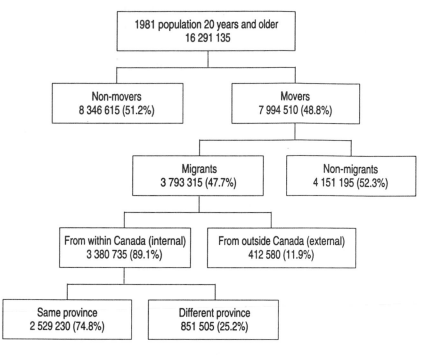

Source: Adapted from Canada, Statistics Canada 1983, table 1.

Definitions:
Non-movers are persons who, on census day, were living in the same dwelling they occupied five years earlier.

Movers are persons who, on census day, were living in a different dwelling than the one occupied five years earlier.

Non-migrants are movers who, on census day, were living within the same census subdivision they resided in five years earlier.

Migrants are movers who, on census day, were residing in a different census subdivision within Canada five years earlier (internal migrants) or who were living outside Canada five years earlier (external migrants).

Canadian permanent list abreast of address changes.

As noted, it is true generally of movements within Canada that the overwhelming majority of transfers are intraprovincial as opposed to interprovincial and that slightly better than one-half of all moves occur within the relatively compact borders of the same census subdivision. However, a move is a move, and in a system with a permanent electoral list of registered voters, every move entails at least one bookkeeping entry. The address corresponding to a name on a list has to be changed regardless of whether the individual has moved across the street or across the country.

Not only are bookkeeping entries needed for correcting altered addresses, but other demographic changes lead to regular requests for additions, deletions or alterations to be made to a permanent roll. These would include additions of citizens who came of age and of naturalized citizens; deletions of voters who died or emigrated; or alterations resulting from changes in voters' names. Based on information provided by Statistics Canada and the Department of the Secretary of State we have estimated the following number of entries would have been needed in Canada to take account of the changes in these categories in 1988:[25]

Additions of newly eligible voters	
18-year-old voters	391 200
naturalized Canadians (18+)	68 000
Removals	
deaths (18+)	182 500
emigration (18+)	30 300
Change of names (marriage or other)	200 000

The total of 872 000 entries would have amounted to one for every 20 voters at the time. Even allowing for a modest overlap in these categories (some new Canadians are 18 years of age when naturalized, for example, and at least one member of a newly married couple typically changes not only an address but often a surname as well), it is fair to assume that easily 800 000 entries would have had to have been made to a permanent electoral roll in 1988 to have taken account of demographic changes in Canada's population over the course of that year.

Because of enumeration it is not necessary in Canada to record this volume of yearly changes; they are captured immediately prior to the election when the voters list is compiled. In Australia or Germany, however, the aim of the permanent list is to record these changes as they occur (or in Britain, to record them once a year), so that at the call of an election, an up-to-date list is ready. As is evident from the earlier discussion of comparative voter registration systems, that objective may be accomplished either through the employment of existing local authorities or through the creation of a national bureaucracy whose sole purpose is to maintain the list.

In addition to assuring the availability of a list of eligible voters, permanent lists have other attractions that must be acknowledged. First, from the perspective of Canada, where from the issuing of the writs to polling day federal elections require a minimum of 50 days to complete, the short election campaigns of countries with a permanent voters list are undoubtedly attractive. In Great Britain, the same period may be as short as 21 days and, in Australia, it may vary between 33 and 58 days, although in two of the three elections of the 1980s, the campaign lasted 36 days (1987 and 1984).[26] In British Columbia, the one Canadian province to use a permanent list for any extended time, the election period is 29 days. The compilation of a voters list by enumeration need not contribute to a campaign as long as 50 days, as witnessed by the experience of some of the other Canadian provinces whose periods between the drop of the writ and polling day may be as short as 29 days (Saskatchewan) or 35 days (Manitoba).

Another associated advantage is the sharing of the list by several levels of jurisdiction, which results in some attendant savings in election administration. This occurs in Britain where the single list is used annually in local elections and, less frequently, in European parliamentary elections, as well as in national parliamentary elections. In Australia, the national register, or roll, is shared by the federal and four state governments; in addition, the Australian list is used for the conduct of referendums. Similarly, lists compiled by local authorities in Germany and France are used in elections at each of those countries' respective levels of government. Indeed, because of its perceived completeness and finality, the permanent list in all of these countries assumes an authority that is not duplicated in Canada, where the voters list is treated as a momentary encapsulation of the electorate.

It is the continuing authority of the permanent list that endows it with an attraction for uses other than elections. In Britain, as noted earlier in this study, the permanent voters list has been associated recently with the introduction of the poll tax or community charge. There are, admittedly, practical reasons for this particular association, since local authorities are responsible for the administration in each instance. Yet the fact that it has been associated with a non-electoral purpose is relevant to this discussion. It raises the question of the uses to which such a list would be put in Canada and, more directly, the issue of privacy, which has also been raised in Australia. Depending on the sources of data used to construct the list (tax or social insurance records as opposed to self-registration), a permanent voters list can be expected to elicit similar unease in Canada. Nor is the alternative use of a permanent Canadian voters list only speculation: at hearings or in material presented to the Royal Commission, it has been suggested that the list could be used to verify the eligibility of party members to vote for candidates and, presumably, delegates to conventions (Guarnieri 1990; Carty 1990, 12–13).

The sharing of a common voters list by federal, provincial and municipal authorities would be convenient for voters, political parties and election officials. For voters, it would remove the confusion that results from the possibility of being enumerated two or three times within the space of a few months. In 1988, a number of eligible electors who were omitted from the federal voters list failed to use the revision process because they believed that their names were already on the list, having been recently enumerated by their province or municipality. For example, on 22 November, the *Calgary Herald* reported that in Alberta "the principal reason for confusion was September's provincial enumeration, which ended just days before the October 14 start of the federal enumeration. There were countless incidents of eligible federal voters ignoring the federal enumeration because they thought the earlier enumeration covered the federal vote." For political parties and candidates at all levels, access to a permanent voters list would mean they could start canvassing before the call of an election. Finally, from the perspective of governments and their election officials, the advantage of a permanent voters list would lie in the presumed economy to be achieved through the reduced costs of a single compilation.

Practical difficulties must be overcome before the benefits of a shared permanent list can be realized, however. These have to do with questions of agreement – on eligibility criteria for all voters (for example, age, residence requirements), on electoral boundaries of constituencies, on information to be included on the list and on the distribution of the list itself. Every permanent list provides for updating, and unless that updating is to be totally dependent upon the voluntary action of the voter, the cost associated with revision (and the benefits derived from it) will have to be shared. Yet a permanent list will be more accurate (and, therefore, more useful for electoral purposes) to one or another level of government the closer the date of revision is to that government's election call. Thus, as Richard Balasko, then acting chief electoral officer for Manitoba, has said: "The timing of the major update of the list would ... have to take account of the likelihood of elections at the several levels of jurisdiction sharing the list" (Balasko 1990, 20). In short, a single permanent voters list applied to Canada's several levels of government would require on the part of all governments a commitment to long-term cooperation. Agreement on standards would only be the first (satisfying) condition; agreement on maintaining those standards would be the second (necessary) one.

The question of who will be ultimately responsible for the list must be resolved. Those who advocate a permanent voters list for Canada, one that would be shared by other jurisdictions, are silent on this matter but their silence implies that for reasons of efficiency that responsibility would rest with federal government officials. This is the experience of Australia. Yet it is not invariably the case, for in Germany, France and Great Britain, local authorities exert a determinative control over the maintenance of the list. As the historical section on Canada's electoral system notes elsewhere in this study, there is precedent for the provinces having control of national voter registration. In theory and in practice there is no obvious impediment to the provinces exercising this responsibility again. In electoral law Canada has borrowed relatively little from the experience of the United States. If control of a permanent list were to be located in the provinces, however, Canada would move much closer to the American model and that, in our view, is problematic. It could lead to surrender of the federal list as well as to differing standards and approaches to list-making. In short, it could undermine central control of Canada's election registration system. American experience suggests that too much decentralization is not a good thing.

The permanent voters list is difficult to evaluate from the perspective of cost. In countries like Britain, Germany or France, the system of voter registration is decentralized among local authorities. The officials who are assigned the job of maintaining the lists are responsible for other local government tasks throughout the year. Moreover, the list is used on various occasions for different elections. In Britain, as well as, presumably, these other European countries, there appears to be little consensus among local authorities about how to allocate costs to these different functions. The result is that such cost figures as appear are incomplete and offer little guidance to those attempting to evaluate the permanent list system. The Pinto-Duschinskys reported that in Great Britain "the overall [annual] cost of registration in 1985 averaged £40 000 per constituency" (1987, 8), while officials in D Division of the Home Office suggested in a telephone conversation with the authors of this study that there is no single answer to the question, since costs vary enormously among districts, with registration in a central district such as Westminster costing close to £200 000 to complete.

Australia, the one country that this study examines (other than Canada) that operates its voter registration from a central headquarters, although through a network of permanent offices nationwide, reported total outlays for roll maintenance for the year ending 30 June 1989 at Aust.$27 206 000. The division of these costs was among salaries ($13.2 million), administration ($1.2 million), enrolment expenses ($7.6 million) and electoral roll review ($6.7 million) (AEC 1990, 46). In 1989–90, a period that encompassed a national election, enrolment expenditures totalled $8 991 000 (ibid.). With an electorate on 30 June 1989 of 10 741 668, the cost per elector to maintain the list was

$0.84. If the financial data for 1988–89 are used, a period that included roll review, the total cost was $14 367 000 – for an electorate of 10 300 798 persons, as of 30 June 1988 – or $1.39 per elector.

By comparison, in 1988 the cost of Canada's federal enumeration and revision, a figure that included travel but not printing expenses, was $27 791 142. The enumerated electorate, including Canadian Forces and public service voters but excluding those sworn in on election day in rural polls, totalled 17 639 001. The per-voter cost in 1988 was therefore $1.58. Cost comparisons between countries and political systems as distinct as those of Canada and Australia must be treated with caution, as a study by Canada's Representation Commissioner demonstrated more than two decades ago (Canada, Representation Commissioner 1968, 54–56), but these statistics do suggest the nature of the contrast between a system that enumerates perhaps once every four years and one that maintains a continuous register and therefore needs continuous expenditures to maintain the electoral roll.

The final question to raise about the permanent list, because it has assumed greater importance in Canadian life since the early 1980s, is the contribution that system of voter registration makes to the promotion of a free and democratic political system. As several Canadian political scientists have noted, Canada is increasingly identified by the public and by academics as a "Charterland" (for example, Cairns 1989), a truth borne out by the 1988 challenges brought under the Charter to exclusionary sections of the *Canada Elections Act*. Is a permanent voters list sympathetic in its operation to this revolution in Canadian values? The systems studied in this report occasion doubt. Consider, for instance, the following limitations on the freedom to register: closure of the lists, perhaps months in advance of polling day (Great Britain); the variation seen among local authorities in the conduct of revisions to the register (Great Britain, France, Australia); compulsory registration (Australia); the use of a national identity card (Germany); and the array of registration requirements among the states for the exercise of the franchise for national elections (United States). To what extent do such requirements encourage or discourage voter turnout, invade privacy, create obstacles for particular categories of voters such as the homeless or the illiterate? Whatever the rationale for these practices – efficiency, protection against fraud – they, and other features of permanent lists, appear to conflict with growing evidence of a desire in Canada for elections that promote a free and democratic system. As our earlier discussion on the problems and shortcomings of enumeration has demonstrated, Canadian voting registration practices and policies are not immune to criticisms but it is doubtful whether adoption of a permanent voters list would improve the conditions that contribute to a free and democratic system.

Anticipatory Enumeration

In evidence before the Royal Commission several interveners advocated what might be called an anticipatory or head-start enumeration. In other words, they wished to see the labour of compiling a voters list through enumeration separated from the "rush once the writ is dropped," when there is "insufficient time for recruitment and training of enumerators, and for actual enumeration."[27] Most proposals for an anticipatory enumeration called for a supplementary enumeration to occur after the election call, although some advocates referred only to "revisions" after the issuance of the writ. Whether those revisions were to be made as a consequence of the initiative of the voter or in response to some reminder by those officials responsible for compiling the voters list was ambiguous in several of the presentations.

In the context of this study, the value of anticipatory, or pre-writ enumeration must be gauged by the degree to which it is deemed to overcome the problems and shortcomings of "post-writ" enumeration. Unlike the different permanent lists examined earlier, such a system requires enumeration, it thus touches directly on the problem of finding enumerators that is encountered by the Canadian system. Yet it is different from the Canadian system because of the fixed timetable set down for enumeration.

When enumeration is linked to the issuance of the writ, the planning and organization that it requires turn on a crucial "unknown" – the date on which enumeration is to begin. With anticipatory enumeration, planning and organization are part of a fixed timetable; those in charge can recruit in advance, plan the training of enumerators and have all the supplies ready. As the *Canada Elections Act* currently stands, the CEO and his or her staff are hostages to fortune as regards timing. As seen earlier in our study, where the government calls a summer election – as it did in 1984 – additional problems can be created in finding and training enumerators. One advantage of a regularized enumeration period that is separate from the election campaign is that those in charge of voter registration need not compete with the political parties for personnel; it is frequently said that parties do not want to nominate their best people as enumerators because it robs them of an important resource in the election campaign. Instead, ROs can build up lists of enumerators with whom they can maintain regular contact, even where the constituency associations formally nominate individuals to act as enumerators. Thus, predictability of the event on the one hand leads to improved competence and experience of personnel on the other hand.

In our earlier discussion of the accuracy and coverage of enumeration in national elections, it was found that in addition to omissions from the list of eligible electors because of careless enumeration, voter registration in Canada falters when it comes to registering groups that are particularly hard to reach such as the disadvantaged (the homeless, the illiterate and the disabled), and the seasonally transient (vacationers, native peoples who spend part of each year on the land away from their dwelling place and students, who spend part of the year in academic institutions). For the first category, problems of registration remain, but anticipatory enumeration allows more time and opportunity than at present to make the personal contact that enumeration has the potential to permit, while for the second category, anticipatory enumeration can reduce the problem of the absentee eligible elector if it is carried out at a scheduled time, preferably outside of the summer and winter months when voters are most likely to be absent.

It must be admitted that in Alberta, the one jurisdiction studied where the voter registration system is based on regularly scheduled enumeration, it is possible for qualified electors to avoid enumeration (that is, fail to have their names on the voters list) and still vote on election day. This provision together with the fact that no record is kept of the number of changes, additions or deletions required to be made to the list at the time of the provincial election means that in the one jurisdiction where anticipatory enumeration occurs, it is difficult to ascertain the accuracy of the voters list when the election is called. It can be said, however, that over 79 000 more names appeared on the Alberta voters list on election day (5 percent of the total electorate) than at the close of the enumeration period in October 1988.

A single enumeration between elections raises an additional concern about the accuracy and completeness of the list generated. This is especially the case in a province like Alberta which in the last decade and a half has experienced rapid and substantial migrations of population, first into the province as a result of economic prosperity and then out of the province when the economy slumped. (In 1984, for the first time in its history and notwithstanding the depressions and drought of the 1930s, Alberta's population suffered a small but absolute decline.) Since it is exactly movements of this kind, especially in metropolitan areas, that have placed pressure on the conduct of federal enumerations and contributed to the problems documented by returning officers and members of the public alike, it is difficult to see how a system of anticipatory enumeration, at least as it operates in Alberta, would satisfy critics of federal enumeration procedure.

Yet criticism of anticipatory enumeration is not heard in Alberta. The Alberta Elections Office reports that most of the calls it receives from the public deal with factual inquiries such as where to vote and how to get on the list. These are the same kind of questions that the Australian Electoral Commission receives from citizens concerned about their enrolment status. In short, people everywhere demonstrate little knowledge or awareness of voting registration procedures. Few actual complaints occur in Alberta over registration practices, largely because voting day registration allows omissions to be rectified if the voter so desires.

On the matter of public perception, it is worth noting that experience at the federal level with a de facto anticipatory enumeration in 1980 also produced very few complaints.

Since the 1980 election was called only nine months after the 1979 election, the chief electoral officer dispensed with the usual door-to-door enumeration and used the official lists from the 1979 election as the preliminary lists. Revision was started right away. A card was mailed to all names on the 1979 official list. The number of revising agents was increased, the period of revision was extended from the usual 7 to 19 days, and the revising agents went door to door in all newly developed areas. The sittings for revision were held for nine days rather than the traditional three.

To prevent double registrations, a special form was prepared to be completed by all those who applied to be added to the list. This allowed the elector's name to be struck off the list for the polling division in which she or he had previously lived.

An information program that cost in excess of $3 million was launched on television, in the press and on radio. The information was placed in all Canadian dailies, most community weekly newspapers and in key ethnic newspapers. This information program consisted of three stages: an invitation for all electors to ensure their names were on the list; information on advance polls, their dates and conditions to vote thereat, and on transfer certificates for the handicapped; and a reminder on the date and hours of polling day and of the right to four consecutive hours off work to vote. This information program was combined with a program to inform the media of election procedures. Elections Canada estimates that the information program cost $0.25 per elector.

In 1980, 656 126 electors were added to the list during revision. This constituted 4.1 percent of the total electorate (in 1984 and 1988, the percentage of names added through revision was 3.1 and 2.2

respectively). The cost of registration in 1980 totalled $9.4 million compared to $23.7 million in 1984 and $27.7 million in 1988. The experience of 1980 was the only deviation from the registration process set down in 1938. Yet, despite the fact there was no enumeration, fewer complaints were heard about omissions and mistakes than in 1979. Anticipatory enumeration seemed to work well even though the degree of accuracy of the 1980 lists remains an open question. This is because the list was not purged of electors who had died or who had moved after the 1979 election but whose names were not struck from the voters list for their old address. It must be recalled, however, that the 1980 election followed the 1979 election by a space of less than nine months. This is not the average length of a Parliament (the next two elections of the 1980s came at four-year intervals). Thus, the relative ease in 1980 of capturing changes in the voters list through an augmented revision period is unlikely to be duplicated in the normal rhythm of parliamentary elections.

Anticipatory enumeration facilitates shorter election campaigns since the bulk of the voters list is already compiled at the time the writ is issued. Alberta does not have the shortest possible campaign among Canadian jurisdictions, but it is among the provinces with the shortest possible period. There are, of course, reasons other than registration for a campaign. But there seems little doubt that if a reduced campaign period is the object desired, then anticipatory enumeration, or a permanent voters list, is preferable to the current system in effect for registering Canada's voters.

In conclusion, both the permanent voters list and anticipatory enumeration provide alternatives that would rectify some of the problems and shortcomings of enumeration. In turn, each system would create new problems or uncertainties in place of the old. Because it has been implemented at a subnational level only, anticipatory enumeration raises a number of questions about its adaptability to a larger, more heterogeneous political unit. The contrast between it and Canada's current enumeration system would seem to lie as much as anything else in the availability of election day registration in the unit where it is practised (Alberta), and in the absence of that provision in federal elections for Canada's urban voters. More liberalized revision practices are one subject to be considered in the final portion of this study on options for reform.

OPTIONS FOR REFORM

We noted in the first section of this study that a voter registration system that is universally accessible, protective of the interests of both the individual and the public, and widely perceived as fair and reasonable is one of the essentials of a free and democratic society. It follows that to be accepted as legitimate, the procedures adopted by a democratic state to produce its lists of voters must themselves be known to be open, fair and free from abuse. So far as we have been able to determine, the record suggests that the system followed in Canada at the federal level since 1938 to enumerate voters and to revise lists has been without major instance of public or private wilful abuse. Fraudulent activity may from time to time have marked other aspects of Canadian politics, but so far it seems not to have become a factor of any significance in registering voters. With respect to the current system's accessibility and fairness, however, it is clear that certain problems do exist and that they will have to be addressed. We will return to that point later in this section.

Our reading of the experience of other countries, of other provinces and territories, and of Canada's federal experience with door-to-door enumeration held at the time of an election, leads us to believe that the Canadian enumeration and revision system is worth preserving in its general form. The figures we have presented with respect both to the accuracy of the electoral population and operational costs demonstrate to our satisfaction that Canada's post-1938 enumeration and revision system is preferable to alternative forms of voter registration. A system that places the onus for registration on the state rather than on the citizen and that is coupled with door-to-door enumeration serves as a personal reminder by the community of the positive value that it places on electoral participation by its citizens. The approach of a pending election is heralded through human contact. Voter registration, like other instruments of government, reflects the values of distinct cultures and draws on unique histories. This helps to explain why it is likely, in our view, that, barring a recognized need for a truly major overhaul, Canada's enumeration and revision system would be as unacceptable to other Western, liberal democratic states as we believe theirs would be to Canada.

Compared to the other registration processes we examined, Canada's system has a greater potential for satisfying one procedural condition that we regard as critical to the legitimacy of a voter registration system. Enumeration possesses the potential for incorporating those with special needs into the eligible electorate. These include electors in hospitals and prisons, those with physical or mental disabilities, and the homeless, the poor and the illiterate. For such people, a system that depends upon self-registration may well have a repressive effect on their willingness or capacity to be included on the list of electors. The Royal Commission on Electoral Reform and Party Financing was reminded of this by the National Anti-Poverty Organization. In their brief "Poor People and the Federal Electoral System: Barriers to Participation" they argued that "any system that shifts, even marginally, the responsibility for voter registration from the state to the elector will have a discriminatory impact on lower income Canadians" (National Anti-Poverty 1990, 6).

The point is worth careful consideration. It is clear that some identifiable classes or groups of otherwise qualified electors are more likely than others to be omitted from the voters list. As a general statement, it can be said that these are persons whose living arrangements are such as to elude the observation of enumerators in their prescribed house-to-house visitation. It should be emphasized that this discussion concerns enumeration per se, not the casting of the ballot: these are distinct actions. While the arguments on behalf of introducing mail-in ballots or mobile voting boxes may be substantial and convincing as an improved means of reaching those Canadians who are otherwise qualified to vote but whose style or condition of life prevents them from exercising their franchise, they are none the less separate arguments from those concerned with improving the enumeration process.

Some electors are missed by enumerators because the location of their residence is not accessible or known to the enumerators or because the times of the visits are not convenient. Persons in shelters or hostels fall into this difficult-to-enumerate category because, as the brief of the National Anti-Poverty Organization has noted, the visiting hours set down in the *Canada Elections Act* coincide with the times "when many hostels and shelters require that the residents leave." Or, again, the Act explicitly excludes from enumeration anyone who has not been "in continuous residence in such lodgings ... for at least ten days immediately preceding the enumeration date." Yet, as the National Anti-Poverty Organization brief observes, "many shelters and hostels do not permit continuous residence for ten-day periods." More fundamental still is the Act's assumption that only those electors with a "house" are eligible for inclusion. By definition, the homeless are excluded.

It would be idle to claim that Canada's system of enumeration does not omit some of the sick, the disabled or the poor from its voters lists. But there is no evidence, or even indictment, that the current process discriminates in any systematic or intentional way against the socially disadvantaged. By contrast, the concern exists, at least for the National Anti-Poverty Organization, that proposals to introduce "a permanent voters list should be carefully examined for their potential impacts upon marginalized and low-income electors." Arguably, enumeration is sufficiently adaptable that its processes can be altered to target specific "marginalized" groups, exactly the type of potential voter which in the new era of the Charter Canadian politicians and the public indicate they want to see incorporated into the political system. The advantages of a voter registration system that does not require citizens in these categories to take the initiative to register to vote are self-evident.

The personal contact between the enumerator and the voter that lies at its base overcomes many of the obstacles inherent in a system of self-registration that depends upon the voter's initiative, commitment and knowledge to keep it current and complete. The omission of any eligible elector from a voters list is undesirable but the omission of distinct and, in all likelihood, already disadvantaged classes of voters because of the registration process is even less tolerable. In his last statutory Report (Canada, Elections Canada 1989b), Canada's former chief electoral officer spoke of some citizens being statutorily disfranchised: those in prisons or those with mental disorders. A system of registration that reversed the onus for getting on the list, by placing it on the elector would consequently, in our opinion, swell the ranks of the disfranchised. Evidence on voter registration in a country such as the United States, where responsibility rests in the first instance with the self-motivation of the voter, indicates that it is the disadvantaged who are most likely not to be registered.

We believe that the strengths of enumeration are sufficiently compelling to warrant reform of Canada's system of voter registration rather than adoption of either a permanent list or what we have referred to here as anticipatory enumeration. Conversely, while variants of these alternatives to enumeration might remedy some of the difficulties experienced with a system of voter registration conducted after the call of an election, in our view they would create more problems than they would solve. The remedy would be worse than the disease that it seeks to cure.

The present enumeration system is more current and more complete in terms of the proportion of eligible voters that it captures than any other system studied, with the possible exception of Germany, and for the very reason that it is compiled immediately before an election through a door-to-door canvass. Enumeration meets these benchmarks because revisions to the voters list are made closer to polling day in Canada than in any other country studied and because, unlike any version of a permanent list, enumeration does not have to deal with the problem of culling the list, that is, weeding out the ineligible voters. Critics of enumeration invariably view the compilation of the voters list from the perspective of inclusion rather than exclusion; yet an accurate list is as much a product of the deletions made to it as it is of the additions. In Australia, the majority of the hundreds of thousands of transactions that regularly occur before a general election are corrections and transfers; this is an activity foreign to the Canadian context because the list is compiled anew at each election.

If as we have argued one of the strengths of enumeration lies in the personal contact made between enumerator and elector and the immediacy between that contact and the general election, that too is where its weakness lies. The heart of the dilemma in making enumeration work well is to find an army of competent persons to do the job in an inordinately short span of time. A related problem is that no matter how short that period, it none the less extends the length of the election campaign (currently a minimum of 50 days, a duration some find unacceptable). Thus, enumeration is subjected to opposing pressures: the need to conduct a more thorough canvass of the electorate but within a shorter election campaign period than is currently the case. The imperatives arising from the first pressure are to preserve or even extend the time devoted to enumeration; those from the second are to reduce the time that enumeration requires to the point even of abolishing it altogether or removing it from the election period proper.

Since we are of the opinion that enumeration is worth preserving, but since we also recognize the constraints under which it currently operates, we propose the following five recommendations to improve the current system.

Personnel

Our study has confirmed the problem of finding qualified enumerators. Since the strength of enumeration rests on the quality of the contact made between the enumerator and the voter, the matter of suitable personnel is crucial to the integrity of Canada's voter registration system. The selection of enumerators rests in the first instance with the political parties and, currently, the parties too often fail to nominate promptly a sufficient number of adequate persons for the job. As long as the present practice obtains, the returning officers are in a difficult if not impossible position, since they cannot meet their responsibility of seeing that enumeration is satisfactorily carried out. For that reason we believe that there is every reason to abandon the exclusive reliance upon partisan nominations for enumerators and to introduce open competition under the supervision of the local returning officers. Advertisements calling for applications from qualified individuals should be permitted and encouraged, and the returning officer should be granted the power to hire as appropriate to his or her needs. Political parties would not, of course, be denied the opportunity of proposing names. That should continue. It is simply that they should no longer enjoy the exclusive right to do so.

We concur with Bill C-79 that the residency and age restrictions placed on the selection of enumerators should be removed. Where it is necessary and desirable, returning officers should be able to go outside their constituency to find qualified persons. Such a reform would not only expand the pool of eligible enumerators in general but it would, along with ending exclusively partisan nominations, allow returning officers to seek out as enumerators individuals with particular skills and aptitudes. Examples of the latter would be those with a knowledge of languages other than English or French (a desirable ability in reaching the hundreds of thousands of naturalized Canadians who do not speak either of Canada's official languages) and those who have experience with such hard-to-enumerate groups as the homeless, the illiterate and the hearing disabled. Similarly, we recommend that the eligible age for enumerators be reduced to include 16- and 17-year-olds. We see no reason why these young people cannot (and should not) be involved in the crucially important step of registering fellow citizens. Of course, we realize that most of these persons will be in school and that the timing of an election during the academic term might prevent their full-time participation in enumeration. But there is no reason why returning officers should be prohibited from considering as eligible 16- and 17-year-olds because of their age.

Granting returning officers the authority to hire 16- and 17-year-olds as enumerators and to go outside their own constituency to find persons to act as enumerators makes sense. The lower age limit should pose no problem to the credibility of the enumeration system given the tasks to be performed; indeed it may actually enhance it if the proper training and encouragement of young, responsible and civic-minded enumerators takes place. It would add 800 000 potential individuals to the pool from which enumerators could be drawn, and it is appealing given the proven willingness of teenagers to take on part-time work. The freedom to hire as enumerators individuals who live outside a riding simply recognizes a sociological fact of life, particularly in large, cosmopolitan, mobile urban areas where facility in a language other than French or English may often be the paramount consideration in choosing individuals to work in certain polling districts. Artificial boundaries such as constituency limits should not impede the returning officers' options to hire persons appropriate to the job wherever they may be found.

At the last general election approximately 88 000 enumerators were required. Since the majority of polls are urban polls, where two enumerators are to be appointed, it appears to us that some economy in personnel could be achieved if the requirement for enumerators to work as a team were abolished and returning officers were granted the discretion to determine the number required for each urban poll. In some instances a single enumerator might be sufficient. A majority of the provinces and territories have such a provision, apparently without difficulty. The *Canada Elections Act* cannot anticipate the number of enumerators required for constituencies of varied size and social heterogeneity but the returning officer is in a position to do so. By the same token, there may be good reasons to appoint a second enumerator in those rural polls where rapid in-migration of exurbanites has changed the settled quality of the area. In such instances the returning officer appears to us best positioned to decide what number of enumerators should be sent into the field.

A final suggestion for increasing the personnel pool would be to remove the financial disincentive that currently discourages individuals who are beneficiaries of income security or unemployment insurance payments from agreeing to assume the job, and to establish a more generous payment schedule by adding a base rate to the existing per name fee. As matters now stand, persons who agree to serve as enumerators and who receive income security or unemployment insurance cheques run the risk either of having their benefits cut or of jeopardizing their payment. We believe voter registration offers a unique opportunity for the average citizen, young through old, to serve his or her country regardless of income or its source. We also believe that a number of social assistance and unemployment insurance recipients would welcome the opportunity to serve as enumerators. Accordingly, we urge the removal of the financial penalties (some of which may fall within provincial jurisdiction) now discouraging the participation of recipients of social assistance. We are of the view as well that federal enumerators should receive a base rate for their work, as is the case with the provinces, which together with a per name rate should make the task more financially attractive.

Matters of Time

Extending Revision

As noted at several points in this study, one of the most frequent sources of complaint about the conduct of elections in Canada is the perceived difficulty of eligible voters omitted from the preliminary voters list in getting on the final list. The relevant provisions of the *Canada Elections Act* are not unduly harsh compared with electoral registration schemes in other countries. (Indeed, we have found Canada more open to make late changes to its list than any of the other national systems with which we compared it.) But there is a perception of hardship and, despite widely differing claims about the numbers of persons affected, we are satisfied that that has been the reality for some Canadian electors. There is also the fact that the federal rules governing revision are less generous than those in the majority of the provinces. Assuming that federal elections continue to be held on Mondays (or even if moved to Sunday, as some persons before the Commission have suggested), we recommend that the period of revision be extended for urban voters to 9:00 PM on the Friday preceding polling day.[28] We also recommend that the same revision period apply to rural voters and that they no longer be eligible to be vouched for on election day at the poll. This change, we realize, would remove the current right of rural voters to be sworn in at the polls. None the less, in an era when equality of treatment is invoked on numerous issues, there is no justification for the Act's current discriminatory provisions as regards election day registration.

It could be argued, of course, that election day registration privileges should be extended to both urban and rural voters, but we do not support this suggestion. It could lead to delay and confusion at the polls, thus detracting from a familiar procedure that in the past has been both simple and quick. (British Columbia's experience in 1986 would seem to support the concern.) Even if it did not, however, we are convinced that it is organizationally desirable to have a two-day break (from Friday evening until Monday morning) between the closing of the lists of electors and the opening of the polls. Not only does this break offer the returning officer and other local election officials the opportunity to pause at the end of one stage and to prepare for the next, it also helps to distinguish what in our view are two important, but separate, acts: registration and voting. The second depends upon the first having been satisfactorily completed. With a revision period extended from the current 17 to our proposed three days before the election, and with adequate notice of the times and ways that an unenumerated voter may get his or her name on the list, in our view sufficient opportunities would clearly exist for all who wish to get on the list to do so.

The experience of Manitoba, the only province with an enumeration system with a record of election day registration in all urban and rural polls, might be cited as evidence against our recommendations. In 1988, 4 percent of the total number of electors were added to the list when they went to vote on election day. In 1990, following a late summer enumeration and revision, the figure was 4.7 percent. If between

4 and 5 percent of the electorate could be added to the lists on election day, why not support election day registration? The answer, it seems to us, lies in our previous recommendation for a substantial expansion of the revision period and for divorcing registration from the election itself. Manitoba, like Canada, currently stops its revision at Day 17 before the election; it allows, in fact, only two days (18 and 17 of the election calendar) for revision, compared with Canada's three. In our opinion, making it possible for electors to get their names on the list from the beginning of the enumeration period (currently Day 38 of the election timetable) up to the close of Day 3 (with a 10-day break between enumeration and revision) will provide ample opportunity for those in the federal jurisdiction who intend to vote. The 1988 and 1990 Manitoba figures would in our view have been substantially lower if the province had had a longer revision period and had allowed revision days closer to the election. As we have noted earlier in our study, the level of interest in an election increases as the polling day draws near. By designing the revision timetable to capture those electors whose interest in, and knowledge of, the election comes late in the campaign (say following a televised debate among party leaders well into the campaign), procedures would be in place to enable them to get on the list should they previously have been missed.

Shortening Campaigns

As we have noted, Canada has its share of critics of long election campaigns. They fault the enumeration process for its part in making campaigns longer than they would wish. For such critics, the lightning speed of Britain's three-week elections (which, as we have pointed out, is due to a permanent voters list subject neither to challenge nor change) apparently holds some attraction. We see no reason to keep the minimum campaign period at its present 50 days if ways could be found to shorten it. It is our distinct impression based on interviews with senior members of Elections Canada's staff that they have some very positive suggestions for cutting back the minimum period to approximately 42 or 43 days while still maintaining a door-to-door enumeration. We recommend a 43-day minimum. A country as geographically large and as socially diverse as Canada needs a sufficient period of campaign time to assess the parties, candidates, leaders and policies and to weigh the alternatives. In our view, six weeks is appropriate to that task.

If improvements of that order could be introduced then clearly one of the concerns of critics of the current timetable would be addressed. It might not be to the satisfaction of all, but it would be an improvement over the present situation. To reduce Canadian campaigns to a minimum of 43 days would be to make them only 10 days longer than the minimum period provided for in Australia, which has a continuous electoral roll. Yet if Elections Canada is correct, Canada could still produce a voters list as accurate as, or more accurate than, that of Australia, and do it without the need to maintain a continuing bureaucracy of over 1 000 persons (based on Australia's experience of 3.5 officials per electoral district).

While discussing Australia and the length of election campaigns it should be said that that country sets a maximum (58 days) as well as a minimum length. Canada, as already noted, has no statutory maximum period for a campaign; the length of the campaign is the prerogative of the government. As long as there is no statutory maximum, debate over reducing the length of the campaign through reform of the enumeration system is somewhat academic.

Returning Officers' Enumeration and Revision Responsibilities

We have concluded that the enumeration and revision responsibilities of returning officers need to be more clearly defined. This was anticipated in 1986 by the White Paper on Electoral Reform and in 1987 by Bill C-79. The section of the *Canada Elections Act* concerning the "Preparation of Lists of Electors" would have been replaced by that legislation. The effect of the new section would have been to state in more explicit terms the responsibilities of the returning officer "for supervising and overseeing the preparation of the list[s] of electors" and "for ensuring that as far as possible every qualified elector ... will be enumerated." Bill C-79 would have been an improvement in this respect. In so far as the revision of lists is concerned, this is a responsibility that the present Act does not delegate to the returning officer. In urban polls, revision of lists is a statutory responsibility of the courts, although in practice many judges delegate revision almost completely to the returning officers. In rural polls, it is the enumerator who serves as the revising agent and the courts are not involved. We suggest treating urban and rural revision of lists equally and specifically delegating that responsibility to the returning officer.

In general it is our view that the returning officers should be given greater authority and discretion to carry out their responsibilities for enumeration. It might be noted as well that rural enumerators under Bill C-79 would have been required to conduct house-to-house enumerations, in contrast to the existing system that permits them total discretion as to how rural lists are compiled. We agree with that proposal. Its effect would be to put rural and urban enumerations on an equal footing and to enhance the reliability of the rural lists.

Bill C-79 also proposed extending the vote to Canadians residing outside Canada. We recommend such a change to ensure the right to vote to Canadian citizens who have resided outside the country for no more than five consecutive years. It would become the chief electoral officer's responsibility to construct and to maintain a voter registry of eligible Canadians who might cast absentee ballots. This strikes us as the most reasonable way of carrying out the registration process. To devolve that obligation onto the returning officer at the constituency level would be to invite differing interpretations of eligibility and to add a potentially time-consuming (though not always a numerically large) burden to those already heavily involved in the local electoral administrative process. Our proposals simply build on the experience of Elections Canada with the lists of Special Voting Rules electors abroad (diplomatic and military personnel and their dependants).

Relaxed Enfranchisement Rules and Enumeration Procedures

Canadians have demonstrated the capacity to give a humane character to their election administration. Electors who are hospitalized in chronic institutions, who are handicapped or who are in veterans' or nursing homes, for instance, are to be enumerated and are assured the right to vote. But more can be done for groups or individuals overlooked in the process. Elsewhere in this report we have noted the impact of the *Canadian Charter of Rights and Freedoms* on Canada's election law. Several of the cases before the courts at the time of the federal election in 1988 would not have been launched had Bill C-79 been approved by Parliament. The denial of the right to vote to federally appointed judges and to the mentally disabled would have been removed by Bill C-79, and certain categories of prison inmates would have been enfranchised. As well, as we have just noted, Canadian citizens living abroad, apart from those already enfranchised in the ranks of the military and the diplomatic corps, would have become eligible to vote. The 1988 court cases demonstrated that challenges under the Charter to the categories of disqualified voters contained in the *Canada Elections Act* have a good chance of succeeding. That may well prove to be true also of challenges launched by non-resident Canadians who invoke section 3 of the Charter, for its characterization of "democratic rights" restricts the franchise according to citizenship, rather than place of residence. The relevance of such an observation comes from the administrative difficulties that a successful challenge by non-residents would present to election officials in the course of an election campaign. In our view, the solution would be to head off such a challenge by accepting the principle that non-resident Canadians be granted the right to vote and that the chief electoral officer maintain the registry. Some aspects of the enumeration and revising processes should be brought more in line with a Charter-aware electorate. As proposed in Bill C-79, for example, enumerators should be obliged to inquire about and make note of any elector's requirement for level access to the poll on election day and revising agents should be available for a further five days to respond to requests of electors to have their names added to, corrected on or deleted from the preliminary list of electors.

Other identifiable groups of persons whose lifestyle may affect detrimentally their opportunity to be enumerated are native people, a number of whom move between town, reserve and remote areas in the course of a single year, and the homeless. For many of these people, making it on to a voters list becomes a matter of chance. For status Indians, one possible reform that we recommend would be to allow enumerators to check a band council's lists for names and locations of its members. This proposal, which was first made before the Commission by a former candidate of native origin, would be a supplementary procedure and would not replace the normal enumeration procedures. We also recommend allowing these same electors to register for proxy voting ahead of an election and to make that proxy valid for the period when they would be absent from their residence in a larger centre. For itinerant native persons, for homeless persons and for others who may lack a permanent address we recommend that the *Canada Elections Act* be changed to allow them to list as their address that of the office of the returning officer in the constituency in which they would vote. For those who reside, from time to time, in shelters or hostels or other quarters provided temporarily for homeless persons, we suggest that, if appropriate to the individuals' circumstances, the address of such a building would suffice for the purposes of enumeration and revision.

Modern Technologies

As early as the 1968 Castonguay Report federal election officials were urging greater use of computers and electronic equipment to prepare lists of electors (Canada, Representation Commissioner 1968). Given the advances in computer technology since that time, surprisingly little has been done to make computers part of the enumeration and revision processes.

Facsimile transmission of election documents, for example, was not legally permitted as recently as 1988. In 1986 Elections Canada contracted with a firm of computer consultants to identify and develop over 30 election-related systems and to select the appropriate hardware to carry these systems. Terminals were subsequently installed at

Elections Canada headquarters, but despite this in the 1988 election it was unusual for computers or word processing to be found in the offices of returning officers.

The *Canada Elections Act* still technically requires enumerators to prepare either a handwritten or a typed list of electors. For those returning officers (67 in all) who in 1988 none the less used data-processing firms to computerize their lists, there was no common software available from Elections Canada. Each firm had to prepare its own software. It is our view that the provisions of the Act pertaining to the preparation of preliminary and official lists should be fundamentally rewritten to permit the fullest possible use of advanced technologies and that appropriate operational and managerial support should be made available to local election officials to ensure a transition to computer technology that is as rapid as possible. Elections Canada clearly intends to move in that direction, and, as of early 1991, has written to all returning officers to inform them of the steps being taken to automate the preparation of lists of electors and the addressing of notices of enumeration in all electoral districts. This has prompted an overwhelmingly favourable response from returning officers. They were found to be very receptive to the idea of using computer technology, welcoming the change in large part as a way of ensuring a measure of quality control on enumeration and the preparation of lists (information provided to Margaret Woodley by Elections Canada 1991).

We also recommend a thorough study, possibly with some pilot projects, of "electoral mapping." Proposed to the Commission at its hearings in Regina by Saskatchewan's chief electoral officer, an electoral mapping information service would provide enumerators with addresses and postal codes at the time of their door-to-door canvass. Linked to a digitized computer mapping system by a postal code, the system supplies enumerators with a list of residences in a given poll. The enumerator's job is to fill in the name of the person(s) residing at that address. The purposes of such address-based mapping are to ensure a greater measure of reliability of the lists and to reduce (in Saskatchewan's case from seven to two) the number of steps required to complete an entry on an official list of electors (Lampard 1990). The proposal warrants careful examination.

It should also be mentioned that it is possible that the current enumeration system could be improved by matching enumerators' lists against some type of aerial residential grid to determine if any blocks, apartment buildings, or other concentrations of voters have been omitted. One explanation for the large number of complaints received from unenumerated electors in 1988 is the absence of any dependable verification procedure by which the work of enumeration can be measured. Such a verification system is worth exploring.

CONCLUSION

To conclude this study we would simply note that in our view the problems attributed to enumeration in Canada are not legion. On the contrary, they are relatively few and quite specific: the principal ones are to find qualified enumerators and, then, to organize and train them in a short period of time. On the basis of the numbers of eligible voters who are omitted from voters lists, or on the basis of convenience whereby revisions can be made to the preliminary list, our best judgement is that the Canadian system of enumeration compares favourably with other systems of voter registration. The recommendations we have presented above are designed to reduce the system's errors and to enhance its convenience.

APPENDIX A

FIFTY-DAY CALENDAR FROM WRIT TO ELECTION (AIDE-MÉMOIRE FOR THE RETURNING OFFICER)

Day 50
Issue of writ.

Day 49
Serve notice to persons entitled to nominate urban enumerators and revising agents.

Day 48
Contact rural enumerators.

Day 47
Prepare enumeration supplies – include specimen list.

Day 46
Issue supplies to rural enumerators.

Day 45
Last day for candidates to nominate urban enumerators.

Day 44
Instruct urban enumerators and issue supplies.

Day 43
Instruct urban enumerators and issue supplies.

Day 42
Instruct urban enumerators and issue supplies.
Prepare notice of enumeration for printing.

Day 41

Instruct urban enumerators and issue supplies.
Prepare notice of enumeration for printing.
Last-minute replacements for enumerators.

Day 40

Instruct urban enumerators and issue supplies.
Send notice of enumeration for printing.

Day 39

Instruct urban enumerators and issue supplies.
Post lists of enumerators in office.
Last-minute arrangements for enumeration.

Day 38

Enumeration begins.
Deal with enumeration problems.
Send lists of enumerators to chief electoral officer (CEO).

Day 37

Deal with enumeration problems.

Day 36

Deal with enumeration problems.
Last day for candidates to nominate revising agents.

Day 35

Deal with enumeration problems.

Day 34

Deal with enumeration problems.

Day 33

Instruct revising agents.

Day 32

Enumeration ends.
Start receiving lists of electors.
Address notice of enumeration.
Correct and reproduce lists of electors.

Day 31

Receive lists of electors.
Correct and reproduce lists of electors.
Address notice of enumeration.
Revising agents start.

Day 30

Address notice of enumeration.
All urban lists must be received from enumerators.
Correct and reproduce lists of electors.
Rural lists must be posted.

Day 29
>   Address notice of enumeration.
>   Correct and reproduce lists of electors.
>   Prepare accounts of enumerators.

Day 28
>   All rural lists must be received.
>   First day to mail notice of enumeration.

Day 27
>   Send lists of electors to CEO.
>   Send copy of lists to candidates.

Day 26
>   Last day to mail notice of enumeration.

Day 22
>   Instruct revising officers and issue supplies.

Day 20
>   Ensure revising officers prepared to start.

Day 19
>   Sitting for revision (urban and rural).

Day 18
>   Sitting for revision (urban).

Day 17
>   Sitting for revision (urban).
>   Last day for rural enumerators to send statement of changes to
>   returning officer.

Day 16
>   If no objections, statement of changes to urban lists to be completed.

Day 13
>   Sittings for revision (objections).

Day 0
>   Polling day.

Source: Canada, Elections Canada 1989a.

APPENDIX B

Figure 8.B1
The electoral hourglass

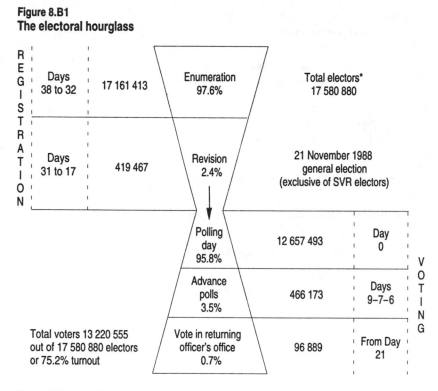

Source: Elections Canada, January 1989.

Note: Days are number of days before polling day.

*Total number of names on the preliminary and revised lists; does not include the 58 121 Special Voting Rules electors.

APPENDIX C

Table 8.C1
British Columbia statistical information

	1 June 1988–1 June 1989	1 June 1987–1 June 1988
Immigrants from other countries	16 416	14 324
Emigrants to other countries	4 350	4 654
In-migrants from other parts of Canada	61 846	57 449
Out-migrants to other parts of Canada	34 387	37 917
Deaths	20 811	20 974
Population 18 years of age only	1 June 1989 1 June 1988 44 200 43 900	1 June 1987 42 400

Source: Gary Weir, Manager of Data Dissemination, Planning and Statistics Division, Ministry of Finance and Corporation Relations, Province of British Columbia.
Note: All categories represent persons aged 19 and over.

ABBREVIATIONS

c.	chapter
R.S.C.	Revised Statutes of Canada
S.C.	Statutes of Canada
s(s).	section(s)

NOTES

This study was completed in April 1991.

In the preparation of this report we have received information and assistance from a large number of election officials at both the federal and provincial levels in Canada. For the foreign sections, we have been helped by Peta Dawson (Australia), Curtis Gans, William Kimberling and Raymond Wolfinger (United States), Michael Pinto-Duschinsky (Great Britain), and K.-H. Nassmacher, Enno Kruse and Hans Michelmann (Germany). Research assistance has been provided by Emily Chernesky, Bruce Cory and Susan Horley (University of Saskatchewan), Kathryn Stoner (Harvard University) and Margaret Woodley (Ottawa). The manuscript has been typed by Marilyn Berger, Susan Briggs-Faust and Lucille Brown. To all of those who have helped, we wish to acknowledge our gratitude with thanks.

1. We have relied heavily on the work of our late colleague, Norman Ward, for our description of voter registration in Canada between 1867 and 1938. Our account of the post-1938 period is based on various public documents. These include the statutory Reports issued by the chief election officer following each federal election, the *White Paper on Election Reform* (Canada,

Privy Council 1986) and Bill C-79, which was introduced in 1987 in the House of Commons but never adopted by Parliament. A brief account of the history of voters lists in Canada is found in Canada, Representation Commissioner (1968, 3–7).

2. In practical terms, however, the naming of enumerators often follows a different course from that laid out in the Act. After trying to seek out the candidates from the previous election, ROs will normally turn to the new candidates whose parties came first and second at the previous election, or to the local party association if a candidate is not yet nominated. The parties tend to submit lists of names rather than designating the enumerator for each poll, and in fact complain that they cannot assign people to polling divisions as they would like.

3. Each of these short (11 pages or less) Working Documents cited in this part of our study carries the following explanatory note: "This summary of issues is based on briefs and testimony received during the Commission's public hearings from March 12 to June 13, 1990 [July 24, 1990 in the case of Nos. 40 ("Disabled and Handicapped Voters") and 36 ("Northern and Remote Ridings")". They were supplied to the authors by the Royal Commission.

4. These data have been corrected and are contained in a memorandum from Louis Lavoie, Director of Operations (Elections Canada) to members of the Management Committee, 26 April 1990 (in authors' possession).

Electors on official list at 1988 general election related to number of persons qualified to vote

Population of Canada	25 923 300
Electors on official list	17 639 001
Canadian citizens aged 18 and over	19 337 880
– non-Canadian citizens aged 18 and over	– 717 500
– inmates	– 50 000
– mentally handicapped	– 20 000
– returning officers	– 295
– CEO and A/CEO	– 2
	787 797

Electors on official list at 1988 general election related to number of persons qualified to vote (cont'd)

Potential electorate	18 550 083
Electors who were not registered	911 082
Percentage of electors registered, 17 639 001 of 18 550 003	95.09
Average number of electors missed per district	3 008
Average number of electors missed per polling division	16

Source: Data for November 1988 supplied by Statistics Canada, prepared in April 1990.

Note: A more recent set of calculations for the Royal Commission found 95.99 percent of electors registered in 1988. Using the same total for the population aged 18 and over but a larger number of non-Canadian citizens, fewer inmates and no mentally handicapped persons (following a Federal Court of Canada judgement in October 1988 invalidating their prohibition from voting), this study found 53 000 additional registered voters (memorandum from Luc Dumont to Michael Cassidy, 12 November 1990).

5. As explained in the previous chapter, revision occurs in urban polls on the 19th, 18th and 17th days before polling and in rural polls at any time after the posting of the preliminary list up to the 17th day before polling. The list in an urban poll is closed after the last day of revision, and an eligible elector who is not on the list at that time is not qualified to vote. Rural voters, however, may be sworn in or vouched for on polling day in order to vote if they are not on the list.

6. Quotations in this paragraph come from Bohuslawsky (1988) and the *Star Phoenix*, Saskatoon (1990).

7. See note 4. The figure cited by Dr. Kholopov would mean an additional 571 002 electors on the official list in 1988, for a total of 18 210 003 persons. Thus, the percentage of electors registered would be 18 210 003 of 18 550 003, or 98.1 percent.

8. We recommend as well two excellent documents comparing, among other aspects of electoral law, voter registration in various Canadian jurisdictions. Both are prepared by Elections Canada: *Compendium of Canadian Electoral Legislation* (1990a) compiled annually by the Director of Operations, and "Survey on Voter Registration: Provincial and Municipal Jurisdictions" (1990c).

9. Information in this section has been provided by provincial election officials in response to questions about principal registration problems experienced and the nature and type of elector complaints on registration.

10. At the time of the 1988 federal election in Montreal Laurier–Sainte-Marie, 59 956 names were on the official lists; following enumeration and revision

for the 1990 by-election the figure was 52 672. The comparable figures for the federal by-election in Oshawa were 63 626 (1988) and 62 005 (1990). The chief electoral officer extended the revision deadline to the Friday before the Monday polling. Revision captured 3.9 percent of the official lists of voters in Sainte-Marie and 2.7 percent in Oshawa. This compares with a national average of 2.2 percent in 1988.

11. As well, there may be a more political explanation for the move to end election day registration. Under the system used in the 1986 British Columbia election, votes by people who registered on election day were not counted on election night. As a consequence two Social Credit candidates who seemed to have been elected on election night lost their seats when this very identifiable group of ballots was added to the total. The Social Credit government may have felt (probably rightly) that people who registered on election day were more likely to be young, mobile, and renters (i.e., more likely to be NDP supporters). The change in the law therefore has the appearance of being partisan.

12. In 1951, North Dakota introduced a scheme whereby elections would be conducted without a list. Precincts are designed so that electoral officials would know the electors, ideally 1 000 in size. To be able to vote the elector must be 18 years of age, a U.S. citizen and must have lived in the precinct for at least 30 days prior to polling day. No identification is required; the elector is asked if he or she is qualified, the name is recorded in the poll book and the elector votes. A person's qualifications can be challenged by an election board member or by a designated political party challenger. If challenged, the elector can sign an affidavit affirming eligibility to vote or just leave the poll. After the election, 10 percent of all affidavits filed for each county are checked for fraud by the county state auditor. If fraud is found in the sample, then all affidavits may be checked at the auditor's discretion. In the 1989 election, 10 000 affidavits were filed, 1 000 were checked, and no fraud was found.

13. The data in the following table suggest that the later that registration is available, including election day itself, the greater the turnout of voters. However, a word of caution in reading too much into the table. The states that have adopted election day registration have generally had a higher turnout than others even before they adopted election day registration, and when examined individually, the three states that adopted election day registration continued to experience a decline in voter turnout, along with other states, after its adoption.

Percentage national turnout in presidential elections for states with and without election day voter registration: 1976–88

	States with election day registration	States without election day registration	Difference
1988	63.68	49.52	14.16
1984	64.66	52.41	12.25
1980	66.54	51.70	14.84
1976	66.88	52.73	14.15

Source: "Voter Registration" 1990, 101.

Note: Figures were calculated for only the last three Presidential elections because prior to the 1976 election only North Dakota had no registration requirement. Percentages shown are of the voting-age population that cast a vote for the highest office.

14. In addition to Bennett's piece in *PS*, see also those by Piven and Cloward (1990), and Gans (1990).

15. Information for this section has been compiled from Council of State Governments (1988, 211); United States, Federal Election Commission (1977, appendix B); Canada, Elections Canada (1975a, 4); and Crocker (1990, 28).

16. See the House Administration Committee Report on Bill H.R. 2190, the *National Voter Registration Act*, in "Voter Registration" (1990, 102–3).

17. "Voting age population includes a great many people who could not possibly vote: millions of aliens who are categorically ineligible to vote; over a million citizens who are ineligible in most states – ex-felons and inmates of prisons and mental hospitals; and, most numerous, citizens who would be eligible if they had taken the step of establishing that eligibility by registering" (Glass et al. 1984, 49).

18. The notable exception is the League of Women Voters (1972) who have explored the option of a door-to-door registration by government officials as one way of improving the American registration system.

19. Gray and Gee (1967) arrived at their figure of completeness (96 percent) for the electoral register on 10 October 1965 by means of a sample survey. In discussing their method, they say: "The basic principle in the design of this type of investigation is that a sample of individuals who were eligible to have been registered should be obtained which is completely independent of the list of electors. The survey, which was designed to investigate the accuracy of the Ten-per-Cent Census taken on April 24th 1966 and commissioned by the General Register Office, provided a particularly suitable opportunity to study the Register of Electors." To the extent that their sample was accurate in 1965, it underlines the deterioration in the completeness of the register in the last quarter century.

20. In its submission to the JSC on "Statistics Relating to Roll Maintenance," the AEC (1988d) said that it "does not consider that failure to enrol or to notify changes of enrolment is at a level which warrants reversion to the penal provisions and practices of the 1950s and 1960s, but were the Joint Standing Committee to believe that a significant problem exists and that this is the appropriate remedy, the evidence of those years is available as some guide to the likely effect of the change. Annual figures varied considerably, but the average for the 16-year period was 13 000 administrative cases and 650 cases taken to court per year which, with the increase in total enrolment since that period, would if the incidence of non-compliance has remained unchanged produce almost twice as many cases in the late 1980s."

21. In the 1990 general election, 441 075 eligible voters failed to cast a ballot, according to information provided by Peta Dawson, Information Section, Australian Electoral Commission, August 1990. We wish to thank Peta Dawson and the Commission for their assistance to the authors in compiling this section of our study.

22. The authors wish to thank Jean-Marc Hamel, the former chief electoral officer of Canada for supplying them with this and a second document (both 1989) from the Ministère de l'Intérieur.

23. The authors are indebted to Dominique C. Tremblay, a researcher of the Royal Commission on Electoral Reform and Party Financing, who undertook the detective work necessary to track down information on the French system of voter registration. Indirectly, we would also like to express our appreciation to those academics and officials in France who shared their knowledge of this topic with Ms. Tremblay.

24. York University (1979). Our thanks to Richard Johnston, Department of Political Science, University of British Columbia, for providing these data.

25. Figures provided by Statistics Canada and Department of the Secretary of State. For reasons peculiar to the year, the 1988 naturalized citizen (18+) category has been averaged over the 1986 and 1988 years. The "change of name" data are almost certain to be conservative estimates, as they have been taken unchanged from the figure given by the chief electoral officer in his 1975 report entitled *Examination of Possible Ways of Reducing the Election Period* (Canada, Elections Canada 1975b).

26. It is relevant to this discussion that election campaign periods grew longer in Australia during the 1980s. Before 1983, the minimum and maximum periods were 14 and 51 days, with the 1983 campaign lasting 29 days.

27. These quotations are taken from a summary of briefs submitted by Duclos and Bujold (1990) and Donald (1990).

28. Bill C-79 included a provision for revisions to the preliminary lists on Days 14, 13 and 12, with a special revising day (for additions only, no deletions or corrections) on Friday, Day 3.

BIBLIOGRAPHY

Aggerholm, Barbara. 1984. "Many Miss Right to Vote." *Winnipeg Free Press,* 30 August.

Aitkin, Don, and Brian Jinks. 1982. *Australian Political Institutions.* Brisbane: Pitman.

Alberta. Chief Electoral Officer. 1988. *Report of the Chief Electoral Officer on the 1988 General Enumeration.* Edmonton.

Australia. *Commonwealth Electoral Act 1918,* No. 27, 1918 (incorporating all amendments by legislation made to 30 June 1980).

———. *Privacy Act 1988,* No. 119, 1988.

———. *Commonwealth Electoral Act 1918* (Memorandum Showing the *Commonwealth Electoral Act 1918,* as Amended by the *Commonwealth Electoral Legislation Amendment Act* 1983).

Australia. Australian Electoral Commission. 1985. *Commonwealth Electoral Procedures.* Canberra: Australian Government Publishing Service.

———. 1988a. "Conduct of the 1987 Election." Submission to Joint Standing Committee on Electoral Matters. Canberra: AEC.

———. 1988b. "Ray Lays 'Dead Voters' Allegations to Rest." *Scrutiny: The Staff Newsletter of the Australian Electoral Commission.* 6 (May): 5, 7.

———. 1988c. "Response to Liberal Party Submission of 31 May 1988 (No. 29)." Submission to Joint Standing Committee on Electoral Matters. Canberra: AEC.

———. 1988d. "Statistics Relating to Roll Maintenance Activities." Submission to Joint Standing Committee on Electoral Matters. Canberra: AEC.

———. 1989a. *Annual Report, 1987–1988.* Canberra: Australian Government Publishing Service.

———. 1989b. *Annual Report, 1988–1989.* Canberra: Australian Government Publishing Service.

———. 1989c. *Scrutiny: The Staff Newsletter of the Australian Electoral Commission.* 10 (July).

———. 1990. *Annual Report, 1989–1990.* Canberra: Australian Government Publishing Service.

———. 1991. *Scrutiny: The Staff Newsletter of the Australian Electoral Commission.* 16 (January): 1–2.

Australia. Joint Select Committee on Electoral Reform. 1983.
Report No. 1. Canberra: Australian Government Publishing Service.

Australia. Joint Standing Committee on Electoral Matters. 1988.
"Is This Where I Pay the Electricity Bill?" *Report No. 2.* Inquiry into
the Report on the Efficiency Scrutiny into Regionalization within the
Australian Electoral Commission. Canberra: Australian Government
Publishing Service.

――――. 1989. "1987 Federal Election." *Report No. 3.* Inquiry into the Conduct
of the 1987 Federal Election and 1988 Referendums. Canberra: Australian
Government Publishing Service.

Balasko, Richard D. 1990. Brief to the Royal Commission on Electoral
Reform and Party Financing. Ottawa.

Bennett, Stephen Earl. 1990. "The Uses and Abuses of Registration and
Turnout Data: An Analysis of Piven and Cloward's Studies of Nonvoting
in America." *PS: Political Science & Politics* 23:166–71.

Bohuslawsky, Maria. 1988. "Missed Voters Lowest in Years."
Winnipeg Free Press, 23 November.

Butler, David, Howard R. Penniman and Austin Ranney, eds. 1981.
*Democracy at the Polls: A Comparative Study of Competitive National
Elections.* Washington, DC: American Enterprise Institute for Public
Policy Research.

Cairns, Alan C. 1989. "Ritual, Taboo and Bias in Constitutional
Controversies in Canada." The Timlin Lecture. Saskatoon.

Calgary Herald. 1988. "Forgotten Voters Angry." 22 November.

Canada. Bill C-79, *An Act to amend the Canada Elections Act,* 2nd Session,
33rd Parliament, 1986–87.

――――. *Canada Elections Act,* R.S.C. 1985, c. E-2, s. 4, Scheds. II, IV, V.

――――. *Canadian Charter of Rights and Freedoms,* s. 3, Part I of the
Constitution Act, 1982, being Schedule B of the *Canada Act 1982*
(U.K.), 1982, c. 11.

――――. *Dominion Elections Act, 1938,* S.C. 1938, c. 46.

――――. *Electoral Franchise Act,* S.C. 1885, c. 40.

――――. *Military Voters Act,* S.C. 1919, c. 34.

――――. *War-time Elections Act,* S.C. 1917, c. 39.

Canada. Bureau of Management Consultants. 1979. *An Assessment of the
Coverage and Accuracy of the Present Method of Voter Enumeration.*
Study prepared for Elections Canada. Ottawa.

Canada. Elections Canada. 1975a. *Contact* No. 13 (1 Oct.).

————. 1975b. *Examination of Possible Ways of Reducing the Election Period.* Ottawa.

————. 1976. *Contact* No. 15 (1 Feb.).

————. 1979. *Contact* No. 32 (1 Oct.).

————. 1988. *Thirty-Fourth General Election, Report of the Chief Electoral Officer.* Ottawa: Minister of Supply and Services Canada.

————. 1989a. Memorandum of Special Assistant to the Director, Electoral Lists. 29 August.

————. 1989b. *Report of the Chief Electoral Officer of Canada as per subsection 195(1) of the Canada Elections Act.* Ottawa: Minister of Supply and Services Canada.

————. 1990a. *Compendium of Canadian Electoral Legislation.* Ottawa.

————. 1990b. Memorandum of Louis Lavoie, Director of Operations, Elections Canada, to members of Management Committee, 26 April.

————. 1990c. "Survey on Voter Registration: Provincial and Municipal Jurisdictions." Ottawa.

Canada. House of Commons. 1937. *Report of the Special Committee on Elections and Franchise Acts.* Ottawa: King's Printer.

Canada. Privy Council Office. 1986. *White Paper on Election Law Reform.* Ottawa.

Canada. Representation Commissioner. 1968. *Report of the Representation Commissioner on Methods of Registration of Electors and Absentee Voting 1968.* Ottawa: Queen's Printer.

Canada. Royal Commission on Electoral Reform and Party Financing. 1990. *Working Documents,* Nos. 1–45. Ottawa: Queen's Printer.

Canada. Statistics Canada. 1983. *1981 Census Canada. Population, Mobility Status, Canada, Provinces, Census Divisions, Census Metropolitan Areas.* 92–907. Table 1-1. Ottawa: Minister of Supply and Services Canada.

————. 1988. *1986 Census Metropolitan Areas and Census Agglomerations: Part 2.* Ottawa: Minister of Supply and Services Canada.

Canadian Association of the Deaf. 1990. Brief to the Royal Commission on Electoral Reform and Party Financing. Ottawa.

Carlson, Richard J. 1974. *Voter Registration Systems in Canada and Western Europe.* New York: National Municipal League.

Carty, Kenneth R. 1990. "Does Canada Need a Permanent Voters' List?" Issue paper prepared for the Royal Commission on Electoral Reform and Party Financing. Ottawa.

————. 1991. "Citizens, Electors, Voters and Parties in Canada or The Case of the Missing Voters List." Round Table on Voter Registration, Center for International Affairs, Harvard University, 9–10 May.

Central Mortgage and Housing Corporation. 1971. *Canadian Housing Statistics*. Ottawa: CMHC.

Chronicle-Herald (Halifax). 1984. "Enumerators Quit Jobs, Head for the Beaches." 13 August.

Coleman, Kevin J., Thomas H. Neale and Joseph E. Cantor. 1990. "The Election Process in the United States." *CRS Report for Congress*, 13 April.

Committee for the Study of the American Electorate (CSAE). 1990. "Creating the Opportunity: Voting and the Crisis of Democracy." Washington, DC.

Congressional Quarterly. 1990. 10 February.

Council of State Governments. 1988. *The Book of States, 1988-1989 Edition*. Lexington: Council.

Courtney, John C. 1988. "Franchise." In *The New Canadian Encyclopedia*. Edmonton: Hurtig.

Crewe, Ivor. 1981. "Electoral Participation." In *Democracy at the Polls: A Comparative Study of Competitive National Elections*, ed. David Butler, Howard Penniman and Austin Ranney. Washington, DC: American Enterprise Institute for Public Policy Research.

Crocker, Royce. 1990. "Voter Registration and Turnout in States with Mail and Motor-Voter Registration Systems." *CRS Report for Congress*, 23 February.

Demichel, A., and F. Demichel. 1973. *Droit électoral*. Paris: Dalloz.

Donald, E. Cameron. 1990. Brief to the Royal Commission on Electoral Reform and Party Financing. Ottawa.

Duclos, Louis, and Rémi Bujold. 1990. Brief to the Royal Commission on Electoral Reform and Party Financing. Ottawa.

Dunlop, Malcolm. 1988. "Enumeration Mistakes Affected Hundreds of Eligible N.S. Voters." *Chronicle-Herald* (Halifax), 23 November.

Farrell, David J. 1988. *Automating the Mark Back of Electoral Rolls*. Canberra: National Technology in Government Conference.

France. Ministère de l'Intérieur. 1989a. *Aide-mémoire à l'usage des délégués de l'administration au sein des commissions administratives chargées de la révision des listes électorales*. Paris.

———. 1989b. *Instruction relative à la révision et à la tenue des listes électorales*. Paris.

Gans, Curtis B. 1990. "A Rejoinder." *PS: Political Science & Politics* 23:175.

Glass, David, Peverill Squire and Raymond Wolfinger. 1984. "Voter Turnout: An International Comparison." *Public Opinion* (6):49–55.

Gray, P.G., and Frances A. Gee. 1967. *Electoral Registration for Parliamentary Elections.* Government Social Survey. London: HMSO.

Guarnieri, Albina. 1990. Testimony before the Royal Commission on Electoral Reform and Party Financing, Ottawa, 12 June.

Jabin, A. 1957. *Guide général des élections.* Paris: Berger-Levrault.

Jackman, Robert W. 1987. "Political Institutions and Voter Turnout in Industrial Democracies." *American Political Science Review* 81:405–23.

James, Deborah S. 1987. "Voter Registration: A Restriction on the Fundamental Right to Vote." *Yale Law Journal* 96:1615–40.

Kholopov, Alexander. 1990. Testimony before the Royal Commission on Electoral Reform and Party Financing, Halifax, 11 June.

Kimball, Penn. 1974. "The Case for Universal Voter Enrollment." In *Issues of Electoral Reform,* ed. Richard J. Carlson. New York: National Municipal League.

Kimberling, William C. 1991. "A Rational Approach to Evaluating Alternative Voter Registration Systems and Procedures." Round Table on Voter Registration, Center for International Affairs, Harvard University, 9–10 May.

Lambie, David, MP (United Kingdom). 1990. Interview. Ottawa, 30 May.

Lampard, Keith. 1990. Testimony before the Royal Commission on Electoral Reform and Party Financing. Regina, 18 April.

League of Women Voters. 1972. *Administrative Obstacles to Voting.* Washington, DC.

Lindell, G.J. 1983. Submission to the Joint Committee on Electoral Reform. Canberra.

Masclet, Jean-Claude. 1989. *Droit électoral.* Paris: Presses universitaires de France.

Massicotte, Louis. 1989. Memorandum from Louis Massicotte (Adjoint special au Directeur, Elections Canada) to Louis Lavoie (Director of Operations, Elections Canada). 11 August.

National Anti-Poverty Organization. 1990. "Poor People and the Federal Electoral System: Barriers to Participation." Brief submitted to the Royal Commission on Electoral Reform and Party Financing. Ottawa.

"National Voter Registration Act." 1990. *Congressional Digest* 69 (April): 98.

New York Times. 1990. "Voter Registration Bill Falls Short in Senate." 27 September.

Percheron, Annick, and Nonna Mayer. 1990. "Les absents du jeu électoral." *Lien social:* 398–401.

Pinto-Duschinsky, Michael. 1991. "Electoral Administration in the United Kingdom." Paper presented at the Round Table Conference on Election Administration in Comparative Perspectives, Vedback, Denmark, 27–28 March.

Pinto-Duschinsky, Michael, and Shelley Pinto-Duschinsky. 1987. *Voter Registration in England and Wales: Problems and Solutions.* London: Constitutional Reform Centre.

Piven, Frances F., and Richard A. Cloward. 1990. "A Reply." *PS: Political Science & Politics* 23:172.

Powell, G. Bingham. 1986. "American Voter Turnout in Comparative Perspective." *American Political Science Review* 80:17–43.

Squire, Peverill, Raymond Wolfinger and David Glass. 1987. "Residential Mobility and Voter Turnout." *American Political Science Review* 81:45–65.

Star Phoenix (Saskatoon). 1990. "Enumerators Said Often Afraid to Enter Poor Neighborhoods." 30 May.

The Times (London). 1987. "Fears over Poll Tax Fail to Discourage Voters Registering." 27 October.

Todd, Jean, and Bob Butcher. 1982. *Electoral Registration in 1981.* Office of Population Census and Surveys. London: HMSO.

Todd, Jean, and Jack Eldridge. 1987. *Electoral Registration in Inner City Areas, 1983-1984.* Office of Population Censuses and Surveys, Her Majesty's Stationery Office. London: HMSO.

Toinet, Marie-France, and Françoise Subileau. 1989. "L'abstentionnisme en France et aux États-Unis: Méthodes et interprétations." In *Explications du vote, un bilan des études éléctorales en France,* ed. Daniel Gaxie. Paris: Presses de la fondation nationale des sciences politiques.

United Kingdom. *Representation of the People Act 1983,* 1983, c. 2, s. 52.

United Kingdom. Home Office. 1984. *Code of Practice for Electoral Registration Officers.* RPA 283. London.

———. 1988. *Guidance for the Use of Canvassers.* RPA 326. London.

United Kingdom. Parliament. 1984. *Government Reply to the First Report from the Home Affairs Committee, Representation of the People Acts, Session 1982–83 HC32-1.* Cmnd 9140. London: HMSO.

United Kingdom. Parliament. Home Affairs Committee. 1983. *First Report from the Home Affairs Committee, Representation of the People Acts, Session 1982–83, HC32-1.* London: HMSO.

United States. Bill H.R. 2190, *National Voter Registration Act,* 101st Congress, 1990.

United States. Federal Election Commission. 1977. *Statewide Registration Systems 1*. Washington, DC: National Clearinghouse on Election Administration.

Ursaki, Don. 1990. Testimony before the Royal Commission on Electoral Reform and Party Financing, Vancouver, 17 May.

"Voter Registration Pros and Cons." 1990. *Congressional Digest* 69 (April).

Ward, Norman. 1963. *The Canadian House of Commons: Representation*. Toronto: University of Toronto Press.

Wilson, Deborah. 1990. "Referendum Bill Stirs B.C. Dispute." *Globe and Mail*, 11 July.

Wolfinger, Raymond. 1991. Correspondence. 5 May.

Wolfinger, Raymond E., and Steven J. Rosenstone. 1980. *Who Votes?* New Haven: Yale University Press.

York University. Institute for Behavioural Research. 1979. *Social Change in Canada: Trends in Attitudes, Values and Perceptions*. Toronto.

Young, Penny. Undated. *Compiling the Electoral Register, 1989*. Office of Population Censuses and Surveys. London: HMSO.

9

ADMINISTRATION AND ENFORCEMENT OF ELECTORAL LEGISLATION IN CANADA

Cécile Boucher

A PROVISION IN CRIMINAL LAW must meet three criteria if it is to be observed and enforced. First, the wording must be clear and unambiguous: there must be no question about the responsibilities imposed. Second, it must be possible to determine whether an offence has been committed and to prove it beyond all reasonable doubt. Third, the punishment must fit the crime. The *Canada Elections Act* is deficient in all three areas.

This becomes apparent when we look at the complaints and prosecutions brought under the *Canada Elections Act*. The complaints received by the Commissioner of Canada Elections after the last two general elections mainly concerned the financing of election campaigns. Less than 10 percent of all those received were brought before the courts. Some complaints, of course, are unfounded, but others cannot be taken further because various provisions of the Act have not been adapted to current circumstances and are thus difficult to enforce, or the terms used are ambiguous. Finally, the fact that offences under the *Canada Elections Act* are subject to criminal prosecution has made the Commissioner of Canada Elections reluctant to prosecute offenders because of the difficulties inherent in establishing a criminal standard of proof.

Sections 259 and 261 of the Act have even been declared unconstitutional under the *Canadian Charter of Rights and Freedoms*. In addition, the chief electoral officer has repeatedly warned Parliament in his annual reports about provisions that might be declared unconstitutional. This problem is becoming all the more serious, since people seem increasingly inclined to find weaknesses in legislation and turn to the courts to advance their rights. Vague, imprecise legislation invites such action.

Compared with other criminal offences, election offences do not warrant the penalties prescribed by the Act. Although harsh, the penalties have failed to increase compliance with the Act and, in our view, since they are disproportionate to the offences they seek to punish, they are inappropriate. It is also evident from case law in this area that the maximum penalties prescribed in the *Canada Elections Act* are almost never imposed and do not deter offenders as legislators intended.

Furthermore, the way elections have been conducted for many years now no longer justifies criminal charges for offences that are essentially administrative. Vote buying, intimidation, casting more than one ballot and corruption are no longer as widespread as they were at the turn of the century. Today, most offences are related to minor or technical issues that are not, in themselves, serious enough to compromise the integrity of the system.

For these reasons, the law should be adapted to the current practices of individuals and groups in the electoral process; the penalties and structure of the Act should be revised, and some terms should be redefined. In addition, an organization should be created with full jurisdiction over all aspects of the Act, so that it may be enforced with greater efficiency and speed. Such a body would encourage greater compliance with the provisions of the Act, especially if offences were no longer subject to criminal proceedings. More flexible procedures would reduce politicians' dissatisfaction with the process of applying the *Canada Elections Act* and ensure their closer cooperation with Elections Canada.

The first section of this study compares the various administrative structures responsible for implementing electoral legislation in Canada with similar organizations in other countries. The second section reviews offences and penalties in those jurisdictions. Finally, the third section describes how the legislation is applied by the various administrative bodies and, specifically, the measures taken when it is contravened. Empirical data enable us to assess the strengths and weaknesses of each structure. In conclusion, we attempt to show that, based on our research, Canada could introduce a more flexible structure and thus significantly improve the effectiveness of our electoral system.

ADMINISTRATIVE STRUCTURES AND ENFORCEMENT OF ELECTORAL LEGISLATION

This first section compares the administrative structure responsible for enforcing the *Canada Elections Act* with similar bodies in other jurisdictions. Various aspects such as staff, powers and relationship with Parliament are examined.

Elections Canada

Elections Canada is the body responsible for implementing the *Canada Elections Act*. This organization, like the Commissioner of Official Languages and the Auditor General, enjoys a special status, since it is answerable only to Parliament. All Elections Canada offices are located in Ottawa, although some decentralization occurs during elections, when local returning officers supervise and administer election activities at the local level. With a core staff of about 50, and a further 50 temporary employees, Elections Canada is a fairly small organization, but during elections it can expand to include more than 200 000 people.

The chief electoral officer (CEO), whose rank is equivalent to that of a deputy minister, is responsible for all aspects of the organization's administration. Elections Canada has four main departments: Operations, Elections Financing, Communications and Human Resources. The office of the Commissioner of Canada Elections forms a separate entity. Although the Commissioner is to some degree responsible to the CEO, and appointed by this person, the Commissioner's decisions do not require the CEO's authorization or approval.

Like all government departments, Elections Canada must submit its annual operating budget to Treasury Board for approval. A standing committee of the House of Commons, currently called the Standing Committee on Elections, Privileges and Procedure, then examines the operating budget and gives final approval. The Committee actually serves as a link between Parliament and the organization of elections, and carries out mandates received from the House of Commons. For the past 30 years, the House has referred all bills concerning the *Canada Elections Act* to this Committee.

The only regular contact between the Committee and Elections Canada occurs in the spring, when the Committee examines the organization's budget. The Committee has until the end of May to object to the way funds have been allocated, and all its decisions and objections must be approved by the House. This is the only time that the CEO and the CEO's principal officials are invited to take part as resource persons in the Committee's work. They also assume this role when amendments to the *Canada Elections Act* are proposed or specific problems arise regarding the legislation.

In practice, the Committee has no real power over the organization of elections and has made no objections to the budget in recent years. The Committee also has no permanent links with Elections Canada. Its role is limited to bringing items it considers relevant to the attention of the House.

Chief Electoral Officer

The CEO is solely responsible for Elections Canada operations. Since the position was created in 1920, the government has had no control over persons appointed to this position, because the appointment is permanent and because the conditions of employment have been removed from government influence. The CEO's political independence is also reinforced by a tradition of impartiality, which dates from the creation of this post. As with judges, the position of CEO demands independence and impartiality (Canada, *Canada Elections Act*, ss. 4–6). The CEO is appointed by the House of Commons after nomination by the government and may be removed from office only by a joint resolution of the House of Commons and the Senate. However, the incumbent must retire at age 65 and may not hold any other concurrent position. The independence of the office is further ensured by the CEO's duties, which are comparable to those of a Federal Court judge. The CEO receives the same benefits as Federal Court judges under the *Public Service Superannuation Act*, and the person's salary is paid out of the Consolidated Revenue Fund.

As additional guarantees of impartiality, the CEO is precluded from voting (Canada, *Canada Elections Act*, s. 51), must communicate with the Governor in Council through a member of the Privy Council designated for the purpose (ibid., s. 4(3)), and is thus not answerable to any specific minister.

Should the CEO be absent or unable to perform the duties of the position while Parliament is not in session, a substitute is appointed by the chief justice of Canada or the most senior Supreme Court justice. The appointment remains in effect until two weeks after the opening of the next session of Parliament (Canada, *Canada Elections Act*, ss. 6, 7).

The *Canada Elections Act* (s. 8) sets out the duties of the CEO in precise terms. It is the CEO's responsibility to ensure election officers comply with the Act and are impartial, to direct and monitor the conduct of elections, and to issue the instructions necessary for effective implementation of the Act.

Aside from the prerogatives conferred by the Act, section 9 assigns special powers to the CEO. Should an unforeseen situation arise, the CEO is permitted to adapt the provisions of the Act accordingly. The receipt of ballots after normal polling hours, however, is not permitted, except when voting has had to be suspended because of riots or other emergencies.

The CEO has several duties related to the financing of election campaigns:

- to register political parties (Canada, *Canada Elections Act*, s. 24);
- to determine and publish the level of allowable election expenses (ibid., ss. 39(2) and 211);
- to authorize the reimbursement of expenses to various election participants (ibid., ss. 241 and 322); and
- to receive returns detailing the expenses incurred by candidates and parties (ibid., ss. 44(3) and 235).

The CEO, in conjunction with the Commissioner of Canada Elections, is responsible for issuing guidelines for enforcing the Act, the most important of which are those concerning the election expenses of registered political parties and candidates. Although these guidelines do not take precedence over the Act, they nonetheless make it possible for those involved to be thoroughly informed of the implications of various sections of the Act, while guaranteeing that they will not be prosecuted if they comply with the provisions.

Within 10 days of the opening of any session of Parliament, the CEO must report to the House on his/her organization's activities since submission of the previous report (Canada, *Canada Elections Act*, s. 195). The report should also include any recommendations for amending the Act.

Assistant Chief Electoral Officer

The assistant chief electoral officer (ACEO) assists the CEO in the performance of the latter's duties (Canada, *Canada Elections Act*, s. 11). The CEO may delegate powers to the ACEO, as authorized by the Act, and the ACEO may replace the CEO when the latter is absent. The assistant chief electoral officer is appointed by the Governor in Council. However, the requirement of guaranteed impartiality imposed on the CEO does not extend to the ACEO, even though this person may be called on to perform certain of the CEO's duties under the Act. Former CEO Jean-Marc Hamel pointed out this fact at the hearings of the Royal Commission on Electoral Reform and Party Financing: "However, the legislature gave the government powers and responsibilities that, in my view, should now be subordinated to the basic principle of independence if it is necessary for the sake of the democratic process. I am thinking in particular of the appointment of the Assistant Chief Electoral Officer" (Hamel 1990, 9).

In practice, the complexity of the electoral process and the delegation of powers to the ACEO have increased in tandem. The Act was amended in 1983 to make such delegation official. The integrity of the process is not threatened by the method of appointing the ACEO at the present time, but if the CEO and the ACEO were to be increasingly required to act jointly, the latter's appointment would have to be shielded from criticism and allegations of partisanship, as a matter of principle and for the sake of consistency.

Commissioner of Canada Elections

The Elections Canada administrative structure also includes a commissioner, whose role is becoming increasingly judicial. The *Canada Elections Act* stipulates that the CEO must appoint a Commissioner of Canada Elections (s. 255), whose main responsibility is to ensure that the provisions of the Act are complied with and enforced. The Commissioner's duties and obligations are, in fact, conferred directly by the Act, and not by delegation from the CEO, as is the case for other members of Elections Canada staff. The Commissioner receives complaints concerning elections and begins legal proceedings as necessary. The Commissioner has been responsible for dealing with all offences under the *Canada Elections Act* only since 1977. From 1974[1] to 1977, the Commissioner's responsibility covered prosecuting campaign financing offences only.

Aside from quasi-judicial duties, the Commissioner is directly responsible for enforcing the Act. For example, the Commissioner is required to inform all individuals concerned of their obligations under the Act, suggest corrective measures for quickly settling minor offences brought to the Commissioner's attention and interpret the Act as required or requested.

Before a prosecution can be instituted under the *Canada Elections Act*, the Commissioner must give consent in writing (s. 256), except in such cases as maintaining order on polling day, personation, ejection of individuals from a polling station or disorderly conduct at public meetings. Although civil actions are allowed in some situations, they also require the prior consent of the Commissioner. The Commissioner does not have the same powers as a commissioner appointed under the *Inquiries Act*, except when an action specifically involves election officers or an extensive inquiry is not required. The Royal Canadian Mounted Police (RCMP) are called upon in other cases, since the Commissioner lacks the power of search and seizure and cannot appear before the courts to request the necessary warrants.

The CEO must direct the Commissioner to investigate all offences that may have been committed by elections officers (Canada, *Canada Elections Act*, s. 257). Decisions made by the Commissioner and CEO are strictly independent of each other. The Commissioner establishes the guidelines on whether to prosecute or not; the CEO ensures that they are followed when complaints are examined. Jean-Marc Hamel described the role played by the CEO with regard to complaints and prosecutions: "My role is to set the policy and terms of reference. My only interest in individual cases is to make sure that the commissioner follows or respects the policy or guidelines. Under no circumstances do I go to the file or have to give any permission or authority, because the commissioner already has that authority in the legislation" (Canada, House of Commons 1988, 24:83).

The Elections Canada policy on enforcing the Act is that every legitimate complaint and every case alleging violation of the Act should be investigated promptly. In cases where the interests of the public and of justice are at stake, the Commissioner will prosecute (permission required by the Act) when there is a good chance that the suit will be successful (Canada, Elections Canada 1989, 38). As will be seen, this policy, combined with procedures resembling those of criminal law, means that few complaints currently result in court action.

Bill C-79

Bill C-79 was tabled in the House of Commons in June 1987. It included most of the recommendations contained in the White Paper on Election Law Reform, which itself repeated many of the recommendations made in various reports submitted by the CEO since 1983 (Canada, Privy Council Office 1986). The bill proposed revising the existing organization and dividing responsibility for implementing the Act among members of a team, the Election Enforcement Commission (Canada, Bill C-79, ss. 70.001–70.016). The bill died on the order paper, and the political appointment of commissioners was undoubtedly one of the most hotly contested aspects of the bill (Surtees 1987).

The Commission was to be made up of a chairperson appointed for a seven-year term by resolution of the House of Commons, and representatives of every party with at least 12 seats in the House, who were to be appointed for three years. A final member, representing the public – to be designated by the Governor in Council upon the recommendation of all parties – would be appointed for a five-year term. Commissioners could only be removed by the Governor in Council at the request of the House. The Governor in Council would also be responsible for setting remuneration.

Under the terms of Bill C-79, the Election Enforcement Commission would have been responsible for enforcing the provisions of the *Canada Elections Act*. It would thus have issued directives regarding the application of the Act, taking over the duties of the Commissioner of Canada Elections and the CEO. The Commission would have been able to ask the courts for powers of search and seizure and could obtain RCMP assistance when necessary. In short, the goal was to simplify complaint procedures and avoid using the RCMP for administrative problems.

Along the same lines, the power to deal with electoral disputes would have passed from the trial courts of each jurisdiction to the Federal Court, so that a more consistent body of case law on elections in Canada could be established (Canada, Bill C-79, s. 1(2)). Provision was also made for repealing the *Corrupt Practices Inquiries Act*, the *Disfranchising Act*, and the *Dominion Controverted Elections Act* (ibid., s. 92).

In summary, the administration of the Canadian electoral system has several distinguishing features. First, Elections Canada is independent of the government. Such independence is, however, fragile, despite the method used to appoint the CEO and the conditions of the incumbent's employment. As the ACEO and returning officers are named by the Governor in Council, they cannot be dismissed by the CEO. In addition, it is impossible for the CEO or Commissioner to appeal decisions pertaining to the application of the Act to a higher court without authorization from the Attorney General of Canada. This feature sharply reduces their authority and independence regarding legal action. Finally, the CEO and Commissioner are the only ones empowered to defend any of their decisions that result in controversy. Although the government indicated its desire to change this system, this initiative failed when the House of Commons did not pass Bill C-79.

Election Administration Structures in Various Jurisdictions

Legislators in some Canadian provinces have chosen to legislate the various aspects of the electoral process by passing three laws: an elections act, a political process financing act and a controverted elections act. Manitoba, Prince Edward Island and New Brunswick have all followed this procedure. However, Newfoundland, British Columbia, the Northwest Territories and Quebec have a single act covering all aspects of the process. Bill C-79 was intended to consolidate all electoral legislation in Canada in a single act. As table 9.1 shows, the financing of election campaigns is the subject of specific legislation in five provinces, whereas acts dealing with contested elections are in force in six provinces.

There is no common reason for the number of laws governing the electoral process. Ontario and New Brunswick have two acts in force (one for financing and one for the administration of an election), resulting

Table 9.1
Electoral legislation in various jurisdictions

Elections Act	Election Finances Act	Controverted Elections Act
Canada	Prince Edward Island	Canada
(Bill C-79)	New Brunswick	Nova Scotia
Newfoundland	Ontario	Prince Edward Island
Prince Edward Island	Manitoba	New Brunswick
Nova Scotia	Alberta	Manitoba
New Brunswick		Saskatchewan
Quebec		Yukon
Ontario		
Manitoba		
Saskatchewan		
Alberta		
British Columbia		
Northwest Territories		
Yukon		

in two separate administrative bodies. These are the only jurisdictions where this has happened. Elsewhere, an abundance of regulations on financing has not prompted the creation of additional bodies. Most jurisdictions where electoral legislation has been revised in the last 20 years have repealed legislation on controverted elections, incorporating it into the provincial elections act.

Administrative Structures in Provincial Jurisdictions

The provinces tend to follow one of two approaches. Either the CEO is solely responsible for applying the Act or the responsibility is shared. As can be seen from table 9.2, the most common arrangement is where the CEO is responsible for applying the Act and relevant legislation in its entirety, i.e., from issuing the guidelines to initiating legal action. This method is found in 10 jurisdictions within Canada.

The federal model, with responsibility shared between the CEO and the Commissioner of Canada Elections, is not used in any of the provinces. In addition, New Brunswick is the only province where someone other than the CEO is responsible for enforcing the *Political*

Table 9.2
Application of electoral legislation in various jurisdictions

Jurisdiction	Responsible for enforcement of the act	Power to investigate	Power to institute proceedings	Limitation periods for instituting proceedings	Judgement
Canada	CEO	Commissioner of Canada Elections (RCMP)	Consent of Commissioner of Canada Elections	6 and 18 months	Trial Court in each province
(Bill C-79)	CEO Elections Enforcement Commission	Elections Enforcement Commission (RCMP or others)	Elections Enforcement Commission	18 months	Federal Court
Newfoundland	CEO	CEO may name an investigator	Anyone	1 year	Supreme Court
Nova Scotia	CEO	CEO (police)	CEO	9 months	Supreme Court and County Court
Prince Edward Island	CEO	Unspecified	Anyone	Unspecified	Supreme Court
New Brunswick	CEO Supervisor of Political Financing*	Supervisor	Authorization of supervisor and someone else	1 year	Court of Queen's Bench
Quebec	CEO	CEO appointment	CEO	2 years	Court of Quebec

Ontario	CEO Election Finances Commission*	Election Finances Commission CEO	CEO and Election Finances Commission	1 year	Depends on case
Manitoba	CEO	CEO	CEO	2 years	Court of Queen's Bench
Saskatchewan	CEO	CEO appointment	Anyone	6 and 18 months	Court of Queen's Bench
Alberta	CEO	CEO appointment	CEO	Unspecified	Supreme Court
British Columbia	CEO	Unspecified	Anyone	1 year	Supreme Court
Yukon	CEO	CEO or other designated person	CEO or elector	6 months	Supreme Court
Northwest Territories	CEO	CEO appointment	CEO must approve	1 year	Supreme Court
United States*	Federal Election Commission Election Crime Branch, Department of Justice	Federal Election Commission Election Crime Branch, Department of Justice	Federal Election Commission (FEC) Department of Justice	3 years	FEC (negotiated settlement) Court
Australia	Australian Electoral Commission	Federal Court	Anyone	Unspecified	High Court Federal Court

*Applies only to financing of the political process.

CEO: Chief Electoral Officer; FBI: Federal Bureau of Investigation; FEC: Federal Election Commission; RCMP: Royal Canadian Mounted Police.

Process Financing Act (s. 14). As mentioned, Ontario, with two Acts, has divided its administrative structure in two, one body dealing with campaign financing (Ontario, *Election Finances Act*) and the other with the electoral process (Ontario, *Election Act*).

In New Brunswick, there is a clear division between the enforcement of the *Elections Act* and that of the *Political Process Financing Act*. The CEO and the Supervisor of Political Financing exercise the same functions in their respective domains, both being answerable to the legislature. The CEO, however, maintains the register of political parties (New Brunswick, *Elections Act*, s. 130). The Supervisor is appointed by the Lieutenant Governor for a term of five years on the recommendation of the legislature (New Brunswick, *Political Process Financing Act*, s. 4). The Supervisor conducts inquiries, has the power to request search warrants (ibid., s. 16) and is the only one who may institute proceedings. The CEO does not have similar powers with regard to the *Elections Act*. The only link between the Supervisor and the CEO is an advisory committee (ibid., ss. 20–29), comprising the CEO, the Supervisor and two representatives from each party (not members of the legislature). The Committee advises the Commissioner on any matters submitted to it.

In Ontario, the Commission on Election Finances (Ontario, *Election Finances Act*, s. 2) ensures that the Act is enforced with regard to the financing of election campaigns. It is, to some extent, partisan in nature, since each elected party appoints two people (not members of the legislature) to the Committee. Two other members, a lawyer and the chairperson, are appointed by the Lieutenant Governor for a term of five years. The CEO is an ex-officio member. The Commission has full powers to investigate and prosecute. It is responsible for all matters related to financing.

Manitoba (*Elections Finances Act*, s. 4) has an advisory committee made up of a representative from each political party. The Committee advises the CEO only on the *Elections Finances Act*. Quebec (*Election Act*, ss. 514–523) and Nova Scotia (*Elections Act*, s. 6) also have similar committees, but their role is limited to advising on the legislation as a whole.

In most provinces, the CEO can appoint a private investigator, who has powers of search and seizure. The CEO, a designated person or the Commission thus controls the investigators' activities, which is clearly not the case at the federal level when the RCMP are called in.

In several provinces, provision is made for instituting a private prosecution independently of the wishes or consent of the CEO or of the organization responsible for enforcing the Act. This is true of Newfoundland, New Brunswick, Saskatchewan, British Columbia and the Yukon.

There are no administrative bodies with powers of adjudication. Those responsible for enforcement may settle minor issues only by issuing warnings so that problems may be rectified. Cases that require prosecution are dealt with by the courts, as at the federal level. All provinces have specified periods within which actions can be taken but, except for Prince Edward Island and Alberta, these are all limited.

The provinces, therefore, tend to follow one of two models: either the CEO has sole responsibility for enforcing the Act or responsibility is shared by more than one person. This can be directly through a commission or the CEO can call on a committee that provides advice on cases that go to court. In all cases, the commissions directly responsible for enforcing electoral legislation have members with party affiliations. Advisory committees also have a partially partisan membership.

A review of the various provincial electoral organizations is relevant because of their composition and mandates. In each case, the legislation stipulates that no particular political party may control the organization's decisions. From this point of view, partisan appointments serve only to maintain close links between the political parties and the organizations responsible for applying the Acts. This ensures that the election organization authorities are legitimized by the political parties, while maintaining a team approach with regard to decision making. To a certain extent, these measures may increase public confidence in the system, and indeed Bill C-79 attempted to borrow some of them. It failed, however, because of the formula proposed for appointing members to the Election Enforcement Commission and the parties' disagreement on the definition of election expenses. The idea of decentralizing powers, as is done in some provinces, is nonetheless valid, and may still be achievable in some other way.

Administrative Structures in Other Countries

Although few countries use models like those in Canada, their experience may illustrate the possibility for changes to Canada's system. We have selected two foreign jurisdictions: Australia and the United States.

This is not an arbitrary selection: the models presented comprise features that could be fairly easily adapted to a new administrative structure in Canada. We consider that such an examination cannot fail to be worthwhile. Both the Australian Electoral Commission and the United States Federal Election Commission offer concepts that could apply in Canada.

In Australia, administration of the electoral process is the responsibility of the Australian Electoral Commission. This body is composed of a chair (a judge), an Elections Commissioner and one other member. All are appointed by the Governor General for a seven-year term. The Commissioner, whose duties are comparable to those of the CEO in Canada, is the only full-time member. A commissioner who no longer meets the appointment qualifications, has missed more than three meetings or does not fulfil his or her functions in an appropriate manner may not continue to sit on the Commission, and will be dismissed by the Governor General (Australia, *Commonwealth Electoral Act*, ss. 8–10, 12).

The Commission's duties are to provide a report to the minister on enforcement of the legislation, perform the duties described in the legislation, keep the public informed about the electoral process, establish guidelines for interpretation of the *Commonwealth Electoral Act*, encourage research on the electoral process and publish documents dealing with its functions (Australia, *Commonwealth Electoral Act*, s. 7). The electoral law does not give the Commission exclusive power to initiate investigations or prosecutions. But, like any voter, the Commission can ask the police to investigate complaints or initiate a prosecution.

Since 1974, the Federal Election Commission (FEC) in the United States has been responsible for enforcing legislation on campaign financing (the *Federal Election Campaign Act*) in that country. The FEC's duties are administrative and quasi-judicial. Its primary function is to ensure the openness of the system, by requiring reports on expenses and monitoring the U.S. legal provisions concerning campaign contributions.

The FEC has eight members. The secretary of the Senate and secretary of the House of Representatives are ex-officio members but do not have voting rights. The six other members are chosen by the President of the United States and confirmed by the Senate. Appointments are for a six-year term. These members are directly affiliated with the two major political parties, but no more than three of them may belong to the same party (U.S., *Federal Election Campaign Act*, s. 437c(a)(1)). To preserve impartiality, members must restrict themselves to performing their duties. In addition, the Commission chairperson and vice-chairperson may not be from the same party; they both serve a one-year term (ibid., s. 437c(a)(5)).

The FEC must meet at least once a month (U.S., *Federal Election Campaign Act*, s. 437d). All meetings are public, except for those dealing with complaints, internal management issues or other confidential matters. The organization has a staff of approximately 250 people and its budget was $15.4 million in 1989 (Federal Election Commission, 1989b, 14). The duties (U.S., *Federal Election Campaign Act*, s. 437c(b)(1)) of the FEC are mainly to provide legal opinions on the interpretation of the Act and regulations on request, to issue forms and examine all complaints. In addition, the FEC must negotiate fines when offences are admitted and institute criminal court proceedings as necessary. The FEC has full responsibility for enforcing the law in civil cases. It is responsible for establishing spending limits for candidates and political committees, which must register with the Commission.

This structure is unique in that the FEC is empowered to deal with civil cases. Its powers (U.S., *Federal Election Campaign Act*, ss. 437d(a), (b), (c), (e)) range from receiving and investigating complaints to instituting proceedings in civil cases. Its powers of investigation enable it to subpoena all necessary documents and witnesses. The FEC also has the power to ask the court to issue orders requiring individuals or groups suspected of offences to comply with the Act.

The Commission must prescribe forms (U.S., *Federal Election Campaign Act*, s. 438), receive reports and hold hearings prior to their publication. Any new rules proposed by the FEC must go to the Senate and House of Representatives, and receive their approval within 30 days. If there is no challenge, rules come into force 10 days after the final date for approval by the two Houses.

The two countries discussed above have established different organizations for enforcing electoral legislation. The Australian system for enforcing legislation is similar to that in several Canadian provinces. It will be noticed, though, that procedures for dealing with complaints and prosecutions under electoral legislation are not the responsibility of the enforcing organization, as in most Canadian jurisdictions. The United States adopts a different approach. The American federal body and its quasi-judicial powers offer an interesting model, because it assumes that there can be two types of offences and that procedures for dealing with complaints may vary, depending on the circumstances. Since offences are civil in nature, they are not subject to criminal proceedings, unlike Canadian practice. The U.S. government also grants regulatory powers to the FEC, thereby granting the administrative authority legal powers recognized by the courts.

ELECTION OFFENCES AND PENALTIES

The effective enforcement of electoral legislation is measured not only by a study of its organization, but also by whether it is clear and precise, with equitable penalties for various election offences. There is great diversity in Canada in this regard. As this section shows, offences and penalties vary from one jurisdiction to another, and their definition has a substantial impact on how the system operates.

Election Offences and Penalties in Canada

The *Canada Elections Act* (ss. 267 and 269) defines three types of violation: offences, illegal practices and corrupt practices. There are specific
penalties for each category. Offences are punishable on summary conviction by a fine not exceeding $1 000 and/or imprisonment for up to one
year. On indictment, the penalty is a fine not exceeding $5 000 and/or
imprisonment for a term not exceeding five years. The Act also makes
provision for a penalty of $25 000 for bodies (Canada, *Canada Elections
Act*, ss. 40, 47, 48, 319–321) such as political parties and broadcasting
companies. The same type of penalty applies in the case of illegal practices, but with the additional deprivation of political rights. The person
convicted is not eligible to be elected to or to sit as a member of the
House of Commons, vote at any election of a member of that House or
hold any office within the appointment of the Crown or Governor in
Council for a period of five years. The same penalty applies for corrupt
practices, but for a period of seven years. Bill C-79 did not propose any
changes in this area.

The loss of the right to vote or to stand for election has never been
enforced, since the cases heard very seldom concerned corrupt practices. Therefore, it is difficult to say whether such penalties would
amount to encroachment on the prerogatives of the House or could be
justified under section 3 of the *Canadian Charter of Rights and Freedoms*.
Furthermore, there is very little case law in this area. The *MacLean* decision (1987) in Nova Scotia would suggest that it is lawful to prohibit an
elected member from sitting, but prohibiting someone from standing
for election may encounter difficulty. However, some reservations about
the *MacLean* case are warranted, since the conviction was not under
the *Canada Elections Act*. It could be argued that more severe punishment
of candidates or elected members is justified, since they must be more
familiar with the Act than other electors.

Civil penalties are relatively rare and can be added to the penalties imposed in criminal court. Examples include loss of salary in the
case of election officers, prohibition from sitting if a candidate's return
has not been submitted, deregistration of a party that does not submit
information required to update its application for registration or does
not appoint an auditor, and loss of reimbursement of election expenses
for candidates and parties if returns are not submitted. Finally, an election may be declared void if irregularities or corrupt practices occurred
that directly influenced the results of the election.

Boyer (1987, 962) considers that the offences/illegal practices/
corrupt practices classification follows the logic that corrupt practices
refer specifically to violations related to *Criminal Code* offences, whereas

illegal practices are more regulatory offences. A review of current offences and penalties runs counter to this reasoning. In Canada, only agents and candidates may be convicted of corrupt practices and then only for certain specific offences, which may be either regulatory or criminal. For example, voting in an irregular manner or influencing the vote of an elector is illegal practice for an elector, but becomes corrupt practice if committed by the candidate or the agent (Canada, *Canada Elections Act*, s. 267(2)). Illegal practices also concern the secrecy of the vote, although they involve election campaign financing in most cases. In short, there seems to be no logical progression whereby penalties increase with the seriousness or consequences of the violation. We consider that the status of the offender is a more important criterion.

The *Canada Elections Act* contains some sections based on past practices that no longer necessarily reflect current regulatory requirements. Its style is heavy and, in many cases, far too detailed; such sections are more difficult for the courts to enforce and they quickly become obsolete.

Finally, violations and attendant penalties are scattered throughout the Act. Offences are often detailed at the end of a series of provisions covering a given subject. Sections 249 to 270 deal with a number of general offences. In many cases, the offences set out in the section on special voting rules[2] have already been included within the text of the Act.

Election Offences and Penalties in Canadian Provinces

As table 9.3 indicates, there are no real similarities in penalties for election offences in various jurisdictions.

Unlike federal election offences, provincial violations classified as offences may not proceed by indictment. Only in Nova Scotia (*Elections Act*, s. 181) and Prince Edward Island (*Election Act*, s. 137) are the financial penalties specified in the Act greater than those for violations at the federal level. The Northwest Territories' (*Elections Act*, s. 225(1)) penalties are identical to federal ones and, indeed, its legislation is closest to federal legislation. In Ontario (*Election Act*, s. 96), Quebec (*Election Act*, s. 565), New Brunswick (*Elections Act*, s. 118(3)) and Alberta (*Election Act*, s. 150), a prison sentence may not be imposed on persons convicted of offences. Imprisonment may vary from three months to two years for illegal acts or fraudulent activities. Except for Quebec (ss. 551–564) and Saskatchewan (*Election Act*, s. 197), no province has set a minimum fine. Saskatchewan also has a minimum period of seven days for imprisonment (ibid., s. 191). New Brunswick (s. 69), Saskatchewan (s. 191) and Newfoundland (*Election Act*, s. 61(1)) impose more severe penalties on election officers who have committed certain offences.

Table 9.3
Procedures and penalties imposed in the political process in Canada

Jurisdiction	Offence		Intermediate category		Corrupt practice
	Summary conviction	Indictment	Summary conviction	Indictment	
Canada	$1 000 and/or 1 year	$5 000 and/or 5 years	*Illegal practice:* May not vote, sit and vote in the legislature and hold office for the Governor in Council for 5 years.	*Illegal practice:* May not vote, sit and vote in the legislature and hold office for the Governor in Council for 5 years.	Candidate and Agent: May not vote, vote or sit in the legislature and hold office for the Governor in Council for 7 years.
Newfoundland	$500 and/or 3 months		*Indictable offence:* $1 000 and/or 6 months *Illegal practice:* $1 000 and costs, loss of right to vote in elections and to be elected to the legislature.	*Indictable offence:* $1 000 and/or 6 months.	$2 000 and costs. Loss of right to vote in elections and to be elected to the legislature.
Nova Scotia	$2 000 and/or 2 years				May not be elected, sit in the legislature and hold office for the Governor in Council for 5 years.
Prince Edward Island	$2 000 and/or 2 years				$200 and/or 3 months. May not sit and be elected and hold office for the Lieutenant Governor and in the civil service for 5 years.

New Brunswick	$200	*Illegal practice:* $500, may not vote, sit and vote in the legislature and hold office for the Governor in Council for 5 years.	$1 000 and/or 1 year, may not vote, sit and vote in the legislature and hold office for the Governor in Council for 5 years. Candidate: 6 years
Quebec	$500		May not engage in partisan work, vote, be a candidate and hold office in the government or the House for 5 years.
Ontario	$5 000		Candidate: May not be a candidate, hold office for the Crown or the Lieutenant Governor for 8 years. Other: $5 000 and/or 6 months
Manitoba	$200 and/or 2 months	*Elections offence:* $2 000 and/or 1 year.	
Saskatchewan	$25 to $1 000 and/or 7 days to 1 year		May not sit, vote, be elected and hold office in a municipality or for the Crown for 8 years.
Alberta	$500		$5 000 and/or 2 years. May not be a candidate, vote, hold office for the Crown for 8 years.

Table 9.3 (cont'd)
Procedures and penalties imposed in the political process in Canada

Jurisdiction	Offence		Intermediate category		
	Summary conviction	Indictment	Summary conviction	Indictment	Corrupt practice
British Columbia	$500 and/or 1 year		*Personation:* Candidate may not sit and vote for the life of the legislature. *Other:* May not vote, stand for or hold office in a municipality, legal office, be a judge for 7 years.		May not vote, stand for or hold office in a municipality, in a law office, be a judge for 7 years.
Northwest Territories	$1 000 and/or 1 year		*Illegal practice:* May not vote, sit and vote in the legislature and hold office for the Governor in Council for 5 years.		Candidate and agent: May not vote, sit and vote in the legislature and hold office for the Governor in Council for 7 years.
Yukon	$2 000 and/or 3 months				$5 000 and/or 1 year, loss of rights, but not specified.

Except in Newfoundland (*Election Act*, s. 120(1)) and federally (Canada, *Canada Elections Act*, s. 267), intermediate violations termed illegal practice, indictable offence or personation are brought before the courts by summary conviction. British Columbia (*Election Act*, s. 262) and the Northwest Territories (*Elections Act*, s. 227) generally impose the same financial penalties and prison terms as those at the federal level, but with the addition of the loss of political rights. In Newfoundland (s. 120(2)), Manitoba (*Elections Act*, s. 164) and New Brunswick (*Elections Act*, ss. 118(2) and 119), however, intermediate categories involve higher fines and longer prison terms, in addition to a loss of political rights. In all these examples, offences in the intermediate categories entail deprivation of political rights for varying periods of time. In Manitoba (s. 164), there are no provisions prohibiting individuals convicted of illegal practices from standing for election or sitting as a member of the legislative assembly.

Corrupt practices are defined in the legislation of all provinces except Manitoba. In the Yukon, the legislature is responsible for deciding whether the candidate may be deprived of political rights if found guilty of a corrupt practice (Yukon, *Legislative Assembly Act*, s. 11(2)). In Ontario (*Election Act*, s. 97(1)), loss of the right to run for office for a period of eight years applies only to candidates, while the section includes the penalty of a prison term for others. In New Brunswick (*Elections Act*, ss. 118(1) and 119), individuals guilty of election fraud are deprived of political rights for six years and candidates for seven years. In Prince Edward Island (*Controverted Elections (Provincial) Act*, s. 107), fines and prison terms are less severe for corrupt practices than for offences, even though the penalty for corrupt practices includes loss of political rights. Ontario (s. 97(1)), Saskatchewan (*Election Act*, s. 183a) and Alberta (*Election Act*, s. 173(2)), where an individual may lose political rights for eight years, have the most severe penalties. Being found guilty of a corrupt practice generally results in the loss of political rights for varying periods of time. There is a tendency to treat agents and candidates more severely.

Canada (*Canada Elections Act*, s. 267(2)) and the Northwest Territories (*Elections Act*, s. 225(2)) differentiate between offenders, considering certain offences to be corrupt practices because they were committed directly by the candidate or official agent. Only candidates and agents can be convicted of election fraud under the *Canada Elections Act*.

Federally, only three financial penalties and two prison terms are possible; provincial statutes contain a far wider variety of penalties. When it is justified by the violation, most jurisdictions try to increase or decrease the penalty, depending on the nature of the offence; this results in perhaps a dozen different levels of penalties in the same statute.

Although they use a system that incorporates two or three types of offences, New Brunswick, Newfoundland, Ontario, Manitoba, Alberta and the Yukon impose increasingly heavy financial penalties and prison sentences where applicable, depending on whether the violation is an offence or a corrupt practice. At the federal level, the only penalty increased is the loss of political rights. Penalties in provincial jurisdictions are much more likely to increase in proportion to the seriousness of the violation.

Quebec is the only province where all offences are listed together in the Act. Unlike other jurisdictions, Quebec legislation defines the penalty and then lists the offences punishable by that penalty. Penal provisions are set out in sections 551 to 569. The sections contain all the types of offence with specific penalties for individuals, candidates and various bodies; the penalties are higher for the last two. Provision is also made for repeat offenders, where the penalties may be doubled or tripled. All financial penalties have a minimum fine. There is a general provision (s. 565) for a maximum fine to punish anything that is not specified as an offence in the Act, but is defined as a prohibition. Provision is also made for the offence of aiding and abetting. Corrupt practices are mentioned in only one section (s. 567).

Saskatchewan is the only jurisdiction where the statute describes the penalty immediately after the offence. This makes the text difficult to read; there is also a great variety of financial penalties.

The Ontario *Election Act* defines penalties under a general provision (s. 96); no mention is made of imprisonment, except for corrupt practices, for which the penalties are more severe. A distinctive feature of this jurisdiction is that it does not include offences contained in the *Criminal Code* (Boyer 1981, 62). In fact, section 91(27) of the *Constitution Act, 1982* gives Parliament exclusive jurisdiction over criminal matters. In 1968, the Select Committee of the Ontario Legislature found that the *Election Act* infringed the exclusive jurisdiction of the federal government by stating that certain infractions were criminal offences. Several sections of the Ontario *Election Act* have thus been repealed, particularly those concerning the use of force and violence, intimidation and undue influence. So far, this seems to be the only province that fears a challenge from federal authorities, since it is the only one to have made these changes.

As with penalties, there is no uniformity in the style and content of electoral legislation from one jurisdiction to the next. Some texts are relatively short and define general principles; others attempt to cover as many situations as possible, in order to avoid the officials responsible for enforcing an elections act having to rely on their discretionary powers. With regard to offences, when the legislation covers aiding and abetting and includes a general provision, the texts are much shorter and usually much easier to read. Quebec and Ontario provide interesting examples of how statutory provisions can be simplified.

Offences and Penalties with regard to Political Financing in Canada
In many jurisdictions, the financing of political activity gives rise to a new category of penalties. Prince Edward Island, Nova Scotia and the Northwest Territories punish offences related to the financing of election campaigns in the same way as other violations, as do federal authorities.

As can be seen from table 9.4, no specific penalties are provided for organizations in Prince Edward Island or British Columbia. No penalties are provided in Newfoundland and the Northwest Territories, because political parties are not recognized.

Table 9.4 also shows that no provision is made for prison terms in Ontario (*Elections Finances Act*, ss. 49–50), Alberta (*Election Finances and Contributions Disclosure Act*, ss. 41–42), Quebec (*Election Act*, ss. 559–560) and Manitoba (*Elections Finances Act*, s. 88). In Quebec (s. 561), New Brunswick (*Political Process Financing Act*, s. 88(1)), Ontario (s. 49) and Alberta (s. 41), organizations and unions are generally punished much more severely ($3 000 to $30 000) than are individuals or parties ($100 to $10 000). Again, indictment exists only under the *Canada Elections Act*.

Quebec (*Election Act*, s. 561), Nova Scotia (*Elections Act*, ss. 164I and 175), Prince Edward Island (*Election Expenses Act*, s. 16) and Manitoba (*Elections Finances Act*, s. 69(3)) are the only jurisdictions to recognize the liability of the party leader when the party is under suspicion, but such liability remains limited to certain sections, including the submission of returns or expenses paid illegally.

Only the Northwest Territories (*Elections Act*, s. 227) and Newfoundland (*Election Act*, s. 120(4)) retain the intermediate category, but Newfoundland no longer uses indictment. Financial penalties and prison terms are the same as those for the election process as a whole. Very few statutes punish election campaign financing offences as corrupt practices. However, when such a penalty does exist, it applies only to candidates and their agents, as is the case at the federal level, in Newfoundland, Quebec, British Columbia and the Northwest Territories.

In Alberta (*Election Finances and Contributions Disclosure Act*, ss. 14.1 and 43), it is an offence to receive contributions illegally and the offender must pay a fine equal to the illegal contribution. There are very few jurisdictions where the penalty is proportionate to the amount of the illegal contribution.

Table 9.4
Procedures and penalties imposed in financing the political process in Canada

Jurisdiction	Offence		Intermediate category		Corrupt practice
	Summary conviction	Indictment	Summary conviction	Indictment	
Canada	$1 000 and/or 1 year Party; $25 000	$5 000 and/or 5 years	*Illegal practice:* May not vote, sit and vote in the legislature and hold office for the Governor in Council for 5 years.	*Illegal practice:* May not vote, sit and vote in the legislature and hold office for the Governor in Council for 5 years.	Agent and candidate: May not vote, vote or sit in the legislature and hold office for the Governor in Council for 7 years.
Newfoundland	$500 and/or 3 months		*Illegal practice:* $1 000 and costs, loss of right to vote in elections.		Candidate: $2 000 and costs. Loss of right to vote in elections.
Nova Scotia	$2 000 and/or 2 years				May not be elected, sit in the legislature and hold office for the Governor in Council for 5 years.
Prince Edward Island	$2 000 and/or 2 years				$200 and/or 3 months. May not sit and be elected and hold office for the Lieutenant Governor and in the civil service for 5 years.
New Brunswick	Union and corporation: $10 000 Other: $1 000 3 months' imprisonment				

Jurisdiction	Fine	Disqualification
Quebec	Corporation: $3 000 to $30 000 Individuals: $100 to $10 000	Party leader, agent and candidate: May not engage in partisan work, vote, be a candidate and hold office for the government or the House for 5 years.
Ontario	Union and corporation: $10 000 Other: $1 000	
Manitoba	Party: $5 000 Other: $1 000	
Saskatchewan	Party: $5 000 Other: $1 000	
Alberta	Union and corporation: $10 000 Other: $1 000	
British Columbia	$200 to $1 000 and/or 6 months	Candidate: May not vote, stand for, hold office in a municipality, in a law office, be a judge for 7 years.
Northwest Territories	$1 000 and/or 1 year	*Illegal practice:* May not vote, sit and vote in the legislature and hold office for the Governor in Council for 5 years. Candidate and agent: May not vote, sit and vote in the legislature and hold office for the Governor in Council for 7 years.

The requirement to report election expenses and the requirement to ensure that allowed expenses are not exceeded are the provisions that best ensure the openness of the system and equal opportunity for parties and candidates. They are also the provisions that are most frequently contravened in the majority of provinces and at the federal level. The greatest variety of penalties and responsibilities for agents, candidates and parties is also found in these two areas.

As table 9.5 shows, Ontario (*Election Finances Act*, s. 48), Manitoba (*Elections Finances Act*, s. 69(1)), Saskatchewan (*Election Act*, s. 210) and Alberta (*Election Finances and Contributions Disclosure Act*, s. 40), together with the federal level (Canada, *Canada Elections Act*, s. 47), are the only jurisdictions that recognize the joint liability of the party and its agent or the candidate and his or her agent when returns are not submitted. No penalty is provided for in Newfoundland and the Northwest Territories because, as political parties are not recognized, they do not have to submit a return.

Nova Scotia (*Elections Act*, s. 164E), Quebec (*Election Act*, s. 562) and Manitoba (*Elections Finances Act*, s. 69(3)) recognize the direct liability of party leaders in such situations, and prevent them from sitting. Only New Brunswick (*Political Process Financing Act*, s. 88.1) recognizes the sole liability of agents when this offence is committed. On the other hand, Quebec, Newfoundland, Nova Scotia and Prince Edward Island do not hold agents accountable if no expense returns are submitted.

A candidate's failure to submit a return is punished differently throughout Canada. In Newfoundland (*Election Act*, s. 121(11)), the candidate is fined $10 per day. In New Brunswick (*Political Process Finances Act*, s. 88.1), the candidate is not permitted to sit or vote in the legislature, in addition to any other penalty. In Quebec (*Election Act*, s. 563), the candidate is not permitted to sit and must pay a fine of $50 per day until the return is submitted. The same fine is imposed on the candidate's agent in New Brunswick. In Ontario (*Election Finances Act*, s. 44(2)(*b*)), the member's seat becomes vacant or the unelected candidate may not stand in a future election and expenses are not reimbursed (ibid., s. 46). In Manitoba (*Elections Finances Act*, s. 19(2)), the party is deregistered, and elected candidates or party leaders may not sit (ibid., s. 69) or, if not elected, may not run in the next election.

It is interesting to note that it is only at the federal level (Canada, *Canada Elections Act*, s. 236(2)) and in the Northwest Territories (*Election Act*, s. 186(2)) that failure to submit an expense report is considered an illegal act or corrupt practice, and punished by depriving the candidate and agent in question of their democratic rights. The *Canada Elections Act*, however, stipulates that deliberate intent must be proven before a candidate or agent can be convicted of an illegal act.

Table 9.5
Maximum penalties for failure to submit an expenses return

Jurisdiction	Parties	Party agent	Candidate	Candidate's agent
Canada	$25 000	$1 000 and/or 1 year or $5 000 and/or 2 years	$1 000 and/or 1 year or $5 000 and/or 2 years Loss of rights: 5 years May not sit	$1 000 and/or 1 year or $5 000 and/or 2 years Loss of rights: 5 years
Newfoundland			$10 per day	
Nova Scotia	Leader may not sit		May not sit	
Prince Edward Island	No reimbursement of expenses		No reimbursement	
New Brunswick	No reimbursement	$50 per day	No reimbursement	$50 per day
Quebec	Leader may not sit $50 per day		$50 per day May not sit	
Ontario	No reimbursement $2 000	$1 000	May not sit No reimbursement Seat vacant $1 000	$1 000
Manitoba	Deregistration Leader may not sit $20 000	$2 000	May not sit if elected If not elected may not stand for election $2 000	$2 000

Table 9.5 (cont'd)
Maximum penalties for failure to submit an expenses return

Jurisdiction	Parties	Party agent	Candidate	Candidate's agent
Saskatchewan	$5 000	$5 000 and/or 6 months	$5 000 and/or 6 months	$5 000 and/or 6 months
Alberta	$5 000	$1 000	$1 000	$1 000
British Columbia	No reimbursement	$200 to $1 000 6 months	$200 to $1 000 and/or 6 months	$200 to $1 000 6 months
Northwest Territories			May not sit $1 000 and/or 1 year Loss of rights: 5 years	$1 000 and/or 1 year Loss of rights: 5 years

Table 9.6
Maximum penalties for overspending

Jurisdiction	Parties	Party agent	Candidate	Candidate's agent
Canada	$25 000	$1 000 and/or 1 year or $5 000 and/or 2 years	$1 000 and/or 1 year or $5 000 and/or 2 years Loss of rights: 5 years May not sit	$1 000 and/or 1 year or $5 000 and/or 2 years Loss of rights: 5 years
Nova Scotia	Party leader: $2 000, 2 years Loss of rights: 5 years	$2 000, 2 years Loss of rights: 5 years	$2 000, 2 years Loss of rights: 5 years	$2 000, 2 years Loss of rights: 5 years
Prince Edward Island		$200 and/or 3 months Loss of rights for 5 years		$200 and/or 3 months Loss of rights: 5 years
New Brunswick		$10 000 and/or 3 months	$1 000 and/or 3 months Seat vacated	$10 000 and/or 3 months
Quebec		$1 000 to $10 000 Loss of rights: 5 years		$1 000 to $10 000 Loss of rights: 5 years
Ontario	Reduction of reimbursement	$1 000	Reduction of reimbursement Seat vacated	$1 000
Manitoba	Reduction of reimbursement $20 000	$1 000	Reduction of reimbursement $2 000	$1 000
Saskatchewan	$5 000	$5 000 and/or 6 months	$5 000 and/or 6 months	$5 000 and/or 6 months
Northwest Territories			$1 000 and/or 1 year	

With regard to election expenses, Manitoba (*Elections Finances Act*, s. 73(1)) and Ontario (*Election Finances Act*, s. 39(4)), as shown in table 9.6, reduce the reimbursement by the amount overspent. Prince Edward Island (*Election Expenses Act*, s. 16(1)(*a*)), New Brunswick (*Political Process Financing Act*, s. 85) and Quebec (*Election Act*, s. 559(1)) do not recognize the liability of parties that exceed the spending limit. Nova Scotia (*Elections Act*, s. 164I(2)) is the only province where the party leader may be fined for this offence; the other provinces do not recognize the leader's liability.

When an official agent exceeds the maximum amount allowed for expenses in Quebec, the judge has the discretionary power to consider the offence a corrupt electoral practice (*Election Act*, s. 567). This discretionary power is not recognized in any other provincial jurisdiction.

Unlike the situation at the federal level, agents in most provinces are penalized in the same way, whether they are acting for a party or for a candidate. New Brunswick (*Political Process Financing Act*, s. 85(3)) and Ontario (*Election Finances Act*, s. 44(2)(*a*)) deal the most severely with candidates since they declare the seat vacant. The *Canada Elections Act* stipulates that deliberate intent must be proved before candidates or agents are deprived of democratic rights because of excessive election spending.

This comparative summary of provincial legislation indicates that the provinces have broader penalties than has the federal legislation, especially with regard to party financing. In addition, corrupt practices relate more to the voting process, rather than to political financing. An assessment of the situation in the provinces shows that the *Canada Elections Act* is not very innovative and provides for few civil penalties, especially for the offences most commonly encountered – failure to submit expense returns and spending above allowable limits. Some provinces offer some very interesting alternatives in this regard.

COMPLAINTS AND PROSECUTIONS: CURRENT SITUATION

In this section, the current situation with regard to complaints, investigations and prosecutions in the electoral process in Canada and in other jurisdictions is examined. An attempt is then made to pinpoint why it is often difficult to deal with complaints and prosecutions in Canada and why there is no incentive to greater compliance with the Act.

Complaints and Prosecutions in Provincial Jurisdictions

Table 9.7 indicates that, Quebec apart, there are far fewer complaints and prosecutions in provincial jurisdictions than at the federal level. But the data should be weighed carefully. The reason why the various provinces show so few complaints is because they do not record complaints that are unjustified or that can be resolved without an investigation.

Table 9.7
**Complaints and prosecutions during the last two elections
in Canadian jurisdictions**

	Complaints		Prosecutions	
Jurisdiction	Last election but one	Last election	Last election but one	Last election
Canada	567	862	115	50
Newfoundland	0	4	0	4
Nova Scotia	n.a.	n.a.	0	2
Prince Edward Island	0	0	0	0
New Brunswick	8	4	0	0
Quebec	591	156	49	29
Ontario	20	127[a]	3	20[b]
Manitoba	1	1	1	0
Saskatchewan	0	0	0	0
Alberta	0	1	0	1
British Columbia	0	0	0	0
Yukon	1	0	0	0
Northwest Territories	1	1	0	1

Sources: Questionnaire sent to chief electoral officers and annual reports of the various jurisdictions. Some complaints and prosecutions relate to offences that occurred outside an electoral period.

[a]Includes 77 complaints related to the Patricia Starr case.

[b]Includes 20 prosecutions related to the Patricia Starr case.

n.a.: not available.

Electoral complaints and prosecutions at the federal level and in Quebec cover the entire Act, i.e., from the voting process to financing election campaigns. In the other provinces, except for Ontario, few offences relate to political financing. Saskatchewan has had no complaints or prosecutions for the last three general elections. One individual, however, received a two-week sentence and was fined $250 for voting under someone else's name in a by-election. This was one of the rare instances where imprisonment was ordered for a breach of an elections act.

All complaints in Ontario concerned breaches of campaign financing rules, but few were serious enough to warrant prosecution. The Starr affair is undoubtedly the most serious case the Commission on Election

Finances has ever had to consider. The accused, who was head of the Toronto branch of the National Council of Jewish Women, was found guilty of making illegal campaign contributions to Ontario Liberal party candidates among others. The Council as such did not, in fact, make contributions. In addition, some local associations submitted falsified financial statements to the Commission. Investigation revealed some 77 irregularities, most of which resulted in prosecutions.

In the Yukon, the only complaint concerned obstructing the work of an enumerator. The one case brought to court in Manitoba concerned overspending on advertising; the accused pleaded guilty and was discharged by the judge. Another complaint concerned government advertising, but it was concluded that no offence had been committed. In Alberta, a candidate was charged under the *Criminal Code* with using false documents; the case is still under investigation. None of the four Newfoundland complaints concerned parties or candidates. One related to advertising on voting day (the accused was fined $100), and another concerned initialling ballots when scrutineers were not present (the person was fined $200).

Quebec provides more extensive data, which can be compared with those at the federal level. Given the relatively high number of complaints and prosecutions in Quebec, a closer examination of the situation is appropriate. As table 9.8 shows, 65 percent of complaints and 82 percent of prosecutions dealt with campaign financing. The most common offence was related to the submission of expense returns, but prosecution resulted in only 2.9 percent of cases. Paying expenses without being an agent is a breach of the Act, and is usually prosecuted (40 percent) in Quebec. Overall, relatively few complaints (approximately 8.3 percent) result in prosecutions, probably because of the method used to record complaints. Frivolous and unjustified complaints are included in this table but, for the most part, these are not investigated closely and files are closed within a few days. Unlike the other provinces, a greater number of complaints and prosecutions are related to political financing.

The criteria used to decide whether to prosecute are the same as in the other provinces: Does prosecution serve as an example? Is it in the public interest? What is the impact on the reputation of the accused? What were the circumstances at the time? In Quebec, except for the general provision, a minimum penalty is always provided for and usually applied to individuals or groups found guilty.

It is difficult to draw any general conclusions as to how complaints and prosecutions are dealt with in Canadian provinces. The CEOs say that few people violate election legislation. The authorities have sufficient

Table 9.8
Complaints and prosecutions instituted under the Quebec *Election Act*,
1985 election

Offences related to:	Complaints		Prosecutions		Prosecutions/ complaints	Penalties
	N	%	N	%	%	$
Fraudulent voting	11	1.9	1	2.0	9.1	100
Time off to vote	26	4.4	0	0.0	0.0	—
Electoral staff	38	6.4	1	2.0	2.6	100
Electoral list and revision	55	9.3	0	0.0	0.0	—
Advertising	44	7.4	0	0.0	0.0	—
Broadcasting	10	1.7	4	8.2	40.0	100
Payment of expenses without being an agent	42	7.1	12	24.5	28.6	100 to 1 000
Expense returns	276	46.7	8	16.3	2.9	50 to 100
Other offences by: parties, agents, candidates	67	11.3	20	40.8	29.9	10 to 150
Other	22	3.8	3	6.1	13.6	100
Total	591	100.0	49	100.0	8.3	—

Sources: Annual reports of the Chief Electoral Officer of Quebec.

discretionary powers to deal with minor offences and, generally speaking, those at fault fall into line upon notification by the organizing body. On the other hand, it seems that officials responsible for running elections in Quebec have much tighter control over the activities of parties, candidates and agents than their counterparts in other provinces. The size of the organization may be one explanation. For example, during the last election the Chief Electoral Officer of Quebec sent formal notices to a number of individuals and groups enjoining them to respect the prohibition on advertising by third parties during the campaign or face prosecution. The number of complaints and prosecutions may also be the result of very detailed regulations, especially with regard to financing, although this can also be found in other provinces where the number of cases is not so high.

Procedure for Dealing with Complaints at Elections Canada

We now turn to the way complaints and prosecutions are handled by Elections Canada, comparing the federal and provincial systems, and also consider the types of alleged violations and their treatment.

Elections Canada has a national network of resource people responsible for advising the Commissioner of minor or local offences that occur during elections. In 1988, most complaints came from individuals or political parties, who submitted them in writing to the Commissioner's office. Others came from the Commissioner's national network, the CEO and Elections Canada personnel, who identified irregularities after checking candidates' and parties' returns.

Complaints are examined first at the Commissioner's office to determine their legitimacy. The RCMP then investigate major cases, while private investigators look into other cases. The results of the investigations are then studied at the Commissioner's office by independent lawyers, the legal adviser for Elections Canada and the Commissioner. If it is necessary to prosecute, the legal adviser then acts as prosecutor. The subject of a complaint, the complainant and the national executive of the party involved are kept informed of progress in the case. Thus the complainant is always notified of the outcome of the complaint (Canada, House of Commons 1988). This process is illustrated in figure 9.1.

The Commissioner has discretionary power at this level. Legal proceedings are not based on a single element in support of an accusation; other circumstances are also taken into account.

The policy of the Commissioner of Canada Elections[3] is based on the following factors (Canada, House of Commons 1988, 20A:15):

- the certainty or likelihood of success – in other words the sufficiency of the evidence to prove guilt beyond a reasonable doubt;
- the exemplary effect of any particular prosecution;
- the nature of the facts giving rise to the offence;
- the effect of a conviction on the individual who is the subject of the case; and
- the extent to which specific provisions of the *Criminal Code* would have to be used to support the enforcement of the *Canada Elections Act*.

The Commissioner consequently enjoys enormous discretionary power in deciding whether to prosecute. In practice, the complex procedure and the need to prove intent in most cases results in a situation where only the most serious cases are brought to court.

For the last four general elections, there has been no consistency in complaints or prosecutions (table 9.9). Complaints have tended to rise since 1979; campaign financing accounted for more than 65 percent of complaints in 1984 and almost 81 percent in 1988. Complaints related to the sale of alcohol and allowing employees four hours off work to vote bring this total to 95 percent. There are very few complaints of

Figure 9.1
Elections Canada procedure for dealing with complaints

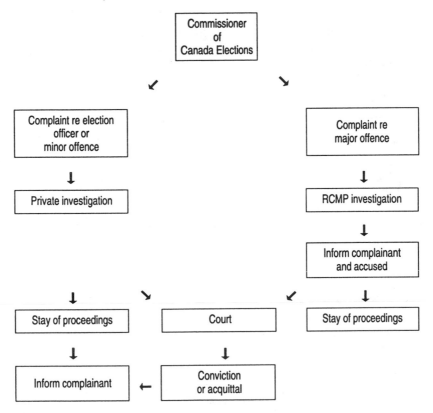

election fraud. An analysis shows that Elections Canada's main problem in enforcing the Act is the financing of election campaigns. If prosecutions for offences for the sale of alcohol are subtracted from the total for 1984, then the number of prosecutions declined during the last two elections, with financing remaining the most common cause.

As tables 9.9, 9.10 and 9.11 show, most apparent violations of the *Canada Elections Act* are committed by the parties, the candidates and their agents and, although complaints have increased in this area, prosecutions have decreased. There are various reasons for this. First, most of the current provisions regarding the financing of election campaigns were introduced in 1974. They were therefore not enforced until 1979 and, as a new election was called so shortly after in 1980, individuals, groups and Elections Canada only became familiar with the Act and its regulations in 1984. That is why the Commissioner was much more cautious about prosecuting between 1980 and 1984. The figures show

Table 9.9
Complaints and prosecutions in Canada (1979, 1980, 1984 and 1988 elections)

Offences	1979 Prosecutions	1980 Prosecutions	1984 Complaints	1984 Prosecutions	1988 Complaints	1988 Prosecutions
Party, candidate, agent, auditor*	63	88	371	28	696	34
Election officer	5	0	14	0	21	1
Election fraud	5	1	7	0	8	3
Time off to vote	4	1	54	1	51	9
Sale of alcohol	15	12	82	82	14	1
Others	2	2	39	4	72	2
Total	94	104	567	115	862	50

Sources: Annual reports by chief electoral officers and unpublished Elections Canada data.

*Most of these cases involved election expenses or election expenses reporting.

that, in 1984, 7.5 percent of financing complaints were prosecuted, compared with 4.8 percent in 1988. The proportion of successful prosecutions increased from 50 percent in 1984 to 70.4 percent in 1988.

Election campaign financing aside, individuals usually comply with the Act's provisions and the electoral process in general. Offences related to allowing employees time off work to vote and the sale of alcohol are not, in our view, reason to question the integrity of the system. Fraud and corruption are no longer common practice in the election of candidates and parties. Other means of influencing voters, such as media use, appear much more effective. With regard to financing offences, the effectiveness of the system is not in doubt because of the number of offences, but rather because of the difficulties created by rigid procedures, the consequences for the individual and ambiguous legislation. Many minor offences thus go unpunished, and individuals and groups have no motivation to comply with the Act. Difficulties in enforcing electoral legislation in Canada are rooted in these factors. Criminal penalties are inappropriate for punishing election offences, and the gravity of the offences committed during the last elections does not warrant their use.

Offences and Enforcement
This section provides a detailed analysis of the problems encountered in dealing with complaints and investigations and in deciding whether to prosecute. We have examined many complaints and prosecutions from the last two elections in order to understand the problems faced

Table 9.10
Complaints and prosecutions, 1984 general election

Offences regarding	Complaints		Prosecutions		Prosecutions/ complaints	Prosecutions leading to conviction
	N	%	N	%	%	%
Parties, candidates, agents*	371	65.4	28	24.3	7.5	50.0
Election officers	14	2.5	0	0.0	0.0	—
Election fraud	7	1.2	0	0.0	0.0	—
Four hours off to vote	54	9.5	1	0.9	1.9	100.0
Sale of alcohol on polling day	82	14.5	82	71.3	100.0	89.0
Others	39	6.9	4	3.5	10.3	50.0
Total	567	100.0	115	100.0	20.3	78.3

*Most of these cases involved election expenses or election expenses reporting.

Table 9.11
Complaints and prosecutions, 1988 general election

Offences regarding	Complaints		Prosecutions		Prosecutions/ complaints	Prosecutions leading to conviction
	N	%	N	%	%	%
Parties, candidates, agents*	696	80.7	34	68	4.9	70.4
Election officers	21	2.4	1	2	4.8	100.0
Election fraud	8	0.9	3	6	37.5	66.7
Four hours off to vote	51	5.9	9	18	17.6	66.7
Sale of alcohol on polling day	14	1.6	1	2	7.1	0.0
Others	72	8.5	2	4	2.8	50.0
Total	862	100.0	50	100.0	5.8	65.9

*Most of these cases involved election expenses or election expenses reporting.

by the Commissioner and the CEO in enforcing the Act.

The definition of election expenses (section 2(1)) is clearly crucial to the enforcement of the *Canada Elections Act* with regard to financing.

The CEO has emphasized this in several reports: "The present definition of *election expenses* is so vague and imprecise that its application to various sections of the Act has become extremely difficult. Problems related to pre-writ expenses, the principle of direct promotion of or opposition to a candidate or a political party (third party advertising), the monies paid to agents and campaign workers, fund raising, opinion surveys and the use of capital assets, to name but a few, must be looked at and clarified" (Canada, Elections Canada 1986, 10).

The problems here arise mainly from the terms used to define election expenses. The expression "for the purpose of promoting or opposing, directly and during an election, a ... party, or ... candidate" makes intent very difficult to prove. Was it the violator's purpose to promote or oppose a candidate? For example, is a survey or poll intended to oppose or to support a candidate or a party? Are letters sent out by parties during their fund-raising campaigns – letters that often refer to "good" or "bad" candidates – intended to promote or oppose a particular party? There are no mutually inclusive or exclusive definitions, such as those found in Quebec and Ontario for example, that allow a clear determination of what is meant by "election expense." Therefore, all new practices adopted by parties must be assessed carefully to determine whether they correspond to an election expense. In the courts, the ambiguities of the Act leave the accused with the benefit of any doubt. This means that the alleged offences cannot be punished, not because there has been no offence, but because there is no clear definition of the violation in question, and the term "directly" is open to interpretation. Such inconsistencies often prevent the Commissioner of Canada Elections from taking a case to court.

A member of Parliament has pointed out the consequences for candidates: "The current Act mentions election expenses, electoral expenses. No one knows what they are. Candidates and members find themselves before the courts only to be acquitted because the Act is not clear. This affects their credibility" (Lavoie 1990, 13).

The expression "election expenses" is used in several provisions, and its ambiguity affects all portions of the Act dealing with the financing of election campaigns. This problem has become more pronounced since 1984, explaining why few campaign financing offences are prosecuted. To gain a better understanding of the problems in enforcing the Act, we reviewed 150 complaints received by Elections Canada. The Commissioner of Canada Elections informed us that none of the complaints received in 1988 regarding election expenses could be pursued, because individuals, agents and candidates also have to work with this ambiguous definition. In many cases, the expenses in question were not election expenses, so no cases went to court.

The two provisions of the Act concerning limitation of expenses and false declarations on an expense return are closely related, because items in excess of the spending limit are usually not included in the return, meaning that the declaration is false.

The policy of the Commissioner of Canada Elections is to prosecute only when overspending involves large amounts and the candidate or party tried to conceal it, proving that the action was intentional (Canada, House of Commons 1988). If information is missing, i.e., the declaration is false, no legal action is taken if the offender agrees to provide the information to the Commissioner.

Such offences are usually committed by candidates and agents, very rarely by the parties and their agents. Moreover, the Commissioner of Canada Elections told us that, in most of the complaints received during the last election, overspending was minimal and would not require prosecution to protect the integrity of the process.

The problem with these offences is not one of overspending and/or false declarations. It is more a question of the joint liability of candidates and their agents. The case law on the subject has not yet given us a clear interpretation of liability.

In *R. v. Roman* (1986), the candidate and agent were accused of exceeding the ceiling on expenses and failing to include those expenses in the return, an illegal act. Judge Zimmerman acquitted the candidate on the following facts: The candidate has an agent and auditor. Therefore there is nothing to prove that the candidate knowingly and deliberately failed in his responsibilities by incurring expenditures that should have been included in the report. The fact that the returns were reviewed by the agent and the auditor shows that the candidate took due care. As to the agent stating that he reviewed and prepared the expense return with due care, the judge held that there was nothing to indicate that the agent was aware of the matter; he was thus acquitted. In this case, the liability of the agent and candidate is established only if one or the other is aware of the expenditures, even though the Act requires that the agent control expenses. In our view, this interpretation leaves unresolved confusion.

In another case involving a candidate (*Baillargeon* 1986), the judge's opinion was quite different. Judge Gagnon emphasized that: "It is clearly not possible for a candidate personally to check every expense incurred in running an election campaign. However, although section 61.1[4] delegates responsibility, simply delegating this task to a competent person does not exonerate the candidate when expenses exceed in the aggregate the maximum election expenses provided for in the Act" (ibid., 15).

In another case, we find a different interpretation of the liability of candidates. In *Baillargeon v. Marin* (1987), Judge Poirier described the candidate's liability:

> The Court must first determine the meaning of the beginning of section 61.1(1), in other words, what do the words: "any other person acting on his behalf" mean? Under section 61.1(1), is the candidate responsible for all election workers in his riding or is he responsible for the people he has hired for his election campaign? The beginning of section 61.1 seems to imply that the candidate is responsible for his official agent and for anyone acting on behalf of the official agent or at least if we apply the *ejusdem generis* rule he would be liable for the actions of any individual who has an official role similar to that of an official agent. Moreover, section 62 paragraph 4[5] provides that only the official agent may pay accounts or make payments for expenses incurred for purposes of the conduct or management of the election and paragraph 3 provides that every person who makes any payment, advance or deposit in contravention of paragraph 4 is guilty of an illegal practice and of an offence. In some cases, riding officials have been charged and some have pleaded guilty or been fined after distributing money illegally to workers on election day. Therefore, the Court seriously doubts that the delegation of responsibility provided for in section 61.1 would extend to all members of the party working to elect a candidate, even as volunteers.
>
> On the other hand, if under section 61.1, the candidate is responsible for any persons acting on behalf of the Conservative party in the riding, then the Court would have to conclude that the candidate-respondent at least knew about the election expenses even if the Court did not find that the overspending was intentional or deliberate. (*Baillargeon* 1987, 10–12)

These three cases give a clear picture of the problems associated with establishing the liability imposed by the Act on candidates and their agents for expenses incurred. In one case, it was held that a candidate is liable, while in the other two cases liability was found to be limited. Therefore, it is almost impossible to decide who is liable since the case law is contradictory. Under the circumstances, it is difficult for the Commissioner of Canada Elections to decide whether the agent or candidate is liable for overspending, thus compounding the confusion.

Expenditures by third parties and identification of printed material (Canada, *Canada Elections Act*, ss. 259 and 261) also affect enforcement of the Act. These two provisions have not been applicable since 1984 because of a decision of the Alberta Court of Queen's Bench (*National Citizens' Coalition* 1984). Mr. Justice Medhurst held that the provisions dealing with regulating the activities of third parties were, prima facie, in violation of the *Canadian Charter of Rights and Freedoms*, and this violation was not justifiable under section 1.

Following the federal government's decision not to appeal this ruling, the CEO did not enforce the two sections, and also decided that it would be unfair to apply them in all provinces except Alberta. This decision was confirmed by the Federal Court in 1988 in a subsequent case (*Riddell* 1989). In that decision, Mr. Justice Muldoon held that there was no evidence to support the argument that democracy would be threatened if section 70.1[6] were not enforced.

Since this section is unconstitutional, it means that Elections Canada can no longer exercise control over the expenses of local associations previously governed by this section. In addition, no provision covers government publications during an election. Therefore, support for a particular minister, for example, could benefit the party in power.

As for section 261 of the *Canada Elections Act*, the French version does not correspond to the English version. In French, the printed material in question includes all third parties, whereas in English it includes only parties and candidates. The provision was found unconstitutional based on the French version.

The prohibition against parties and candidates broadcasting and publishing during a fixed period (ss. 213 and 48) also creates problems for Elections Canada. For broadcasting, it is often difficult to prove whether the candidate or the party acted properly or participated in the event in question. If the message is not sufficiently direct, it may not fall within the definition of election expenses. There is also often confusion as to whether the election of a candidate or the candidate's personal business is being promoted, especially when the person concerned owns a company.

As far as publication in a periodical is concerned, the CEO pointed out, in one of his reports, how easy it is to circumvent the legislation because the definition of "periodical" is a publication published at intervals not exceeding 31 days. Periodicals falling outside this limit can therefore be used (Canada, Elections Canada 1984, 23).

In addition, the prohibition on broadcasting and publication only applies to candidates and not to individuals trying for nomination. Because of this inconsistency, someone who does not have the status of a candidate cannot be charged. In other cases, arrangements for advertising have already progressed too far when an election is called for proceedings to be instituted. These factors explain why there were many complaints (54) in 1988, but only eight charges laid.

Under current policy, the Commissioner of Canada Elections no longer prosecutes police complaints under section 251, prohibition of the sale of alcohol on polling day. This provision is both inconsistent and unfair because, during by-elections, particularly in urban areas, alcohol can often be easily purchased in an adjacent riding. In addition, the provision does not apply to advance polls. As indicated in *Parkdale Hotel Limited* (1986, 516), "The argument that any particular provision of the statute might be obsolete, or that public or private opinion does not consider any such provision necessary, is not the key to its validity." In the same vein, "if Parliament can set up liquor control and temperance measures at large, it can certainly control for purposes of its own elections the dispensation of liquor on election day" (ibid.).

The maximum for notices of meetings for candidates and parties to be spent (s. 214) is also unclear. Candidates are subject to a fixed maximum of 1 percent, whereas parties have no limits imposed; this is a clear advantage for candidates associated with parties (Canada, Elections Canada 1984, 23).

As for the provisions concerning hours off for voting (s. 149), the French and English versions of the law are not the same. In English, the provision seems to apply only to employees paid on an hourly basis whereas, in French, the provisions apply to everyone.

Advertising in a polling station (s. 158) is also difficult to consider as an offence because the English version does not correspond to the French. According to the English version, it is not an offence to display posters at a school since the section mentions only the inside and outside walls of the polling station itself and not the building in which it is located. The policy of the Commissioner of Canada Elections in this regard is to request the RCMP to remove advertising material.

Election expenses paid by someone other than an official agent (s. 217) were the subject of 80 complaints in 1988, but did not result in any prosecutions. This provision has posed many problems. First of all, section 217 requires that all electoral expenses, not just election expenses, be controlled by the agent but, once again, the French and English versions do not correspond. The French states that expenses may be paid by someone else whereas, in English, they may be paid only by the agent. The Commissioner's policy is not to prosecute if the people involved have not attempted to conceal such matters. In the opinion of Commissioner Allen, this is a technical offence, with no need for criminal prosecution.

Submission of returns by candidates (s. 238) is another provision that is difficult to apply. Of the 127 complaints received during the last election, most concerned delays of a few days because of the mail. In many instances, candidates' expenses were under $1 000, which is usually less than an auditor's fees. The Commissioner's policy is not to prosecute in such cases.

One of the deficiencies of the *Canada Elections Act* is that it does not exclude prosecution under the *Criminal Code*. The absence of general provisions[7] similar to those in provincial jurisdictions (Alberta, *Election Act*, s. 150(1); Quebec, *Election Act*, s. 565; New Brunswick, *Political Process Financing Act*, s. 88(1); and Ontario, *Election Finances Act*, s. 49) and the fact that the Act does not cover aiding and abetting,[8] although there are such provisions in other jurisdictions,[9] require the *Code* to be invoked in such cases. In addition, the *Criminal Code* contains provisions related to the electoral process such as corruption[10] and the destruction of election documents.[11]

The *Canada Elections Act* recognizes only the liability of the person committing an offence. The one counselling the offence is not held responsible, and there is no provision covering conspiracy. Elections Canada has always been most reluctant to use the *Criminal Code*. Commissioner Gorman said so on several occasions when the House of Commons Standing Committee on Elections, Privileges and Procedure was hearing the facts in the Masse case. If the minister had been prosecuted, he would have been prosecuted under section 21 of the *Criminal Code*, which covers aiding and abetting. Commissioner Gorman stated:

> Regarding the use of the *Criminal Code*, even though the *Canada Elections Act* provides for summary conviction and indictable offences, and for imprisonment as a penalty, it is not a criminal statute. I have always felt that it would be inappropriate in most cases for me to seek the support of the *Criminal Code* to enforce the provisions of the *Canada Elections Act*, thus criminalizing what are in essence regulatory offences. (Canada, House of Commons 1988, 20:25)

While it is possible to use the *Criminal Code* to charge and convict an offender, it is Elections Canada policy to avoid using a very complex procedural code that imposes harsh punishment on the offender because such a prosecution has serious consequences for the accused without any deterrent effect. In actual fact, the problem with the current Act is that, since prosecution is so complex, no action is taken unless the gravity of the offence warrants setting the procedure in motion.

The penalties imposed in criminal court also highlight the fact that courts of law have little interest in elections cases. Offences are punished by small fines that bear no direct relationship to the nature of the offence. For example, a party that does not submit a return is liable to a fine of only $500 and may continue its activities; the provision does, however, ensure the openness of the system. Table 9.12 shows that, despite the apparent severity of the penalties provided for in the Act, imprisonment and the loss of political rights are seldom imposed and fines are minimal.

The review of how complaints are dealt with shows that Elections Canada's access to the courts is hampered by a number of legal constraints. In addition, judges generally impose minimal fines in cases involving elections offences. Criminal proceedings give the accused the benefit of the doubt in situations where, for example, the ambiguity of the term "election expenses," differences between the French and English versions and the lack of precision with regard to individual liability make conviction difficult. While these problems are specifically related to the wording of the Act, they are accompanied by others regarding administrative structure and procedure.

It must be remembered that the Commissioner does not have the powers of an investigator appointed under the *Inquiries Act*, except in

Table 9.12
Fines imposed on conviction, 1984 and 1988 general elections

Offences	Less than $100	$100	$200	$250	$300	$400	$500	$800
Advertising by a candidate during blackout period	X							
Advertising by a party during blackout period				X				
Overspending by a candidate		X						
Overspending for notices of meetings				X				
Expenses paid by someone other than agent		X	X					X
Failure of candidate to submit expense return	X					X		
Failure of party to submit expense return							X	

the case of election officers (Canada, *Canada Elections Act*, s. 257). In other cases, the Commissioner must use the services of the RCMP, and this poses two problems: (1) Electoral offences are not a first priority for these officers and therefore the procedure takes a long time. Cases investigated by the RCMP remain open for an average of one year, whereas those dealt with directly by Elections Canada remain open for an average of one month;[12] (2) The RCMP are immediately identified with criminal cases, which means that being the subject of a police investigation has a direct repercussion on the reputation of the person concerned.

Jean-Marc Hamel has pointed out the disadvantages of a police investigation:

> Complaints received during an election alleging that a candidate has committed an offence must be handled judiciously, as the person's chances of being elected could be adversely affected if it became known that he or she was under police investigation. The same problems occur following the election, when an investigation deals with a complaint against an elected official. One cannot overlook the possible harm done individuals because of the assumption of guilt too often associated with police investigation. Even though the Charter presumes persons innocent until they are found guilty by a court of competent jurisdiction, reality tells otherwise. (1990, 14)

A police investigation has a considerable impact on an individual. Elections Canada has no control over investigators' activities; as Hamel says, this can adversely affect the election of a candidate or the reputation of a member after election.

Another problem mentioned by Commissioner Allen was the separation of powers between the CEO and the Commissioner. In certain cases, directives issued by the CEO are not consistent with the Commissioner's criteria for instituting proceedings. During the 1988 general election, confusion arose about how candidates' representatives were to be identified at polling stations. The Commissioner decided not to punish any such offences.

Recommendations for Enforcing the Act Made at Hearings of the Royal Commission on Electoral Reform and Party Financing

Recommendations and comments made on the enforcement of the *Canada Elections Act* during the Royal Commission hearings indicated that those involved in the process would like the current structure and procedures changed.

Three major points became clear from the submissions made (table 9.13). In general, all those concerned were in favour of changing current

Table 9.13

Submissions on the structure and enforcement of the *Canada Elections Act* during hearings of the Royal Commission on Electoral Reform and Party Financing

Proposals	Number of submissions
Act should be more strictly enforced and offences more severely punished	5
Enforcement of the Act should be the sole responsibility of CEO	9
Complaints should be dealt with more quickly	8
Adjudication by administrative tribunal	13
Decision by the Federal Court	6
Candidate should be notified when he/she is subject of an investigation	3
RCMP should remain responsible for investigations	3
A body other than the RCMP should investigate	34
RCMP should investigate only criminal cases	16
Opposed to the creation of a commission as proposed by Bill C-79	3
Creation of a commission on election financing	4
In favour of the creation of a commission	15
Commission should consist of members appointed by resolution of the House of Commons	4
Serious violations of the Act should be prosecuted under the *Criminal Code* and in Provincial Court	15
Decriminalization of the Act	18
No decriminalization of the Act	3

CEO: Chief Electoral Officer; RCMP: Royal Canadian Mounted Police.

procedures for enforcing the Act, with particular emphasis on the investigations conducted by the RCMP. For various reasons, including the slowness of the procedure and the harm caused by criminal investigations to personal reputations, those involved would like another body, a commission or investigator, responsible to Elections Canada, which would investigate regulatory offences.

Interest was also expressed in establishing an administrative tribunal with the power to adjudicate purely regulatory offences.

Finally, the creation of an electoral commission was favoured. This body would have the power to enforce the Act just as the CEO, the Commissioner of Canada Elections, the RCMP and the trial courts do now. Insofar as is possible, it would incorporate some of the powers held by these authorities.

Although most of the people who commented on this issue advocated structural changes, the desire for changes in investigation methods was even more vigorous. Opinion differed to some extent on the powers and duties to be attributed to an electoral commission.

In short, and judging by the submissions, there is a desire for greater flexibility and efficiency in the complaints procedure and judicial process.

Current Situation

An analysis of the current situation on the enforcement of the *Canada Elections Act* reveals the following:

- Terms concerning offences and throughout the Act in general (see the definition of election expenses) are poorly defined, often preventing Elections Canada from instituting proceedings.
- There are shortcomings in the Act, sometimes requiring the authorities to bring an action under the *Criminal Code.*
- Various provisions of the Act are not enforceable because they are unconstitutional (cf. the *Canadian Charter of Rights and Freedoms*).
- Several sections of the Act are obsolete.
- The English and French versions differ.
- Sanctions are too severe for minor offences, leading the courts to impose only minimal penalties.
- Police investigations (RCMP) may harm personal reputations, in addition to being time-consuming.
- Elections Canada is not empowered to negotiate or deal with minor offences without going before the courts.
- There is a lack of interest on the part of judges in trial courts in dealing with offences that are basically regulatory.
- It is difficult to establish proof in court because of the ambiguity of the Act and the requirement to prove intent.
- The costs of often fruitless legal proceedings are extremely heavy for the government.
- Differing decisions handed down by the trial courts in each of the territories and provinces create inconsistent case law.
- The Commissioner requires the Attorney General's permission before going to appeal. The Attorney General is an elected official who may have to judge his or her own party colleagues in the House of Commons.
- The political parties, Elections Canada, candidates and members of Parliament all indicate a desire to see the Act amended.

PROPOSAL FOR A NEW STRUCTURE FOR ELECTIONS CANADA

The problems encountered in enforcing the *Canada Elections Act* and their effect on how the system operates have been analysed in previous sections. This section evaluates the application of administrative law procedures to breaches of the *Canada Elections Act*. Suggestions for a new administrative structure for the electoral process are then put forward, including new standards and a new legislative framework.

Separating the Electoral Process from the Judicial Process

Current procedures for dealing with violations of the Act come under the criminal law. Section 11(*d*) of the *Canadian Charter of Rights and Freedoms* guarantees that every individual is presumed innocent until proved guilty beyond all reasonable doubt. The burden of proof follows from this presumption of innocence. The Crown must therefore offer proof and, if the Act is unclear or imprecise or if there is insufficient evidence, the accused has the benefit of the doubt. Proof of the offence must be based on two elements: the physical element, i.e., the tangible effect of the offence or action (*actus reus*), and the mental element (*mens rea*) or intent. Section 7 of the Charter provides that everyone has the right not to be deprived of the right to liberty and security of the person except according to the principles of fundamental justice. In the vast majority of cases, intent must be proved in cases subject to imprisonment. The accused is entitled to the benefit of the doubt and the accused's actions may not be taken as a proof of intent. Most offences in the current *Canada Elections Act* are subject to these two provisions, because they come under criminal law and assume a deprivation of liberty.

In law, there are three ways in which offences may be dealt with before the courts. (1) An absolute liability offence does not require proof of intent if the facts alleged by the Crown have been proved; conviction is automatic. Care may not be cited as a defence. This type of offence must be handled cautiously to ensure that there is no conflict with section 11(*d*) of the *Canadian Charter of Rights and Freedoms* regarding the presumption of innocence. (2) In a strict liability offence, the Crown does not necessarily have to prove intent in order to institute proceedings, but the defence may raise the question during the trial; it may show that it has taken due care to avoid committing an offence. (3) In a *mens rea* offence, the Crown must prove intent.

Currently, most offences under the *Canada Elections Act* are subject to the *mens rea* test and, in many cases, it is hard to prove intent because of the difficulty, if not impossibility, of discerning the offender's objective. Under administrative law, absolute liability and strict liability are more appropriate because it is difficult to prove the state of mind of the accused, as the minor and often technical nature of the offences makes the burden of proof a very heavy one (Côté-Harper et al. 1989, 338). Webb notes the same difficulties:

The forms of regulatory offence currently most prevalent (absolute and strict liability) were originally created by courts and legislatures in an attempt to address behaviour which was not subjectively intended but was nevertheless potentially harmful. Traditional criminal offences – where the prosecution is required to establish beyond a reasonable doubt both the *actus reus* and the *mens rea* of the offence – have proven to be impractical in this regard, because of the limited scope of behaviour they address (that is, subjectively intended behaviour) and the virtual impossibility of the prosecution being able to prove fault in regulatory contexts (that is, where only the accused is likely to have the information upon which a finding of fault could be based). (1989, 420–21)

The difficulty in suiting criminal procedure to regulatory matters has been raised by those directly involved with the administration of the electoral process. In addition, the fact that very few prosecutions have been instituted in electoral cases compared with the number of complaints received can be explained in part by the need to use criminal procedure.

A number of reasons are currently being put forward justifying the decriminalizing of offences or violations of various regulations and laws. Factors suggesting that a more flexible administrative procedure would be more effective in ensuring that the Act is obeyed and enforced include ever-growing government involvement through regulations, the inadequacy of procedures provided by the *Criminal Code* and the tendency of Western nations to remove offences from the judicial process.

Sieghart (1980) noted that, in several countries, including Austria, Great Britain, Germany, Greece and the United States, offences fall into two categories. *Criminal Code* offences are those where an individual is wronged or a real risk exists. Regulatory offences represent an abstract risk, arising from a deviation from the law, and require a provision designed to protect society as a whole.

In fact, these categories encourage compliance with the legislation, by enabling the rapid processing of cases and placing an intermediate step between the criminal law and the offenders. As Healy says:

The aim of regulation, in general terms, is enhancement of the public welfare through the prevention of harm or the promotion of specific goods ... The prevention of harm is also one of the aims of the criminal law but it does not follow that any legal sanction for the prevention of harm is a criminal offence. The prevention of harm is a rationale or justification that supports legal sanction without reference to the criminal law. (1990, 7)

Penalties for regulatory offences are intended to correct a situation and redress wrongs; they are also intended to encourage compliance with the provisions. The criminal model seems increasingly inappropriate for non-criminal offences because of the rigidity of the procedure, the virtual absence of negotiation and the costs involved. Authorities are reluctant to punish minor offences and those where intent cannot be proven beyond a reasonable doubt because of the high cost in human and material resources.

Although Deysine (1982) deals specifically with electoral corruption, she clearly describes what happens when offences are inconsistent with penalties: the latter are never imposed. The resulting lack of control causes people to lose confidence in the system and to become apathetic about the process.

Experience suggests that administrative tribunals and the decriminalization of offences are the preferred options for enforcing the *Canada Elections Act*. Administrative tribunals are able to hear and decide rapidly cases that arise when enforcing laws, to specialize, and to offer lower costs and a simple procedure based on a hearings process (Gosselin 1989).

In our opinion, such features, together with a proper regulatory procedure, would make it possible to enforce the Act more effectively. Disputes would be settled more quickly, *mens rea* would be required only in specific cases, the range of penalties would be better suited to minor and major offences and it would be possible to settle disputes out of court. The administrative procedure would also protect individuals who have committed minor or regulatory offences from being investigated by the RCMP or being charged and sentenced in a criminal court. It would also mean that cases could be handled more quickly and at a lower cost.

Moore (1990, 1–2) discusses the advantages of using civil proceedings to deal with criminal offences. When the nature of the offence does not justify criminal proceedings, the deterrent effect is eliminated because of the procedural constraints provided in the *Criminal Code*. The penalties imposed are too severe (often imprisonment), which means that the standard of proof is higher (obligation to prove intent), with the result that prosecutors are reluctant to charge offenders. There are always long delays. The impact on the reputation of the accused is enormous. The advantage of civil proceedings is that cases are dealt with promptly since proof is easier to establish, and the procedure is less harmful to the reputation of the accused. In all cases, a higher level of compliance and better enforcement of the Act result.

Examples of Administrative Structures

Four typical examples illustrate the advantages of using such an administrative system to enforce the *Canada Elections Act*. The only example dealing with electoral matters is the U.S. Federal Election Commission (FEC). The other examples are the Ontario and Quebec securities commissions and the Canadian Human Rights Commission. Once again, these choices are not arbitrary. The administrative procedures followed by these organizations are pertinent to this study. The sharing of powers within the FEC demonstrates that it is possible to grant quasi-judicial powers to an administrative authority in electoral matters through negotiated agreements. The securities commissions provide the advantage of structures that enjoy procedural flexibility for settling disputes, as well as powers of adjudication. The Human Rights Commission differs from the other models in that it provides two distinct structures – one to allow for negotiated settlements between the parties and the other to decide on cases that cannot be settled out of court.

Dealing with Complaints and Prosecutions Instituted by the FEC

In the United States, the FEC is responsible for receiving complaints from organizations and voters on election campaign financing matters. The FEC cannot deal with anonymous complaints (U.S., *Federal Election Campaign Act*, s. 437g(a)(1)). Any decision to institute proceedings, investigate or negotiate a settlement must be made with the consent of at least four FEC members (ibid., s. 437g(a)(4)(A)(i)), i.e., the majority of members with voting rights. This procedure is illustrated in figure 9.2.

The fine imposed in the case of a conciliation agreement is up to $5 000 or an amount equal to any illegal contribution or expenses. If the Commission finds that the offences were committed knowingly and intentionally, the maximum penalty is doubled (U.S., *Federal Election Campaign Act*, s. 437g(a)(5)(B)). The decision to transfer the case to the prosecutor without any attempt at conciliation is also made by four FEC voting members (ibid., s. 437g(a)(5)(C)). In most cases, the FEC tries to arrive at a conciliation agreement, rather than take legal action. Civil proceedings can be begun if the conciliation agreement is not honoured by the parties at issue. If it is impossible for the FEC to negotiate a settlement, it may transfer the case to the court in the judicial district where the offence was committed. The penalties will be the same as those imposed by the FEC (ibid., s. 437g(a)(b)(6)).

If the FEC refuses to act on complaints, the court can direct the Commission to do so. It is then possible to appeal to the Court of Appeal and the final judgement may be taken to the Supreme Court. A

Figure 9.2
Federal Election Commission procedure for dealing with complaints and prosecutions

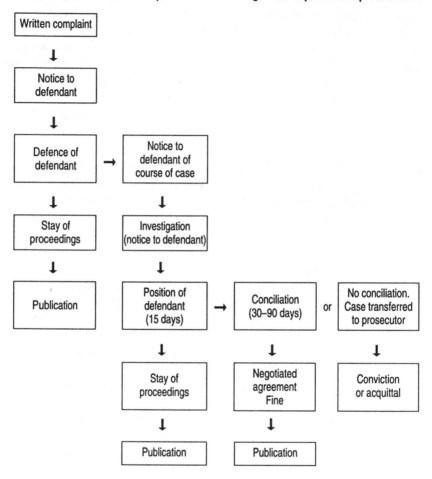

maximum of three years is allowed for action taken by the Commission or court (U.S., *Federal Election Campaign Act*, s. 455).

The reason why the FEC's system is relevant to this study is its use of civil action for settling cases promptly. This procedure, which is far more flexible than that in Canada, facilitates enforcement of the legislation without recourse to the courts, yet without totally excluding them. The system makes it easier to deal with and punish offences, since it is the FEC that interprets and formulates the guidelines. Suspects may also present their case before going to conciliation or before the courts.

Nevertheless, the FEC has its critics. The most frequent criticisms are lack of impartiality, excessive delays, a lack of respect for freedom of expression and arbitrary decisions. There is a reluctance to investigate and to prosecute when large numbers of people and political personalities are involved. However, Alexander and Haggerty note that:

> These explanations suggest that at least part of the blame for the commission's alleged lack of impartiality may be due to the complexities of the law, the commission's relative lack of resources, and the desire of Congress to ensure that members are not subject to random audits. Nevertheless many critics remain unconvinced. They continue to maintain that the FEC commissioners, political appointees all, are reluctant to step on the toes of those who are responsible for their appointments and their agency's appropriations. (1987, 45)

In general, there is some controversy over the Commission's effectiveness. Some observers consider that this body is "toothless," while others suggest that the fact that political parties nominate Commission members compromises its impartiality. It has even been stated that Commission members cannot act effectively because they are too concerned about their own appointment. In addition, the lengthy procedures involved in hearing witnesses and others involved cause delays, meaning that decisions have little deterrent effect when a significant period of time elapses between a complaint being filed and a decision being made.

Despite these difficulties and criticisms, FEC penalties following conciliation (table 9.14) are, all things being equal, higher than those imposed by Canadian criminal courts.

Part of the FEC's administrative structure is the Election Crimes Branch (ECB), which is part of the Public Integrity Section of the Criminal Justice Division of the Justice Department. This body was set up in 1980 to ensure enforcement of the elections act at the national level. The ECB must approve all investigations and criminal prosecutions, and it is directly involved in their day-to-day management.

The ECB is responsible for prosecuting four types of offence:

- Electoral fraud: interference with ballots, vote counting, stuffing ballot boxes.
- Failure to declare contributions and expenses. These violations involve large sums of money and intentional misconduct.
- Patronage involving public employees.
- Violations of federal restrictions governing lobbies.

Investigations are conducted by the Federal Bureau of Investigation (FBI), under the supervision of the ECB. Complaints are made to the FBI, and the ECB decides whether it is necessary to prosecute. The ECB may

Table 9.14
Examples of penalties imposed by the FEC after negotiated settlement, 1989–90

Defendant	Violation	Penalty ($)
Group	Excessive and prohibited contributions	3 500
Group	Transfer of non-federal funds to a federal account	1 200
Group	Return not registered and containing false information	5 000
Individual	Excessive contributions	250
Group	Return not submitted within time limit	300
Group	Return not submitted within time limit	1 200
Group	Return not submitted within time limit	8 750
Group	Return not submitted within time limit	375
Group	Return not submitted within time limit	1 000
Group	Return not submitted within time limit	3 400

impose fines of $25 000 or 300 percent of the amount involved in the offence. Approximately 150 cases are prosecuted every year.

The dual jurisdiction used in the United States has significant disadvantages. Moore (1990, 5) pointed out the problems inherent in such a procedure. Witnesses refuse to testify to avoid their testimony being used at another level. Investigations continue, even if the case is being prosecuted at two levels. Testimony gathered during civil proceedings can be used at the criminal level, with the result that penalties can be imposed in both the criminal and civil cases, which is contrary to the fundamental rights of an individual.

Although the FEC and the Department of Justice (DOJ) agreed to a memorandum of understanding (U.S., Department of Justice 1988, 80–81) establishing rules for cooperation, the problem of dual jurisdiction remains. The memorandum sets out the following directives:

- The FEC is responsible for minor and unintentional violations.
- The DOJ is responsible for serious and intentional violations.
- The FEC must transfer all cases involving serious and intentional violations to the DOJ.
- The DOJ must transfer minor violations to the FEC.

There is a degree of competition between these two authorities, which complicates matters. Canadian legislators should be aware of this problem, because cases involving dual jurisdiction could make all

Commission decisions inoperative, thus making the administrative body both expensive and ineffective.

Quebec Securities Commission

The Commission des valeurs mobilières du Québec (CVMQ or the Quebec Securities Commission) (Quebec, *Securities Act*, ss. 277–300) is made up of seven commissioners appointed by the government for a five-year term. Only the chair and the two vice-chairs hold their positions full time. Commission members may be dismissed by the minister responsible only on the recommendation of the Court of Appeal. Their remuneration is fixed by the government and may not be reduced. The quorum of the Commission is two members and the chair has the deciding vote.

The Commission is relatively independent of the government. The government's control over the Commission is mainly by means of an annual report on the Commission's activities (Quebec, *Securities Act*, s. 302), in which recommendations may be made for amending the *Securities Act*.

The Commission's principal function (Quebec, *Securities Act*, s. 276) is to ensure the smooth operation of the securities market in Quebec. The Commission is responsible for enforcing the Act and regulations. It has responsibility for supervision, control and information, and its decisions have the same effect as those of a court of law. The type of decisions rendered by the Commission gives it the status of an administrative tribunal.

The Commission consists of four branches: information, administration, market registry and legal affairs. The chair has overall responsibility for these four branches. Since Commission staff members hold their power by delegation, the Commission is empowered to review decisions made by its personnel.

All complaints concerning the securities market in Quebec are filed with the Commission, which is exclusively empowered to authorize its staff to conduct an investigation. If Commissioners authorize an investigation, the director of legal affairs controls the procedure, acting independently of the Commission. The director names investigators, who have the required powers. The results of the investigation are then submitted to the Commissioners, who may close the case, call hearings or refer the case to the courts.

Hearings allow defendants to present their position before the Commission, which also exercises its powers of adjudication at that time. Only civil penalties are imposed, including voiding contracts (Quebec, *Securities Act*, s. 214), nullifying transfers (ibid., ss. 215, 217 and 222), temporarily suspending securities brokers or consultants and drawing up a code of ethics (Commission des valeurs mobilières du Québec 1989a, 2). Although the *Securities Act* allows the Commission to impose fines, the Commission does not do so.

The Commission must institute proceedings within two years of being informed of offences, which include:

- failure to observe the terms of a Commission decision;
- failure to fulfil an undertaking with the Commission;
- failure to furnish, within the prescribed time, information or a document required by the *Securities Act* or regulations;
- failure to appear after summons, to refuse to testify or to refuse to send or remit any document or thing required by the Commission or an agent appointed by it in the course of an investigation (Quebec, *Securities Act*, s. 195); and
- submission of false or misleading information (ibid., ss. 196–197).

The Commission may impose the following penalties: a fine of $500 to $10 000 for an individual, as well as imprisonment of one month to two years; a fine of $500 to $25 000 in other cases (Quebec, *Securities Act*, s. 202). The same penalties apply to breaches of the regulations.

A person may appeal decisions made to the Quebec Court, before three judges (Quebec, *Securities Act*, ss. 324–330). Such an appeal does not suspend execution of the decision, however, unless the judges or the Commission decide otherwise. The Quebec Court of Appeal may, on request by one of the judges of the Quebec Court, review the Commission's decision. The Superior Court may issue an injunction under the *Securities Act*, at the request of the Commission.

Approximately 100 charges are laid per year by the Commission, with convictions in 99 percent of cases.[13]

Ontario Securities Commission

The Ontario Securities Commission (OSC) is similar in some ways to the Quebec Commission, especially in its mandate and powers. However, their administrative structures are different.

The Ontario Securities Commission is divided into five relatively distinct departments (OSC 1990, 6–8). The first level consists of the Commission, a statutory tribunal made up of a chair, two vice-chairs and up to eight other members, all appointed by the Lieutenant Governor in Council (Ontario, *Securities Act*, s. 2). The chair acts as chief executive officer. Two members constitute a quorum. The Commission's functions are as follows: it formulates policy, sits as an administrative tribunal, reviews decisions made by the Executive Director or the Executive Director's staff, hears appeals from decisions made by self-regulatory organizations and makes recommendations to the government for changes to legislation. Attached to the Commission is the Office of the Secretary, which assists with hearings.

The second level is made up of Commission staff, coordinated by the Executive Director. The branches at this level are Accounting, the Office of the General Counsel, the Finance Division, Capital Markets, International Affairs, Human Resources and Enforcement.

The Ontario Securities Commission has administrative responsibility for ensuring the competence and integrity of registrants, reviewing and distributing disclosure documents and enforcing the Act, together with its power of investigation.

The Commission's powers are as follows (OSC 1990, 6):

- to suspend, cancel or impose terms on registration, or reprimand registrants;
- to grant or deny exemptions from provisions or requirements of the Act to groups or individuals;
- to cease trading of any security;
- to order that funds be frozen or ask the court to appoint a receiver;
- to order audits of registrants;
- to establish and maintain standards for financial reporting requirements and proxy solicitation; and
- to grant recognition to self-regulatory organizations and review their rules as required.

Enforcement Branch receives complaints and investigates them (Ontario, *Securities Act*, ss. 11–17). Commission and tribunal staff work independently of each other when dealing with complaints and investigations. The Executive Director and the Director of the Enforcement Branch thus have exclusive responsibility for deciding whether to investigate or to institute proceedings. Although a Commissioner may take part in discussions on these decisions, he or she has no authority in this area. In practice, proceedings are instituted only with the consent of the chair of the Commission.

When a person or an organization is seen to have contravened the *Securities Act* or to have committed an offence under the *Criminal Code*, an investigator is appointed and may examine the books of the person concerned. The investigator has the power to call witnesses and require the presentation of relevant exhibits; these powers are the same as those of the Supreme Court of Ontario. The investigator may seize the required documents. The Commission may then appoint an expert to examine the documents. When the investigation indicates that the Act has been contravened and an offence has been committed under the *Criminal Code*, the Commission must submit a complete report to the minister, who may order an investigation and appoint an investigator. The investigation is held in secret. In many cases, however, the issue is resolved through an agreement between the offender and the Commission instead of being taken to court.

Proceedings must be instituted within a year of the Commission's being informed of an offence (Ontario, *Securities Act*, s. 3(4)).

The Commission may review its own decisions and those of its staff. The Director must notify the Commission at once of any refusal to register; the Commission (Ontario, *Securities Act*, s. 8) then has 30 days to call a hearing and review the decision, if necessary. The person or company concerned also has 30 days to request that the Commission review the Director's decision.

Commission decisions may be appealed to the Divisional Court (Ontario, *Securities Act*, s. 9). An appeal does not prevent the decision from being enforced, unless the Commission or court decides otherwise. Upon appeal, the Divisional Court[14] may make decisions on matters that relate to the Commission's mandate. The Commission may modify the court's decisions to make them fit the circumstances.

It is an offence to give the Commission distorted facts, contravene the provisions of the *Securities Act* and its regulations or fail to obey the directives issued under the *Securities Act* and its regulations (Ontario, *Securities Act*, s. 118). The penalty is a fine of not more than $1 million and/or imprisonment for not more than two years. In the case of a corporation, the director, officer or person responsible is also guilty of violating the Act and is liable, on summary conviction, to the same penalties.

Canadian Human Rights Commission

Staff take complaints at the Canadian Human Rights Commission (CHRC). An investigation follows and the file is submitted to the Commission for decision. However, the staff try to settle disputes before submitting them to the Commission. The complainant and the person or organization against whom the complaint has been made are given an opportunity to look at the results of the investigation and to provide additional information or observations before the matter is forwarded to the Commission.

The Commission may decide to:

- approve the ruling if one has been made;
- dismiss the complaint if it is not substantiated;
- appoint a conciliator to reach a settlement which, in turn, is subject to approval; or
- send the case to the Human Rights Tribunal (CHRC, undated, 5).

The Human Rights Tribunal is completely independent of the Commission. Its members work part time and participate in only a few cases a year. For each case, the decision is made by a panel of one to three members. The chairperson of the panel chooses the members for each proceeding from among all members of the Tribunal. Members participating in a hearing may require the accused to

- cease the discriminatory practices;
- take the necessary steps to remedy the effects of the discrimination;
- restore the rights or privileges lost; and/or
- pay a maximum fine of $5 000 (CHRC, undated, 6).

Decisions can be reviewed by the Federal Court and also the Supreme Court.

These four examples of administrative structures have certain features in common. First of all, the decisions of the administrative tribunals may be appealed in courts of law. It is possible in all cases to transfer the proceedings directly to the courts. The advantage of these administrative bodies lies in their ability to deal with ordinary problems quickly, without, however, precluding the involvement of the courts when more serious cases arise. Another feature of these bodies is the fact that the members of the commissions are specialists. The various commissions studied all possess various means whereby people may become informed of current rules. Wide powers of investigation are given in each organization. Hearings of witnesses or others involved usually result in quasi-judicial decisions by the Commission. This procedure allows the authorities to learn about the disputes and to make the necessary decisions. An out-of-court settlement is always preferable to formal legal action.

In addition, the enabling legislation of these organizations is extremely precise regarding the appointment of members, procedures, time periods and delegation of powers. In most cases, the people appointed to sit on the tribunals have the same prerogatives as magistrates in courts of law.

Canada Elections Commission[15]

The objective sought when proposing a new structure for Elections Canada is greater flexibility and thus effectiveness in the administrative management and enforcement of the *Canada Elections Act*.

The Election Enforcement Commission, as set out in Bill C-79, already included a number of elements designed to partially remove the process from the legal system. The current demand to make procedures more flexible and the fact that very few violations of election laws are related to fraud lead us to believe that the proposals in Bill C-79 did not go far enough. Under the bill, the Election Enforcement Commission would have mainly performed the same duties as those currently carried out by the Commissioner of Canada Elections, i.e., deciding to conduct investigations or initiate legal action following the alleged violation of the *Canada Elections Act*. The major change proposed by the bill was granting search and seizure powers to private investigators, thereby avoiding the necessity of calling on the RCMP. Despite this reform, all legal action would have been initiated before a court of law. The Commission would not have had any conciliation powers aimed at avoiding fruitless legal action.

An assessment of the obstacles faced by Elections Canada and others concerned leads to the conclusion that a new structure is essential, enjoying the power to conduct investigations and act as an administrative tribunal for violations under the current Act pertaining to administration of the voting process and election campaign financing. The models presented indicate that grouping such functions is possible. The Quebec Securities Commission, for example, reserves the exclusive power to call for investigations, even if it does delegate the duty of conducting these investigations to the head of legal affairs. In the Ontario Securities Commission, on the other hand, the Executive Director and Director of Enforcement are responsible for deciding whether an investigation is to be conducted and for laying charges.

In our opinion, the experience of the Canadian Human Rights Commission shows clearly the necessity of not structuring a tribunal in such a way that it is concerned solely with adjudication functions. In this context, there would be no specialization of members, because there would not be enough cases on which they had to adjudicate. These factors explain why it would be preferable to give the Canada Elections Commission the administrative duties currently performed by Elections Canada, along with all responsibilities pertaining to the enforcement of the Act.

To bolster the confidence of all participants, particularly that of the political parties, it is essential that the latter participate in appointing

Commission members. The appointment of commissioners by political parties, as practised in Ontario and the United States, might not be practical for a federal structure. Thus, it is suggested that commissioners be named by a resolution of two-thirds of the House of Commons. The CEO, who would chair the Commission, would be appointed for a seven-year renewable term. The other six members would be appointed for a renewable five-year period. Two vice-chairs would be appointed to full-time positions and the other four members to part-time posts. The initial appointments for three of these members once the new structure is established would be for a seven-year period to ensure continuity. Commission members would obviously continue in their positions as long as no successor has been selected. Dismissals should be conducted in the same manner as appointments.

This method of appointing Commission members would ensure that individuals or groups subject to Commission decisions would be treated impartially. For this purpose, appointment and dismissal procedures, remuneration, fringe benefits and the immunity members would enjoy should be set out in the Act. This would also increase the confidence of the political parties in a relatively autonomous structure independent of the government of the day. To ensure the highest degree of impartiality, commissioners and managers could not be employed by a political party, nor could they be members of or contributors to a political party. Members could be recruited from among the university community, the legal profession or retired judges, for example. However, the conditions ensuring members' independence and impartiality would nonetheless allow for the recruitment of commissioners with a political background.

The scope of the Commission's mandate clearly justifies having two full-time vice-chairs, who would also serve to counterbalance the authority of the CEO. One vice-chair, in conjunction with the authorities responsible for conducting investigations, could make decisions regarding action on complaints. The other vice-chair could be responsible for hearings and public meetings. The other four part-time commissioners would be primarily concerned with negotiating settlements. Seven commissioners appear sufficient to ensure representation of various points of view on the Commission. In addition, with responsibility resting on several members, we believe that such a measure could only increase the credibility of an organization that is now under the responsibility of a single official, the CEO.

Unlike the current organization – Elections Canada – the Commission would have wide-ranging administrative and quasi-judicial powers. It would act as an administrative tribunal for complaints filed against individuals and parties. It would have the right to review all decisions made by its staff. The Commission would also act as a board of directors for Elections Canada. All the functions currently exercised by Elections Canada or the CEO would be transferred to the Commission. As with the Ontario and Quebec securities commissions, the powers of the CEO and Commission staff would be granted by delegation. In the future, positions taken and recommendations made to Parliament by Elections Canada would come from the Commission, even if the CEO were often their originator.

The CEO's administrative duties would be broader than is now the case. The Canada Elections Commission would be responsible for issuing guidelines for enforcement of the Act and should consult with political parties concerning various issues. It would also be empowered to formulate regulations. It would convey to Parliament any suggestions for changes in the Act. It would also be more accessible to the public, because it would have a mandate to hold public hearings. The Commission would also inform and raise public awareness with regard to the electoral process.

The Commission would submit an annual report to Parliament. As is now the case, this report would be sent to the Speaker of the House of Commons to be tabled immediately. The Commission could also act in an advisory capacity to the Standing Committee of the House of Commons responsible for matter related to elections. The Commission's proposed regulations would be forwarded to the House of Commons, and not submitted for Cabinet approval.

The Commission would submit non-statutory expenditures for Treasury Board approval, as do all government departments.

When processing complaints and legal action, the person responsible for conducting investigations would have a decisive role. Complaints would be referred to that person's office, as happens with the Commissioner for Canada Elections at present. The complainant would be informed by the Director if no action were taken on a complaint. At the request of the person accused of an infraction, the decision not to pursue the case would be made public.

When an in-depth investigation is required, the person directing the operation could request the services of an investigator who would have powers of search and seizure, granted by the Federal Court. Depending on the circumstances, the RCMP could investigate, at the request of the Commission. The investigations director would inform the CEO if the preliminary investigation seemed to indicate that a serious breach of the Act had occurred. The CEO would then assign a commissioner who, with the investigations director, would make subsequent decisions

Figure 9.3
Proposed procedure for dealing with electoral complaints

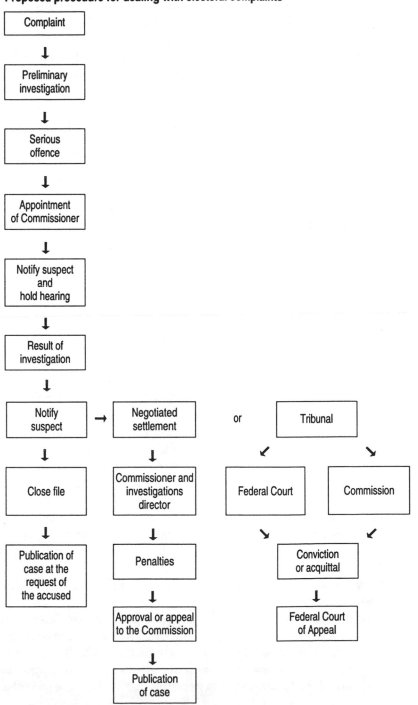

related to the case. Proceedings would be instituted only upon a joint decision of the investigations director and the designated commissioner. If there is disagreement, another commissioner would be asked to settle the matter. The procedure is shown in figure 9.3.

The proposal that more than one person should be involved in deciding whether to prosecute or conduct an in-depth investigation is based on two factors. First, the Commission's guidelines for the interpretation and enforcement of the *Canada Elections Act* must be consistent with the criteria and guidelines applied by the investigations director in deciding whether to proceed with a complaint. The designated Commissioner can ensure such consistency exists. In addition, the current procedure whereby only the Commissioner of Canada Elections can make the decision to prosecute has been criticized upon occasion. The Masse case is an example. If the decision is made collectively, the responsibility is shared and presumably the decision would be less open to criticism. The same justification applies for negotiated agreements.

When a relatively minor matter can be settled by negotiation between the parties, the investigations director should negotiate a settlement for later approval by the Commission; it would then be made public. More serious cases would involve both the director and a commissioner designated for that purpose.

When prosecution or a negotiated settlement is involved, the names of the parties and the nature of the offence should be made public. Other investigations would remain confidential, unless otherwise requested by the parties affected. Cases must be kept confidential until concluded to protect the reputation of the persons involved. An investigation during an election campaign may hinder a candidate's election or, when members have been elected, damage the person's reputation and work. Hearings guarantee that the individual named in a specific complaint may be heard before the case becomes public. The need to publish the results of a case that goes before the Commission is based on the fact that the public should be certain that the individuals or groups charged either have their names cleared or are punished. We believe publication of these results would be beneficial. It can increase public confidence in the system and also make political participants more aware of the penalties that they may suffer in violating the *Canada Elections Act*.

Offences or violations may be prosecuted before either the Commission or the Federal Court. The designated commissioner or investigations director would determine which body is appropriate.

A predetermined number of commissioners should be appointed by the chair of the Commission to hear the cases (or by the vice-chair if the chair is absent). Commissioners who were party to the investigation could not take part in the hearing. When the Commission uses its quasi-judicial powers, it would have the full authority of a court of law, including the ability to request documents and set costs. The Commission should issue its decision in writing, and could review such decisions on request. An appeal from a Commission decision could be brought before the Federal Court of Appeal on issues involving the Commission or on questions of law if a motion is filed within 30 days of the decision being rendered.

The Commission would always try to reach a negotiated settlement before instituting formal proceedings. The hearing would also enable the accused to present their case. The powers of the investigations director would be broad enough to permit screening out of unfounded complaints and those that might overburden the Commission's operations.

As part of its powers to enforce compliance with the *Canada Elections Act*, the Commission could prohibit refunds of expenses to a candidate or party or remove a party from the register, thereby removing its ability to issue receipts for campaign contributions. It could also have a Federal Court enforce its orders.

Serious cases would be referred to Federal Court. One of the reasons why the Federal Court was established as it is today was to "resolve the problems which arose due to the possibility of contradictory judgements of different superior courts exercising judicial review of the same decision" (Pépin and Ouellette 1982, 379). The Federal Court's jurisdiction is limited to matters related to the federal administration and cases that come within the exclusive jurisdiction of Parliament. Selection of the Federal Court has several advantages: decisions would be more consistent, and lawyers could specialize in this field; parties could then hire the same lawyer to defend different cases across the country, making a defence more effective and reducing costs. In addition, the Federal Court sits in various locations across Canada, making it accessible at reduced cost.

In conclusion, the proposed administrative structure could reduce delays and costs while increasing efficiency in enforcing the Act. Being able to appeal a decision of the Commission to a court of law would guarantee individuals and groups that their cases will be dealt with impartially. The fact that regulations, guidelines, investigations and prosecutions would be conducted by the same body makes it possible to ensure procedural consistency. The flexibility of this structure would increase compliance with the Act. In addition, the Commission could act promptly without the procedural constraints imposed by the *Criminal Code*, also promoting greater compliance with the *Canada Elections Act*.

Offences and Penalties[16]

The *Canada Elections Act* defines a series of offences and, except for companies, imposes fines and prison sentences, without any distinction as to whether the offence is regulatory or criminal. The proposed structure could not function in this way.

Under legal rules, regulatory offences are, by their very nature, accessory to a statute, and hence "breaches of a statute." On the other hand, criminal offences relate directly to the basic values of society, and are specified as "violations."

The *Canada Elections Act* makes provision for both types of offences. Although an analysis of complaints and prosecutions in Canada over the last few decades indicates that fraud is no longer widespread and corruption is no longer a decisive factor in political victories, it is nevertheless essential that the *Canada Elections Act* contain provisions covering fraud, together with penalties severe enough to act as a deterrent. We believe that cases involving fraud and corruption should continue to be dealt with through the judicial process. In the provinces and other jurisdictions, provision is made for more severe penalties for "corrupt practices." There are two reasons why this type of offence must be prevented. First, individuals must be deterred from committing offences of this type; second, the public must be assured that such practices are punishable by law because confidence in the system rests mainly on public perception. In reality, the need to call upon the judicial process to prevent corrupt practices relies equally on the perception of individuals and the existence of repressive measures in the legislation.

Knaub (1970) established a classification that makes electoral fraud readily definable:

- Fraud that affects the freedom of the elector and is intended to deceive the elector.
- Corruption: To procure advantages to win votes.
- Attempts to influence or put pressure on an elector.
- To vote twice, or to vote under a false name; incorrect registration on the electoral list.

In addition, the *Criminal Code* is a reliable guide in determining which offences are criminal, such as perjury, defamatory libel, intimidation, personation, assault and corruption.

Offences Dealt with by the Courts

Violations embodying several characteristics are grouped in this section. Prosecutions would be conducted in Federal Court, without the

Commission being involved. After conducting an investigation, the investigations director and a commissioner would give reasons for either dismissing the complaint or instituting legal proceedings. Only the Commission could take legal action related to the *Canada Elections Act*. This condition is necessary to protect candidates and political parties that might be brought before the courts during an election campaign to face charges that subsequently prove groundless.

With one exception, the penalties imposed would not include imprisonment. As already stated, violations should be strict liability offences in order to reduce the burden of proof on Elections Canada. Several Canadian provinces no longer impose a prison sentence for this type of offence. In our view, offences of this type are usually not very serious and, in practice, the courts do not impose prison sentences.

On the other hand, since the courts often impose modest fines as punishment, we believe that a minimum fine of $100 is justified to maintain a deterrent effect. The maximum fine of $5 000 corresponds to that currently imposed when proceeding by indictment.

A general offence describing intention has been inserted in this section. We believe that such a provision is necessary so that authorities can prosecute serious cases where proof of intent is required, without resorting to the *Criminal Code*. The gravity of such offences justifies prison sentences, fines and loss of the right to be elected or sit in the House. The Crown would be required to prove intent to achieve conviction. Unlike the current Act, the loss of voting rights would no longer be a penalty, because the right to vote is a fundamental right, and would be unlikely to deter someone firmly set on committing a violation.

Aiding and abetting would be included in the offences judged before the courts. The Commission could also have recourse to Federal Court to punish contempt for Commission orders.

In our opinion, the legislature should review the wording of the Act as a whole. As it now stands, many sections of the Act cover the same offence. For example, making a false statement, under oath and otherwise, appears in five provisions, and secrecy of the vote is dealt with in nine paragraphs. In addition, most of the offences in the section on special voting rules are already mentioned in the main body of the Act. Provincial legislation provides examples of how the wording of the Act could be clarified and simplified.

In this section, we recommend the repeal of certain sections of the Act including: offences related to proxy voting (Canada, *Canada Elections Act*, s. 146), illegal arrangements related to reproduction of election documents (ibid., s. 69) and a general provision for advance polls (ibid., s. 301(c)). Most of the offences should be set out in clearer language in sections that are more general, without referring to specific situations.

It is important to note that, in the first category of violations judged before the Federal Court, the persons targeted are primarily electors. The second category targets the parties, candidates and agents. Finally, there will be a greater number of instances where agents, candidates, broadcasters and employers fall under the exclusive jurisdiction of the Commission.

Table 9.15 lists violations judged before the Federal Court. Those cited in the tables are mostly from the *Canada Elections Act*.

Table 9.15
Offences dealt with by the courts

Offence committed by	Nature of the offence	Comments
	Penalty: $500 to $5 000	
Anyone	Illegal arrangements concerning a contract (new provision)	
Anyone	Obstructing an election officer in the performance of his or her duties (71(3))	This provision should be extended to all election officers because now it covers only obstruction of an enumerator or a revising agent.
Anyone	Making a false statement concerning the conduct, personal character or withdrawal of a candidate (90) (264)	These two sections should become one, since they cover the same topic.
Anyone	Secrecy of the vote (129) (II, 103(*a*))	This section should be simplified since it now covers nine paragraphs and it is repeated in the schedule of special voting rules. The Quebec legislation (s. 557) provides a good example.
Anyone	Making an untrue statement or false declaration, or illegally vouching for an applicant (147(4)) (236(2)) (301(*a*)(*b*)) (II, 103(*d*)(*e*))	A new general provision should be created to make the text easier to read.
Anyone	Approaching a poll while armed (156(1))	
Anyone	Offences involving election documents (249)	This offence should also be written in simpler language since it now consists of 12 paragraphs.

Table 9.15 (cont'd)
Offences dealt with by the courts

Offence committed by	Nature of the offence	Comments
Anyone	Undue influence and corruption (250) (252(*g*)) and (253)	These two sections should become one and the language should be simplified.
Anyone	Personation (252(*a*)(*b*)(*c*)(*d*)(*e*)(*f*)) (II, 103(*c*))	This section should be simplified and included with a more general section.
Anyone	Inducing an elector not qualified to vote (252(*g*))	
Anyone	Undue influence (253) (II, 103(*a*)(*b*))	These sections should become one general section.
Anyone	Preventing a public meeting (260)	
Anyone	Inducing persons to make false oath (263)	
Anyone	Personation of an election officer (IV, 14)	
Election officer	Manipulating election documents (249(1)(*h*))	
Election officer	Administering an oath by mentioning a disqualification that does not apply (122(4))	

Penalty: $1 000 to $10 000
Two years' imprisonment
Loss of the right to sit or to stand in the next election

Anyone	Knowingly committing an offence to vary the result of a vote (new provision)	

Note: Numbers in parentheses refer to sections of the *Canada Elections Act*.

Offences Dealt with by the Courts and the Commission

Offences that have been the subject of most of the complaints received by Elections Canada in the past few years fall into the second category. These are primarily concerned with financing election campaigns, and most could be settled by conciliation or the administrative tribunal. However, it is essential to ensure that serious violations can be judged in a court of law. This explains why there are different penalties, depending upon the tribunal.

Table 9.16 shows that penalties differ depending on the offence.

Table 9.16
Offences dealt with by the courts and the Commission

Offence committed by	Nature of the offence	Additional penalty	Comments
	Penalty		
	Commission: $0 to $5 000; Court: $500 to $10 000		
Anyone	Advertising prohibited in polling station (157) (158)		The prohibited area should be defined.
Anyone	Destroying or removing election documents or posters of candidates and parties (262) (266)		
Anyone	A breach of the Act for which no penalty is provided (new provision)		Necessary to punish all offences not expressly provided for in the Act.
Anyone	Ineligible person signing the candidate's nomination paper (78(3))	If the person is elected, the election is declared void.	
Candidate's agent	Exceeding the limits of expenses for a candidate (39(1)), (208(2))		
Candidate's agent	Failing to file a return of expenses for a candidate (47(1)), (236(3))		
Candidate's agent	Making a false statement or submitting incomplete information in the return (47(1)), (236(3))	Two years' imprisonment (court only)	
Candidate	Making a false statement or submitting incomplete information in the return (47(1)), (236(3))	Two years' imprisonment, loss of right to sit or stand in the next election (court only)	
	Penalty		
	Commission: $0 to $5 000 or 200% of the value of the illegal contribution		
	Court: $500 to $10 000 or 200% of the value of the illegal contribution		
Anyone	Not paying contributions out of his or her own funds (36(1)(a) (2))		
Anyone	Not paying contributions only to the agent (36(1)(a) (2))		
Anyone	Making a payment other than through the agent or without authorization (36(1)(b)), (217(3)) (259(1))		

Table 9.16 (cont'd)
Offences dealt with by the courts and the Commission

Offence committed by	Nature of the offence	Additional penalty	Comments
Anyone	Exceeding the limit of expenses for notices of meetings (214(2))		To be fairer, the limits should be defined for parties. The section should also deal with persons who want to be elected.
Candidate	Exceeding the limit of expenses for a candidate (208(1))	Two years' imprisonment. Loss of the right to be elected or to sit in the House of Commons (court only)	

Penalty
Commission: $0 to $5 000
Court: $500 to $10 000

Party's agent	Exceeding the limit of expenses for a party (39(1))		Penalties are more severe than those imposed on a candidate's agent.
Party's agent	Failing to file a return (47(1))		Penalties are more severe than those imposed on a candidate's agent.
Party's agent	Submitting false information or incomplete information in the return (47(1))	Two years' imprisonment	Penalties are more severe than those imposed on a candidate's agent.

Penalty
Commission: $0 to $5 000 or 200% of amount overspent
Court: $500 to $10 000 or 200% of amount overspent

Party	Exceeding spending limits (40(2))		
Party	Making a false statement or submitting incomplete information (47(1))		

General provisions

Anyone	Failing to comply with an order of the Commission (new provision)	Commission: $0 to $5 000 or contempt of court Court: $0 to $5 000 and a maximum of two years' imprisonment	

Table 9.16 (cont'd)
Offences dealt with by the courts and the Commission

Offence committed by	Nature of the offence	Additional penalty	Comments
Anyone	Aiding and abetting: When two or more persons together form an intention to carry out an unlawful purpose and to help each other achieve it, and any one of them, in carrying out the common purpose, commits an offence, each of them is a party to that offence.	Punishable by the same penalty imposed on the person who commits the offences.	Section 21(2) of the *Criminal Code*. Provision is similar to section 566 in the Quebec *Election Act.*
	Penalty		
	Commission: daily fine, after 30 days' loss of rights		
Party	Failing to file a return (47(2))	$1 000 per day. Loss of rights to reimbursement, deregistration and loss of party status in the House of Commons.	Additional time may be granted by the Commission.
Candidate	Failing to file a return (236(3))	$100 per day. Loss of rights to reimbursement of expenses and of deposit.	Additional time may be granted by the Commission.

Note: Numbers in parentheses refer to sections of the *Canada Elections Act*.

An effort has been made to establish a direct link between the nature of the offence and the penalty. Thus, offences involving money or expenses are generally penalized proportionately, usually by a fine of 200 percent. The proportional nature of the fines allows the penalty to be tied directly to the seriousness of the violation. For example, under the current Act, a party might exceed the spending limit by $1 million, incurring a maximum fine of $25 000. With the schedule shown in table 9.16, the penalty could be as much as $2 million. This type of proportional penalty is found in the United States.

To encourage individuals and parties to comply with the Act, imprisonment would be stipulated when false information is supplied in expense reports. This penalty is more severe than that for failing to submit a report or for exceeding permissible expenses. Such a measure would encourage individuals to report the activities of candidates and parties clearly.

Because of the Commission's specialization in electoral matters, it is considered advisable not to set minimum penalties to punish these violations, because the Commission should be at liberty to assess the penalties to be imposed. The logic would be different for the Federal Court, because the violations referred to it would be very serious, which presupposes that the appropriate fines should be greater than the proposed minimum of $500.

Offences Dealt with by the Commission

This section covers essentially regulatory offences, involving the rules applying to the electoral process per se. In addition, in cases such as employers allowing time off work to vote, or advertising during blackout periods, the problem can be resolved by direct and prompt intervention on the part of the Commission. There are minimum penalties for broadcasting offences only, to maintain a deterrent effect; otherwise, no minimum has been suggested in order to allow the Commission enough latitude in making its decisions. Table 9.17 illustrates the system.

This proposed classification of offences and penalties may well improve enforcement of the Act if, at the same time, the Act is restructured and clarified, with fewer references to specific situations. This would make it possible to avoid reliance on the *Criminal Code,* by adding provisions on aiding and abetting and general provisions for the Commission and Federal Court. In addition, the classification has been adapted to the new structure of Elections Canada, which requires removing implementation of the Act from the judicial process to some extent.

Table 9.17
Offences dealt with by the Commission

Offence committed by	Nature of the offence	Additional penalty	Comments
	Penalty: *Commission: $0 to $5 000 or 200% of the value*		
Official agent	Failing to identify the agent's printed material (261(2))		
Political party or candidate	Publishing or advertising during blackout period (48(1))		
	Penalty: *Commission: $1 000 to $25 000*		
Broadcaster	Offences concerning broadcasting (307 to 321)		
Anyone	Broadcasting outside Canada (303(1))		

Table 9.17 (cont'd)
Offences dealt with by the Commission

Offence committed by	Nature of the offence	Additional penalty	Comments
	Penalty: *Commission: $0 to $5 000*		
Election officer, candidate or non-elector	Acting as an agent for a candidate or a party without being eligible (35(3))		
Election officer, candidate, agent	Acting as an auditor without being eligible (42(2))	Return is void.	
Election officer	Registering an ineligible person on an electoral list and not registering an eligible person (71(2)), (203(1)), (IV(19)), (V(8))		
Election officer	Refusing to remit election documents after having been relieved of his or her duties (96(2)), (IV(75)), (V(26))		
Employer	Refusing to allow four hours to vote (150(1))		
Returning officer	Refusing to declare an elected person duly elected (194)	Loss of right to payment.	
Official agent	Failing to appear before the Commission or to make reports required by the Commission (239)		
Official agent	Paying the claims in a time period longer than three months (221(3))		

Note: Numbers in parentheses refer to sections of the *Canada Elections Act*.

Table 9.18 summarizes the complaints and actions undertaken by Elections Canada for the 1988 election, classified as above. The results show that, if all complaints had been acted upon, the Commission would have dealt with about 93 percent of the cases. If the 49 actions initiated by Elections Canada had been handled under the current system, 84 percent of cases would have been decided by the Commission. In short, creating new categories of violations and assigning quasi-judicial powers to the Commission would greatly reduce the number of *Canada Elections Act* violations taken before the courts.

Table 9.18
Processing of complaints and prosecutions

Violation	Complaints	Prosecutions	Complaints (# in each category)			Prosecutions (# in each category)		
			Court	Double	Commission	Court	Double	Commission
Financing of election campaigns by registrants	655	33	–	400	255	–	1	32
Third parties	74	0	–	–	74	–	–	–
Scrutineers	21	1	21	–	–	1	–	–
Election fraud	16	3	16	–	–	3	–	–
Employer	51	9	–	–	51	–	–	9
Other	31	3	20	9	2	3	–	–
Total	848	49	57 (7%)	409 (48%)	382 (45%)	7 (14%)	1 (2%)	41 (84%)

Note: This table shows how complaints and prosecutions related to the 1988 general election would have been classified under the new provisions proposed in this study. Complaints (14) and prosecutions (1) in 1988 concerning the sale of alcoholic beverages on election day are not included in this table. All figures are for the 1988 general election.

CONCLUSION

This study provides abundant evidence of the fact that the enforcement mechanisms in the *Canada Elections Act* are obsolete. We have seen very rigid procedures dominated by criminal law and a proliferation of offences and penalties that no longer reflect current needs in supervising the electoral process. The findings are clear. Although electors, candidates, agents and parties generally comply with the Act and fraud is uncommon, the procedural mechanisms used in enforcing the Act do not guarantee compliance, particularly where the financing of political activity is concerned.

The problems noted are a direct result of the criminalization of penalties and the ambiguity of the Act. Complaints rarely result in prosecutions, because the authority to conduct investigations is limited, criminal investigations are harmful to the reputation of an individual and penalties are often disproportionately harsh. In addition, although the *Canada Elections Act* has now been in force for 15 years, basic problems of interpretation have not been resolved because case law is both sparse and inconsistent and the guidelines issued by Elections Canada are imprecise because of deficiencies in the Act. Moreover, given current conditions, it would be difficult to clarify or improve this situation within the framework of the current law.

To make enforcement of the Act more effective, one option would be to remove the enforcement process from the judicial system. Although decriminalization assumes that electoral offences will be dealt with less severely, there are several factors that, on the contrary, might make the consequences of committing an offence more serious. An example would be penalties that are directly proportionate to the seriousness of the offence. If the process were removed only partially from the judicial system, it would still be possible to go directly to a court of law that can impose prison sentences in cases of fraud or matters serious enough to require greater penalties than those available to an administrative tribunal.

In short, if the legislation described in specific and precise terms the prerogatives of those involved, it would be easier to intervene promptly. Offences could be dealt with either through negotiated settlements or decisions made following a procedure applicable to minor offences and to those affecting the integrity of the system. The ability to deal easily with alleged offences would certainly encourage greater compliance with the Act. It would also ensure that the Canadian electoral process is based on rules that are properly applied, thus ensuring openness and fairness.

ABBREVIATIONS

Alta. L.R.	Alberta Law Reports
c.	chapter
C.S.P.	Court of Sessions of the Peace
D.L.R. (4th)	Dominion Law Reports, Fourth Series
F.C.	Federal Court Reports
Ont. Prov. Ct.	Ontario Provincial Court
Pub. L.	Public Law
Q.B.	Court of Queen's Bench
R.S.A.	Revised Statutes of Alberta
R.S.B.C.	Revised Statutes of British Columbia
R.S.C.	Revised Statutes of Canada
R.S.M.	Revised Statutes of Manitoba
R.S.N.	Revised Statutes of Newfoundland
R.S.N.B.	Revised Statutes of New Brunswick
R.S.N.S.	Revised Statutes of Nova Scotia
R.S.N.W.T.	Revised Statutes of Northwest Territories
R.S.O.	Revised Statutes of Ontario
R.S.P.E.I.	Revised Statutes of Prince Edward Island
R.S.Q.	Revised Statutes of Quebec
R.S.S.	Revised Statutes of Saskatchewan
R.S.Y.	Revised Statutes of Yukon
S.N.B.	Statutes of New Brunswick
S.Q.	Statutes of Quebec
s(s).	section(s)
T.D.	Trial Division
U.K.	United Kingdom

NOTES

This study was completed in August 1991.

I would like to thank Yvon Tarte, Louis Massicotte and George Allen of Elections Canada whose invaluable help made this study possible. I would also like to thank Jean-Marc Hamel for his judicious comments on previous versions of this document.

In this study, quoted material that originated in French has been translated into English.

1. The position of Commissioner of Canada Elections was created in 1974.

2. Special rules governing elections are set out in Schedule II of the *Canada Elections Act*. These rules define various means whereby members of the Canadian armed forces, veterans, public servants on duty outside Canada, and their spouses and dependants living with them may exercise voting rights.

3. J.O. Gorman is the former Commissioner of Canada Elections.

4. Corresponds to section 208 of the current Act.

5. Corresponds to section 217 of the current Act.

6. Corresponds to section 259 of the current Act.

7. General provision contained in section 126 of the *Criminal Code:*

   (1) Every one who, without lawful excuse, contravenes an Act of Parliament by wilfully doing anything that it forbids or by wilfully omitting to do anything that it requires to be done is, unless a punishment is expressly provided by law, guilty of an indictable offence and liable to imprisonment for a term not exceeding two years.

   (2) Any proceedings in respect of a contravention of or conspiracy to contravene an Act mentioned in subsection (1), other than this Act, may be instituted at the instance of the Government of Canada and conducted by or on behalf of that Government.

8. Section 21 of the *Criminal Code* states that:

   (1) Every one is a party to an offence who

     (*a*) actually commits it;

     (*b*) does or omits to do anything for the purpose of aiding any person to commit it; or

     (*c*) abets any person in committing it.

   (2) Where two or more persons form an intention in common to carry out an unlawful purpose and to assist each other therein and any one of them, in carrying out the common purpose, commits an offence, each of them who knew or ought to have known that the commission of the offence would be a probable consequence of carrying out the common purpose is a party to that offence.

9. Such as in the election laws of Nova Scotia, Prince Edward Island and Quebec.

10. Section 121(2) of the *Criminal Code:*

    Every one commits an offence who, in order to obtain or retain a contract with the government, or as a term of any such contract, whether express or implied, directly or indirectly subscribes or gives, or agrees to subscribe or give, to any person any valuable consideration

(*a*) for the purpose of promoting the election of a candidate or a class or party of candidates to Parliament or the legislature of a province; or

(*b*) with intent to influence or affect in any way the result of an election conducted for the purpose of electing persons to serve in Parliament or the legislature of a province.

Section 748(3) and (4) of the *Criminal Code:*

(3) No person who is convicted of an offence under sections 121, 124 or 418 has, after that conviction, capacity to contract with Her Majesty or to receive any benefit under a contract between Her Majesty and any other person or to hold office under Her Majesty.

(4) A person to whom subsection (3) applies may, at any time before a pardon is granted to him under section 4 of the Criminal Records Act, apply to the Governor in Council for the restoration of one or more of the capacities lost by him by virtue of that subsection.

11. Section 377 of the *Criminal Code:*

(1) Every one who unlawfully

   ...

(*c*) destroys, damages or obliterates an election document or causes an election document to be destroyed, damaged or obliterated, or

(*d*) makes or causes to be made an erasure, alteration or interlineation on or on an election document,

is guilty of an indictable offence and liable to imprisonment for a term not exceeding five years.

(2) In this section, "election document" means any document or writing issued under the authority of an Act of Parliament or the legislature of a province with respect to an election held pursuant to the authority of that Act.

12. Estimated data based on a sampling of 150 complaints received by Elections Canada for the 1988 general election.

13. Estimate obtained by Roland Côté, Commissioner and Vice-President of the Quebec Securities Commission.

14. The Divisional Court of Ontario hears cases regarding administrative law.

15. The administrative structure described below was developed by Robert
    Gabor, a commissioner with the Royal Commission on Electoral Reform
    and Party Financing.

16. The classification of offences described below was developed jointly by
    Michael Cassidy, research coordinator for the Royal Commission on
    Electoral Reform and Party Financing, and the author of this study.

INTERVIEW

George Allen, current Commissioner of Canada Elections, Ottawa, 24 April
1991.

BIBLIOGRAPHY

Alberta. *Election Act*, R.S.A. 1980, c. E-2.

———. *Election Finances and Contributions Disclosure Act*, R.S.A. 1980, c. E-3.

Alexander, H.E., and B.A. Haggerty. 1987. *Administration and Enforcement:
Financing the 1984 Election.* Lexington: Lexington Books.

Australia. *Commonwealth Electoral Act, 1918*, as amended 30 September 1990.

Baillargeon v. Maltais, C.S.P. Qué. (District de Mingan), No. 650-01-001050-
855, 1986.

Baillargeon v. Marin, C.S.P. Qué. (District de Gaspé), No. 130-27-00058-865,
1987.

Boyer, J.P. 1981. *Political Rights: The Legal Framework of Elections in Canada.*
Toronto: Butterworths.

———. 1987. *Electoral Law in Canada: The Law and Procedure of Federal,
Provincial and Territorial Elections.* Toronto: Butterworths.

British Columbia. *Election Act*, R.S.B.C. 1979, c. 103.

Canada. Bill C-79. *An Act to amend the Canada Elections Act*, 2nd Session,
33rd Parliament, 1986–87.

———. *Canada Elections Act*, R.S.C. 1985, c. E-2.

———. *Canadian Charter of Rights and Freedoms*, Part I of the *Constitution Act,
1982*, being Schedule B of the *Canada Act 1982* (U.K.), 1982, c. 11.

———. *Canadian Human Rights Act*, R.S.C. 1985, c. H-6.

———. *Constitution Act, 1982*, being Schedule B of the *Canada Act 1982*
(U.K.), 1982, c. 11.

———. *Corrupt Practices Inquiries Act*, R.S.C. 1985, c. C-45.

———. *Criminal Code*, R.S.C. 1985, c. C-46.

———. *Disfranchising Act*, R.S.C. 1985, c. D-3.

————. *Dominion Controverted Elections Act*, R.S.C. 1985, c. C-39.

————. *Inquiries Act*, R.S.C. 1985, c. I-11.

————. *Public Service Superannuation Act*, R.S.C. 1985, c. P-36.

Canada. Elections Canada. 1984. *Report of the Chief Electoral Officer as per subsection 59(1) of the Canada Elections Act*. Ottawa: Minister of Supply and Services Canada.

————. 1985. *Report of the Chief Electoral Officer as per subsection 59(1) of the Canada Elections Act*. Ottawa: Minister of Supply and Services Canada.

————. 1986. *Report of the Chief Electoral Officer as per subsection 59(1) of the Canada Elections Act*. Ottawa: Minister of Supply and Services Canada.

————. 1989. *Report of the Chief Electoral Officer as per subsection 195(1) of the Canada Elections Act*. Ottawa: Minister of Supply and Services Canada.

————. 1991. *Report of the Chief Electoral Officer as per subsection 195(1) of the Canada Elections Act*. Ottawa: Minister of Supply and Services Canada.

Canada. House of Commons. Standing Committee on Elections, Privileges and Procedure. 1988. *Minutes of Proceedings and Evidence*. Ottawa: Queen's Printer.

Canada. Privy Council Office. 1986. *White Paper on Election Law Reform*. Ottawa: Queen's Printer.

Canadian Human Rights Commission. Undated. *Your Rights: Filing a Claim with the Canadian Human Rights Commission*. Ottawa.

Commission des valeurs mobilières du Québec. 1989a. *Le marché des valeurs, section 1*. Québec.

————. 1989b. *Rapport d'activités 1988–1989*. Québec: Bibliothèque nationale du Québec.

Côté-Harper, Gisèle, Antoine D. Manganas and Jean Turgeon. 1989. *Droit pénal canadien*. 3d ed. Cowansville: Éditions Yvon Blais.

Deysine, A. 1982. "Political Corruption: A Review of the Literature." *European Journal of Political Research* 8:447–62.

Federal Election Commission. 1988. *Federal Election Campaign Laws*. Washington, DC.

————. 1989a. "The Election Crimes Branch." *FEC Journal of Election Administration* 16:20–21.

————. 1989b. "The Federal Election Commission." *FEC Journal of Election Administration* 16:14–17.

————. 1990. "Compliance." *FEC Journal of Election Administration* 16 (3): 13–15.

Germany. *Act regarding Political Parties*, 24 July 1967.

————. *Federal Elections Act*, dated 7 May 1956, as amended by the 5th Act to amend the *Federal Elections Act*, dated 20 July 1979.

Gosselin, J.F. 1989. "L'alchimie des Chartes vue de l'intérieur du tribunal administratif: le retour du Cheval de Troie?" In *Tribunaux administratifs à la lumière des Chartes*, ed. Quebec Bar Association. Cowansville: Éditions Yvon Blais.

Hamel, J.M. 1990. Brief to the Royal Commission on Electoral Reform and Party Financing. Ottawa.

Healy, P. 1990. *For a Model of Regulatory Offences: Compliance and Regulatory Remedies*. Ottawa: Department of Justice.

Inkster, N. 1990. Testimony before the Royal Commission on Electoral Reform and Party Financing. Ottawa.

Knaub, Gilbert. 1970. *Typologie juridique de la fraude électorale en France*. Paris: Dalloz.

Lavoie, J. 1990. Brief to the Royal Commission on Electoral Reform and Party Financing. Ottawa.

MacLean v. Nova Scotia (Attorney General) (1987), 35 D.L.R. (4th) 306 (T.D.).

Manitoba. *Controverted Elections Act*, R.S.M. 1987, c. C-210.

————. *The Elections Act*, R.S.M. 1987, c. E-30.

————. *The Elections Finances Act*, R.S.M. 1987, c. E-32.

Moore, L. 1990. *Civil v. Criminal Enforcement: Working out the Problems*. 1990 COGEL Conference. Anchorage.

National Citizens' Coalition Inc./Coalition nationale des citoyens v. Canada (Attorney General) (1984), 32 Alta. L.R. (2d) 249 (Q.B.).

New Brunswick. *Controverted Elections Act*, R.S.N.B. 1973, c. C-21.

————. *Elections Act*, R.S.N.B. 1973, c. E-3.

————. *Political Process Financing Act*, S.N.B. 1978, c. P-9.3.

New Democratic Party of Canada. 1990. Submission to the Royal Commission on Electoral Reform and Party Financing. Ottawa.

Newfoundland. *Election Act*, R.S.N. 1990, c. E-3.

Northwest Territories. *Elections Act*, S.N.W.T. 1986 (2), c. 2.

Nova Scotia. *Controverted Elections Act*, R.S.N.S. 1989, c. 96.

————. *Elections Act*, R.S.N.S. 1989, c. 140.

Ontario. *Election Act*, R.S.O. 1990, c. E-6.

————. *Election Finances Act*, R.S.O. 1990, c. E-7.

————. *Securities Act*, R.S.O. 1990, c. S-5.

Ontario Securities Commission (OSC). 1988. *Annual Report 1988.* Toronto: Queen's Printer.

———. 1990. *Annual Report 1990.* Toronto: Queen's Printer.

Parkdale Hotel Limited v. Canada (Attorney General), [1986] 2 F.C. 514.

Pépin, G., and Y. Ouellette. 1982. *Principes de contentieux administratifs.* 2d ed. Cowansville: Éditions Yvon Blais.

Prince Edward Island. *Controverted Elections (Provincial) Act,* R.S.P.E.I. 1988, c. C-22.

———. *Election Act,* R.S.P.E.I. 1988, c. E-1.

———. *Election Expenses Act,* R.S.P.E.I. 1988, c. E-2.

Quebec. *Election Act,* S.Q. 1989, c. 1.

———. *Securities Act,* R.S.Q., c. V-1.1.

Quebec. Directeur général des élections du Québec. Commission de la représentation électorale du Québec. 1986. *Rapport annuel 1985–1986.* Québec.

———. 1987. *Rapport annuel 1986–1987.* Québec.

Quebec. Directeur général des élections du Québec. 1988. *Rapport annuel 1987–1988.* Québec.

———. 1989. *Rapport annuel 1988–1989.* Québec.

———. 1990. *Rapport annuel 1989–1990.* Québec.

R. v. Roman and Donkin, Ont. Prov. Ct., Zimmerman J., 19 June 1986.

Riddell v. Hamel, [1989] 2 F.C. 434.

Saskatchewan. *The Controverted Elections Act,* R.S.S. 1978, c. C-32.

———. *Election Act,* R.S.S. 1978, c. E-6.

Sieghart, P. 1980. *Breaking the Rules: The Problems of Crimes and Contraventions.* London: International Commission of Jurists, British Section.

St-Germain, G. 1990. Brief to the Royal Commission on Electoral Reform and Party Financing. Ottawa.

Surtees, L. 1987. "Broad Powers for Proposed Election Panel Assailed." *Globe and Mail,* 4 August.

United States. *Federal Election Campaign Act of 1971,* Pub. L. 92-225, 7 Feb. 1972.

United States. Department of Justice. 1988. *Federal Prosecution of Election Offenses.* 5th ed. Washington, DC.

Webb, K.R. 1989. "Regulatory Offences, the Mental Element and the *Charter:* Rough Road Ahead." *Ottawa Law Review* 21:419–78.

Yukon. *Controverted Elections Act,* R.S.Y. 1986, c. 33.

———. *Elections Act,* R.S.Y. 1986, c. 48.

———. *Legislative Assembly Act,* R.S.Y. 1986, c. 102.

CONTRIBUTORS TO VOLUME 10

Cécile Boucher	Research Analyst, RCERPF
John C. Courtney	University of Saskatchewan
Yves Denoncourt	Research Analyst, RCERPF
Patrice Garant	Université Laval
Kenneth Kernaghan	Brock University
Pierre Landreville	Université de Montréal
Lucie Lemonde	Université de Montréal
David Mac Donald	Senior Research Analyst, RCERPF
Peter McCormick	University of Lethbridge
David E. Smith	University of Saskatchewan
Jennifer Smith	Dalhousie University

ACKNOWLEDGEMENTS

The Royal Commission on Electoral Reform and Party Financing and the publishers wish to acknowledge with gratitude the permission of the following to reprint and translate material:

The American Enterprise Institute for Public Policy Research; American Political Science Association; Stephen Earl Bennett; Cambridge University Press; Commonwealth of Australia; Congressional Digest Corporation; Maurice Cranston; Elections Canada; National Civic League; Oxford University Press; Random House, Inc.; Peters, Fraser & Dunlop; University of Toronto Press.

Care has been taken to trace the ownership of copyright material used in the text, including the tables and figures. The authors and publishers welcome any information enabling them to rectify any reference or credit in subsequent editions.

Consistent with the Commission's objective of promoting full participation in the electoral system by all segments of Canadian society, gender neutrality has been used wherever possible in the editing of the research studies.

THE COLLECTED RESEARCH STUDIES*

---

* The titles of studies may not be final in all cases.

COMMISSION ORGANIZATION

CHAIRMAN
Pierre Lortie

COMMISSIONERS
Pierre Fortier
Robert Gabor
William Knight
Lucie Pépin

SENIOR OFFICERS

Executive Director
Guy Goulard

Director of Research
Peter Aucoin

Special Adviser to the Chairman
Jean-Marc Hamel

Research
F. Leslie Seidle,
  Senior Research Coordinator

Coordinators
Herman Bakvis
Michael Cassidy
Frederick J. Fletcher
Janet Hiebert
Kathy Megyery
Robert A. Milen
David Small

Assistant Coordinators
David Mac Donald
Cheryl D. Mitchell

Legislation
Jules Brière, Senior Adviser
Gérard Bertrand
Patrick Orr

Communications and Publishing
Richard Rochefort, Director
Hélène Papineau, Assistant
  Director
Paul Morisset, Editor
Kathryn Randle, Editor

Finance and Administration
Maurice R. Lacasse, Director

Contracts and Personnel
Thérèse Lacasse, Chief

Editorial, Design and Production Services